Photoshop

RESTORATION & RETOUCHING

FOURTH EDITION

Katrin EISMANN

Wayne Palmer *Dennis* Dunbar

Photoshop Restoration & Retouching, Fourth Edition

Katrin Eismann, Wayne Palmer, Dennis Dunbar

New Riders
www.peachpit.com

New Riders is an imprint of Peachpit, an imprint of Pearson Education, Inc.
To report errors, please send a note to errata@peachpit.com

Executive Editor: Laura Norman
Editors: Cari Jansen and Victor Gavenda
Production Editor: David Van Ness
Copyeditor: Scout Festa
Proofer: Scout Festa
Compositor: Kim Scott, Bumpy Design
Indexer: James Minkin
Cover Design: Aren Straiger and Chuti Prasertsith
Interior Design: Kim Scott, Bumpy Design
Cover Photographs courtesy of (from top): Hildenbrand Family Collection, George Simian, Wayne Palmer, William Short, Katrin Eismann, Mody Family Archives, Teri Campbell, and Palmer Family Archives

ISBN-13: 978-0-321-70101-5
ISBN-10: 0-321-70101-1

1 18

To all of our parents and grandparents who passed on to us family memories that we cherish and that we will pass on to future generations.

—Katrin

To my family, whose numerous photos I have raided for examples. To my dear wife, Pam, whose support has been immeasurable. And last but not least, to my daughter, Amanda, who was an infant when the previous edition of the book was written and who is now a young woman.

—Wayne

To my wife, Amy, who spurs me on with her support and encouragement. To those who helped me at the beginning of my professional career, Charles James and Joe Berndt. And to all those who continue to inspire me, thanks for the support that sparks our desire to keep learning and creating.

—Dennis

ACKNOWLEDGMENTS

Writing a book initially seems like a secluded undertaking, but the very task of researching and seeking expert insights into any topic changes the process from solitary to collaborative. Over the years, we have learned from countless Photoshop experts, engineers, artists, students, and especially my readers, whose questions and comments always challenge me to be clearer and remain relevant. Thank you to Ken Allen, Tom Ashe, the late Mark Beckelman, Carrie Beene, Russell Brown, Shan Canfield, Jane Conner-ziser, Douglas Dubler, Seán Duggan, Bruce Fraser, Allen Furbeck, Greg Gorman, Mark Hamburg, Gregory Heisler, Art Johnson, Scott Kelby, Julieanne Kost, Schecter Lee, Dan Margulis, Andrew Matusik, Pedro Meyer, Bert Monroy, Myke Ninness, Marc Pawliger, Phil Pool, Andrew Rodney, Jeff Schewe, Kristina Sherk, Eddie Tapp, Chris Tarantino, Leigh-Anne Tompkins, Lee Varis, John Warner, Lloyd Weller, Ben Willmore, and Lorie Zirbes for putting up with last-minute emails, phone calls, and questions from us.

Thank you to the numerous contributors who make this fourth edition so valuable. Readers, photo enthusiasts, and imaging professionals from all around the world are featured in these pages and listed in the Appendix. You were all wonderful to work with, generous with your images and techniques, and understanding of my production deadlines. *Merci, vielen dank, gracias,* and thank you!

Calling this book a fourth edition is not accurate—this really is a brand-new book. We reviewed every single technique, substituted many images with better examples, and increased the number of advanced techniques throughout the entire book. Our primary goal was to write a book that readers of previous editions would find valuable enough to purchase and feel they got their money's worth.

—Katrin

In addition to all the worthy folks mentioned by Katrin, I'd like to thank the editors who kept this project on course through a voyage that lasted several years: Cari Jansen, who cracked the bottle of champagne over the bow of the ship and launched it on its way, and Victor Gavenda, who came onboard when the vessel was caught in the Doldrums and steered it safely into port.

—Wayne

The phrase "It takes a Village" reminds me how all of us in this industry could not possibly grow and thrive without the sharing and guidance of others. I'd like to thank those who helped me along the path as I learned about image making and retouching: William James Warren, who first introduced me to compositing by hand in the darkroom; Charles James, who first taught me retouching on a computer; Daniel Ecoff, who put up with countless questions as I was learning; Dan Margulis, whose writings on color correction I have read for nearly 30 years; and my friends and peers who continue to share and inspire continued growth in this work: Pratik Naik, Sef McCullough, Eric Tolladay and Lisa Carney.

—Dennis

ABOUT THE AUTHORS

Katrin Eismann specializes in interpretive travel, still life, and portrait photography. She is an internationally respected artist, a teacher, and the co-author of *Photoshop Restoration & Retouching, Photoshop Masking & Compositing, The Creative Digital Darkroom,* and *Real World Digital Photography*—all of which have been translated into numerous languages. She received her BFA degree in photographic illustration from the Rochester Institute of Technology and her MFA degree in design at the School of Visual Arts and in 2005 was inducted into the Photoshop Hall of Fame. Her images have been featured in numerous books, magazines, and group and solo exhibitions. Katrin is the founder and chair of the Masters in Digital Photography department at the School of Visual Arts in New York City, and she has never met a pixel she didn't want to change.

Katrin hopes someday to take photographs that require no color correction, retouching, cropping, dodging and burning, or enhancement of any kind, but in the meantime she'll keep learning (and teaching) Photoshop.

Wayne Palmer has had a passion for photography all his life. He has a degree in education from Bloomsburg State College, but his interest in photography kept him in the darkroom as much as the classroom. After graduation, he worked for Guardian Photo, Inc., for 13 years in the marketing of photofinishing services on a national level.

Wayne started his own business, Palmer Multimedia Imaging, in 1994, offering custom photographic, videographic, and digital photo restoration services. He has worked with Photoshop since version 3, and previously used Aldus PhotoStyler. A self-described AV nerd, Wayne enjoys sharing his knowledge of photography, digital imaging, and computers. He teaches Photoshop, Photoshop Elements, and digital photography in the continuing education department of the Pennsylvania College of Technology.

Dennis Dunbar is *the* Photoshop magic behind countless movie posters and commercial images. Dennis teaches workshops around the world, sharing professional strategies and professional insights into retouching and compositing that are accessible to both beginners and advanced users.

Contents

FOREWORD

I first became acquainted with Katrin Eismann at a Thunderlizard Photoshop conference in Chicago back in 1997, where she gave a presentation on restoring and retouching grayscale images using Photoshop 4.0. As I was developing a new business concentrating on that type of work, she had my attention.

Two years later, Katrin was presenting a more involved lecture on restoring images at another Thunderlizard conference, in Orlando. She was also scheduled to present a similar program later in the week at the Photo Expo trade show in New York City. I was attending both events and emailed her asking if she would be giving the same lecture at both events. She got back to me saying there would be some overlap, but I could be her guest for the second event—an offer I was happy to accept! Afterward, I introduced myself and that was the start of a long-term friendship. Katrin told me she was writing a book specifically about photo restoration and if I had any good examples, she might include them. Well, I did...and she did, and that was the first edition of *Photoshop Restoration & Retouching*.

We kept in touch and two years later the publishers wanted to update the book. Katrin asked me to come onboard as her technical editor. To say the least, I was honored! That invitation opened the door to more technical editing roles, not only for her books, but for those by a number of other authors.

In 2005, the publishers felt there was a need for another update and this time Katrin asked me to come onboard as her co-author, which was a very humbling experience. This role also got me on the beta-testing team for Photoshop, and that led to my joining the prerelease programs of several other applications.

But it was a very important year for me for another reason. My wife and I adopted a little girl from China. Traveling to China required a visa, and there is a Chinese consulate in New York City. Katrin had invited me to attend an Adobe event in NYC to announce the upcoming release of Photoshop CS2. I welcomed the idea, as not only could I attend the event, but I could also take passports to the Chinese consulate for the visa, which I understood would be processed the same day. Much to my chagrin, the person behind the counter took the passports and said come back Friday. It was Monday. I didn't live near NYC, so this would have involved a more than eight-hour round trip just to pick them up. I told Katrin of my predicament and she generously offered to pick them up and ship them to me. Our friendship was cemented.

Fast-forward to the present and many changes have taken place. Katrin has had me help her on several other projects over the years. Photography and videography have become so commonplace that the quality of imagery from a phone can rival what used to require a standalone camera. Photoshop has gone through numerous revisions, and the sister program Lightroom was launched. Even the book industry is not what it once was as more and more people rely on the Internet for information and the number of books being published has shrunk. And on a personal note, my daughter, who was just learning to walk while I was working on the last edition, is now headed to high school.

What hasn't changed in that time is the type of restoration work being done. Printed photos are still torn, water damaged, stuck to glass, and faded. And people want to look their best in photos, regardless of accuracy. What *has* changed is that Photoshop has new tools that can make the work go faster.

Work on this edition of the book began over three years ago, and at one point it looked like it was going to be tabled. Busy schedules put us behind, and Katrin finally said she did not have the time to finish it. To avoid the efforts already exerted being lost, she turned the project over to me to complete.

The editors of *Popular Photography* magazine credited the previous edition as the best book for learning Photoshop (and it was ultimately translated into seven languages). I was a long-time subscriber of the now discontinued publication, so I took great pride in that endorsement and trust that this version will maintain that reputation.

Katrin, thank you for your friendship and for trusting me to care for your baby.

—Wayne R. Palmer

INTRODUCTION

Has this happened to you? You're looking through a cluttered drawer and as you reach into the back you find an old photo. It's small and tattered, but as soon as you pull it out the memories come flooding back. You pause for a moment to remember who is in the photo and where it was taken. Most of us do not have a photographic memory—but we do have actual photographs that have frozen the time of our family and community history. These images are our memory treasures, and they deserve to be cared for and shared with family and friends as prints, in email attachments, and on social media.

Currently, the most popular camera is your smartphone, and the convenience of a phone camera to take and share pictures has changed the actual experience of photography for all of us. Of course there is no film in your phone, but that does not mean that film is dead. While the essence, the meaning of the film image is not dead, the actual medium is dying a slow death as it fades, degrades, and is eaten by pests. Save the photos. Get them out of the damp basement or dry, hot attic. Take them out of those corrosive cardboard boxes and put them into archival storage sleeves and boxes. Do your best to store them somewhere cool and dry (relative humidity of 20 to 50 percent). If you really want to be all digital, scan or digitally photograph the film and original prints to create digital masters.

THE IMPORTANCE OF IMAGES

Our photographs contain our memories and our legacy, and they connect us to our family and friends. Even if they are cracked, yellowed, or damaged, we don't throw them away. No matter how tattered or faded a photograph is, it still helps us remember and learn about the past. The combination of image, emotion, and memory is fascinating. With the addition of one component to this mixture—Photoshop—you can make faded colors rich again, remove damage, and clean up mold, making images as clear and crisp as the day they were taken. With the skilled use of Adobe Photoshop as presented in this book, you can fight the ravages of time and, more importantly, share the memories with your family and friends.

As you can see by paging through this book, not all the pictures and examples featured here are historical. Many of the examples are images captured with the latest digital cameras or that came from leading photo studios. It would be ideal to capture perfect images that would not require any color correction or image transformations to, for example, straighten a building, but photographic reality often works against our best intentions. In fact, when Katrin takes pictures she often "sees" the Photoshop interface in her viewfinder—meaning Photoshop is a great tool to have (so to speak) in your camera bag. Working with contemporary images is addressed in Chapters 8 ("Portrait Retouching"), 9 ("Beauty Retouching"), and 10 ("Product, Food, and Architectural Retouching").

THE IMPORTANCE OF LEARNING

Time, practice, and patience—you can't be good at a sport, cook a gourmet meal, or restore an image without them. There will be frustration, anger, and muttering, generally along the lines of "Why do I even bother... this looks terrible... I might as well just stop right now." Please turn off that noisy, no-good critic (whom we all have in our heads). Shut the voice down and keep practicing. Just as you learned to master a hobby, sport, or language, you'll learn to master and enjoy Photoshop restoration and retouching.

There is no magic pill, instant quality button, or make-it-better keystroke. It takes time, dedication, curiosity, and a hint of stubbornness to get past the missteps and misclicks. Every image you work on today teaches you strategy and skills for the image you'll open tomorrow.

IS THIS BOOK RIGHT FOR YOU?

This book is right for you if you love images or work with photographs as a dedicated amateur or full-time professional. You may be a historian, a photographer, a librarian, a teacher, a multimedia artist, a designer, an artist, or the grandparent who wants to share the best photos with the rest of the family. This book addresses salvaging historical images and righting the contemporary images that have gone wrong: the missed exposures, the poor color balance, the busy and distracting background, or the inevitable wrinkle, pimple, or extra pounds that just drive you crazy every time you look at that photo.

This book is *not* for you if you don't have the time, curiosity, and patience to read through the examples, try them out, and then—just as I push my students—take the techniques further by applying them to your own images.

You have three ways to learn the techniques presented in this book:

- By reading the examples and looking at the images.
- By downloading the provided images from the Peachpit website (see the section "Downloading the Images") and, with the book in hand, re-creating our steps.
- By taking the techniques shown here and applying them to your own images. As you work, you'll need to adjust some of the tool or filter settings to achieve optimal results. It is exactly at that moment, when you are working with your own images, that you're really learning how to restore and retouch images.

This is not an introductory book. To get the most out of it, you should be comfortable with the fundamentals of Photoshop, know where the tools are and what they do, and be familiar with common tasks, such as how to activate a layer or save a selection.

THE STRUCTURE OF THE BOOK

This book is divided into three primary areas:

- Improving tone, contrast, exposure, and color
- Removing dust and mold, and repairing damage
- Professional portrait, beauty, and product retouching

In fact, the book is structured in the same way you should work with your images, starting with a brief overview of Photoshop essentials, file organization, and the tools a retoucher needs. It then works through tonal and color correction (the first things to focus on when retouching an image), followed by chapters on dust and damage removal; portrait, product and architectural retouching; and the techniques professional retouchers use in the fashion and glamour business.

Each chapter starts with a brief overview of what will be covered in the chapter and starts with a straightforward example that leads to more advanced examples. You may be tempted to jump to the more advanced sections right away, but we don't recommend it. Our teaching and chapter structure serve the purpose of building up the tools and techniques, and the introductory examples serve as the foundation for the advanced examples. Similarly, the chapters on tonal and color correction serve as the foundation for the portrait and beauty retouching chapters. Do we expect you to read the book from cover to cover? Of course not! Page through the chapters so you can see how the book and the retouching workflow are structured, find examples that are similar to the images you are working on, and then work your way through the book.

★ NOTE Please visit this book's Access Bonus Content page at peachpit.com, where you can download many of the images featured in the book (for instructions on how to access the page, see the section "Downloading the Images"). These images are for your personal use only and should not be distributed by any other means or used to promote any business of any kind.

Numerous professional retouchers, teachers, and photographers have generously shared images and examples, many of which are posted on the Access Bonus Content page. We did feature some images for which we were not able to procure permission to post the files, so those have not been posted on the page. Call us old-fashioned, but we respect international and US copyright laws; the copyright of all images remains with the originator, as noted throughout the book. Please do not email the publisher or us to request images that are not posted. We cannot send them to you. You don't want us to go to jail, do you?

In cases where we didn't have permission to post specific images on the Access Bonus Content page, you can use similar images from your own photo albums or collections to follow along. Although you won't have the exact image we are using in the book, the problems being corrected are universal, so we are sure you'll be able to learn the techniques by working with similar images. After all, we're sure you will be branching out to your own problem files sooner rather than later.

Last but certainly not least, let me introduce my two co-authors, Wayne Palmer and Dennis Dunbar. Wayne is the owner of Palmer Multimedia Imaging and has been doing digital photo restoration for over 20 years and is a photographer in his own right. Dennis Dunbar is the Photoshop magician behind countless movie posters and commercial architectural, product, and glamour images.

We wish you a lot of fun as you bring back image memories and take your contemporary photographs to a higher level.

Best regards,

—Katrin Eismann, Wayne Palmer,
and Dennis Dunbar

DOWNLOADING THE IMAGES

Your purchase of this product in any format includes access to the downloadable images mentioned throughout the book. To access the images:

1. Go to *www.peachpit.com/register.*
2. Sign in or create a new account.
3. Enter this number in the ISBN field: **9780321701015**
4. Click Submit.

You will be taken to your My Registered Products page, where you will find that this book has been added. Click the Access Bonus Content link to go to the page containing the image download links.

Part I

WORKSPACE & WORKFLOW

Chapter 1

EQUIPMENT, INPUT, AND RAW PROCESSING

Before you set off on a well-deserved vacation, we imagine that you plan and prepare. We imagine that you read up on your destination, make sure you have all the required paperwork, pack for the expected weather, and of course make sure that someone will water your plants while you're away so you can fully enjoy your vacation.

Similarly, preparing your work environment, planning workflows, and considering a backup strategy will allow you to enjoy working on restoration and retouching projects and concentrate on the job at hand.

In this opening chapter, we'll cover the following indispensable foundations:

- Workspace and equipment essentials
- Input workflow
- Raw processing
- Backup strategy

Restoration and retouching takes more than being a fast mouse-clicker. Good retouchers understand that the images they are working with are very important to the client, a family member, or the person in the picture. Before you start a retouching project, take a moment to consider that the pixels represent real people and real events—they're more than a collection of dark and light specks of digital information. It's your job to bring back memories from faded, cracked, and damaged originals. This is a weighty responsibility, and keeping that in mind throughout the restoration and retouching process helps you see the image with empathy and care.

WORKSPACE AND EQUIPMENT ESSENTIALS

Your work environment and the tools you work with have a great influence on how enjoyable and efficient your restoration and retouching work will be. Theoretically you could do high-end client work at the local copy shop, but that guy glancing over your shoulder and asking for the model's phone number isn't going to help your concentration one bit.

FIGURE 1.1 Professional retouching area, courtesy of CyanJack in NYC. © *2016 CyanJack*

Your retouching studio or work area is a place you'll be spending a lot of time, so it makes sense to invest the time and money to make it as comfortable and productive as possible. You do not need to remodel your home or build an addition; we're just suggesting you consider a few improvements that can make your workplace a nicer and more efficient place to be.

Environment and Lighting

The retouching environment should be a quiet area away from distractions and foot traffic. A room without windows would be good choice, but we realize that working in a bunker may not be the most appealing idea. Be aware that windows allow the light levels in your work environment to change throughout the day, which will affect your perception of the image. Paint the walls a neutral gray and set up the lighting so that there aren't any reflections showing in the monitor. In FIGURE 1.1, you see a retouching work area that is built into a corner. The L-shaped configuration enables the retoucher to get a lot of work done without having to get up. As you can see in FIGURE 1.2, a daylight-balanced GTI Graphic Technology lightbox (www.gtilite.com) provides a well-illuminated area to study originals and prints. To make the retouching area more focused, keep your bookkeeping, paperwork, and social media distractions on a separate computer.

Furniture

It always amazes us that people will spend thousands of dollars on computer equipment and then put it all on a cheap folding table they found in the basement.

FIGURE 1.2 Viewing prints in controlled light is essential when evaluating prints. © *2016 SVA Digital Photography*

Even worse are some of the rickety chairs people sit in to work on the computer. After a few hours they wonder why their necks or lower backs are so sore. Katrin prefers a chair with armrest support—and as Wayne points out, if you use a chair with arms, the arms must be able to slide under the desk. If the chair's arms keep you away from the desk, you have to reach for the keyboard and mouse. After a few hours of this, you will develop muscle aches. Working on standing desks is gaining in popularity, as the health implications of hours of sitting are not positive. Look for a standing desk that allows you to quickly adjust the height, such as the Varidesk Pro Plus 48.

A good table without harsh edges, preferably one that angles down to the point where your arms rest on the table, and a chair with lower back and arm support are essential retouching equipment. Just think of it: Over the course of a few years, you'll probably replace your computer a few times. How often do you need to replace a good working table and professional chair? Not very often, so making the investment in good furniture that fits you will pay off in health and well being for years to come.

FIGURE 1.3 Before image restoration. Yvonne Lessard (left) and her sister Laura Plante in Saint-Évariste, Québec, Canada in 1964. © *Plante Family Archive*

Speaking of health, you should know that uninterrupted intensive computer use can be bad for your eyes, back, wrists, and more. You can avoid many aches and pains if you watch your posture, vary your computing activities, take frequent breaks, and hydrate. An important tip for retouchers is to use these frequent breaks to focus your eyes on something in the distance. For more information about steps you can take to make your work area and work habits as healthy as possible, please visit www.healthycomputing.com.

As Allen Furbeck told me, "Restoring this image for my friend and colleague Tom Ashe took me about 30 hours. Most of my time was used to carefully adjust dozens of curves, and it required that my eyes remain fresh. I needed to take breaks to avoid straining my eyes" (**FIGURES 1.3** and **1.4**). Please see Chapter 4 to see how Allen restored this image. You need to take breaks and return to your work with a fresh eye.

FIGURE 1.4 After image restoration which included taking breaks. Photo by Grace Rousso © *Plante Family Archive*

Computer Equipment

Adobe has done a fantastic job in developing and releasing Adobe Photoshop CC for both OS X and Windows. So does it matter which computer platform you use? Yes, it does. It should be the operating system that you're most comfortable with. Each operating system has its own interface and ways of managing files, memory, software, and more. Wayne prefers working with Windows, and Katrin and Dennis have a preference for Mac OS X. Thankfully, Photoshop is Photoshop is Photoshop, and the few differences between Photoshop on a Mac and Photoshop on Windows won't alter the skills and techniques you need to know to do restoration or retouching magic.

We're often asked whether you need a desktop computer to do high-end retouching or restoration work or if a laptop will do. Laptops offer tremendous processing power, and just as with a desktop system, you'll need to invest in external hard drives for backup and scratch disks. Most importantly, we recommend that you use an external high-quality color monitor with your laptop when doing color-critical work.

Spending money on computer equipment requires research and planning. If you are about to build a workstation for retouching with Photoshop, consider these variables:

- **CPU speed:** The higher the speed, the faster the computer. Photoshop CC is 64 bit and requires a multicore Intel processor (Mac) or a 2 GHz or faster processor (Windows). Be careful to watch the internal bus speed as well; the fastest CPU (central processing unit) will not produce the performance increases you expect if the internal bus speed, which communicates between the CPU and other system components, such as memory, is slow. Current computers are equipped with multiple cores, and for most users, the increase in performance that more than six to eight cores offers is not worth the increase in cost.

- **RAM:** Photoshop uses RAM (random-access memory) to process image information, and if there is not enough RAM available Photoshop uses hard drive space (referred to as scratch disk) to process the image. RAM is much faster than a hard drive, so the more RAM you have allocated to Photoshop, the better it will run. How much RAM do you need? As much as you can afford! Take into account that you'll often have more than one image open and that as you add layers, your RAM requirements will increase. Adding more RAM to a computer is the easiest way to increase Photoshop's performance. Photoshop shares the RAM that is installed on your computer with the operating system and other applications that are running. So when in doubt, buy more RAM!

  By default, Photoshop allocates 70 percent of the available RAM to Photoshop, which you can increase to 100 percent *if* Photoshop is the only other open application. It is safer to increase the RAM allocation in 5 percent increments, restarting Photoshop and seeing how it performs.

  TIP You can see how efficiently your computer system is running by selecting Efficiency from the status bar at the bottom left of the document window. A reading of less than 100% tells you that the functions you are performing are being written to the scratch disk, which is always slower than working in RAM.

- **Hard drive space:** This is a classic "bigger is better" proposition as long as you are choosing from the highest-performance drives. Photoshop performs better with fast, clean (defragmented) hard drives to write data to. When Photoshop runs out of RAM, you should, given the choice, go with fast drives, preferably SSDs (solid state drives) connected via USB 3.0 or 3.1. Ideally, use one hard drive for the computer operating system and applications, at least one for image file storage, and additional drives as scratch disks.

- **Scratch disks:** The scratch disk is free hard drive space that Photoshop uses as temporary memory after it fills the RAM with image processing. The scratch disk space needs to be unfragmented and free of clutter. Setting the scratch disk to a drive other than the drive that contains your operating system helps optimize the performance of Photoshop and your computer (FIGURE 1.5). A fast scratch disk is very helpful when working on a laptop, which in most cases has only one internal drive. Photoshop supports up to 64 exabytes of scratch disk space on up to four

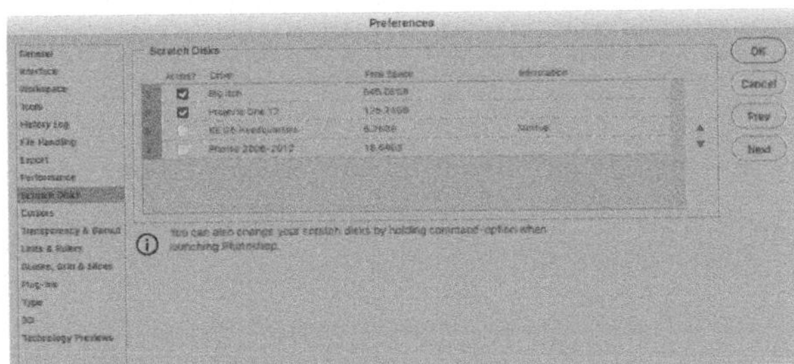

FIGURE 1.5 Set the Photoshop scratch disk to a fast, empty hard drive. Katrin calls her Scratch disk the Big Itch.

volumes, with an exabyte equaling 1 million terabytes, a value none of us have ever reached.

- **Monitor:** This is the visual component of your system, and no matter how fast or sexy your CPU is, if you are not happy with the image your monitor produces, you will not be happy with your workstation. A good monitor will outlast one or two upgrades of your CPU. The only limitation on the effective life of a monitor is the accuracy of the color it produces, which usually degrades in three to five years.

We recommend you use a color-critical graphic-quality display connected to your laptop or desktop computer. Glossy displays, such as those used on the iMac and MacBook Pro, are not conducive to color-critical image editing because they are glossy, which causes distracting reflections and makes them harder to calibrate. We recommend the NEC MultiSync PA242W, PA272W, or PA302W. These are 24", 27", and 30" displays, respectively. All are custom measured at the factory, with measurements hardwired into the display, and they perform optimally with the NEC SpectraView hardware and software calibration.

No matter how good the monitor is, it will not be an accurate representation of your image unless it is calibrated. Fortunately, basic calibration software is available on your operating system. On Windows, you can use Calibrate Display Color (type "calibrate display" in the Search box). On Mac, use the Apple Display Calibrator (System Preferences > Displays > Color). Both programs use the judgment of the person calibrating the monitor in the evaluative process. For more accurate profiling, invest in a monitor calibration system, such as the X-Rite i1Display Pro (**FIGURE 1.6**) or the Datacolor Spyder, to physically

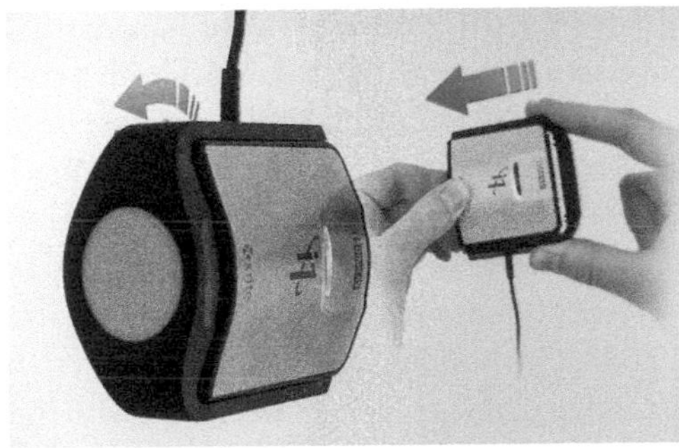

FIGURE 1.6 Calibrating the monitor with an X-Rite i1Display Pro. © *2016 Katrin Eismann*

and accurately calibrate your monitor at least once a month or before starting an important project.

For color management information, we recommend the book *Color Management & Quality Output*, by Tom P. Ashe, a color management and photographic print authority.

+ TIP To have two monitors running on the same computer, your computer needs to be able to support a second video card, or you can replace your existing card with one that supports dual display. Install the new card and use the display settings to determine which monitor will be your primary monitor. You can just drag images and panels back and forth between them.

+ TIP To decrease reflections and distractions, build a monitor hood with black quarter-inch foam core board, Velcro, and black gaffers tape, as shown in **FIGURE 1.7**, or visit www.photodon.com to purchase a monitor hood.

FIGURE 1.7 A homemade monitor hood cuts down on reflections. © *2016 Katrin Eismann*

• **Pressure-sensitive tablet:** An absolute must. A pressure-sensitive tablet lets you work with a stylus, and it feels just like working with a pencil or brush. The harder you push, the thicker the stroke. Wacom is the leader in this technology, and their progressive improvements of these devices continue to be impressive. Wacom tablets range from small (active size 12.6×8.2 inches) to large (19.2×12.5 inches). Most photographers and retouchers work best with the medium (active size 15×9.9 inches) tablets.

• **Backup or archive system:** You should always back up your work, as well as your system settings. This is a discipline that will make you feel very smart when you need the backup (or very stupid if you did not back up your files). Redundant (RAID) or USB 3.0 or 3.1 drives are the best option for backups. We address backup strategy at the end of this chapter.

You should have at least three backups of your image files: desktop, local, and offsite. The desktop backup is the files and hard drives you are currently working on and need quick access to. Local backup includes all files on the desktop hard drives and additional recent (within 6 month) files that are stored on hard drives that may be stored in your office or home. Offsite backup is a comprehensive backup of all your files, stored (you guessed it) either online or offsite; for example, Katrin stores her offsite hard drives in her office in Manhattan. Please see "Backup Strategy" later in this chapter for additional information.

• **Printers:** The quality of inkjet printers is skyrocketing while the costs are nose-diving. The current choice of print media, from high-gloss to roughly textured fine art papers, can add a beautiful note to your images. Before buying a printer, consider the number and size of the prints you'll need to make, because maintaining and calibrating a printer may not be worthwhile if you need only a few prints a year.

INPUT WORKFLOW

You might think that the first step of a restoration project would be to scan or photograph all the original prints or film, but before you start it is best to evaluate the originals and prioritize the task at hand. This is especially important if you are the family archivist who inherited the boxes of old prints, negatives, or slides and now want to scan or photograph the originals to restore and share with your family and friends (**FIGURES 1.8** and **1.9**).

FIGURE 1.8 Take the time to sort boxes of prints. © *2010 Katrin Eismann*

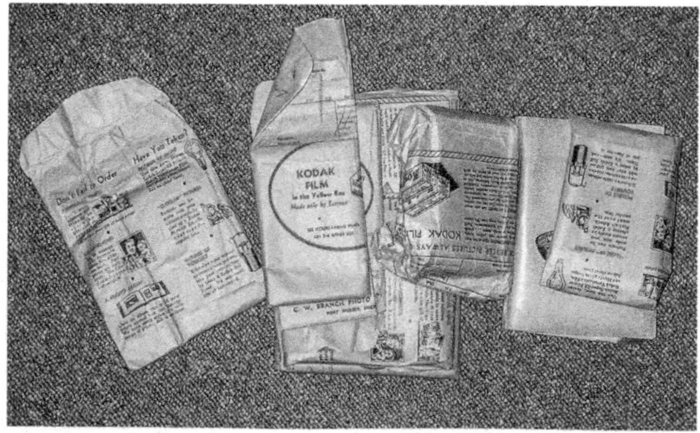

FIGURE 1.9 Consider yourself lucky if you have the original film—so many people throw the filmstrips away. © *2010 Katrin Eismann*

Prioritize Your Time and Effort

Scanning is important, time consuming, and, in our opinion, also very boring. We understand your excitement as you find an old box of prints (**FIGURE 1.10**) and exclaim with the best intentions, "I'm going to scan all these photos and send them to the family!" In our experience, your best intentions will evaporate as the scanning becomes more and more tedious. Start by sorting and prioritizing the images.

Take the time to identify the A, B, and C images, with the A's being the "must input" images: those with the greatest family value or those that you won't have access to for a long time. B images are those that others will appreciate, and C images are those that you want to input but don't necessarily need to restore, print, or share immediately. This rating system can be disregarded when you find those silly or embarrassing gems that are ideal for Throwback Thursday (#TBT) Facebook posts (**FIGURE 1.11**)!

FIGURE 1.10 This jumble of family photos needs to be organized and prioritized before scanning. © *2015 Katrin Eismann*

Scanning priority should go to the following:

- Photos that you have possession of for only a short time. For example, you may be visiting a family member and have limited access to the family photo archive. Use your digital camera or smartphone to photograph the prints, preferably in soft, diffused daylight.
- Fragile originals that are disintegrating and need to be handled with great care. Make sure to capture loose pieces of the prints and then use Photoshop to piece the puzzle back together.
- Originals that include close family members or that can serve as a visual legacy resource when interviewing older family members about family history or ancestry.
- Your most emotionally important images.

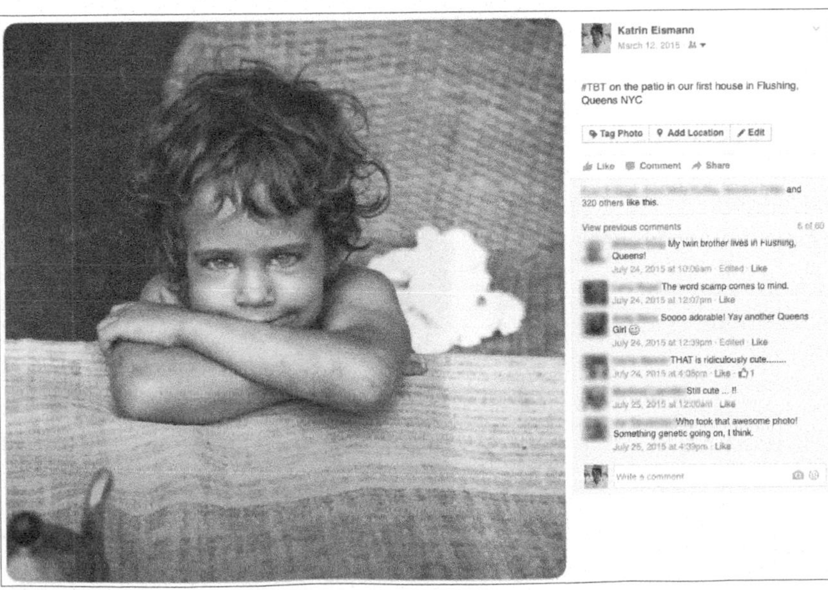

FIGURE 1.11 Sharing Throwback Thursday photos is fun and sometimes embarrassing! © *1959 Alexander P. Eismann*

Scanning Resolution vs. Print Resolution

The nomenclature that scanners and printers use to describe digital information is not identical, which is a potential source of mystery and confusion. Scanner resolution values are in the 1200–6400 samples per inch (spi) or pixels per inch (ppi) range. Photographic printer resolution is based on dots per inch (dpi) and the most common inkjet output resolutions are 240 dpi, 300 dpi, and 360 dpi. 240 dpi works well for inkjet prints on softer, watercolor matte surface papers that have greater dot gain (the amount by which ink spreads), and 300 or 360 dpi works well for the harder, glossier baryta papers, which show less dot gain.

If your final output is destined for offset printing in a magazine or book, the final files will typically be printed at 133 lpi (lines per inch), or at 150 lpi for a book such as this (if you are holding the paper edition right now). For optimal results for offset printing, submit files with twice the number of pixels per inch as the line screen; for example, 266 ppi for a magazine or 300 ppi for a book.

For images that do not require extensive restoration or retouching, scan the original in at 10 to 20 percent larger than final output; this allows for straightening and cropping. For images that are very damaged and require extensive restoration, scan at 50 percent larger than the final output requires. After restoring the higher resolution file, downsize it to the print size; this will also help conceal telltale restoration or retouching artifacts. The biggest possible scan is not always the best scan, as overly large scans are cumbersome to work with and can actually be so detailed that every speck of dust or scratch is faithfully captured, which will make more work for you later on.

To calculate how much resolution you need to scan or capture, use the general guidelines in TABLE 1.1 and the Photoshop New dialog.

To determine the amount of information you need to input for a specific optimal print size, use the New dialog box (**File > New**), enter the Width and Height values in inches or centimeters, enter the Resolution value (FIGURE 1.12), and then change the unit of measurement to pixels to determine the required pixel amounts (FIGURE 1.13).

TABLE 1.1 **Print Resolution**

TYPE OF PRINT	PRINT RESOLUTION IN PIXELS PER INCH
Continuous tone	200 or 400 ppi
Inkjet with matte media	180 or 240 ppi
Inkjet with luster or glossy media	240, 300, or 360 ppi
Weekly magazine	133 lpi — scan in 266 ppi
Glossy magazine or book	150 lpi — scan in 300 ppi

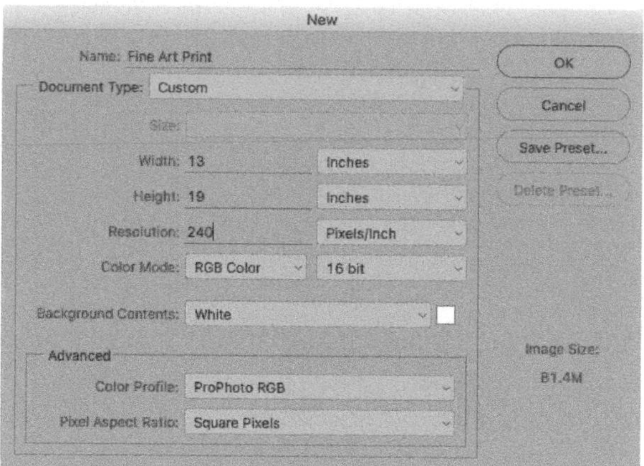

FIGURE 1.12 Photoshop New dialog box set to inches to determine print size and resolution.

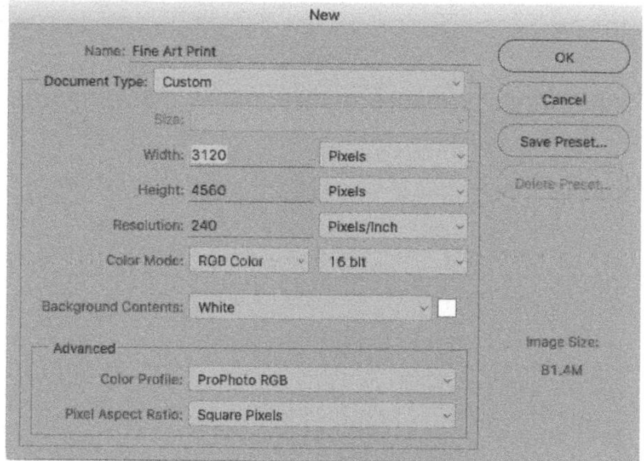

FIGURE 1.13 Photoshop New dialog box set to pixels to determine minimum scanner resolution.

TIP When determining the resolution of the scan, concentrate on the size of the longest side of the image, because the shorter side will fall into place.

How much quality to you really need? The easiest answer would be the highest-quality/biggest file possible. But in all honesty, do you really need to photograph the originals with a full-frame 42 MP (megapixel) digital camera for social media posting? Doubtful. Calculate a reasonable amount of image information, and then use a scanner or camera that can deliver that quality. FIGURE 1.14 shows several input examples of the same file, when viewed at 100 percent in Photoshop.

When printed to scale with identical print resolution, each print will look good with the lower resolution files being used for making smaller print than the higher resolution files. The online scan and smartphone prints are smaller than the high-end camera and scanner files.

CAUTION The size and quality of the original will greatly influence the quality of the final output. A small, scratched, faded print will never make an outstanding large-format fine art print. In fact, over-scanning a textured or highly damaged print will only result in a large file with less-than-useful image information—bigger isn't always better.

How much equipment and space do you have to scan or photograph? Sorting and handling a lot of prints takes space and patience. Break the project into manageable steps—have a reasonable goal to input X number of prints or scans per input session. If space or lack of equipment is a challenge, consider using an online input service such as Legacybox (legacybox.com), addressed later in this chapter, or Scan My Photos (www.scanmyphotos.com).

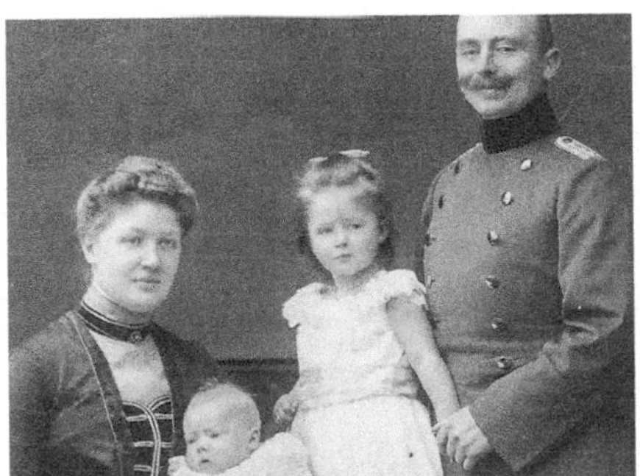

Photographed with an Apple iPhone 6+ (8 MP)

Photographed with the point-and-shoot Sony RX-100 Mark4 (20.1 MP)

Legacybox scan

Photographed with the full-frame Sony Alpha a7R2 (42.4 MP) with a 55mm lens

Scanned with an Epson scanner

FIGURE 1.14 The same antique print photographed with a variety of digital cameras, scanned, and input via an online service.

• When do you need the digital files? It would be great to have all the time in the world, but clients and family seem to want restoration work yesterday. If time is on your side, consider the previously mentioned online input services.

• How delicate are the images? This is a critical evaluation point; delicate originals will never get better over time. Handle them very carefully, preferably with archival white cotton gloves, and store them in a climate- and humidity-controlled environment—meaning get them out of your basement, garage, or attic!

• Are any of the originals wet, moldy, insect infested, or damaged by rodents? This is a critical issue you need to address as soon as humanly possible. Often the random cardboard boxes your family stored photos in are damaging the prints because they release toxic gases or attract rodents (**FIGURE 1.15**). If you cannot get to scanning the photos, please consider placing the prints into archival acid-free boxes, available online via Archival Methods (www.archivalmethods.com) and Gaylord Archival (www.gaylord.com).

FIGURE 1.15 Rodent damage requires that prints be moved into new, clean, acid-free boxes as quickly as possible.

Eradicating Mold, Mildew, and Fungus

The best way to avoid mold, fungus, and mildew problems is to store your photographs in a humidity-controlled environment with a relative humidity of 20 to 50 percent. According to Henry Wilhelm's book *The Permanence and Care of Color Photographs* (Preservation, 1993), available as a free download at www.wilhelm-research.com/book_toc.html, the problem lies in the fact that "gelatin, the major component of the emulsion of films and prints, is unfortunately an excellent nutrient for fungi." To make matters worse, insects are attracted to fungus, and they're more than happy to munch on your valuable photographs too. A strong vinegar smell or a white powdery residue is a telltale sign of an image suffering serious deterioration.

Removing Fungus and Mold

When working with film you may be able to stop the fungus attack by gently cleaning the film with a cotton swab and Kodak film cleaner. Then scan in the film and use the Clone Stamp and healing tools to rid the world of this evil. There is a good chance that fungus has already done its damage, and its removal may not reveal any useful information.

On the other hand, removing mold from a print should be done only by a professional photo conservator because the mold or fungus can grow deeply into the paper fibers. Do not try to wash, clean, or treat original prints unless you can live with the fact that anything you do to the original print might actually damage the paper more than the mold already has. The examples in **FIGURE 1.16** show a variety of damage caused by Superstorm Sandy, which hit the New York City area in late October 2012.

Handling Wet or Damaged Photos

Water damage caused by broken pipes, floods, or storm damage is among the most daunting challenges you may face. Of course, as your home is suffering flooding due to a hurricane or violent storm, your family's safety is your first priority. But when you have a moment, consider these suggestions from the Operation Photo Rescue website:

1. Carefully lift the photos from the mud and dirty water. Remove photos from waterlogged albums, and separate any prints that are stacked together, being careful not to rub or touch the wet emulsion of the photo surface. Remove photos from plastic sleeves in albums as soon as possible.

Cracking

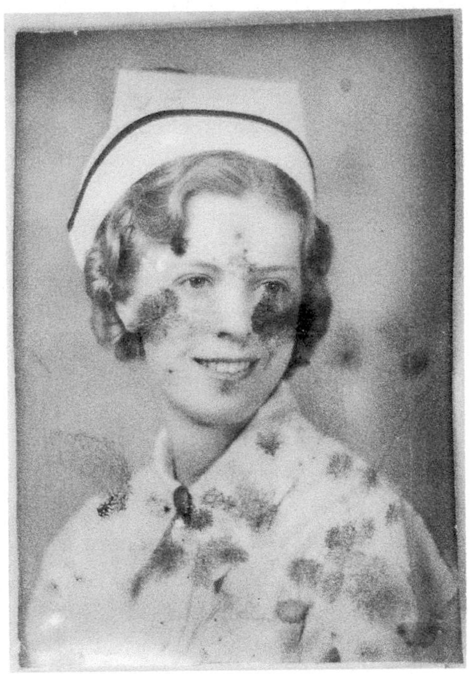
Mold

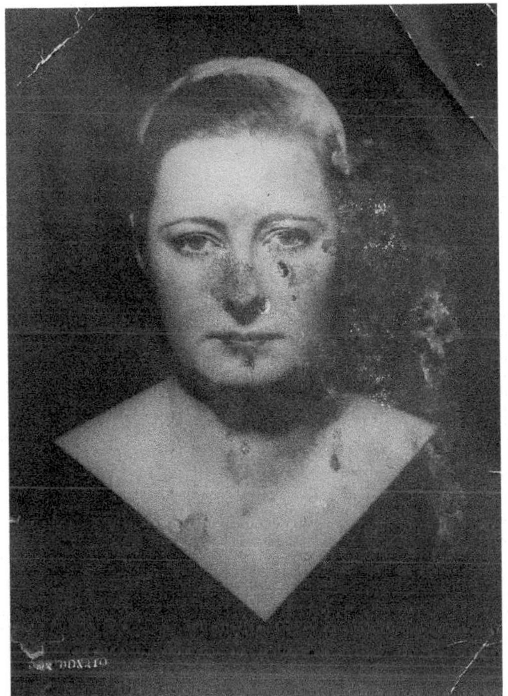
Mold and cracking

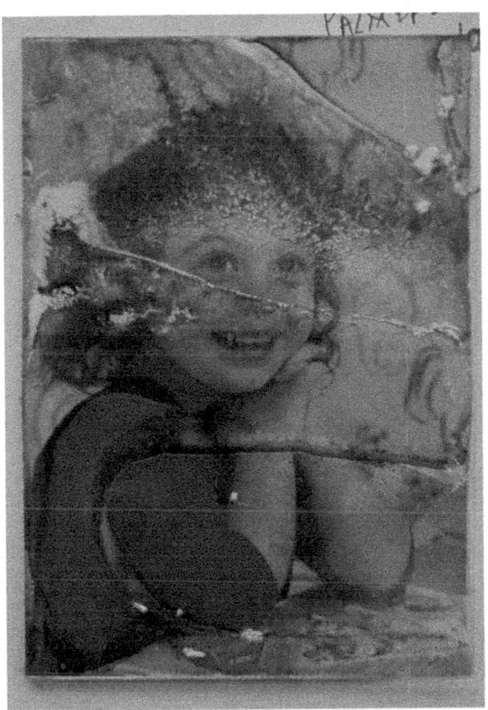
Mold and cracking

FIGURE 1.16 Damaged photos

2. If the prints are very dirty, gently rinse them in clear, cold water to wash away the coarsest dirt. Do not rub the print with anything, including your well-meaning fingers. Be sure to change the water frequently.

3. If you have time and dry space, lay each wet photo face up on any clean blotting paper, such as paper towels. Don't use newspapers or printed-paper towels, as the ink may transfer to the wet photos. Change the blotting paper every hour or two until the photos dry. If possible, do your best to dry prints indoors, as sun and wind will cause photos to curl more quickly.

4. If you don't have time right away to dry the damaged photos, rinse them to remove any mud and debris. Carefully stack the wet photos between sheets of wax paper, and seal them in a Ziploc-type plastic bag. If possible, freeze the photos to inhibit damage. This way, photos can be defrosted, separated, and air-dried later, when you have the time and space to do it properly.

ADDITIONAL TIPS FOR HANDLING WATER-DAMAGED PHOTOGRAPHS

Try to get to flood-damaged photos within two days or they will begin to mold or stick together, making saving them much less likely.

- Begin with photographs for which there are no negatives or for which the negatives are also water damaged.

- Photos in frames need to be saved when they are still soaking wet; otherwise, the photo surface will stick to the glass as it dries and you will not be able to separate it without damaging the photo emulsion. To remove a wet photo from a picture frame, keep the glass and photo together. Holding both, rinse with clear flowing water, using the water stream to gently separate the photo from the glass.

- It is important to note that some historical photographs are very sensitive to water damage and may not be recoverable. Older photographs should also not be frozen without first consulting a professional conservator. You may also want to send any damaged heirloom photos to a professional photo restorer after drying.

Input Options

A flatbed scanner used to be the go-to option for inputting, or digitizing, prints, but with the improvement of digital camera image quality, photographing prints, books, and three-dimensional originals is the more popular choice. But as addressed here, flatbed and film scanners still have their place in the restoration workflow.

Scanning

It is difficult to make a general recommendation on scanners because they vary from very poor to very good and from cheap to expensive. Many restoration artists have a mid-level flatbed scanner that is capable of scanning up to 11×17-inch prints. Look for a scanner that captures at least 12 bits of data, and keep an eye on the optical resolution of the scanner—it should be at least 2400 pixels per inch for scanning prints. We use the Epson Perfection V800 photo color scanner, which boasts a resolution of 6400 ppi for film scanning or 4800 ppi for reflective objects and prints.

If you envision scanning old film, which may be in non-standard formats, consider a scanner that has a transparency adapter option. Be sure that it comes with a variety of film holders for the different possible sizes of film. If you will be retouching newer images captured on film, consider a separate film scanner or look into working with a professional photo lab for sharper, high-bit scans with finer detail. In all honesty, most photographers and image collections are using digital cameras to input their valuable originals, as addressed later in this chapter.

Essential Flatbed Scanning Workflow

Take the time to familiarize yourself with the scanning software that comes with your scanner, and make some test scans to identify the optimal settings for your needs. With an Epson Perfection photo color scanner and the included Epson Scan software, our scanning workflow is as follows:

1. Clean the scanner bed by blowing off any dust or dirt, or use a soft cloth dampened with monitor or glass cleaner to wipe the platen clean. Never spray

ESSENTIAL SCANNING TIPS

- Always start with clean originals and a clean scanner. It is much faster to blow off dust with a Rocket blower or to clean the scanner platen glass than to clean up or dust-bust the digital file later.
- When you're using a flatbed scanner, do not close the lid, which would apply pressure to delicate originals and most likely damage them.
- If an original is too large for the scanner, scan it in pieces and include 20 percent overlap. Then use Photomerge, or layers with layer masks, to blend the parts together. When scanning a large original in sections, always scan all parts in the same orientation to ensure that the tonality and reflectivity remain consistent.
- Avoid applying automatic sharpening during the scanning process, as it is more challenging to restore or retouch overly sharpened files.
- Scan antique originals in RGB, as often one of the channels will yield a good black and white image for further restoration.
- The old adage "Scale up in hardware and scale down in software" still rings true. It is best to capture more image information than required during input, and if a smaller file is needed, use Photoshop to scale the file down. But it is not recommended to scale a smaller file up and expect optimal image quality or results.
- We prefer to scan with lower contrast to ensure that all highlight and shadow details are maintained.

cleaner directly onto the scanner glass, as the liquid may leak into the scanner.

2. Review the scanner software preferences to make sure that the images will be scanned into either the Adobe RGB or ProPhoto color space. For critical scanning projects, create a scanner profile by scanning an IT8 scanner test target and building a scanner-specific color profile.

3. Turn off any automatic sharpening—often called Unsharp Mask—as it is easier to restore or retouch images that are not overly sharpened.

4. Place the original on the scanner bed with the long edge of the print in alignment with the scanner head (FIGURE 1.17). This orientation allows more of the original to be captured with the pure optical resolution of the scanner versus the stepper motor resolution.

5. For highest-quality scans, make high-bit scans (in this example, 48-bit versus 24-bit scans), which will yield high-bit files that have greater tonal information; this is especially important in the delicate highlight and shadow image areas. Scanning high-bit files will require you to save the scan as a TIFF. If you

FIGURE 1.17 Position the image on the scanner with the longer side of the print in alignment with the scan head.

are scanning for social media or basic family email sharing, scanning as a 24-bit file and saving as a JPEG is fine.

6. Upon making a preview scan, make sure that the original is straight and correctly oriented. It takes very little effort to straighten or flip a print on the scanning bed (**FIGURE 1.18**), and it will save you Photoshop time and will result in better scans.

FIGURE 1.18 Straightening a print on the scanner takes a split second and results in higher-quality scans.

7. Adjust the histogram so that the black and white points are not clipped (**FIGURE 1.19**) by moving the black point and white point sliders just to the outside of their respective histograms areas. Clipped highlights or shadows are image areas in which the image information has been forced to pure white or black, and no amount of Photoshop magic can restore image information that was not captured to begin with.

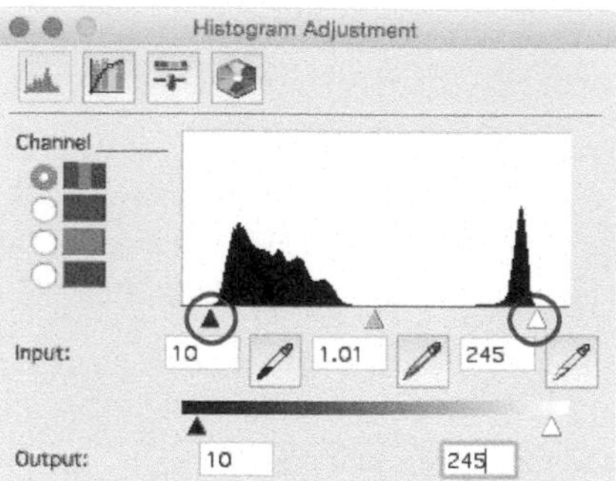

FIGURE 1.19 Moving the black point and white point to just where the histogram starts.

8. Before doing the final scan, check the resulting file size. Base the desired file size on the amount of restoration work the image needs and the final output size (see the advice on page 10, earlier in this chapter).

9. Make the final scan, and save the file before removing the original from the scanner bed.

Depending on your scanning software, you may opt to apply color correction, descreening, or dust removal. We have had good results with automatic color correction (**FIGURE 1.20**) on faded or sepia prints and with descreening offset-printed originals (**FIGURE 1.21**). We cover descreening in more detail in the Chapter 5 section "Reducing Offset Moiré." Note that color correction of film scans in which the dye couplers in the film have burst, causing extreme or uneven color casts, is much more challenging. Please see Chapter 4 for techniques to improve and correct color.

FIGURE 1.20 Test the automatic color correction results for your scanner. © *Wiedersheim Family Archive*

Scanning without descreening

Scanning with descreening

FIGURE 1.21 The descreening option may be helpful for quick or low-resolution work, but descreening may blur important details. © *Tom P. Ashe*

FIGURE 1.22 SilverFast's iSRD scans the image in RGB and infrared and then compares the scans to remove the dust and damage. © *Mark Segal,* Scanning Workflows with SilverFast 8, SilverFast HDR, Adobe Photoshop Lightroom, and Adobe Photoshop

Third-Party Scanning Software

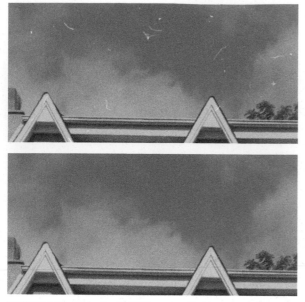

Many professionals use SilverFast, a third-party scanning software that allows for refined scanning control and includes very sophisticated infrared dust and scratch removal (iSRD). iSRD is a very efficient dust and debris remover in which the scanner scans the original twice—once in RGB and once in infrared—to capture the dust, damage, and scratches. The software then compares the RGB and infrared scans and removes the damage via an automatic cloning and healing algorithm while maintaining image detail (FIGURE 1.22). The SilverFast descreening controls are very sophisticated and produce excellent results (FIGURE 1.23).

The learning curve of SilverFast requires dedication, but it can be better managed with the excellent PDF book *Scanning Workflows with SilverFast 8, SilverFast HDR, Adobe Photoshop Lightroom, and Adobe Photoshop*, by Mark Segal.

Gang Scanning

Scanning similar originals at the same time can reduce print-handling time, which in turn can reduce potential damage. Place the originals on the scanner with approximately half an inch between each original, and make one large scan (FIGURE 1.24).

FIGURE 1.23 SilverFast descreening options allow for greater control. © *Mark Segal,* Scanning Workflows with SilverFast 8, SilverFast HDR, Adobe Photoshop Lightroom, and Adobe Photoshop

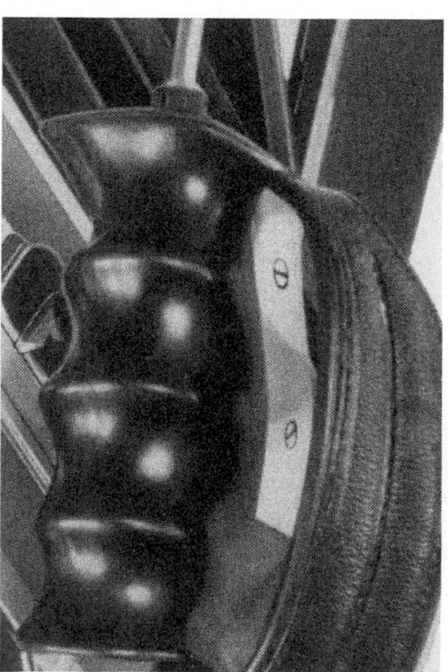

Without descreening

With descreening

FIGURE 1.24 Scanning similar images at once saves time and reduces handling.

To have Photoshop automatically separate the image files:

1. Choose **File > Automate > Crop and Straighten Photos**.

2. Save and name each file with the family or client name and a unique sequential number (FIGURE 1.25).

FIGURE 1.25 Photoshop can automatically separate the gang scan into individual files.

Digital Cameras

We find ourselves scanning prints less and less because scanning can introduce glare and reflections, which are nearly impossible to retouch. In many cases, antique originals are often too large, fragile, or three-dimensional to scan with a standard flatbed scanner. Use a digital camera to input delicate and reflective originals. In FIGURE 1.26, you see Operation Photo Rescue volunteers cataloging, inputting, and restoring a wide variety of prints damaged during Hurricane Sandy.

FIGURE 1.26 Operation Photo Rescue volunteers hard at work. *© 2013 Katrin Eismann*

Museums and historical collections are working with high-resolution medium-format cameras (30–100 megapixels) to digitize their sensitive artwork and archives. Scott Geffert, senior imaging manager at the Metropolitan Museum of Art, says, "The adoption of objective capture practices (verified exposure, calibration, resolution, and other image technical attributes) has enabled the museum to ensure quality and consistency of reproductions using any number of camera brands. Artwork reproduction imaging practice is based upon "scene-referred" imaging, where accuracy to the original scene is the goal, as opposed to the more common "output-referred" or pleasing film-like renditions built into most cameras and raw processing software. Scene-referred images are ideal for long-term archiving and can be repurposed to any current and future medium."

Regional practices such as the US FADGI (Federal Agency Digitization Guidelines Initiative) and the European Metamorfoze Preservation Imaging Guidelines are currently moving together toward a unified ISO (International Standards Organization) standard. The Metropolitan Museum of Art is leading the way in this standardization effort.

Creating a reliable workflow for input can be based on a tripod with a horizontal extension arm, a copy stand or as Katrin uses a Quadra-Pod™ forensic copy stand as seen in **FIGURE 1.27**.

35mm digital cameras are a fabulous copying solution, with full-frame cameras available for $1500 and (of course) seemingly countless prosumer cameras with interchangeable lenses bragging 20-plus megapixel sensors; both types can capture amazing detail and image quality. **FIGURE 1.28** shows a sophisticated copy stand setup, with the target ensuring that the camera is level and calibrated.

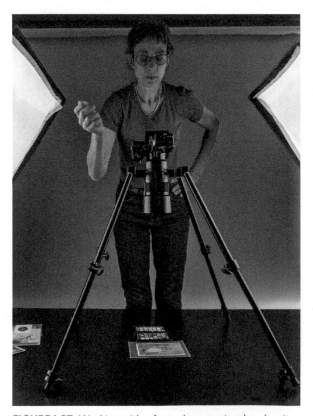

FIGURE 1.27 Working with a forensic copy stand makes it very easy to copy antique prints. © *2016 Marko Kovacevic*

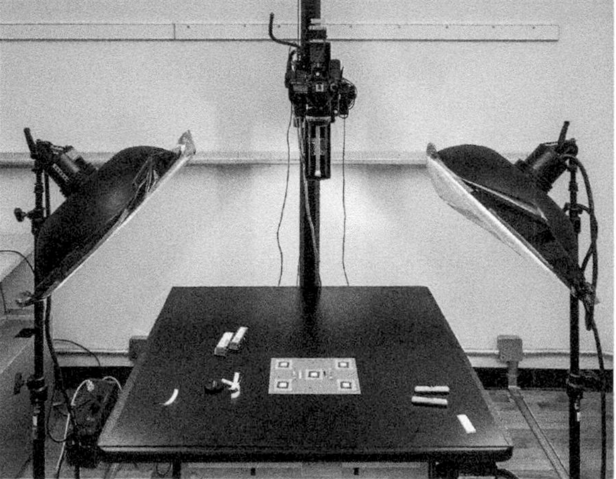

FIGURE 1.28 Professional copy stand with GoldenThread calibration target. © *2013 Katrin Eismann*

Depending on the image size required, you can shoot originals with a smartphone, a point-and-shoot, or a 35mm camera. For social media posting, a smartphone is certainly adequate. For prints smaller than 8×10 inches, a good point-and-shoot provides plenty of information. A higher-quality camera with an outstanding lens captures the information to do the finest restoration work. In fact, many of the examples featured in this book were digitized with a digital camera rather than scanned.

To ensure consistent results with digital copy work, do the following:

- Use a soft, diffused light source or two lights that are positioned at a 45-degree angle to the original.
- Make sure that the light evenly illuminates the original. Measure the light at the four corners and center of the print using a light meter, and adjust the light accordingly.
- Use either a copy stand (which looks like the column of an old enlarger, with a tripod head that allows the camera to point straight down) or a four-legged forensic copy stand, which is what Katrin uses.
- Make sure that the camera is parallel to the original by placing a small bubble level on the camera back and adjusting the camera angle to level.
- Include a known reference in each shot, such as a Kodak 21-step wedge or the edge of an X-Rite Color Checker (FIGURE 1.29).

FIGURE 1.29 Include in the image a standard color reference, such as the X-Rite Color Checker.

- Set the camera to a low ISO, such as 100 or 200, shoot in the raw file format, and set the camera white balance appropriately. In fact, almost any white balance setting is better than Automatic, as using a fixed white balance will make the digital copy work more consistent and easier to color correct.
- If possible, use a macro lens or a 50mm or higher focal length lens.
- Test your lens to see at which f-stop it is sharpest; in most cases, that will be around f/11. There is rarely an advantage to shooting at f/16 or f/22, as those f-stops do not ensure that the image will be sharper—in fact, they might make the image less sharp than f/8 or f/11.
- To reduce camera shake, use a cable or a digital release, shoot tethered to operate the camera from your computer, or as a last resort, use the camera's self-timer to take the picture. If you are using a larger, heavier DSLR, see if using the mirror lock-up feature helps reduce camera vibration.

A little bit of care and attention to detail before using your camera as a scanner will pay off a great deal later. It is very irritating to finish a lot of copy work only to see that the images are soft, unevenly lit, or crooked.

TIP For additional information on using your camera as a scanner to input prints and film, please visit www.dpbestflow.org/camera/camera-scanning and read Mark Segal's article on camera scanning at luminous-landscape.com/articleImages/CameraScanning.pdf

Outsourcing

Admittedly, scanning or doing copy work is not our favorite pastime. If time allows, gathering and sending your originals to Scan My Photos, Legacybox, or a local scanning service may be a good option.

Scanning Services

We submitted a wide variety of originals to Legacybox—including black & white and color prints, slides, and tintypes (historical photos that were captured as a positive on thin sheets of tin)—and in about six weeks received the originals back, along with digital files (FIGURE 1.30). Note that we sent the box and paid for the service as a normal customer. We received no special service or treatment.

FIGURE 1.30 Working with Legacybox is straightforward. © 2015 Katrin Eismann

Compared to the process of making our own scans (FIGURE 1.31), in our opinion the Legacybox process took too long, and the scans were too high in contrast and also too small—each print scan JPEG was about 2 MB, and we could print them as 5×7-inch prints at 240 ppi (FIGURE 1.32). The medium-format film scan JPEGs came in at 5 to 6 MB, and we could print them at 8×10 inches at 300 ppi.

Local Services

Having a service bureau or professional photo lab do copying, scanning, and printing for you can be a good alternative, especially when you are just starting out and need to stagger your equipment expenses. Working with a service bureau also gives you access to high-end equipment and services that you may need only once in a while.

FIGURE 1.31 Scanning yourself allows you to control tonality and file size.

FIGURE 1.32 Legacybox scans are fine for making small prints or for social media sharing.

Ask your local camera or photo store if they offer scanning or printing services. I took a framed print to Ernst Camera Shoppe in Port Huron, Michigan, and had it scanned and duplicate prints made for family members (FIGURE 1.33). When I picked up the print, the owner proudly pulled out the first edition of this book—how sweet is that!

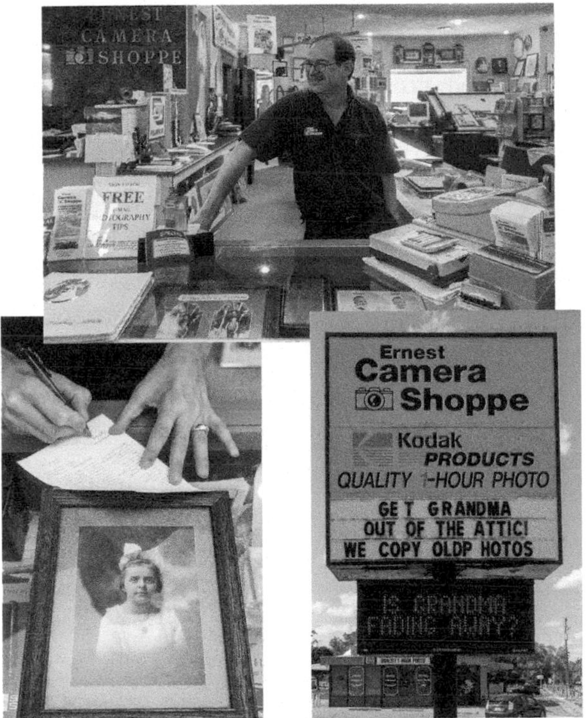

FIGURE 1.33 Working with a local camera store is a great way to reduce equipment costs. © *2015 Katrin Eismann*

RAW PROCESSING

Countless online tutorials and many books address working with Adobe Camera Raw (ACR) and Adobe Photoshop Lightroom to process JPEG, TIFF, and raw files. For in-depth and trusted information, we rely on Martin Evening, Julieanne Kost, Peter Krogh, and Rob Sylvan for best practices and comprehensive workflow recommendations. With the caveat that we can dedicate only a few pages to raw processing, we will share the essential skills and tools to use to process both scanner files and raw files so that you bring the best file into Photoshop for additional restoration or retouching.

ACR and Lightroom are powerful tools that complement Photoshop's greatest assets: layers, masks, filters, and precise selections. Use Adobe Bridge with ACR or Lightroom to organize your files and folders; apply primary global image corrections such as straighten, crop, tonality, color, and contrast; apply local corrections such as dust or blemish removal; or darken or lighten image areas with a gradient.

The biggest advantage of ACR or Lightroom over Photoshop is that they are "parametric image editors," meaning that they save the changes you apply to an image in its XMP (extensible metadata platform) file without ever changing the actual image file. Photoshop, however, is a pixel editor. When using Photoshop, you are truly working on the rendered file and changing actual image information. The advantages of parametric image editing (PIE) are that you can make changes more quickly and have the ability to undo changes, even long after you quit the application.

We understand that more and more people are using ACR and Lightroom for their image processing, but when it comes to pixel-level restoration or retouching, Photoshop is still king or queen of the hill.

When working with scanner files or camera files, we start our image processing in ACR or Lightroom to straighten and correct color, contrast, and tonality, as addressed in the following step-by-step tutorials.

Katrin is a total Lightroom aficionado but we know that many restoration artists and designers use Adobe Bridge to manage their files and therefore we have opted to show you raw processing with Bridge and ACR. Lightroom's image-processing engine is exactly the same as ACR's, albeit with a different interface; we are sure that savvy Lightroom users will be able to follow along.

Processing Scanner Files

The primary goal is to create a tonal- and color-corrected file that you can then take into Photoshop for additional restoration. In ACR, you can process one or many files simultaneously, or, if the scans are very similar, you can select all the images and the change you apply to the active file will automatically be applied to all selected files.

ch1_scan_1.jpg
ch1_scan_2.jpg
ch1_scan_3.jpg

1. In Bridge, select all three files and choose **File > Open in Camera Raw** or press Cmd-R/Ctrl-R.

2. Starting with the topmost image, use the Straighten tool to draw along the bottom edge of the image (**FIGURE 1.34**), dragging from the leftmost side of the line to the rightmost side to straighten the image.

+ TIP ACR can be thrown off by large unimportant areas in the image, such as image borders or cardboard that images were mounted on. Therefore, we recommend that you straighten and crop the image in ACR before applying color or tone corrections.

3. Use the crop handles to refine the crop, and click the Hand tool to accept the crop.

4. Repeat steps 2 and 3 for the remainder of the images to refine the crop for each image.

5. Now that each image is straight and cropped, it's time to apply color and tonal corrections. In the filmstrip, select all three images. Click the topmost image, and Shift-click the bottom image.

Notice that the top image has a blue line around it, meaning it is the active image, whereas the other images are highlighted. Any change you apply to the active image will simultaneously be applied to all active images.

FIGURE 1.34 Straighten and crop the image before applying global processing.

6. To neutralize the brown color cast, select the White Balance tool and click an area that you think could be white. In this example, the bow on the left woman and the man's shirt are good candidates to have originally been white. Click once on either the bow or the shirt to remove the color cast (FIGURE 1.35).

7. Take a look at the histogram. Notice that the primary information is in the center and that there is no true shadow or highlight information, a classic symptom of old, faded, low-contrast images.

When working with old prints, you will notice a great loss of contrast in the original image, created when the shadow areas become lighter and the lighter areas become darker.

8. Click the Auto menu (FIGURE 1.36), and ACR will set the dark and light points and adjust contrast and exposure.

9. In some cases, ACR may add a bit too much pop for historical images, so we recommend moving the

FIGURE 1.35 Use the White Balance tool to neutralize color casts.

FIGURE 1.36 Starting the image corrections by clicking Auto often creates very acceptable results, and it's a time saver!

Exposure slider slightly to the left and zeroing out the contrast correction by typing 0 (zero) into the Contrast field.

10. Depending on the original and your subjective taste, reduce the Vibrance or Saturation slider to –20 to –30 to remove unwanted brown/sepia tone (**FIGURE 1.37**).

★ NOTE With monochrome-toned images, adjusting the Vibrance or Saturation sliders creates similar results. When working with color images, especially ones with skin tones, use Vibrance to refine image saturation, as it automatically keeps skin tones from being changed.

11. Now that all three images are acceptable in terms of color, contrast, and tonality, take a moment to inspect each image and crop and fine-tune the Basic tab parameters as needed (**FIGURE 1.38**).

12. Continue to the following section to learn our recommendations for saving ACR-processed files, or click Done to automatically write the changes to the XMP metadata and exit ACR.

FIGURE 1.37 Carefully adjust the Exposure, Contrast, and Vibrance settings to best render the original look of the antique image.

FIGURE 1.38 Crop and refine each image as needed.

Saving and Renaming Files in ACR

After correcting scans in ACR and returning them to Bridge, you could open that TIFF or JPEG file and do the finer restoration work. But we don't recommend that, as it is always better to work on a duplicate file that you've saved into a work in progress (WIP) folder.

After processing images in ACR, click Save Image (in the lower-left corner of the ACR interface) to save a separate version of the file with a new name—one that has WIP after the original scan name. Select TIFF from the Format menu. For less important projects, we save TIFFs using Adobe RGB (1998) as the color space and 8 Bits/Channel as the bit depth; but for the most critical projects, we use ProPhoto RGB and 16Bits/Channel as the Color Space settings (FIGURE 1.39).

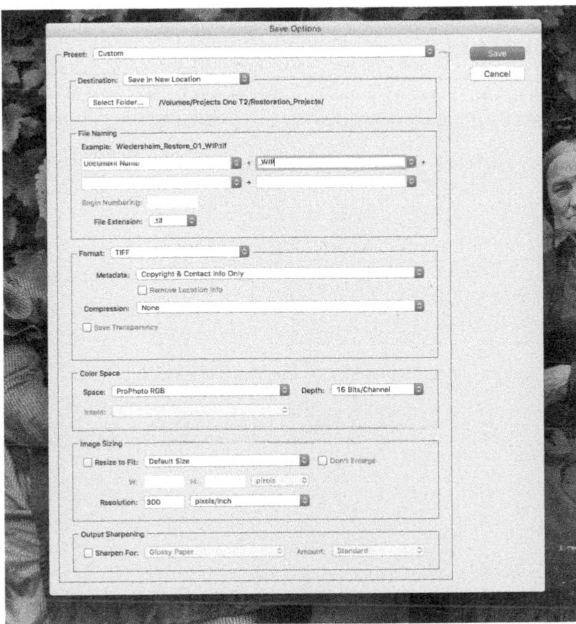

FIGURE 1.39 Save the images as TIFF files to create new files to restore in Photoshop.

Synchronizing ACR settings

The more you work with ACR, the more you'll discover that excellent image processing on one image would look great on other images. To synchronize or apply ACR settings from one image to others within ACR, follow these steps:

1. In the ACR filmstrip, click the best-processed image. Then press Cmd-A/Ctrl-A to select all the images.

2. In the upper-right corner of the ACR filmstrip, select Sync Settings from the Filmstrip panel menu.

3. In the Synchronize dialog box, select a subset from the Subset menu, or select and deselect the options you wish to apply to the other images (FIGURE 1.40). In the example shown here, Katrin opted to deselect Crop, as each image required a different crop.

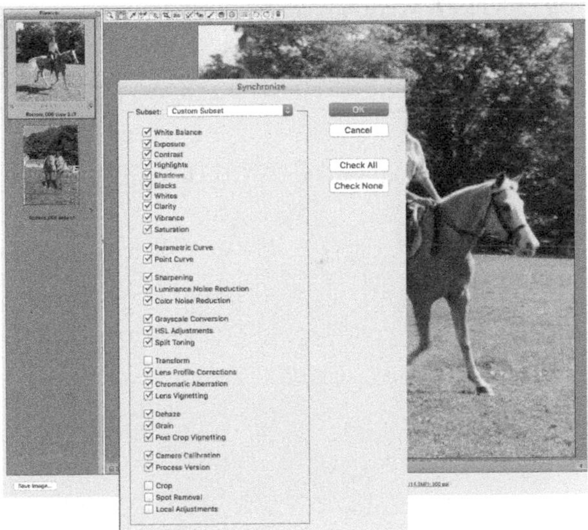

FIGURE 1.40 Synchronizing ACR adjustments with two or many images to speed up image processing.

4. You may need to review the applied changes to each image and refine ACR as needed.

5. Click OK to update the other images, and either Save and rename the files or click Done to return to Bridge.

Synchronizing ACR settings and processing is very helpful to speed up your image workflow.

Synchronizing ACR settings in Bridge

ACR never changes the file, and it writes the adjustments to an XMP sidecar file, which you can take advantage of to quickly apply ACR adjustments to a great number of images without even opening ACR!

ch1_tintype_01.jpg
ch1_tintype_02.jpg
ch1_tintype_03.jpg
ch1_tintype_04.jpg
ch1_tintype_05.jpg
ch1_tintype_06.jpg

1. Select one representative image that is similar to the other images, and use ACR to adjust it (**FIGURE 1.41**). Click Done to exit ACR.

FIGURE 1.41 Use ACR to process a representative image.

2. In Bridge, Ctrl-click/right-click the adjusted image, and select Develop Settings > Copy Settings (**FIGURE 1.42**).

3. Select the similar images, Ctrl-click/right-click, and select Develop Settings > Paste Settings (**FIGURE 1.43**) to bring up the Paste Camera Raw Settings dialog box, which is exactly the same as the Synchronize dialog box. Select or deselect settings, and click OK.

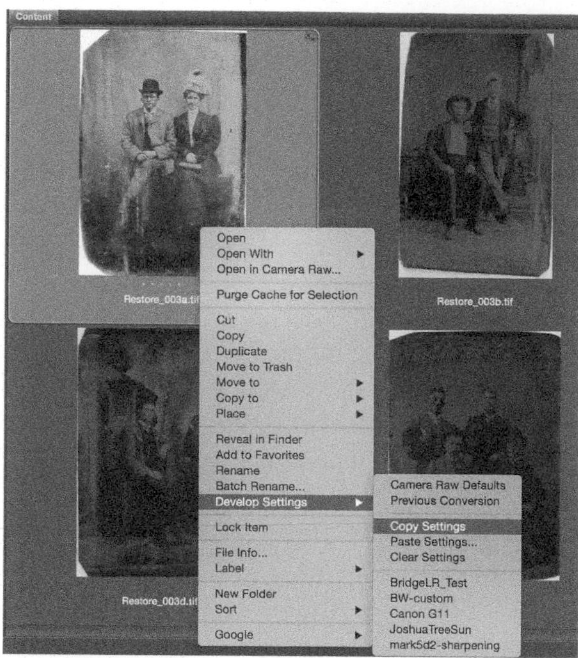

FIGURE 1.42 Copy the Develop settings.

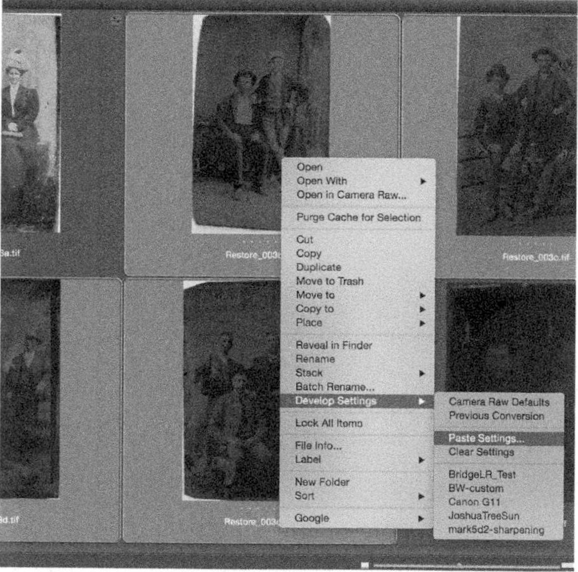

FIGURE 1.43 Select similar images and paste the Develop settings.

In the blink of an eye, the images will be adjusted with the pasted settings. If needed, select any images that may need further refinement, and open and process them in ACR, as we show in the following step.

4. In our example, one tintype of two young men was lightened a bit too much. In Bridge, select just that image, press Cmd-R/Ctrl-R to open ACR, and reduce the Exposure correction and straighten out the image (FIGURE 1.44).

FIGURE 1.44 After pasting the Develop settings, fine-tune image-specific settings.

Syncing and copying and pasting settings are great ways to speed up your workflow. If you need to get back to the original file, in Bridge Ctrl-click/right-click the adjusted image and select Develop Settings > Clear Settings.

Processing Digital Camera Files

Processing digital camera files is the moment when you take the original camera files and interpret them to best reflect your photographic intent, either objectively, by using a known reference, or subjectively, by adjusting the image to your personal standards. In the following section, we process some digital copy work and also a portrait to introduce additional capabilities within ACR.

Processing Digital Copy Work

When you're doing digital copy work, we recommend including a known color reference, as in FIGURE 1.45, where Katrin included the grayscale section of the X-Rite ColorChecker. Whether you're working on location (FIGURE 1.46) or in the studio (FIGURE 1.47), including an X-Rite ColorChecker in an establishing shot provides a known reference that you can use to build a camera profile or, in conjunction with the ACR White Balance tool, to bring the image into a known neutral state.

FIGURE 1.45 Include a known standard with copy work.

FIGURE 1.46 The X-Rite ColorChecker Passport Photo should be illuminated with the same light as the subject, but for white balance purposes it doesn't even need to be in focus. © *2014 Katrin Eismann*

FIGURE 1.47 Use an X-Rite ColorChecker to record the color temperature of your studio lights. © *2014 Katrin Eismann*

 **ch1_copywork.dng**

Let's practice using the color reference in the following example (FIGURE 1.48).

1. Open the *copywork.dng* file in ACR, and select the White Balance tool. Click the second square from the right (FIGURE 1.49). It is important to use the second square because that is the "white with detail" swatch on which Thomas Knoll, co-inventor of Adobe Photoshop and ACR, bases an accurate white balance.

2. Select the Straighten tool, and drag along the bottom edge of the image. Then use the crop handles to bring the crop in, to frame the image. At this point you can crop out the X-Rite ColorChecker, although many restoration artists leave it to control the quality of the print output. Click the Hand tool to accept the crop (FIGURE 1.50).

3. Click Auto.

FIGURE 1.48 Before and after ACR adjustments

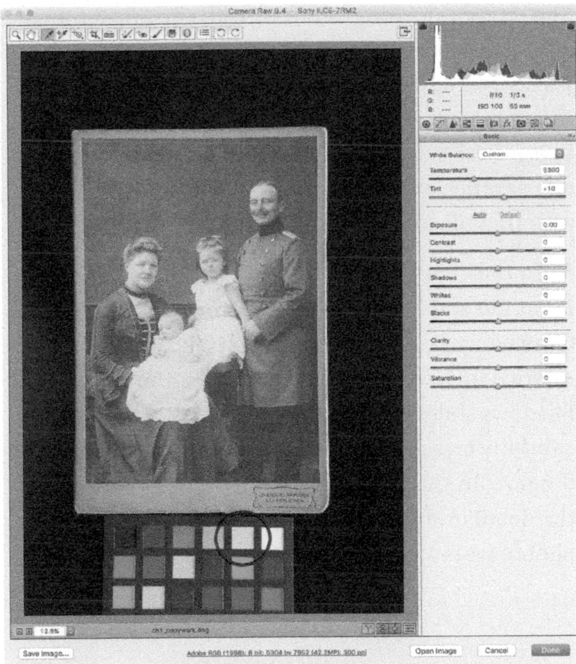

FIGURE 1.49 Use the White Balance tool on the second white square.

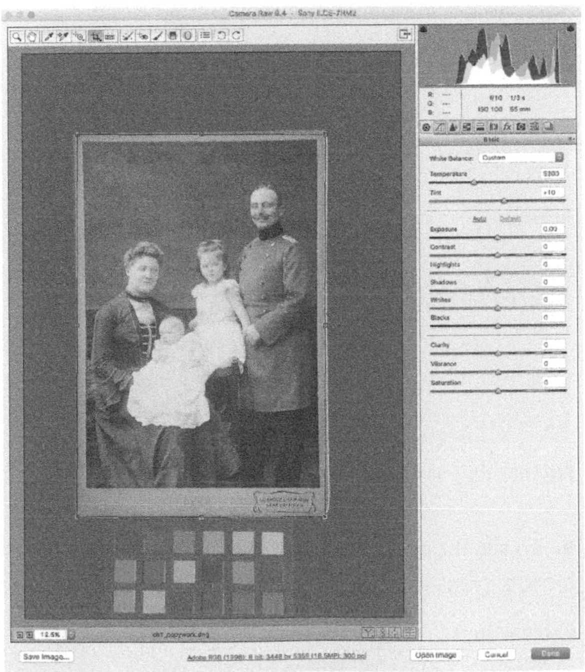

FIGURE 1.50 Straighten and crop the image.

This time we'll take a closer look at adjusting the Basic tab settings to refine the image processing.

Take a look at the image and notice that it is a bit flat, without rich shadows. Now look at the histogram; notice that the leftmost area—the blacks and shadows—don't contain a meaningful amount of image information (FIGURE 1.51). Without darker shadows or, as some people would say, rich blacks, an image seems to float off the surface and lacks the visual guts more commonly referred to as contrast or punch. Considering that this is an old print of a loving family scene (we know it is loving because the image is of Katrin's great grandparents with her grandmother as a young girl), the shadows don't need to go to pure black, but deeper, richer shadow tones will improve the overall image.

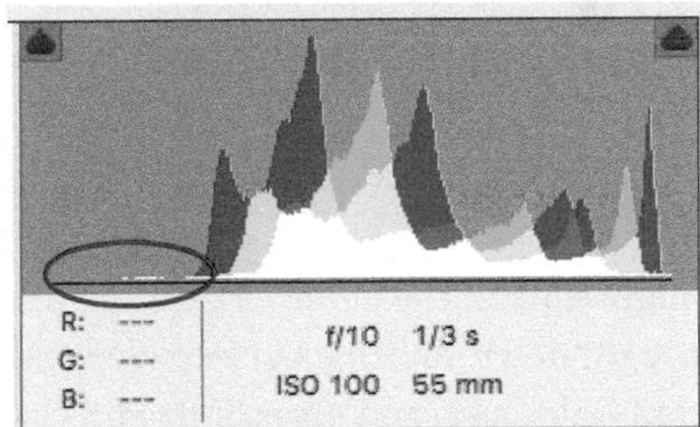

FIGURE 1.51 Study the histogram to understand image tonality.

4. To deepen the shadows and darker areas, drag the Shadow slider to the left; since this example is so flat, we moved the Shadow slider all the way to –100.

5. Click in the Blacks field, and press Shift and tap the Down Arrow key to change the value in ten-point increments. In this example, six taps made the image look much better.

6. To see a progress comparison, tap the Q key or click the small split view icon (FIGURE 1.52). Continue tapping Q to cycle through additional view options.

FIGURE 1.52 Compare your progress by tapping the Q key.

7. The highlights in the children's white dresses need to be brought down to bring back some detail. Click in the Highlight field, and press Shift and tap the Down Arrow key three times to move the highlights down to –79 (FIGURE 1.53).

FIGURE 1.53 Reducing highlight values to restore detail in the white clothing

The image is looking better already. To add a bit more snap or contrast, you could either adjust the Contrast value in the Basic tab or use the dedicated Tone Curve tab, which is what we recommend. Interestingly, these two curve controls are independent of one another, meaning you can adjust one without affecting the other.

8. In the Tone Curve tab, you could either use the Point tab and select Medium Contrast from the Curve menu or, for more control, click the Parametric tab. In the Parametric tab use the Blacks and Shadows sliders to darken the shadow area, and then carefully increase the highlights to create a modified S-curve. In this image, it is important to maintain the detail in the children's clothing and not force the lighter areas areas to paper white (FIGURE 1.54).

FIGURE 1.54 Refine the image with parametric curves.

9. To see the effect that just the curves adjustment is having, press Cmd-Option-P/Ctrl-Alt-P.

Curves in ACR, Lightroom, and Photoshop are tremendously powerful; entire books, classes, workshops, and lectures have been dedicated to working with curves. We work with curves throughout the upcoming chapters.

10. Select the Detail tab to see whether editing Noise Reduction settings is effective. In this example, even dragging the Luminance slider all the way to 100 does not yield meaningful results—and our rule of thumb is "if a control isn't helping an image, then using it is hurting it." Therefore, zero out the Luminance and Color sliders, and move on to the HSL/Grayscale tab.

11. To reduce the overall sepia color cast, click the Saturation tab and, rather than trying to guess which colors make up a color cast, click the Targeted Adjustment tool in the toolbar. Select Saturation or press Cmd-Option-Shift-S/Ctrl-Alt-Shift-S (**FIGURE 1.55**). On the studio backdrop, drag downward or to the left to reduce the sepia; we would leave a hint of the color, as shown in **FIGURE 1.56**.

FIGURE 1.55 Access the Saturation Targeted Adjustment tool.

FIGURE 1.56 Reduce the saturation of the sepia color cast.

For this image example, we will jump over Spilt Toning, as adding toning is a creative interpretive decision that can better be added after the restoration work is complete.

12. In the Lens Corrections tab, select the Profile tab and make sure that Enable Lens Profile Corrections is selected. In the Color tab, select Remove Color Aberration (**FIGURE 1.57**). The Manual tab corrections are very useful but are best used for architectural, landscape, or geometric images; for images with people or no distinct linear reference, they can be skipped over.

FIGURE 1.57 Check that the lens corrections are being applied.

At this point, the image looks very good and you can either click Done to return to Bridge, which saves the ACR settings with the image, or use Save Image to save a TIFF that we'll clean up. We'll continue sharing information and tips on working with ACR in the following section and as we process a contemporary portrait.

+ TIP Press Cmd-Option-P/Ctrl-Alt-P repeatedly to preview the effect that an individual ACR panel is having on your image.

ACR Effects

The Effects tab contains controls for Dehaze, Grain, and Post Crop Vignetting—all useful controls when used judiciously. Dehaze removes aerial and perspective haze and adds a hint of contrast; it's not recommended for antique images that should remain true to their original character. Grain and vignetting are also useful but are best applied after restoration or retouching work is complete. Adding grain is addressed in the Chapter 5 section "Returning Image Texture," and vignetting is covered in Chapter 7.

Camera Calibration

The Camera Calibration tab offers tremendous controls; it is divided into three sections:

- Process determines which Adobe Camera Raw engine is used to develop the images, with the most recent being the best choice.
- Camera Profile determines initial color and tone rendering (FIGURE 1.58). It is similar to, in the days when you bought a roll of film, choosing a color negative or a slide file with more or less contrast and saturation, as best suited for your subject and lighting conditions. When you create custom profiles, they show up at the bottom of the Camera Profile list.

★ NOTE Different file formats, camera bodies, and scanners will show different camera profiles in the Name menu in the Camera Calibration tab.

- The Shadows and Primary sliders allow you to fine-tune a camera profile and shift colors creatively.

TRY IT Build your own camera color profile by photographing an X-Rite ColorChecker Passport Photo in raw, saving the file as a DNG (Digital Negative file format), and using the free ColorChecker Passport Photo software to build a camera- and lighting-specific camera profile (FIGURE 1.59). This is a very straightforward process and recommended if you are shooting many images in similar lighting.

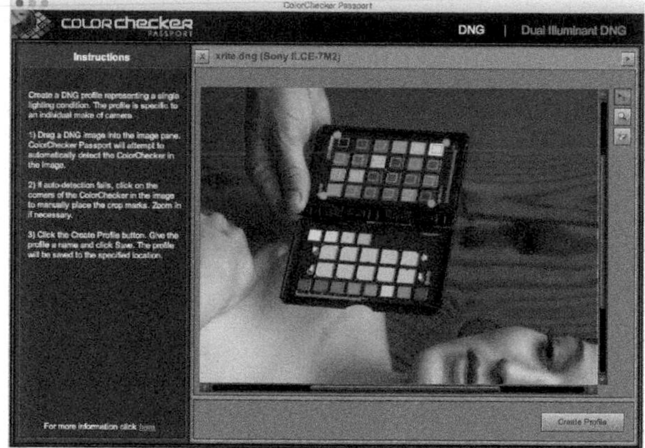

FIGURE 1.59 Building a camera profile is straightforward.

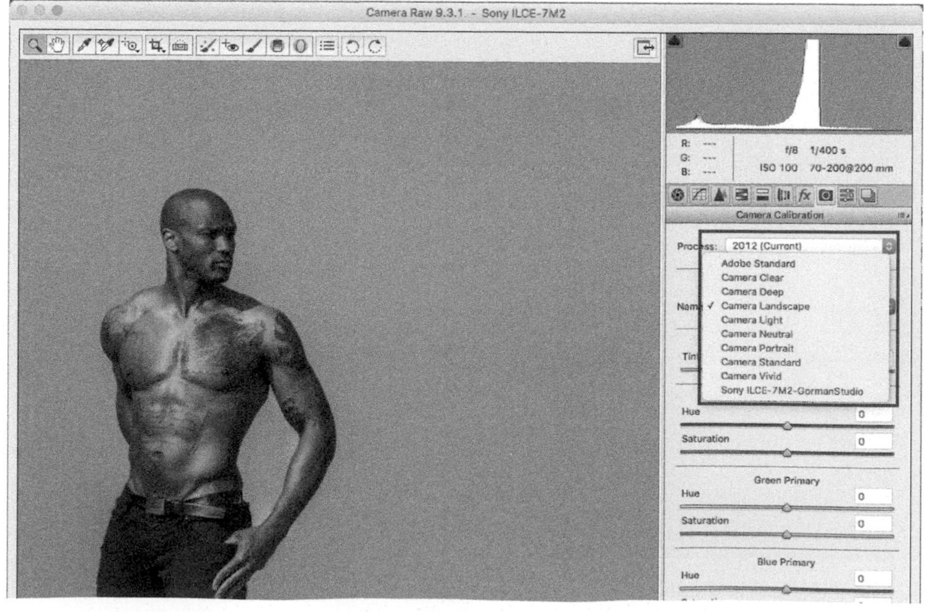

FIGURE 1.58 Each camera profile creates a subtly different base image rendering. © *2014 Katrin Eismann*

TRY IT In the Camera Calibration tab, view the different camera profiles to see the effect they have on your images. For older images, a less contrasty rendering such as Adobe Standard may be more appropriate, and for landscape or architectural work a punchier rendering such as Camera Clear or Camera Deep may be more pleasing.

Presets

The Presets tab is where you create and save either settings that you want to use later or settings you use again and again. For example, if you are constantly applying the same sharpening or grayscale conversions, a preset can save you time.

To create and save ACR settings:

1. In ACR, apply the desired changes to a representative image, such as a landscape, a portrait, or a detailed still life (**FIGURE 1.60**).
2. Click the Camera Raw Settings menu in the top right of any of the tabs, and select Save Settings.
3. Name the preset clearly. For example, start all noise reduction preset names with NR or Noise Reduce.
4. Select the settings you need to create the preset from the Preset menu or by selecting and deselecting the settings in the Save Settings dialog box.
5. Click Save. ACR saves the settings as a preset in the correct CameraRaw Settings folder.
6. To use a preset, select Apply Preset from the Camera Raw Settings menu or, even more easily, click the name of the preset in the Presets tab (**FIGURE 1.61**).

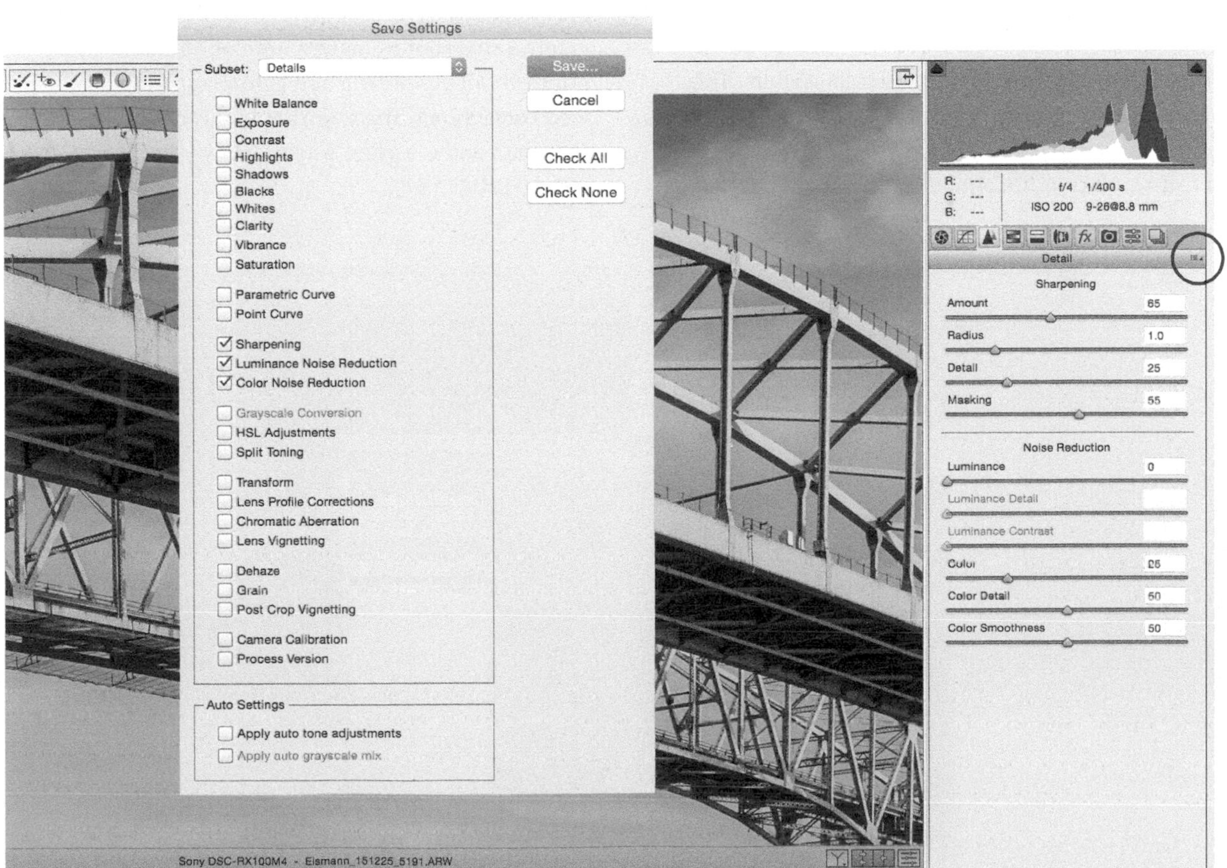

FIGURE 1.60 Creating ACR presets to speed up image processing

FIGURE 1.61 Applying an ACR preset to an image

Snapshots

The final image adjustment tab is Snapshots. This is where you can save work in progress, similar to saving a version of a file but without actually saving a full-resolution file onto your hard drive. We often create a snapshot to make a note of how a file looks after overall processing and before applying localized corrections. The snapshot is saved with the file metadata and is a great way to study your processing steps (**FIGURE 1.62**).

FIGURE 1.62 Use snapshots to create version notes, which can each be adjusted and exported. © *2015 Katrin Eismann*

Original

Basic processing

Retouch and enhance

Selective dodging

Creative toning

FIGURE 1.63 Exploring basic to creative image processing with Adobe Camera Raw © *2015 Katrin Eismann*

Processing a Studio Portrait

Processing a portrait in ACR allows you to apply global tonal, contrast, color, and sharpening to the image. In addition, you can take advantage of the local adjustment tools—including the Spot Removal, Red Eye Removal, Adjustment Brush, Graduated Filter, and Radial Filter tools—to apply localized enhancements and corrections. Working with the Spot Removal, Red Eye Removal, and Adjustment Brush tools is addressed in Chapter 8, and in the following section we delve into working with the Graduated and Radial filters.

Working with portraits allows you to make many creative decisions. Natural or edgy? Color or black and white? A moody dark tone and color, or light pastel? Browsing fashion or high school senior portraits on Flickr or SmugMug can make your head spin with possibilities. A number of photographers and service providers sell ACR and Lightroom presets to create stylized photographic looks, but if you play enough with the sliders and settings you'll be able to create your own custom looks and presets that make your images shine.

In the following tutorial, we address some of the ACR controls we haven't used yet and also show you how to add creative effects, as seen in the progression from original to natural to creative processing (**FIGURE 1.63**).

ch1_portrait.dng

1. Click the shadows and highlights clipping warning icons in the histogram to see if there are any under- or overexposed areas (**FIGURE 1.64**). As you can see, there seem to be overexposed areas on her forehead. But before adjusting exposure, let's see how adjusting white balance and choosing a more appropriate camera profile can improve an image quickly and easily.

2. This image was photographed in mixed light, as Katrin was shooting the portrait with a studio strobe and softbox during a video shoot, which required a continuous light source for the video cameras. When faced with challenging white balance, select Auto from the White Balance menu (Basic tab), which analyzes the image and often does a good job of determining reasonable color (**FIGURE 1.65**).

FIGURE 1.64 Check exposure via the shadows and highlights clipping warnings.

FIGURE 1.65 Auto white balance often creates a good starting point.

3. The image is overall still a bit cool. Use the White Balance tool to click on her front tooth, which brings the image into a good neutral color range (**FIGURE 1.66**).

TRY IT Also try adjusting the Blue/Yellow and Green/Magenta sliders to fine-tune the white balance.

4. Click the Camera Calibration tab to see how selecting a different camera profile can make images pop with very little effort. For this image, Camera Deep and Camera Portrait both look good, and you could use either depending on your preference. We like both, leaning toward the slightly more open Camera Portrait rendering (**FIGURE 1.67**).

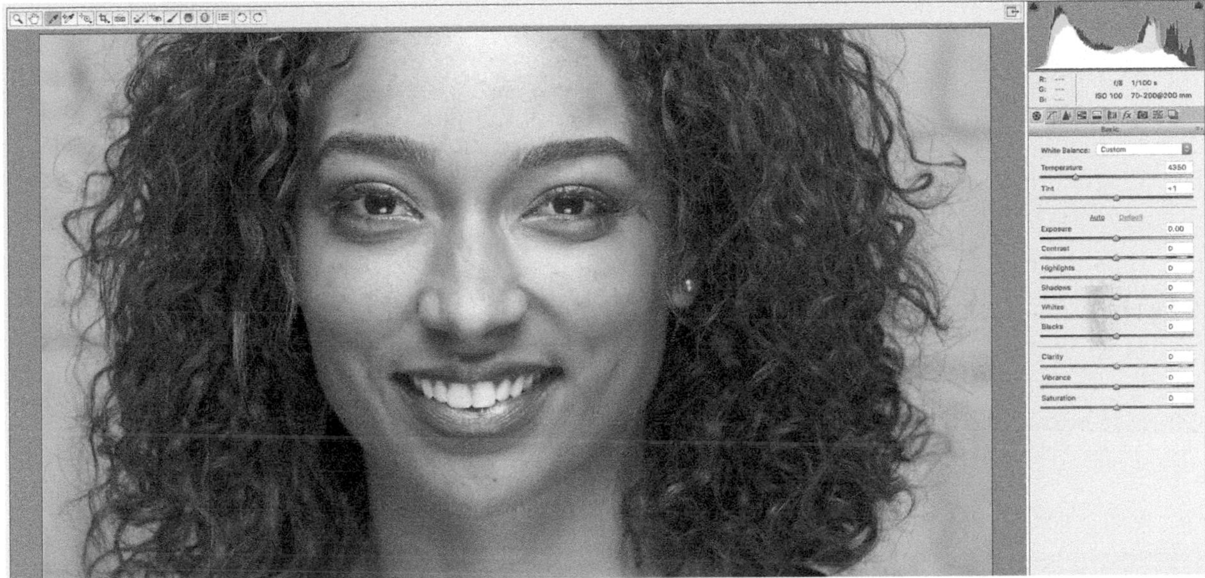

FIGURE 1.66 Further subtle white balance refinement warms the model's skin tone.

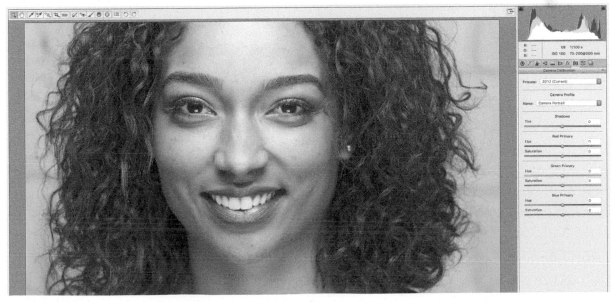

FIGURE 1.67 Check which camera profile creates the best results.

5. Now that the overall image is pleasing, return to the Basic tab to refine the exposure and tonality. When processing portraits, being light-handed and allowing the person to look lively is flattering. With a very slight increase (+.25) in Exposure and a slight opening up of the Shadows (+15), the portrait begins to have a glow to it that best reflects the positive energy of the model (**FIGURE 1.68**).

6. Select the Tone Curve tab, select the Point tab, then select Medium Contrast from the Curve menu to add pleasing tonal contrast to the image (**FIGURE 1.69**).

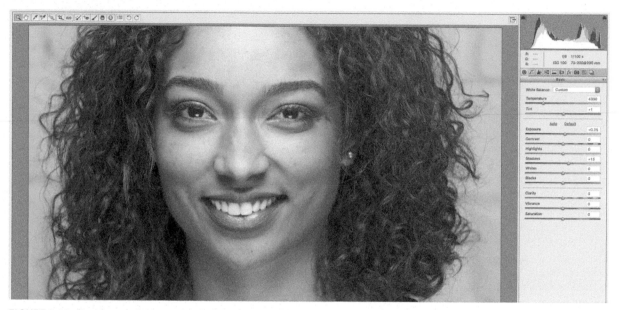

FIGURE 1.68 Opening up the exposure and shadows a bit

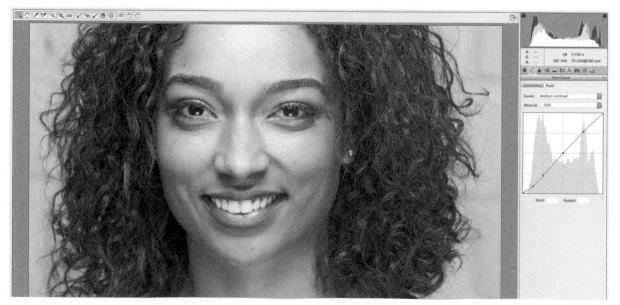

FIGURE 1.69 Adding a hint of pleasing contrast

Input Sharpening

Sharpening in the raw developing process needs to be subtle and controlled. Input sharpening, also referred to as capture sharpening, is used to offset any softness that the sensor anti-alias filter or lens may add.

How much sharpening to apply depends on the camera and lens combination and how much detail and tonal variation/frequency the image has. High-frequency images contain a great deal of detail and many tonal differences (for example an image of the inside of a fine watch). Low-frequency images are less complex (a good example would be a foggy landscape). High-frequency images look good with slightly more sharpening, and softer, less visually complex images do not require as much sharpening. Portraits are often both high and low frequency, with the eyes, lips, and hair being high frequency and the skin being a low-frequency area.

Our example image was shot with a Sony Alpha a7R II mirrorless digital camera, which does not have an anti-aliasing filter on the sensor; Katrin used a very sharp lens, so this file doesn't require a great deal of ACR sharpening. As shown in FIGURE 1.70 we used Amount 75, Radius 0.9, Detail 14, and Mask 80.

Control the sharpening effect via four sliders:

- **Amount** determines the strength of the sharpening, with a range of 0 to 150. In all honesty, we rarely go much above 80; stronger sharpening can be applied and better controlled with the next three sliders.
- **Radius:** Digital sharpening is an edge-contrast boost, and the Radius slider controls how far from the edge the sharpening will take place. Radius settings of 0.75 or lower are best for high-frequency-information images, and higher settings can be used for low-frequency images.
- **Detail** applies halo suppression to the Radius setting to contour the edge enhancement. Lower values apply less halo suppression, and higher values apply more. Many times we find ourselves bouncing back and forth between the Radius and Detail sliders to refine the sharpening effect.
- **Masking** is an additional suppression control that protects areas with less detail—such as skin, sky, and flat surfaces—while creating a high-contrast edge mask that allows the edges to be sharpened. Press Option/Alt to watch the mask as it's built on the fly.

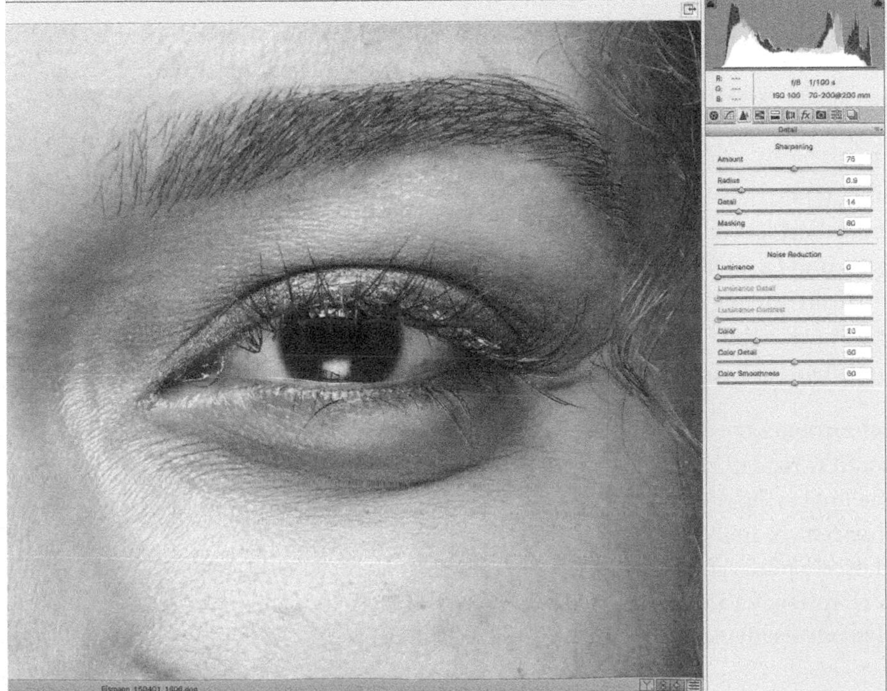

FIGURE 1.70 Input sharpening needs to be subtle.

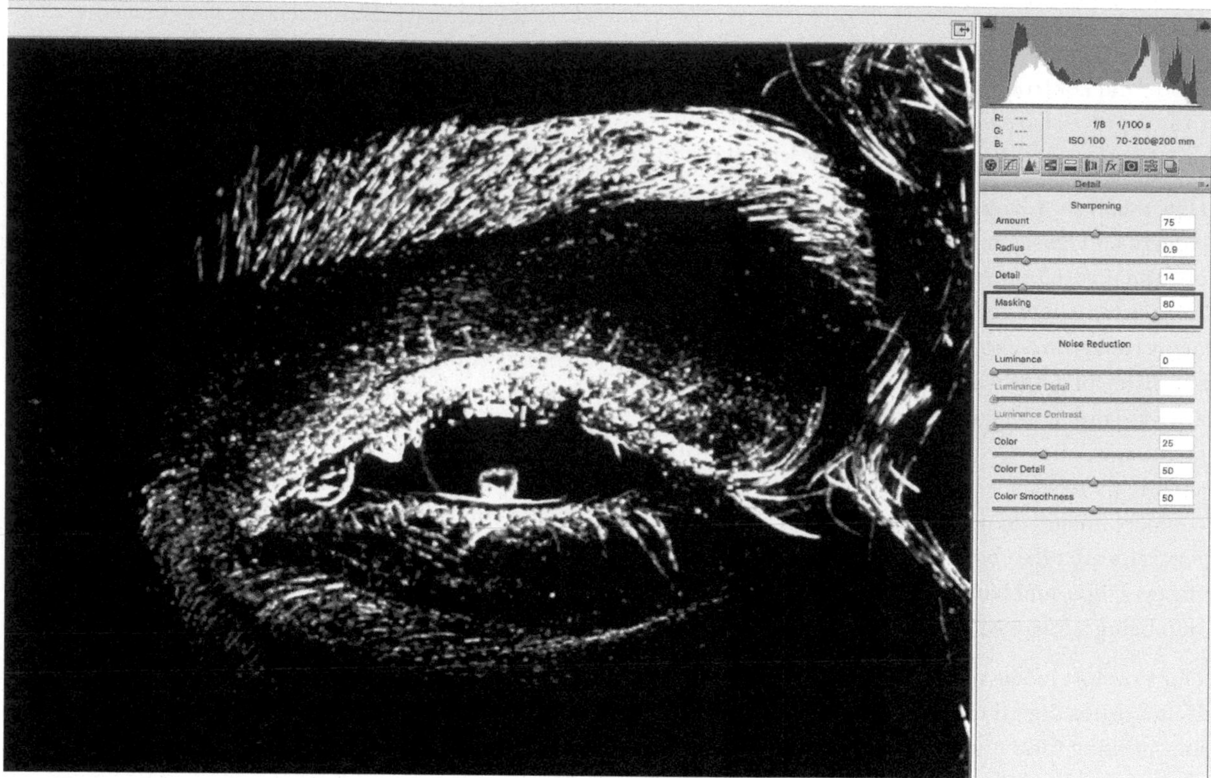

FIGURE 1.71 Black areas are not sharpened.

The white areas will be sharpened and the black areas protected from any sharpening (FIGURE 1.71).

TIP Press Option/Alt when adjusting each sharpening slider to better see the impact of the adjustment.

When applying input sharpening to portraits that will be further retouched in Photoshop, less is more because it is easier to retouch skin and facial features that aren't overly sharpened. Final sharpening of eyes, lips, and other important features is part of the retouching process, as shown in Chapters 8 and 9.

Localized Corrections and Enhancements

At this point, our example portrait is rendered naturally and we could continue improving the image with the local image enhancement tools, apply creative effects, or open it in Photoshop for refined retouching. To continue our exploration, let's stay in ACR to do a bit of cleanup and creative enhancement.

Before you head off into the creative aspects of ACR, we recommend taking a snapshot, which is a note in progress of where the file is at the moment. Creating a snapshot of the image at this point is a great way to get back to a natural image; said another way, sometimes our creative explorations are less than successful, and it's nice to know that you can return to "good" by clicking the Basic Processing snapshot in the Snapshots tab.

1. Select the Snapshots tab. In the lower-right corner, click the New Snapshot icon (it looks like a piece of paper). Name the new snapshot *Basic Processing*, and click OK.

2. Use the Crop tool to reduce the extraneous edges and to center her a bit better (FIGURE 1.72).

3. Tap over the few spots or skin flecks with the Spot Removal tool set to Heal, a small (3- to 5-pixel) brush size, and at 37 Feather and 100 Opacity (FIGURE 1.73).

FIGURE 1.72 Cropping recomposes the portrait.

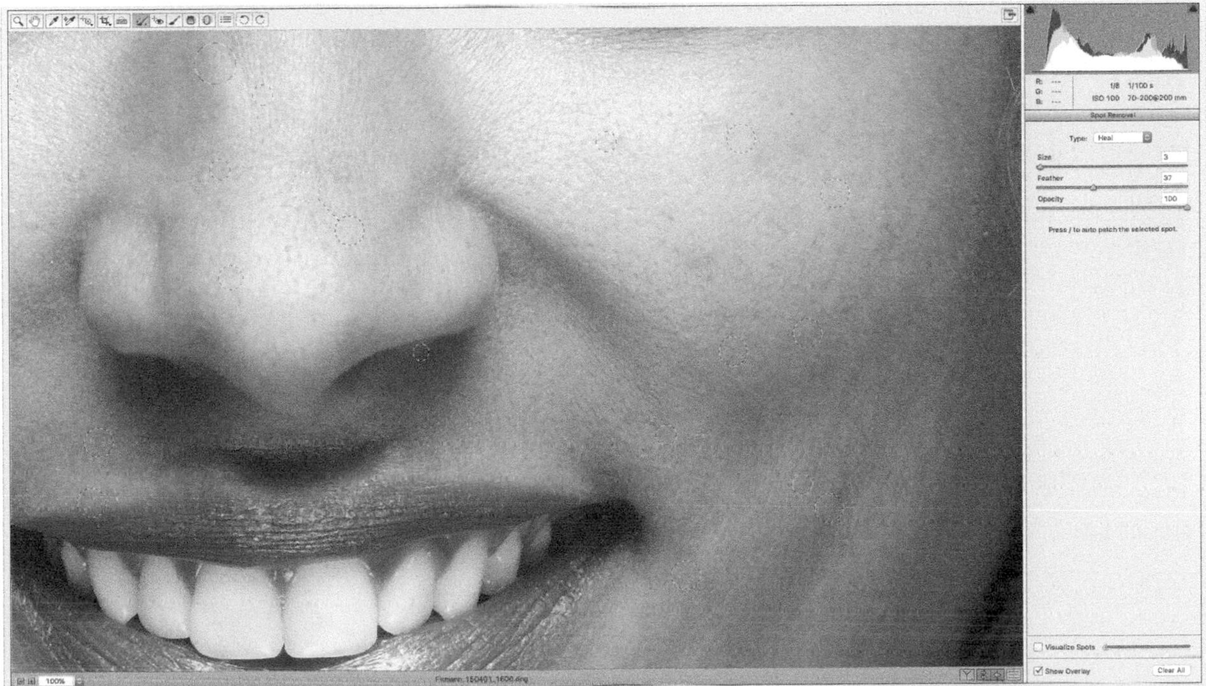

FIGURE 1.73 Use the Spot Removal tool to remove obvious spots, blemishes, moles, and stray hairs.

4. Use the Adjustment Brush with a +0.40 Exposure and +15 Clarity to brush over her eyes to make them a bit brighter and clearer (**FIGURE 1.74**). Click the Hand tool to accept the changes.

5. Make a second snapshot and name it *Basic Retouch*.

Darkening the edges of a print, also referred to as vignetting, keeps the viewer's eye from wondering off to the print edge and simultaneously brings the visual focus back to the center of the image; in this case, the woman's face gains greater visual importance.

6. Select the Radial filter, and while pressing Option/Alt, drag from her nose outward to pull an oval shape over her face (**FIGURE 1.75**). Reduce the Exposure to at least –1.00, and if the center of the image is being darkened rather than the outside, scroll to the bottom of the controls and select Outside.

Professional retouchers work with lightening (dodging) and darkening (burning) to smooth skin, balance tonality, and create pleasing contours. For high-end professional retouching, you would use dodge and burn techniques with Photoshop layers, but for a quick pick-me-up you can use the ACR Adjustment Brush tool.

7. Set the Adjustment Brush's Exposure +1.10, and make sure that the feather is at 75. Brush over the dark circles under her eyes, near the bridge of her nose, in her smile lines, and a bit under her lower lip (**FIGURE 1.76**).

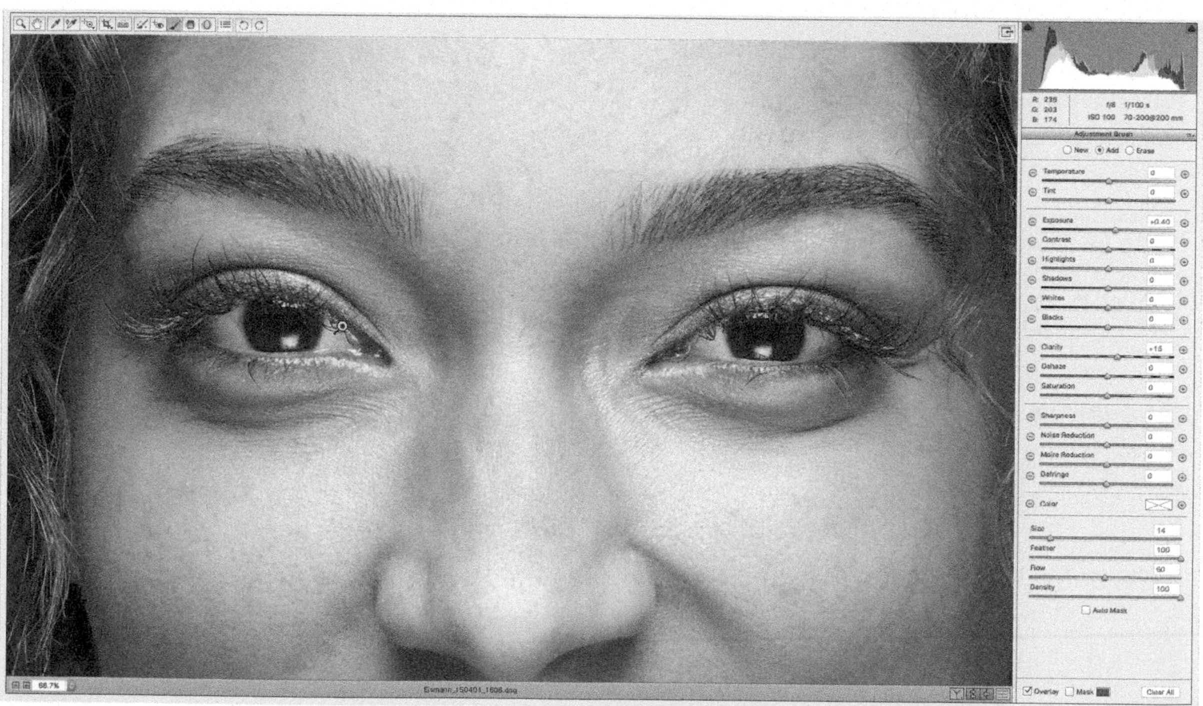

FIGURE 1.74 Brushing in exposure and clarity to enhance eyes

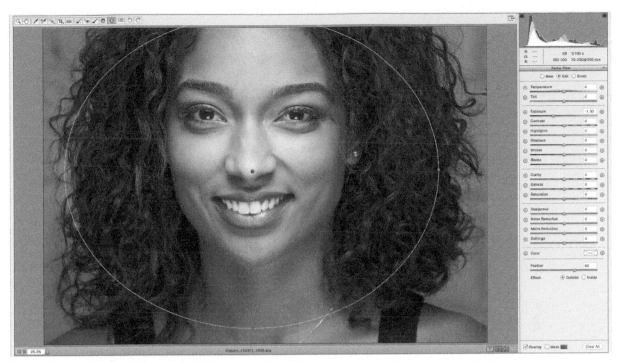

FIGURE 1.75 Darken image edges with the Radial gradient.

FIGURE 1.76 Selective dodging, or lightening, under eyes and lips helps contour the face.

FIGURE 1.77 Erase unwanted Brush strokes as needed.

8. To see where the brush effects takes place, select Mask (as circled in **FIGURE 1.77**). To erase unwanted brush strokes, press Option/Alt. This changes the Adjustment Brush tool to the Eraser tool.

9. Make a third snapshot, name it *Dodge*, and get ready to experiment with black and white conversion and refined toning.

Creative Effects

The beauty of working in ACR is that any change can be refined or deleted, which allows us to experiment long into the night. Of course you can lose even more sleep playing with—we mean working with—Photoshop. To wrap up our raw processing lesson, let's get a bit more creative and convert the image into black and white and then add subtle toning.

10. Select the HSL/Grayscale tab, and select Convert to Grayscale.

11. Rather than guessing which colors to lighten or darken, click the Targeted Adjustment tool and select Grayscale Mix, or press Cmd-Option-Shift-G/Ctrl-Alt-Shift-G.

12. Position the Targeted Adjustment tool on her forehead, and drag up carefully to emphasize her face, as you would on a photo shoot (**FIGURE 1.78**).

13. To better frame the image, click the existing Radial filter and reduce the Exposure to –1.55 and the Sharpness to –60 (**FIGURE 1.79**).

Toning a black and white image adds depth and is usually done by adding opposite colors to the lighter and darker tones; for example, you would warm the highlights and cool the shadows. To apply toning, you could use the Split Toning tab, but the Tone Curve tab offers greater control over where the toning takes place.

FIGURE 1.78 Use the Targeted Adjustment tool to refine the black and white tonality.

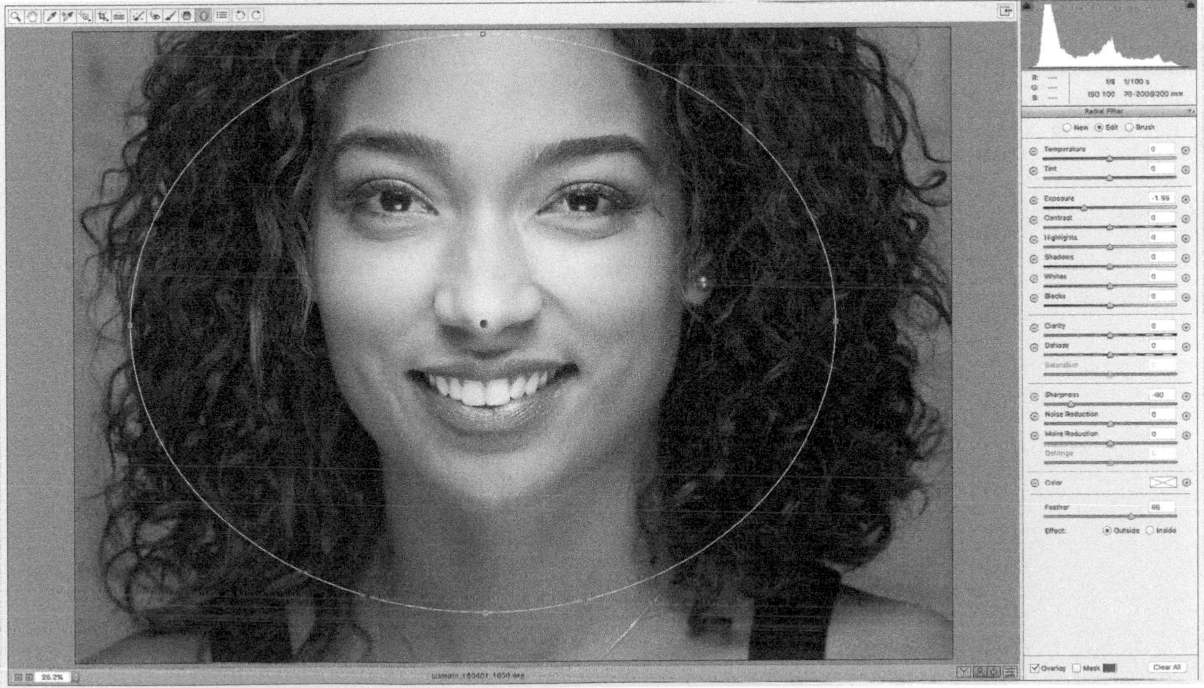

FIGURE 1.79 Experiment with the Radial gradient to darken and soften image edges.

14. In the Curves tab, click the Point tab, and from the Channel menu select Red. Click the midpoint and drag up ever so slightly. To avoid toning the shadow areas, add a lock by adding an additional point on the curve at the three-quarter tone intersection (**FIGURE 1.80**).

15. Select the Blue channel, click the three-quarter tone, drag up ever so slightly, and lock the midtones by adding another point on the curve (**FIGURE 1.81**), which protects the lighter tones from becoming blue.

16. Tap Q to cycle through the before-and-after comparisons (**FIGURE 1.82**). Make sure to save a preset for any creative and toning effect you like.

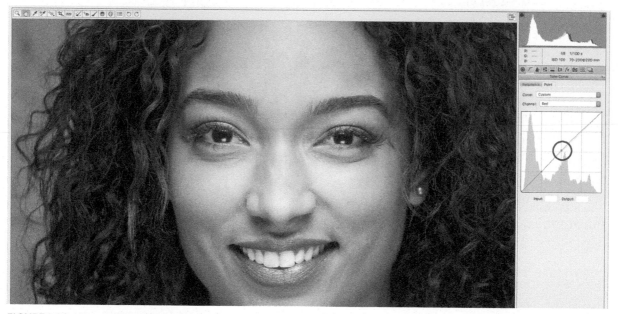

FIGURE 1.80 Warming highlights with a Red curve

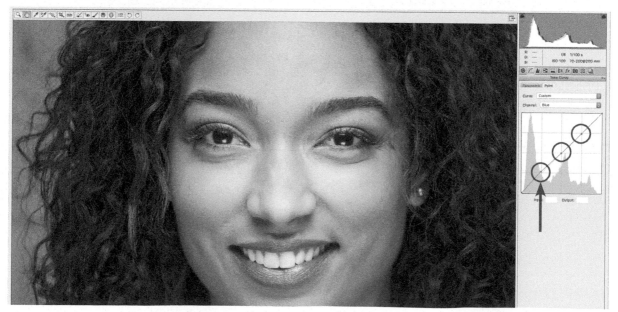

FIGURE 1.81 Cooling shadows with a Blue curve

FIGURE 1.82 Tap the Q key to cycle through before and after views.

In conclusion, use ACR or Lightroom to make a lot of images look very, very good with global color, tonality, and contrast adjustments and some retouching, and work with Photoshop to make a few images perfect with careful cloning/healing, filters, and layers.

BACKUP STRATEGY

It's not a question of *if* a hard drive will fail; it is really a question of *when* a hard drive will fail. If you have a backup strategy, when a hard drive fails or is lost, stolen, or damaged, you will feel very smart; if you don't, you will feel miserable, depressed, and—OK, you get it. The best strategy is to build in redundancy; we take our cue from photographer and workflow expert Peter Krogh, who developed the 3-2-1 approach:

- Three identical copies
- Two different hard drives or media
- One offsite or online copy

With the prices of hard drives dropping and the speed of cloud-based backup increasing, it is wise to create "a set it and forget it" backup system. A reliable backup system eliminates human error and is software based. On a Mac, Katrin uses CarbonCopyCloner, and on PC you can use SyncBack. Set the software to mirror hard drives automatically; for example, every 24 hours at a specific time. For the offsite copy, use a third hard drive that you really keep offsite: at your workplace, in a neighbor's house, or even in a bank safe deposit box—wherever you can access it once a week to swap it with an updated hard drive.

★ NOTE CDs and DVDs are no longer cutting edge, because they will disintegrate, and most computers being sold today don't support CDs or DVDs.

If you have a fast and reliable Internet connection, use a cloud-based system such as Google Drive or Amazon Cloud Drive. Professional cloud-based services such as Backblaze, CrashPlan, and Carbonite automatically back up your files and applications and store them safely for recovery in case of a disaster. If you're on a Mac, make sure Time Machine is turned on. On Windows, get in the habit of using Windows' backup and system restore features to back up files and applications. The world of operating software changes very quickly, so please research the most current software and services; it will allow you to rest well at night knowing that your important photographs and files are redundantly backed up.

CLOSING THOUGHTS

The one thing that no computer, book, or class can give you is the passion to practice, learn, and experiment with the skills and techniques it takes to be a good restoration artist or retoucher; it requires more than removing dust or covering up a wrinkle here and there. Restoration enables you to give someone cherished memories that have faded over time. Retouching and restoration is a fantastic hobby and a challenging profession, so let's dive in and get to work.

Chapter 2

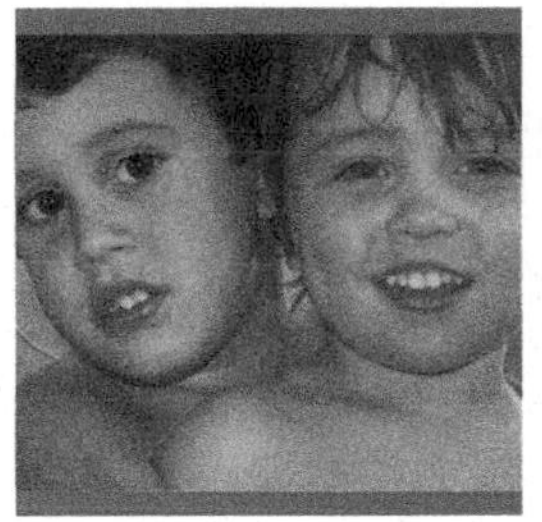

PHOTOSHOP AND PHOTOSHOP ELEMENTS ESSENTIALS

Put three people in a room and give them each the same Photoshop problem and 30 minutes, and Katrin bets that they'll each come up with a different way to solve the problem. The variety of approaches that Photoshop allows can be frustrating or invigorating, depending on how much you like to explore and experiment. What separates a casual Photoshop user from a power user? In most cases, it's experience and the ability to visualize the final outcome of the project. To power users, Photoshop is transparent—the interface practically disappears as they work to create the retouched or restored image. For novices, Photoshop can be so overwhelming that they get lost finding tools, commands, and controls. Even though they might get the image done, it will have taken them a lot longer than necessary.

Learning to move quickly through Photoshop helps you be a better retoucher because you can concentrate on the image instead of the software.

In this chapter, you'll learn about

- Preferences, color settings, and workspaces
- Tools, quick keys, brushes, and navigation tips
- Layers, masks, and blending modes
- Translating Photoshop into Photoshop Elements

Restoration and retouching takes more than being a fast mouse-clicker. Good retouchers understand that the images they are working with are very important to the client, a family member, or the person in the picture. Before you start a retouching project, take a moment to consider that the pixels represent real people and real events—they're more than dark and light specks of digital information. It's your job to bring back memories from faded, cracked, and damaged originals. This is a weighty responsibility, and keeping that in mind throughout the retouching process helps you see the image with empathy and care.

PREFERENCES AND COLOR SETTINGS

Adjusting Photoshop's preference settings lets you control the application's look and feel, performance, and many other settings to best fit your workflow and maximize your computer's processing capabilities. In the following pages, we offer suggestions for preference settings, but we also understand that you'll adjust settings to best fit your personal needs. For the most current and trusted performance recommendations, we respect and follow Jeff Tranberry, Adobe Chief Customer Advocate, who worked on the Photoshop product development and digital imaging teams for many years: https://helpx.adobe.com/photoshop/kb/optimize-photoshop-cc-performance.html.

Preferences

Improve Photoshop's efficiency by setting the application preferences and color settings. On an Apple computer, you'll find these settings under **Photoshop CC > Preferences** and **Edit > Color Settings**. On Windows they are under **Edit > Preferences** and **Edit > Color Settings.**

In the following section we prefer not to burn valuable page space by reviewing every single preference category and setting but will concentrate on the ones that affect Photoshop's performance in relationship to restoration, retouching, and working with photographic images.

General: Select Show "Start" Workplace When No Documents Are Open to have quick access to recent or often-used files. Deselect Export Clipboard to save time and memory when a large image file is copied when jumping (often accidentally) over to a different application.

Interface: Sets the overall look of Photoshop in terms of color theme, interface text size, and channel and menu highlight color. Many people use the Light Gray color theme, as it contrasts less with images, allowing you to make more accurate color saturation and tonal decisions (FIGURE 2.1). Others use Medium Gray to see details and pick up on problem areas, such as blown-out highlights. Carrie Beene, who retouches high-end beauty product advertisements, says, "I use the Dark Gray interface. Black is too stark, and the lighter ones are too bright for the best color corrections to me" (FIGURE 2.2). We prefer to use the Medium Gray or Dark Gray color theme. Black is too reflective, especially when working on a glossy monitor, and Light Gray is too bright.

History Log: Off by default, it can be a useful way to track the time and settings used on an image. Edit Log Items set to Sessions Only tracks the time an image is opened and closed. Concise tracks the steps, and Detailed records the steps and all settings used. Additionally, you need to decide whether to record these steps onto separate text document, into the file metadata, or both. Katrin used the History Log feature when a client in a science-related field required a complete record of what she did to an image.

Performance: RAM and Scratch Disk settings are addressed in the Chapter 1 section "Computer Equipment." History States settings allow for multiple steps of undo, and anyone doing restoration or retouching work knows that those mouse clicks and brush strokes add up quickly, which is why we recommend you increase the History States setting to at least 100. It can be increased to 1000, which we do not recommend, as that requires a very large scratch disk and, in our opinion, creates an unwieldy History panel record. High-end retoucher Timothy Sexton explains, "I set History to 20 steps. If I realize an error after 20 steps, I am too far ahead by that point, so it's not worth it to me to have more than 20. In the History

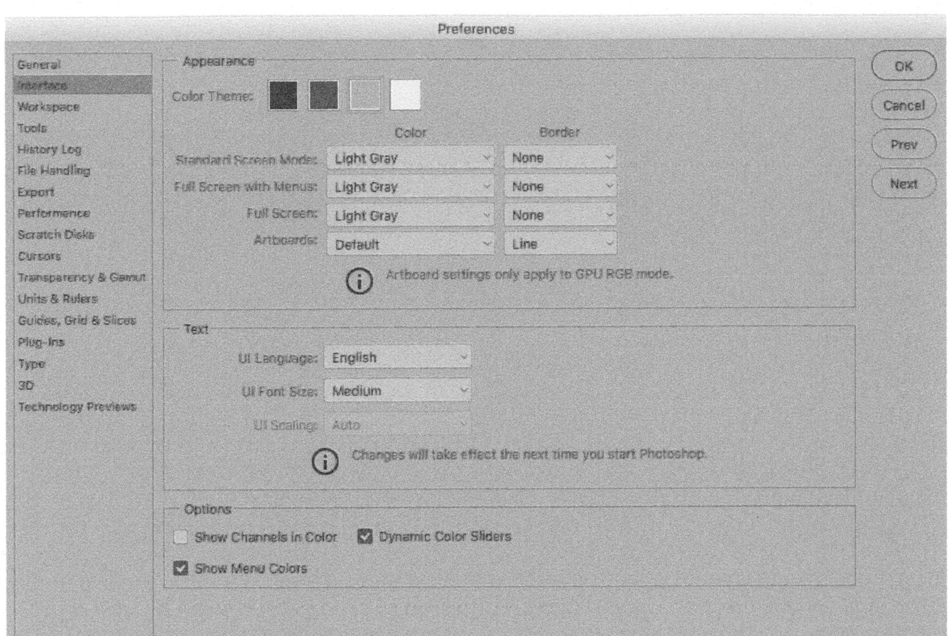

FIGURE 2.1 Adjusting Photoshop's interface preferences, such as color theme and text settings.

FIGURE 2.2 New York City-based retoucher Carrie Beene prefers the Dark Gray interface. © *Rick Day Photography*

panel, I use a non-linear history so I don't accidentally toggle back in history and then lose everything." Like Tim Sexton, Carrie Beene keeps the History States setting at 20 steps: "Working with layers allows me to undo anything I have done beyond 20 steps. Also, at 20 steps you never have to scroll your history, which I don't like doing," she says.

Chris Taratino, a professional retoucher, says, "I have my History always set for 100 states, Cache Levels at 2, and Cache Tile Size set to 1024k. In Photoshop itself, the History panel is set to automatically create the first snapshot, automatically create a new snapshot when saving, and allow non-linear history" (**FIGURE 2.3**).

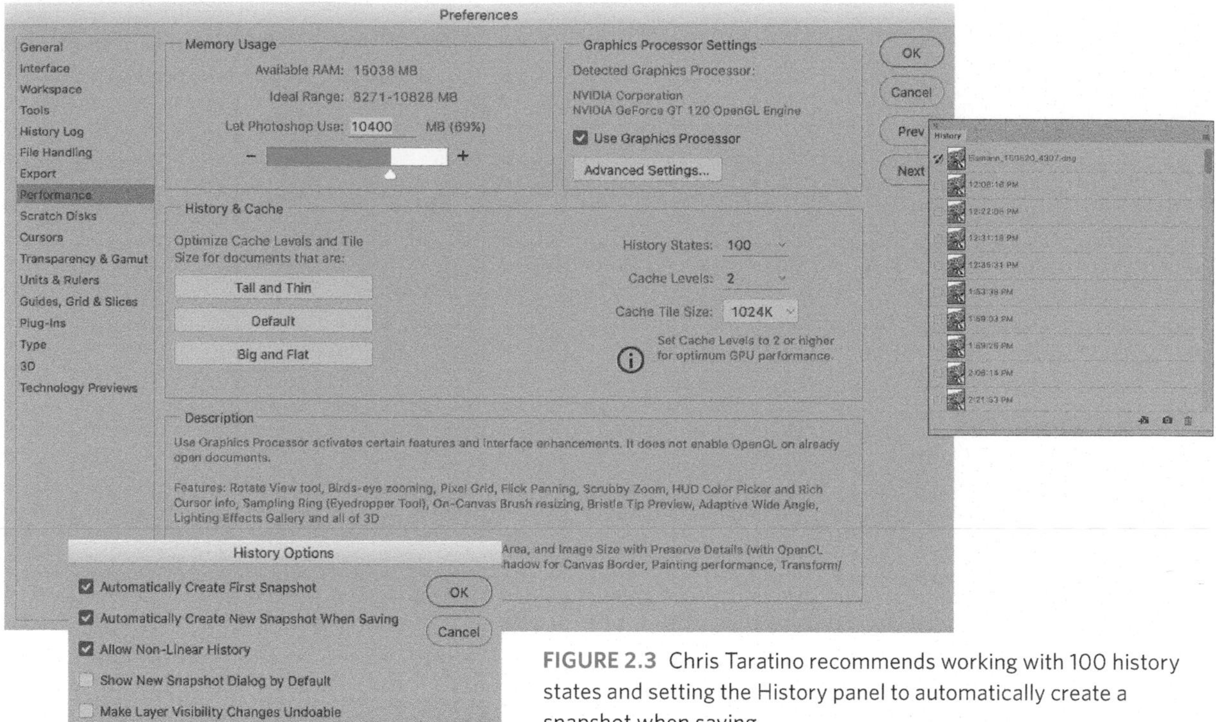

FIGURE 2.3 Chris Taratino recommends working with 100 history states and setting the History panel to automatically create a snapshot when saving.

Cursors: Control the default look of painting and other cursors. For greatest accuracy, set Painting Cursor to Full Size Brush Tip, with Show Crosshair in Brush Tip selected. For other cursors, decide whether the icon or a crosshair works best.

+ TIP You can change any tool, such as the Eyedropper or Crop tool, to an accurate crosshair by tapping the Caps Lock key. Tapping the key again returns the tool to its previous look.

Color Settings

The color space determines the size of the color gamut (that is, the number of colors Photoshop will work in). Think of color spaces as boxes of crayons—sRGB is the smallest box of crayons and is suitable for web display, and Adobe RGB and ProPhoto RGB have thousands more colors of crayons and are best suited for files that are destined for print. ProPhoto RGB is best suited for high-bit-depth files, and Adobe RGB is good for working with 8-bit files destined for offset printing. To access color settings, choose **Edit > Color Settings.**

As Dennis explains, "I work for a wide variety of clients, and in regard to color spaces it is important to be flexible. So while my default color space is Adobe RGB, I often work in whatever color space the client prefers. Most of the time this is Adobe RGB, then sRGB, and on the rare occasion ProPhoto. Real-world colors fit very comfortably inside the Adobe RGB gamut, where I am less likely to run into gamut or banding problems." Wayne works with (said politely) less than optimal photos and scans, and he says, "In my line of work, I work with a lot of faded and poorly taken care of images. So working in a color space larger than what a print has to offer, or what your printer is capable of, is not useful to me. So I stick with Adobe RGB."

Discussions on color spaces have caused many sleepless nights, and we asked high-end commercial and glamour retouchers to see which color space they work in. Carrie Beene says, "I work in ColorMatch or

HISTORY PANEL: MORE THAN MULTIPLE UNDOS

On the most basic level, the History States feature allows you to step backward and forward in as many steps as are set in **Preferences > Performance > History States**. For example, setting History States to 50 will keep track of 50 changes to each open Photoshop document, such as each click with the Clone Stamp or Healing Brush tool, adding a layer, using a filter, and so on. As soon as you make the fifty-first change, the record (not the effect) of the first change will disappear from the History panel. You can step backward by clicking the history state in the History panel or pressing Cmd-Option-Z/Ctrl-Alt-Z to go back one step at a time; press Cmd-Shift-Z/Ctrl-Shift-Z to step forward. When you reach the set number of history states, you can of course keep working, but the previous changes are replaced in the History panel by the new steps. Think of the History panel as a conveyer belt, with each bucket holding one change; the conveyer belt is only as long as the number of states set in the History States option.

Using the History panel for multiple undos is useful, but if you step backward a few steps and then apply (for example) a new brush stroke, all the steps that came after the new brush stroke will be lost. To allow for greater flexibility, you can enable non-linear history in the History panel menu, which allows you to step backward, apply a new stroke or effect, and maintain the previous history steps.

On the bottom of the History panel you will find the Create New Document From Current State icon, which lets you create a new document that you can work on, and the Create New Snapshot icon, which creates a record (snapshot) of the document at that moment.

The History panel has partners in the toolbar: the History Brush and the Art History Brush tools, which allow you to paint from a history state by clicking the small square to the left of the history state or snapshot and then painting. Experiment with history painting and blend modes to create unique effects. The History Brush is a wonderful tool, but it is not omnipotent, and anything that changes the image resolution is Kryptonite to the History Brush, including cropping, making Image Size, Canvas Size, Color Mode, and Bit depth changes, and rotating (except for square images that are rotated exactly 90 or 180 degrees).

Most importantly, please understand that history and snapshots are lost (that is, sent to pixel heaven) when the document is closed. History is a great feature, as it allows you to back away from undesired Photoshop decisions, and everything that is recorded in History is between you and Photoshop. So the next time you make a mistake, such as saving a version of the file without layers, do not panic and do *not* close the file—rather, open the History panel, click the command previous to Flatten Image, and then save the file. History to the rescue!

Adobe RGB, as my client prefers. These color spaces are middle of the road: not too big, not too small, and easiest to convert files into CMYK without problems." Timothy Sexton says, "I work in Adobe RGB, with CMYK set to U.S. Web Coated SWOP v2. Adobe RGB is a very capable color space, and I have never had any problems with converting to the CMYK profiles that my clients require" (**FIGURE 2.4**). Katrin and Chris Taratino set up their color settings identically, and as Chris says, "I only work in ProPhoto color space with 16-bit files. Since ACR and Lightroom can export out to ProPhoto, I prefer to work with what those applications support."

For additional information about Photoshop color management, please visit https://helpx.adobe.com/photoshop/topics/color-management.html.

Workspaces and Navigation

Setting up the Photoshop interface is similar to organizing your kitchen or workbench. In both cases, tools need to be in a logical place. Photoshop's workspaces remember which panels are displayed, how they are grouped, and where they are displayed. They can also include keyboard shortcuts, menus, or toolbar customizations.

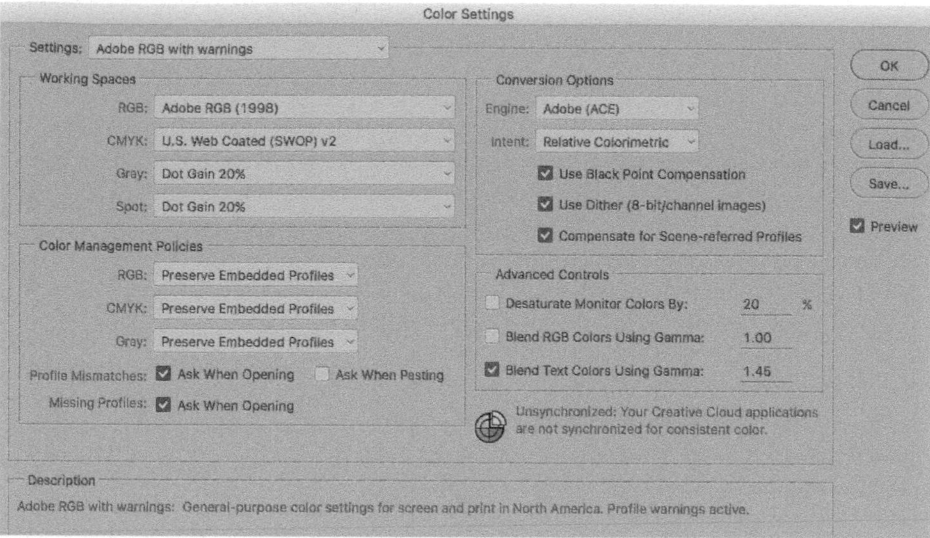

FIGURE 2.4 Set the Color Settings options to best suit your workflow.

To save time and reduce frustration, take advantage of the ability to save and recall custom workspaces. Every time you quit Photoshop, the panel positions are remembered, and the panels will be in the same place when you launch Photoshop again. If you're like us—working late into the night moving panels to get the work done—the last position of the panels probably isn't the best position for getting back to work the next morning.

Customizing Workspaces

Setting up and saving custom workspaces that reflect the task at hand is well worth the effort. For example, Katrin's primary workspace includes the Layers, Channels, Paths, Adjustments, Info, and Histogram panels. Timothy Sexton, who has retouched hundreds of celebrity portraits for countless magazine covers, has his workspace spread across two monitors (FIGURE 2.5), with all relevant tools and panels close at hand.

To create a custom workspace:

1. Position and group the panels as desired.
2. Choose **Window > Workspace > New Workspace** or select New Workspace from the Workspace Switcher in the application bar.
3. Name your workspace and click Save.

After creating additional workspaces, you can access them from the **Window > Workspace** menu or select them from the Workspace Switcher in the application bar.

To delete a workspace, choose **Window > Workspace > Delete Workspace**. To reset a workspace, choose **Window > Workspace > Reset**. Reset restores the active workspace to how it was saved originally. The Start workspace shows when no images are open in Photoshop.

Photoshop also includes a set of default workspaces created for particular types of work, including Motion, Painting, and Photography. Selecting one of the default workspaces is a great place to start when creating your own workspaces.

We asked some high-end retoucher friends to share their Photoshop workspace setups with you. As Chris Taratino explains, "I used to use a dual-monitor setup, but with my main monitor now being 30 inches wide, it became impractical. I now have panels on each side, with the image in the center of the screen (FIGURE 2.6). I frequently hide the panels to utilize the entire screen and have the panels set to pop out upon mouseover. Like all retouchers I use a Wacom tablet, but I use mine with an Art Pen for the rotation control it offers. The other tool I utilize daily is the Leap Motion

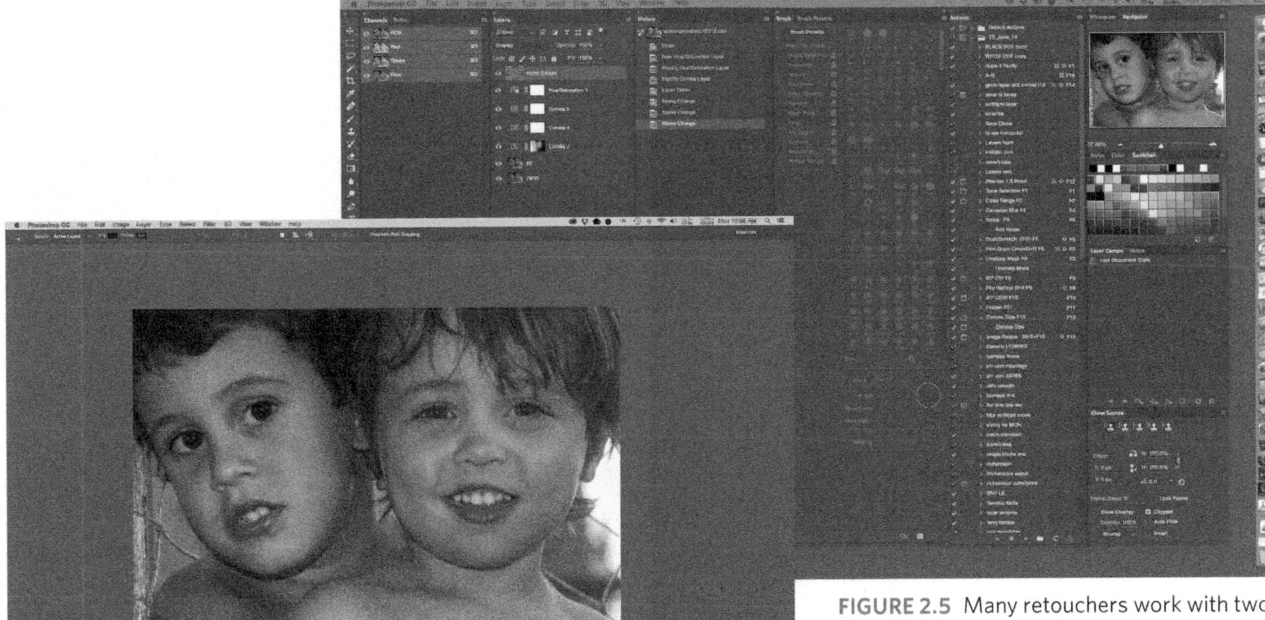

FIGURE 2.5 Many retouchers work with two monitors—one for the image and one for the Photoshop panels.

Controller (www.leapmotion.com/), which tracks my hand motions. It doesn't interact directly with Photoshop, but with the help of BetterTouchTool (www.boastr.net), I can assign gestures to actions and the Leap Motion will put those in motion (FIGURE 2.7). For example, I like to have two windows of an image open at the same time set to different zooms that update as I work. With the twirl of a finger, my image is opened in a new window, the workspace is split into whatever I might need, zooms are automatically adjusted, and my main window is chosen again and ready to begin work. Because of the Leap I can better utilize my standing desk by moving away from my monitor and still have access to my keyboard."

TRY IT Taking a few moments to arrange the panels is similar to setting up your workspace in a traditional studio: Brushes go over here and camera equipment goes over there. Position the panels in relation to how often you use them, with the more important ones—Layers, Channels, and Info panels—close at hand.

THE WORKSPACE VIEW

Your monitor is your work table. Keeping it organized and neat will pay off in time saved and frustration reduced. Learning to use every bit of your monitor's real estate can make a small monitor seem a lot larger and make a large monitor seem even more expansive.

- Take advantage of your monitor's real estate by working in either Full Screen Mode With Menu Bar or Full Screen Mode. Tap F to cycle through the viewing modes, or choose **View > Screen Mode**.
- Consider working with a two-monitor system, with the second monitor for many Photoshop panels, Adobe Bridge, or Lightroom. The second monitor can be less expensive or used, as you won't be doing any critical color correction or retouching on it.
- Experiment with changing the display resolution using your operating system's Display settings. If you can comfortably read the menus at a higher resolution, you will greatly expand your working space.

FIGURE 2.6 A 30-inch monitor offers plenty of space for the image and the Photoshop panels.

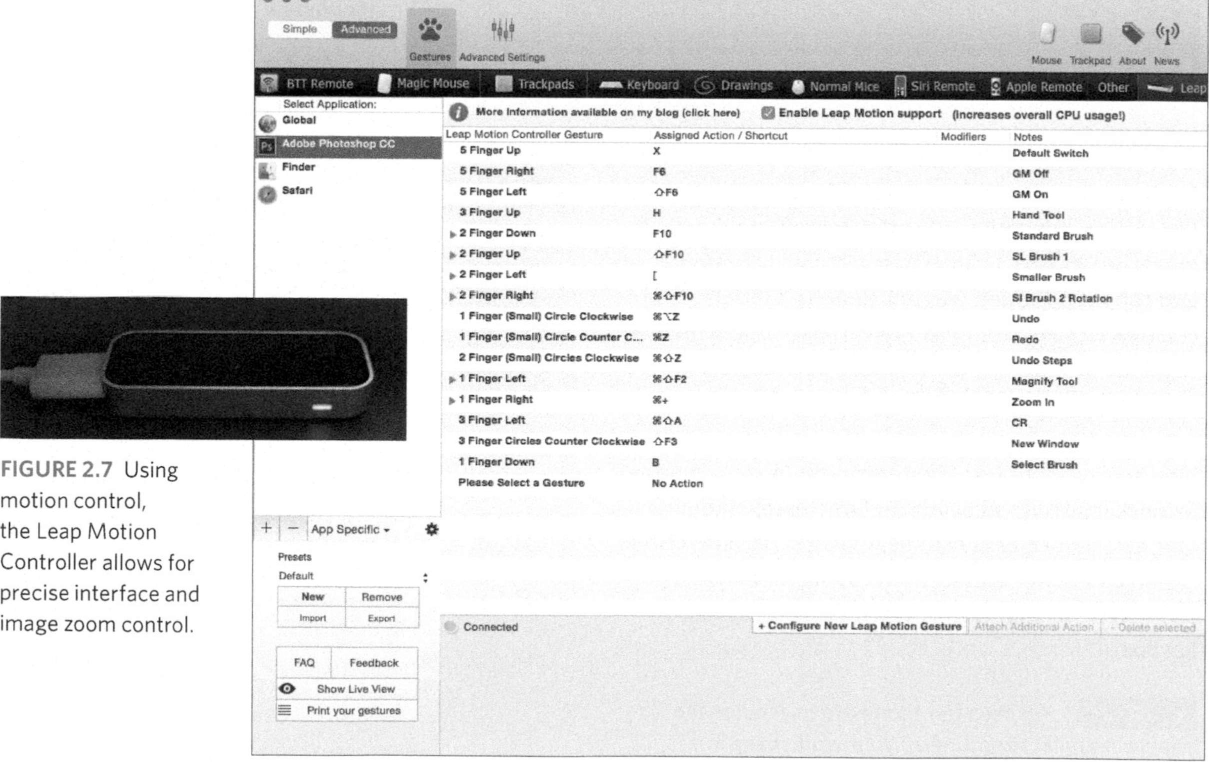

FIGURE 2.7 Using motion control, the Leap Motion Controller allows for precise interface and image zoom control.

Customizing Menu Commands

Photoshop offers numerous ways to navigate through a file and a plethora of shortcut keys to choose tools and open menus. Do you need to know them all? Of course not. There are over 600 of them! Should you learn how to activate the tools that you'll be using every day? Absolutely. If you use a tool or command three or more times a day, learning its keyboard shortcut saves time. Additionally, if you access a filter or sequence of commands more than three times a day, learning how to create an action or a custom keyboard command is a good idea.

Choose **Edit > Keyboard Shortcuts** or **Edit > Menus** to view any established keyboard shortcut or to create your own custom shortcuts. As Adobe has used up practically every possible keyboard combination, you will probably bump an existing command to create your own. But don't worry; you can always change the keyboard shortcuts back to their default settings. For example, Katrin uses **Select > Color Range** a lot, so she modified the command menu to use Cmd-Option-K to open the Color Range dialog box (FIGURE 2.8). To achieve this, she mapped Cmd-Option-K to Select > Color Range and clicked Accept. Many of the command keys are already assigned, so you'll need to decide whether the established shortcut or your desired command key is more useful. Keep in mind that setting up a shortcut that is assigned to another command in Photoshop will remove the shortcut from the original command.

TRY IT Find a menu command that you use quite often, and assign a shortcut to it using **Edit > Keyboard Shortcut**.

TIP Consider saving customized shortcuts as a new set. Click the Create New Set Based on Current Shortcuts icon in the Keyboard Shortcuts and Menus dialog box.

PANEL TIPS

- When working with a single monitor, have as few panels open as possible.
- Tap the Tab key to hide or show all panels, including the Tools panel and options bar, at once.
- Shift-Tab to hide all panels while keeping the Tools panel onscreen.
- Pull unnecessary nested panels out of their groups and close them. For example, the Styles panel is seldom used in restoration or retouching work. If you separate and close it, it won't pop up with the other docked panels.
- Decide on an ideal panel placement for your workflow. This saves time when hiding and showing panels, because they will reappear exactly where you positioned them. Save the ideal placement as a workspace with a logical name. Use the workspace switcher in the application bar to toggle between workspaces.
- On Windows-powered touch devices, the Modifier Keys panel (**Window > Modifier**) lets you access frequently used modifier keys: Shift, Ctrl, and Alt.

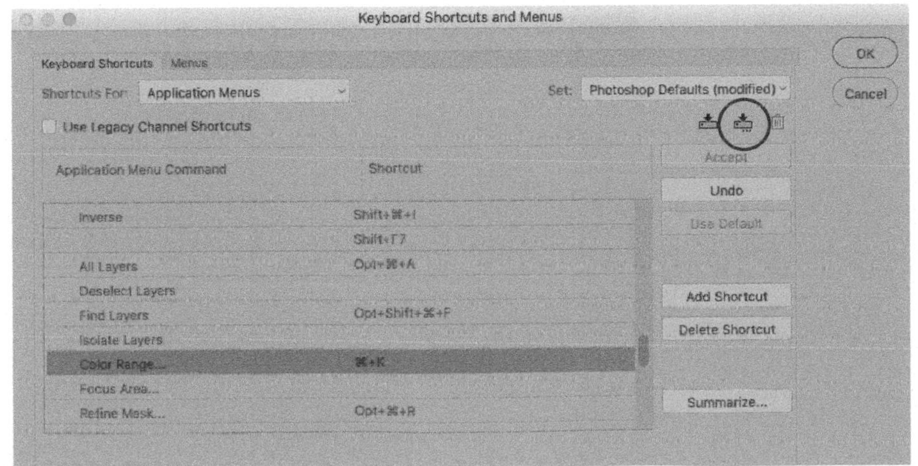

FIGURE 2.8 Customize menu commands for commands you use often, and create a new set based on current shortcuts.

Customizing Your Toolbar/Tools panel

Photoshop is used as an imaging tool by photographers; graphic, mobile, and web designers; illustrators; and forensic and medical imaging professionals. Each user has tools that they use every day and other tools that they never touch. You can customize your toolbar (sometimes referred to in the Help file as the "Tools panel") to show only your most important tools and reorder or regroup the tools you use frequently by following these steps:

1. Choose **Edit > Toolbar**, or select Edit Toolbar from the three dots (•••) below the Zoom tool, to open the Customize Toolbar dialog box.
2. Drag the tools that you do not use to the Extra Tools column (FIGURE 2.9).
3. Rearrange tools or tool groups in the Toolbar column by dragging them into position. For example, the tools you use the most could be grouped closer to the top of the toolbar.
4. Save the edited toolbar as a preset, and click Done to enjoy your personalized toolbar.

To access the extra tools, long-press the Edit Toolbar icon in the Tools panel and select the tool (FIGURE 2.10). To restore the Tools panel to Photoshop defaults, choose **Edit > Toolbar** and click Restore Defaults.

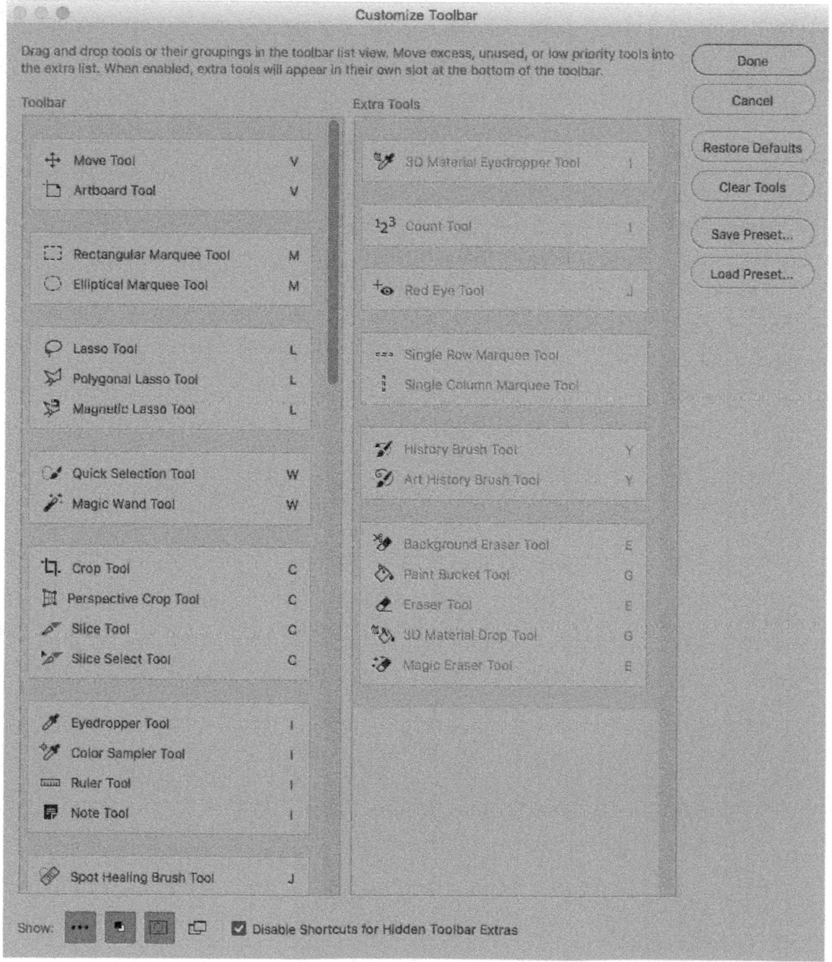

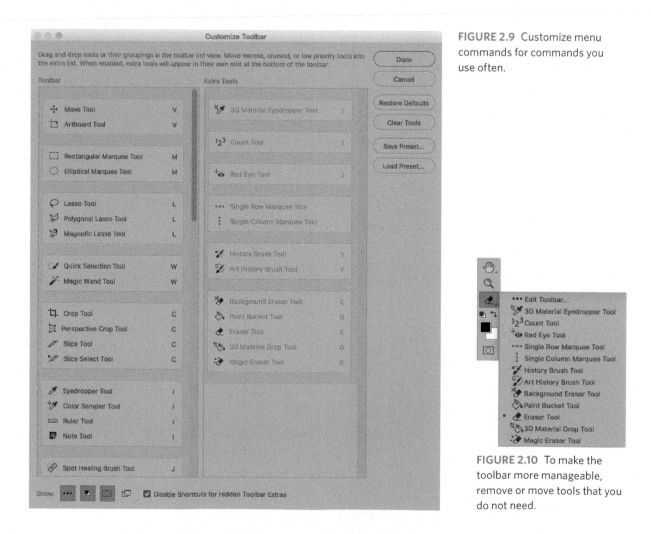

FIGURE 2.9 Customize menu commands for commands you use often.

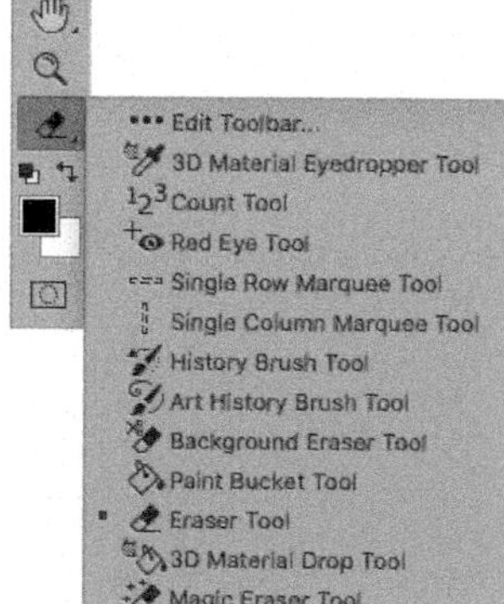

FIGURE 2.10 To make the toolbar more manageable, remove or move tools that you do not need.

Efficient Image Navigation

Take some time now to learn the following Photoshop shortcut keys and navigation techniques. Launch Photoshop, and open an image that is at least 10 to 20 MB. The reason we suggest practicing with a 10–20 MB file is that you will really appreciate the ease of navigation when you are working with an image that is larger than your monitor can display.

To be an efficient retoucher or restoration artist, learning to move through an image and zoom in and out quickly is essential. Critical retouching is done at a 100% or 200% view, as shown in FIGURE 2.11, which means that you are seeing only a part of the entire file. Zooming in to and out of a file allows you to see how the retouched area is blending in with the entire image.

Navigation and Viewing Shortcuts

Use any of the following techniques to determine image view size.

To view an image at 100% and see image details, do one of the following:

- Double-click the Zoom tool (magnifying glass) in the toolbar.
- Press Cmd-Option-0/Ctrl-Alt-0. Note: That's a zero, not the letter O.
- Press Cmd-1/Ctrl-1, as listed in the View > 100% menu.
- Spacebar-Ctrl-click/Spacebar-right-click and choose 100%.
- Enter 100 in the zoom percentage window in the lower-left corner of the file and press the Return/Enter key.

To zoom out and see the entire image:

- Double-click the Hand tool.
- Press Cmd-0/Ctrl-0. Note: Again, this is a zero, not the letter O.
- Spacebar-Ctrl-click/Spacebar-right-click and select Fit on Screen from the contextual menu.

To zoom in and out fluidly with any active tool:

- To zoom in: spacebar-Cmd/spacebar-Ctrl and press and hold anywhere on the image; or tap Z to select the Zoom tool, and press and hold on the image.
- To zoom out: spacebar-Option/spacebar-Alt and press anywhere on the image; or tap Z, click the image, and press Option/Alt to zoom down to a desired view magnification.

★ NOTE With the Zoom tool active and Scrubby Zoom selected in the options bar, you can also zoom in and out fluidly by dragging to the right or left.

FIGURE 2.11 Memorize how to zoom in to and out of an image efficiently. © *KE*

- To change the zoom level in preset increments:
  - To zoom in: Cmd-+/Ctrl-+
  - To zoom out: Cmd--/Ctrl--

+ TIP To simultaneously zoom in or out on multiple images, add the Shift key to the use of the Zoom tool. This also works for the techniques listed previously that access the Zoom tool through shortcuts.

★ NOTE If the fluid zoom doesn't work, ensure that the Animated Zoom option is selected in Preferences > Tools and that your graphics card supports these operations.

To pan through an image:

- On both Windows and Macintosh, pressing the spacebar converts any tool (except the Type tool, if you are actively entering text) into the Hand tool, which enables you to pan through an image. This works only if the image is larger than your monitor can display. You can also use the Navigator panel, covered at the start of Chapter 5, to pan around an image.

To navigate in and compare multiple open files:

1. Choose **Window > Arrange > Tile All Horizontally** or **Tile All Vertically** (FIGURE 2.12).
2. Click the document tab for one file and zoom in to the area or detail you are interested in.
3. Choose **Window > Arrange > Match All** and all files will jump to exactly the same location and zoom (FIGURE 2.13).

FIGURE 2.12 Tile multiple images to quickly line them up. © *KE*

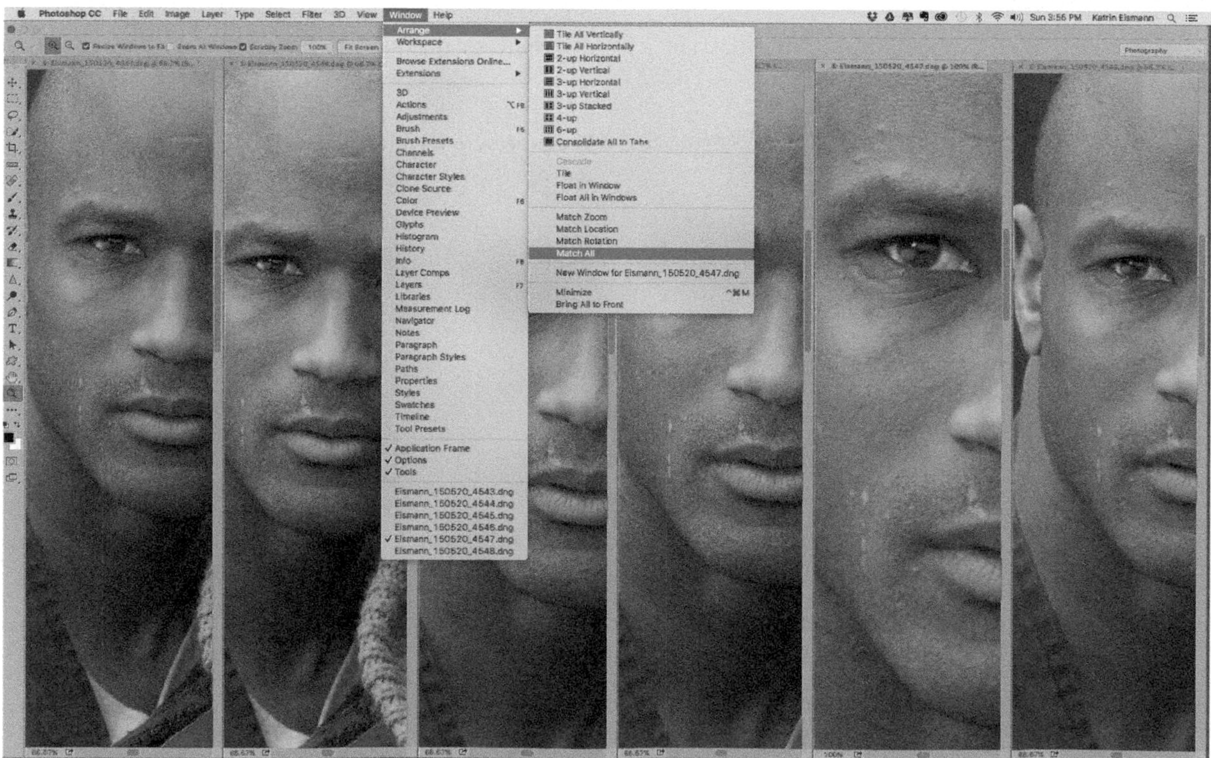

FIGURE 2.13 Match image zoom and location to compare multiple files. © *KE*

FIGURE 2.14 To compare multiple images, press Shift-spacebar to scroll or scrub through all open images. © *KE*

4. To scroll through all images at once, press Shift-spacebar and drag. The cursor will become the Hand tool and you can scroll through all open documents (FIGURE 2.14).

If you have an extended keyboard, you can review an image that is too large to fit entirely in the document window using only the keyboard. This is useful when inspecting the image for dust or scratches or when inspecting a high-resolution glamour portrait. To see every detail, start by zooming to 100% view, or 200% when working on a high-resolution display, and use these shortcuts to adjust the viewing area one screen width or height at a time:

- Tap the Home key to jump to the upper-left corner.
- Tap the End key to jump to the lower-right corner.
- Tap Page Down to move down one full screen.
- Tap Page Up to move up one full screen.
- Tap Cmd-Page Down/Ctrl-Page Down to move one screen width to the right.
- Tap Cmd-Page Up/Ctrl-Page Up to move one screen width to the left.

Use Rotate View for Easier Editing

The Rotate View tool is a fantastic feature for working at an angle in order to make detailed restoration, painting, drawing, or retouching work easier. Phil Pool, owner of Omni Photography, provides his aviator customers with the unique service of allowing them to see themselves pilot their own plane in the air. This is done by compositing a masked version of the plane sitting on the ground into an aerial photo. Phil uses the Pen tool to make an initial selection. He finds it easier to work from the top to bottom of the screen, so he uses the Rotate View tool to put the plane into the easiest position for creating the path (FIGURE 2.15). Using the tool's keyboard shortcuts, he can switch back and forth to keep rotating the plane to continually make a vertical selection.

When working on an image's finer details, work in full-screen mode at 100% zoom level and use the Rotate View tool to adjust the image angle as needed:

1. Tap F to enter full-screen mode and change the zoom level to 100%.

2. Tap R to select the Rotate View tool (grouped with the Hand tool).

3. Drag to rotate the image.

4. Click Reset View in the options bar to set the rotation angle back to 0 degrees.

FIGURE 2.15 Use the Rotate View command to get into the corners of a restoration or digital illustration.
© Phil Pool - Omni Photography

If all these navigational tips are starting to get jumbled, remember that you don't need to sit down and memorize them all at once. Learn the ones you use all the time—including the most often used tools and how to hide and show panels—and you'll be working like a power user in no time.

TOOLS, QUICK KEYS, AND BRUSHES

Tapping the appropriate letter on the keyboard activates a specific tool in the Tools panel. In most cases, the first letter of the tool's name is the letter to tap, such as B for the Brush tool or M for the Rectangular Marquee tool. There are exceptions to the first-letter rule, such as J for the Spot Healing Brush tool, and V for the Move tool. FIGURE 2.16 spells out the letter commands you use to access each tool.

To see and learn the tool tips, position your mouse over a tool. A tool tip appears, listing the name of the tool along with its keyboard shortcut, as shown in FIGURE 2.17. By default, the tool tips are enabled. If you don't see the tool tips, press Cmd-K/Ctrl-K to display the Preferences dialog box, and in the Tools category select Show Tool Tips.

As you can see in FIGURE 2.18, some tools are grouped. For example, the Dodge, Burn, and Sponge tools all share one spot in the Tools panel. Cycle through the tools by pressing the Shift key as you tap the tool's shortcut key until you reach the desired tool. TABLE 2.1 lists all the nested shortcuts you'll need for retouching and restoration.

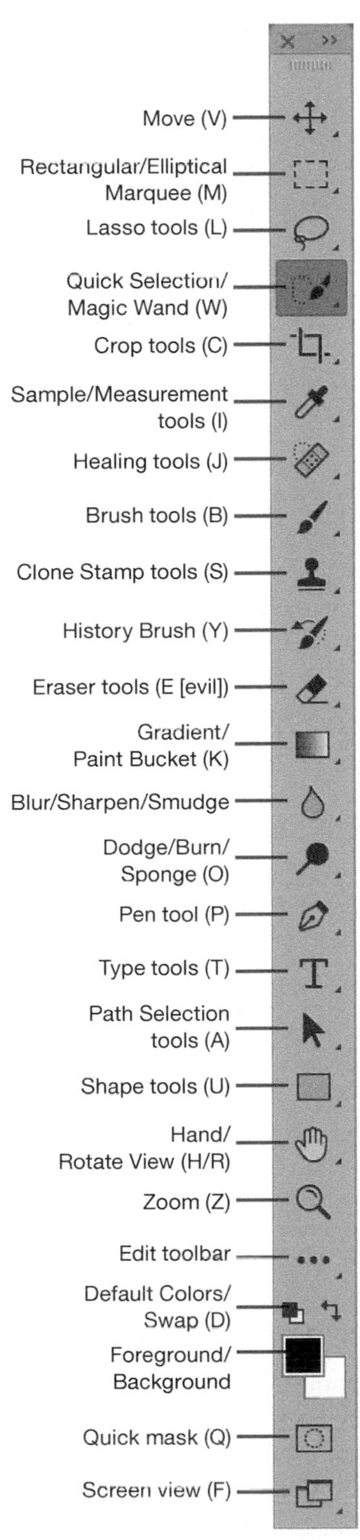

FIGURE 2.16 Learn the quick keys of the tools you use most often.

TABLE 2.1 Grouped Tools

TOOL	SHORTCUTS
Move	Shift-V cycles between the Move tool and the Artboard tool.
Marquee	Shift-M cycles between the Rectangular and Elliptical Marquee tools.
Lasso	Shift-L cycles through the Lasso, Polygonal Lasso, and Magnetic Lasso tools.
Quick Selection	Shift-W cycles through the Quick Selection and Magic Wand tools.
Sampler tools	Shift-I cycles through the Eyedropper, 3D Material Eyedropper, Color Sampler, Ruler, Note, and Count tools.
Spot Healing Brush	Shift-J cycles through the Spot Healing Brush, Healing Brush, Patch, Content-Aware Move, and Red Eye tools.
Brush	Shift-B cycles through the Brush, Pencil, Color Replacement, and Mixer Brush tools.
Clone Stamp	Shift-S cycles through the Clone Stamp and Pattern Stamp tools.
History Brush	Shift-Y cycles between the History Brush and Art History Brush tools.
Eraser tool	Shift-E cycles through the Eraser, Background Eraser, and Magic Eraser tools. (Think E for *evil*, as erasing pixels is destructive.)
Gradient	Shift-G cycles through the Gradient, Paint Bucket, and 3D Material Drop tools.
Blur	No shortcut for Blur, Sharpen, and Smudge tools.
Dodge	Shift-O cycles through the Dodge, Burn, and Sponge tools.
Pen	Shift-P cycles between the Pen and Freeform Pen tools.
Path Selection	Shift-A cycles between the Path Selection and Direct Selection tools.

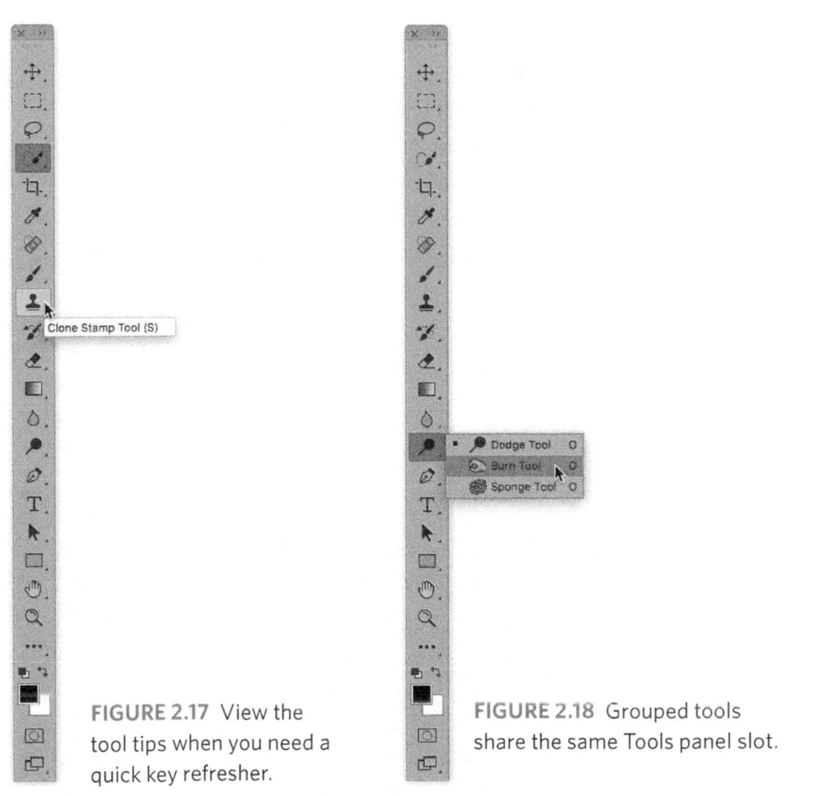

FIGURE 2.17 View the tool tips when you need a quick key refresher.

FIGURE 2.18 Grouped tools share the same Tools panel slot.

+ TIP Press Shift and the tool's keyboard shortcut to toggle through the tools in a tool group. For example, Shift-L selects and toggles through the Quick Selection/Magic Wand tools. Note that the Use Shift Key for Tool Switch option must be selected in **Preferences > Tools** for this to work.

★ NOTE If you would rather repeatedly tap the tool's shortcut key (without pressing Shift) to cycle through the tools in a tool group, press Cmd-K/Ctrl-K and deselect Use Shift Key for Tool Switch.

Quick Keys

For all intents and purposes, Photoshop is identical on both the Macintosh and Windows platforms. Throughout this book we've used both commands, with Macintosh before Windows. For example, undoing the last step would read Cmd-Z/Ctrl-Z. In general, the Macintosh Command (Cmd) key would be used where the Windows Control (Ctrl) key is, and you'll find that the Mac Option key maps to the Windows Alt key. Where the right mouse button is used on Windows, Control is used on the Mac.

Photoshop was developed to be used with two hands: one on the keyboard and one on the mouse. The time you save by using keyboard equivalents to access a tool or command and to navigate through a file will make you a more efficient retoucher. Additionally, using the keyboard rather than the mouse reduces the total number of repetitive mouse clicks that can add up to the pain, aggravation, and lost productivity of repetitive-motion injury.

Knowing the keyboard shortcuts to access tools, change settings, and control panels enables you to concentrate on the image. For example, imagine that you are retouching a file and need to access the Clone Stamp tool, decrease the brush size, increase the hardness, and change the brush opacity to 50%.

The manual method involves selecting the Clone Stamp tool, opening the Brush panel, finding (we mean guessing) the right brush size and hardness, selecting the Opacity value, and entering 50.

The shortcut method entails tapping the letter S (for Stamp). To decrease the brush size, tap the left bracket ([) key, or Ctrl-Option-drag/Alt-right-mouse-drag left. To increase the hardness of the brush, press Shift and tap [, or Ctrl-Option-drag/Alt-right-mouse-drag down to visually determine hardness. Then tap 5 to set the opacity.

It's a faster way to get the same results! In fact, it takes longer to write this out than it does to do it.

Visit https://helpx.adobe.com/photoshop/using/default-keyboard-shortcuts.html for a downloadable Keyboard Shortcut Reference.

Brushes

When using painting tools such as the Brush, Clone Stamp, History Brush, or Eraser tool, changing the tool's opacity can assist in performing more subtle retouches. You can change the tool's opacity by entering the required value in the options bar, but you don't need to highlight the Opacity setting in the options bar to do so:

- Enter a number from 1 to 9, and the tool's opacity setting changes to the corresponding value. If you enter 1, the opacity changes to 10%; enter 9 and it changes to 90%. Enter 0 to set the opacity to 100%.
- You can set finer values by quickly entering the precise percentage. For example, entering 1 and 5 would set the opacity to 15%.

To change a painting tool's flow, which is how fast the "paint" builds up, press Shift and enter a number.

When using the exposure tools (Dodge, Burn, Sponge) or blur tools (Blur, Sharpen, Smudge), the opacity settings are represented by Exposure and Strength percentages in the options bar. Thankfully, the same command to dial in a setting applies.

To change brush size or hardness via the keyboard for any of the painting, exposure, or blur tools use these shortcuts:

- Left bracket ([) decreases brush size and maintains hardness and spacing settings.
- Right bracket (]) increases brush size and maintains hardness and spacing settings.

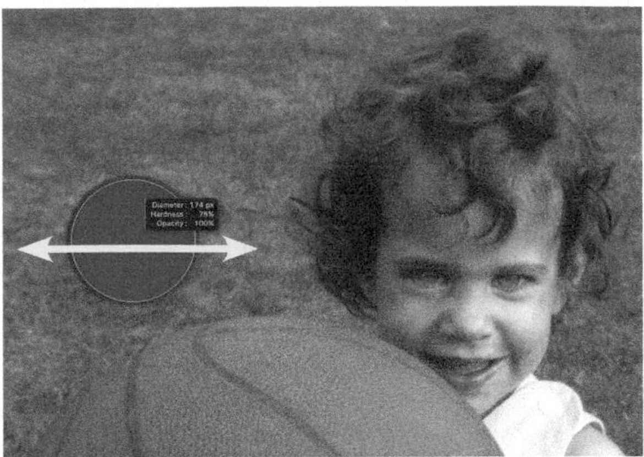

FIGURE 2.19 Interactively controlling brush size is very useful for retouching and restoration work. © *A.P Eismann*

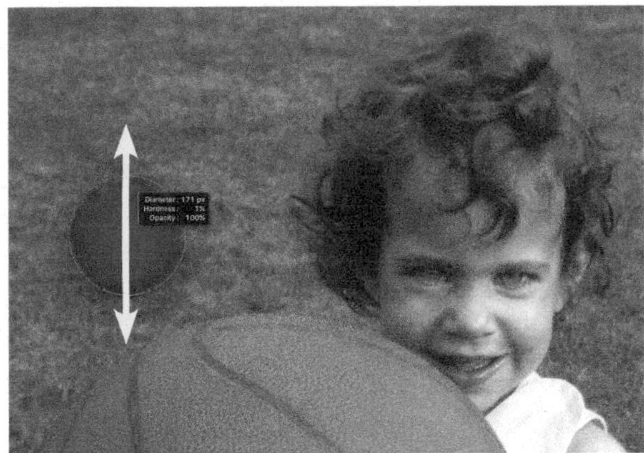

FIGURE 2.20 Controlling brush hardness size.

- Shift-left bracket ([) decreases brush hardness and maintains size and spacing.
- Shift-right bracket (]) increases brush hardness and maintains size and spacing.

To change brush size or hardness interactively for the painting, exposure, or blur tools, try this:

- Press Ctrl-Option (Mac) or Alt-right-mouse (Windows) and drag left or right to decrease or increase brush size (FIGURE 2.19) and up or down to decrease or increase brush hardness (FIGURE 2.20). As Julieanne Kost explains, "I prefer these shortcuts even though they are a bit more complex than tapping the left or right bracket keys, as many international keyboards do not have brackets."

FIGURE 2.21 The context menu of a selection tool with an active selection. © *A.P Eismann*

Brush and Tool Context Controls

Every Photoshop tool includes context-sensitive menus that you access by Ctrl-clicking/right-clicking directly on the image. These menus give you tremendous control over each tool. Shift-Ctrl-clicking/Shift-right-clicking brings up different context menus.

For some tools, the context menu will change depending on the state of the tool or file at the time. For example, notice the difference between the context menu for any selection tool with and without an active selection (FIGURES 2.21 and 2.22).

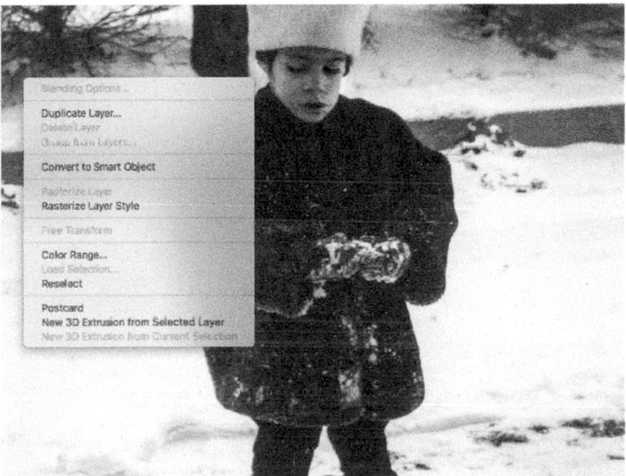

FIGURE 2.22 The context menu of a selection tool without an active selection.

While you are using the painting, exposure, and sharpening tools, Ctrl-click/right-click to bring up the Brush Presets panel and select a brush preset or to edit brush size or hardness (**FIGURE 2.23**). Shift-Ctrl-click/Shift-right-click to bring up the tool's blending modes context menu (**FIGURE 2.24**). Blending modes control how colors and settings applied to tools interact with the pixels they paint over; you'll see them used extensively in upcoming chapters.

The context menus for the healing tools differ from the painting tools. With the Spot Healing Brush tool active, Ctrl-click/right-click to access the tool's specific brush settings menu (**FIGURE 2.25**). Pressing Shift-Ctrl-click/Shift-right-click lets you choose the blending modes (**FIGURE 2.26**).

TRY IT Rather than going through the menu of every tool here, I suggest you open an image and go through the context menus of each tool. Also try adding the Shift key to see what additional context controls appear for the active tool.

TIP Julieanne Kost gives the following tip: Ctrl-click/right-click the tool icon in the options bar (officially called the Tool Preset Picker) and choose Reset Tool or Reset All Tools to set the tool options to their default state. This shortcut is a great way to troubleshoot why a tool might not be working the way that you think it should—perhaps you changed the tool's blending mode or feather the last time you used it and have forgotten to set it back. Please note that this shortcut doesn't reset the visibility or grouping of the tools, only their options.

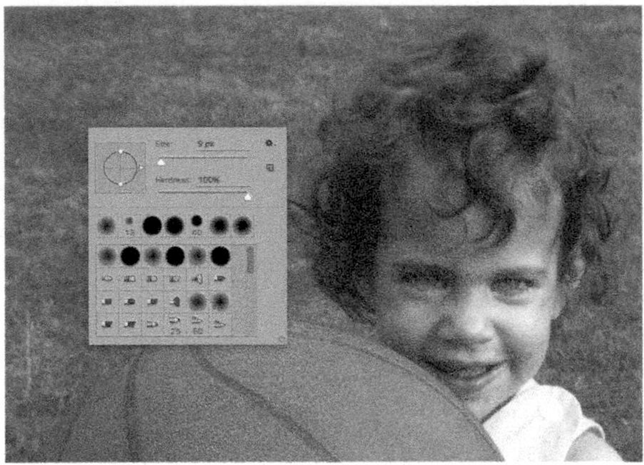

FIGURE 2.23 Avoid a trip to the Brush panel—Ctrl-click/right-click to bring up the Brush presets picker.

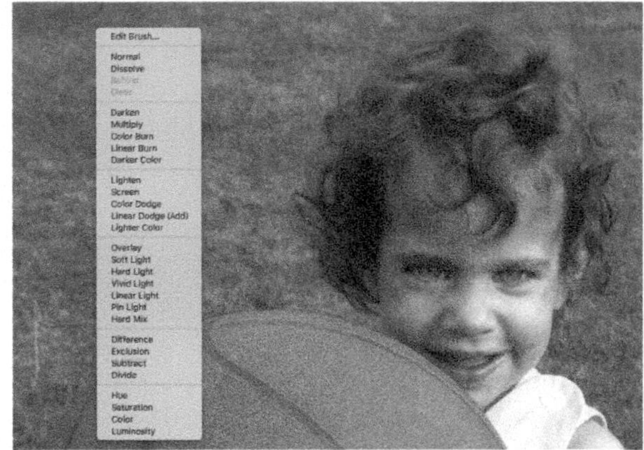

FIGURE 2.24 Change brush blending modes on the fly via the context menu.

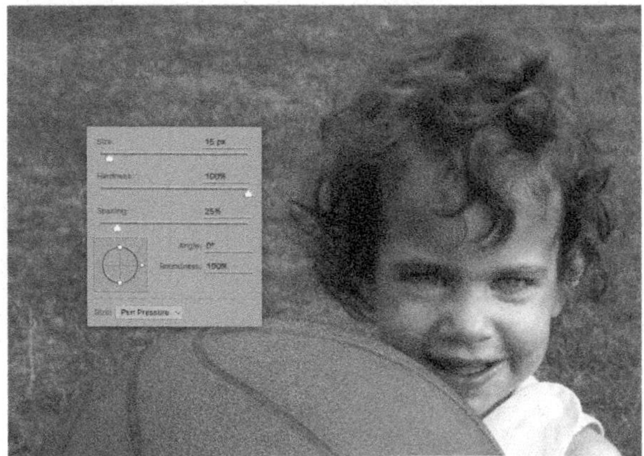

FIGURE 2.25 The context menu for the healing tools.

FIGURE 2.26 The context menu for the blending modes for the healing tools.

LAYERS, MASKS, AND BLENDING MODES

For a retoucher, layers are the most important feature in Photoshop, and throughout this book you will be working with the Layers panel and using nine different types of layers.

Background layer: This is your original image information, the pixels captured at scanning or photographing time. The Background layer should be treated as carefully as your original camera files and print or film originals. Never, ever retouch directly on the Background layer. It should remain as pristine as the day you scanned or photographed it (FIGURE 2.27). Do we sound adamant about this? You bet. The Background layer is your reference, your guide, your before and after. Do not touch it. To maintain the Background layer's integrity, either duplicate it (not recommended, as this doubles the file size) or use Save As to back up the original file before undertaking any color correction, retouching, or restoration—or better yet, use layers to work nondestructively.

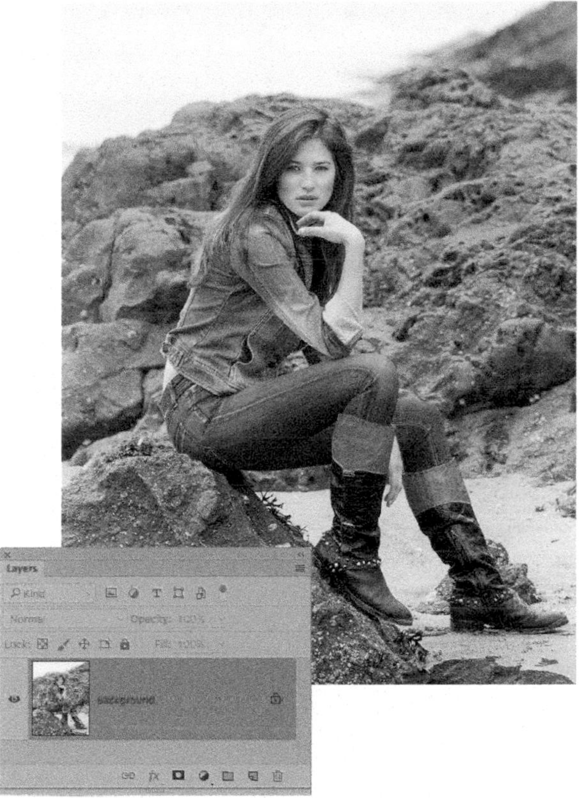

FIGURE 2.27 The Background layer is the original and should never be worked on or changed in any way. © *KE*

Duplicate layers: In the Layers panel, select the layer to duplicate. Choose **Layer > Duplicate**, or drag the layer to the New Layer icon at the bottom of the Layers panel. This creates an exact copy, in perfect registration, which you can work on and retouch without affecting the original data. Press Cmd-J/Ctrl-J to duplicate a layer. As mentioned, duplicating the Background layer doubles its file size, so we don't recommend it unless it is the only way to work nondestructively.

Copied layers: Many times you don't want or need to duplicate the entire Background layer, because you need only a portion of a layer to work on. In those cases, select the part of the image you want to use and choose **Layer > New > Layer via Copy** or press Cmd-J/Ctrl-J. Photoshop copies and pastes the selection onto its own layer and keeps the newly created layer information in perfect registration with the original data (FIGURE 2.28).

FIGURE 2.28 Copying parts of images to new layers saves file size and creates a dedicated layer on which to refine image elements.

FIGURE 2.29 Image adjustment layers are one of Katrin's favorite Photoshop features and allow for unlimited color and tone correction and enhancement.

Adjustment layers: Adjustment layers enable you to apply global and selective tonal and color corrections (FIGURE 2.29). We will use them extensively in Chapters 3 and 4 to improve image tone and color, in Chapters 5 and 6 to repair damaged images, and in Chapters 8 and 9 in the professional portrait and beauty retouching workflows.

Empty layers: Photoshop represents empty layers with a grid pattern (transparency). Think of these empty layers as a clear sheet of acetate on which you paint, clone, heal, and blur without affecting the pixel data of the layers underneath (FIGURE 2.30). You can use an empty layer to make quick notes on retouching or repair that needs to be done (FIGURE 2.31). All

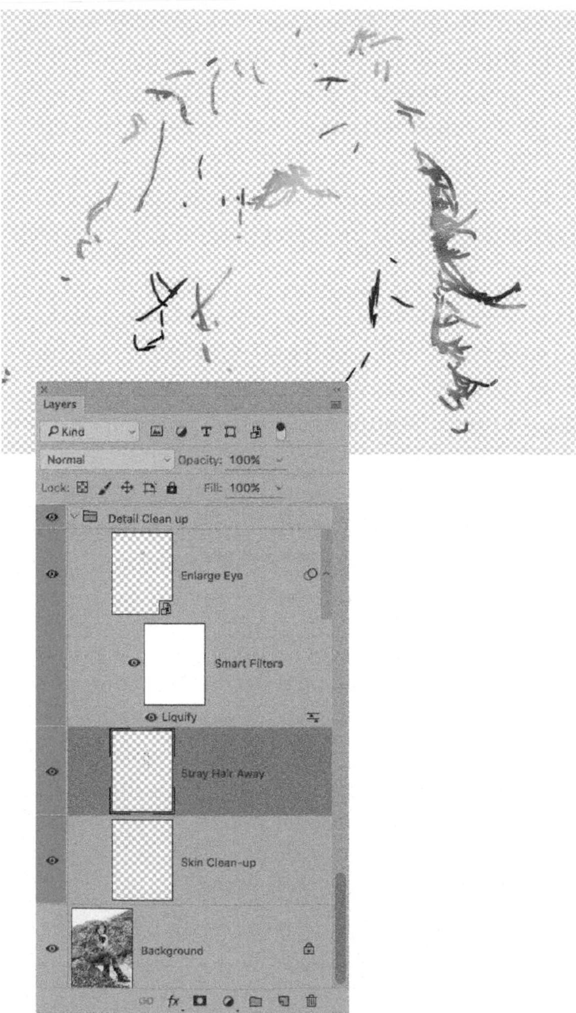

FIGURE 2.30 Work on empty layers to keep retouching, cleanup, and repair on a separate layer.

FIGURE 2.31 Make quick notes on an empty layer.

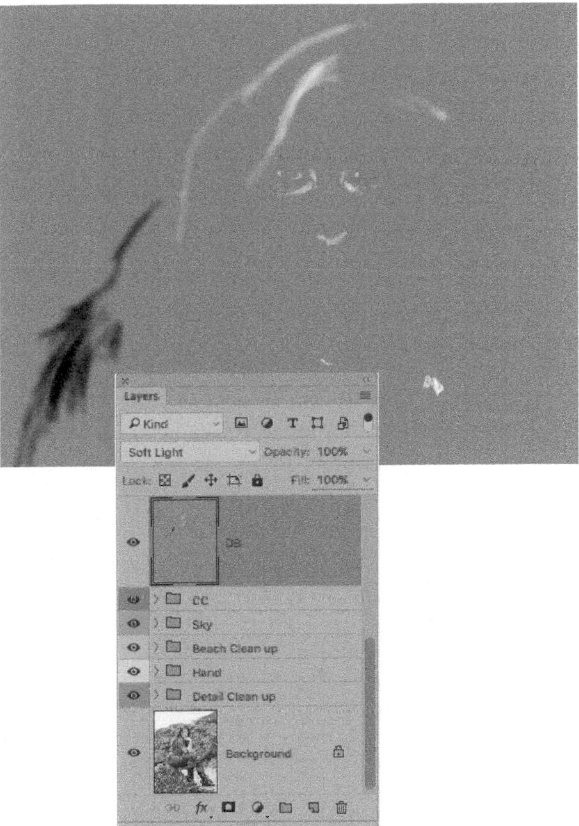

FIGURE 2.32 Neutral layers are ideal to dodge and burn to correct tonality and even out skin texture.

three of us use empty layers extensively, as they allow you to work nondestructively and, best of all, erase or delete parts of the repair or retouch and try again to achieve better results.

Neutral layers: Photoshop doesn't "see" the blending mode neutral colors of white, gray, or black when they're used in combination with specific layer blending modes. We'll be using neutral layers to apply subtle and dramatic tonal improvements (FIGURE 2.32) and sharpening effects throughout the restoration and retouching process.

Fill layers: Fill layers enable you to add solid color, gradient, or patterned fills as a separate layer (FIGURE 2.33). The solid color fill layer, combined with blending modes and layer opacity, is useful when you are coloring and toning an image.

FIGURE 2.33 Use fill layers to experiment with color, gradients, and patterns.

Merged layers: As the number of layers increases, it is often easier to work on a Work in Progress (WIP) layer, which is a flattened layer created with all visible layers you have been retouching (**FIGURE 2.34**). To create a new merged layer with image information, select the topmost layer in the Layers panel and press Cmd-Opt-Shift-E/Ctrl-Alt-Shift-E.

Smart Objects: Reference data from the original file rather than rendered pixels, which allows both flexibility and quality.

- Use Smart Objects when bringing in raw camera images from ACR or Lightroom to maintain the raw processing flexibility.
- Choose **Layer > Smart Object > Convert into Smart Object** before using image adjustments—including our favorite, Shadows/Highlights—or when transforming layers or partial layers (for example, when replacing heads that need to be transformed to best fit into a photograph). A Smart Object layer can be transformed over and over again without diminishing image quality (**FIGURE 2.35**).

FIGURE 2.34 Merged layers are a great way to mark retouching progress.

FIGURE 2.35 Converting a layer to a Smart Object allows you to repeatedly resize the layer without diminishing the image quality.

FIGURE 2.36 Smart Filters allow you to adjust and refine filter settings as often as needed.

- Choose **Filter > Convert for Smart Filters** to use Photoshop filters, whose settings and masks you can refine as often as needed to perfect your images (FIGURE 2.36).

The best aspect of layers is that they all (with the exception of the Background layer) support layer masks, blending modes, opacity and fill changes, and advanced blending options—features you'll be working with throughout the book to retouch and restore images.

Layer Naming and Navigation

Layers enable you to build up a retouch. In many cases, a retouching project can take 5, 10, 20, or more layers to finish. Relying on the generic Photoshop name, such as Layer 1 or Layer 1 Copy, to identify layers is a sure way to be confused and frustrated as you try to find the layer you need to work on. It takes only a moment to name your layers as you build up a retouch, which enables you to identify and activate the correct layer quickly and easily.

Additionally, you can access layers by Ctrl/right-clicking with the Move tool. The context menu that appears gives you instant access to all visible layers that have nontransparent pixels at the pointer position. As shown in FIGURE 2.37, the context menu reveals all layer names that have pixel information at the exact point where the mouse is. Best of all, by selecting the required layer name, the layer is activated—even if the Layers panel is not open at the time.

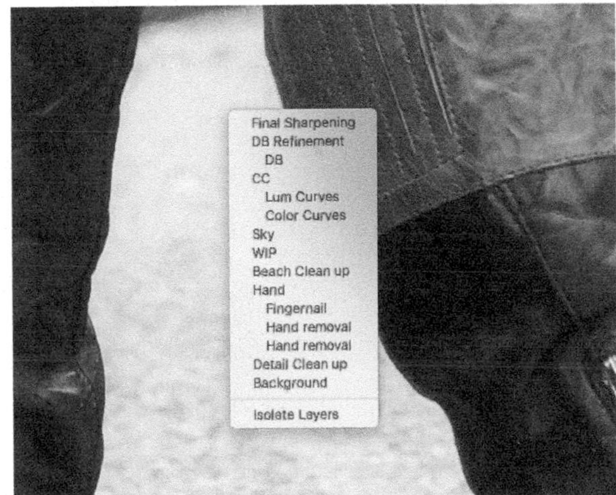

FIGURE 2.37 Naming layers is essential for managing complex retouch and restoration projects.

To name a layer, double-click the existing name in the Layers panel and type a meaningful name. It takes only a moment to name a layer, and it will save you countless minutes of confusion and frustration.

TIP To move layers up and down the Layers panel, use the command keys Cmd-[/Ctrl-[to move layers down and Cmd-]/Ctrl-] to move layers up.

Working with Layer Groups

In Photoshop, you can create up to 8000 layers including layer styles, something that requires a way to organize and manage layers more efficiently. Layer groups, shown in FIGURE 2.38, are folders in which you can place related layers. The groups can be expanded or collapsed by clicking the expansion arrow to the left of the group name. Layers can be moved around within the group by dragging them. A layer group can be moved around within the layer stack by dragging it up or down in the Layers panel.

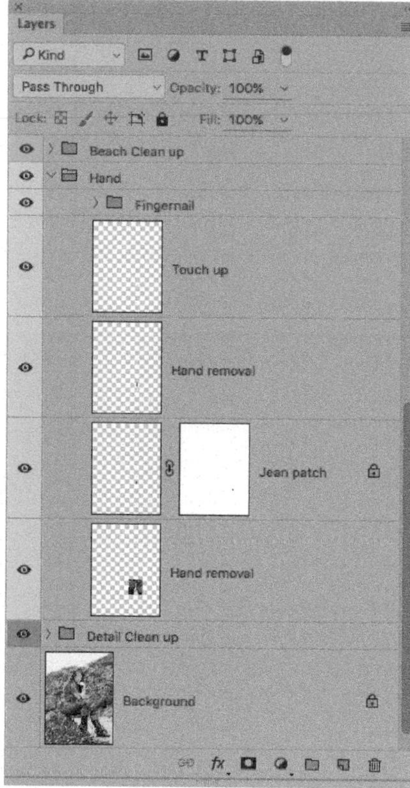

FIGURE 2.38 The many layers you create when retouching are much more manageable as color-coded layer groups.

There are two ways to create a layer group:

- Select New Group from the Layers panel menu, name the layer group, and then drag the desired layers into the group.

- In the Layers panel, select the layers you would like in a layer group by Shift-clicking them (to select adjacent layers) or Cmd-clicking/Ctrl-clicking them (to select layers that are not directly next to each other). Select New Group From Layers from the Layers panel menu (or press Cmd-G/Ctrl-G) to place the selected layers into the new layer group. Add additional layers to a layer group by dragging them into the desired layer group.

There are three ways to delete a layer group:

- Drag the layer group to the trashcan icon at the bottom of the Layers panel. This deletes the entire layer group without showing a warning dialog box.

- Select Delete Group from the Layers panel menu. The dialog box in FIGURE 2.39 then gives you the choice to cancel the operation, delete the group, or delete the group and the group's contents.

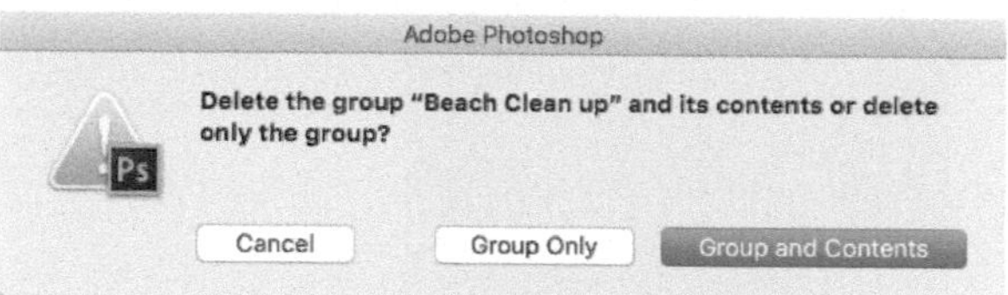

FIGURE 2.39 You can delete the group and the contents or only the group.

- Cmd-drag/Ctrl-drag the layer group to the trashcan to delete the layer group without deleting the contents of the group. The layers that were in the group remain in the document in the order in which they appeared in the group. You can also select the group and choose **Layer > Ungroup Layers** to delete the group and retain the contents.

Color-code layers to identify layer relationships quickly, and lock layers to prevent accidental edits to image data, transparency settings, and layer position.

To color-code a layer:

1. Select the layer in the Layers panel.
2. Ctrl-click/right-click the layer and choose a color from the context menu.

Organizing, naming, or color-coding layers and layer groups takes only a moment, but it can save you a lot of time in hunting for the layer you want to work on. Creating and using consistent names for layers and layer groups is imperative to an efficient workflow.

If you work with a partner, on a team, or as part of a production workflow, you'll especially need to use layer names. Imagine that you're working on a complicated retouching project and, for some reason, you can't come to work to finish the retouch. If the layers are well named, someone else on your team will be able to open the file, find the layers that need additional work, and finish the project. However, if the layers are all over the place, not named, or not in layer groups, it will take a while for someone else to figure out where to begin. In the worst-case scenario, a very important layer might be ruined or deleted. Enough said—name your layers!

Flattening and Discarding Layers

We recommend being a conservative Photoshop retoucher with a large hard drive and a lot of RAM. Don't throw away layers unless you know that they are absolutely wrong or unnecessary. Keep all production layers with a file because you never know whether a mask or tidbit of information from a layer will be useful later in the project or when the client changes his or her mind. By clicking the eyeball in the view column on the left side of the Layers panel, you can hide a layer whenever you like. Flatten an image only after doing a Save As and only as the very last step before sending a file to the printer or taking a file into a page layout program.

WORKING WITH PHOTOSHOP ELEMENTS

Photoshop Elements is considered Photoshop's little sibling. It is primarily geared toward amateurs, and it has fewer features and a simpler interface than Photoshop. Photoshop Elements users may wonder whether they can use it to work through the types of examples demonstrated in this book. The short answer is yes. Photoshop Elements offers the same basic tools as Photoshop, but there are some limitations. Let's explore some of the similarities and differences.

Photoshop Elements Background

Photoshop Elements is designed for those who do not need the extensive web, prepress, design, and video features of Adobe Photoshop, and want to improve their images quickly. With each Photoshop Elements release, new features are added, making Photoshop Elements more and more similar to working with Photoshop to retouch and restore images.

In the US, you can buy Photoshop Elements at big-box office supply stores, online as a standalone application, or bundled with Adobe Premiere Elements, a video editor. With Photoshop Elements and Adobe Premiere Elements, many users would have all the tools necessary for photo or video editing. Wayne has used and been a fan of Photoshop Elements for many years.

Photoshop Elements comes with the Photo Editor, used for image editing, and the Organizer, which has features similar to Bridge and Lightroom, such as the ability to sort, rate, and add keywords to images and videos. It also includes a search engine. Like Lightroom, it uses a catalog to organize files and ratings, track changes, and perform a number of nondestructive editing tasks, such as tonal and color corrections. In addition, tasks like printing, creating slide shows, or sharing on social media are available without entering the Elements Editor (FIGURE 2.40). If after working with Photoshop Elements you feel the need for the additional features of Lightroom, you can upgrade the Photoshop Elements catalog to a Lightroom catalog.

★ NOTE To import a Photoshop Elements catalog into Lightroom, launch Lightroom and choose **File > Upgrade Photoshop Elements Catalog**. Note that catalogs created in older versions of Photoshop Elements might not be upgradable; you'll first need to upgrade them to a newer version of Photoshop Elements.

Photoshop Elements Walkthrough

When you launch Photoshop Elements, a Welcome screen appears from which you can launch the Photo Editor, the Organizer, or the Video Editor (FIGURE 2.41).

To open a recently opened file or start a new file from the Welcome screen, just click the disclosure triangle next to Photo Editor.

FIGURE 2.40 Photoshop Elements includes the Organizer, which is used for keeping track of files, sorting, rating, and minor edits. Its catalog is similar to Lightroom's.

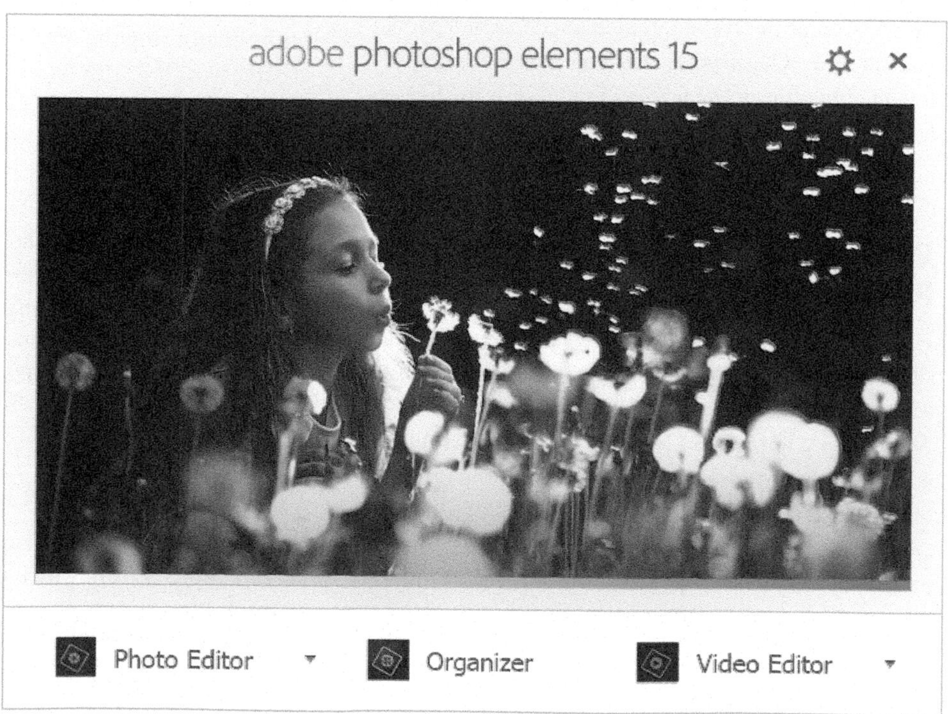

FIGURE 2.41 The Welcome Screen in Photoshop Elements presents options for opening the Photo Editor, the Organizer, and the Adobe Premiere Elements Video Editor.

★ NOTE The Adobe Premiere Elements Video Editor is offered as a choice even if it is not installed. Clicking the Video Editor option launches a window offering the option to install it or to download a trial version.

+ TIP You can set Photoshop Elements so that it bypasses the Welcome screen and launches your application of choice: Click the gear icon on the Welcome screen, select an application, and click Done (FIGURE 2.42).

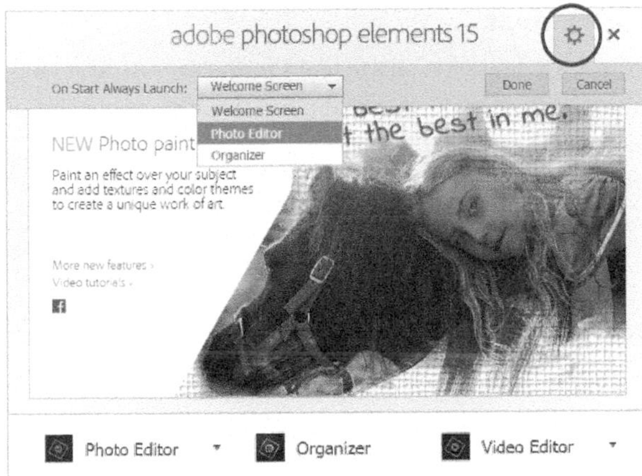

FIGURE 2.42 To always open the Photo Editor when launching Photoshop Elements, change the startup settings from the Welcome screen.

Once the Photo Editor is launched, Photoshop Elements offers a tabbed interface with eLive, Quick, Guided, and Expert options. The Quick, Guided, and Expert options are editing modes.

eLive

eLive is the default view when Photoshop Elements is launched for the first time. It offers Photoshop Elements tutorials, which are continuously updated, and search and help options. Upon subsequent launches, Photoshop Elements opens to the last-used interface (FIGURE 2.43).

Quick Mode

As its name implies, Quick mode provides an abbreviated set of editing tools and quick fixes. On the left of the document window is a panel offering basic tools, including the Quick Selection, Red Eye Removal, Whiten Teeth, Spot Healing Brush, and Crop tools. On the right are options for performing quick adjustments to exposure, lighting, color, and so on. Click the disclosure triangle next to any option to see its settings. For example, Color has settings for Saturation, Hue, and Vibrance; click a thumbnail to apply its settings to the image (FIGURE 2.44).

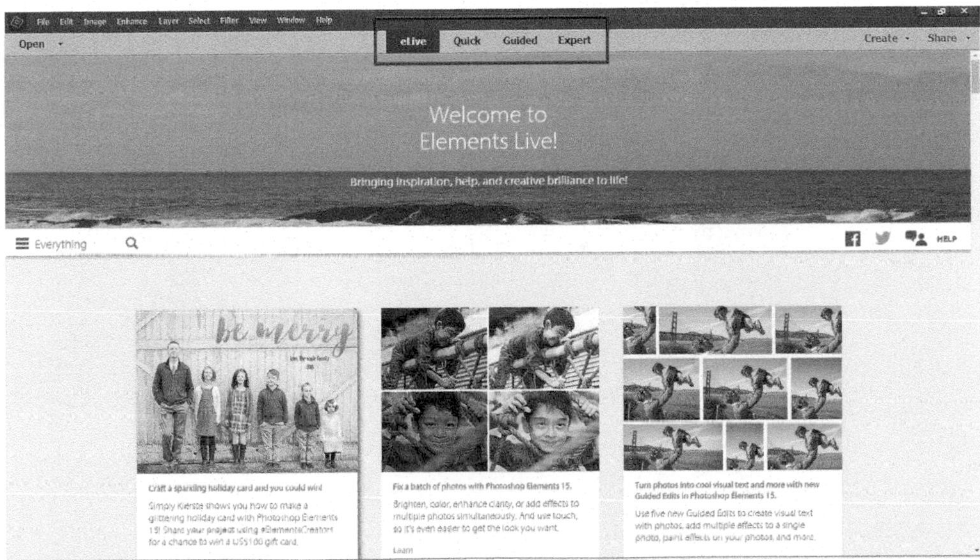

FIGURE 2.43 The eLive interface presents web-based tutorials. Click the Quick, Guided, or Expert tab to choose an editing mode.

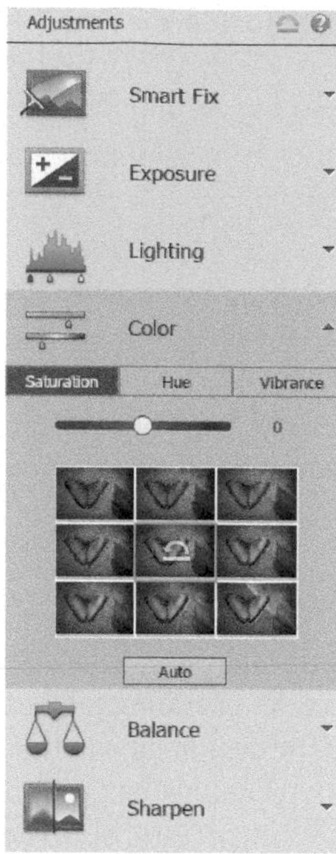

FIGURE 2.44 Quick mode shows a basic tools panel (left) and an Adjustments panel (right) that offers a variety of user-friendly correction tools with real-time previews.

Guided Mode

Guided mode provides step-by-step tutorial assistance in the following categories: Basics, Color, Black & White, Fun Edits, Special Edits, and Photomerge (which creates panoramic images). Each category has several subjects that walk the user through the necessary steps to complete a task (FIGURE 2.45).

Click an editing topic within a category to experience the complete walkthrough for an image you want to edit.

Expert Mode

Expert mode looks a little like Photoshop. At first the interface may look very basic, but upon opening the History, Layers, or Info panel, to name a few, you'll see that underneath the simpler interface lies the heart of Photoshop (FIGURE 2.46).

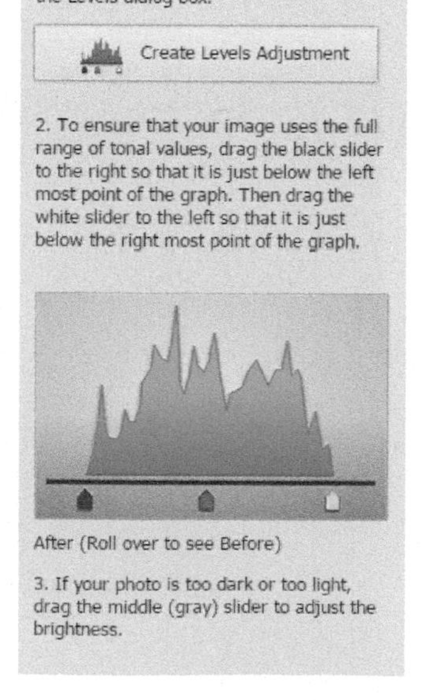

FIGURE 2.45 Guided mode provides step-through tutorial assistance.

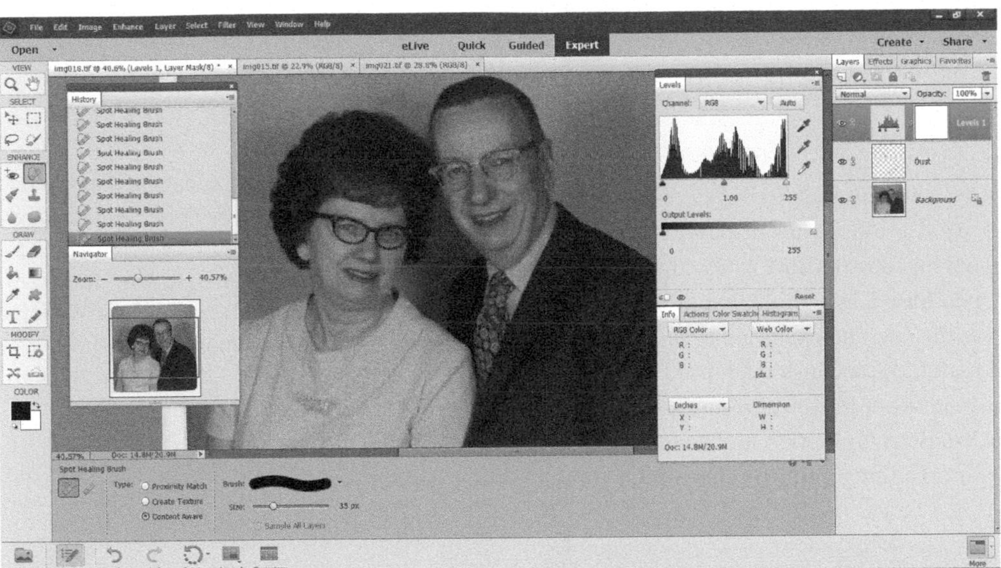

FIGURE 2.46 After you open a few panels, Expert mode looks similar to Photoshop.

Comparing Photoshop Elements and Photoshop

The similarity between Photoshop and Photoshop Elements will be obvious once you're in Expert mode. Photoshop Elements has many of the same tools and features. It has tabbed windows and adjustment layers, it supports masking, it has many of the same filters and similar panels, and it even uses many of the same keyboard shortcuts as Photoshop.

Images appear in tabbed document windows and are detachable, just like in Photoshop. The look and feel of the Photoshop Elements workspace is customizable, with panels that can be shown or hidden.

Click the More button, in the lower-right corner, and select Custom Workspace to switch from the basic workspace to a custom workspace that allows you to float panels that are normally docked and organize the workspace to your liking (**FIGURE 2.47**).

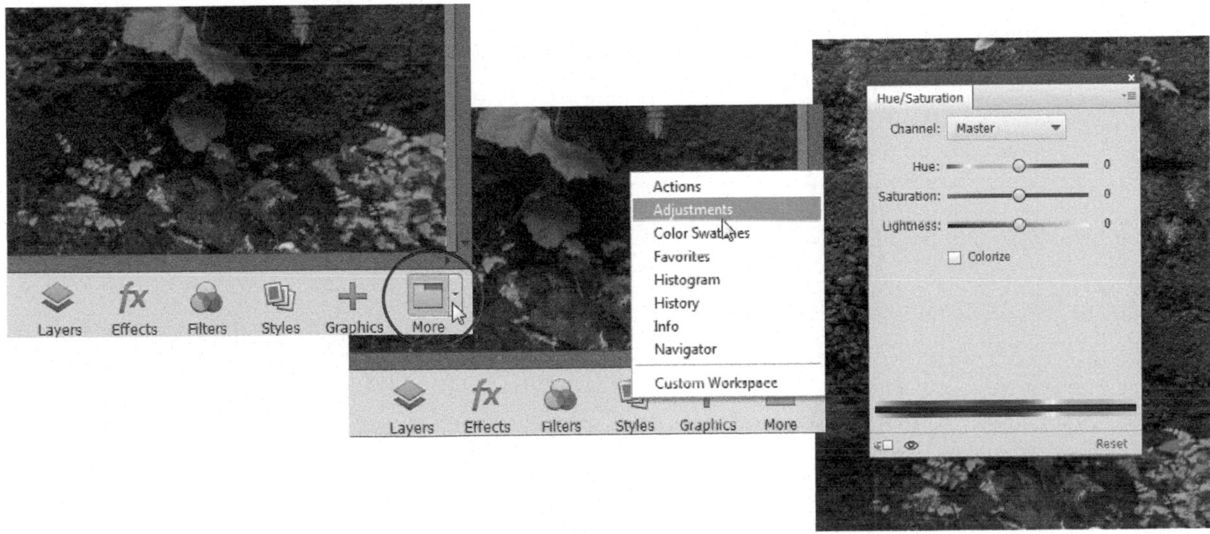

FIGURE 2.47 Click More to access additional panels, and select Custom Workspace to personalize the interface.

★ NOTE Photoshop Elements does not have a provision for saving custom workspaces, so a program crash or a resetting of the preferences will return the workspace to its default layout.

One thing you'll notice is that the actual work area is smaller than Photoshop's, as along the bottom of the interface are additional buttons (FIGURE 2.48). Click Photo Bin to show open files. Click Tool Options to access the settings for the currently selected tool; these settings often match the settings referenced in Photoshop's options bar. Other buttons here provide quick access to the Organizer, an option for rotating files, and an option for arranging multiple open files.

+ TIP To gain a larger work area, hide the Photo Bin or Tool Options panels by clicking the corresponding button in the bottom panel.

★ NOTE Photoshop Elements supports the playing of Photoshop actions (**Window > Actions**). Actions are a series of commands or tasks that were recorded and that can be played back on other images. You can't create actions in Photoshop Elements. Select Load Actions from the Actions panel menu to import Photoshop actions into Photoshop Elements. Photoshop actions will work as long as the action uses features found in Photoshop Elements.

FIGURE 2.48 A panel at the very bottom contains buttons for quick tasks and access to other panels.

PROCESSING CAMERA RAW FILES

Photoshop Elements also comes with a Camera Raw editor. It resembles a lighter version of Adobe Camera Raw (ACR) and handles basic adjustments. Open and edit multiple images individually, or simultaneously by clicking the Select All button (**FIGURE 2.49**).

To edit Camera Raw images:

- Choose **File > Open in Camera Raw;** or, from within the Organizer, right-click the image and choose Edit with Photoshop Elements Editor, which will open the Camera Raw dialog.

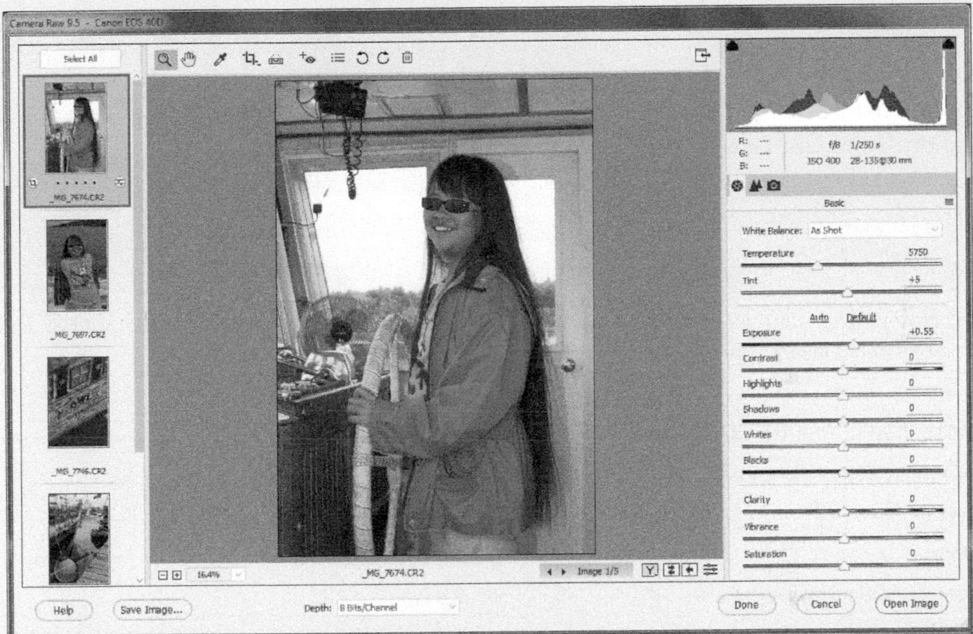

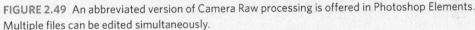

FIGURE 2.49 An abbreviated version of Camera Raw processing is offered in Photoshop Elements. Multiple files can be edited simultaneously.

An experienced Photoshop user using Photoshop Elements might notice the absence of standard Photoshop features such as the Channels and Paths panels, the Patch and Pen tools, and the Content-Aware Scale and Warping options. Sometimes missing features are located under different menus; for example, Sharpen filters are listed under the Enhance menu, and the Canvas Size and Image Size commands are found by choosing **Image > Resize**. Some commands have slightly different names. Curves are not available as a standalone adjustment (destructive editing); to apply curves, choose **Enhance > Adjust Color > Adjust Color Curves.**

Despite the absence of the full set of selection of tools found in Photoshop, Photoshop Elements is a capable editor and can take on difficult restoration tasks. The image in **FIGURE 2.50** had a very large stain that was removed using some of the same tools found in Photoshop and was restored using layers to maintain a nondestructive workflow.

TABLE 2.2 provides a comparison of the features in Photoshop Elements and Photoshop.

FIGURE 2.50 Photoshop Elements offers nearly the same number of nondestructive workflow options as Photoshop, including layers, adjustment layers, and masks.

TABLE 2.2 **Photoshop Elements vs. Photoshop features comparison**

INCLUDED IN PHOTOSHOP ELEMENTS	ADDITIONAL PHOTOSHOP FEATURES
Layers and Layer groups	Layer sorting, advanced locking and fill options
Clone Stamp tool	Clone Source panel
Spot Healing Brush and Healing Brush tools	Patch tool
Content-Aware Fill	Content-Aware Scale
Curves and Black & White conversions as standalone adjustments (Enhance menu)	Curves, Black & White, and Color Balance adjustment layers
Masking for layers and adjustment layers	Quick Mask and Color Range selections
Actions are playable only	Batch and script automation
Abbreviated ACR	Full ACR controls and Camera Raw Filter
Blending modes	Channel access
Filter Gallery and Correct Camera Distortion	Liquify and Vanishing Point filters
Limited Smart Object through the Place command	Smart Filters and Smart Objects
Color Modes Bitmap, Gray, Indexed, or RGB	CMYK, or Lab Color mode
8 bit and limited 16-bit image handling	8, 16, and 32-bit image handling
Basic selection of adjustment layers	Curves, Color Balance, Black & White, Exposure, and Vibrance adjustment layers
Color workspace s-RGB and Adobe RGB only	Custom color workspaces and proof preview
Lasso tools, Quick Selection tool	Full Pen and Path access
Auto Haze Removal as standalone filter	Haze removal as part of camera raw
Basic scale, skew, rotate, freeform, and transform controls	Warp transformation and Puppet warp
Custom brushes and patterns	Bristle brushes and dedicated Brush Panel
	Customizable shortcuts, interface and workspaces

Photoshop Elements has some features that Photoshop does not. For example, an automatic red-eye removal (Auto Correct) and the equivalent of red-eye removal for pets (Pet Eye), which can be useful in eliminating the ghostly green reflections often seen in animal images taken with flash. Pet Eye is an option under the Red Eye Removal tool (FIGURE 2.51).

Photoshop Elements does include a number of the same tools as Photoshop, and technically it is a variant of Photoshop, but some of those features are inaccessible. This has opened the door to a secondary market of plug-ins that tap into those hidden features. One such plug-in is called Elements+ (www.elementsplus.net). It provides access to many hidden features—like Curves, Color Balance, and Quick Mask—by adding a few menu items and an additional panel in the Effects tab. Although it does not convert Photoshop Elements into a full-blown version of Photoshop, it does make the program more versatile (FIGURE 2.52).

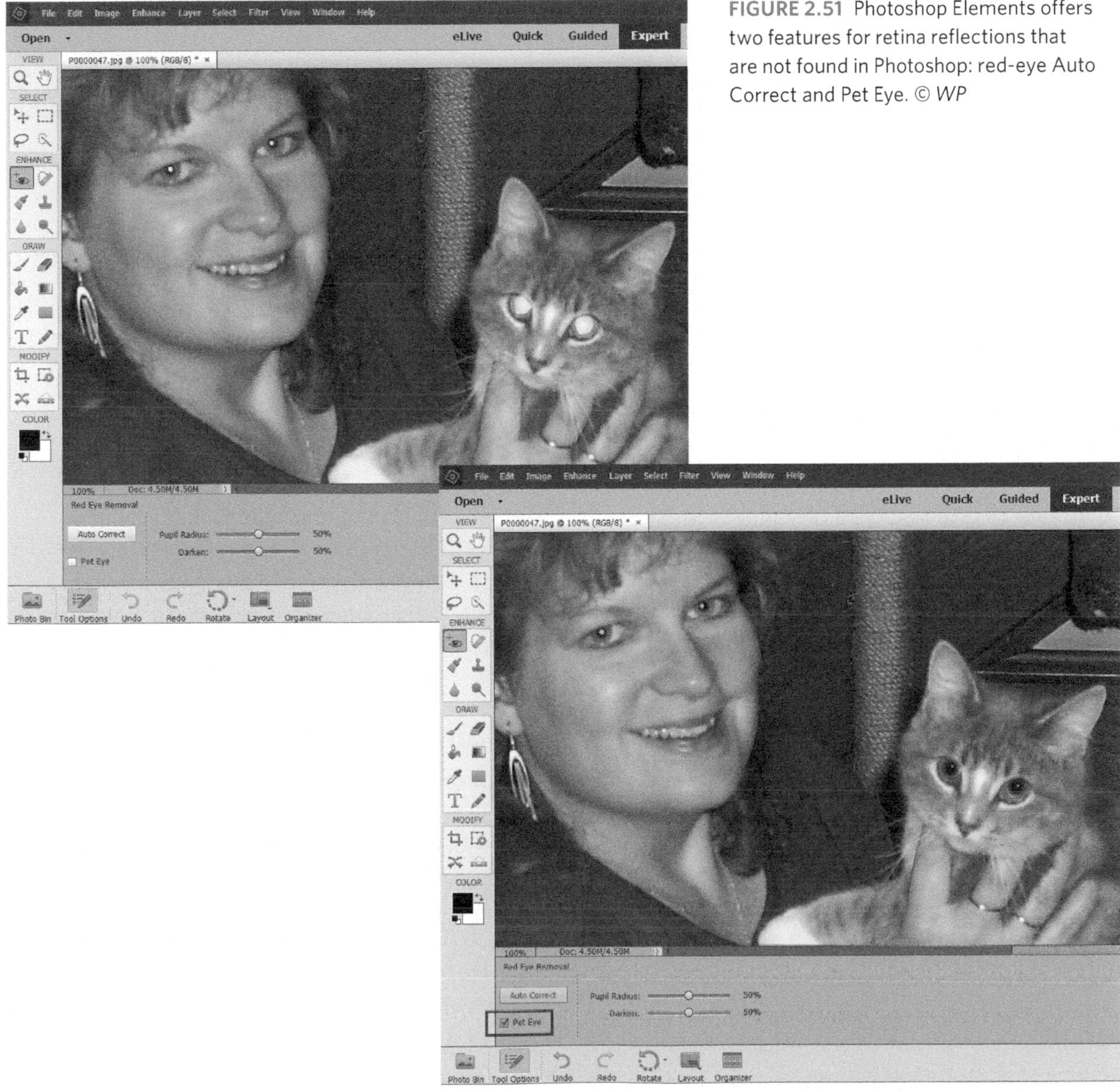

FIGURE 2.51 Photoshop Elements offers two features for retina reflections that are not found in Photoshop: red-eye Auto Correct and Pet Eye. © *WP*

FIGURE 2.52 Elements+ adds several Photoshop features to Photoshop Elements, allowing you to, for example, work with a curves adjustment layer.

Photoshop Elements has a lot of competition from free applications. One, called Pixlr, (www.pixlr.com/editor), runs within a browser. Another, Gimp (www.gimp.org), is available as an open source program.

Perhaps the biggest competitor is Adobe itself, through repeated solicitations to switch to Photoshop, both inside the Photoshop Elements interface and on the Photoshop Elements website. When the Adjust Color Curves feature is used, an offer to switch to Photoshop is found in the interface. The Photoshop Elements website promotes switching to the Creative Cloud Photography plan, with a side-by-side comparison of features and a mention of the minor price difference between the two. Despite the offers to switch, there are advantages to using Photoshop Elements—including the simpler interface, which is uncluttered by unneeded Photoshop features.

Many of the techniques in this book can be done in Photoshop Elements. If methods are presented that use tools found only in Photoshop, alternative methods, workarounds, downloadable actions, and third-party plug-ins can assist.

CLOSING THOUGHTS

The one thing that no computer, book, or class can give you is the passion to practice, learn, and experiment with the skills and techniques it takes to be a good retoucher. Retouching is more than removing dust, or covering up a wrinkle here or there. Retouching enables you to give someone cherished memories that have faded over time. Retouching and restoration is a fantastic hobby and a challenging profession, so let's dive in and get to work.

Part II

TONE, EXPOSURE & COLOR

IQUIFY • CAFFEINE • PERSPECTIVE CROP • COLOR CORRECTION • SHARPENING • RETOUCH STRAT
AYER MASK • SEPIA TONING • HANDLING DELICATE ORIGINALS • DUST & SCRATCHES FILTER • CO
NGE • NOISE FILTERS • CONTENT AWARE MOVE • NOISE REDUCTION • FOOD RETOUCHING • LOCAL CO
RRECTION • PRODUCT RETOUCHING • CONTENT AWARE SCALE • WHITE BALANCE • NONDESTRUC
TING • RESTORATION WORKFLOW • HEALING TOOLS • CURVES ADJUSTMENT LAYER • TRANSFORMATIO
ROPPING • DODGE AND BURN • ENVIRONMENT AND LIGHTING • PERSPECTIVE CORRECTIONS • EXPOS

Chapter 3

EXPOSURE CORRECTION

Times have changed. We now see the immediate results of our photography on the LCD screens of our cameras and phones. But we are still disappointed by pictures that are too light, too dark, or just way off because the camera did not meter what we considered important or the flash didn't illuminate adequately. All these problems can be traced back to incorrect exposure. Although modern cameras have sophisticated light meters and exposure controls, strong backlighting or well-intentioned but incorrect camera settings can fool these modern wonders into making the wrong exposure.

Correcting exposure in digitally created images can prove to be a challenge, but correcting exposure with already printed photos or slides can put one's Photoshop skills to the test. Older images are subject to the ravages of time, and were often displayed in strong sunlight or stored improperly. With the transient nature of most color photographic substrates, these factors can wreak havoc on your fondest memories. When pictures fade, they no longer contain any rich blacks or pure whites, and they often suffer from odd color shifts.

In this chapter, you'll work with grayscale and color images to

- Use Levels and Curves adjustments to improve image contrast
- Use blending modes as an alternative to adjustment layers
- Apply tonal improvements to selective areas
- Work with Smart Objects and Smart Filters for nondestructive editing

EVALUATING IMAGE TONE AND PREVISUALIZING THE FINAL IMAGE

Taking a moment to evaluate the tone of an image is tremendously important. In that moment, you should identify the tonal character of the image and imagine how the image would ideally look after you're finished editing it. This technique, called previsualization, was developed by the black-and-white photographers Ansel Adams and Edward Weston. By imagining the final image, you create a goal to work toward. For example, in Photoshop you open a dark file. Your previsualization would be "I want the image to be lighter." Having a visual goal in mind helps you stay focused and not distracted by the many options that Photoshop offers.

An image's tonal character can be light, dark, or average, also called high key, low key, or medium key, respectively. Subject matter and how much light was in the original scene determine the tonal character of the image. If you're not sure which tonal type the image you're looking at belongs to, choose **Window > Histogram** to open the Histogram panel.

A histogram is a graphical representation of the pixels in the image, plotting them from black (on the left) to white (on the right). The greater the number of pixels in the image at a specific level, the taller the histogram is at that point. Knowing this, you can look at the histogram of any image and can tell where the majority of the pixel information falls.

When editing the tones, it is helpful to recognize which tonal type of image you're working with so you don't apply extreme tonal corrections (FIGURE 3.1). For example, if you are working with a high-key image in which the histogram is biased to the right, it wouldn't make any sense to darken the image just so that the histogram looks more balanced. By becoming familiar with what the tonal values represent—the shadows, midtones, or highlights of an image—you'll learn which areas of the histogram need to be adjusted to either lighten or darken the image.

CUSTOMIZING THE HISTOGRAM PANEL

With color images, the Histogram panel can be set to display the distribution of pixels in a variety of ways for both RGB and CMYK images.

First, choose Expanded View or All Channels View from the Histogram panel menu, and then choose one of these options from the Channel menu:

- RGB or CMYK to show a composite of all the channels
- Individual R, G, or B (or C, M, Y, or K) channels
- Luminosity, to show the luminance of the composite channel
- Colors, which shows all the color channels superimposed

The histogram in the Levels or Curves dialog box or the Adjustments panel is limited to RGB or CMYK composite or the individual R, G, or B channels or C, M, Y, or K channels.

Assessing Tone with the Measuring Tools

Evaluating the image on a calibrated monitor in a controlled viewing environment (see Chapter 2 for recommendations on setting up a studio) is essential when retouching. If you are unsure about your monitor or your visual assessment of an image, rely on the Eyedropper and Color Sampler tools and the Info and Histogram panels to evaluate and measure image tone and to track changes as you work. The Eyedropper is a digital densitometer that you can use to measure tonal and color values at specific locations in the image. The Color Sampler tool is nested with the Eyedropper tool in the Tools panel and is used to add fixed measuring points, as addressed in the next section. Keeping your eye on the Info panel is an essential habit while editing tone, contrast, and color.

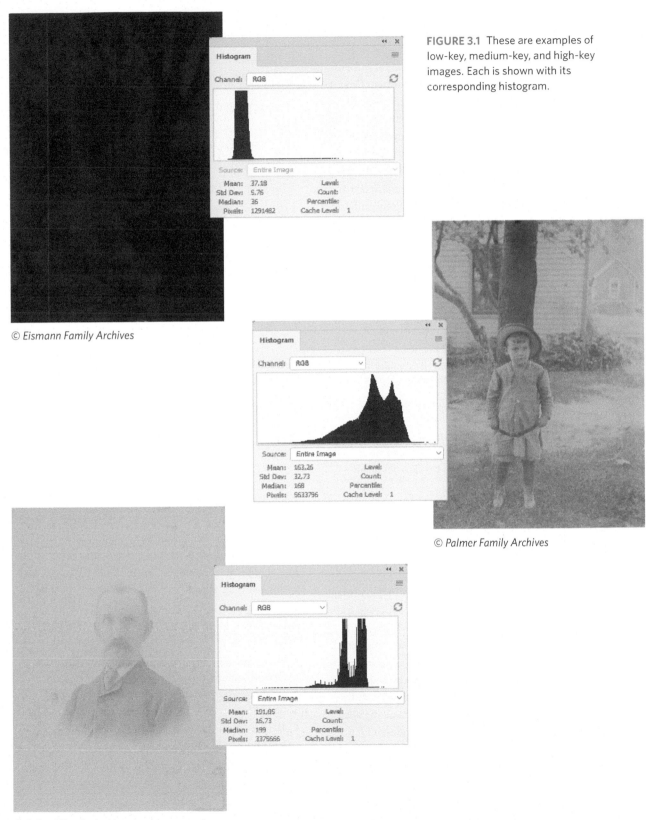

FIGURE 3.1 These are examples of low-key, medium-key, and high-key images. Each is shown with its corresponding histogram.

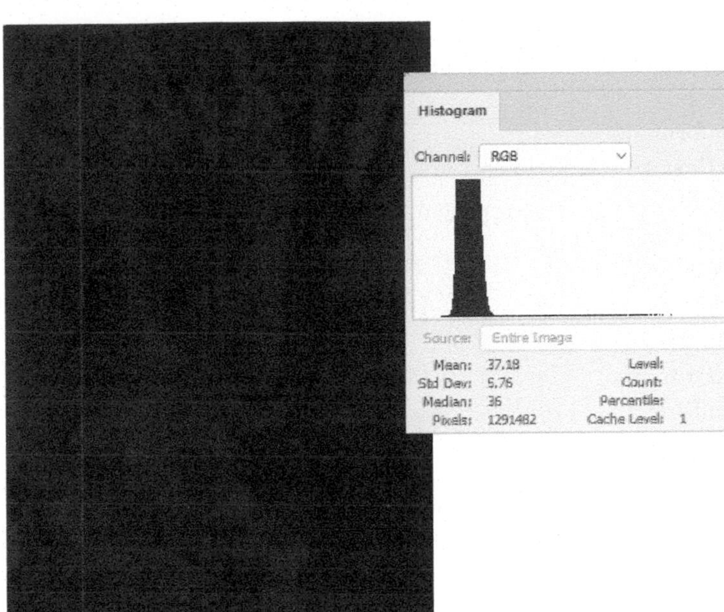

© Eismann Family Archives

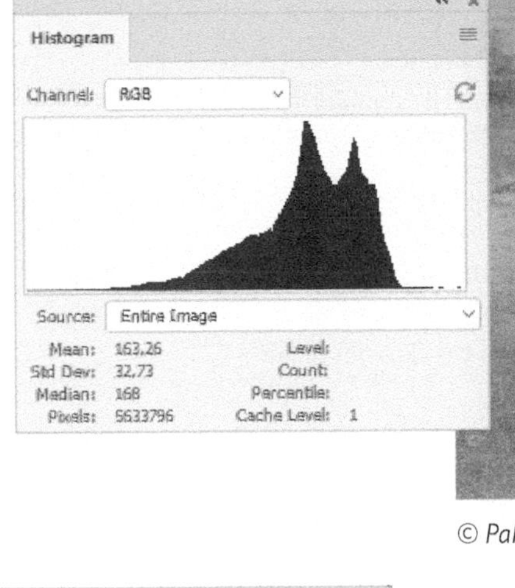

© Palmer Family Archives

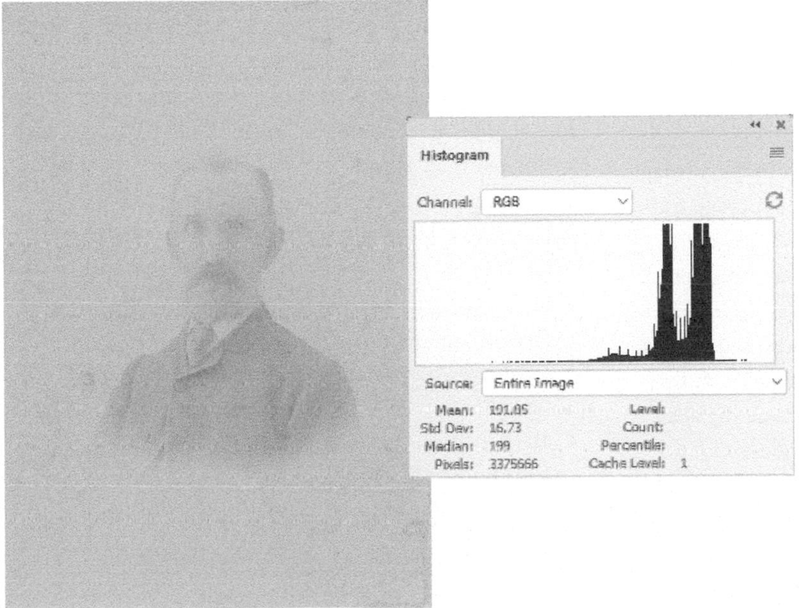

© Palmer Family Archives

Select the Eyedropper tool, and on the options bar choose 3 by 3 Average from the Sample Size menu (FIGURE 3.2), which also sets the sampling size, in pixels, for the Color Sampler tool. The pixel information is displayed in the Info panel. If the panel is not visible, press F8. In the Panel Options of the Info panel, set the first readout to reflect Actual Color and the second readout either to suit your own preferences or to reflect your final output. To set readouts in the Info panel, click the tiny triangle next to the eyedropper and drag to your desired readout. Or from the Info panel menu, choose Panel Options and select your desired settings. For example, if you are going to use offset printing, choose CMYK Color from the Mode menu for the second color readout. Photographers who are familiar with the zone system prefer to use grayscale (K) to read the black tonal-output values (FIGURE 3.3).

FIGURE 3.2 Use the 3 by 3 Average option to sample a small region of the image.

TIP Choose Point Sample from the Sample Size menu when viewing an image at 100% or larger to ensure that the sample chosen is the correct pixel.

CUSTOMIZE THE INFO PANEL

To make the Info panel easier to read, set the secondary readout to display grayscale values. That gives a single scale that ranges from 0–100 and removes some of the digital clutter from the panel.

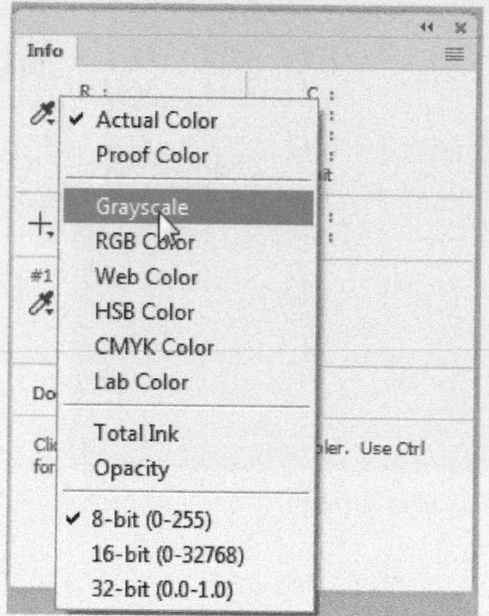

FIGURE 3.3 Click the tiny triangle next to the secondary readout eyedropper and choose Grayscale to simplify the Info panel display.

Tracking Tonal Changes with Color Samplers

Color samplers are lockable probes (up to four) that you can tack onto an image in the image editing process. You can place up to four samplers in each image. Each color sampler has a number and a corresponding area in the Info panel. You can move any color sampler at any time, as long as the Color Sampler tool is active. These four color samplers can be used to measure and track shadows, midtones, highlights, and a fourth tone of your choice. In FIGURE 3.4, I've placed three color samplers to track image highlights, shadows, and midtones. But color samplers can do something even better: while you're actively adjusting tonal values, the color samplers provide readouts of before and after values. In the Info panel (FIGURE 3.5), the number before the slash is the original value, followed by the edited value. As soon as you click OK to any adjustment layer, the before/after readout behavior reverts to the single readout. Color samplers automatically disappear when you select other tools and reappear when you activate the Eyedropper or Color Sampler again.

NOTE There are multiple ways to remove color samplers.

- With the Color Sampler tool active, hold down Option/Alt and move the cursor over the color sampler; when you see the scissors icon, click and the color sampler will be removed.
- Right-click while the cursor is over the color sampler and choose Delete from the context menu.
- Simply drag the color sampler outside the image.
- To remove them all at once, click Clear in the options bar.

FIGURE 3.4 Use color samplers to track the tonal values of the image.

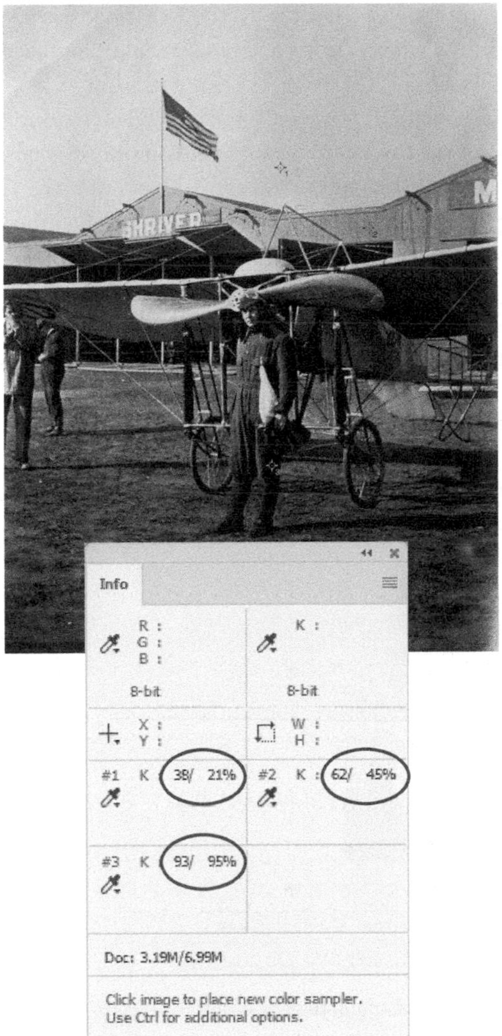

FIGURE 3.5 After you adjust the exposure of the image, the Info panel shows both the original and new values. © *Palmer Family Archives*

The Histogram Panel

The Histogram panel (FIGURE 3.6) should look familiar to digital photographers who have explored the playback features of their camera or phone or who have used scanning software. In short, the Histogram panel is a bar graph displaying the tonal values of pixels in an image, ranging from dark to light. The Histogram panel has multiple display options for showing RGB values, individual channels, luminosity, and colors. Additionally, the panel can be set to measure the entire image, a selected layer, or an adjustment composite. Further options include two sizes for the panel and an expanded view that can show individual channels in either black or color.

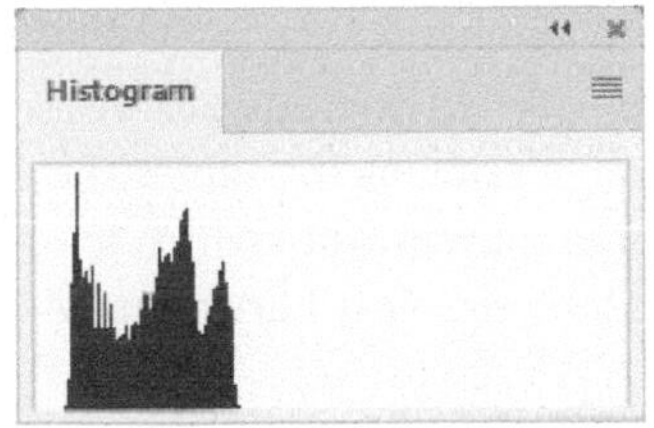

FIGURE 3.6 The default, Compact view of the Histogram panel

We recommend you work with the Expanded view (FIGURE 3.7), which shows a 256-step scale. Compact view shows only 100 tones and is not accurate enough for critical tonal editing. Even when working in 16-bit files, the Histogram panel still only displays 256 values, which may sound restrictive. But if the Histogram panel could show true high-bit, the interface would have to be 256 times larger to accommodate the 65,536 levels of brightness. The Histogram panel can also be expanded to show individual channel information in a variety of ways (FIGURE 3.8).

TIP The Histogram panel displays cached tonal values. After you make changes to an image, click the circular arrows in the upper-right corner of the Histogram panel to force Photoshop to update the values in the cache and to refresh the display.

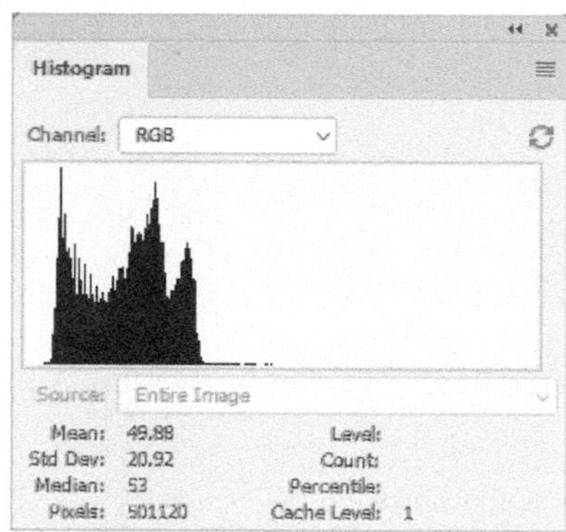

FIGURE 3.7 The Expanded view of the Histogram is more accurate than the Compact view.

The Histogram panel is updated in real time while adjustments are made. FIGURE 3.9 shows a dark image, the Histogram panel for that image, and the Properties panel for an unedited Curves adjustment layer (the histogram is displayed behind the curve). FIGURE 3.10 shows the result of lightening the image. While you're making adjustments, the Histogram panel displays before and after values, with light gray showing the original data and black showing the after adjustment data. Note that the histogram within the Curves Properties panel remains the same. The Histogram panel has three sources from which it can create the graph; be sure to select Entire Image

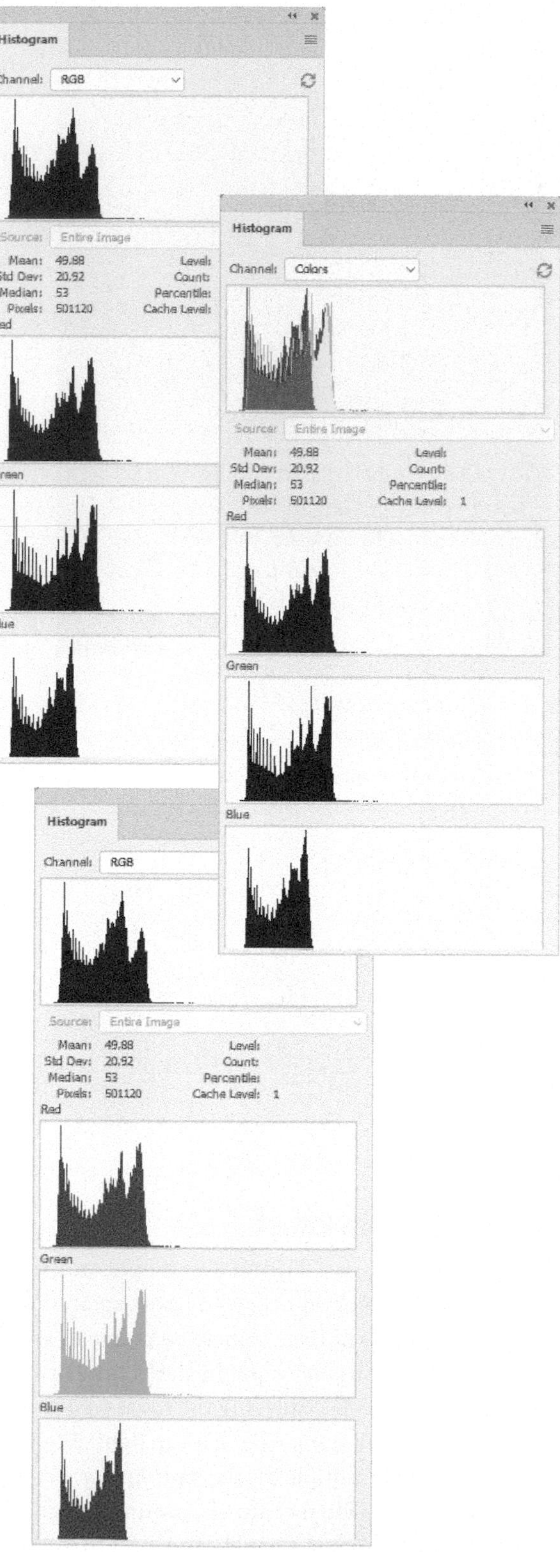

FIGURE 3.8 When the Histogram panel is in Expanded view, multiple options are available for displaying color channel information.

FIGURE 3.9 The histograms in the Curves adjustment layer Properties panel and the Histogram panel are identical before making adjustments. © *Palmer Family Archives*

FIGURE 3.10 After an adjustment is made, the Histogram panel updates to display before and after graphs.

or Adjustment Composite to include all layers. Like other panels, it is customizable to meet your needs and available screen real estate.

+ TIP The Levels and Curves dialogs and adjustment panels include histograms, but it's best to refer to the Histogram panel because it updates when adjustments are made.

+ TIP Use the RGB Channel option in the Histogram panel for a simple monochromatic readout.

The Importance of Adjustment Layers

Whether you work with Levels or Curves adjustments or any of the other supported image-adjustment features, we insist (yes, we all insist) that you use adjustment layers, one of the very best features in Photoshop. The same adjustments can be located on the Image > Adjustments submenu, but those adjustments permanently alter the pixels. Adjustment layers enable you to make nondestructive changes to your image. You can change and refine tonal and color adjustments as many times as needed without altering the underlying layer's original data until you choose to apply them by flattening the image. Adjustment layers sit on top of the image and apply the adjustment math to the pixel information without permanently changing it, making them a fantastic tool with which to experiment with, refine, redo, and learn from tonal and color adjustments.

The list of adjustment layers is long, but the ones most frequently used for tonal and color correction are Levels, Curves, Vibrance, Hue/Saturation, Color Balance, Black & White, and Photo Filter.

+ TIP It is also possible to use the adjustment commands on the Image > Adjustments submenu nondestructively. That requires converting the layer on which you want to use them into a Smart Object, as explained in Chapter 5. The advantage is that several adjustments can be applied and grouped as a single layer. The disadvantage is that all those adjustments must live under a single layer mask.

FIGURE 3.11 shows a very dark tintype image and the histogram displayed in the Levels dialog box (accessed by choosing Image Adjustments Levels). FIGURE 3.12 shows the improved image after making adjustments using Levels before closing the dialog. FIGURE 3.13 shows the histogram after the Levels dialog is reopened. Notice that the histogram takes on the appearance of a comb with gaps. These gaps could result in a noticeable banding effect in an image. No amount of readjusting will return the histogram or the image to its original state. By contrast, FIGURE 3.14 shows the result of the histogram when using Levels on an adjustment layer. The histogram remains in its original state (because the actual pixels in the image haven't been changed), and nondestructive changes can continue to be made *ad infinitum*. Again, this is why the Histogram panel is important—adjustment layer histograms do not update.

★ NOTE We don't recommend using either the Brightness/Contrast command or adjustment layer, even though it has been improved from its legacy form. Levels and Curves offer better control and use more sophisticated mathematics to apply the tonal changes. We also don't recommend Exposure, even though it sounds like a logical choice. Exposure is designed primarily for tweaking 32-bit HD images.

The benefits offered by working with adjustment layers include the following:

- They enable you to make tonal corrections without changing or degrading the source image data until you flatten the image.
- Their opacity can be adjusted. By lowering the adjustment layer's opacity, you reduce the strength of the tonal or color correction.
- They support blending modes. Blending modes mathematically change how layers interact with the layer below them. They are a great aid in restoration work because they enable you to improve image tonality quickly.
- They are resolution independent, enabling you to drag and drop them between disparately sized and scaled images.

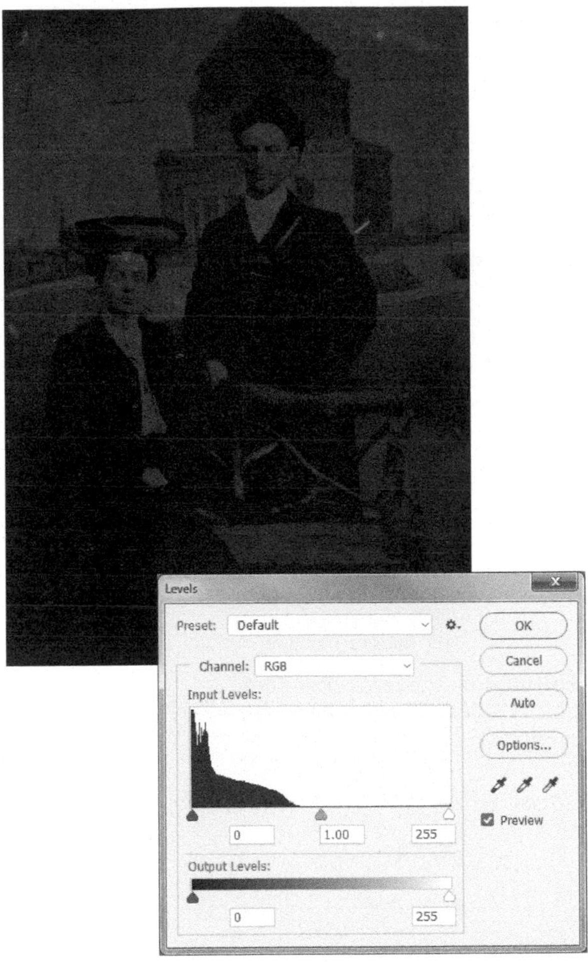

FIGURE 3.11 The histogram for this tintype reveals information only on the darker end of the scale.
© Palmer Family Archives

FIGURE 3.12 A dramatic improvement can be made by just moving the white and gray sliders.

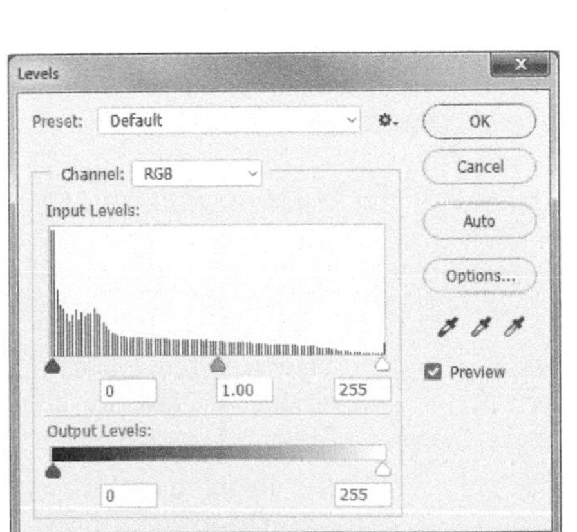

FIGURE 3.13 When the Levels dialog box is reopened, a new histogram shows the potential problems.

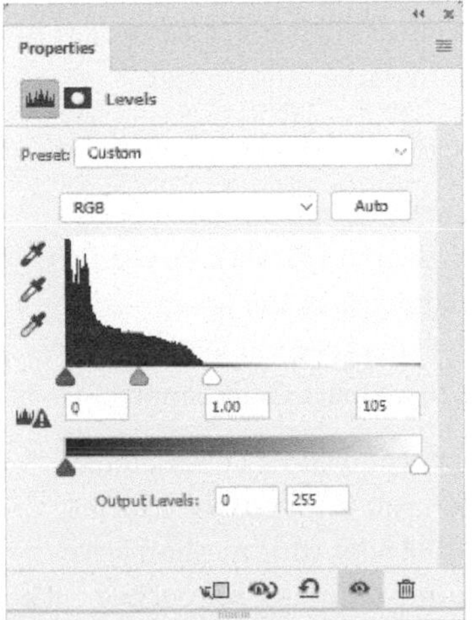

FIGURE 3.14 By using a nondestructive adjustment layer, the image can be changed without permanently changing the image's original information.

- They include layer masks, with which you can hide and reveal a tonal correction with the use of selections or painting.
- They are especially helpful when making local tonal, contrast, and color adjustments to parts or smaller areas of an image.
- If you don't like an adjustment, just throw the offending adjustment layer into the Layers panel trash and start over.
- They add very little to the size of the file.
- They work equally well in 8-bit and 16-bit files.

+ TIP If the adjustment feature you want to use is not available as an adjustment layer, it can still often be used nondestructively by first converting the image layer into a Smart Object. If that is not an option, duplicate the layer as a backup before applying a destructive edit.

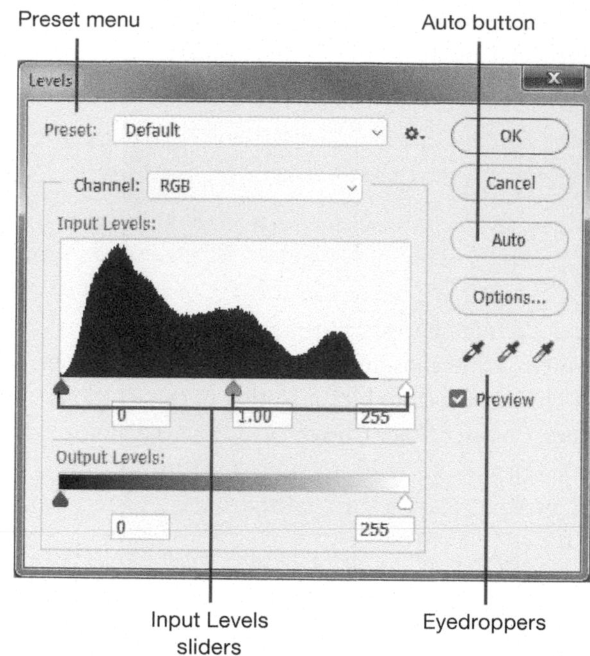

FIGURE 3.15 The Levels dialog box

MASTERING TONALITY WITH LEVELS

Working with Levels adjustments enables you to influence three tonal areas of an image: shadows, midtones, and highlights. You can use the input sliders and the black-point or white-point eyedroppers to place or reset black or white points. The gray eyedropper is not available when you are working with black-and-white images; it is used to find neutral points in color images. Often, you can make an image pop right off the page just by setting new white and black points and moving the midtone gamma slider (to the left to lighten or to the right to darken the image).

You can access the Levels controls in two ways:

- Choose **Image Adjustments > Levels** to open the Levels dialog box, seen in FIGURE 3.15. But this method changes actual pixels in the image—it's *destructive*—and so we don't recommend it unless you convert the layer to a Smart Object first.
- Open the Layers panel and add a Levels adjustment layer, which gives you access to the Layers Properties panel (FIGURE 3.16). This method leaves the underlying pixels in your image untouched—it's *nondestructive*.

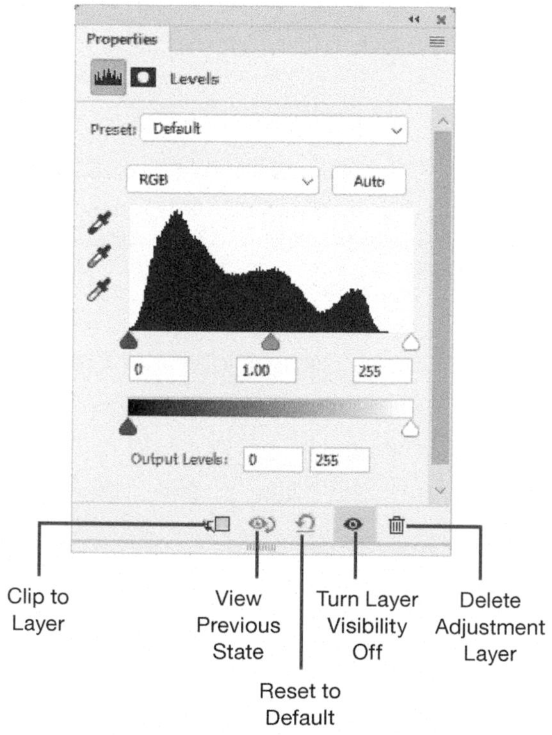

FIGURE 3.16 When Levels are used as an adjustment layer, the Properties panel offers these additional features.

The most important Levels controls to enhance image tone are these, all of which are addressed in greater detail in this chapter:

- Presets: Choose a standard set of adjustments from the Preset menu or use them to recall saved settings.
- Auto button: Use the Auto button to prompt Photoshop to apply one of four types of auto corrections, as explained in Chapter 4. You can choose which setting Photoshop uses by clicking the panel menu icon and choosing Auto Options or by Option/Alt-clicking the Auto button. Either of these actions opens the Auto Color Correction Options dialog box; select one of the algorithms listed there. If the image is in grayscale as opposed to RGB, there are no choices for algorithms.
- Eyedroppers: Use the eyedroppers to set white and black points for both black-and-white and color images, and use the neutral gray eyedropper to define a neutral tone in color images.
- Input Levels sliders: Use the highlight and black sliders to determine the black and white points by moving the relevant slider to the area of the histogram where the light or dark information starts.

Levels used as an adjustment layer offer these additional options.

- Clip to Layer applies the adjustment to the layer directly below.
- View Previous State.
- Reset to Default.
- Turn Layer Visibility Off.
- Delete Adjustment Layer.

Working with the Black and White Point Sliders

FIGURE 3.17 shows an image that is badly faded with age. The areas that should be white have gotten darker and the shadows are not a rich black, which reduces the contrast and makes the print unattractive and tonally flat, as shown by the narrow range of tonal values in the histogram. Use the following technique to darken the shadows, brighten up the highlights, and return a broader range of tonality. The corrected image (FIGURE 3.18) has snap to it.

FIGURES 3.17 and 3.18 © *Palmer Family Archives*

Upon opening the image, click the Create New Fill or Adjustment Layer icon (sometimes called the "Oreo cookie" or "yin yang symbol") at the bottom of the Layers panel (FIGURE 3.19). From the list of adjustment layers, choose Levels.

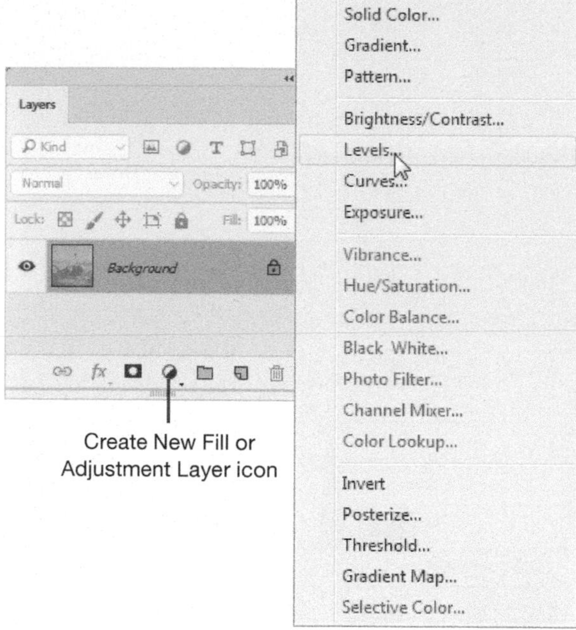

FIGURE 3.19 Click the Create New Fill or Adjustment Layer icon to access adjustment layer options.

TIP A faster way to create an adjustment layer is to click the icon for the desired adjustment on the Adjustments panel. Hover your mouse over the icon to cause the name of the adjustment to appear in the upper-left corner of the panel (FIGURE 3.20).

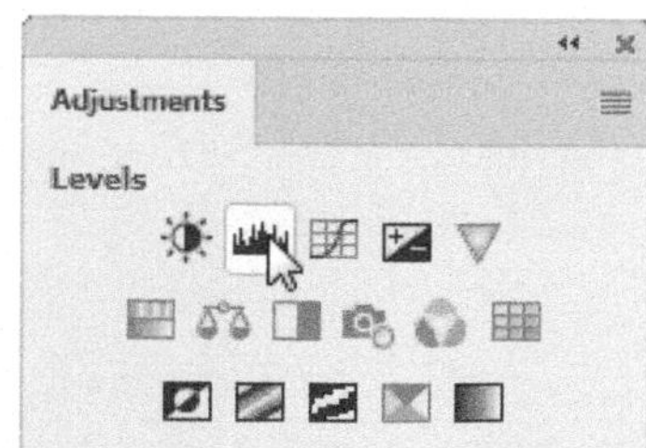

FIGURE 3.20 The Adjustments panel offers fast access to creating an adjustment layer.

The Levels adjustment layer we just added resides above the background layer and does not destructively change the image (FIGURE 3.21). FIGURE 3.22 shows the narrow tonal range of the image inside the histogram of the Levels adjustment.

NOTE When you're working with scanned prints, the histogram can show spikes at either end of the graph, indicating exposure information that is not part of the image. This can be caused by a scan that includes the print's border, the scanner bed, or perhaps even part of a photo album page.

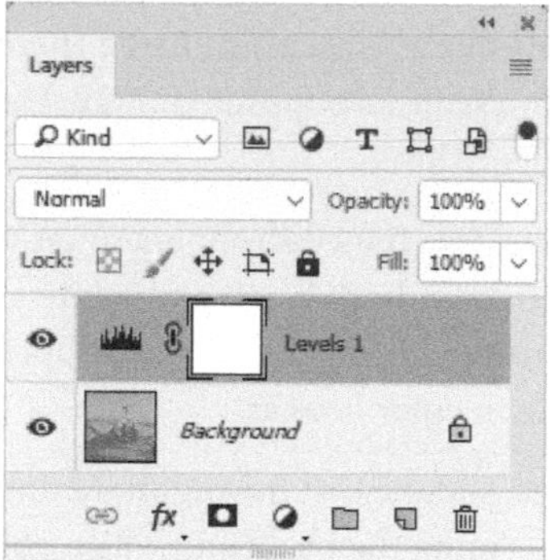

FIGURE 3.21 Adjustment layers float above the background layer and are used to make nondestructive edits.

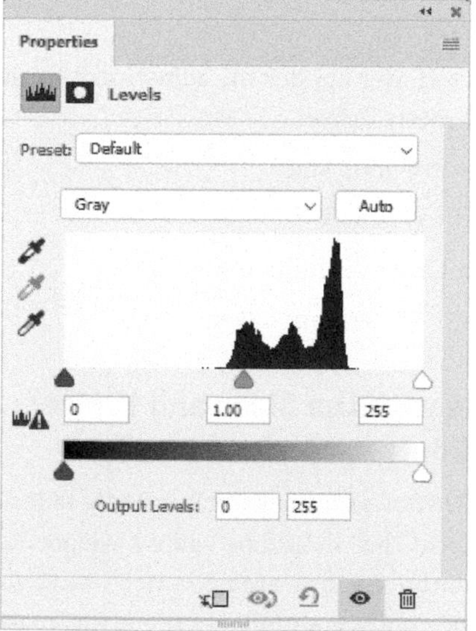

FIGURE 3.22 Before adjustments, the Levels histogram replicates the Histogram panel.

1. Drag the black triangle on the far left side of the histogram to the right until it is under the left edge of the graph, as shown in FIGURE 3.23.

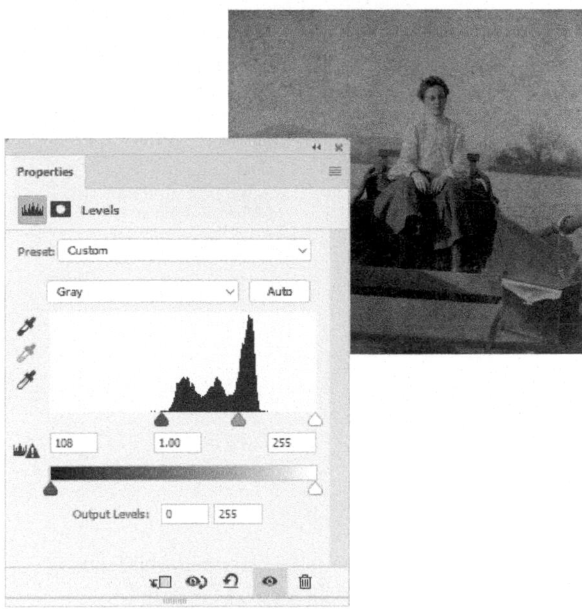

FIGURE 3.23 Moving the black slider to the right makes the image darker.

2. Drag the white triangle to the left until it is under the right edge of the graph, as shown in FIGURE 3.24.

FIGURE 3.24 Moving the white slider to the left makes the image brighter.

Adjusting the tonal range of an image will often reveal damage that may not have been noticeable prior. Repairing the correction of any revealed damage will be addressed in later chapters.

+ TIP Adjusting the tone of an image may also shift the color, boost the saturation, or both. Blending modes will be addressed later in the chapter, but changing the blending mode of the Levels adjustment layer to Luminosity will keep any color in the image more natural. Additional options for monochromatic images include using the tint option with a Black and White adjustment layer or using the Colorize option with a Hue/Saturation adjustment layer and choosing a hue that is similar to the original.

! CAUTION Dragging the white or black sliders too far into the white or black area of the histogram may clip important information to pure white or pure black. Evaluate the image and the image histogram to see where the image information falls, taking care not to clip tonal values that should be kept. Again, using adjustment layers keeps any clipping from being permanent.

Working with the Midtone Slider

When working with faded images, using the black and white point sliders to add contrast is a good starting point. If, after using them, the image is too dark, adjust the midtone slider to the left to lighten the image; if the image is too light, move the midtone slider to the right. The photograph shown in FIGURE 3.25 was stored improperly and has lost all contrast, while FIGURE 3.26 shows the improved image after adjusting all three sliders.

ch3_schoolboys.jpg

1. As in the last example, create a Levels adjustment layer (FIGURE 3.27) and drag the black and white sliders to the edges of the information in the histogram (FIGURE 3.28).

FIGURES 3.25 and **3.26** © *Palmer Family Archives*

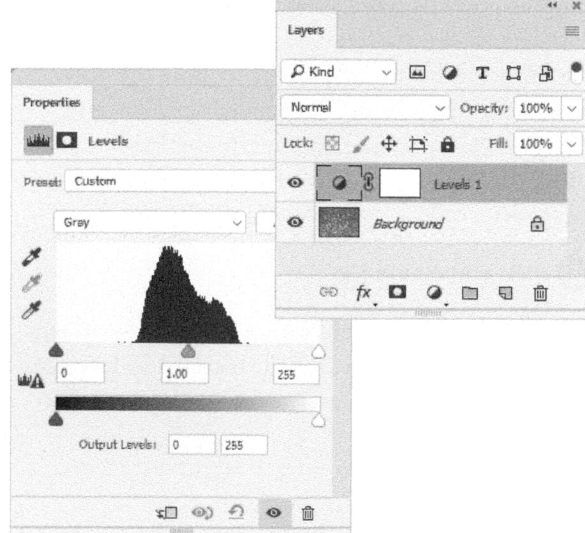

FIGURE 3.27 The histogram shows the image to be tonally flat.

FIGURE 3.28 Adjusting both the black and white sliders improves the image, but makes it a bit too bright.

2. The image is greatly improved but is now a bit too light and could use a little more help. Slide the midtone slider to the right to darken the midtones (**FIGURE 3.29**).

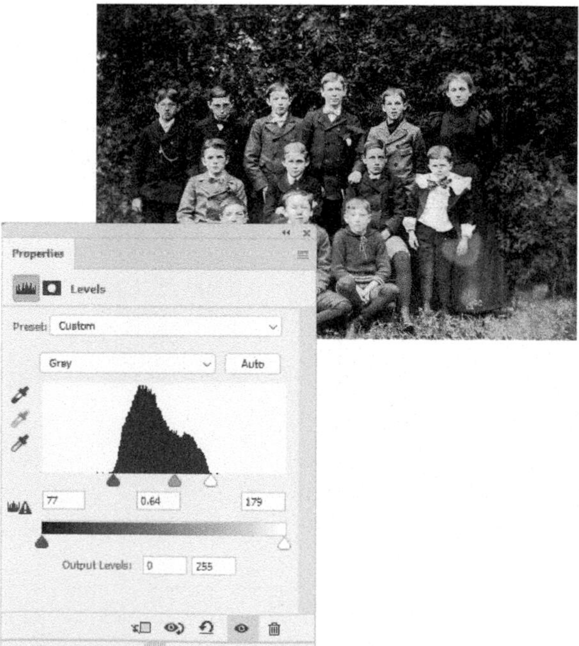

FIGURE 3.29 Adjusting the midtones vastly lowers the brightness level, improving the image.

Working with Levels Eyedroppers

When working with historical images or photographs for which you don't have personal knowledge of the tones or color, you can use your visual memory to improve tone. FIGURE 3.30 shows a classic photo that lacks the needed contrast. By redefining the white and black points with the Levels eyedroppers, the image is speedily improved, as shown in FIGURE 3.31.

FIGURES 3.30 and 3.31 © *Palmer Family Archives*

One of the challenges with setting new white or black points with an eyedropper is that it is very easy to select a point that is not the actual lightest or darkest point, resulting in some of the tonal information being clipped. Clipping the white points is particularly noticeable in printing.

ch3_dinner_party.jpg

1. Open the Info panel and set one of the readouts to Grayscale.

2. Create a Levels adjustment layer, which displays the narrow Histogram graph (FIGURE 3.32).

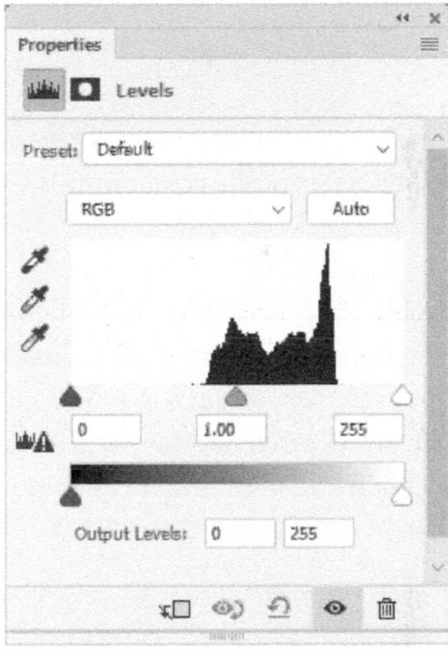

FIGURE 3.32 The histogram shows a narrow range of tonal values.

3. Select the white eyedropper and move it over the image. Locate the brightest spot in the image by watching the readout on the Info panel. The tablecloth is without detail and the Info panel shows a K value of 26%. Click in the image where the Info panel readout shows the brightest reading (this will be the tablecloth) (FIGURE 3.33).

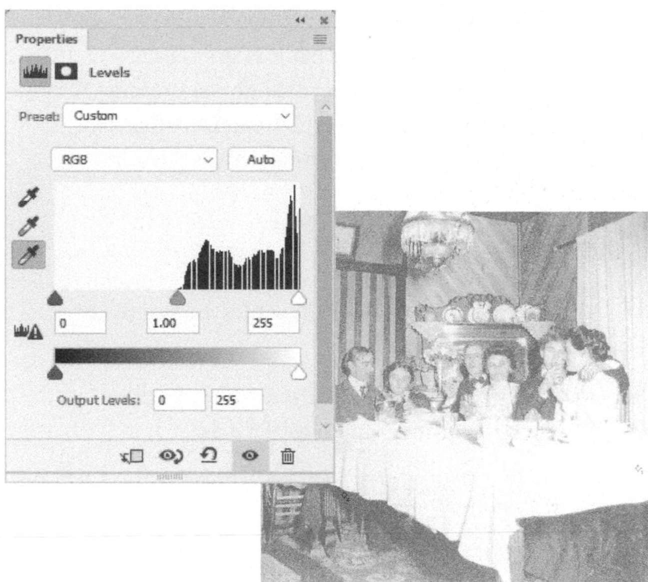

FIGURE 3.33 Setting the white point on the overexposed table cloth

4. Select the black eyedropper and look for the darkest area in the image. It is tempting to just click the black shoe, but that would turn the shoe completely black and clip some other shadowed areas that have details. The shadowed area under the table is a good spot to set the black point (FIGURE 3.34).

FIGURE 3.34 Setting the black point to the shadow under the table brings out the contrast possible in the image.

TIP To assist in finding the areas that will be clipped by the sliders, hold down the Option/Alt key while moving either slider, or from the panel menu choose Show Clipping for Black/White Points.

CURVES AND CONTRAST

After you're comfortable working with Levels, Curves adjustments are the next tool to add to your Photoshop repertoire. The advantage of Curves is that they can give you up to 16 points to influence the tonal values of an image, whereas Levels allow you just three (highlight, midtone, and shadow points) (FIGURES 3.35 and 3.36).

- Preset: Use the presets from the drop-down menu for a number of standard changes or to recall saved settings.
- Channel Selection: Access the individual channels, primarily used for color correction.
- Auto: Use the Auto button to prompt Photoshop to apply one of four types of auto corrections, as explained in Chapter 4. You can choose which setting Photoshop uses by clicking the menu icon and choosing from the list of algorithms, or Option/Alt-click the Auto button to have the same menu appear. If the image is in grayscale as opposed to RGB, there are no choices for algorithms.
- Eyedroppers: Use the eyedroppers to set white and black points for both black-and-white and color images, and use the neutral gray eyedropper to define a neutral tone in color images.
- On-Image Adjustment tool: Use this tool to select the area for tonal adjustments.
- Edit points: Use to add points to the curve for modification.
- Draw Curve: Use to manually draw a curve.
- Smooth: Use to round out a curve.
- Black and white sliders: Use to set black/white points.

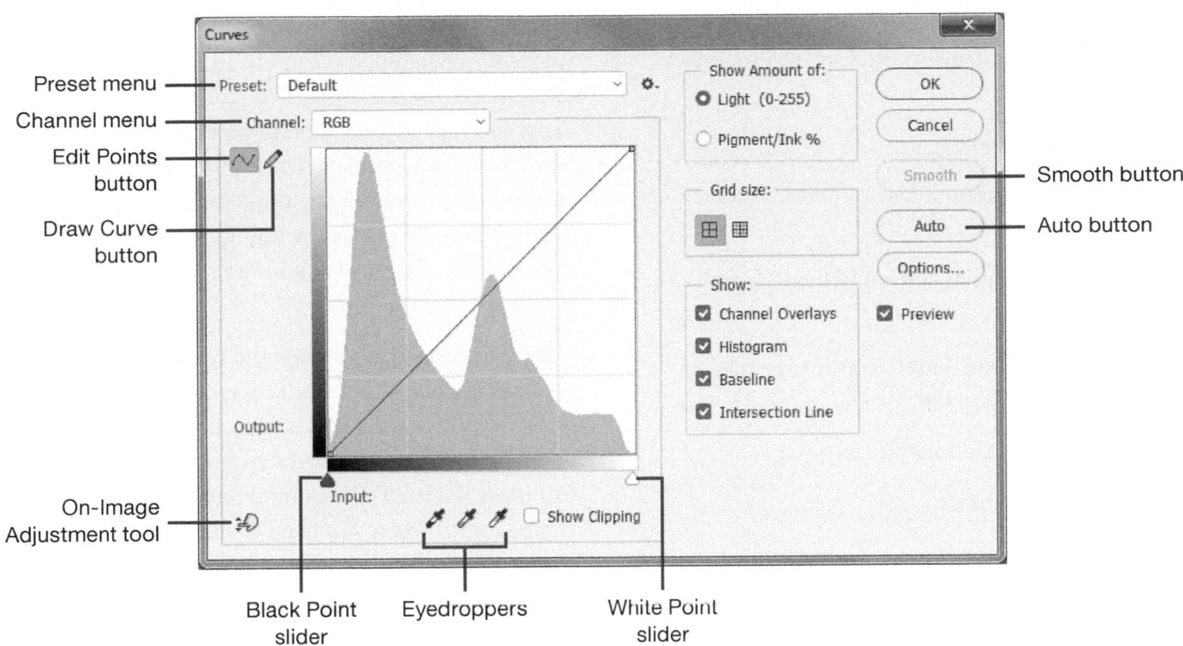

FIGURE 3.35 Curves as a normal adjustment has a larger interface but a smaller set of options.

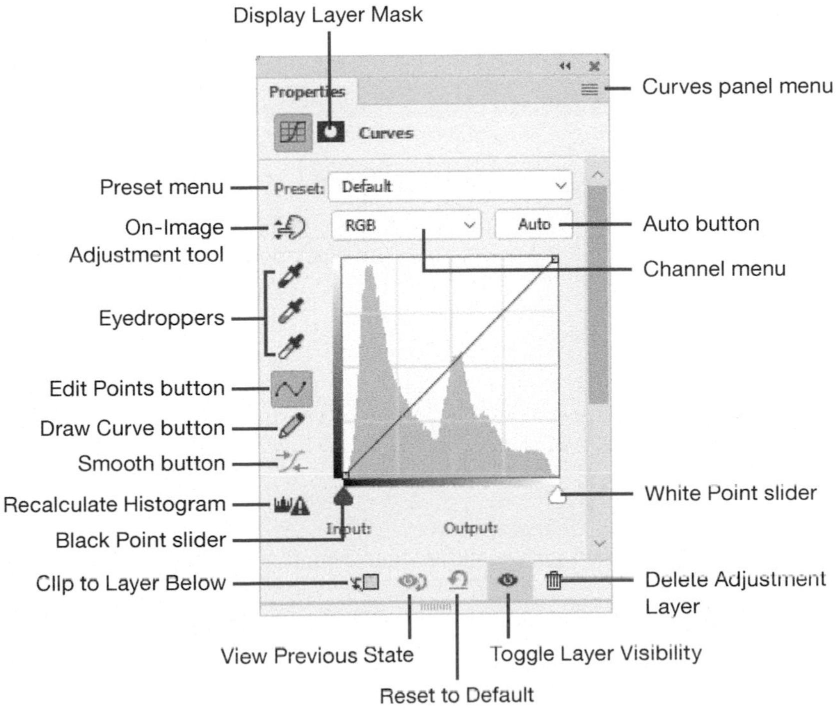

FIGURE 3.36 Curves as an adjustment layer has all the same features.

If you use Curves as an adjustment layer, you gain these additional controls in the Curves Properties panel:

- Display Layer Mask.
- Recalculate Histogram: Use to make a more accurate histogram
- Clip to Layer: Applies the adjustment only to the layer directly below.
- View Previous State: Hold down to see image before adjustment is made.
- Reset to Default: Undoes all changes.
- Toggle Layer Visibility.
- Delete Adjustment Layer.
- Curves panel menu.

You can customize the display of Curves data to suit your needs. In the Curves Properties panel, choose Curves Display Options from the panel menu to open the Curves Display Options dialog box (FIGURE 3.37) (the options are always visible in the Curves dialog box).

By default, the Curves graph displays a range of tonal values (0–255), but you can opt to display a range of pigment/ink percentages (0–100). From Katrin's experience, people with prepress experience prefer the ink percentage scale, while photographers prefer the tonal value scale—the same values used in Levels. The 0–255 scale places the highlights on the shoulder (upper part) of the curve and the shadows on the toe (lower part) of the curve.

Note that choosing between the two not only reverses the black to white order, but also changes the numeric value of the scales. You also have the option of changing the graph grid size from quartertones to a more detailed grid in increments of 10%, which can be useful when you need to make a minor tonal correction.

TIP Hold down Option/Alt and click anywhere in the graph to switch between a quartertone grid and a 10% percent increment grid.

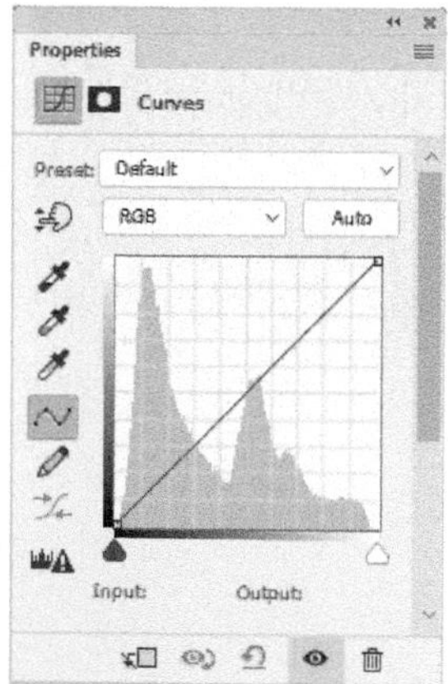

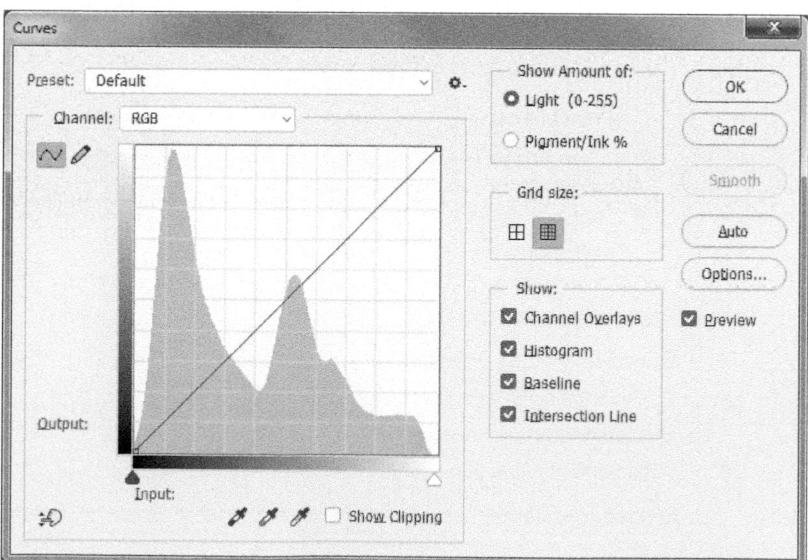

FIGURE 3.37 Changing the display of the Curves Properties panel and the Curves dialog box. The grid is set to 10% increments; compare to Figure 3.36, where the grid is set to quartertone increments.

Improving Contrast with Curves

Just as Levels had several ways to improve contrast, Curves does as well, plus a few more tools that makes Curves one of the most powerful ways of correcting tone and color. Let's explore a number of the options Curves has to offer.

On-Image Adjustment Tool

At first, Curves can appear pretty intimidating, which is why many users start with Levels. The On-Image Adjustment tool within Curves is a simple way to adjust an image, understand how the tool works, and gain confidence in the use of Curves. Just select the tool and click in the area where you want to alter the tone. This will place a point on the curve. Drag up to brighten that area or down to darken it. Let's try it out on an image whose tonal range was flattened when the camera's light meter averaged the light it received from the scene (**FIGURES 3.38** and **3.39**).

 **ch3_beach_waves.jpg**

Follow these steps to use the On-Image Adjustment tool to quickly improve an image.

1. Create a Curves adjustment layer and select the On-Image Adjustment tool.

FIGURE 3.38 A tonally flat image © *WP*

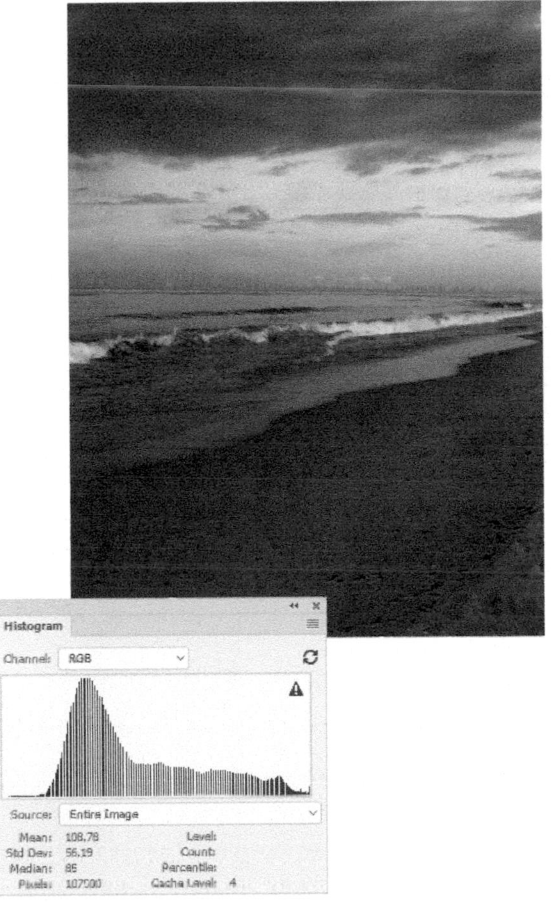

FIGURE 3.39 Using the On-Image Adjustment tool quickly restores the original beauty of the fading light.

2. Locate the brightest point in the picture, which is the breaking waves and place the mouse pointer over it. Drag upward to brighten the image (FIGURE 3.40). It is OK to let the curve go up against the top of the graph, as there is no information in the graph where the line touches the top of the scale; otherwise, the image would most likely be brightened too much. Note that there is a point placed on the curve.

FIGURE 3.40 Dragging upward with the On-Image Adjustment tool (circled) lightens the image.

3. Locate the darkest area in the image, which looks like the dark wave not far from where the bright point was sampled. Drag down until a nice contrast is created (FIGURE 3.41). Going too far will turn shadowed area to total black.

FIGURE 3.41 Dragging down with the On-Image Adjustment tool darkens the image.

Bringing Detail with Curves

The best aspect of Curves is the control you have over the many points of tonal information. With Curves, you can quickly enhance image contrast by applying a classic S curve (which is what was created in the last exercise), or you can spend more time with the interface and use bump points to bring out selected tonal details, as we'll do with the next image.

ch3_bearded_man.jpg

Creating a classic S curve is a normal way to create contrast. Now let's try it by placing and adjusting the points on the curve.

FIGURE 3.42 shows another family heirloom that has aged significantly. The image is tonally flat, as seen in the narrow amount of data displayed in the histogram. This image will require a very steep S curve due to the small tonal difference between the highlights in the man's shirt and the shadow of

FIGURES 3.42 and 3.43 © *Eismann Family Archives*

his coat. Setting the white and black points, as with Levels, and then putting multiple points on the curve allows the midtones to be adjusted to bring out more contrast, as shown in FIGURE 3.43.

1. Create a Curves adjustment layer and open the Curves Display Options dialog. Select the Light option. This will have the histogram display information the same way as Levels, with black on the left and white on the right (FIGURE 3.44).

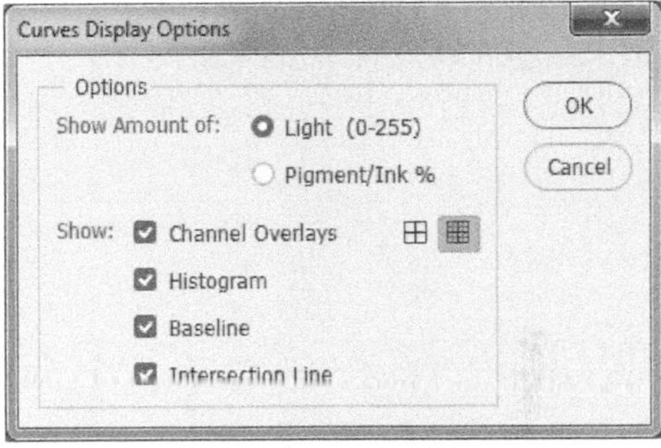

FIGURE 3.44 Set the Curves Display Options dialog to show the amount of light at each point in the image.

2. When working with such flat originals, start by moving either the highlight or shadow point along the top or bottom of the curve to deepen the shadows or lighten the highlights (FIGURE 3.45).

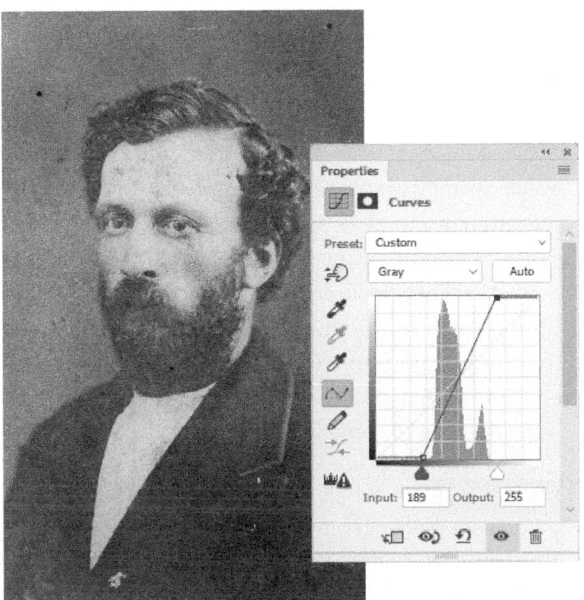

FIGURE 3.45 Adjusting the white and black points brings noticeable improvement.

3. This has made a noticeable improvement, but the addition of a few more points can refine the contrast. Place a third point partway up from the black point and then a fourth point part way down from the white point. Nudge each new point toward the center of graph to pick up what little contrast is left (FIGURE 3.46).

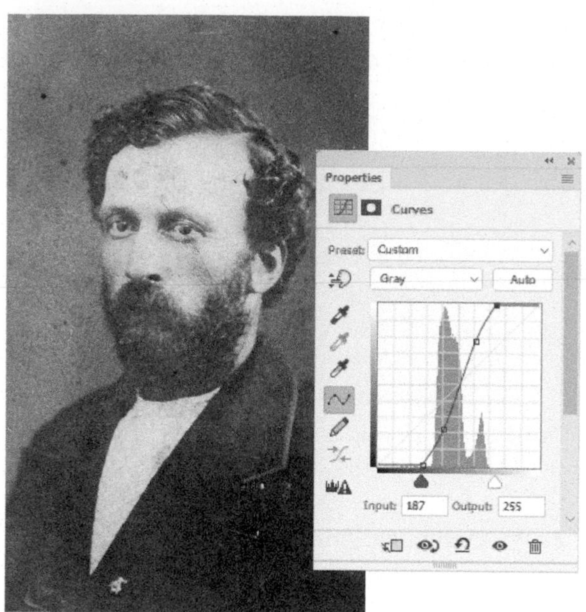

FIGURE 3.46 Make slight adjustments to the additional points on the curve to improve contrast.

TIP Points on the curve can be nudged by selecting the point and using the arrow keys on your keyboard.

When using Curves, keep an eye on the Info and Histogram panels as you are adjusting contrast and tonal values. You don't want to force the dark areas so far down that they become pure black. Conversely, you want to keep some details in your highlights, so don't force bright areas to 0%. The only values that should be completely white are specular highlights, such as reflections on chrome bumpers.

! CAUTION When using Curves to increase contrast, there is always a tradeoff. Adding contrast in one area takes tonal information away from another. Making radical adjustments can lead to posterization (abrupt changes in tone) in the flat areas of the curve.

TRY IT The two workhorses for tonal correction are Levels and Curves. Now that you have the basics for adjusting tonality in an image, try both Levels and Curves to improve this very faded old image (FIGURES 3.47 and 3.48).

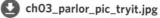

ch03_parlor_pic_tryit.jpg

FIGURES 3.47 and 3.48 © *Palmer Family Archives*

WORKING WITH BLENDING MODES

With the exception of the Background layer, every Photoshop layer, including adjustment layers, supports blending modes, which influence how a layer interacts with the layers below it. This happens on a channel-by-channel basis, so blending modes can in some instances simultaneously lighten and darken. For retouching work, blending modes simplify and speed up tonal correction, dust cleanup, and blemish removal. The blending modes are arranged into functional groups, as labeled in FIGURE 3.49 and reviewed in TABLE 3.1.

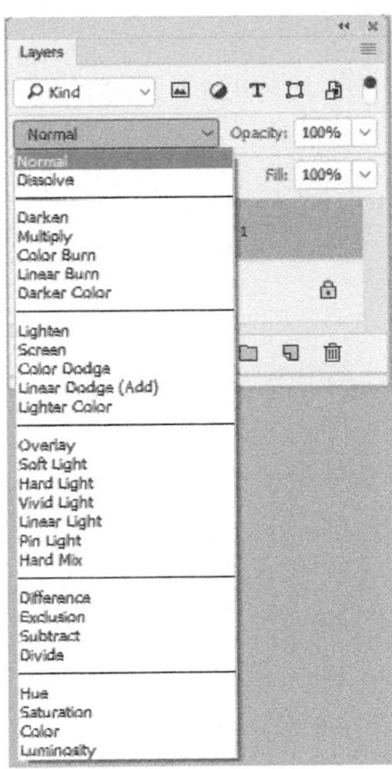

FIGURE 3.49 Blending modes are most easily accessed by way of the Blend Mode menu in the Layers panel.

TABLE 3.1 **Blending Modes Explained**

BLENDING MODE	DESCRIPTION
Normal	Combines the two sources based on opacity.
Darkening Group	The effect will be progressively stronger as the tones become darker.
Darken	Compares the two sources and replaces light pixel values with dark.
Multiply	Darkens the entire image and is useful to add density to highlights and midtones. It is especially useful for overexposed or very light images.
Color Burn	Results in a darker image with increased contrast.
Linear Burn	Strong combination of Multiply and Color Burn; forces dark values to pure black.
Lightening Group	The effect will be progressively stronger as the tones become darker.
Lighten	The opposite of Darken, it compares the two sources and replaces the darker pixels with lighter pixels.
Screen	Lightens the entire image. Use it to open up or lighten dark image areas and to bring out tonal information in underexposed images.
Color Dodge	Decreases contrast of areas lighter than 50% gray while preserving black values.
Linear Dodge	Combination of Screen and Color Dodge; forces light areas to pure white.
Contrast Group	Used to boost image contrast.
Overlay	Multiplies dark values and screens light values, which increases contrast but without clipping to pure white or black.
Soft Light	Combination of Dodge, which lightens the light values, and Burn, which darkens the dark values. Adds less contrast than Overlay or Hard Light.
Hard Light	Multiplies the dark values, screens the light values, and increases contrast dramatically.
Vivid Light	Lightens the values above 50% gray by decreasing the contrast and darkens the values below 50% gray by increasing contrast.

continues

TABLE 3.1 **Blending Modes Explained** *(continued)*

BLENDING MODE	DESCRIPTION
Contrast Group *(continued)*	
Linear Light	Combines Linear Burn and Linear Dodge; lightens the values above 50% gray by increasing the brightness and darkens the values below 50% gray by decreasing brightness.
Pin Light	Combines Darken and Lighten to replace pixel values. Always very contrasty; used for special effects and, less often, to create masks.
Hard Mix	Lighter values lighten and darker values darken to the point of threshold and extreme posterization.
Comparative Group	
Difference	Reveals identical pixel values as black, similar values as dark, and opposite values are inverted.
Exclusion	Similar to Difference but with less contrast. Blending with black produces no change, and white inverts the compared values to be rendered as gray.
Image Component Group	Only active in color mode images.
Hue	Combines the luminance and saturation of the underlying layer with the hue of the active layer.
Saturation	Combines the luminance and hue of the underlying layer with the saturation of the active layer.
Color	Reveals the color of the active layer and maintains the luminance of the underlying layer.
Luminosity	Is the opposite of Color and maintains the luminosity information of the active layer in relationship to the color underneath.

In the following exercises, you'll work with the most important blending modes to solve tonal problems. The best thing about working with blending modes is that they are completely reversible, enabling you to experiment to achieve the desired result. To access the blending modes, use the Blend Mode menu in the Layers panel.

Using Multiply to Build Density

One of the more difficult exposure problems to remedy is overexposure. There is nothing to bring back once an image reaches the upper end of the exposure scale. This is one reason correct exposure becomes very important when using the JPEG file format for recording images and is one of the best reasons for using the Camera Raw format.

Photographer Amanda Steinbacher normally shoots a few test shots for exposure before commencing with a model shoot. An overexposed image like the one in FIGURE 3.50 is often sent to the digital recycle bin. But by using blending modes, even overexposed images can sometimes be rescued (FIGURE 3.51).

 **ch3_overexposed_model.jpg**

In this exercise we will use adjustment layers, as in previous examples, but instead of tweaking the adjustment controls we will simply change the blending mode.

1. Create a Levels adjustment layer. Note that you can choose most any adjustment layer, keeping in mind that you are not using the layer's controls but simply using the layer as a method for changing the blending mode.

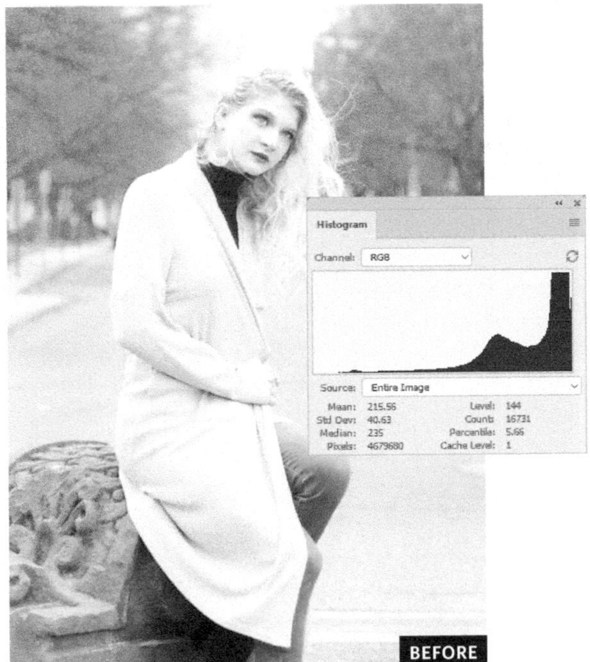

FIGURES 3.50 and **3.51** © *Amanda Steinbacher, Amanda Steinbacher Photography*

2. In the Layers panel, choose Multiply from the Blend Mode drop-down menu. The image is noticeably improved, as seen in **FIGURE 3.52**.

FIGURE 3.52 An adjustment layer with Multiply chosen from the Blend Mode menu darkens the image.

3. The effect of a blending mode can be multiplied by duplicating the adjustment layer. Duplicate the Levels adjustment layer to amplify the effect, as seen in **FIGURE 3.53**.

FIGURE 3.53 Duplicating the adjustment layer multiplies the effect.

4. At this point, the darkening effect might have gone a little too far, as the shadowed areas have filled in to near total black and the color has become oversaturated. Adjust the opacity of the second Levels layer to 50%, which reduces the effect (**FIGURE 3.54**).

FIGURE 3.54 Multiple layers set to Multiply mode saved this image.

TIP The same effect can be created by duplicating the image layer and changing the blending mode, but the file size is doubled. Adjustment layers add very little to the overall file size.

Using the Screen Blending Mode

Just as a blending mode can be used to darken an image, it can also be used to lighten. Tintype photography was very popular in the 1860s and 1870s, although the technology was used for many years later. Often these images darken with age, and just using blending modes can make major corrections (**FIGURES 3.55** and **3.56**).

ch03_tintype_with_fingerprint.jpg

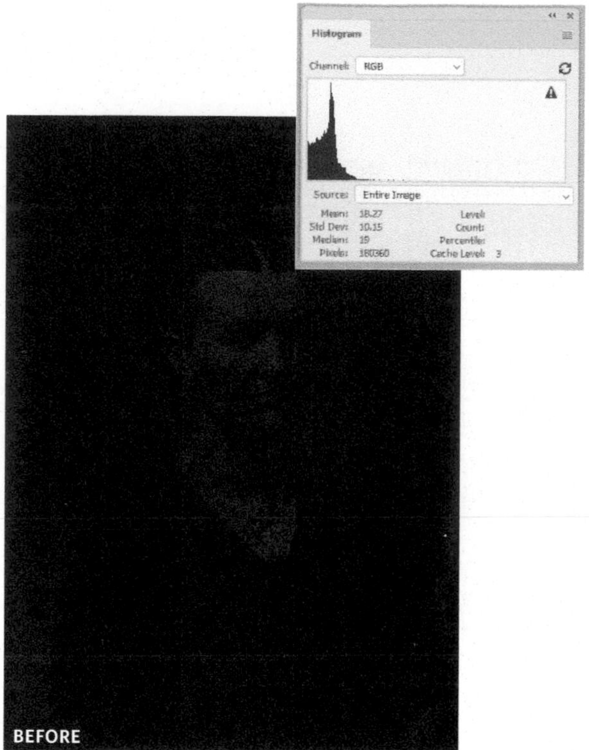

FIGURES 3.55 and **3.56** © *Palmer Family Archives*

1. Create a Levels adjustment layer and change the blending mode to Screen. The image already looks better (**FIGURE 3.57**).

FIGURE 3.57 An adjustment layer with the blending mode set to Screen starts to lighten the image. © *Palmer Family Archives*

2. As in the last example, duplicate the adjustment layer to double the effect (**FIGURE 3.58**).

FIGURE 3.58 Duplicating the adjustment layer multiplies the effect.

3. The image is greatly improved but could use a bit more brightening. Duplicate the layer a second time. Now it is a bit too bright (**FIGURE 3.59**), but as in the last example, using an adjustment layer with a blending mode is not all or nothing. Lower the opacity of the last duplicated layer to 40%, as shown in **FIGURE 3.60**, to tone it down.

FIGURE 3.59 Duplicating the adjustment layer a third time brightens the image too much.

FIGURE 3.60 Lowering the opacity of the top adjustment layer to 40% gives us the image we want.

The lightened picture reveals a number of areas that need to be cleaned up as well as a very pronounced fingerprint. Techniques will be presented in future chapters for repairing all the newly appearing damage.

APPLY LOCAL CORRECTIONS

Techniques presented so far in this chapter have been for applying global changes, or changes to the entire image. Many times it is only a smaller area or section of the image that needs to be addressed. In the following sections we cover methods for making corrections to smaller sections.

Transitioning a Tonal Correction

In this desert landscape photo, the late afternoon sun was blocked by a mountain range, causing a shadow to fill in the foreground (FIGURE 3.61). The camera's meter averaged out the contrasting areas, creating a flat look. By using an adjustment layer with a blending mode, and with a gradient applied to the layer mask, the late afternoon dramatic effect is returned (FIGURE 3.62). Use the following steps to put some punch back into the picture.

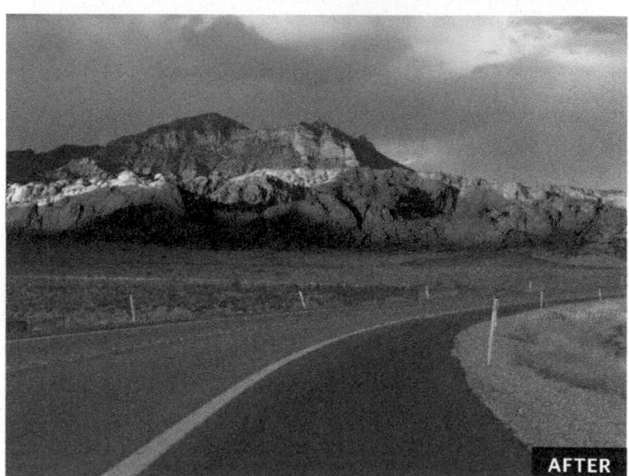

FIGURES 3.61 and 3.62 Before and after. © *WP*

ch3_redrock_shadow.jpg

1. As in previous examples, create a Levels adjustment layer, not to make any adjustments but simply to apply a blending mode. Choose Multiply to darken the image, as seen in FIGURE 3.63.

FIGURE 3.63 The Multiply blending mode darkens the entire image. © *Wayne R. Palmer*

2. Now the mountainous area has some depth to it, but the foreground has become too dark. Select the Gradient tool (G) and be sure the gradient type is set to Linear. Reset the Foreground/Background colors to their defaults by pressing the letter D. If the foreground color is not set to white, press the letter X to swap the two.

3. Making sure the layer mask on the adjustment layer is active, click near the bottom of the red mountain range and drag down into the gray level ground. When you release the mouse button, a transition will appear in the mask, from white (at the point where you clicked) to black (where you released), partially blocking the effect. If the transition of the effect is too abrupt, try again, creating a more gradual transition by making a longer stroke with the Gradient tool. Each time a new gradient is made, it replaces the previous one. Creating a mask, as seen in FIGURE 3.64, should make for a natural transition and a much more dramatic image (FIGURE 3.65).

FIGURE 3.64 Masking part of the adjustment layer applies the effect only to the mountains.

FIGURE 3.65 The more gradual the transition in the mask, the more believable the result.

+ TIP To see the layer mask at full size, hold Option/Alt and click the mask icon in the Layers panel.

4. Just to kick it up a notch and make the image more dramatic, duplicate the adjustment layer. This will make it too dark, but reduce that layer's opacity to 22% for a nice rich image.

Basing Tonal Corrections on Selections

Fill flash is a common photographic technique used to fill in shadows in broad daylight. In FIGURE 3.66 you can see by the catch light in the subject's eyes that flash was used. But apparently the flash did not have enough power to overcome the ambient light. By selecting just the couple and using a Curves adjustment layer, the couple can be made to look like a powerful enough flash was used (FIGURE 3.67). Here are the steps.

FIGURES 3.66 and 3.67 © *WP*

 **ch3_beach_couple.jpg**

1. With the file open in Photoshop, select the Quick Selection tool and change the brush size to 30. Start dragging over the couple; the tool will automatically select similarly colored areas like the shirts and shorts. Hold down Shift to keep adding to the selection. Hold down Option/Alt to deselect areas. The final selection should look like FIGURE 3.68.

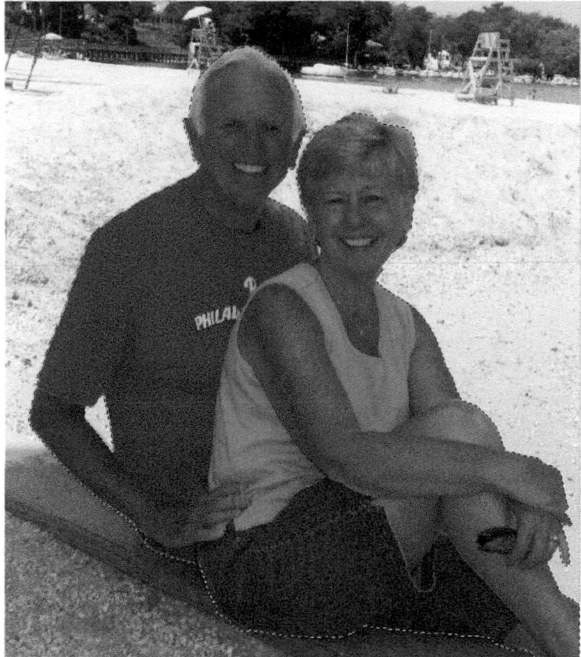

FIGURE 3.68 The Quick Selection tool makes an easy selection of the couple to separate them from their surroundings.

2. Once the selection is complete, click the Create New Fill or Adjustment Layer icon in the Layers Panel and choose Curves. The adjustment layer will be made, with the selection turned into a mask (FIGURE 3.69).

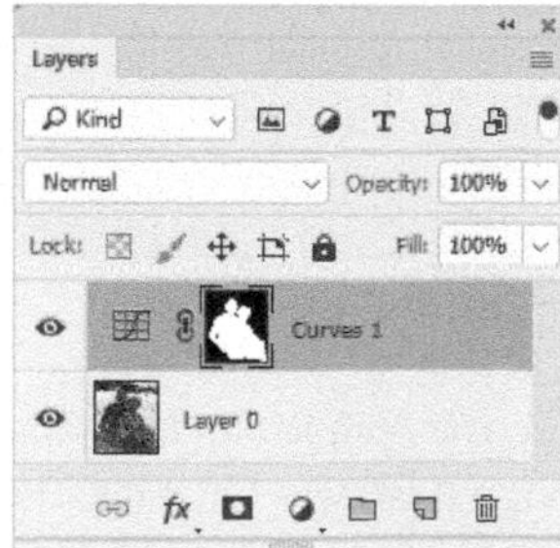

FIGURE 3.69 The selection becomes a layer mask when an adjustment layer is created.

3. Click in the middle of the Curves graph and drag upward to brighten the couple to a believable level, as shown in FIGURE 3.70.

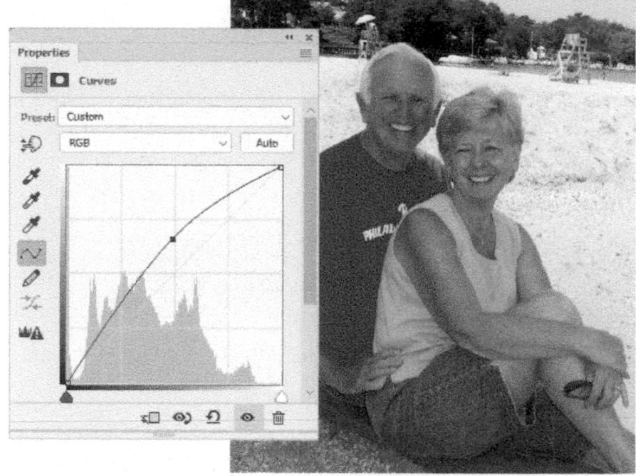

FIGURE 3.70 A minor change to the midtones of the curve balances the lighting of the couple with the background.

TIP In this image the Quick Selection tool made a good selection, which left no telltale transitional area between the adjusted and original areas and gave a realistic effect. For some images the selection will need to be refined further to lead to a believable result; creating such a selection can be one of the more arduous tasks in Photoshop.

Nondestructive Dodge and Burn

Although most of the image looks to be exposed correctly, late afternoon sun behind the little girl causes her face to be shadowed (FIGURE 3.71). A little fill light would be an improvement, and sometimes only small areas need help (FIGURE 3.72).

Using the Dodge tool would be a way of brightening up the dark areas, but unfortunately the Dodge, Burn, and Sponge tools have no options to allow them to be used nondestructively. Unlike many of the other tools in the Tools panel, the Dodge tool cannot be used on a separate layer to keep changes from being destructive. But a workaround to imitate the effect is to use a blending mode on a separate layer.

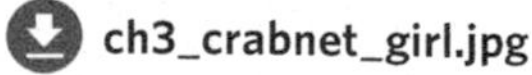

ch3_crabnet_girl.jpg

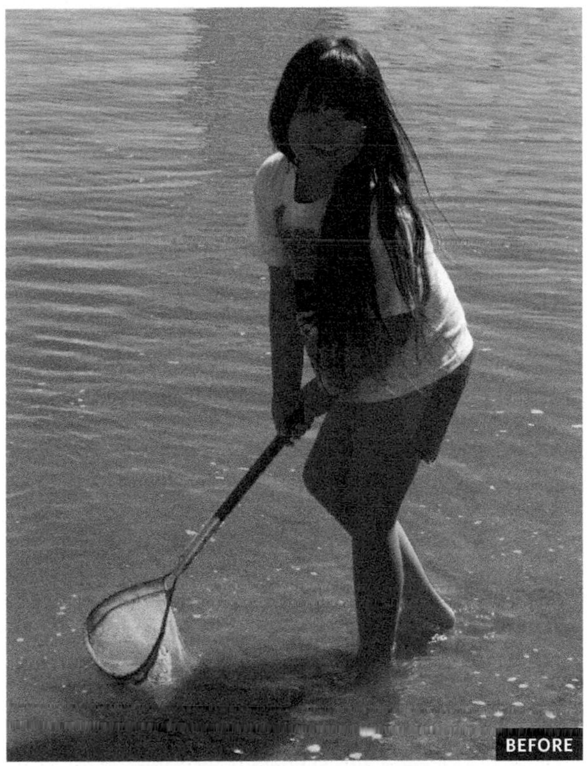

FIGURES 3.71 and **3.72** Before and after. © *WP*

1. Create an empty layer on top of the layer to be adjusted, and change the blending mode to Overlay. Name the layer *Dodge* (**FIGURE 3.73**).

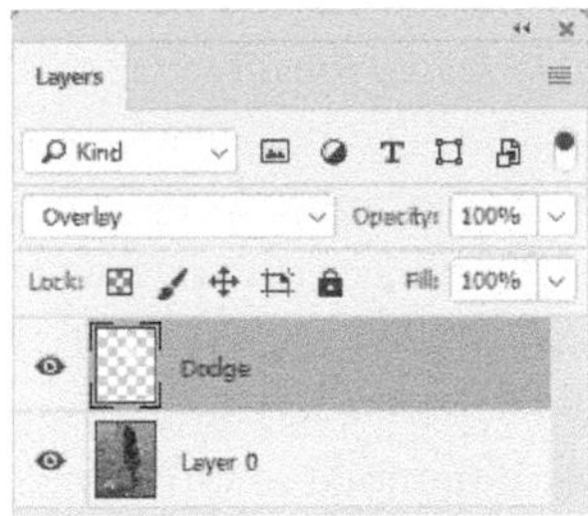

FIGURE 3.73 An empty layer with the blending mode set to Overlay becomes the basis for nondestructive dodging and burning.

TIP Some users prefer to fill this layer with 50% gray so that edits are clearly visible when the layer is viewed by itself. Not doing so makes it easier to undo modifications by simply erasing them.

2. To simulate the dodge effect, select the Brush tool (B), choose a 200-pixel soft-edged brush, and lower the brush's opacity to about 10%. This is not a hard-and-fast number, but stay with lower opacities that build up the effect gradually.

3. With the foreground color set to white, brush over the girl's face and down over the shadowed areas to brighten them. Build the effect up by making multiple strokes. Make the brush smaller as you work down the extremities. If you go too far with the effect or spill out into the water, just use the Undo command, or use the "evil" Eraser tool (in most cases we don't recommend it because it acts destructively) as an undo brush (**FIGURE 3.74**).

FIGURE 3.74 Painting white with a low-opacity, soft-edged brush lightens the girl's face.

+ TIP Continuously painting while not releasing the mouse button or lifting a stylus will put down the same amount of paint, which is useful if you want to apply an even amount of brightness. It is through successive strokes that you build up the effect.

4. A common photographic technique to draw the viewer's eye to the subject is to darken the image's corners, a process called vignetting. To keep dodging and burning separate, create a new empty layer, change the blending mode to Overlay, and name the layer *Burn* (FIGURE 3.75).

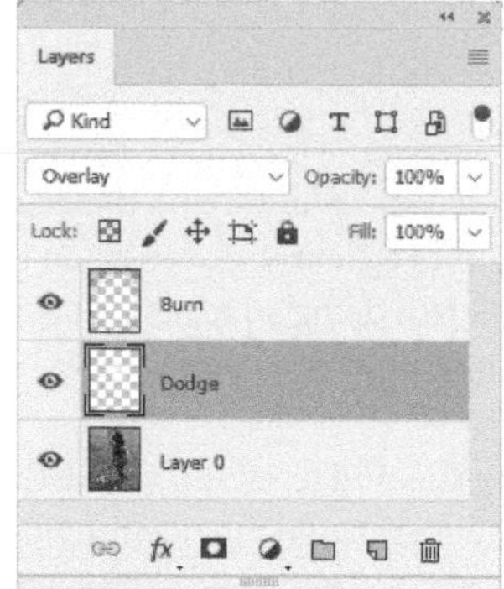

FIGURE 3.75 Using separate layers for dodging and burning keeps the effects from interfering with each other.

5. Sometimes the vignetting effect is dramatic; other times it is a little subtler, in which case the viewer may not even be aware of the effect. To take the subtle route, select the brush, set the color to black, lower the opacity to 4%, and change the brush size to 600 pixels. Draw across the four corners of the image, building up an effect that draws your eyes toward the subject. Repeated strokes will build up the burn effect (FIGURE 3.76).

+ TIP Create separate layers for dodging and burning to make modifications simpler.

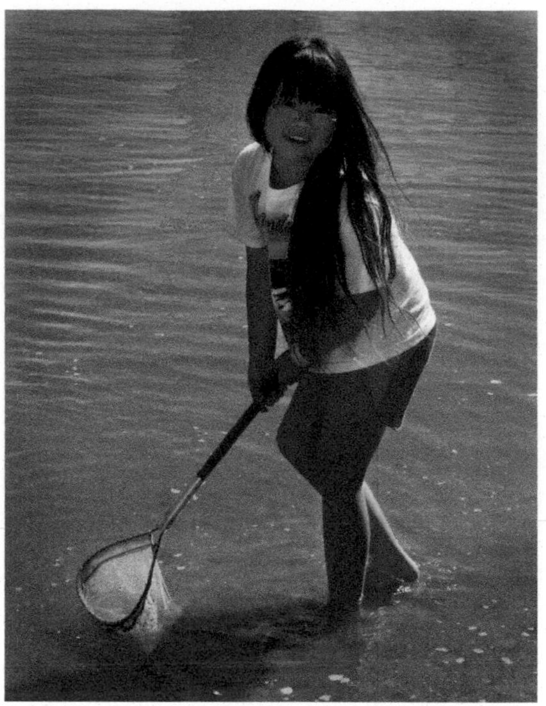

FIGURE 3.76 After a little burning and dodging and the addition of a vignette, this subpar image is now quite respectable.

OTHER TECHNIQUES

Double Processing

Even the best camera meters can be fooled by extreme lighting conditions. Even with high-bit information, it can be difficult to bring out all the tonal information in a single image. Lightening one area may result in the loss of information in another, and the same for darkening.

Processing a file twice and taking the best of both exposures by putting them together is a solution Wayne has used. In this image, he wanted to show the magnificent stone work while also showing the stormy clouds. It did not seem possible to get the best of both in one processed file. So he processed the image twice in Adobe Camera Raw (ACR), once for the bright areas (FIGURE 3.77) and once for the dark (FIGURE 3.78).

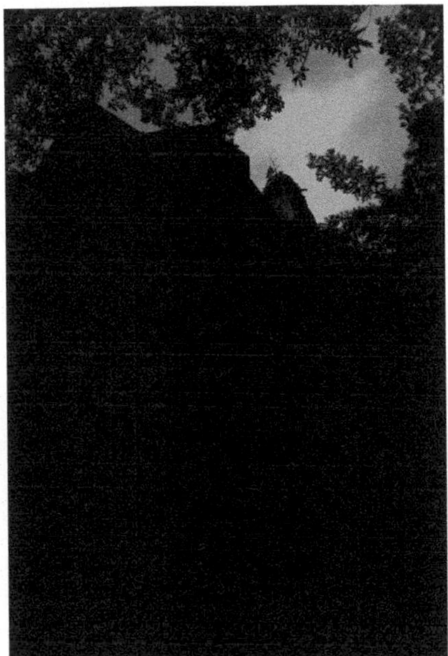

FIGURE 3.77 The file was first processed in ACR to enhance the brighter areas of the image.

FIGURE 3.78 A second version of the file was made to improve exposure in the darker areas. © *WP*

Both versions were imported into the same Photoshop file, with the image emphasizing the darker areas (the second version) layered on top of the other.

Using the Color Range dialog, a selection of the sky was made relatively easily (FIGURE 3.79). However, when the selection was inverted and converted into a mask, the difference between the two layers was jarring (FIGURE 3.80).

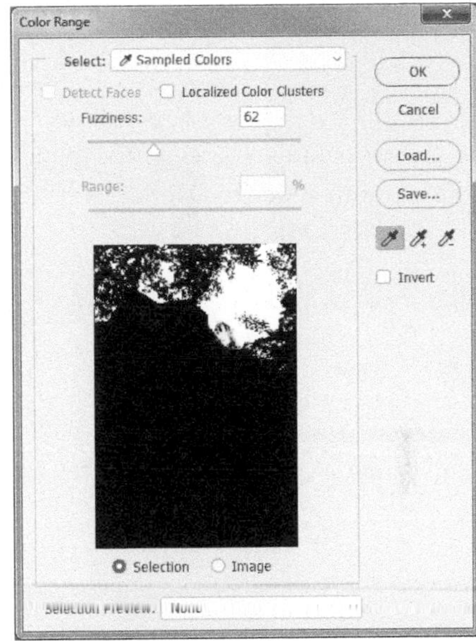

FIGURE 3.79 Using the Color Range dialog box to select the sky

FIGURE 3.80 When the two versions of the image were first composited, the boundary was harsh.

By blurring the edges of the mask with the Gaussian Blur filter (FIGURE 3.81) and then making a few minor brush strokes on the mask, the two images came together believably, as shown in FIGURE 3.82.

FIGURE 3.81 Softening the mask edge by blurring and painting

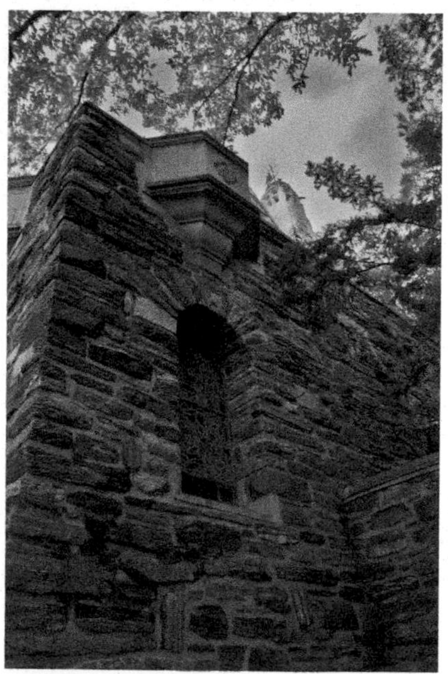

FIGURE 3.82 The composite after working on the mask

TIP This technique could also be attempted by using masks on adjustment layers. But if you have access to the raw file, you will be able to make better initial images by using the original high-bit data.

Shadows/Highlights to the Rescue

When confronted with a processed image that suffers from poor exposure, a Shadows/Highlights command might just be the feature to use without the need for masks or duplicate layers.

FIGURE 3.83 has a very high contrast ratio between the valley floor and the mountains in the distance. Although the darker areas are acceptable, the brighter areas are overexposed.

FIGURE 3.83 This image from a scanned negative suffers from an overexposed background. © *Pamela J. Herrington*

Follow these few steps to keep the image from being a washout.

ch3_zion_narrows.jpg

1. To use Shadows/Highlights nondestructively, convert the layer to a Smart Object. This can be done by choosing Filter > Convert for Smart Filters or by opening the Layers panel menu and choosing Convert to Smart Object (FIGURE 3.84).

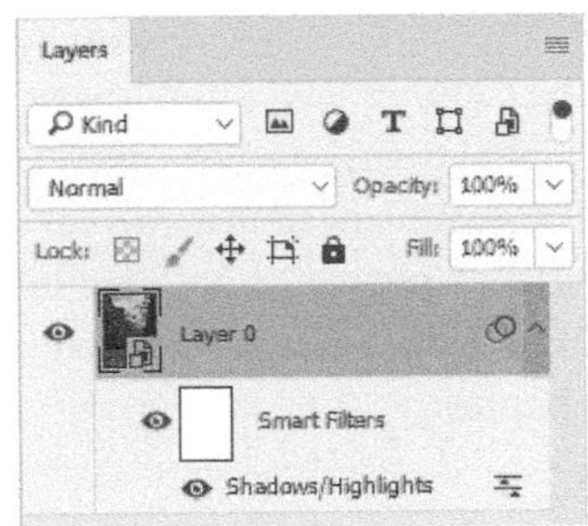

FIGURE 3.84 Converting the layer to a Smart Object makes editing with Shadows/Highlights a nondestructive process.

2. Choose **Image > Adjustments > Shadows/ Highlights**.

3. In the Shadows/Highlights dialog, select Show More Options.

4. Even though the shadows appear fine, they will look a little better if you move the Amount slider in the Shadows section to 17%.

5. The Highlights section of the tool needs addressing the most. Moving the Amount slider to 73% makes the mountains visible again. Leave the Tone and Radius settings at their default values.

6. Under Adjustments, move the Color slider to +50 to give a little boost to the color of the sky. Click OK to accept the changes (**FIGURE 3.85**).

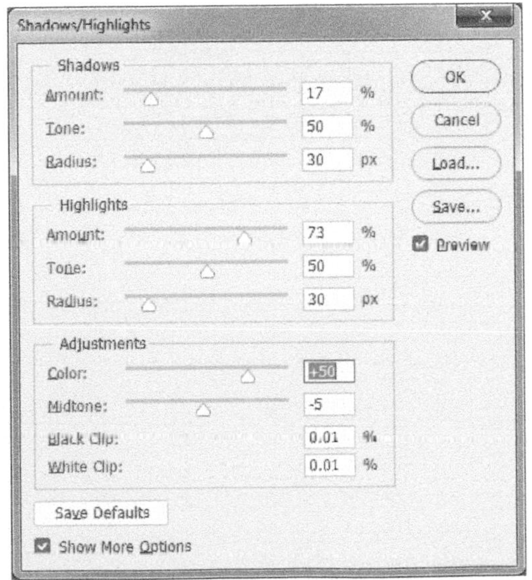

FIGURE 3.85 The Shadows/Highlights dialog box showing our adjustments

The result is shown in **FIGURE 3.86**.

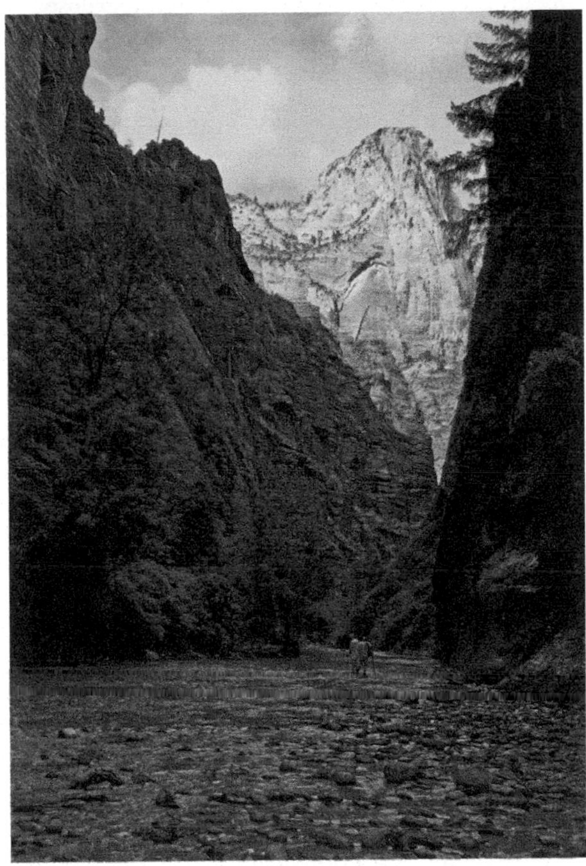

FIGURE 3.86 The Shadows/Highlights command can be very useful in restoring images that suffer from exposure issues.

Camera Raw Filter

An old western movie cliché goes, "There's a new sheriff in town." That expression might apply to the Camera Raw filter. It can be used on any type of file and does not have to be accessed outside Photoshop. Having access to all the tone controls inside one interface makes processing files much easier. You do not have to make a decision as to what specific adjustment tool you want, as you can switch back and forth between the ones you like. Where Levels is divided into three tonal areas, Camera Raw has four. If you like using Curves or applying selective changes, that's all there and much more. But before abandoning all the other techniques and using the Camera Raw filter, consider these caveats:

- It cannot bring back high-bit data if the file has already been converted to 8 bit. So an overexposed image cannot have details brought back, as would be possible with a raw file.
- Used directly on the layer, it becomes a destructive tool. This can be avoided by converting the layer to a Smart Object or Smart Filter. But that leads to another hurdle.
- Painting tools, which include cloning and healing, cannot be used directly on a layer converted to a Smart Object or Smart Filter. This is actually OK, as you would want to keep your edits separate as part of a nondestructive strategy. But it provides a complication. If a tonal or color change is later made to the Smart Object or Smart Filter, upper layers may no longer match. There are workarounds, but they involve multiple steps that wouldn't be necessary using the more conventional methods shown in this chapter.

Even though you can do local adjustments and corrections in the Camera Raw filter, it is probably best to use it for global tonal or color corrections, saving Photoshop's more advanced features for removing dust and scratches and doing detailed local corrections. The Camera Raw filter is covered in more detail in the next chapter.

CLOSING THOUGHTS

At this point we have provided numerous strategies on how to handle images with exposure issues. Often, tonal corrections are just the beginning of the image-editing process. Tonal corrections often reveal damage to an image that has been neglected, as seen in several examples in this chapter. Tonal corrections may also show that the color of an image needs to be addressed, which is the subject of the next chapter.

Chapter 4

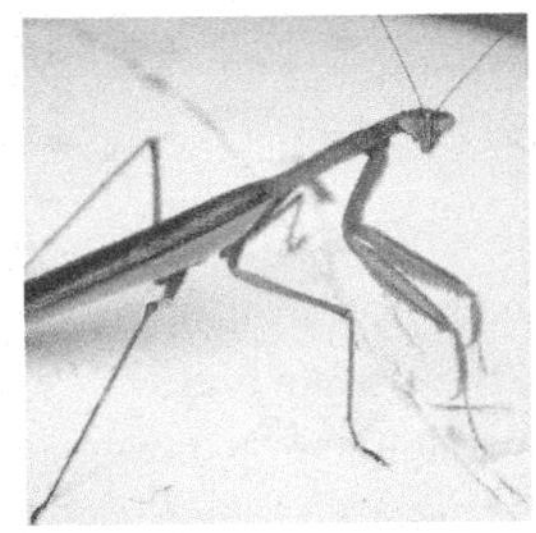

WORKING WITH COLOR

We are very sensitive to color, and our eyes are tremendous tools for seeing and comparing what seems like an infinite variety of hues. The emotional and subliminal importance of color in our world cannot be denied. For retouchers, being sensitive to color values can make the difference between a so-so print and a print that looks as vibrant as the memories it represents.

The importance of color challenges us to work with our visual memory in combination with the best that Photoshop has to offer: Adjustment layers, the Info and Histogram panels, painting and selection tools, and blending modes. In this chapter, you work with color images to learn

- Additive and subtractive color correction
- Global color correction with Levels and Curves
- Selective color correction and restoring color in historical photographs
- Correcting color temperature problems
- Matching, replacing, and changing color

Many of the tools and techniques discussed in Chapter 3, “Exposure Correction,” serve as the foundation for working with color. I highly recommend that you review that chapter before diving into the wonderful world of color.

COLOR ESSENTIALS

There are two types of color in the world: additive and subtractive. In the additive world, a light source is needed to create color. When the primary colors (red, green, and blue) are combined, they create white, as shown in FIGURE 4.1. Your monitor is an example of an additive color device.

In the subtractive world, color is determined by the absorption of light. When the secondary colors cyan, magenta, and yellow are combined, they create black-brown, as shown in FIGURE 4.2. Printing ink on paper is an example of subtractive color. In creating inks for print, impurities in the pigments result in a muddy black-brown when cyan, magenta, and yellow are combined. To achieve rich shadows and pure blacks, black is added in the printing process, which also cuts down on the amount of the more expensive color inks used.

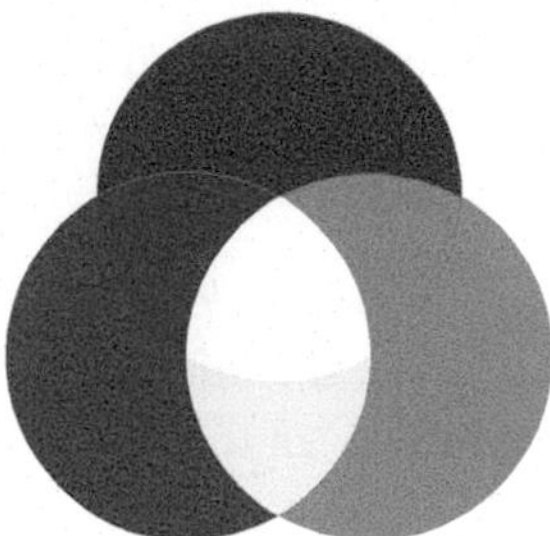

FIGURE 4.1 The additive color system is formed by the primary colors: red, green, and blue.

FIGURE 4.2 The subtractive color system is formed by the secondary colors cyan, yellow, and magenta.

Combining additive primaries yields the subtractive primaries, and combining the subtractive primaries creates the additive primaries. You can see this change where the circles overlap in each of the examples. For the retoucher, understanding this relationship of opposites can be very useful when identifying and correcting color problems. For example, if an image is too blue, you have two ways to approach the problem: either increase the yellow (which is the opposite of blue) or decrease the blue in the image. Both yield the same result: an image with less blue.

In digital imaging, the four most common color modes are RGB, CMYK, Lab, and HSB.

RGB (for red, green, and blue) mode uses the additive color system that monitors, scanners, and digital cameras use. The advantages to color correcting and retouching in RGB include smaller file sizes, the fact that equal values of red, green, and blue will always result in neutral gray, and the fact that a larger RGB color space, like Adobe RGB (1998) or ProPhoto RGB, allows the file to be converted into multiple gamuts and repurposed for multiple final output destinations.

CMYK (for cyan, magenta, yellow, and black) mode uses the subtractive color system. Many people (especially those with prepress or printing experience) prefer doing color correction and retouching in CMYK because they are more comfortable with CMYK color values, and editing colors that are in the same gamut as your printer can help avoid unhappy surprises after the ink hits the paper.

+ TIP Why K for black? It is often said K is used because the B is already used to specify blue in the RGB mode, but the real reason is that in the printing industry K stands for key or key plate, as black holds the image detail.

Lab is a three-channel color mode in which the black-and-white L (lightness) channel information has been separated from the color information. The lightness (also called luminosity) component is measured from 0 to 100. The *a* channel carries green to red, and the *b* channel carries blue to yellow information; each can range from +127 to –128. Lab is a device-independent color space used by color management software and by Photoshop when converting RGB files to CMYK. Color correcting in Lab is a delicate task, because the slightest move on the a or b channel can result in a very strong color shift. On the other hand, Lab is a useful color mode when you are adjusting exposure or cleaning up color artifacts, as both can be addressed in the lightness channel.

HSB stands for hue, saturation, and brightness. Hue refers to the color, brightness refers to the amount of light in the color, and saturation determines the amount of color. You can take advantage of HSB to emphasize or deemphasize color in portrait retouching.

Color Spaces

Don't confuse the color modes described above with *color space*, which is the range of colors that a camera can record, a monitor can display, or a printer can print (FIGURE 4.3). Photoshop uses independent color spaces, which are containers for your colors similar to imaginary boxes of crayons and which come in many different sizes and styles. The largest box of crayons could represent the total number of colors visible to the eye—a range that cannot be displayed or printed. Different color spaces have smaller boxes of crayons or boxes that may contain a different mix of colors have been developed to reflect the different environments in which color is visible or printable. Many designers prefer to use a smaller box of crayons like ColorMatch when the image is going to offset press because a CMYK press has a limited color gamut. Many photographers use Adobe RGB, which is a larger color space that works well for inkjet printing, or ProPhotoRGB, which is ideal for working with 16-bit files from raw files.

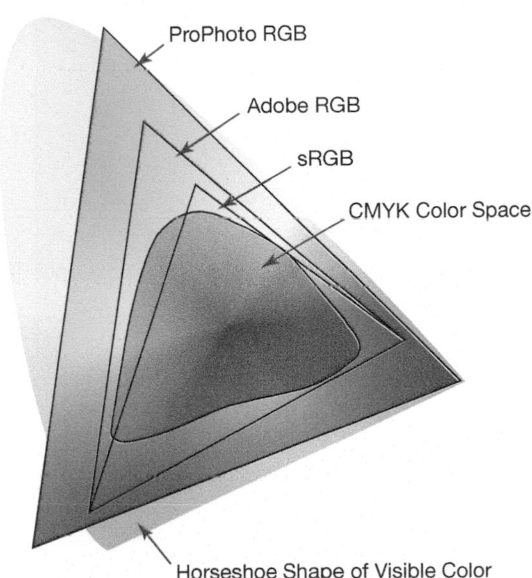

FIGURE 4.3 Color spaces define the range of colors a device can display.

Color spaces vary from printer to printer and even with different types of paper and inks. Photoshop can be set to display the color space used for output along with out-of-gamut warnings for the devices being used. Why work in a color space that cannot be fully displayed in print or on a monitor? The reason is that we don't know what the future holds and what may be a limit now may not be in the future.

IDENTIFYING AND CORRECTING A COLOR CAST

The color correction process always starts by identifying the color cast. You have to know what the problem is before you can apply a solution. A color cast, also called a shade or tinge, is easier to identify in lighter or neutral image areas. For example, a white shirt or a gray sidewalk would be good places to look for a color cast, although they can also be apparent when something is supposed to be black and is not. When evaluating an image for color, find a neutral reference: something that should be white, nearly white, or gray. If it looks, say, slightly blue, then you know that the image has a blue cast. Clearing up the color cast in the lighter and neutral areas usually takes care of most of the required color correction work throughout the entire image. Oddly enough, many photo editing apps now offer effects that simulate the old-time color casts this chapter addresses removing.

If you look at an image and your mind says something is not right color wise, then perhaps there is a cast. Some color casts may be minor to the casual observer, but they are critical in industries like apparel, where a common reason for returns is an item not matching what was advertised.

Undesired color casts occur when the photographer used the wrong type of film for the type of light or had the wrong white balance setting, or when a picture has faded over time. In older film-based images, color casts are common. Most film was white balanced for daylight, meaning bright overhead sun, so images recorded under different lighting often have casts. Images taken under incandescent light turned orange, while images taken under fluorescent light have a blue cast. And film processors pumped out images at very high rates of speed, making usable, but not the most color-accurate, prints.

FIGURE 4.4 The undesirable color cast in this print was caused by age or improper storage. © *KE*

FIGURE 4.5 The wall behind the children has a blue/green cast but should be white. © *WP*

FIGURE 4.6 The white areas have an undesired reddish cast. © *WP*

Here are three examples of undesirable color casts. FIGURE 4.4 shows the extreme color cast from fading due to improper storage. In FIGURE 4.5 the wall behind the two children should be white, but has a bluish green cast that carries over to the faces. FIGURE 4.6 has a nice warm glow, but in reality the white areas should be neutral, as the image was recorded closer to noonday sun.

TIP Sometimes what appears to be a color cast might simply be oversaturation of one color; simply lowering the saturation of that color can correct it.

Consider the Light Source

If any part of an image contains white, gray, or black, it should not be too difficult to use Photoshop's numerous options to neutralize a color cast. But if an image has multiple sources of different types of light or has faded unevenly, correction will be more challenging.

Even though a color may not appear correct, sometimes it actually is. FIGURE 4.7 depicts orange snow. But in this image the light source is from a sodium vapor street lamp, which does emit an orange glow, making this photo fairly close to accurate.

FIGURE 4.7 Despite the orange cast, this image is a fairly accurate representation of the scene because the illumination comes from lights that emit an orange color. © *WP*

Sometimes, getting rid of a color cast may not be the best solution. The pride in this father's expression (FIGURE 4.8) is subdued by the multi-colored stage lights, which create a complex scenario for color correction. There are several areas in the photo that would be considered color neutral and would be a basis from which to correct color. But as seen in FIGURE 4.9, none of the attempts make much improvement, and the color still does not look correct, because the subjects were not photographed under neutral lighting (FIGURE 4.10). In situations like this, a better solution might be to simply convert the image to black and white, which draws attention to the expressions of the subjects and away from the narrow depth of field (FIGURE 4.11) which throws the father a little out of focus.

FIGURE 4.8 An image taken under multiple types of light sources may not be totally color-correctable. © *WP*

FIGURE 4.9 In some cases, making color corrections based on what is perceived as neutral does not yield acceptable results.

TIP Always shoot in color, even if the end result is to be black and white. Having access to the color channels for the conversion to black and white will offer more interpretive potential than using a camera's black and white setting.

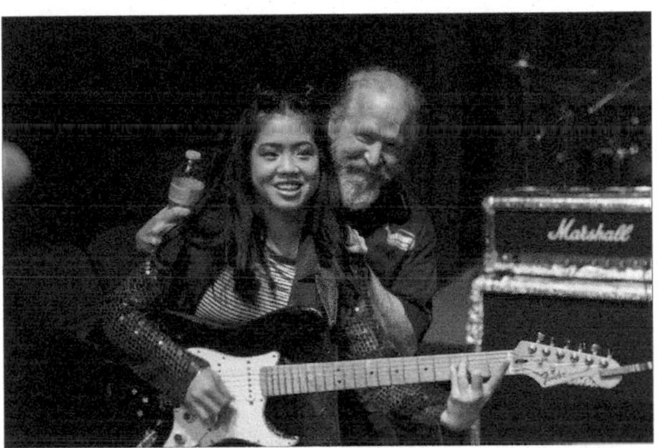

FIGURE 4.10 Even with multiple corrections, the color is still off because the subjects were not under neutral light.

FIGURE 4.11 In difficult lighting situations, a black and white version of the image might be a better solution.

ARE ALL COLOR CASTS EVIL?

There are only two types of color casts in the world: those that enhance the image and those that detract from it.

Fine art child photographer Sonya Adcock uses color casts to help create moods or evoke emotions. Examples include the cold feeling from the blue tint of a snowy, overcast day or the the golden tones of early morning window light (**FIGURES 4.12** and **FIGURE 4.13**).

FIGURE 4.12 The blue and green tones convey coolness. © *Sonya Adcock*

FIGURE 4.13 The abundance of reds and yellows conveys warmth. © *Sonya Adcock*

Finding Neutral

The tools used to identify a color cast are your visual memory, the Info panel, the individual image channels, and practice. Color casts that are similar, such as blue and cyan or magenta and red, can take a bit of practice to identify correctly. If you have a color cast in your highlights, nine times out of ten you'll have a color cast in the entire image. Just because color casts are harder to see in dark areas doesn't mean they're not there. Once you have identified the color cast, think globally and take care of the general problem first. Fortunately, correcting the big problem usually takes care of many of the smaller problems along the way.

Memory Colors

We know that grass is green, the sky is blue, and clouds are white. We refer to these as memory colors, as we know what they should look like. And our brain may assign those colors to things even though an image may show something very different. We use the term color correction because we use our memory of color for the basis of choosing what looks correct.

+ TIP The longer something is viewed, the less noticeable a color cast becomes. Occasionally step away from a color correction project and come back with a fresh set of eyes.

Info Panel

Just as the Info panel was important in making tonal corrections, it is equally important with color corrections. Place the Eyedropper over an area that should be color neutral and read the RGB values in the Info panel. Correctly balanced neutral colors have equal values of RGB, while images with a color cast do not. Darker neutral areas have lower RGB values and lighter ones have higher RGB values. Without even seeing the image, you can tell from the readout (FIGURE 4.14) that the measured area has a strong color cast.

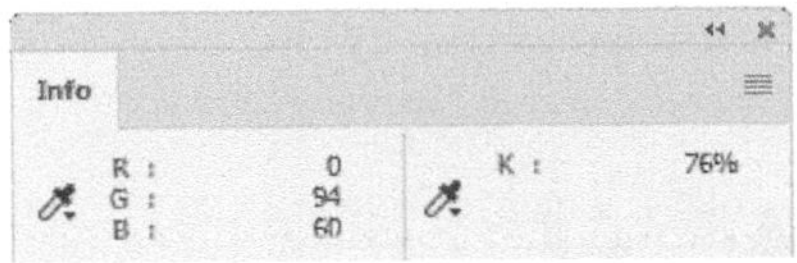

FIGURE 4.14 The Info panel can signal the presence of a color cast.

Channels and Practice

Through the rest of this chapter we will be exploring different color correction methods that work by altering individual channels, similarly to how tonal corrections were made. As with all of Photoshop's tools, the best choice comes with practice and experience.

GLOBAL COLOR CORRECTION

In assessing what would benefit from color correction, the choice is whether a correction needs to be applied to the entire image or just to a portion. We will first address the entire image (referred to as *global*), and then we will explore applying corrections selectively.

Despite the numerous options we will cover for having Photoshop automatically correct color, if you want to become proficient at color correcting you will need to become familiar with the primary colors of each color mode. One way to do so is to remember the order in which the two are listed: RGB and CMYK. The orders of the letters are their color opposites. The opposite of red is cyan, green's opposite is magenta, and the opposite of blue is yellow. If cyan and magenta aren't colors you are familiar with, just keep in mind their opposites in RGB. If a picture is too green, you want to adjust the color in the opposite direction, which is magenta (FIGURE 4.15).

Red ←→ Cyan
Green ←→ Magenta
Blue ←→ Yellow

FIGURE 4.15 Learn the RGB and CMY relationships to better understand color correction.

The Auto Corrections

Identifying a color cast is the first step in color correction; finding the best tool to correct it is another. Photoshop offers options ranging from one-click correction to complex multistep operations. In general, you should take control over the results, but there are images for which the auto correction features do an excellent job. FIGURE 4.16 was taken through tinted glass, and the camera's auto white balance setting did not compensate for it, resulting in a strong greenish-blue tint. To see how powerful the Auto Color command can be, follow these few steps and view the result (FIGURE 4.17).

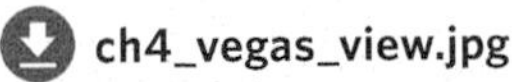

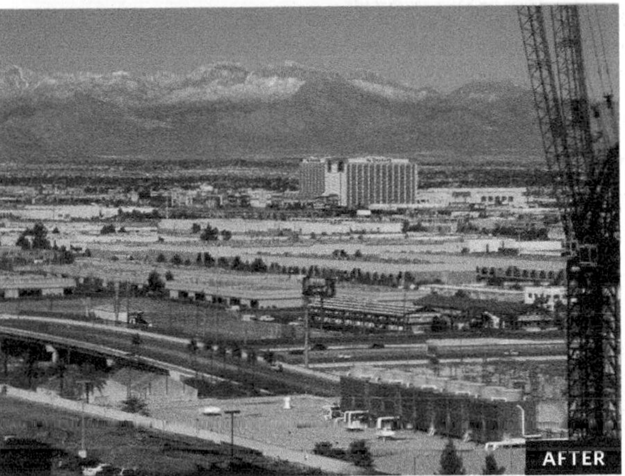

FIGURES 4.16 and 4.17 Before and After. © *WP*

1. To protect the original image, duplicate the background layer by pressing Cmd-J/Ctrl-J.

2. Choose **Image > Auto Color.**

As you can see, the correction is dramatic, and if color correction were always that simple, we could conclude this chapter. But Auto Color can also be a hit-or-miss proposition, and it does not allow for user input. Let's explore Photoshop's more advanced controls, which include nondestructive automatic color-correction options.

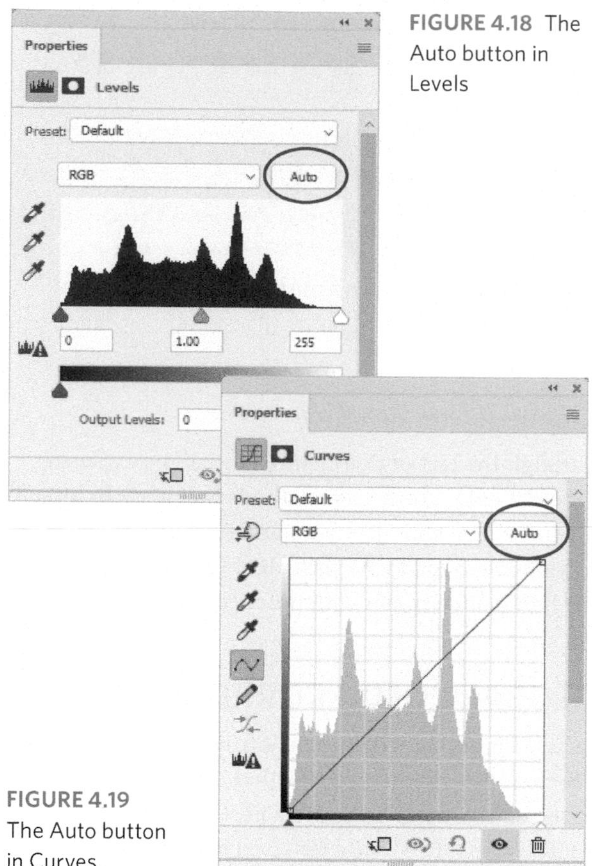

FIGURE 4.18 The Auto button in Levels

FIGURE 4.19 The Auto button in Curves

Automatic Color Corrections with Levels or Curves

Both Levels and Curves adjustment layers allow you to correct color automatically by simply clicking the Auto button in the Properties panel (FIGURES 4.18 and 4.19). By using automatic color correction in an adjustment layer you will keep the changes nondestructive. If you add one of these adjustment layers to the previous image and click the Auto button, you will get a different result. That is because Curves and Levels offer different algorithms for automatic color correction.

Improving Automatic Color Correction

To change the algorithm used by the Auto button in Curves or Levels, open the Auto Color Correction Options dialog in the appropriate Properties panel (FIGURE 4.20). To open the dialog, choose Auto Options from the Properties panel menu or Option/Alt-click the Auto button. You have a choice of four auto color algorithms: Enhance Monochromatic Contrast, Enhance Per Channel Contrast, Find Dark & Light Colors, and Enhance Brightness And Contrast. In addition there are options for snapping neutral midtones, targeting colors, and setting clipping levels, as covered in Chapter 3. The option used by the Auto Color command is Enhance Per Channel Contrast with Snap Neutral Midtones selected. Remember that there is often no quick fix to a problem, and experimentation is the way to learn which options will work best for different images.

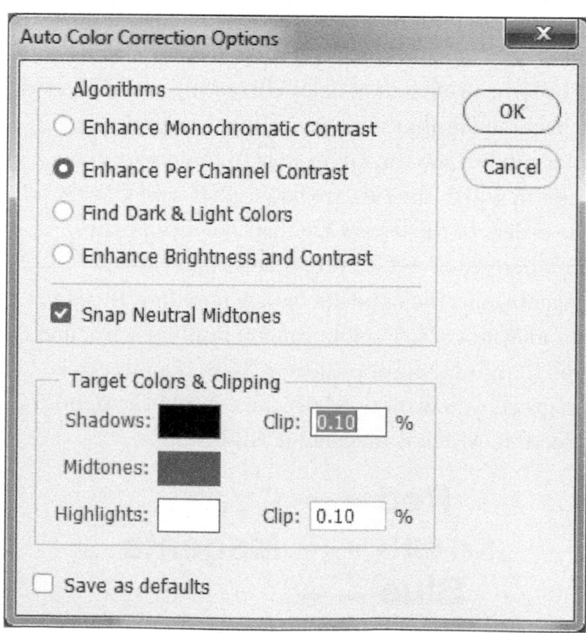

FIGURE 4.20 Using Auto for color correction inside Levels and Curves offers more options.

Targeting Automatic Color Correction

Since automatic color correction evaluates the entire image, it may not always work as expected. Extraneous white borders or torn edges, like those in FIGURE 4.21, can undermine its accuracy. To avoid unexpected results, either crop the file before using Auto Color or make a selection of an area with a variety of tonal variants and apply auto color through a Levels or Curves adjustment layer. If the result is satisfactory, delete or hide the mask to apply the result to the rest of the image. Follow these steps to get great results, as in FIGURE 4.22.

FIGURES 4.21 and 4.22 Before and after. © *The Beckleman Family Archives*

ch4_couchcouple.jpg

1. Use the Marquee tool to select the important area of the image. (Auto Color will use this area for its calculations.) In this example, it would be the faces of the couple in FIGURE 4.23.

FIGURE 4.23 Select the important part of the image.

2. Add a Levels adjustment layer, which will automatically include a mask that hides the unselected area.

3. In the Levels Properties panel, Option/Alt-click the Options button and try the different algorithms. As seen in FIGURE 4.24, Enhance Per Channel Contrast with Snap Neutral Midtones selected creates the best results.

FIGURE 4.24 Auto Color generates a better result when a smaller portion of the image is evaluated.

4. To apply the correction to the entire image, fill the mask with white, delete it, or simply turn it off by Shift-clicking the mask (FIGURE 4.25).

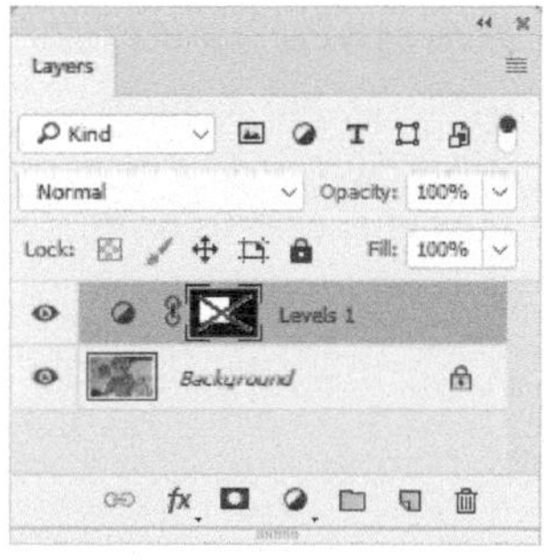

FIGURE 4.25 Turn off the mask to apply the color correction to the entire image.

USE ADJUSTMENT LAYERS TO ALLEVIATE COLOR PROBLEMS

Photoshop offers a number of features that can be used to correct color. Adjustment layers, sometimes coupled with layer masks, are best choice for making re-adjustable and nondestructive edits. Let's go through some of the most useful ones.

Correcting Color Temperature with the Photo Filter

Our eyes don't see color temperature while taking a photograph because our brain balances light to white no matter how cool or warm the light really is. These color casts show up when the auto white balance drifts from image to image, so a series of images taken at the same time can have color shifts because of how the camera evaluates the lighting for each image. This why it is so valuable to shoot in raw, as an incorrect white balance setting can be corrected in editing, if for some reason it's not possible to take the time to set the white balance manually when taking the image.

Back in the days of film, there was no easy way to adjust what we now refer to as white balance or color temperature. Most film was color balanced for daylight, and images recorded in lighting other than midday sun would reveal color casts. Many times a photo lab could correct for casts in the printing of color negative film, but transparency film needed to have the color correct prior to capture. The photographer would add color filters to the lens to add the color that would be missing from the light source.

The Photo Filters adjustment simulates the effect of adding color correction filters. In addition, they can be used for effect, as shown earlier in the chapter.

The sky was overcast when the image in FIGURE 4.26 was taken, giving it what is referred to as a cool look. Notice that the stone in the barn wall has a bluish cast. Follow these steps to apply a warming filter to convey a late afternoon sunny effect, as seen in FIGURE 4.27.

 ch4_horsebarn.jpg

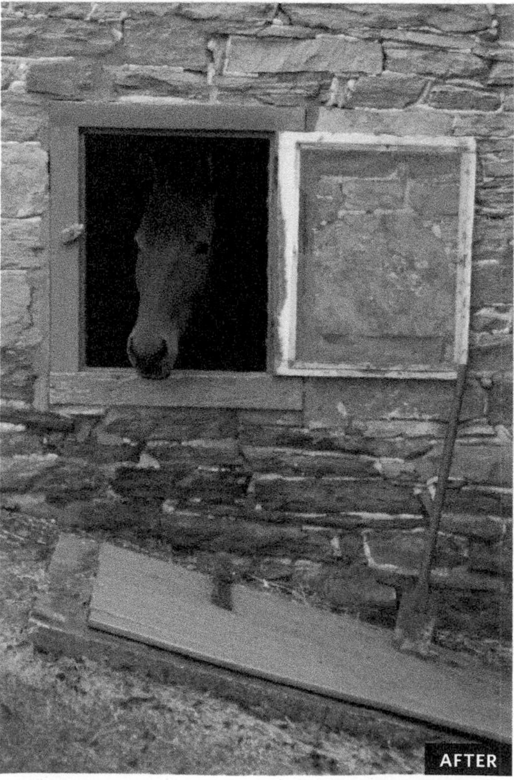

FIGURES 4.26 and 4.27 Before and after. © *WP*

1. Add a Photo Filter adjustment layer. From the Filter menu, choose Warming Filter (85). Be sure the default of Preserve Luminosity is selected, as shown in FIGURE 4.28.

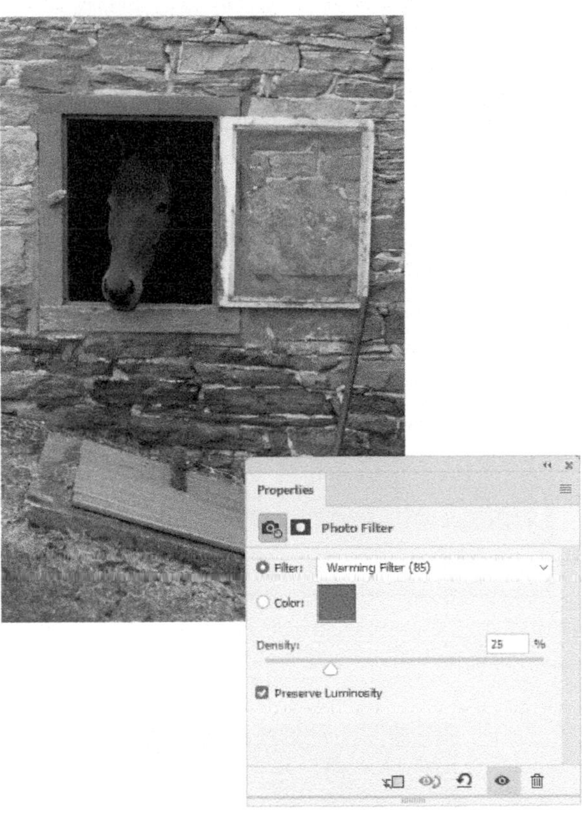

FIGURE 4.28 The default setting for the Warming filter removes much of the blue cast.

2. The effect can be increased by using the Density slider, but a faster option is to just duplicate the adjustment layer by pressing Cmd-J/Ctrl-J.

TRY IT FIGURE 4.29 was taken in a small museum and the objects were illuminated under incandescent light, causing an orange cast. The lighting does create a warm feeling, but it is not an accurate representation of the scene. Adding blue to the image would neutralize the cast. Add a Photo Filter adjustment layer and explore the Cooling filters, experimenting with the Density slider, to eliminate the cast (FIGURE 4.30).

 **ch4_museum.jpg**

FIGURES 4.29 and 4.30 Before and after. © *WP*

TIP Don't confuse these color correction filters with the color filters that are used in black and white photography to increase the contrast of specific colors. That effect can be achieved with the Black and White or Channel Mixer adjustments.

NOTE Photoshop is not an excuse for bad photography. It is always better to set the correct white balance in the camera, especially when capturing in the JPEG format. As I've said many times, if the picture is taken correctly, there will be less work to do on the computer and a smaller chance of unnatural results.

In the previous examples, we used photo filters "straight out of the box" to correct color casts. In the following example, I show a more advanced technique to correct a color cast with the same adjustment. The strong tungsten lighting was not corrected by the digital camera's white balance and the resulting image was overly yellow (FIGURE 4.31). With a few Photoshop steps, I was able to change the color temperature to a more neutral daylight appearance, as you see in FIGURE 4.32.

Using a Photo Filter adjustment layer will compensate for the undesired color temperature of the light by filtering the image with the opposite color.

FIGURES 4.31 and 4.32 Before and after. © *WP*

ch4_yellowlobby.jpg

1. Add a Photo Filter adjustment layer.

2. Make no changes in the Properties panel, and click the color swatch to open the Color Picker. Check the Layers panel. Sample an area of the image displaying the strong color cast you want to correct (see FIGURE 4.33).

3. In the Color picker, invert the Lab a and b values by inserting or deleting minuses. This change (FIGURE 4.34) is not as dramatic as in the last example, because we didn't change the intensity.

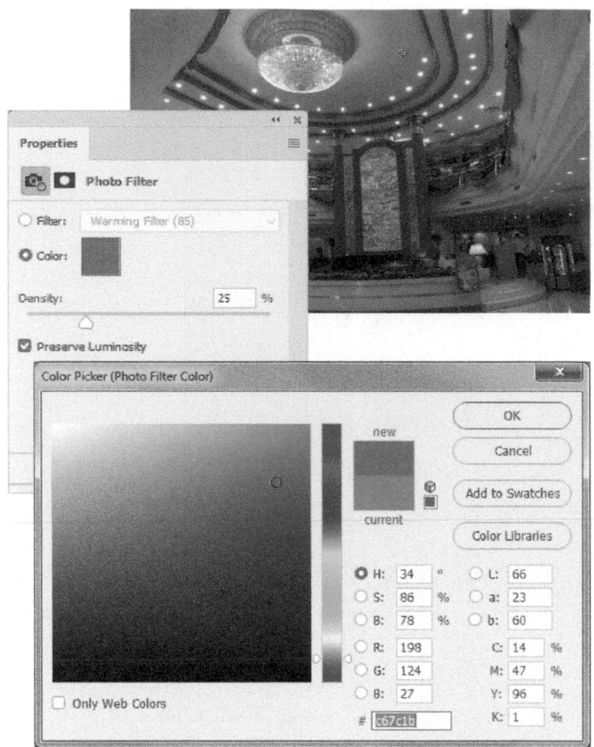

FIGURE 4.33 Select the offending color with the Eyedropper tool.

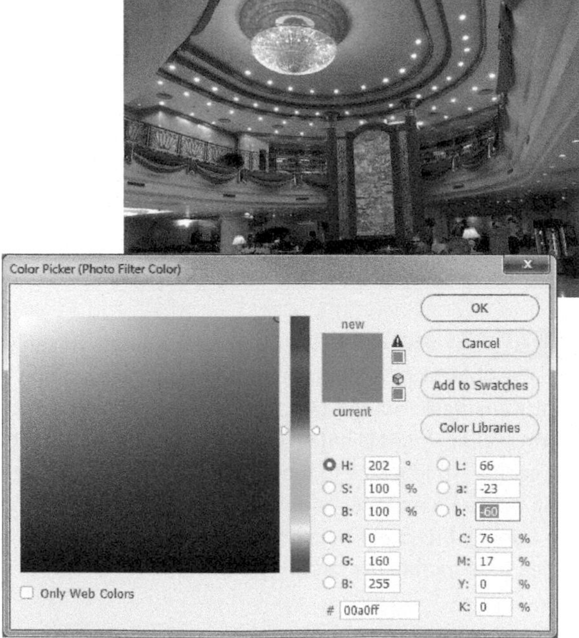

FIGURE 4.34 Invert the a and b color values.

4. Click OK to close the Color Picker. Use the Photo Filter Density slider to fine-tune your correction, as in FIGURE 4.35.

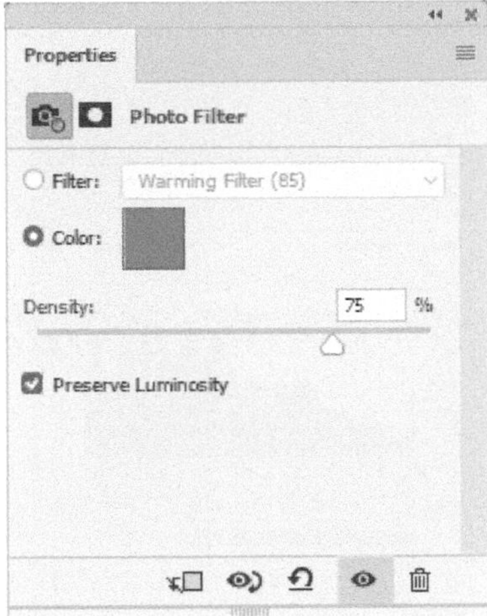

FIGURE 4.35 Increasing the percentage on the Density slider will intensify the effect.

Levels, Curves, and the Gray Eyedropper

Levels and Curves can be used to make very intricate adjustments by working with the individual color channels. Use the gray eyedropper to remedy color casts if a neutral gray area exists in the image.

Inside the Levels and Curves dialog boxes there are three eyedroppers. In Chapter 3, the white and black eyedroppers were covered. The middle eyedropper, gray, is used to establish what should be color neutral.

TRY IT This slide scan (found on a Kodak Photo CD) of a lion giving a raspberry to the photographer (FIGURE 4.36) has a strong green cast. Add a Levels or Curves adjustment layer and use the gray eyedropper to remove the cast. Be sure the Sample Size setting for the Eyedropper is larger than Point Sample and experiment, as there are multiple areas that appear to be gray (FIGURE 4.37).

FIGURES 4.36 and 4.37 Before and after. © *WP*

Adjusting Channels in Levels

Auto correct can sometimes be a matter of trial and error. And the gray eyedropper works well if you know something in the image is truly neutral gray. When neither method seems to work, it is time to take a more hands-on approach by adjusting each of the color channels.

In the late '70s and early '80s, photofinishers using Agfa paper and chemistry often experienced color shifting after only a few years. Fortunately, this did not affect the negatives processed during that time, only the prints made. Traveling portrait studios that set up shop in big-box stores were popular during that time. Prints purchased from those studios did not include a negative, so the customer saw their images start to fade after a few years with no way to get them reprinted again. Such is the case with FIGURE 4.38, which has shifted to primarily orange. Follow these steps to breathe life and color back into the faded print (FIGURE 4.39).

FIGURES 4.38 and 4.39 Before and after. © *Davis Family Archives*

ch4_brothers.jpg

1. Create a Levels adjustment layer. The Histogram in FIGURE 4.40 shows that there is a full range of tonality.

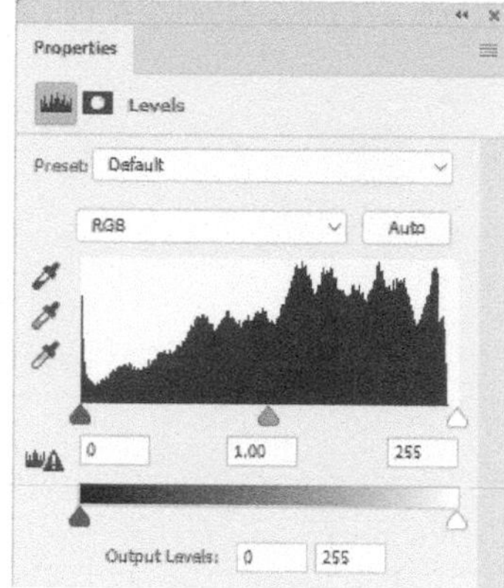

FIGURE 4.40 The histogram shows a full range of exposure in the RGB mode.

2. Open the channel menu and choose the Red channel (or press Option-3/Alt-3). Notice that the histogram in this channel does not show exposure information across the entire graph. Slide the black slider to the right until the point where the histogram starts to rise above 0; the output reading will be 113, as shown in FIGURE 4.41. Already the image has lost most of its red cast.

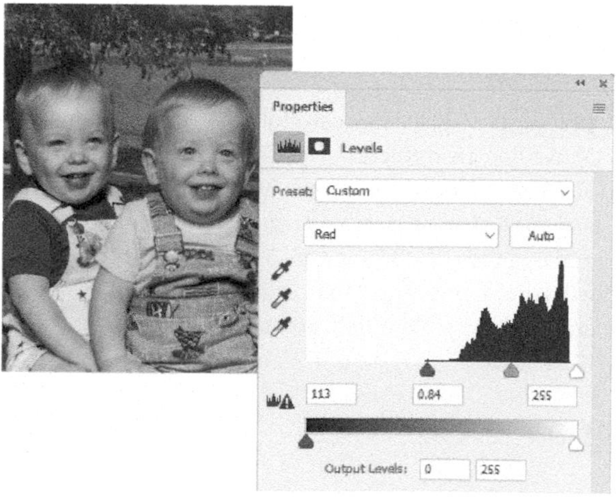

FIGURE 4.41 Adjusting the red channel removes a majority of the red cast.

3. Visit the channel menu again and choose Green (or press Option-4/Alt-4). This channel's histogram shows full exposure information across the graph but would benefit from the blacks being emphasized a little. Adjust the black slider to 14. Nudge the midtone slider to 1.04. Leave the white slider alone, as adjusting it only makes the image brighter than needed (FIGURE 4.42).

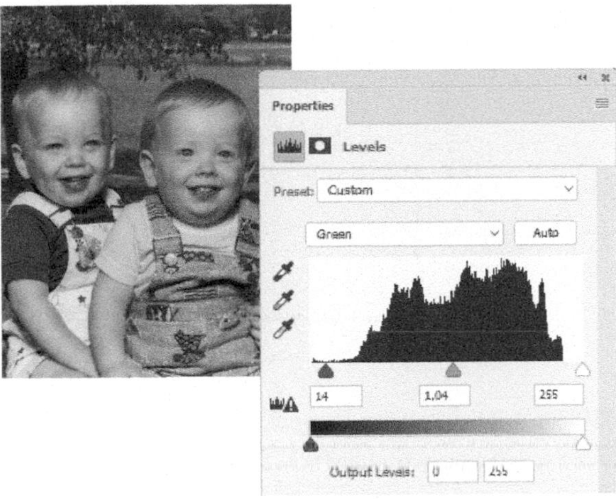

FIGURE 4.42 The green channel shows full exposure range, but a little adjustment to the blacks improves the color.

4. Choose Blue from the channel menu (Option-5/Alt-5). Again, the histogram does not extend across the entire scale. Move the white slider to the point where the graph drops to 0, which is at 197, as shown in FIGURE 4.43.

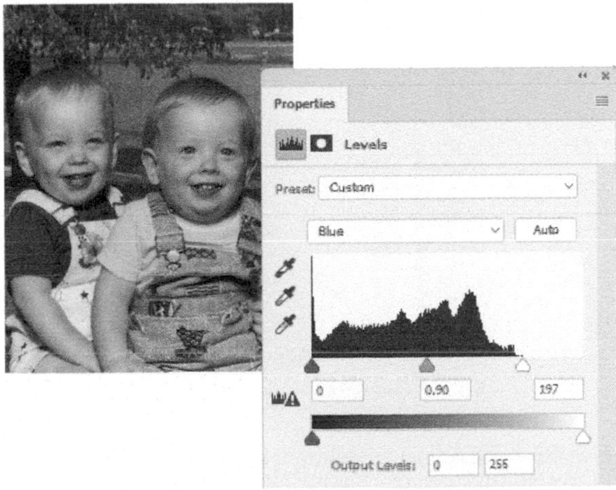

FIGURE 4.43 A final adjustment to the blue channel restores the remaining color.

Ironically, after the color has been corrected, neutral gray areas are revealed, which would have made the correction a simpler task.

Adjusting Channels in Curves

FIGURE 4.44 has a nice warm glow from the colored lights, but it is not an accurate rendition of the scene. The image was taken using tungsten film, which boosted the colors. If you roll the Eyedropper tool over the snow—areas that should show nearly equal readings of red, green, and blue—the red and blue channels indicate a strong imbalance. Curves has individual channel adjustments for addressing color, just like Levels. But Curves can make more detailed corrections, as with tonality adjustments. Follow these steps to make the snow look more natural, as seen in FIGURE 4.45.

FIGURES 4.44 and 4.45 Before and after. © *WP*

1. Add a Curves adjustment layer; its histogram shows a full range of tonality (**FIGURE 4.46**).

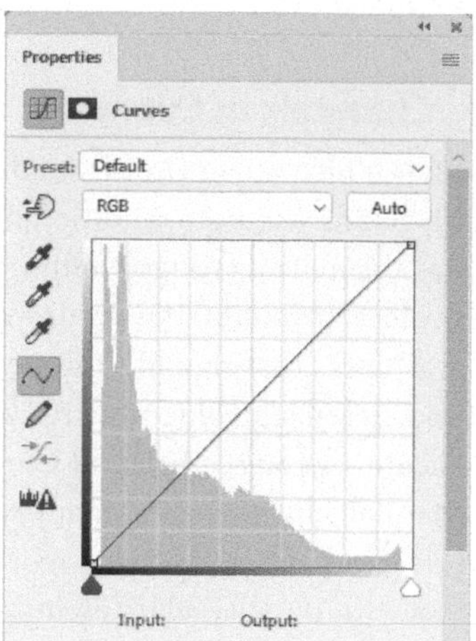

FIGURE 4.46 The histogram shows that the image has been exposed properly.

2. Open the channel menu and choose Red (or press Option-3/Alt-3). Recall that the image needs a reduction in red in order for the snow to look white. Drag the center of the Curves line toward the lower-right corner. Stop when the Input field reads 140 and Output reads 106 (**FIGURE 4.47**).

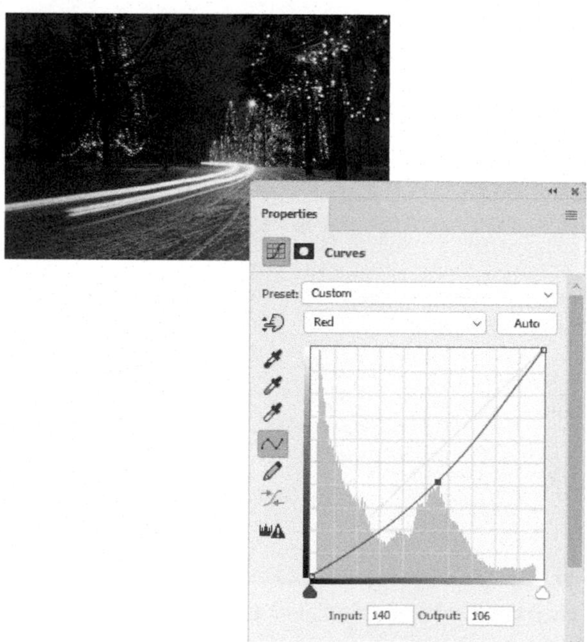

FIGURE 4.47 Adjusting the curve in the red channel removes most of the red.

3. Switch to the Green channel by pressing Option-4/Alt-4. There does not appear to be much green in the image, and the green channel histogram shows a pretty even distribution of information, so make no changes (**FIGURE 4.48**).

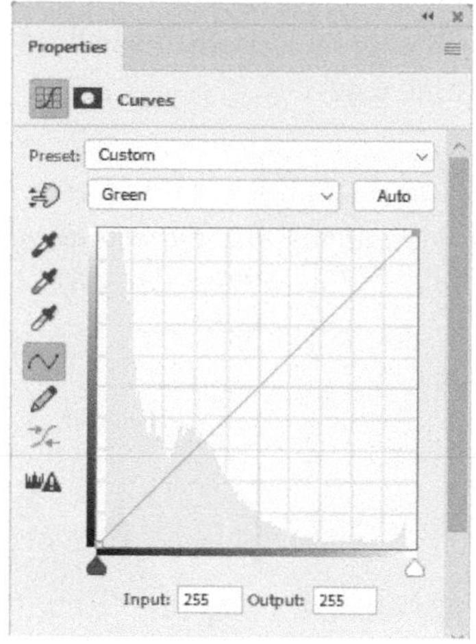

FIGURE 4.48 The green channel is fairly well represented in the graph and needs no adjustment.

4. Lastly, switch to the Blue channel (Option-4/Alt-4). Again, the histogram looks fine, but drag the center of the curve toward the lower-right corner. This moves the color away from blue and toward yellow. Stop when the Input value reaches 138 and the Output value reaches 114 (**FIGURE 4.49**).

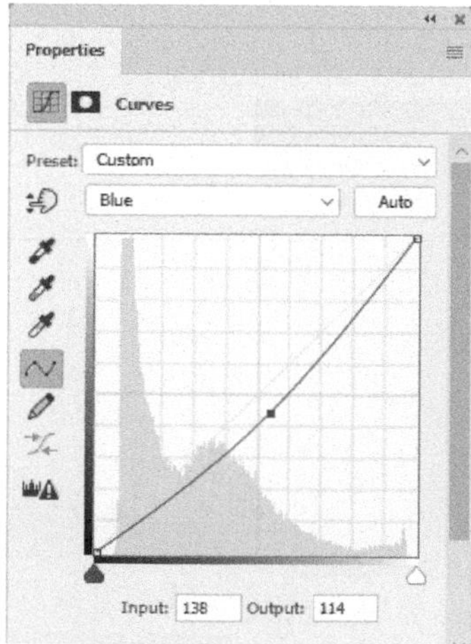

FIGURE 4.49 A final adjustment to the blue channel removes the remaining color cast and makes the snow white.

TIP Correcting both tone and color balance inside a single Levels or Curves adjustment can be a little confusing. Use separate adjustment layers for each.

Divide and Conquer

The Lab color mode is not as intuitive to work in as RGB or CMYK. It has been described as intimidating by Dan Margulis, who has written an entire book dedicated to working with it: *Photoshop LAB Color: The Canyon Conundrum and Other Adventures in the Most Powerful Colorspace (2nd Edition).*

Dennis has devised a method that borrows the concept of working with Lab and has almost all the power of color correcting, but it does so without leaving RGB or CMYK. (Dennis uses this technique in several of the projects in Chapter 8.) He uses the concept of separating color and tone using Curves in conjunction with blending modes (FIGURES 4.50 and 4.51).

FIGURES 4.50 and 4.51 Before and after. © *WP*

To address tonality, he adds a Curves adjustment layer, renames it **Tone**, sets the blending mode to Luminosity, and sets the white and black points (FIGURE 4.52). Any changes affect only the image's brightness while its color remains the same.

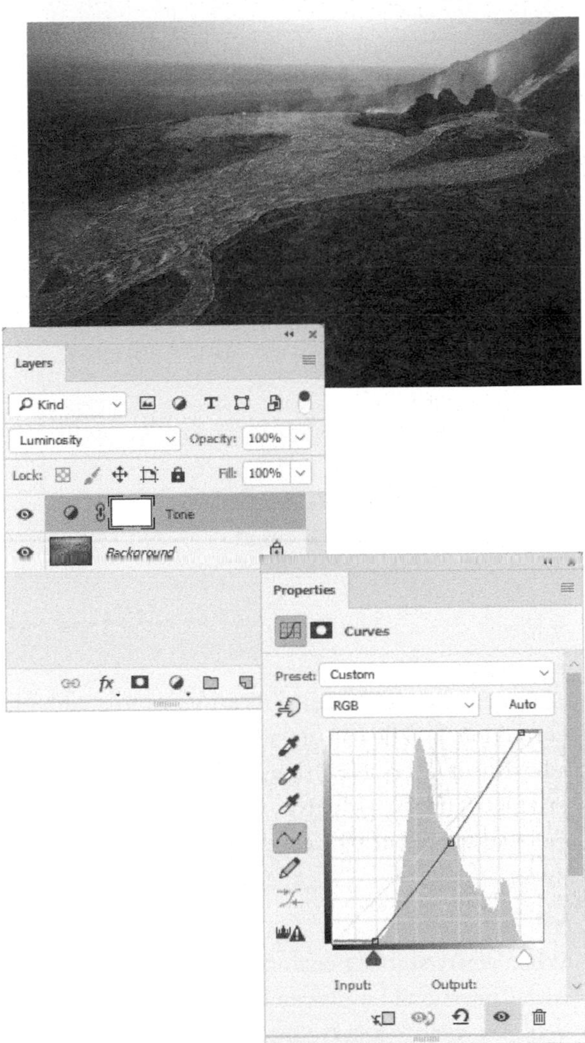

FIGURE 4.52 With the Curves blending mode set to Luminosity, only the tonal value is changed.

For color, he creates a second Curves adjustment layer (renamed **Color**) and sets the blending mode to Color. From there, he accesses the individual channels to correct color. Any changes affect only color, and the tone remains unchanged (FIGURE 4.53).

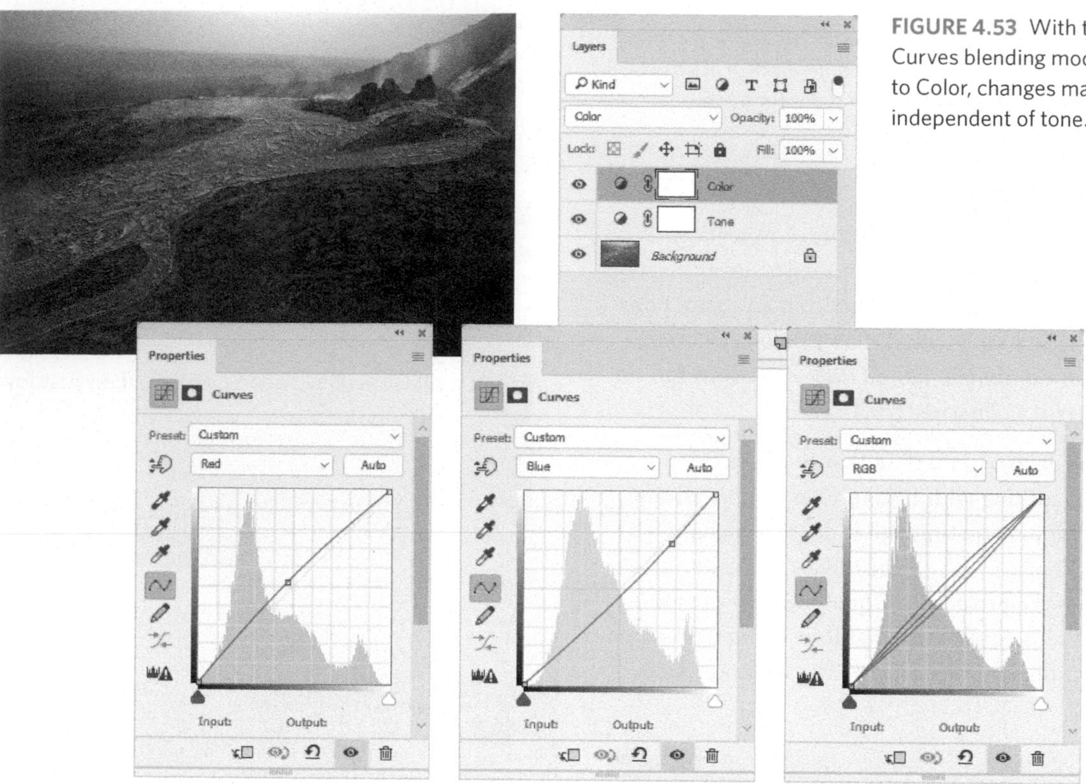

FIGURE 4.53 With the second Curves blending mode set to Color, changes made are independent of tone.

This technique has become Dennis's go-to method for correction, and he uses an action to generate the two adjustment layers. He also uses this method when colorizing an image, as it gives very smooth transitions and makes the borders less detectable.

Color Balance

When you're starting out, addressing color issues with Curves and Levels can be a little intimidating. You may want to reserve them for tonal corrections and use a dedicated adjustment for color. The Color Balance adjustment is straightforward in that it all six colors of the RGB and CMY modes are visible at the same time, making it simpler to correct color without having to jump to different channels. The down side is that there is no histogram built into the Color Balance adjustment for easy monitoring, so you would need to use the Histogram panel or Info panel or just eyeball it.

This old family photo has yellowed with age. Follow these short steps to return the original color (**FIGURES 4.54** and **4.55**).

ch4_group_photo.jpg

1. Add a Color Balance adjustment layer.
2. As the image is most noticeably yellow, drag the Yellow/Blue slider toward Blue, stopping at +21.
3. Carefully drag the Magenta/Green slider toward Magenta to –3.
4. Drag the Cyan/Red slider to the left to –15, as shown in **FIGURE 4.56**.

FIGURES 4.54 and **4.55** Before and after. © *Palmer Family Archives*

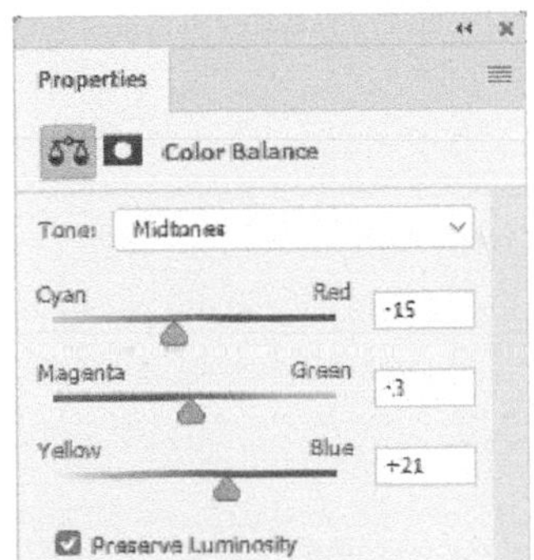

FIGURE 4.56 The Color Balance adjustment provides access to the primary colors of RGB and CMY in a single interface, which can make color correction simpler.

Hue/Saturation

Hue/Saturation is a little less intuitive than Color Balance. It also has three sliders, but they work in a different fashion. The Hue slider changes overall color, the Saturation slider changes the intensity of color, and the Brightness slider is self-explanatory. A minor adjustment with the Hue slider can create a dramatic color change, making it a little tricky for global color corrections. Wayne uses this adjustment to address color casts that remain after other color correction methods have been used or when just lowering intensity of one color corrects a problem.

In this image, we will use the gray eyedropper to first remove most of the color cast and then use the Hue/Saturation adjustment to selectively eliminate the remaining blue cast (**FIGURES 4.57** and **4.58**).

 **ch4-blue_snow.jpg**

FIGURES 4.57 and **4.58** Before and after. © *WP*

1. Create a Levels or Curves adjustment layer, select the gray eyedropper, and click the road in front of the house. This makes a dramatic improvement, but the snow still has a blue cast (**FIGURE 4.59**).

FIGURE 4.59 The gray eyedropper removes most of the blue, but there is still a cast to the snow.

2. Add a Hue/Saturation adjustment layer. Select the On-Image Adjustment tool, find a spot in the blue shadows, and drag to the left until the blue is gone. Alternatively, you could open the menu under the Preset menu, choose Blues, and then drag the Saturation slider to –80, as shown in **FIGURE 4.60**.

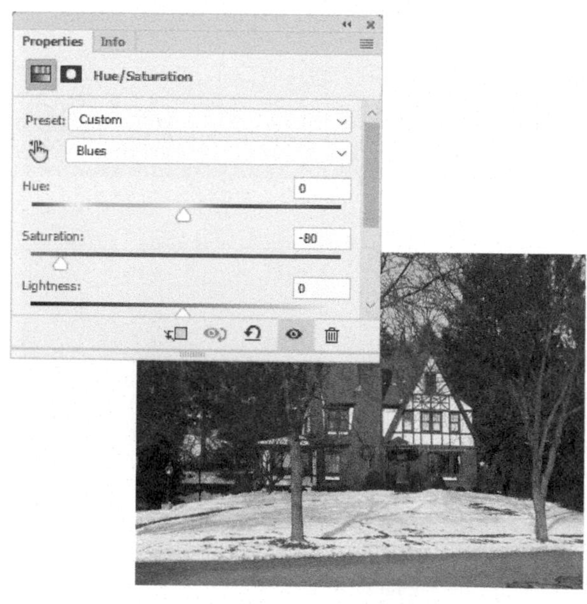

FIGURE 4.60 The remaining blue cast is removed by lowering the saturation level of blue.

3. Unfortunately, the blue sky is now also gone, but it can be restored by adding a gradient to the mask of the Hue/Saturation adjustment layer. Click the mask icon of the Hue/Saturation adjustment layer, press D to select the default colors of black and white, and make sure that white is the foreground color.

4. Select the Gradient tool (G), and remember that with masking black conceals and white reveals. Drag upward a short distance (**FIGURE 4.61**) on the chimney and the blue will return to the sky while leaving the snow neutral.

FIGURE 4.61 The black part of the gradient on the Hue/Saturation mask hides the saturation adjustment and so returns the blue to the sky.

Camera Raw Filter

Learning your way around the color correction tools in Photoshop can take time, patience, and experience. It's like being in a master chef's kitchen—you may not know the best tool for any particular task, and with all the options to choose from, it can be overwhelming.

Instead of being compartmentalized, as adjustment layers are, the Camera Raw filter offers all the tools you need for tonal and color correction inside one interface. There is no need to jump back and forth between different adjustment layers just to tweak a setting.

If you have processed raw files in Adobe Camera Raw (ACR), you are already familiar with the interface. And if you are a Lightroom user, the Camera Raw filter offers the same tools but in a tabbed layout.

The Camera Raw filter contains one special tool not found anywhere else: the White Balance tool. Unlike the gray eyedropper tool found in Levels and Curves, the White Balance tool works on any area that should be color neutral. It does not have to be gray; it works on white or black as well.

In this image of a praying mantis (**FIGURES 4.62** and **4.63**), the insect was standing on a piece of wood painted white, but the camera's auto white balance shifted it toward blue. Unlike other examples in this chapter, this image has no neutral gray area to base a correction on, and using the black or white eyedroppers from Levels and Curves would change the exposure. This is where the White Balance tool shines.

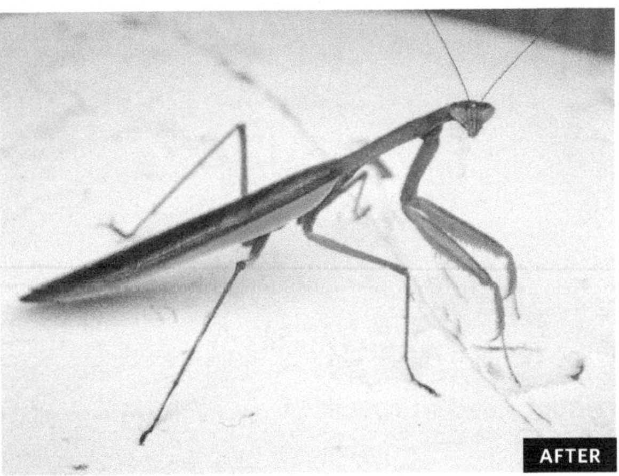

FIGURES 4.62 and **4.63** Before and after. © *WP*

ch4_mantis.jpg

Using Camera Raw as a Smart Filter keeps it from being destructive.

1. Convert the Background layer to a Smart Object by right-clicking it in the Layers panel and choosing Convert to Smart Object; or choose **Filter > Convert for Smart Filters**.

2. Choose **Filter > Camera Raw Filter**; the Camera Raw dialog box opens. Select the White Balance tool (marked by an eyedropper icon) in the Tools panel along the top of the interface, as seen in **FIGURE 4.64**.

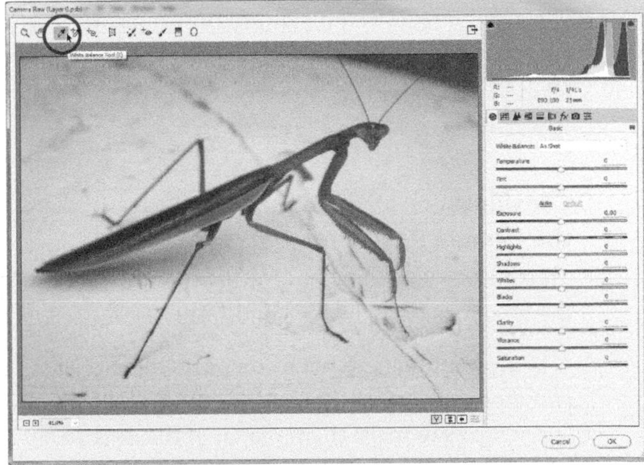

FIGURE 4.64 The White Balance tool in the Camera Raw filter can be used on anything that should be color neutral—white, gray, or black.

3. Click anywhere in the image where the background appears to be white, and the blue cast will vanish. Similarly, click in any of the dark areas. You will get slightly different variations (FIGURE 4.65); the best result is subjective.

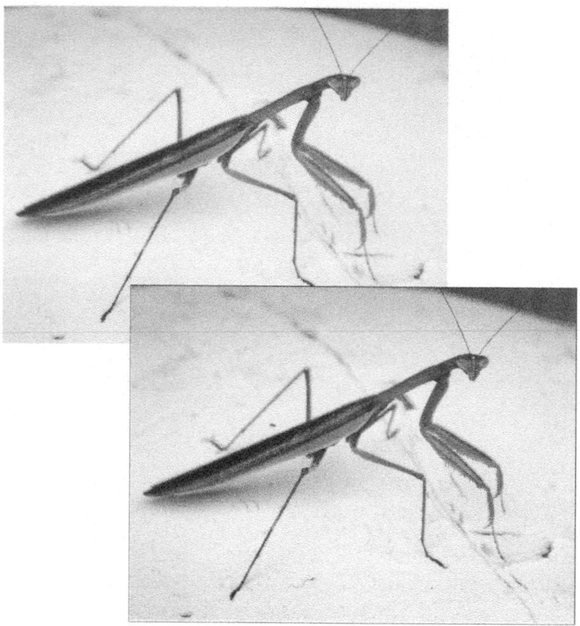

FIGURE 4.65 Clicking white areas in the image removes the blue cast.

With all the correction tools in one interface, the Camera Raw filter might be the go-to option for color correction. And if color is all that needs to be fixed, it would be a good choice, because when the Camera Raw filter is applied to a Smart Object it is nondestructive.

Considerations When Using the Camera Raw Filter

The Camera Raw filter can complicate the workflow if the final image will involve multiple layers.

- When putting together a composited image, it is common to adjust the tones and colors of the different layers to make them match. If the layer to be adjusted is a Smart Object, the changes will not be visible inside the composite until the Camera Raw filter is exited.
- Cloning and healing (topics for upcoming chapters) cannot be applied directly to a Smart Object. They must be made on a separate layer, which is part of a nondestructive workflow. If the Smart Object's color or tone is adjusted later, the upper layers (which would contain cloned or healed information) would no longer match. The changes made inside the Smart Object layer can be saved and then applied to those additional layers if they too are converted to Smart Objects and the adjustments imported into the Camera Raw filter.

To avoid these challenges, this filter might be best reserved for images in which tone and color correction are all that is needed, or those corrections can be finalized before proceeding on a project.

SELECTIVE COLOR CORRECTION

Until now, you've worked on global color correction, but an image can have different problems in different areas. Sometimes one part of the image will be fine and another area's color is way off. Differing color casts can arise due to poor storage conditions, mixed lighting when the photo was originally taken, or misprocessing. Always start with a global color correction, and then select the remaining problem areas and apply local color correction.

Correcting Multiple Color Issues

There are many times when you have to take pictures in mixed lighting situations—such as an office with fluorescent ceiling lights and windows that are letting in daylight, or as shown in FIGURE 4.66, a group shot where the majority of the space is lit with flash but the background is a combination of outdoor and tungsten light. The flash was not up to full charge and slightly underexposed the subject; the camera's white balance also gave it a blue cast. Photographs with mixed lighting are confusing because our eyes naturally neutralize color temperature without us being aware of it. To correct for the mixed lighting, a combination of Photo Filter layers with adjustment masks worked selectively to create the image in FIGURE 4.67.

 **ch4_mixedlighting.jpg**

FIGURES 4.66 and **4.67** Before and after. © *Stephen Rosenblum*

1. Add a Levels adjustment layer, select the white eyedropper, and click the sugar packets in the foreground. The people now look better, but the background lighting is too yellow and even more distracting, as shown in **FIGURE 4.68**.

FIGURE 4.68 A Levels adjustment layer quickly enhances the family but draws too much attention to the background.

2. Use a soft black brush on the Levels adjustment layer mask to paint out the background, as seen in **FIGURE 4.69**. The mask does not have to be very precise, as there would be a little bit of natural blending between the light sources.

FIGURE 4.69 Painting on the layer mask returns the background to its original color and exposure.

3. Cmd/Ctrl-click the Levels adjustment layer mask to load the mask as a selection, then press Cmd-Shift-I/Ctrl-Shift-I to invert the selection (**FIGURE 4.70**).

FIGURE 4.70 Loading the mask as a selection

4. Add a Photo Filter adjustment layer, choose Cooling Filter (82) from the Filter menu, and lower the Density to 15% to neutralize the color cast (**FIGURE 4.71**).

FIGURE 4.71 The Cooling filter neutralizes the color cast of the background.

5. To darken the background a bit, Cmd/Ctrl-click the mask of the Photo Filter adjustment layer to load the selection of the background. Add a Levels adjustment layer, and move the midtones slider to the right to reduce the brightness of the background and highlight the family, as shown in FIGURE 4.72.

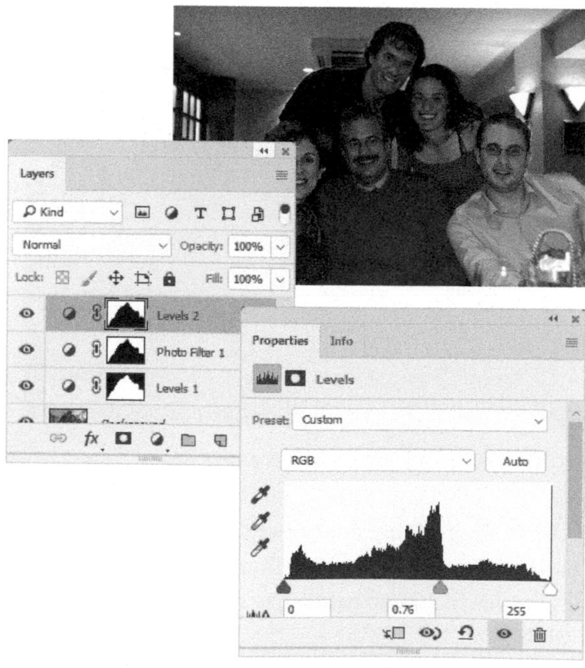

FIGURE 4.72 Using the same selection and lowering the background brightness draws more attention to the subjects.

MATCHING, CHANGING, AND REPLACING COLORS

Photoshop offers a number of tools for matching, changing, and replacing colors. Let's explore those tools and learn their strengths and limits.

Matching Colors Across Images

The Match Color command allows you to replace the colors in one image with the colors in another. This can include the entire image, specific layers, and selections within images. In FIGURE 4.73, notice that the two images are similar in subject matter but the color is noticeably different, even though they were taken at about the same time. In FIGURE 4.74, the magenta color cast has been removed with the Match Color command.

FIGURES 4.73 and 4.74 Before and after. © *WP*

ch4_dragon1.jpg
ch4_dragon2.jpg

1. With both images open, select the one that has the color you want to change, and duplicate the Background layer to prevent a destructive edit. Choose **Image > Adjustments > Match Color** to open the Match Color dialog box. Start the correction by using the Source menu in the Image Statistics section to choose the file you want to match, as seen in FIGURE 4.75.

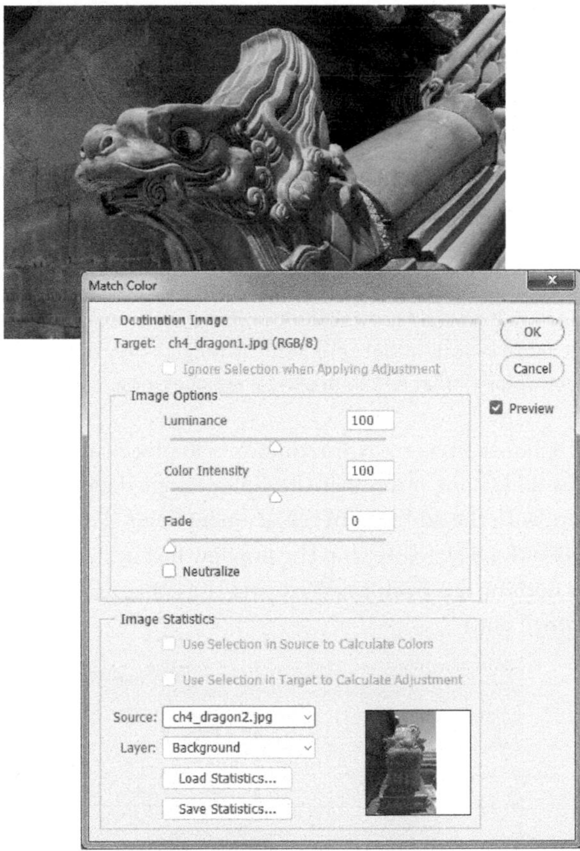

FIGURE 4.75 Choose the source image.

2. Use the Luminance slider to improve overall tonality and the Intensity slider to increase or decrease the color saturation, as seen in FIGURE 4.76. When you're satisfied, click OK to close the dialog box.

Match Color works well for matching colors in the selected areas of two images. Be sure the selection is correct, and be sure to work on a duplicate layer.

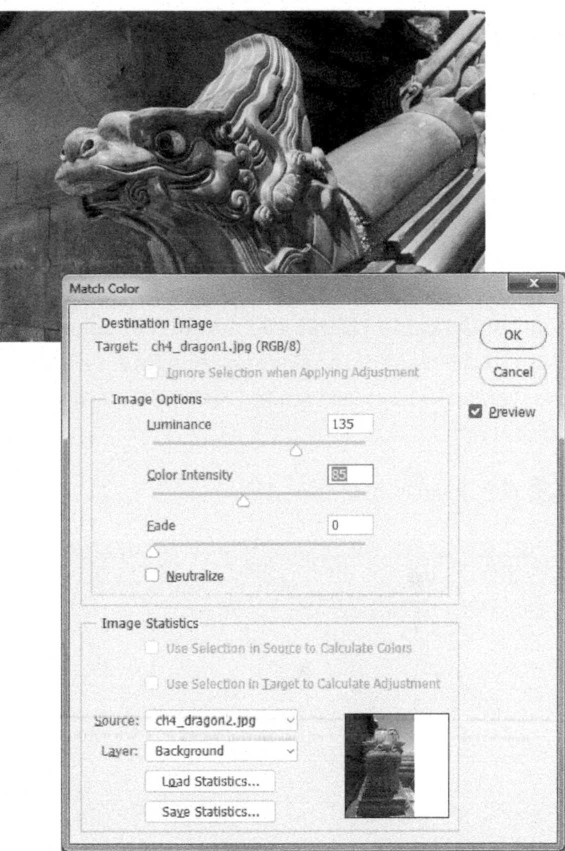

FIGURE 4.76 Adjust Luminance and Color Intensity to fine-tune the correction.

Replacing Colors

The primary Photoshop features for replacing color are the Replace Color command (found under Image > Adjustments) and the Color Replacement tool (nested with the standard Brush tool). They perform essentially the same task, but the Replace Color command uses Color Range to select the area to recolor, whereas the Color Replacement tool uses a brush to define and simultaneously recolor an area. Both tools work directly on the layer, so be sure to duplicate the layer before proceeding. Both have their benefits, and your choice depends upon how difficult it is to isolate the area you want to recolor. If you choose the Replace Color command and have multiple areas of similar color but don't want to change them all, you will want to make a rough selection of the area you do want to change before entering the command.

TIP The effect of the Color Replacement tool or the Replace Color command is directly related to the brightness value of the subject. The closer the brightness is to white or black, the less noticeable the effect. The closer the brightness value is to 128, in RGB mode, the more it will match the color you have chosen to use for replacement.

Let's use the Replace Color command to change the color of the car in FIGURE 4.77. Its current color is close to the color of the sky, and changing it match the woman's jacket, as seen in FIGURE 4.78, would be fun.

ch4_bluecar.jpg

FIGURES 4.77 and 4.78 Before and after. © *WP*

1. Open the file and duplicate the Background layer.

2. The color of the sky is very close to the color of the car. Use the Rectangular Marquee tool to make a rough selection around the car, as in FIGURE 4.79, to avoid changing the color of the sky.

FIGURE 4.79 Make a general selection of the area you want to change.

NOTE When I say a "rough" selection, I really mean it. It doesn't matter if other parts of the image are included in your initial selection, as long as they do not have color similar to the area you are changing.

3. Choose **Image > Adjustments > Replace Color**. The dialog box resembles the Color Range dialog box, with the addition of replacement color sliders (FIGURE 4.80). (Note that the preview box is black, as nothing has been selected, and the controls are zeroed out.)

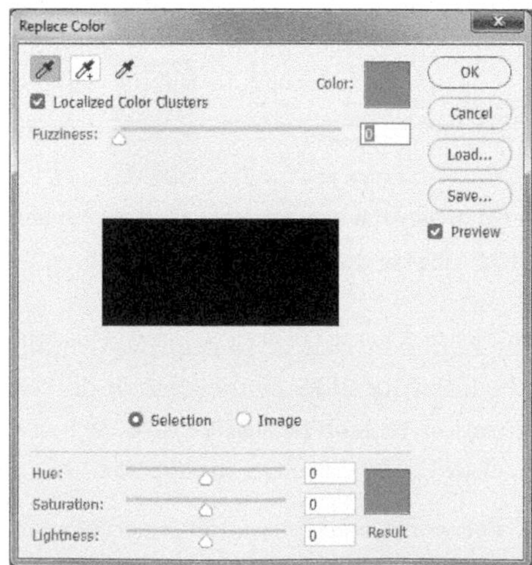

FIGURE 4.80 The Replace Color dialog box contains two (unlabeled) sections: Selection and Replacement.

4. With the eyedropper, drag over the blue in the car and watch the resulting selection in the dialog box. Hold down the Shift key and drag over the entire car to pick up as many of the blue shades as possible, without picking up the woman's jeans. Use Option/Alt, or select the eyedropper with the minus sign, to deselect areas. Increase the fuzziness to include more similar blue colors, as shown in FIGURE 4.81.

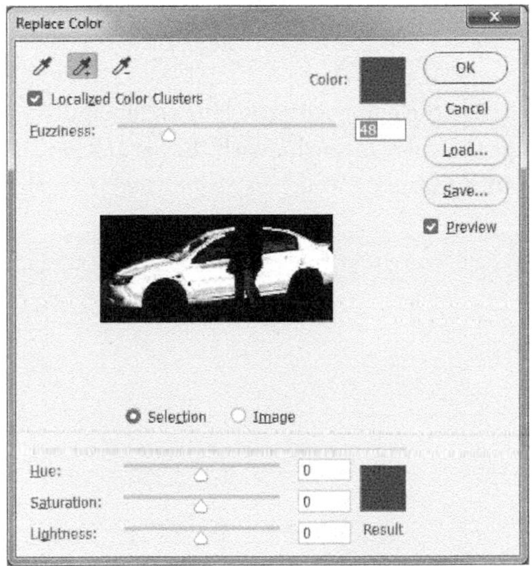

FIGURE 4.81 Use the eyedropper to select the colors to be replaced.

5. Once you have made the color selection, use the lower portion of the dialog box to change the color. Use any of the three sliders to change the replacement color, or click the Result color box to open the Color Picker. With either option, you will have a live update in your image when you choose a new color. Staying in the main dialog box enables you to use the eyedropper to add areas for color. Slide the Hue slider over to a nice purplish color, and use the Saturation slider to tone down the color's intensity, as seen in FIGURE 4.82.

6. Click OK to accept the color change, and then press Cmd-D/Ctrl-D to deselect.

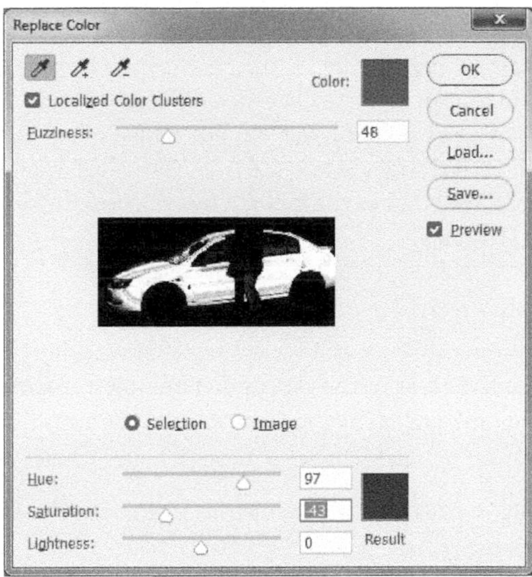

FIGURE 4.82 Use the Hue, Saturation, and Lightness sliders to control the color change.

7. The farther away you move from the original color, the more attention you will have to give to the selection. If your selection did pick up some of the other blues in the image, such as in the woman's jeans and the car windshield, add a layer mask and paint with black to protect those areas (FIGURE 4.83).

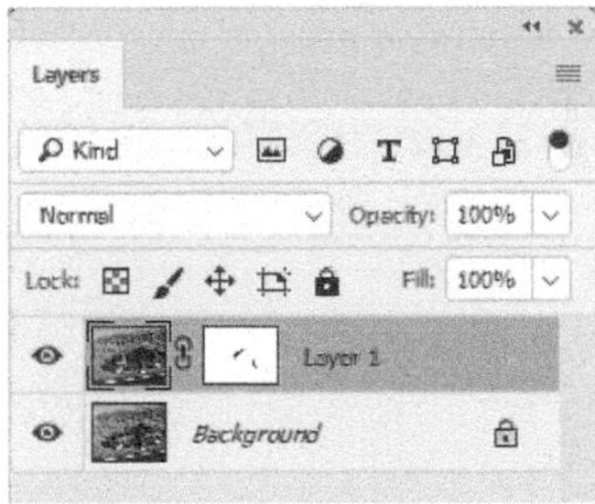

FIGURE 4.83 Use a layer mask to touch up any areas that were unintentionally changed.

TRY IT As you work more and more with Photoshop, you'll learn there are multiple ways to accomplish the same task. Here is another method for changing the color of an object and includes the option of letting you change your mind later (FIGURES 4.84 and 4.85).

color_change.jpg

FIGURES 4.84 and 4.85 © *WP*

1. With the Quick Selection tool, select the red areas of the vehicle (FIGURE 4.86).

FIGURE 4.86 The Quick Selection tool makes fast work of selecting the vehicle's color.

2. Create a Hue/Saturation adjustment layer and be sure Colorize is selected. A mask is automatically generated, and any changes will fall inside the selected area (FIGURE 4.87).

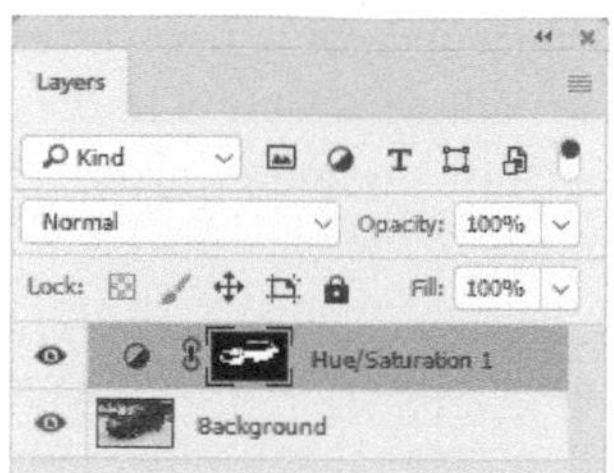

FIGURE 4.87 Upon creating the Hue/Saturation adjustment layer, a mask is generated, limiting the area to be recolored.

3. Change the color with the Hue slider, and change the color intensity with the Saturation slider (FIGURE 4.88).

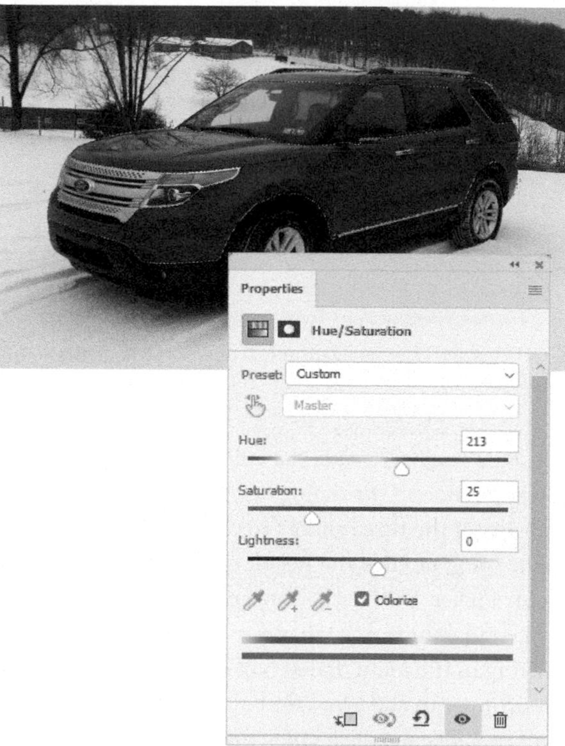

FIGURE 4.88 Use the Hue and Saturation sliders to change to a new color.

4. If the selection is not perfect, paint white on the mask to enlarge the area and paint black to hide any over spills.

This method offers the advantage of being able to easily change the color by simply revisiting the Hue/Saturation adjustment and moving the sliders to a new color.

Changing Color in Lab Color Mode

Editing color in the Lab Color mode has the advantage that the luminosity of the image is not affected. I often turn to this technique when clarity and flexibility are required. In this example, I wanted to change the color of the sign on the truck (FIGURE 4.89) to make it stand out even more (FIGURE 4.90).

ch4_shrimptruck.jpg

1. Convert the image to Lab Color by choosing **Image > Mode > Lab Color**.

2. Use the Polygon Lasso tool to select the sign. Add a Curves adjustment layer.

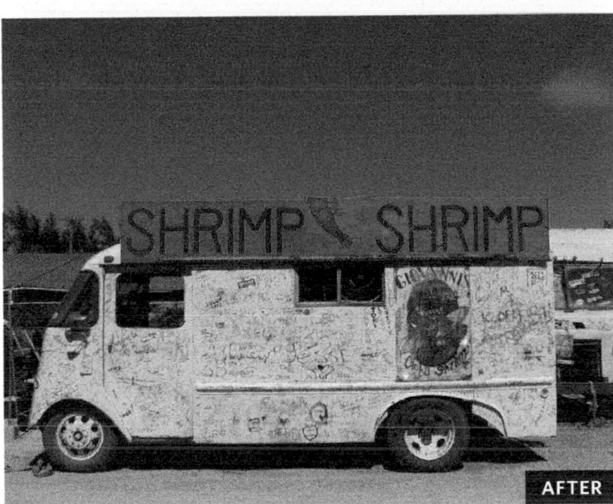

FIGURES 4.89 and 4.90 Before and after. © *KE*

3. In the Curves Properties panel, choose a from the channel menu. Slide the end points of the curve in the a channel to change the color of the sign, as in FIGURE 4.91. Keeping the a and b curve lines straight will change the color and yield more predictable results.

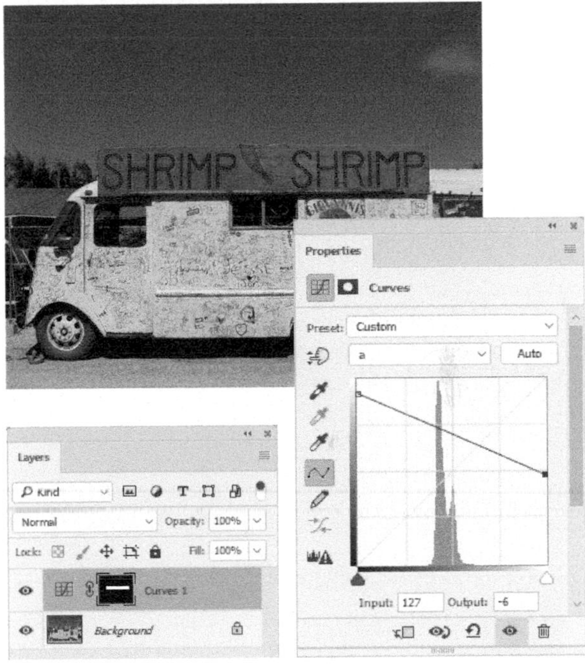

FIGURE 4.91 Use Curves and the Lab Color mode for subtle color changes.

TIP Converting between color modes, like RGB to Lab, is not always a "damage-free" process. Duplicate the file before proceeding, or use the Save As option, to keep the original file intact.

Transferring Color Corrections

If you have invested time into making a color correction and have used adjustment layers, the correction can be applied to another image that needs the same correction. There are several ways to do this.

- Many adjustment layers have the option to save and load presets. In the adjustment layer, open the panel menu and choose Save [adjustment] Preset. Switch to the other image. Create the same type of adjustment layer, and then choose Load [adjustment] Preset from the panel menu (FIGURE 4.92).

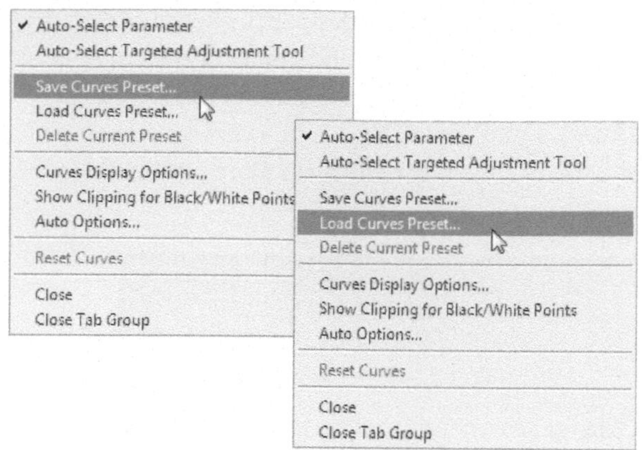

FIGURE 4.92 For many adjustment layers, the settings can be saved and reapplied to another image.

- Choose **Window > Arrange** so all the images to be adjusted are visible. Drag the adjustment layer of the corrected image from the Layers panel to each non-corrected image, as shown in FIGURE 4.93.
- One more method, which is a little trickier, can be done while the images are in tabbed mode. Drag the adjustment layer to the tab of the image you want to adjust. Do not release the mouse button. Wait until Photoshop brings that image to the front, and then drop the adjustment layer on the other image (FIGURE 4.94).

FIGURE 4.93 Adjustment layers can be dragged from one image to another.

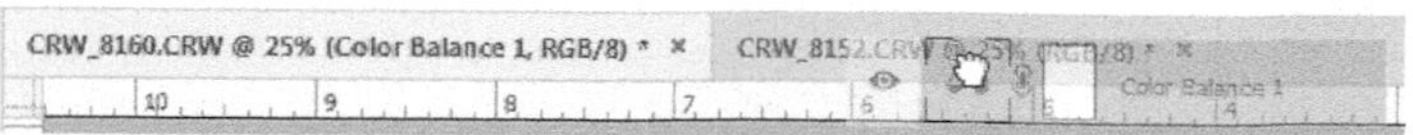

FIGURE 4.94 Adjustment layers can be dragged and dropped from one image to another while in tabbed view.

Colorizing Images

There are times when, despite using the best color correction tools, the color is still not the best and painting back a missing color is an easier solution. And there are times when an old black and white photograph can be colorized for a refreshing look. There are multiple ways to do this, and just adding a few colors can often breathe life into an old image. Lorie Zirbes, of Retouching by Lorie, has worked in the traditional field of photo retouching as well as in digital and truly enjoys colorizing images, as seen in this revitalized image of the farmer and tractor (FIGURES 4.95 and 4.96). Let's examine a number of different colorizing methods as well as the Color blending mode, which is essential to making them work.

FIGURES 4.95 and 4.96 Before and after. © *The Haskett Family Archives. Colorization by Lorie Zirbes*

Understanding the Color Blending Mode

In its simplest form, you could add color to an image by using the Brush tool and painting over the subject, but doing so just covers up what is underneath. Lowering the opacity of the brush, or painting on an empty layer with lowered opacity, is an improvement, but the tonality changes. The Color blend mode becomes very useful, as it allows the addition of color but does not change the tonality of the image, which is similar in concept to Lab color mode.

The key to understanding how the Color blend mode works is knowing that the intensity of the color changes the closer or farther away it gets from 50% gray. In areas that are gray, the color will be very noticeable, while areas closer to white or black will not be. And that is why the Color blend mode works so well. One color can produce many different shades, depending upon the tonal range. FIGURE 4.97 demonstrates this. The top bar of red simply covers the gradient below it. But when that red bar's blend mode is changed to Color, it creates multiple shades of red, with the most intense color produced when the gradient beneath is at 50% gray.

FIGURE 4.97 The Color blending mode creates multiple shades from a single color when combined with a range of multiple tones.

With this understanding of the Color blending mode, you have multiple ways to add or change color in an image.

★ NOTE It may be obvious, but an image in Grayscale mode cannot be colorized until the mode is changed to one that supports color.

BEYOND GLOBAL AND SELECTIVE CORRECTIONS

The color corrections covered in this chapter have only needed a few steps. Many times, the path to a color corrected image is much more involved and will require creativity and problem solving. One of the more difficult challenges in correcting color is an image that has faded unevely (**FIGURES 4.98** and **4.99**).

FIGURES 4.98 and **4.99** Before and after. © *Goldberg Family Archives*

Alan Cutler needed to use multiple layers to restore this unevenly faded image. He first created a Levels adjustment layer that corrected most of the color through the middle of the image, but it did little for the faded edges. He built the image up with multiple layers containing different tonality changes, each showing only small sections through masks. This was followed by several adjustment layers targeting specific areas, like the faces (**FIGURE 4.100**).

FIGURE 4.100 It took multiple layers of corrections to return the original color.

In another wonderful example, Alan used the same methodology to restore the cheerleader image (**FIGURE 4.101**), but at first could not get the colors to be as vibrant and exact. He was able to accomplish this (**FIGURE 4.102**) by painting color back into the image (**FIGURE 4.103**), in a process we will address in the next section.

Although a standard workflow can be used to tackle basic tonal and color corrections, there is no clear-cut answer for every image. Trial and error may be the only answer. Such is the case for **FIGURES 4.104** and **4.105**. Allen Furbeck wanted to maintain the old look of the image (also seen in Chapter 1) while also removing the fading caused by the print having been displayed in a frame with an oval mat. It might have been easier to simply crop the image to the faded oval and just work from there, but Allen wanted to restore the entire image. After 30 hours, multiple renditions, and 150 layers (**FIGURE 4.106**) (which, to show them, would require a fold-out page), he achieved the result he was looking for. This may be way beyond the time a commercial retoucher could spend or could charge a client for, but it goes to show what can be done with enough time and perseverance.

FIGURES 4.101 and 4.102 Before and after. © *The Right Image*

FIGURE 4.103 Painting color into the image was the last step in restoring the vivid colors (right).

FIGURES 4.104 and 4.105 Before and after. © *Plante Family Archives*

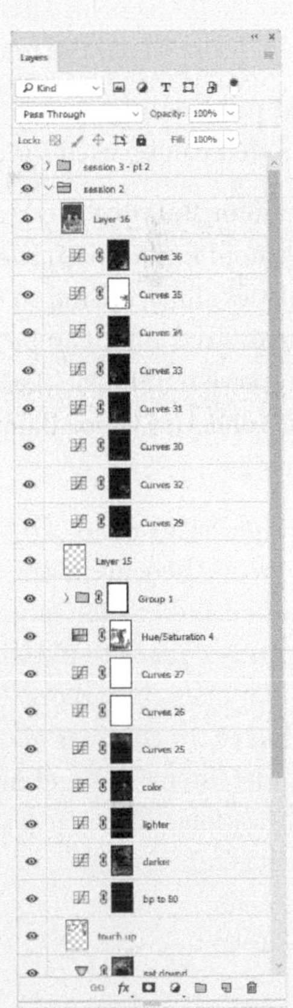

FIGURE 4.106 One hundred fifty layers were created in restoring this image (right).

Colorizing Methods

The most direct method is to use the Brush tool set to Color mode to paint the desired color. The strength of the color can be controlled by the opacity of the brush. To prevent this from being destructive editing, create an empty layer and instead change the layer's blending mode to Color. Color intensity can be controlled through either the brush or the layer's opacity setting. Using a different layer for each color helps keep things organized and makes it easier to change your edits.

TIP The Color blending mode is an option for many painting tools and adjustment layers.

And as we have discovered with other tasks, Photoshop offers multiple ways to accomplish the same task. But perhaps the best way to add or alter color is to use selections along with adjustment layers and layer masks. Select the area to be changed, and add an adjustment layer (it will include a mask defined by the selection); the color alteration is confined to the selection. From there, the mask can tweaked.

Let us examine some different color adjustment layers that can be used for colorization

- **Color Balance** is certainly a way to start, but if you are not familiar with the color wheel and the color relationships, having to move multiple sliders to get the desired color can be a little confusing. Selecting Preserve Luminosity keeps the color from changing the tone. Use Color Balance for more subtle color changes.

- **Hue/Saturation** can be the easiest way to change color, as there are fewer controls. There is one slider for hue and one for saturation. The third slider, for lightness, tends to flatten contrast and is not useful for changing colors. Be sure the Colorize box is selected. In contrast to Color Balance, the colors can be intensified and made very bright by using the Saturation slider. Use a separate adjustment layer for each color.

- **Solid Color** adjustment layers can be a little more intuitive, and Wayne recommends this method when you need more exact color control or when making a large number of color changes. Make your selection, add a Solid Color adjustment layer, and then select the desired color from the Color Picker. Finally, change the adjustment layer's blending mode to Color. The advantage of this method is the ease with which a color can be changed. Reopen the Color Picker inside the adjustment layer, and as you drag through the color field, the image updates in real time. For small areas that would only require a brush stroke or two, it would be easier to bypass the adjustment layer. For example, if a color had been applied to a face and you wanted to add a different color to the lips or eyes, just create an empty layer, set the blending mode to Color, and paint. As long as that layer is on top, it will cover any color below it. Just use caution to paint between the lines.

With any of these color changing methods, the work is nondestructive and colors can be easily altered. Wayne has found this to be important, as the use of color is very subjective and a customer may have different thoughts about what looks correct.

TIP Often, just one color can be used in multiple locations, resulting in different shades because of tonality changes.

In this image, Lorie Zirbes used colors described by the client's recollection to create a great memory (FIGURES 4.107–4.109).

TRY IT Numerous methods for altering color have been presented in this chapter, from individual channel adjustments in Levels and Curves to adjustment layers specifically designed for targeting colors. See what works for you.

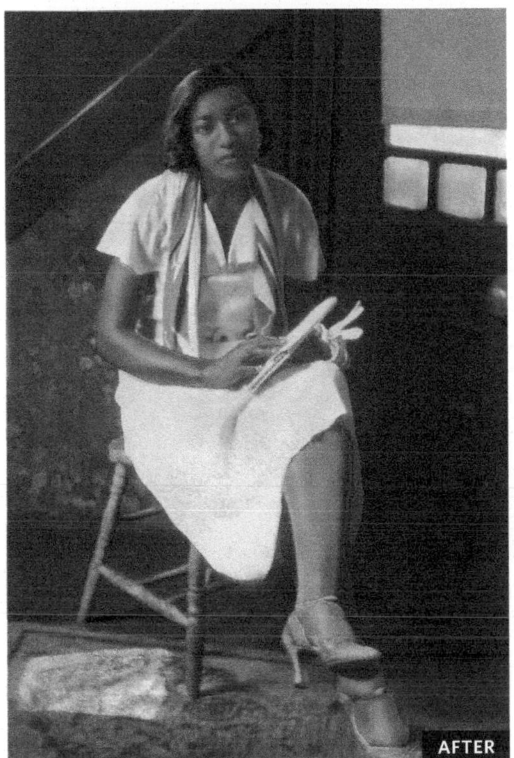

FIGURES 4.107 and 4.108 © *Gafford Family Archives*

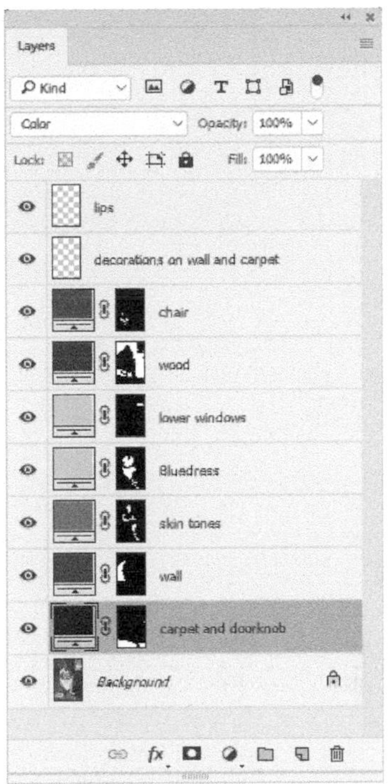

FIGURE 4.109 Lorie used a separate Solid Color fill layer for each color, each with a layer mask and the blending mode set to Color. This technique is completely nondestructive and offers the option of easily changing colors.

Working Backwards: Keeping a Color Element in a Black and White Image

An artistic photo technique is to put one color element in a black and white image to draw attention. We have covered how to colorize a black and white image. It is even simpler to have a color element inside a black and white image when the image was originally in color (FIGURES 4.110 and 4.111).

 **the_apple.jpg**

1. Use the Quick Selection tool to select the apple, as shown in FIGURE 4.112.

FIGURES 4.110 and 4.111 © *Sonya Adcock*

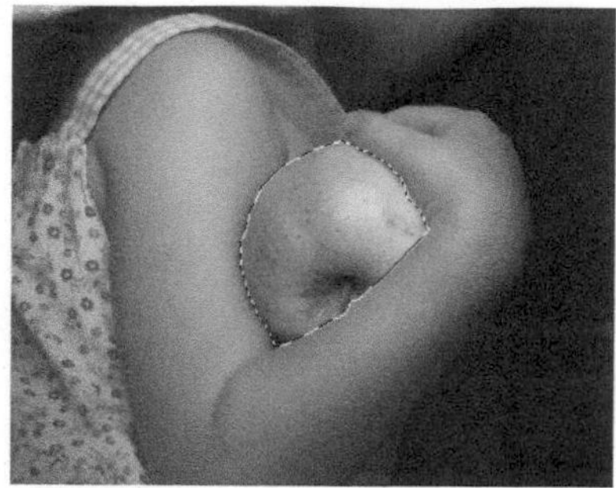

FIGURE 4.112 The Quick Selection tool easily picks up the edges of the apple.

2. In the Layers panel, add a Black & White adjustment layer, which will turn the apple to monochrome, leaving the rest of the image in color (FIGURE 4.113).

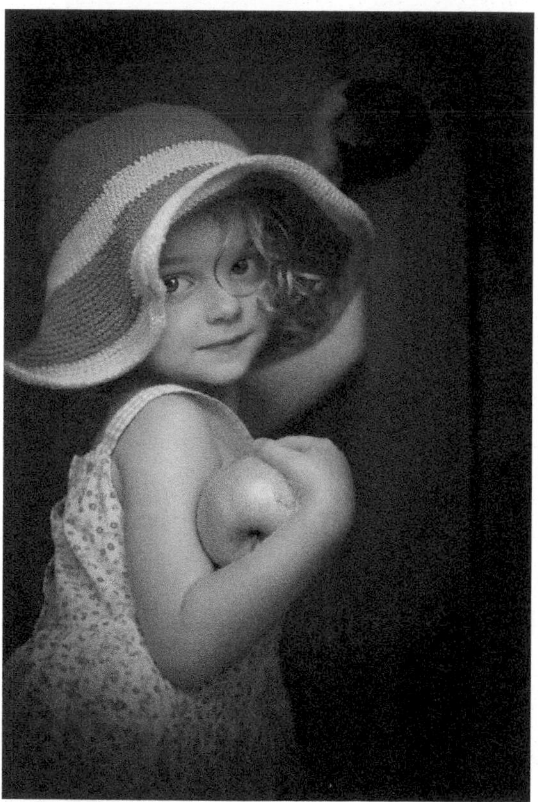

FIGURE 4.113 Because the apple was selected when the adjustment layer was created, the effect is the opposite of what is desired.

3. Be sure the layer mask is active, and press Cmd-I/Ctrl-I to invert the mask (FIGURE 4.114).

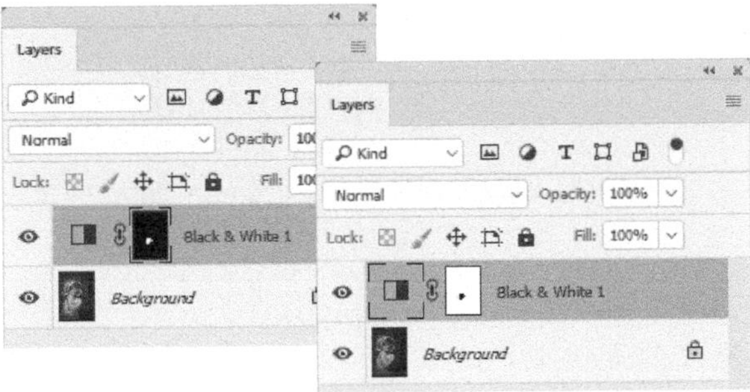

FIGURE 4.114 Invert the mask.

4. The edge of the colored area is a little noticeable. Run the Gaussian Blur filter on the mask at a level of 8 pixels to soften the edge (FIGURE 4.115).

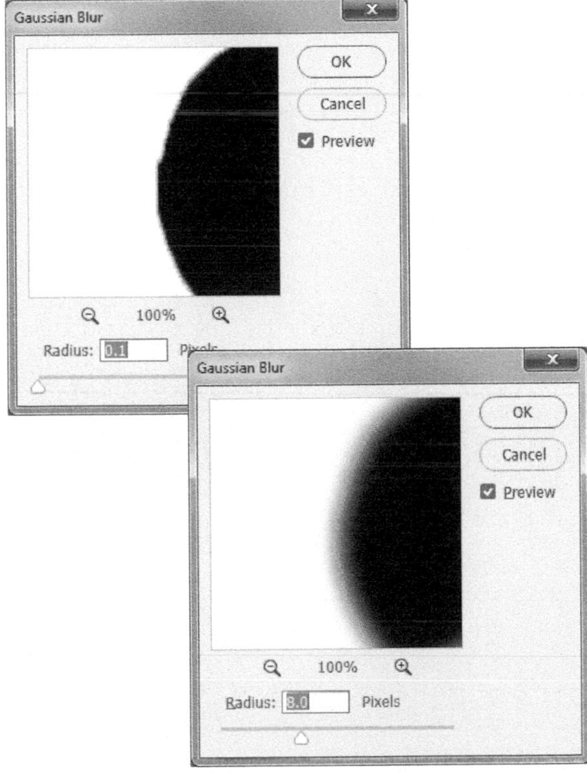

FIGURE 4.115 Blurring the mask creates a smooth transition from color to black and white.

The technique was very popular a few years ago and was used so much it became something of a cliché, but it was a good one and is easy to create.

CLOSING THOUGHTS

The importance of good color—pleasing color—cannot be overestimated. Trying out the techniques in this chapter on your own images will teach you more than any book. So open up some images and learn to really see color—to remove it, add it, change it, or accentuate it—but keep in mind that "good color" is subjective. But it's all important.

Part III

RESTORE, REPAIR & REBUILD

CAFFEINE • PERSPECTIVE CROP • COLOR CORRECTION • SHARPENING • RETOUCH
MASK • SEPIA TONING • HANDLING DELICATE ORIGINALS • DUST & SCRATCHES FILTER •
NOISE FILTERS • CONTENT AWARE MOVE • NOISE REDUCTION • FOOD RETOUCHING •
PRODUCT RETOUCHING • CONTENT AWARE SCALE • WHITE BALANCE •
RESTORATION WORKFLOW • HEALING TOOLS • CURVES ADJUSTMENT LAYER •
DODGE AND BURN • ENVIRONMENT AND LIGHTING • PERSPECTIVE CORRECTIONS •
CORRECTION • HAIR MASKING

Chapter 5

DUST, MOLD, AND TEXTURE REMOVAL

Dust—it is everywhere. It collects on our shelves, under beds, in computers, and on computer screens. And unfortunately, it often becomes a part of our photographs, as dust gets into our digital cameras and hangs tight on prints and film emulsions. Dust has long plagued photographers working in the wet darkroom, and sadly it still torments us in the digital darkroom.

Mold is another common reason for damage and spots on old prints, which were often made with gelatin (a natural protein derived from animals) and vegetable dyes, ideal food for hungry mold. To add insult to injury, cracks, tears, dirty fingerprints, careless spills, and less than optimal handling or storage will wreak havoc on your photographic memories.

In this chapter we will break out the cleaning equipment and address

- Working nondestructively
- Cleaning digital camera files
- Filters and channel extraction for dust removal and reduction
- Working with the Clone Stamp tools and healing tools
- Reducing silvering, moiré, and textures

So let's get down to basics and explore the digital feather-dusting tools of Photoshop.

TAKING IN THE BIG PICTURE

Before you grab the Clone Stamp tool you need to accurately see where the dust or spot problems are. Depending on the file size and your monitor resolution, you may not be able to view the file accurately. When an image is first opened in Photoshop, the view can be very deceptive. You will see the entire image, and in most cases, the image is zoomed out to a level not suitable for retouching.

To clean up the nitty-gritty details, you need to see the nitty-gritty details. Be prepared to zoom in to the image and work at pixel level, and inspect the image at 100% or even 200% if you are working on a high-resolution or Retina display. Otherwise, defects may not be visible, because the screen is displaying an abbreviated version of the file.

TIP Commit to memory these keyboard shortcuts to easily zoom in to and out of an image.

- Cmd-+/Ctrl-+ to zoom in and Cmd--/Ctrl-- to zoom out work in Photoshop, Lightroom, Photoshop Elements, and even many web browsers.
- Cmd-0/Ctrl-0 to zoom out to see the entire image, and Cmd-Option-0/Ctrl-Alt-0 to instantly zoom to 100% view. That is zero, not 'O'.
- Tap the Z key to activate the Zoom tool, press and hold on the image to zoom in to the image, and press Option/Alt to zoom out.

ch5_eatingapple.jpg

Open the eating-apple image, look at the document tab, and notice the percentage at which the image is displayed. At first glance, the image may look fine (FIGURE 5.1). But zoom in to 100% and use the Hand tool to move around within the document window. Note the abundance of specks throughout the image that were not visible when the image was first opened. This is why it is very important to inspect the image at 100%, as anything visible at this view could possibly be seen in print.

When you're zoomed in on an image, and especially one that is particularly high resolution, it can be easy to lose your bearings. This is where the Navigator panel (**Window > Navigator**) can be handy. This panel, when enlarged by dragging out any corner beyond its default size, can also be used as a second view of the image (FIGURE 5.2). The view continuously updates to show changes made, so progress and editing location can be easily monitored. Dragging the red box (the proxy preview area) in the Navigator panel will reposition the area being worked on. This can be particularly useful when you need to check the entire image before making a print or submitting to a client.

FIGURE 5.1 At first glance this image appears to be fine; upon closer examination, dust is revealed. © *Eef Jansen*

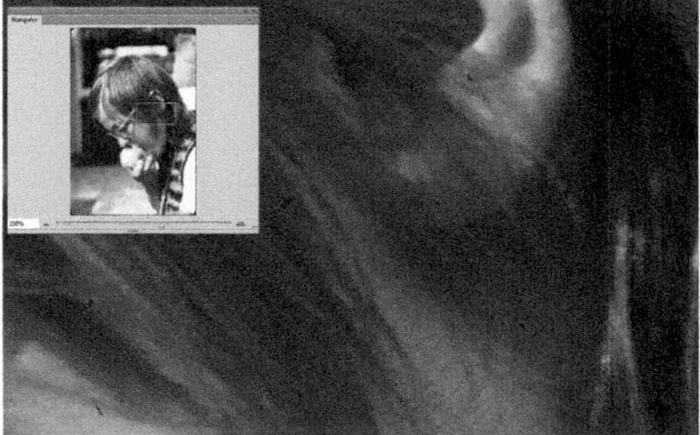

FIGURE 5.2 The Navigator panel, enlarged beyond its normal size, is a helpful reference when working on a small part of an image.

WORKING NONDESTRUCTIVELY

Nondestructive editing is an overall strategy of working in Photoshop that allows you to backtrack your steps and, more importantly, edit without permanently changing image information. In short, nondestructive editing means that tools and tool options are used such that changes can always be undone. Photoshop provides many ways to work nondestructively.

Permanently altering or deleting pixels may result in having to rework an image because something important was removed or altered. Sometimes even the most insignificant spot in a picture may be important, which Wayne, long before he adopted a nondestructive philosophy, learned first-hand when having to redo work for a valuable client (FIGURE 5.3).

To work nondestructively, use:

- **Duplicate layers.** Work on a copy of the Background layer when making edits, such as content-aware scaling, using the Dodge or Burn tools, or non-smart filters, that would otherwise be a destructive edit.
- **Adjustment layers.** Keep tonal and color corrections separate from the background layer, permitting readjustments throughout the editing process.
- **Empty layers.** Use painting, cloning, and healing tools that have the option to put edits on blank layers above the layer being edited.
- **Layer masks.** Hide elements of a layer or parts of an adjustment layer through masking. Editing the mask later can reveal elements again if needed.
- **Smart Objects and Smart Filters.** Convert a layer to a Smart Object before applying any filter, adjustment, or transformation so you can edit settings later without damaging the original image.

Some may argue that working with the History Brush tool and recording snapshots through various stages of work in the History panel allows for nondestructive editing. However, there is one critical caveat in that the contents of the History panel, which includes states, are not retained when the file is closed. This may not be a concern if you complete a restoration in one sitting and the file will never be revisited, but

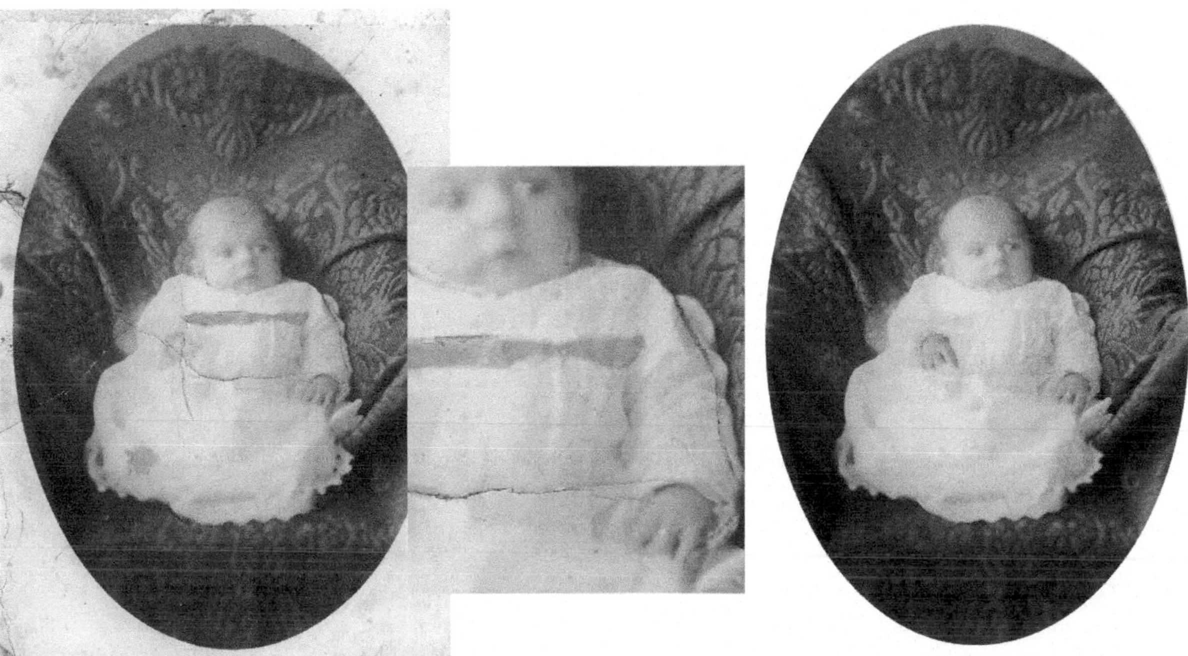

FIGURE 5.3 The white spots on the hand of baby were assumed to be part of the damage. In reality, they were reflections from family rings the child was wearing and an important aspect of the picture. By working nondestructively, removed items can be easily returned.

it becomes problematic if further changes or corrections are desired at a later time. History states can be saved as separate files, but there are more efficient methods for working nondestructively and managing your progress (FIGURE 5.4).

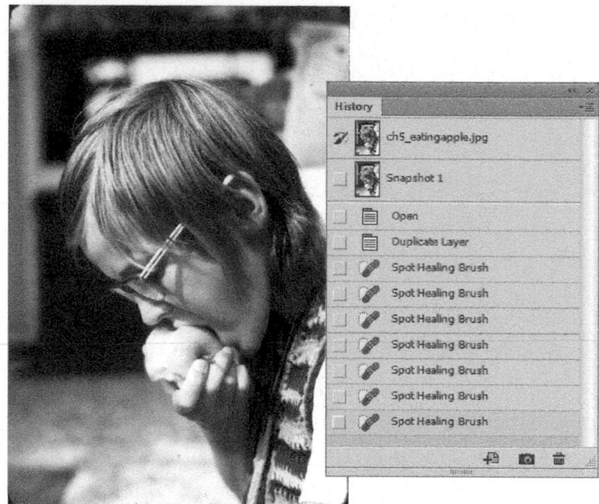

FIGURE 5.4 The History panel and snapshots keep track of steps taken when editing images, but they are lost when the file is closed.

Duplicate Layers

The easiest form of nondestructive editing is simply duplicating the Background layer. Working with duplicate layers within the same document is a more efficient method to use when any of the Background layer information is going to be changed through filters or painting tools. Duplicate the layer and work on it, keeping the Background layer undisturbed. The Background layer can be used for progress reference by turning upper-layer visibility on and off, and sections of it can be copied and pasted over unsatisfactory edits. To duplicate the Background layer, choose **Layer > Duplicate Layer**, drag the Background layer to the New Layer icon in the Layers panel, or press Cmd-J/Ctrl-J (FIGURE 5.5).

★ NOTE Duplicating a pixel-based layer such as the Background layer will double the file size and is not recommended when an empty layer can just as easily and more efficiently serve as a canvas for the cloning and healing brushes.

FIGURE 5.5 The first step in nondestructive editing is to work on a duplicate of the Background layer.

Working on an Empty Layer

The Spot Healing Brush tool, the Healing Brush tool, the Clone Stamp tool, and even the Blur, Sharpen, and Smudge tools include the option Sample All Layers (or a variant, Current & Below or All Layers), which allows changes and repairs to be put on an empty layer above the Background layer. Since the changes are on a separate layer, they are easily refined by erasing or deleting the changes and trying again. Using this method, as opposed to duplicating the entire layer, also keeps the file size smaller because the layer with the changes is not the same amount of data as the Background layer. We all use empty layers all the time in both restoration and retouching work, and we'll work through some useful examples in this chapter.

Working with Adobe Camera Raw

As explained in the following section, you can use Adobe Camera Raw (ACR) and, in a similar vein, Lightroom to clean up sensor dust and standard dust spots on film or print scans. The nondestructive beauty of ACR is that it never actually changes a file, and all changes can be reversed by opening the raw file in ACR or Lightroom again. Files processed in ACR can be opened in Photoshop as Smart Objects, keeping changes nondestructive.

★ NOTE If you save a rendered JPEG, TIFF, or PSD file out of ACR or export it out of Lightroom, then the changes are "baked into" the pixels and are not reversible.

DUST ON DIGITAL CAMERA FILES

Dust is not just a relic of musty photo history; even in the newest digital cameras with interchangeable lenses, it still plagues us. Each time you change the lens, dust may settle on the camera sensor and block the light, ending up as a small dark spot or squiggle on the image. Sensor dust is fairly straightforward to diagnose, as it is usually in the same place in consecutive pictures and is most often visible on detail-free areas such as blue skies (FIGURE 5.6). Some cameras include sensor-cleaning capabilities, but that is no guarantee that the sensor will remain dust free.

FIGURE 5.6 Sensor dust is easily identifiable because it is in the same place in different images. © *John Troisi*

Dust Removal with ACR

ch5_clouds1.dng
ch5_clouds2.dng
ch5_clouds3.dng

Dust spots can be removed from raw, TIFF, and JPEG files in ACR and Lightroom. Open the first of the cloud images in Photoshop to launch ACR, and follow these steps to remove unwanted dust.

1. Select the Spot Removal tool and position (don't click) the brush over a dust spot you need to remove. Drag the Size slider to increase or decrease the brush size until it is slightly bigger than the spot (FIGURE 5.7). Alternatively, tap the left bracket ([) or right bracket (]) key to change the brush size.

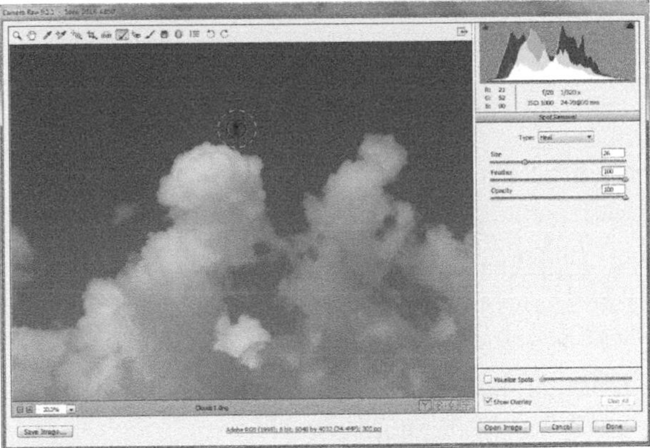

FIGURE 5.7 Using the Spot Removal tool in ACR can be faster than trying to remove the spot in Photoshop.

TIP The brush does not have to be round; to remove an oblong piece of dust, just drag the cursor over the spot.

2. Position the pointer (a blue-white circle) over the spot to remove, and click.

3. The blue-and-white circle changes into a red-and-white circle to signify the area that needs dust busting. A second circle (green-and-white) shows which part of the image is used to conceal the dust. If you do not like results, drag the green-white circle to an area that would be a better cleanup source for the dust spot, or press the forward slash key (/) to sample a different area (FIGURE 5.8). You can also adjust the size by dragging the edge of the circle.

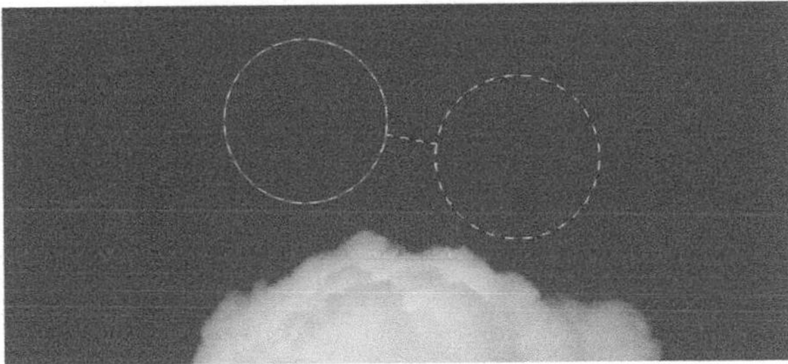

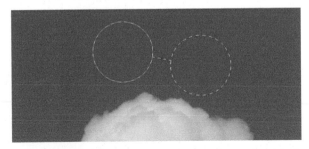

FIGURE 5.8 The Spot Removal tool can make quick work of annoying sensor dust.

4. If you don't like any of the results, Option/Alt-click the red-and-white or green-and-white circle to delete the edit. You can also click the red-and-white circle and press Delete.

AVOID CAMERA SENSOR DUST

The best way to keep the camera sensor clean is to never, ever change lenses, which, as we know, is not realistic. Here are a few tips to reduce the amount of dust on the sensor.

- Avoid changing lenses unnecessarily. Every time the lens is removed, dust and other contaminants can enter the camera.
- Avoid changing lenses in an environment that is dusty, windy, or sandy.
- Turn the camera off during lens changes. This turns off the electrostatic charge on the sensor, which can attract dust.

+ TIP To locate additional spots more easily with the Spot Removal tool, select the Visualize Spots option to locate sensor dust. Drag the slider to adjust the threshold.

5. Repeat steps 1 through 4 for any other dust spots.

6. To open the image into Photoshop, click Open Image; to work nondestructively in Photoshop, press Shift and click Open Object to open the image as a Smart Object in Photoshop.

+ TIP Rather than manually moving the green-white source circle, press the forward slash key (/) to have ACR or Lightroom choose a different source area.

+ TIP ACR features can be used on non-raw files. In Photoshop, convert the layer to a Smart Object and choose **Filter > Camera Raw Filter**.

Fixing Multiple Images in ACR

As we mentioned, if you have dust on one camera file it will most likely be on adjacent files. Thankfully, once dust has been removed in one image in ACR (or Lightroom), the same fixes can be easily applied to multiple images *if the dust spot is in the same location and the sampled area is similar for all images*, as explained here:

1. Start by opening the three cloud images by selecting **File > Open,** which will automatically launch Camera Raw (FIGURE 5.9). Click any one of the image thumbnails, and use the Spot Removal tool to clean up the dust.

2. From the Filmstrip, select the image you retouched, then choose Select All from the Filmstrip panel menu, or use the keyboard shortcut Cmd-A/Ctrl-A. Select Sync Settings from the same menu. Select only the Spot Removal option in the Synchronize dialog box (FIGURE 5.10) and click OK.

FIGURE 5.9 In Adobe Camera Raw, the same spot removal can be applied to multiple images.

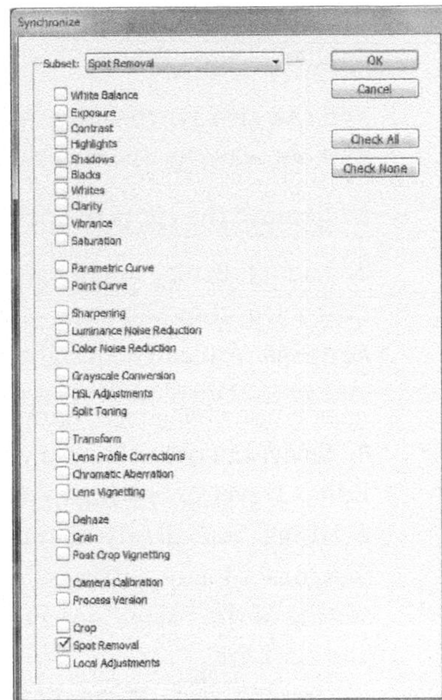

FIGURE 5.10 When removing dust from multiple files by using the Sync Settings feature in ACR, be sure to select only the Spot Removal option.

CLEANING THE CAMERA SENSOR

If you notice sensor dust and repeated camera cleanings do not remove it, you can clean the sensor yourself, with the following caveat: do it very carefully. If you are at all unsure about cleaning the sensor yourself, bring the camera to a camera store or service center for cleaning.

1. Invest in a bulb blower (**FIGURE 5.11**). Navigate to your camera's cleaning settings, which will lock up the mirror and not charge the sensor.

2. Hold the camera so that the sensor is facing down, and use the bulb blower to apply a few gentle puffs of air to dislodge the dust.

3. After cleaning the sensor, take an image of a light, solid object, like a very smooth white wall or a blue sky, using f/11 or f/16 to get a narrower beam of light, which creates a more noticeable shadow. Taking the image out of focus will make the dust stand out. Open the file in ACR, Lightroom, or Photoshop, and if the spot is still there try cleaning again. Keep in mind that the dust speck will be in the opposite position on the sensor from the location in the image. The image is reversed and upside down, so up is down and left is right (**FIGURE 5.12**).

FIGURE 5.11 A bulb blower, which produces a mild burst of air, is the first level of removing dust from a sensor.

FIGURE 5.12 The dust resides behind the mirror and is located in the position opposite from where it is seen in the image. Never use canned or compressed air to clean a sensor.

The changes made in the cleaned-up image will be applied to the others.

You can also synchronize ACR settings to images without actually opening them in ACR.

1. Remove the spots in one image in ACR.

2. Launch Bridge and locate the fixed file. **Choose Edit > Develop Settings > Copy Camera Raw Settings.** You can also right-click the edited image and select **Develop Settings > Copy Settings.**

3. Select the other images with similar spots. Choose **Edit > Develop Settings > Paste Camera Raw Settings.** You can also right-click and select **Develop Settings > Paste Settings.** Select the Spot Removal setting in the Paste Camera Raw Settings dialog box and click OK.

In both situations, the changes can be undone, as all editing in ACR is nondestructive.

The beauty of working in ACR with raw files is that you can apply changes across both horizontal and vertical images. ACR takes into account the orientation of the image and the cleanup will be applied to match the rotation of the image—pretty cool!

DOS AND DON'TS OF SENSOR CLEANING

Never, ever use canned or compressed air on the sensor, as it may contain chemicals that can contaminate the sensor and create a much worse problem.

If a simple blower does not work, consider investing in a cleaning kit, which may consist of specially designed brushes, a magnifying scope, and even a small vacuum. If none of these methods is successful in removing the dust, then as a last resort use a one-time wet wipe system specially designed for the camera's sensor (**FIGURE 5.13**).

If the thought of this process brings up skittish feelings, search out a professional camera repair facility. Contact the camera manufacturer and keep an eye out for local photo conferences, where camera manufacturers often offer free sensor cleaning.

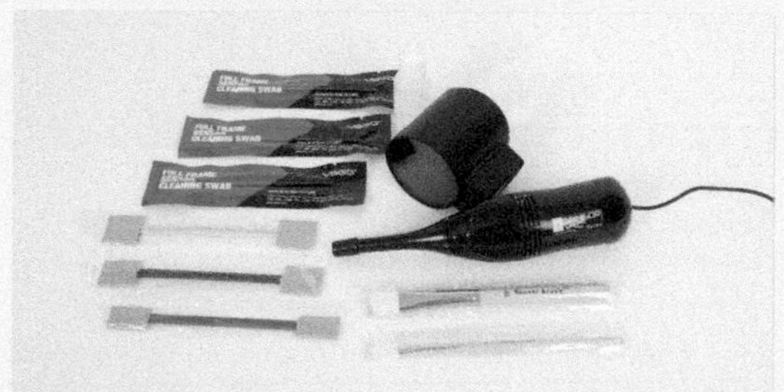

FIGURE 5.13 A complete cleaning kit is the way to go for the do-it-yourselfer.

LESS WORK, MORE RESULTS

It may be very tempting to clean up every itty-bitty dust spot by hand—well, it may be tempting for about 15 minutes! Try these quick tips to restore an image with the Crop tool and content-aware scaling to clean up an image and reduce the amount of delicate handwork needed.

The Crop Tool as Restoration Tool

One of the simplest ways to restore an image is to crop out the damage if it is in an unimportant part of the picture. If a corner is broken off or has faded from being in frame, a simple crop could minimize or possibly eliminate a lot of extra work.

When working with the Crop tool to remove unimportant image areas in a nondestructive manner, make sure that the Delete Cropped Pixels option is deselected in the options bar. With this option disabled, image information is not deleted when cropping; rather, the unwanted material is simply hidden from view. To adjust the crop, drag the visible image within the crop. To bring back all the hidden information, choose **Image > Reveal All** or start a new crop outside the existing one.

 **ch5_portrait_1930.jpg**

To try this out, open the portrait image. Notice that the image has several different stages of fading, particularly from being in a frame that was not rectangular. The important part of the image is not faded, so cropping would be a quick fix (**FIGURE 5.14**).

FIGURE 5.14 This image can be helped just through cropping. © *Palmer Family Archives*

1. Select the Crop tool. In the options bar, click Clear to make sure no fixed-size settings are selected. Also be sure that Delete Cropped Pixels is unselected to keep the crop nondestructive.

2. To set the new crop area, drag from the upper-left corner, excluding the white area, down to the lower-right corner, cropping away the other faded areas of the image.

3. Press Return/Enter or click Commit (checkmark) in the options bar to apply the crop (FIGURE 5.15).

FIGURE 5.15 Cropping all faded material out creates an unwanted end result, as too little headroom is left. Retain the needed headroom when cropping and use the retouching tools discussed to fix the remaining issues.

4. If the crop is not perfect, click the Crop tool to display the edge handles again, and drag the corner or edge handles to the desired crop area. You can reposition the image within the crop area by dragging within the crop boundary. Remember that the information is only being hidden and hasn't been deleted (if Delete Cropped Pixels is unselected) (FIGURE 5.16). Press Return/Enter once more to commit the crop.

FIGURE 5.16 Crop the picture to leave some headroom.

TIP When cropping an image that will be printed or framed, selecting a crop size preset in the options bar can be very helpful and can avoid custom framing expenses.

Restoration with Content-Aware Scale

Content-aware scaling can be useful in covering up dust in images if there is sufficient good material from which to sample. The scan of the slide in FIGURE 5.17 shows dust spots that have settled into the emulsion and would not blow off. Fortunately, there is enough image area that does not have marks to make cleanup a breeze (FIGURE 5.18).

ch5_overlook.jpg

1. Duplicate the Background layer to keep the changes nondestructive.

FIGURES 5.17 and 5.18 © *David Palmer*

2. Select the Rectangular Marquee tool, and create a selection of the entire middle of the picture above the woman's head, as seen in FIGURE 5.19.

FIGURE 5.19 A selection is made of an area not covered with dust.

3. Choose **Edit > Content-Aware Scale**, or press Cmd-Option-Shift-C/Ctrl-Alt-Shift-C. A marquee selection with handles will appear.

4. Drag the center handle upward to the edge of the image (FIGURE 5.20).

FIGURE 5.20 Using content-aware scaling, the selected area expands and covers up the dust.

5. Click Return/Enter to accept the change, or click the checkmark in the options bar.

6. Choose **Select > Deselect**, or press Cmd-D/Ctrl-D, to deselect.

Often the desired final size of an image is one that will fit a standard frame size. Content-aware scaling can be very useful in resizing an image (within reason) without creating visible artifacts or distortion. Katrin was presented with a cute image that needed to fit a preset size for a greeting card (FIGURE 5.21). By using Content-Aware Scale, she was able to squeeze the main subjects closer together without noticeable distortion, especially for the desired output size (FIGURES 5.22 and 5.23).

+ TIP Limit the amount of scaling to about twice the area selected to avoid visible distortion.

FIGURE 5.21 This image was just a little too wide for its intended need, marked by the guide line. © *KE*

FIGURE 5.22 Using Content-Aware Scale, the image can be transformed to a new aspect ratio.

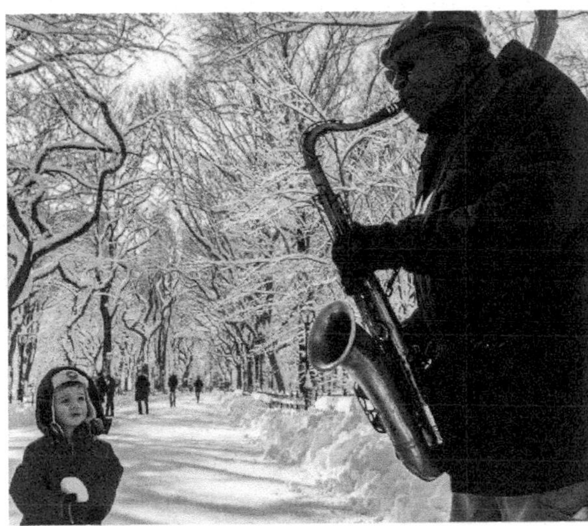

FIGURE 5.23 The final image is resized without any visible distortion. © *2013 Katrin Eismann*

WORK SMART NOT HARD

Several filters in Photoshop reduce and combat dust, but they all have one limitation: they do not replace the discernment of a caring or trained eye. Filters cannot distinguish between unimportant dust spots and things that you would like to retain, such as a highlight in an eye.

Photoshop's filters used to be considered destructive editing, and applying filters to duplicate layers was the way to preserve one's progress. Now, through the use of Smart Filters, Photoshop filters are thankfully nondestructive, and applied settings can be edited even after the file has been closed. Smart Filters allow filters to be applied, adjusted, turned off, stacked as multiple filters, and masked without the original pixel information being altered. The one limitation of Smart Filters is that certain types of editing, like using any of the painting tools directly on the layer, are not possible, but then again, that would be destructive editing.

To use Smart Filters, convert the layers you want to apply the filter to into a Smart Object. Choose **Filter > Convert to Smart Filter**, or Ctrl-click/ or right-click the selected layers in the Layers panel and select Convert to Smart Object (FIGURE 5.24). In the Layers panel, the layer thumbnail icon changes to indicate that the layer is a Smart Object (FIGURE 5.25).

FIGURE 5.24 Converting a layer to a Smart Object

FIGURE 5.25 This little icon in the Layer thumbnail indicates that it is a Smart Object. The double circle indicates that a filter has been applied. When a filter is applied to a Smart Object, the Smart Filter is visible by default. Click the arrow on the right to hide or make visible the filters that are applied.

ch5_dustykitty.jpg

Open the cat image, convert the Background layer to a Smart Object, and let's explore the dust-busting filters.

Despeckle Filter

Choose **Filter > Noise > Despeckle** to apply the Despeckle filter. Click the Smart Filter visibility icon to toggle the filter on and off. The change is very minor and may require zooming in past 100% to see a difference. As the name implies, a speck is very small, and this tool blurs the tiniest of spots determined to be dust. Since the Despeckle filter doesn't offer any control, we rarely use it—it either works or it doesn't, and it feels like a hit-or-miss filter.

Median Filter

The Median filter offers some control over the radius of pixels that it affects. Choose **Filter > Noise > Median.** Press and release the mouse button on the filter preview to see a before and after view. Start with the slider set to 1, and drag the slider to the right while observing the changes. You can also enter a pixel amount directly into the Radius field. By the time 4 pixels is reached, the image has been significantly blurred (FIGURE 5.26).

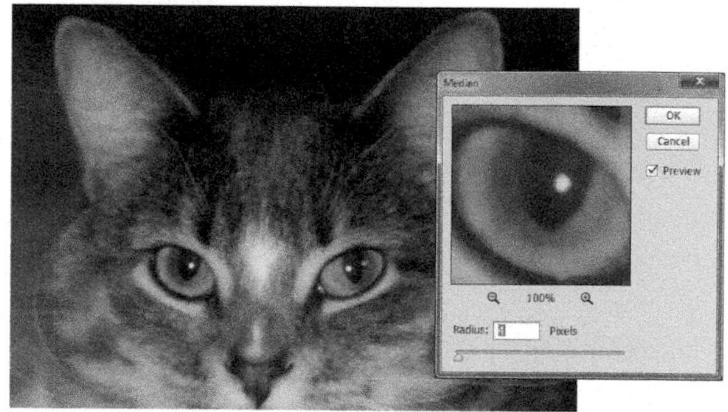

FIGURE 5.26 This close-up view of the cat's eye shows how the filter blurs the image.

The Median filter is useful when there is nothing of similar size to be retained in the image, such as highlights in eyes or individual strands of hair.

Dust & Scratches Filter

The Dust & Scratches filter is most useful for annihilating unwanted elements, such as small dust specks and lines, but it has its limitations as well. If images could be fixed with the simple application of a filter, this book would be rather short.

Choose **Filter > Noise > Dust & Scratches** to show the Dust & Scratches dialog box. As with the Median filter, there is a Radius slider to control the size of pixels that will be affected. Drag the Threshold slider all the way to the right to undo the effect of the Radius slider. Getting the best result is a balancing act between the two controls; start with just enough radius to eliminate dust, and then nudge up the threshold to bring back desired detail.

TIP There is no single solution for applying the Dust & Scratches filter. In a high-resolution image, the Radius setting would likely be higher than in a low-resolution setting, and generally a higher threshold with a lower radius seems to give the better result when dust-busting.

ch5_dustykitty.jpg

As the name implies, a mask is used to hide things. With the use of a filter mask, you can apply any filter more selectively (FIGURES 5.27 and 5.28):

FIGURE 5.27 The Dust & Scratches filter shows how dust can be removed while retaining some of the detail.

FIGURE 5.28 Smart Filters also provide masks so that you can apply the filter to only part of an image.
© Pamela J. Herrington

MINIMALIST RESTORATION

Sometimes fully restoring a photo takes away from its ambience.

Rod Mendenhall (www.rodmendenhall.com) has had a camera of one sort or another in his hands for over 40 years, including many years of darkroom experience. He made the switch to digital over a decade ago, and although he sometimes misses the wet darkroom, he finds the digital darkroom just as challenging as the chemical darkroom, and sometimes more so.

Rod had a photo of his mother that he repaired, but he stopped short of carrying out all the possible corrections. In his words, "My intent with the photo was to repair the physical damage only and leave the ragged edge as it was (FIGURES 5.29 and 5.30). I did not want to color correct, try to sharpen the image, or perform any other corrections. I wanted it to look as old as it was. Retouching the photo and improving the quality such that it looked more accurate or "perfect" would not do the image justice, in my opinion. When someone looks at the resulting image, I want them to get a sense of the time and place in which the image was captured. The hairstyle and clothing will give the viewer a sense of that. But leaving the natural fading and softness of the image helps to drive home the time period in which the photo was originally captured."

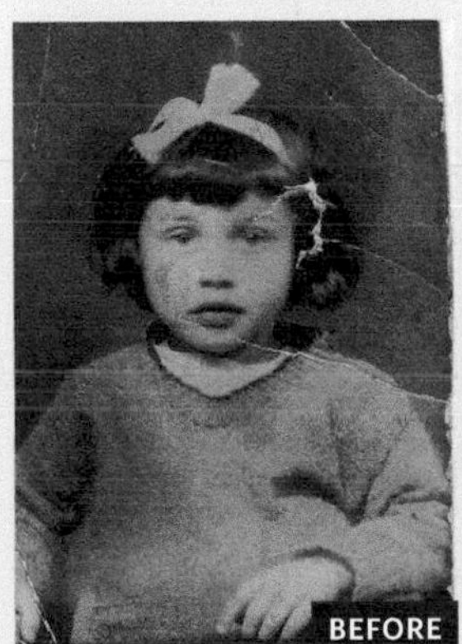

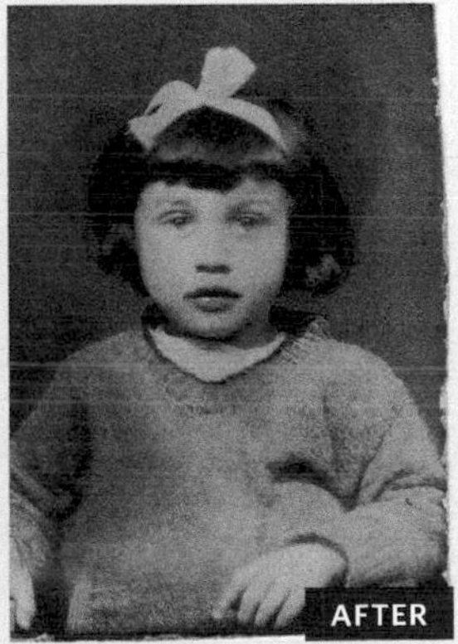

FIGURES 5.29 and 5.30 *© Rod Mendenhall*

1. Select the Background layer.

2. Choose **Filter > Convert for Smart Filters.**

3. Choose **Filter > Noise > Dust & Scratches.**

4. Set Radius to 4 and reduce Threshold to from 10 to 15.

5. Click the Filter Masks thumbnail to select it.

6. Select the Brush tool and a size of around 500 pixels, make sure the foreground color is black, and paint over the eyes, nose, and the ears to conceal parts of the filters effect.

★ NOTE There is no single setting for the Dust & Scratches filter that will work for all images. In general, the higher the resolution of the file, the more aggressive you can be with the settings. The decision rests in the acceptable amount of detail removal.

The downside of the Dust & Scratches filter, as with the Despeckle and Median filters, is that it ultimately blurs the image and will often remove the grain or texture, giving the image an unnaturally smooth look. Later in the chapter, a technique will be explained for how to put grain back into a picture.

Applying filters to layers that are converted to Smart Objects offers significant advantages in the nondestructive workflow:

- The filter can be revisited at any time, and readjusted by double-clicking the filter name in the Layers panel.
- You can adjust the blending options associated with the filter (blending modes and opacity) by double-clicking the Edit Filter Blending Options icon to the right of the filter name.
- Smart Filters offer the option of masking. A filter can be applied to just a part of a layer, and that selection continually tweaked by adjusting the mask.

CHANNEL EXTRACTION

An image channel is how Photoshop builds image information. A grayscale image is made up of a single channel, and an RGB image is made up of three color channels: red, green, and blue. The combination of these three channels creates the millions of colors we see. For the purpose of restoration work, individual image channels can reveal or conceal bothersome dust and damage in a picture. Frequently, but not always, the noisy or dirty channel is the blue one.

Selecting the Cleanest Channel

The little Lisa image (FIGURE 5.31) suffers from stains from an accidental spill or perhaps uneven developing. Even though the image is black and white, it was scanned as color.

FIGURE 5.31 The stains in this image can be rooted out by using just one of the image's channels. © *Mody Family Archives*

ch5_little_lisa.jpg

To see which channel is most useful, do the following (FIGURE 5.32):

1. Choose **Window > Channels** to show the Channels panel.

2. Click the Red, Green, and Blue channels to observe the different grayscale interpretations.

In this image, the green channel shows the least damage.

+ TIP You can also use the keyboard shortcuts listed in the Channels panel to observe the grayscale interpretation of each channel. This is called a *channel walk*. Press Cmd-3/Ctrl-3 for the Red channel, Cmd-4/Ctrl-4 for the Green channel, and Cmd-5/Ctrl-5 for the Blue channel. Cmd-2/Ctrl-2 returns you to the combined RGB view.

FIGURE 5.32 Exploring the different channels reveals three different interpretations of the image, and one of them barely shows the stain now. © *Mody Family Archives*

TIP Scan black and white or monochromatic images in RGB mode, and then extract the cleanest and best channel to work on.

Extracting the Cleanest Channel

With the Green channel selected as the cleanest one, the next step is to turn it into its own file:

1. Click the Green channel in the Channels panel, and press Cmd-A/Ctrl-A to select the channel. Then press Cmd-C/Ctrl-C to copy the channel.

2. Choose **File > New**, and click OK to create a new document.

3. Press Cmd-V/Ctrl-V to paste the copied channel into the image.

4. Choose **File > Save As** to save the newly created grayscale file with a new name.

TIP You can also select the Green channel, choose **Image > Mode > Grayscale**, and click OK to the discard the other channels.

A tonal adjustment brightens the image (FIGURE 5.33) and hides some of the remaining damage, but there are still a few marks to clean up. Using methods that will be presented in following sections will result in stain-free image (FIGURE 5.34).

FIGURE 5.33 A tonal adjustment hides more of the remaining damage.

FIGURE 5.34 The rest of the visible damage is removed with the Clone Stamp and healing tools.

A CHANNELS WORKAROUND FOR PHOTOSHOP ELEMENTS

Photoshop Elements users, this is one area that separates Elements from Photoshop. Elements does not offer an easy way to directly access channel information. Author Richard Lynch offers this solution in his book *The Hidden Power of Photoshop Elements*.

1. Create a new layer at the top of the layer stack.
2. Fill the layer with a primary color of the channel to filter for (R = 255, 0,0; G = 0, 255, 0; B = 0, 0, 255).
3. Set the layer to multiply. This will filter the image for the color you filled.
4. Add a Hue/Saturation layer.
5. Choose the color of the fill (red, green, or blue, as per step 2).
6. Drag the Lightness slider all the way to the right.
7. Merge the visible result to a new layer by pressing Shift-Cmd-Option-E/Shift-Ctrl-Alt-E.

Returning the Ambience

The original image had a bit of nostalgia because it looked a little yellowed. Using the channel extraction method returns the image to a true grayscale file, giving it more of a stark look. Adding a little tone will return the old-fashioned feel. Follow these steps, which can also be used for creating a sepia tone.

1. Convert the image back into an RGB image by choosing **Image > Mode > RGB**. The image will not look any different. Note that the Channels panel has four identical displays of the separate and combined channels, but now a color tone can be applied (FIGURE 5.35).

2. At the bottom of the Layers panel, click the Create New Fill or Adjustment Layer icon and select Hue/Saturation.

3. In the Properties panel, select the Colorize option.

4. Enter 32 for Hue to give the image a brownish cast.

5. Drag the Saturation slider to 18 to control the intensity of the cast and recapture the older look (FIGURES 5.36 and 5.37).

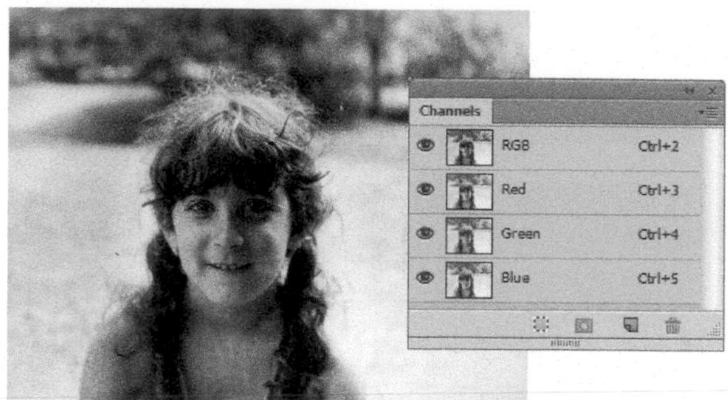

FIGURE 5.35 To add the original color tone back into the image, first convert the grayscale image back to RGB.

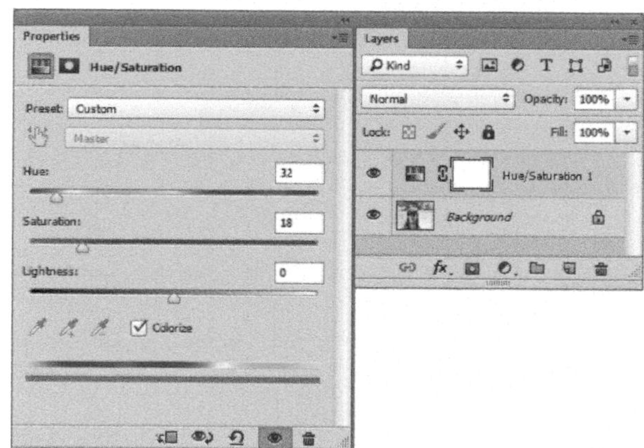

FIGURE 5.36 Sepia or a similar colorization can be added with a Hue/Saturation adjustment layer when the Colorize option is selected.

FIGURE 5.37 The original color tone has been put back into the grayscale image.

REMOVING SPOTS, FUNGUS, AND MOLD

So far the techniques shown are useful for applying global changes to damaged images. Now it's time to get down into the mainstay of restoration work: the Clone Stamp tool and the healing tools.

Using the Clone Stamp Tool

Since the earliest days of Photoshop, the Clone Stamp tool has been the go-to tool for restoring and repairing images. It is basically a copy-and-paste brush, with a sample being taken from a good part of the image and painted over a damaged part.

ch5_dustyman.jpg

Notice the minor amount of dust throughout the picture. The dust spots are larger than some of the details in the image. The Despeckle, Median, and Dust & Scratches filters would blur important details before the dust spots could be hidden. So it's time to roll up our sleeves to conceal bothersome dust.

1. In the Layers panel, click the New Layer icon (FIGURE 5.38).

FIGURE 5.38 This typical old image shows some minor dust spots. Create a new empty layer on top of the Background layer for nondestructive cloning. © *Palmer Family Archives*

2. Choose the Clone Stamp tool from the Tools panel, and in the options bar select Current & Below from the Sample menu. This will place all cloning onto the new layer and keep the Background layer untouched.

The Clone Stamp tool has two options for where it pulls its sampling point from: aligned and non-aligned. With the Aligned option unselected, the Clone Stamp tool will repeatedly pull information from the same sampled point. With the Aligned option selected, the sampling point will keep relocating, moving in tandem to the position of the cursor.

3. Select Aligned in the options bar so that the cursor doesn't always sample from the same area, which is the best choice for most pictures. Sampling from the same spot repeatedly may create an unnatural-looking pattern.

4. Choose a brush size slightly larger than the spot to be removed. Wayne prefers a brush with the hardness set to 0. Hard-edged brushes generally will leave visible unnatural lines in the image, giving the appearance of a finger running through wet paint.

5. Move the cursor to an area that would be a good replacement for where the spot is. Press Option/Alt. The cursor will take the appearance of a target. Click to sample that area, and release the key (FIGURE 5.39). Move your cursor to the spot to be removed and click again. Notice that the sampled area is visible inside the brush, allowing for precise placement of copied material.

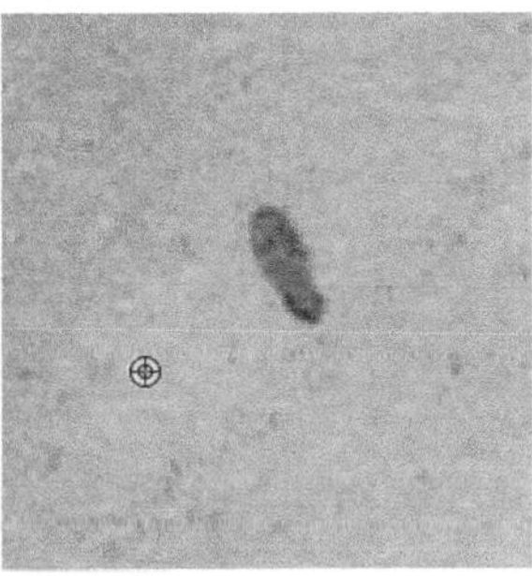

FIGURE 5.39 Choose an area to sample that looks similar to what is being covered up.

FIGURE 5.40 As the changes are made on a separate layer, they can be erased if the look is not satisfactory.

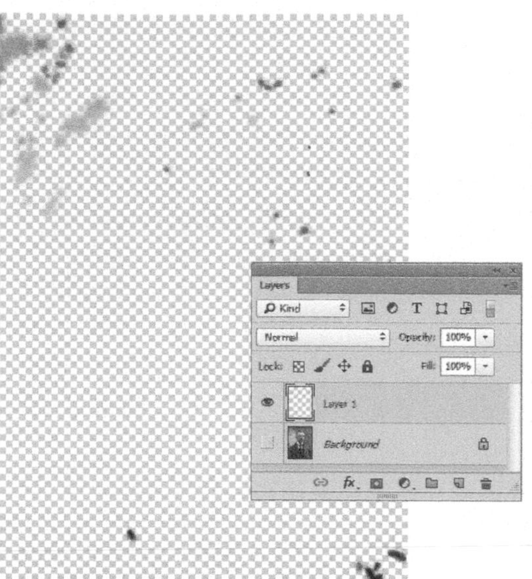

6. Repeat the process throughout the image, resampling as necessary. Choose the resampling point carefully so that it matches the area you're trying to repair. Adjust the size of the brush to match the size of the spot being removed. Use the tool in a dabbing fashion, as opposed to a brush stroke, and resample frequently to avoid a smudgy look or pattern buildup in the image.

With all the changes being placed upon the newly added layer, the Background layer is unchanged. Work can be evaluated by turning the clean up layer off and on (**FIGURE 5.40**). If some of the cloning does not look realistic, use the Eraser tool to erase that area of cloning and try again.

The blending mode of the Clone Stamp tool can be changed to lighten or darken so that only light or dark spots are removed. In this image, switching the blending mode to Lighten makes fast work of removing the dark spots and ultimately changes less of the picture (**FIGURE 5.41**).

TIP Use your cloning concentration carefully, and do not waste time taking out unimportant dust that may be cropped out or unseen in the final print.

TIP Consider reducing the Clone Stamp tool's Opacity setting in the options bar so that the touchups blend in better with their surroundings.

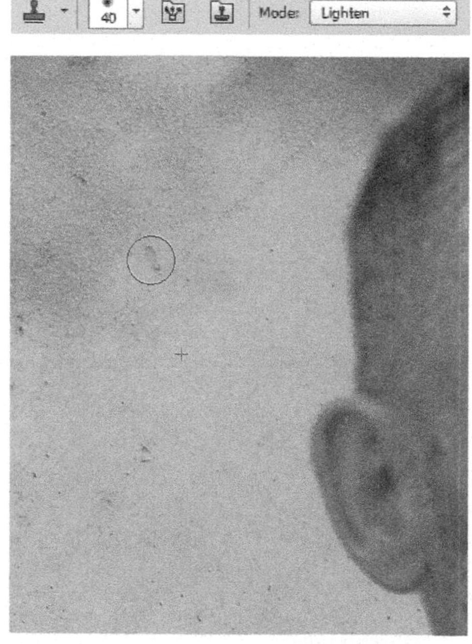

FIGURE 5.41 Using the Lighten blending mode with the Clone Stamp tool targets only spots that are dark.

The Clone Source Panel

With the Clone Stamp tool, every time a new sample is taken the previous sample is replaced. There may be times when it would be beneficial to have more control over the Clone Stamp tool. For example, you might want to reduce the size of the clone source you paint with so that the cloned pixels better match that part of the image you are fixing. With a clone source captured in the Clone Source panel, you can adjust additional settings, such as angle and size. Once they're set, painting with the Clone Stamp tool applies these settings for the active clone source.

The Clone Source panel is not visible by default. Choose **Window > Clone Source** or click the Clone Source panel icon in the options bar to show it. The Clone Source panel provides an option to save up to five different sample points. These points do not have to come from within the image you are working on. Just as with the Clone Stamp tool, you can sample from another opened image.

The image in FIGURE 5.42 is in need of plenty of stain removal, but perhaps the most troubling part is one is that one eye is partly obliterated. By choosing the good eye as the source and flipping it in the Clone Source panel (FIGURE 5.43), the bad eye can be covered up. Additionally, brushes do not always have to be round, and by changing the roundness to more oval in the Brush panel (FIGURE 5.44), a better clone source was sampled. By cloning onto an empty layer, the eye can be further nudged into place with the Move tool and arrow keys.

FIGURE 5.42 This image's most noticeable damage is to one eye. © *Palmer Family Archives*

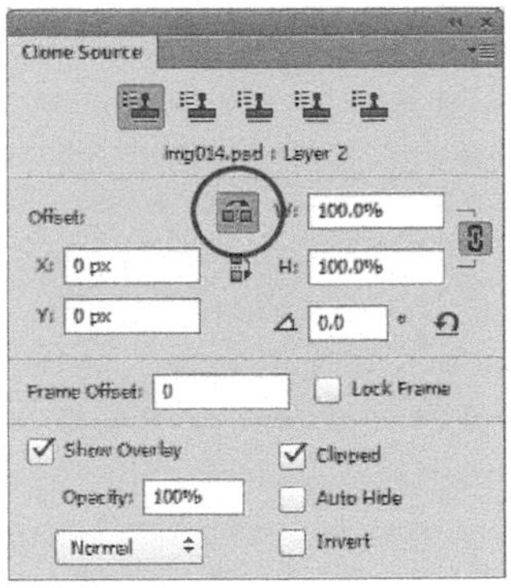

FIGURE 5.43 The Clone Source panel can flip the source.

FIGURE 5.44 Brushes do not have to be round; in the Brush panel a more elliptical brush is better for cloning the eye.

+ TIP Photoshop has a plethora of brushes of different shapes; the Internet offers infinitely more, or you can simply make your own. Any object or selection can be turned into a brush by choosing **Edit > Define Brush Preset**. Keep in mind that brushes can only be grayscale.

The Clone Source panel also offers options for rotating and scaling the sampled source, as well as options for how the brush is viewed. Having the ability to scale or rotate a sample source can be useful when retouching, as it allows you to select sample points from an area in the image that does not precisely match the size or angle requirement for the dust or scratch you are trying to remove. Adjusting the settings for the clone source allows you to better match the size or angle requirement when using the Clone Stamp tool.

Using the Healing Tools

The healing tools (Spot Healing Brush, Healing Brush, Patch, and Content-Aware tools) differ from the Clone Stamp tool in that rather than simply painting duplicate material, they generate the replacement information by analyzing the surrounding areas, and the result maintains texture and tone. On first examination, the healing tools seem like they would replace the Clone Stamp tool, as they seem to be the Clone Stamp tool on steroids, but they are different tools with their own strengths and weaknesses, and they repair images in different ways.

Spot Healing Brush Tool

The Spot Healing Brush tool, as implied by the name, is designed to remove spots, isolated areas such as bothersome wires, and skin blemishes (FIGURES 5.45 and 5.46). With the Spot Healing Brush tool you do no need to determine the sample point like you do with the Clone Stamp Tool. Simply paint with the Spot Healing Brush over the spot you want to remove. When the mouse button is released, the area inside the brush is filled with surrounding material from outside the brush. Click with the Spot Healing Brush tool to quickly fix spots, or use a brush stroke on larger areas. The longer the stroke, the larger the area the brush samples, and sometimes this creates bizarre results, which you can undo with Cmd-Z/Ctrl-Z. Additionally, different results are obtained when painting in different directions.

FIGURES 5.45 and 5.46 © *Palmer Family Archives*

ch5_spotted_man.jpg

1. Select the Spot Healing Brush tool. Since the healing tools are grouped, you may have to cycle through the healing tools by pressing Shift-J to bring up the Spot Healing Brush.

2. To work nondestructively, create a new empty layer above the Background layer, and select Sample All Layers in the options bar.

3. Locate spots in the image, and with the Spot Healing Brush tool click or drag over the spot and release (FIGURE 5.47). Be sure to totally include the spot to be removed within the brush stroke for the best result. Use caution when running this tool along areas that you want to preserve, like the nose and collar. Accidentally painting into these areas can create a smear. Thankfully, any of the fixes can be undone with Cmd-Z/Ctrl-Z or by switching to the Eraser tool and erasing the less-than-optimal repairs.

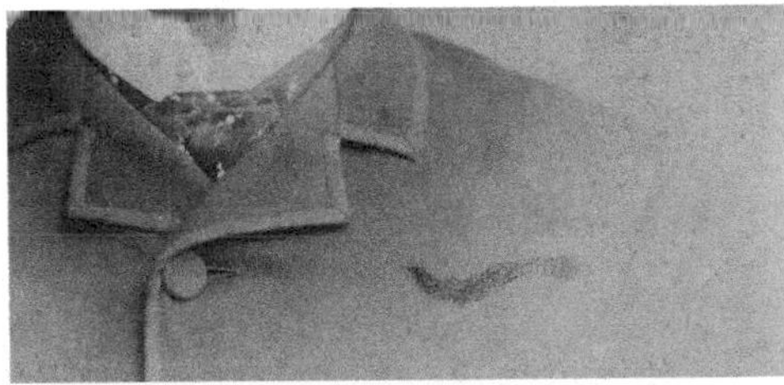

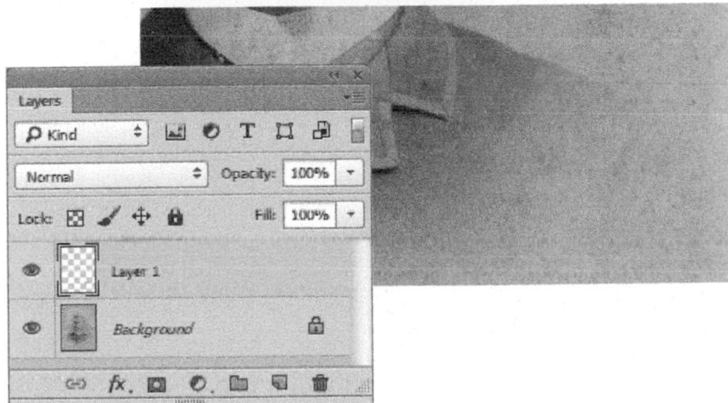

FIGURE 5.47 The damage in this image will be more easily tackled with the Spot Healing Brush tool.

4. In this example, the spot that runs over the man's collar and into the neck is beyond what the Spot Healing Brush tool can successfully fix. It will smudge the image. Switch to the Clone Stamp tool for precise repair to maintain the line of the collar. The repair can be put on the same layer.

TRY IT Try using the Clone Source panel in conjunction with the Clone Stamp tool to repair the spot that runs over the man's collar and into the neck by adjusting the angle of the source.

You might notice that in a number of areas the grain pattern has been disturbed and there are areas that look smooth (FIGURE 5.48). Depending on the size of the output, this may not be noticeable. Save this image as a PSD, and name it *spot_repair.psd*. Later, we'll explain a technique for putting grain back into an image.

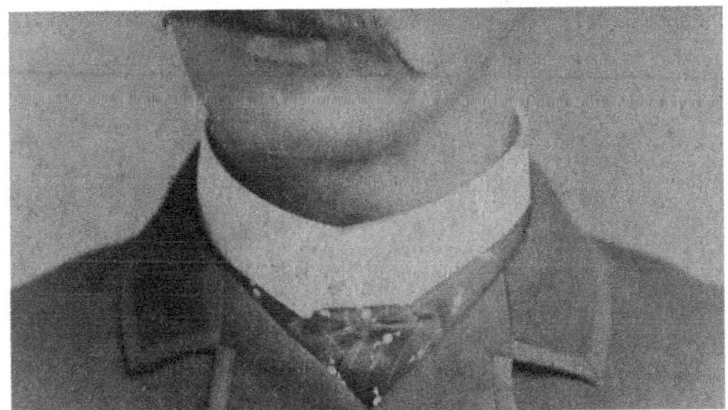

FIGURE 5.48 Repairing an image can remove its grain, giving it a smudged look, as on the left side of this image.

! CAUTION Use caution when using the Spot Healing Brush tool on large areas. The longer the brush stroke, the farther away the tool pulls its sample from, which can produce very undesirable results.

TIP The direction you move the brush can also control where the sample is made. Consider running the brush in a different direction to produce a different result.

Healing Brush Tool

The Healing Brush is best used to repair larger areas of damage and when you need to control where the source information is sampled from. Operate the Healing Brush the same way as the Clone Stamp tool. Start by Option/Alt-clicking to sample, and then brush over the area to be fixed (FIGURES 5.49 and 5.50).

FIGURES 5.49 and 5.50 © *Palmer Family Archives*

ch5_brother_sister.jpg

1. Create a new empty layer.
2. Select the Healing Brush tool, and select Current & Below from the Sample menu in the options bar.
3. Look at the different size scratches and set a brush size a bit larger than the scratch or dust spot to be removed.
4. Move the cursor off to the side of the scratch or dust spot and a bit to the left of the damage. Press Option/Alt, and then click to sample the good information.
5. Drag over the area to heal. After the stroke is made, the healing process will take place. Try not to clean up too much in one stroke. Keep in mind where the Healing Brush tool is pulling information from. If it does not match the area to be healed, erase and try again; only a small change is being made on the layer (FIGURE 5.51).

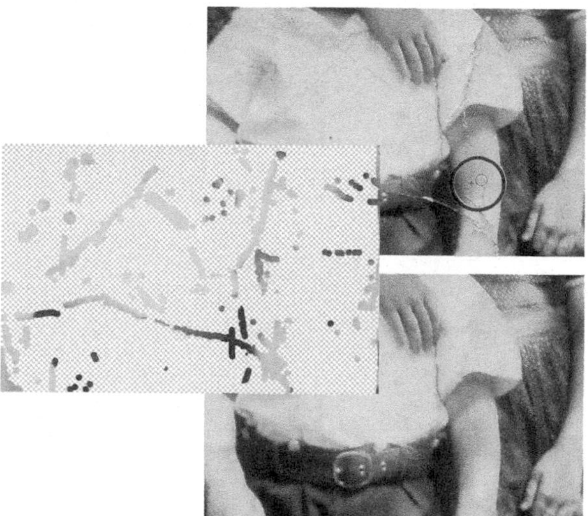

FIGURE 5.51 The view of the top layer with the background layer turned off after all the repairs are done.

TIP As you paint with the Clone Stamp tool or Healing Brush tool, a plus (+) indicates where the source information is pulled from.

6. Frequently sample areas that resemble what is to be repaired. In the little girl's dress, sample the polka dots to make that pattern in the heal.

7. In the boy's shirt, change the blending mode for the Healing Brush tool from Normal to Lighten in the options bar so that only the dark areas are changed. Likewise, change the blending mode to Darken to fix the light scratches against the dark background.

The beauty of the Healing Brush tool is how well it blends in the surroundings. If there are any noticeable abnormalities, resample and run the brush again with a different size; however, the more strokes taken to remove an object, the greater the chances of creating a patterned or altered look.

TIP Don't forget about the brush blending modes. In this image, polluted with spots, setting the blending mode to Darken got rid of the lighter spots with ease but maintained the darker areas such as the ridges in the sweater.

Filters, Clone Stamp, and Healing Brush Team

Now that the basics are covered, you can clean up images by teaming up the filters with the Clone Stamp and Healing Brush tools to get the best out of each.

The Dust & Scratches filter can be used for large unimportant areas. The Clone Stamp and Healing Brush tool work in different ways. Use the Clone Stamp tool for details and areas that need to be preserved, such as spots or smudges that cross areas of different shading of fine detail, and use the Healing Brush tool for less important areas, such as spots in the background.

TRY IT Let's practice the strategies covered to clean up the image of the family (FIGURES 5.52 and 5.53).

1. Convert the layer to a Smart Object.
2. Use the Quick Selection tool to select the background behind the subjects.
3. Choose **Filter > Noise > Dust & Scratches**. A radius of 9 gets rid of most the distracting damage.
4. Create new empty layer.
5. Select the Healing Brush tool, select Current & Below from the Sample menu in the options bar, change the blending mode to Lighten, and then address the remaining darker spots and stains on the background.
6. As you move into the clothing and facial areas, change the blending mode to Darken (to work on lighter spots) or Normal, depending on what type of spots are to be removed. Remember that if you don't like a result, undo and try again or erase the change. Using blending modes reduces the amount of the image actually changed.
7. As you get closer to the more important area of the faces, switch to the Clone Stamp tool if the Healing Brush tool smudges important detail.

ch5_family_of_four.jpg

FIGURES 5.52 and 5.53 © *Palmer Family Archives*

Patch, Content-Aware, Move, and Red Eye Tools

The other tools grouped with the Spot Healing Brush tool are designed for tackling issues other than dust, cracks, or blemishes The Patch tool uses the Healing Brush engine without the need to sample or brush and is best used to repair larger damaged areas.

The Content-Aware Move tool provides the option to move an object or person within a picture and have Photoshop fill in the area it was moved from. Both of these tools are covered in greater detail in Chapter 6. The last tool in this nested bunch is the Red Eye tool, discussed in Chapter 8. It eliminates the demon eyes so commonly found in flash pictures taken with point-and-shoot cameras.

+ TIP The Blur tool is often an overlooked dust-busting tool. Similarly to the Clone Stamp tool and the healing tools, it can make nondestructive corrections on a new empty layer. Set the blending mode to Darken to target light spots, or to Lighten to target darker dust and mold spots.

MANAGING GLARE, TEXTURE, MOIRÉ, AND COLOR ARTIFACTS

Taming print texture, moiré, and color artifacts has caused many sleepless nights for restoration artists, retouchers, and graphic designers. The challenge is to reduce or eliminate these bothersome patterns while maintaining the important image information. Read on to learn how to reduce the problem before even opening the image in Photoshop, how to work with the Image Size dialog to remove moiré, and just as important, how to add grain texture back into the image to cover telltale restoration tracks.

Reducing Problems Before Restoration

The idea of always being able to fix things in Photoshop is not a good philosophy. It is best to take the time to get the best photo or scan possible to avoid additional work. This may involve changing angles, changing lighting, or removing an image from the wall or taking it out of a frame. Often Wayne will simply take an image outside and photograph it under natural light to avoid complications from studio lighting.

Reducing Glare

Images that are behind glass, not flat, or silvering do not lend themselves to being scanned. In these cases, we recommend photographing the image at an angle to avoid the glare and using either the transform tools or the Perspective Crop tool to correct the shooting at an angle.

Katrin was faced with the difficult task of trying to photograph a painting and had no control over its location or the lighting. Colin Wood provided her this idea for how to correct the annoying light reflection spot (FIGURE 5.54): photograph the image at an angle that doesn't show the reflection, and then correct the non-square image using Perspective Crop tool (FIGURES 5.55 and 5.56).

FIGURE 5.54 Photographing this painting straight on resulted in distracting reflections. Taking the photo at an angle eliminated the glare, and then the picture was straightened with the Perspective Crop tool. © *KE*

FIGURES 5.55 and 5.56

Once the image was open in Photoshop, Katrin selected the Perspective Crop tool, which is grouped with the Crop tool. She clicked each corner of the picture, starting with the upper-left corner, followed by the lower-left, lower-right, and upper-right corners. Then she fine-tuned the position of the perspective grid that appeared by selecting one of the handles and dragging it into position (FIGURE 5.57). Finally, she pressed Return/Enter to commit the perspective crop.

FIGURE 5.57 With the Perspective Crop tool active, the border of the non-square image is defined.

TIP To keep the softening of the image to a minimum, Katrin used the sneaky method of opening the raw file at twice the resolution needed. Before using the Perspective Crop tool, she sized the image down (**Image > Image Size**) by selecting Bicubic Sharper from the Resample menu in the Image Size dialog box.

Reducing Silver Mirroring

Silver was used in both film and prints. With time and less-than-optimal storage conditions, silver mirroring can appear as a bluish, shimmering cast in the darker areas of an image; it is especially visible when viewed at an angle.

ch5_collegeportrait.jpg

Scanning images like this with a flatbed scanner can be problematic, as the silver reflects the light directly back. Therefore, it is best to avoid capturing the silvering when the image is scanned or photographed. In this image, the silvering is very noticeable, especially in the darker areas; it was made more so when the light of the scanner bounced off it directly (**FIGURE 5.58**). By tilting to minimize the glare and by photographing the image rather than scanning it, Wayne was able to record a usable image (**FIGURES 5.59** and **5.60**).

FIGURE 5.58 Silver showing through in images can be highly reflective, making scanning difficult. © *Palmer Family Archives*

FIGURE 5.59 By photographing the image at an angle, the reflections are minimized.

FIGURE 5.60 The image can be straightened in Photoshop.

To square the image back, Wayne used the following steps (**FIGURE 5.61**):

FIGURE 5.61 Using guides to help return the image back to square, and Warp mode to transform to the guides with real-time feedback

1. Press Cmd-J/Ctrl-J to duplicate the Background layer.
2. From the rulers (**View > Rulers**), drag horizontal and vertical guides over the image.
3. Choose **Edit > Free Transform**, and click the Warp icon ( ) in the options bar to change to Warp mode.

Warp mode transforms in real time, giving feedback as to how much the image can be transformed without distortion.

4. Drag the corners or the control points to warp the image to the guides, and press Return/Enter to commit the warp.

5. Once the image is square, use the guides to crop.

If an image has already been digitized and the silvering effect is present, the reflections will often have a blue cast, as seen in FIGURE 5.62. This technique can be used to minimize the effect.

FIGURE 5.62 This image has already been scanned, so getting rid of the reflections through tilting the image is not an option. © *Hildenbrand Family Collection*

ch5_silvered_children.jpg

1. Choose **Select > Color Range** and choose Blues from the Select menu. Click OK to create an active selection, and click OK once more if a warning message appears (FIGURE 5.63).

TIP If choosing Blues from the Color Range menu does not work, try manually selecting the affected areas with the Sampled Colors option.

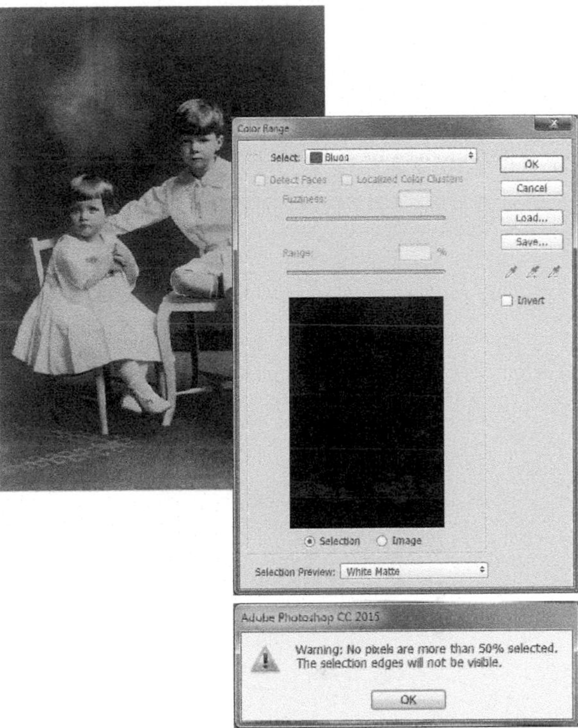

FIGURE 5.63 Use Color Range set to Blues to select the blue reflections.

2. Add a Levels adjustment layer. Don't make any tonal changes, but change the blending mode to Difference to darken the blue reflection (FIGURE 5.64).

The type of adjustment layer used is not important, as you are only using the blending mode.

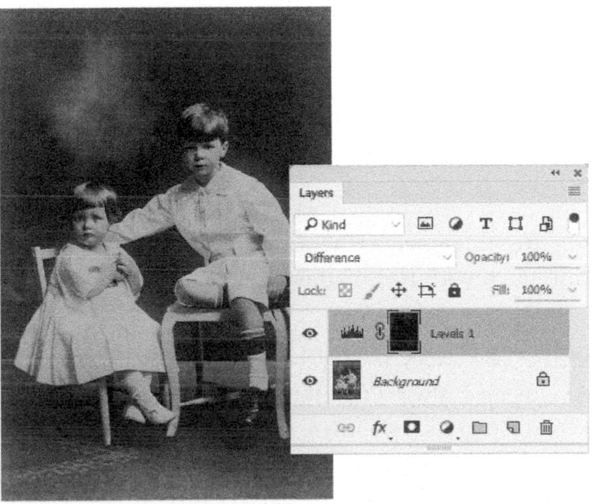

FIGURE 5.64 An adjustment layer with the blending mode set to Difference tones down some of the blue reflections.

3. Some of the blue has been removed. Duplicate the adjustment layer by pressing Cmd-J/Ctrl-J, which removes more blue. Repeat several times until as much blue is removed as possible without making the dark areas of the image look blotchy (**FIGURE 5.65**).

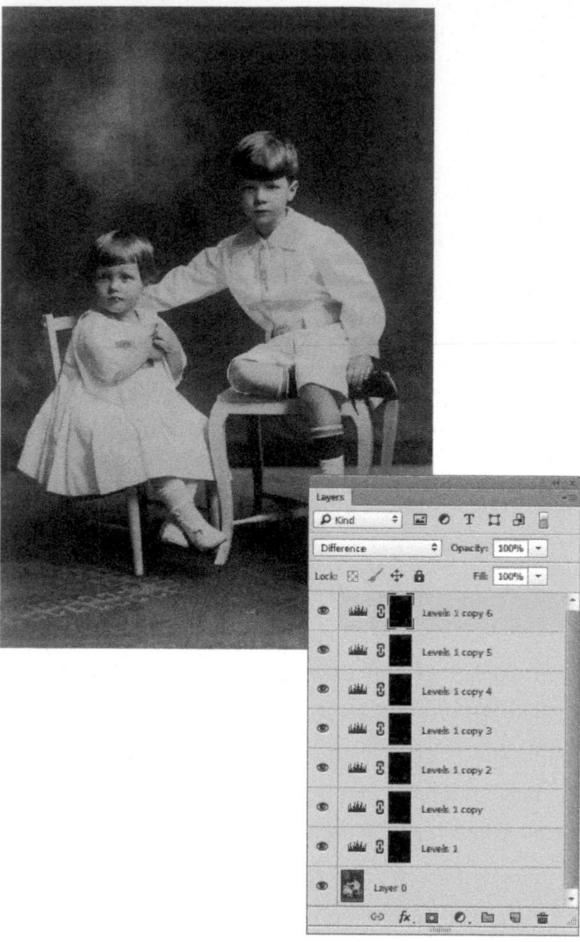

FIGURE 5.65 Duplicating the adjustment layer several more times greatly reduces the amount of the silver blue effect.

As with all restoration work, individual results will vary. In some images, the silvering can be completely eliminated with this method.

Reducing Paper Texture and Print Patterns

In years past it was common to print photographs on textured papers with linen, stipple, hatch, or pebble surfaces. As pleasing as these textures were to the original print, the textures are very problematic when it comes to scanning or photographing the prints. When the image is captured by either method the texture will also be captured and can be distracting. The smaller the original print, the greater the problem because the paper texture is larger relative to the image information. When dealing with textured prints, the Surface Blur filter can help.

The senior portrait example featured here is a realistically hand-colored black and white photograph that is sadly marred by the pattern of the paper (**FIGURE 5.66**).

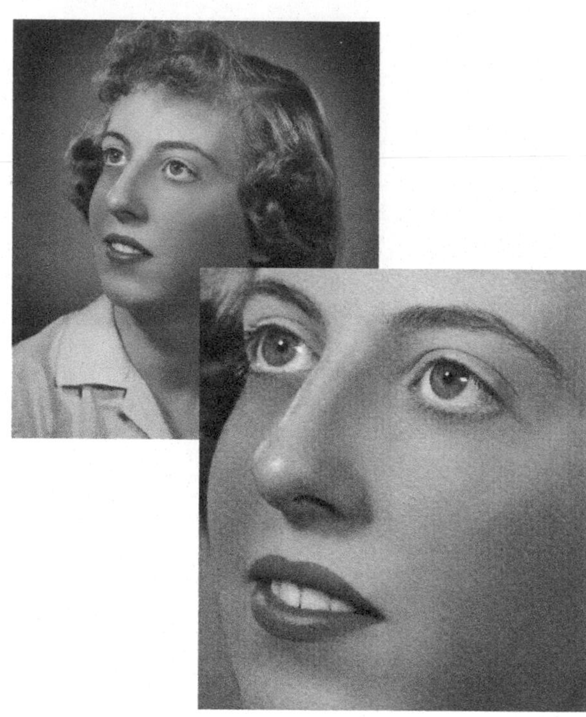

FIGURE 5.66 This colorized portrait has a distracting pattern in it from being printed on textured paper. © *Palmer Family Archives*

ch5_seniorportrait.jpg

1. Choose **Filter > Convert for Smart Filter** to convert the Background layer to a Smart Object.

2. Choose **Filter > Blur > Surface Blur**, set the Radius to 6 and the Threshold to 16, and click OK.

The Radius controls the range of pixels that is effected by the filter where it spots tonal differences. The Threshold puts a break on the filter, by not affecting any pixels with a tonal difference less than the set value.

The pattern is minimized while keeping the blurring to a minimum. Using the controls is a delicate balancing act between removing the unwanted pattern, dust, or distractions and obliterating important details (FIGURE 5.67).

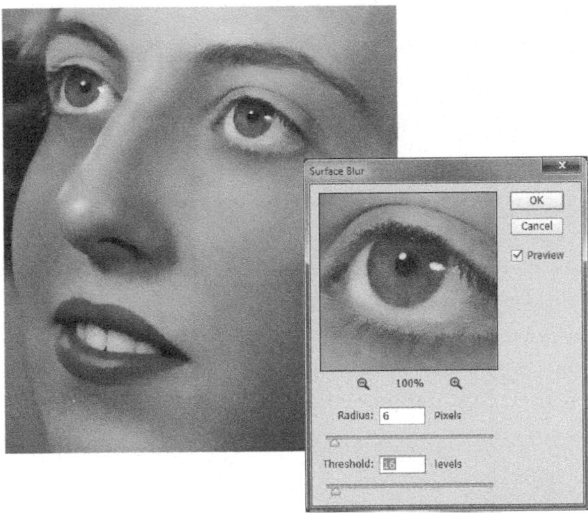

FIGURE 5.67 The texture can be minimized by applying the Surface Blur filter.

To control where the pattern removal takes place, take advantage of the Smart Filter mask to conceal the surface blur of essential image areas.

3. To bring back essential image information, click the Smart Filter mask. With a soft-edged black brush, paint over the eyes and the edge of the mouth to conceal the surface blur effect (FIGURE 5.68).

FIGURE 5.68 Masking the important areas returns sharpness to the key areas.

The result shows how well the paper texture is reduced, and the essential parts of the face still look sharp (FIGURE 5.69).

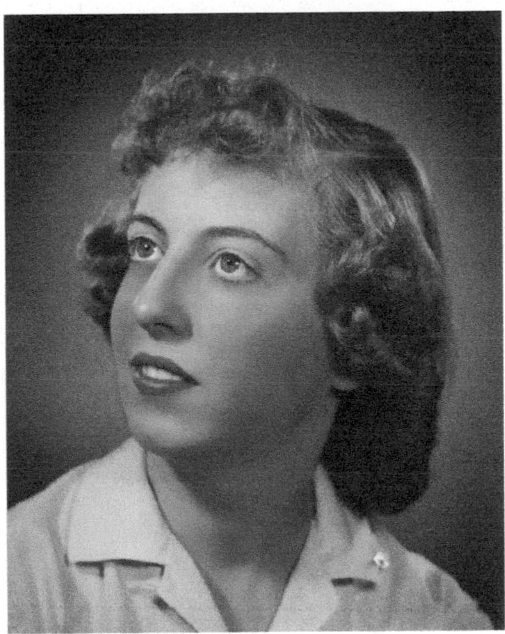

FIGURE 5.69 The pattern has been minimized, with with her eyes and mouth kept sharp.

Reducing Offset Moiré

A magazine or newspaper image consists of tiny little dots that create the illusion of a continuous-tone photograph. These images look sharp from a distance but not so much when enlarged. The de-screening option in a scanner's software is the best way to get rid of the dot patterns as addressed in Chapter 1. If that is not an option, use this process to downsize the image, and then use Photoshop's interpolation process to generate new information to minimize the dot pattern.

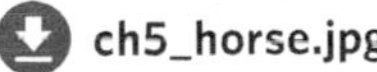
ch5_horse.jpg

In this image from a printed calendar (FIGURE 5.70), notice the pattern from commercial offset printing and note that the picture does not hold a lot of detail, even when zooming in. However, the pattern can be reduced or eliminated by removing the space between the dots and having Photoshop fill in the space by replicating the remaining information.

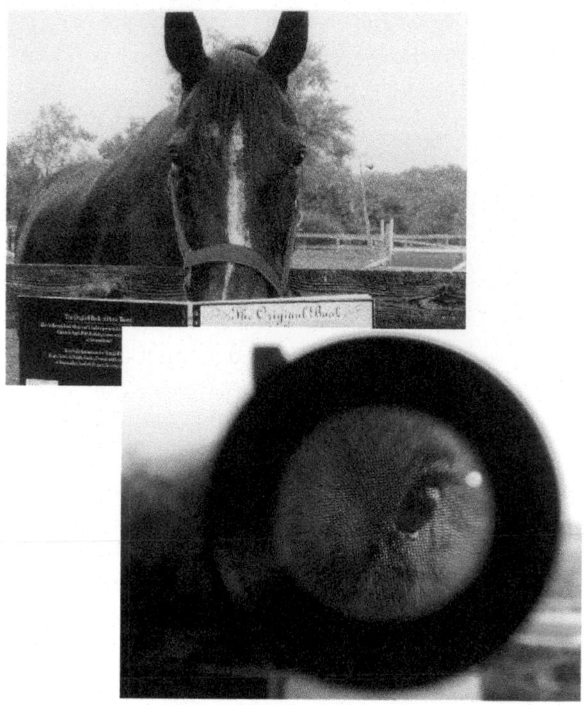

FIGURE 5.70 This image from a printed calendar shows the signs of being screened. When viewed through a loupe, the dot pattern is more noticeable. © *Pamela J. Herrington*

1. Press Cmd-–/Ctrl-– to zoom out until the pattern is no longer visible on the screen, which should be about 50%. Depending on your monitor, the zoom level may vary. Take note of the zoom level that is listed on the document tab.

2. Choose **Image > Image Size** and change the unit of measurement for Width and Height to Percent. Select Resample and choose Automatic from the menu. Change the percentage to 50, and Click OK (**FIGURE 5.71**).

★ **NOTE** The selected downsize percentage is based on the zoom level at which the pattern is no longer visible onscreen.

3. Choose **Image > Image Size** again, select Resample, and change the Width and Height percentage to 200 to size the image back up to the original size. Click OK. Photoshop will resize the image to its former dimensions and the image interpolation will create new information, getting rid of the visible pattern that was present (**FIGURE 5.72**).

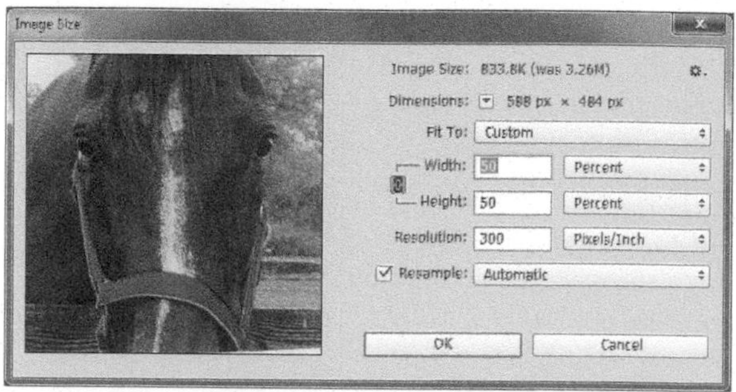

FIGURE 5.71 Reducing the file size by the same amount at which the pattern is not viewable on the screen runs the dots together. © *Pamela J. Herrington*

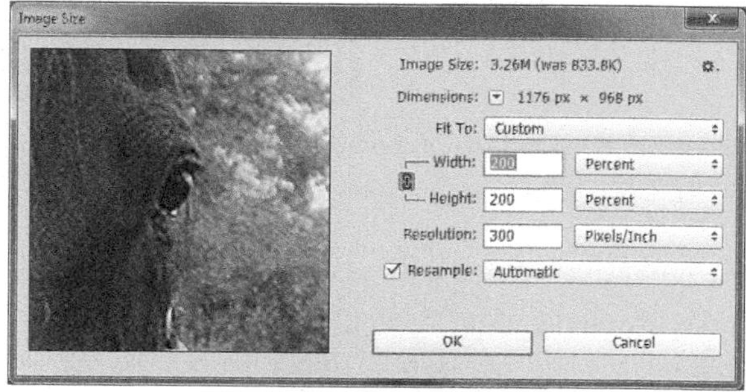

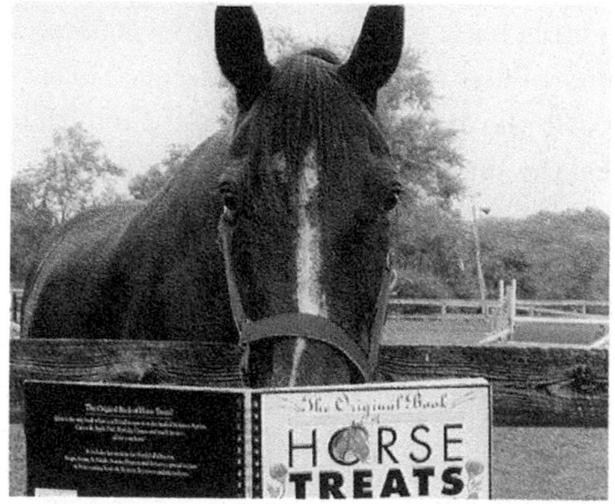

FIGURE 5.72 Returning the file to its original size through interpolation, the pattern is minimized. © *Pamela J. Herrington*

+ **TIP** Downsizing and upsizing an image can also be used to hide dust.

Reducing Digital Camera Noise

In the days of film, visible grain was for some a negative side of high-speed films or underexposed images. Unfortunately, this characteristic has carried over to the digital age and is called *noise*. When a camera's ISO setting is increased, the signal the camera sensor receives is boosted, creating two possible types of noise that are often visible in the darker sections of the image: luminance noise, which can give an image a gritty look like film grain, and chrominance noise, which shows up as colors that do not match the surrounding colors.

When recording images as JPEGs, the camera decides how to handle the noise and will probably produce an image that is less pleasing than what can be achieved with raw processing. Most point-and-shoot cameras, including smartphones, do not offer raw capture options and instead use JPEG. This is when the Reduce Noise filter can be useful.

ch5_backstage_guitars.jpg

1. Zoom in to 100% or 200% and inspect the bodies of the guitars, observing the chromatic digital noise caused by shooting in low light and at a high ISO (FIGURE 5.73).

FIGURE 5.73 At first glance, the noise in this image is not noticeable. On closer inspection, the noise is very distracting. © *WP*

2. Choose **Filter > Convert for Smart Filters**.
3. The Reduce Noise filter is a processor-intensive filter, so it can be helpful to determine the best settings on a smaller section of the image.
4. Using the Rectangular Marquee tool, select a small area of the image that clearly shows the noise.
5. Choose **Filter > Noise > Reduce Noise**, and drag all the sliders to the left.

As with most Photoshop noise reduction filters, finding the best settings—those that create the best balance of noise reduction while maintaining image information—requires experimentation and observation.

6. Drag the Strength slider to 8 to reduce the size of the noise. The color of the noise is still noticeable. Drag the Reduce Color Noise slider to 50%. Drag the Preserve Details and Sharpen Details sliders to 5% to bring back a bit of sharpness (FIGURE 5.74).

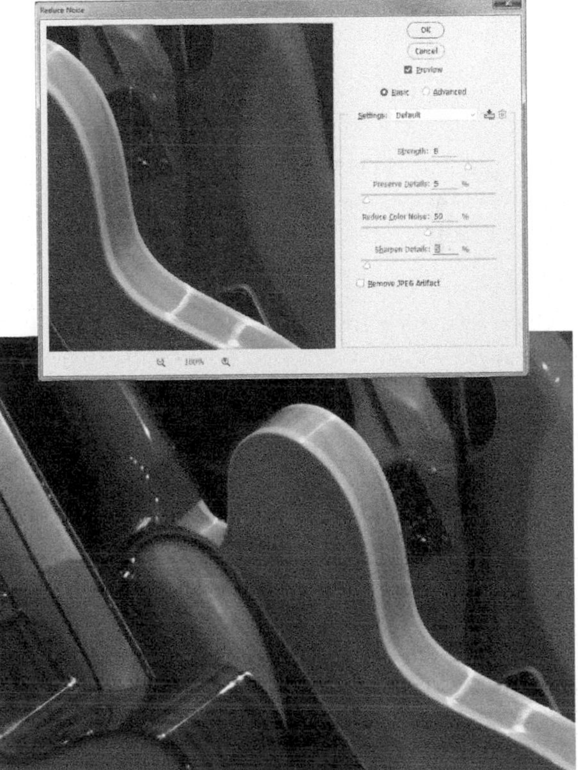

FIGURE 5.74 This after view inside the Reduce Noise filter shows how much noise can be reduced by finding a balance of settings.

7. Click OK to apply the settings to the small area selected, press Cmd-Z/Ctrl-Z to undo the effect, and press Cmd-D/Ctrl-D to deselect the selection.

8. Press Cmd-F/Ctrl-F to apply the last-used filter to the entire file. Be patient, as this filter often takes a bit longer than others to process.

Returning Image Texture

No matter what technique is used to remove dust from an image, maintaining the grain or noise pattern can be challenging. Overzealous cloning and healing can disrupt the original grain or noise patterns, giving the image an uneven look. So after

NOISE AND RAW FILES

An advantage of recording raw is that the amount of noise can be controlled before the image is processed. This image of the New York skyline late in the day is plagued with noise from being shot at a high ISO. A close-up view of the cloud shows the extent of the noise (**FIGURE 5.75**).

By making adjustments in the Details tab in ACR, the noise can be dramatically reduced (**FIGURE 5.76**) and becomes the starting point for editing the image in Photoshop.

FIGURE 5.75 This image has a lot of noise due to the high ISO used. © *KE*

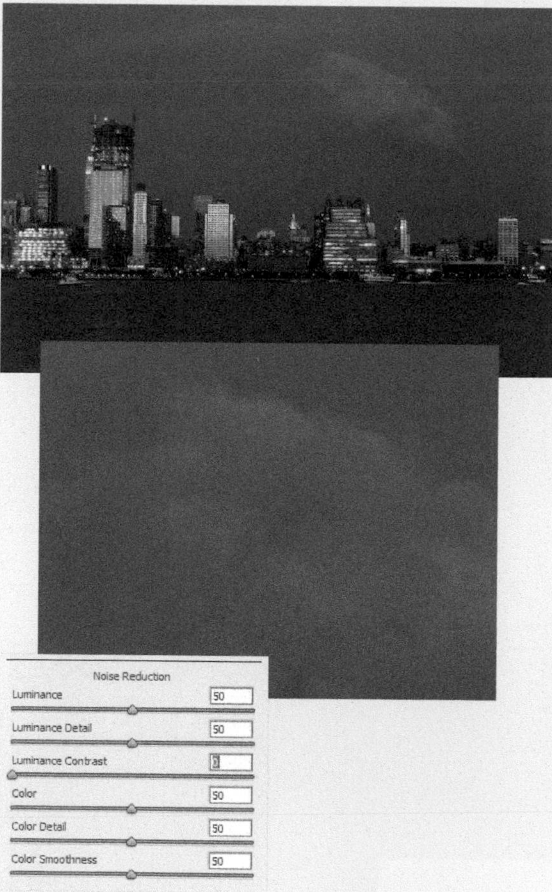

FIGURE 5.76 Using the Noise Reduction options of ACR can minimize the noise.

an entire chapter of providing methods of removing texture and noise from pictures, here is a nondestructive method to put noise or film grain back in (FIGURES 5.77 and 5.78).

1. Open the *spot_repair.psd* image you retouched and saved earlier in this chapter, zoom in, and observe how certain spots of the image show no grain; they look smooth, unlike the rest of the picture.

2. Create a new layer above the topmost layer and set the blending mode to Overlay.

3. Choose **Edit > Fill,** select 50% Gray from the Contents menu, set the blending mode to Normal, set Opacity to 100%, and click OK. The layer is now filled with 50% gray.

4. Choose **Layer > Smart Objects > Convert to Smart Object**, to convert the layer to a Smart Object.

5. Choose Filter > Noise > Add Noise. Drag the Amount slider until the noise size matches the grain in the image. Set Distribution to Uniform, and select the Monochromatic option. Click OK (FIGURE 5.79).

To fully match the grain in the retouched photo, you might need to apply some blur to the noise you've just added.

FIGURES 5.77 and 5.78

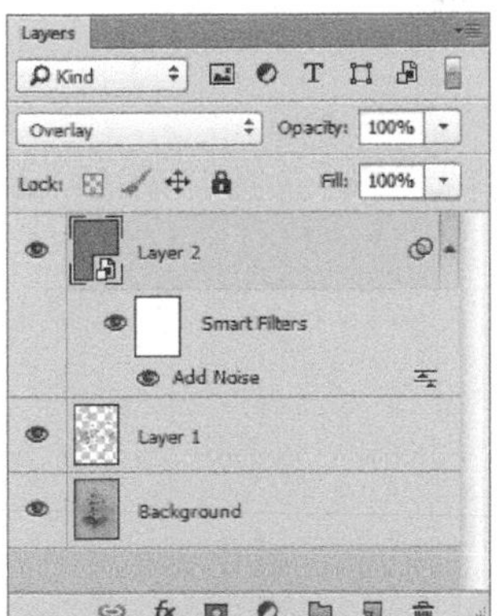

FIGURE 5.79 Simulated grain can be added back with the Add Noise filter.

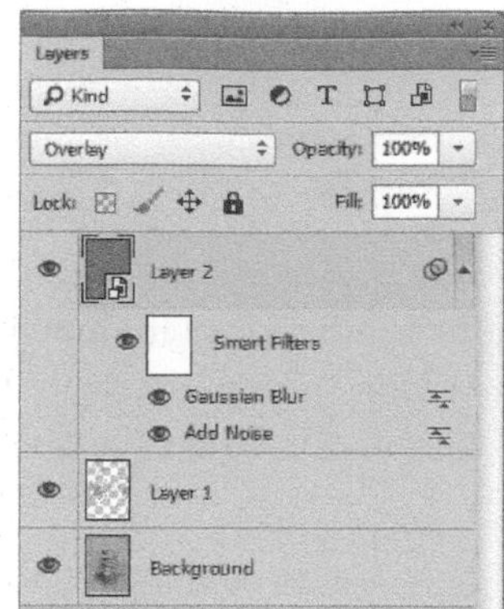

FIGURE 5.80 To reduce the sharpness of the grain, apply the Gaussian Blur filter.

6. Choose **Filter >Blur > Gaussian Blur**. Drag the slider to remove sharp edges on the newly created grain to match the existing grain. Click OK (FIGURE 5.80).

By applying the Noise filter as a Smart Filter, you can return and tweak your grain to be the best match possible, and if you do not want to apply the grain to the entire image, use the masking options within the Smart Filters to refine grain creation.

TIP If the grain is too strong or appears overpowering, use the Opacity slider in the Layers panel to lower the intensity of the grain.

CLOSING THOUGHTS

Removing spots is usually just one part of the image restoration process, and the basics for doing this have been covered in this chapter. Sometimes the work can be a little tedious, as there often is no quick fix to remove spots and it requires the discrimination of a trained eye. Sadly, images all too often face more severe damage. Methods to tackle these issues are explored in the following chapter.

Chapter 6

DAMAGE CONTROL AND REPAIR

We love our photos, and sometimes it seems we love them a bit too much for their own good! We carry them in our wallets, tape them into photo albums, and glue them into frames. All this well-meant mistreatment can cause serious rips, tears, and lost pieces. Additionally, antique documents, such as birth and marriage records, also show fading and wear and tear as they are repeatedly folded and unfolded. In addition to wear-and-tear damage, photos can have unwanted lens distortion and perspective issues caused by the lens used on the camera.

In this chapter, you'll learn to:

- Fix serious rips and tears
- Repair missing parts in images
- Retouch in a perspective plane
- Repair antique documents
- Correct lens distortion and perspective

DAMAGE ASSESSMENT

Before selecting the Clone Stamp tool and setting off to work on an image, review the damage and the repairs to be done and assess which repairs are achievable using Photoshop's repair and retouching tools.

For example, the tintype in FIGURE 6.1 is almost black. A tonal adjustment shows that there's still a face there, but not much else (FIGURE 6.2). When fixing an image, you should replace the damaged areas with image details that are believable. If the image does not contain enough good areas to sample from, the result may not be satisfactory. There will be times when a considerable amount of image restoration fails to show satisfactory improvements. Using the Clone Stamp tool and healing tools to restore damaged spots in pictures, as seen in the previous chapter, works in some areas, but on critical areas, such as a person's face, corrections may change the person's appearance.

When only a limited amount of repair can be done to an image, take a realistic assessment of what a repair might do:

- When it comes to damage to faces, it may be possible to fill in the damage, but replacing or pushing pixels around can make the person in the photo unrecognizable.
- A partial face flipped over to cover damage may repair an image, but the result may not resemble the person in the image.

When restoring images professionally, also consider a client's budget. Some restoration projects may require much more time and effort than the client is willing to pay for. Sometimes, the amount of repair that can be done is limited, but the image still stirs an important memory even if not seen in the image (FIGURE 6.3). Wayne calls these "memory images," as they hold a special meaning for the client even if the image cannot be fully restored.

FIGURE 6.1 This tintype image is nearly black.

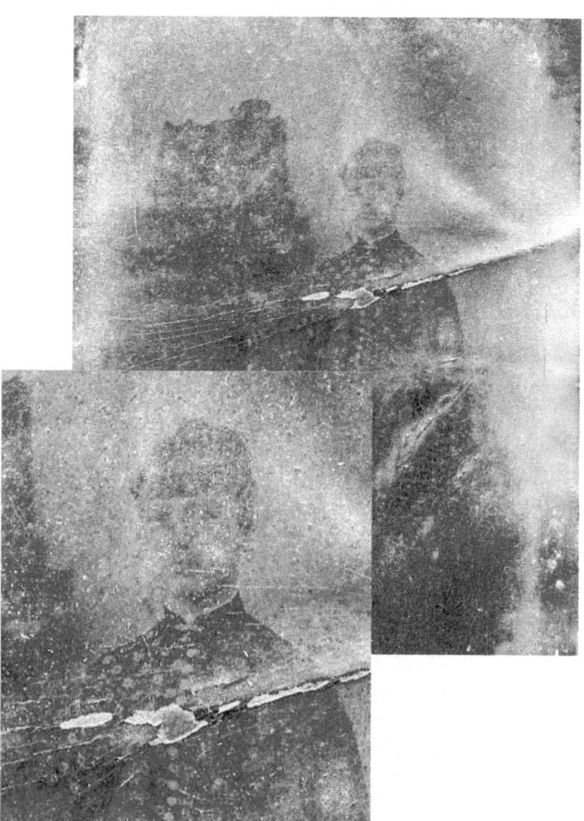

FIGURE 6.2 Tonal corrections reveal that there is still an image, but there is not enough information to make an accurate representation.

Problem Solving

Photo restoration involves problem solving: deciding what tools and steps produce the best result. Discovering what works best for a particular image might take a bit of trial and error.

Some repairs require a creative license. The military picture in FIGURE 6.4 had been rolled up for years; the emulsion cracked in multiple places, running through a number of the individuals' faces. With several of the faces nearly gone and nothing to use for reference, borrowing faces from other locations in the image and putting them into the severely damaged faces results in a restored image, even if it is not historically accurate (FIGURE 6.5).

FIGURE 6.3 This photo was damaged by being kept in a wallet; much can be cleaned up, but the faces are mostly gone.

FIGURE 6.4 This print had been curled up for years and had extensive cracking. Many of the faces are unrecognizable.

FIGURE 6.5 The image was repaired, but liberty was taken with replacing some of the faces.

FIGURE 6.6 This framed image had fallen and had become attached to the glass. *©Smith Family Archive*

FIGURE 6.7 Removal of the glass took longer than the restoration.

FIGURE 6.8 With the amount of damage reduced, the result is more satisfactory.

Sometimes it is approaching things differently. The image in FIGURE 6.6 was stuck to the broken glass, and it looked like it would require quite a lot of time to repair all the lines created by the shattered glass. Wayne used his darkroom experience and soaked the print in warm water for several days to separate the glass from the print, resulting in a new starting image (FIGURE 6.7). The result was much more satisfactory than if all the cracks had to be filled in (FIGURE 6.8).

! CAUTION Before attempting to soak prints attached to glass in water, use extreme caution, have customer permission, have darkroom experience, and ensure you have backup scans of the print. Wayne was able to determine that the paper used for the print was resin-coated, meaning it was sealed by two polyethylene layers and could withstand being submerged. Re-soaking an ordinary fiber-based print will most likely destroy it.

ELIMINATING CRACKS, RIPS, AND TEARS

The image in FIGURE 6.9 had been torn. Fortunately, all the parts were present, and after scanning the parts, the digital puzzle pieces could be put back together and the remaining cracks filled in (FIGURE 6.10).

 **ch6_broken_print.jpg**

Let's walk through the steps for putting this image back together.

1. Select the Lasso tool and draw a selection around the upper-right piece of the broken image. Press Cmd-J/Ctrl-J to copy the selected image piece onto a new layer.

2. Return to the Background layer. Repeat the selection and copy-to-layer steps for the other two pieces (FIGURE 6.11). Make sure you return to the Background layer for each piece before copying the selection to a new layer, to avoid the frustration of trying to copy nothing!

FIGURE 6.9 This image is a digital puzzle. *@Eckhart Family Archive*

FIGURE 6.10 Fortunately, there are no missing pieces and only minor repairs are needed.

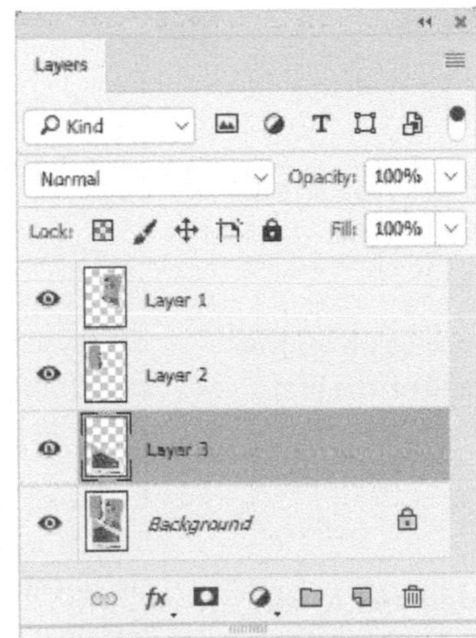

FIGURE 6.11 When selecting the separate pieces, keep the selection away from the image edges to ensure that you copy all the important image information.

3. Turn off the visibility of the Background layer.

The extra information of the scanner bed and remnants from the back of the broken image need to be removed next.

4. Click the upper-right part of the layer to activate it, and select the Magic Wand tool. Set Tolerance to 20, deselect Contiguous in the options bar, and then click the white area outside the image to create a selection (FIGURE 6.12). If the selection isn't correct, choose **Select > Deselect** and adjust the Tolerance level and try again. You can also add to the selection by Shift-clicking areas; subtract from a selection by Alt/Option-clicking areas.

FIGURE 6.12 On each layer, the extra material needs to be removed.

★ NOTE The Magic Wand Tolerance value controls the range of colors that is selected based on the first pixels you click. Higher Tolerance values select more tones and colors, and lower values make smaller, more precise selections.

5. Press Option/Alt and click the Add Layer Mask icon at the bottom of the Layers panel to hide the selection.

6. Repeat steps 4 and 5 for the other two layers (FIGURE 6.13).

+ TIP To hide the selected image area when creating a new layer mask from a selection, Option/Alt-click the Add Layer Mask icon at the bottom of the Layers panel.

FIGURE 6.13 Mask out the information of the scanner bed using a layer mask.

7. To refine the edges of each image piece, select the layer mask for the first part and with a soft-edged brush, paint with black over the edges to hide any remaining unwanted elements and fine-tune the mask. Repeat this step for the other two layers.

8. Select the first layer and choose **Edit > Free Transform** or press Cmd-T/Ctrl-T. Position the cursor outside one of the corner handles to rotate the puzzle piece and straighten it up. Drag the piece into position and press Return/Enter to commit the transformation (FIGURE 6.14).

FIGURE 6.14 Rotate each piece using Free Transform.

9. Repeat the move and transform step for the other two parts. Sometimes changing the stacking order of the layers is helpful to create the best alignment and merging. When finished, a fine crack remains visible between the three parts (FIGURE 6.15).

FIGURE 6.15 Careful arrangement of the three pieces reveals that the damage is not that extensive.

At this point, the information not needed in the final image can be hidden.

10. Select the Crop tool. In the options bar, click Clear to make sure no fixed-size settings are selected, and ensure that Delete Cropped Pixels is unselected to so that the crop doesn't delete pixels but rather hides them. Drag from the upper-left corner of the photo to the lower-right corner, cropping away the outside area and border, and press Return/Enter to apply the crop (FIGURE 6.16).

FIGURE 6.16 Cropping off the outside border reduces the amount of cleanup and repair required.

When working on a complex restoration that has many layers, it can sometimes be difficult to follow all the layers. To make layer management easier, combine all those layers into a new work in progress layer.

11. Select the top layer. Press Cmd-Option-Shift-E/ Ctrl-Alt-Shift-E to merge the three visible layers into a new single layer. Name this layer *WIP* (Work In Progress) (FIGURE 6.17).

TIP The Merge Visible command works well when you want to merge a number of layers. Start by hiding the layers you want to exclude from the merge, then use the keyboard shortcut Cmd-Option-Shift-E/ Ctrl-Alt-Shift-E to merge the visible layers into a single new layer.

FIGURE 6.17 Combining the three layers into a Work in Progress layer simplifies layer management.

12. Create a new empty layer on top of the assembled pieces, and name it *Fixes*. Use the Clone Stamp, Healing Brush, or Spot Healing Brush tool to fill in the thin cracks that remain (FIGURE 6.18). Ensure that the Sample option in the options bar is set to Current & Below or Sample All Layers.

FIGURE 6.18 The repairs are kept on their own separate layer. This keeps them nondestructive and easy to improve on or edit later.

FILLING IN MISSING PARTS

The best restoration results are obtained by using a combination of tools. Learning more about each tool's strengths and weaknesses makes your work expedient. For example, the healing tools work well in areas on which you want to perform touchups that retain texture and lighting, such as spots or blemishes in backgrounds or on faces or clothes. The Clone Stamp tool is better suited when you want to duplicate and retain parts of an image—like a chin line or a coat lapel—that might disappear with the healing tools. The Spot Healing Brush and Healing Brush tools can generate seemingly random and different results based upon which way the brush is stroked.

This image with a missing top piece can be repaired by repeating information already in the image (FIGURES 6.19 and 6.20).

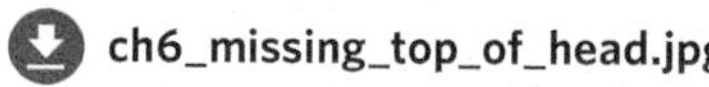
ch6_missing_top_of_head.jpg

1. Use the Quick Selection tool to create a selection of the missing top section. Paint with the tool over the area you want to select. Option/Alt-click the Add Layer Mask icon in the Layers panel to hide the selected area. The Background layer is automatically unlocked and renamed Layer 0 (FIGURE 6.21).

FIGURE 6.19 The top piece of this image was missing.
©Piper Family Archives

FIGURE 6.20 Straightforward cloning was used to rebuild most of the image information.

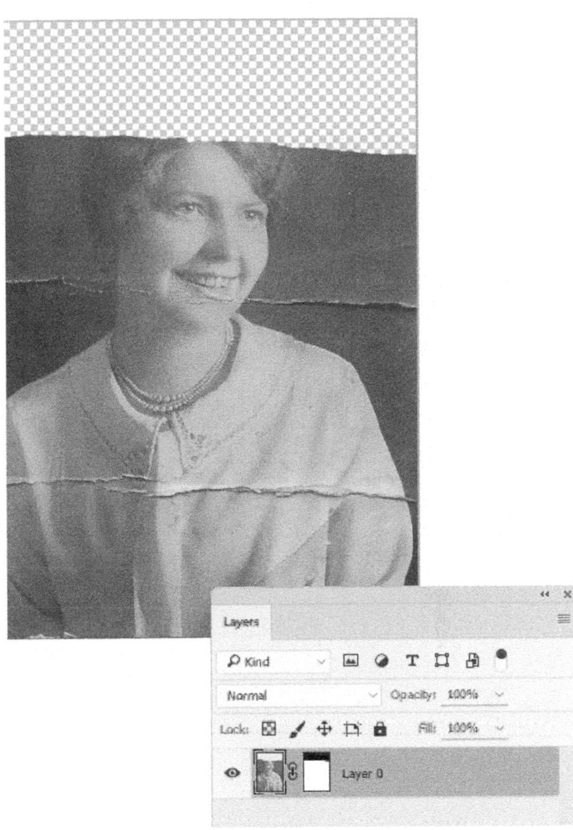

FIGURE 6.21 Use a mask to hide the section that needs to be replaced.

TIP To increase or decrease the brush size on the Quick Selection tool, tap the right or left bracket keys. To remove parts from the selection, press Option/Alt and paint over the areas. To add parts to the selection, press Shift and paint over the areas.

2. Create a new empty layer and name it *fixes*.

3. The healing tools could disturb or remove the lines of the chin, the lip, and the edge of the blouse. Use the Clone Stamp tool to repair the cracks around those areas, with Sample in the options bar set to Current & Below (FIGURE 6.22). Then use a small Spot Healing Brush tool set to Sample All Layers to clean up the remaining cracks or telltale clone patterns.

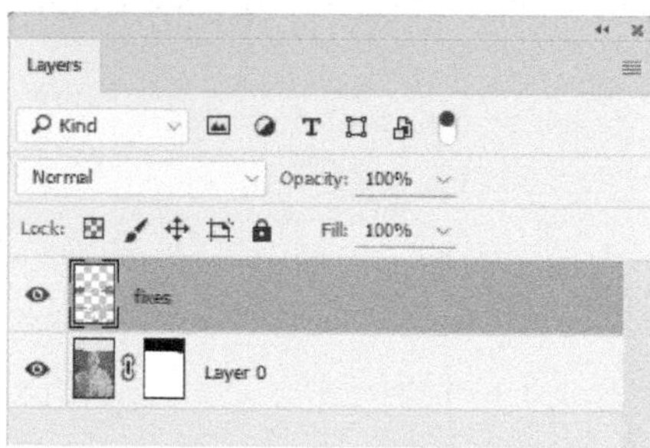

FIGURE 6.22 Put the repairs on their own layer to work nondestructively.

4. Create a new empty layer below Layer 0 and name it *fill in background.*

5. Select the Clone Stamp tool, and set the Sample option to All Layers in the options bar. Sample the area to the right of the woman's face, and with the Aligned option deselected, to ensure the sample area is the same for each brush stroke, paint in missing the backdrop (FIGURE 6.23).

6. Once the missing section is filled in, look for any repeating patterns and use the Spot Healing Brush tool to conceal them.

The most challenging part of this image is creating the remainder of the woman's head.

FIGURE 6.23 Fill in the missing areas by cloning from good sections.

7. Create a new empty layer, named *head top*, above the fixes layer. With the Lasso tool, create a selection in the shape of her hair (this will be filled in with Photoshop hair in the next step) (FIGURE 6.24).

FIGURE 6.24 With the Lasso tool, create a selection that will define where the head should be.

8. With the Clone Stamp tool, carefully sample the patterns in the hair and fill in the selection until the head is complete.

★ NOTE Using a selection constrains the area you can use Clone Stamp tool in, thereby protecting the areas outside the selection.

✚ TIP To get the best result with the Clone Stamp tool, use the Clone Source panel (**Window > Clone Source**) to change the angle or size of the clone source as you paint.

9. Choose **Select > Deselect** and, with the Blur tool with blending mode set to Darken in the options bar and Sample All Layers selected, smooth the edges where the hair blends into the background (FIGURE 6.25).

For the final touchups, it's again easier to work with all the layers merged into a WIP layer.

FIGURE 6.25 Clone the head fill-in on its own layer and blur the edges.

10. Select the top layer, and press Cmd-Option-Shift-E/Ctrl-Alt-Shift-E to merge the layers into a single layer. Name the layer *WIP*. Create a new empty layer above the WIP layer and name it *more fixes*.

11. With the Spot Healing Brush tool set to Content-Aware and Sample All Layers selected in the options bar, paint over the streaks and uneven areas in the image to smooth these areas out (FIGURE 6.26).

FIGURE 6.26 A few final touchups are needed with the Healing Brush tool. Keep changes on separate layers so edits can be undone.

As a final correction, we'll remove the yellow color cast, which ages the image, and enhance the contrast to add a bit of visual pop.

12. Add a Black & White adjustment layer, accepting the default setting, to return the print to its original black and white appearance.

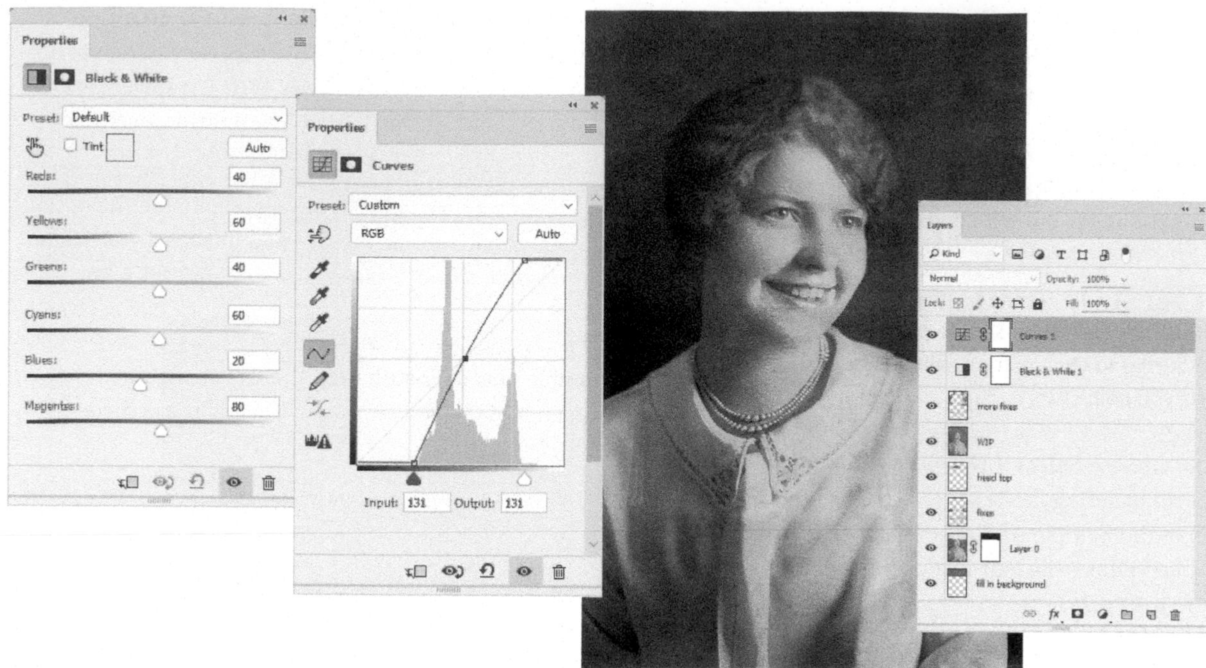

FIGURE 6.27 Adding Black & White and Curves adjustment layers to apply the final tonal adjustments breathes life back into the image.

13. Add a Curves adjustment layer, and drag the black and white points toward the ends of the histogram to increase the contrast. Add a point to the middle of the curve and drag it up to increase the brightness (FIGURE 6.27).

Cloning, Healing, and Recycling

Over time, photos are exposed to changes in temperature and humidity, and they suffer dirt, dust, mold, or light exposure, all of which lead to image deterioration. Framing images behind glass is one way to help them last longer. Unfortunately, if a photograph is behind glass without the inclusion of a mat or spacer, it can stick to the glass, as was the case with this image (FIGURE 6.28). It was damaged even further once it was separated from the glass.

It is a message worth repeating: It often takes a combination of tools to perform a satisfactory restoration. To repair this image required copying and pasting of its parts, combined with careful cloning and healing (FIGURE 6.29).

 **ch6_couple_on_sailboat.jpg**

There is no easy way around it—roll up your sleeves, zoom in to 100% (or higher if you are working on a high resolution display), and use the Navigator panel to keep track of the area you are repairing as you work methodically through the image.

1. Add a new empty layer, named *Fixes*.

2. Use the Clone Stamp tool, with Sample set to Current & Below, to clone over the easier sections of the sky and water on the left side of the image.

3. Use the Healing Brush tool, with Sample All Layers set in the options bar and Aligned selected, to retouch the additional sections onto the empty layer, even filling the areas of the missing shrouds (ropes used on a sailboat), which is addressed in step 4. When done, the empty layer is far from empty, as about a third of the image is replaced (FIGURE 6.30).

FIGURES 6.28 and 6.29 Before and after.
©Claster Family Archive

FIGURE 6.30 This is the major amount of necessary repair, shown on its own layer.

Use the Healing Brush tool to touch up areas that do not contain significant details, such as the sky and the scratches on the clothing. The direction in which you paint controls what type of information is used to touch up the damaged areas. If you don't see the desired result, undo the last brush stroke and paint in a different direction or resample from a different location. Use the Clone Stamp tool for more specific areas, such as the face and shoreline.

The shrouds (ropes) were missing in the area over the couple's head. Fortunately, there is enough material on an undamaged section with which to complete the repair.

4. Use the Polygonal Lasso tool to make a tight selection over a section of the rope, as seen in FIGURE 6.31.

With the Polygonal Lasso tool, click each of the four corners of the area to be reused. If your point is not where you want it, press Delete to undo the last click. Press Escape to remove the selection if you need to start over. Remember to complete the selection by returning to the point of origin.

FIGURE 6.31 The Polygonal Lasso tool makes a precise selection of the rope to be reused.

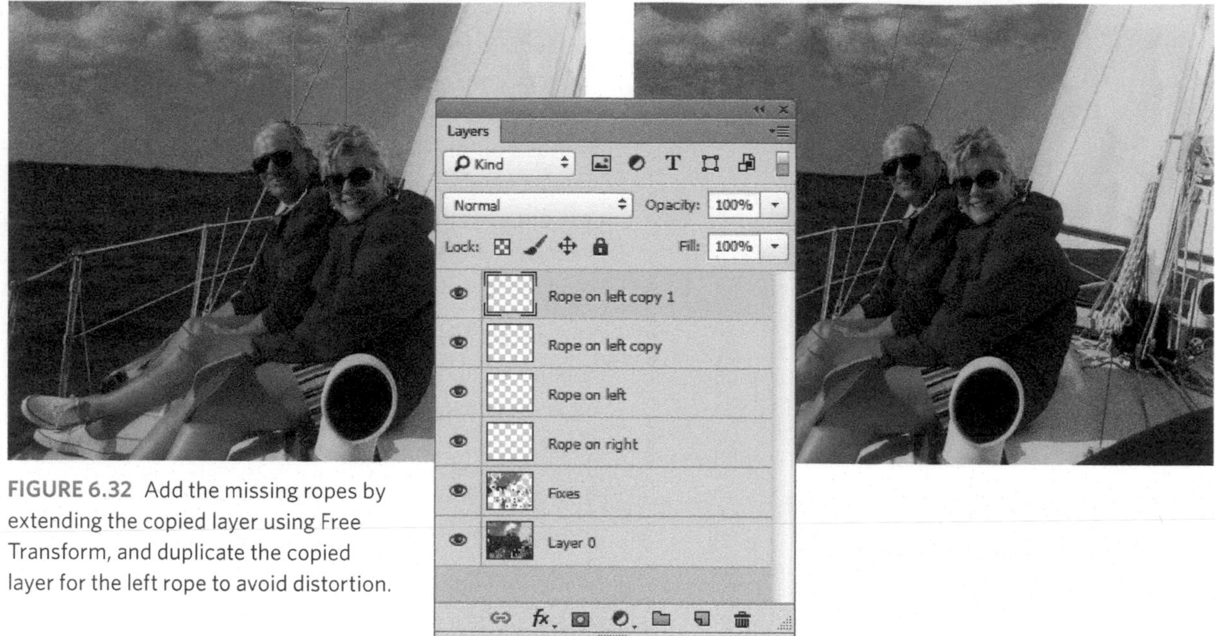

FIGURE 6.32 Add the missing ropes by extending the copied layer using Free Transform, and duplicate the copied layer for the left rope to avoid distortion.

5. With the selection active, click the Background layer and press Cmd-J/Ctrl-J to copy the selection into a new layer named *Rope on right*. Position the layer above the Fixes layer.

6. Use the Move tool to drag the rope into place above the man's head. The rope is a little short of reaching the edge of the image. With the Free Transform tool, press Cmd-T/Ctrl-T extend the rope to the edge of the picture.

7. Repeat the steps 4–6 for the rope on the left, naming the layer *Rope on left.* Instead of stretching the rope using Free Transform, which would result in distortion because of the extent the rope needs to be stretched, duplicate the rope on left layer twice and reposition the sections to run to the edge of the image (FIGURE 6.32).

To make the image level, straighten the horizon.

8. Merge all the layers into a new layer at the top of the stack (press Cmd-Option-Shift-E/Ctrl-Alt-Shift-E), and name the layer *Straightened.*

9. With the Ruler tool (hidden under the Eyedropper tool in the Tools panel), drag a line along the water's edge to establish the horizon. In the options bar, click Straighten Layer. Turn off the visibility of the lower layers, which reveals that there is information missing in the four corners.

TIP To hide all layers except the Straightened layer, Option/Alt-click the eye icon of the Straightened layer.

10. Duplicate the Straightened layer and name it *Filled in corners.* A crop would be a quick fix but would also cut down the size of the image and remove most of the woman's legs. Fill in the corners by choosing **Edit > Transform > Warp**. Click a corner handle and drag it outward and away from the outside edge so the image covers the gap created by straightening. Repeat the steps for the other three corners (FIGURE 6.33).

11. Finally, the image is a little flat in contrast. Add a Levels adjustment layer above all the other layers, and click Auto to give it a little boost (FIGURE 6.34).

It might be easier to leave the ropes out of the image, but sometimes attention to detail can make a restoration better.

TIP Use the arrow keys within the Move tool to precisely nudge an object into proper placement.

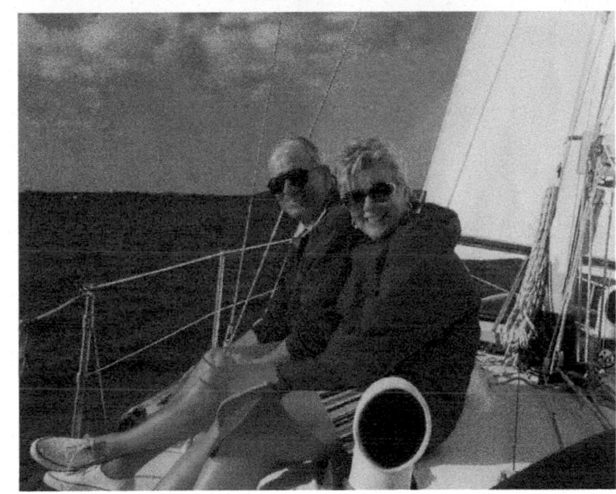

FIGURE 6.33 Use the Ruler tool to level the horizon, and fill in the corners with Free Transform using the Warp option.

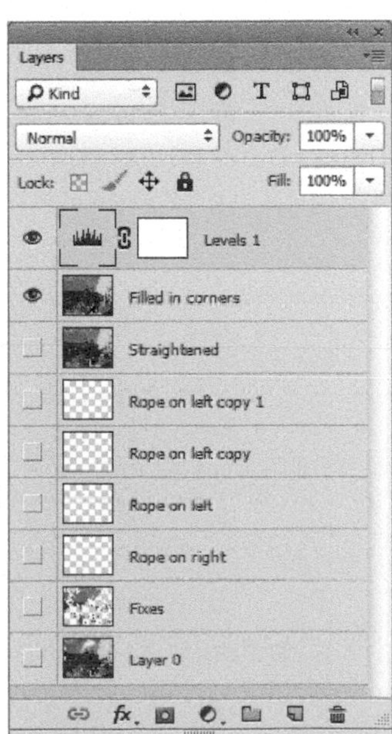

FIGURE 6.34 An Auto Levels adjustment brightens up the flat look.

MAKE WORKING WITH LAYERS EASIER

There may be times when the number of layers in a project is overwhelming (**FIGURE 6.35**). There are several ways to tackle this issue.

One is to put layers into groups, which is like creating folders for multiple layers (**FIGURE 6.36**). Click the Create a New Group icon at the bottom of the Layers panel. Layers can then be dragged into the folder. The group can be expanded or contracted, revealing the contents, by clicking the triangle next to the folder icon. Name the groups for easier identification, as you would layers.

Another method is to filter layers so you see only those layers that match the selected filter type. For example, you can filter layers based on their name, the kind of layer (adjustment, type, shape, etc.), or the blending mode that's applied.

Wayne likes filtering layers he is actively working on: He starts by selecting the layers in the Layers panel he wants to isolate, then clicks the Turn Layer Filtering On/Off icon at the top of the Layers panel to enable the filter. From the filter menu he then chooses Selected. Click the Turn Layer Filtering On/Off icon once more to return the visibility of all layers (**FIGURE 6.37**).

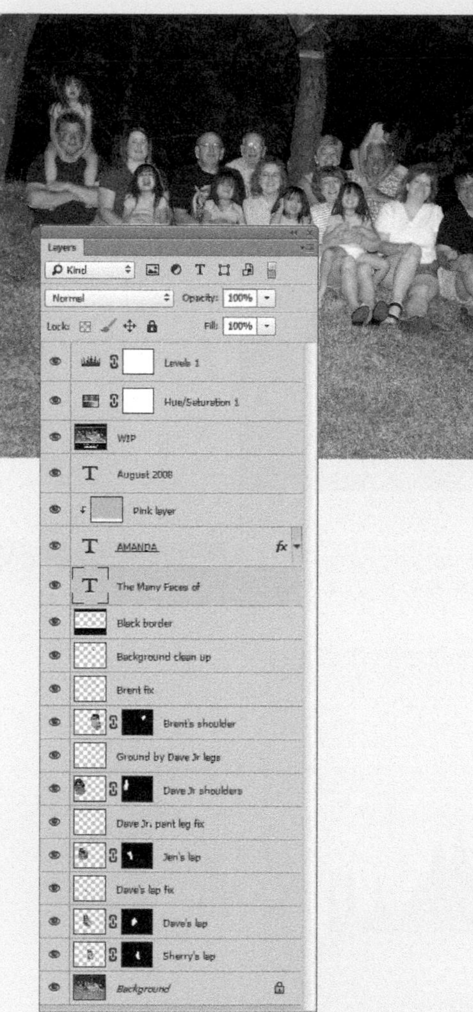

FIGURE 6.35 Sometimes the number of layers is overwhelming. ©*WP*

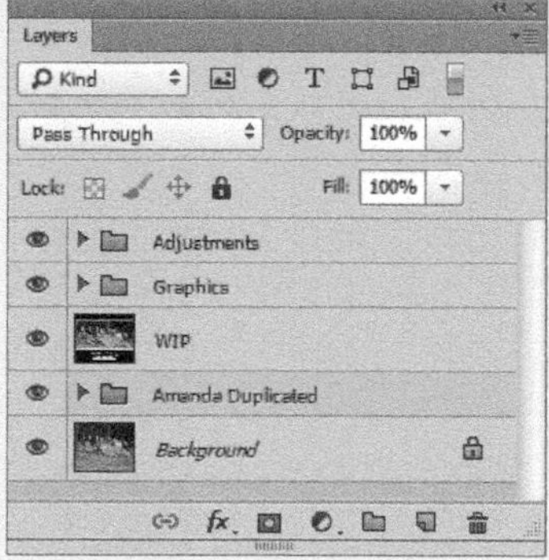

FIGURE 6.36 Layers can be bundled together in groups; select the layers and click the folder icon.

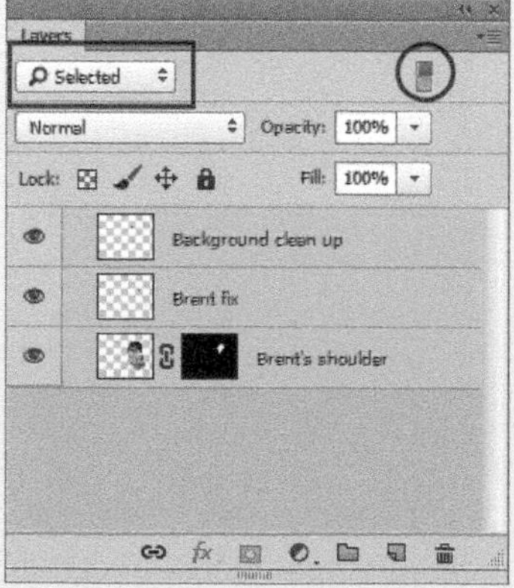

FIGURE 6.37 Selecting only the layers desired for edit and choosing Selected hides all other layers. Clicking the on/off button returns the visibility of the hidden layers.

Patch Tool

The Patch tool is best used to repair or replace larger, less important image areas such as backdrops, walls, and skies. The Patch tool works in two different modes, as selected in the options bar:

- **Normal** requires pixel information to work and matches texture, lighting, and shading with the adjacent areas. To work nondestructively, make sure to work on a duplicate layer.

- **Content-Aware** has the added benefit of allowing you to work on an empty layer (when Sample all Layers is selected in the options bar), and it works well in most cases. Content-Aware also adds two options: Structure, which controls how strongly patterns are matched, and Color, which controls how much the color is blended.

A higher Structure value matches the patterns in the original image more and works better when retaining patterns is important. A lower value creates a softer result. A higher Color value retains more of the patched area's color, giving a smoother transition between the patched area and the rest of the image. For the best result you'll likely need to experiment with these settings. Although Content-Aware mode works nicely in most cases, including when matching patterns, there might be times when blurring of the patched area edges gives an unsatisfactory result. In that case, undo the patch and use Normal mode instead. In Content-Aware mode, use the Patch tool to select the area to patch, and then drag the selection to the replacement area.

To repair an area in Content-Aware mode, use the Patch tool to select the area, drag that selection to an area that would be a good replacement, and release the mouse. Choose **Select > Deselect**.

In Normal mode there are two ways to work with the Patch tool:

- Select Source in the options bar, use the Patch tool to select an area you need to repair, and then drag that selection to an area that would be a good replacement. This is similar to how Content-Aware mode works.

- Select Destination to work in the opposite manner. First select an area that would make a good patch, and then drag it over the area to be replaced.

Let's jump in and take the Patch tool for a spin to see how it works on a real-world image. This image suffers from multiple stains but can be fixed easily with the Patch tool and a final touchup with the Healing brush (FIGURE 6.38). The idea behind the Patch tool is to drag good areas to bad areas or vice versa, but it appears this image has only bad areas. However, you can use the Healing brush tool first to create good source material for the Patch tool to work with (FIGURE 6.39).

FIGURE 6.38 This image looks like it needs a lot of time for repair. *@Palmer Family Archives*

FIGURE 6.39 The Patch tool makes fast work of the stains.

ch6_patch_example.jpg

1. Duplicate the Background layer.

This image does not have a good area to use as a sample for a patch, but one can be made by first healing a small area.

2. Select the Spot Healing Brush tool and set the blending mode to Lighten in the options bar. In the upper-right corner of the image, paint in a circular area that is large enough to be used for a sample patch (FIGURE 6.40).

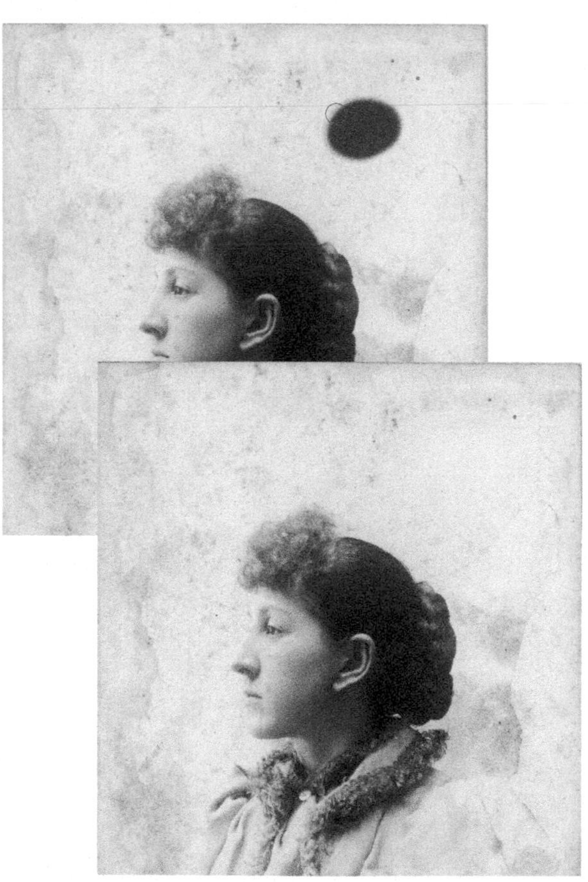

FIGURE 6.40 Use the Spot Healing Brush set to Lighten mode to clean up a small area.

3. Select the Patch tool, set mode to Normal, and click Destination in the options bar. Drag (similar to using the Lasso tool) around the repaired area from step 2, and then use the Patch tool to drag the selected area to a stained area (FIGURES 6.41 and 6.42).

FIGURE 6.41 Use the cleaned area as the starting sample for the Patch tool.

FIGURE 6.42 The fixed area is dragged over an area that needs to be cleaned up.

4. Repeat the process throughout the rest of the background, being careful not to have the patch affect the woman or her dress (FIGURE 6.43).

+ TIP If the Patch tool leaves smudges or noticeable changes, try increasing the Diffusion setting in the options bar, which widens the area being patched and creates a better blend.

FIGURE 6.43 Repeatedly dragging the clean patch cleans up the background.

★ NOTE The patch tool will generate a different result each time the patch is moved and thus avoids creating a noticeable pattern buildup. If the patch moves outside the image, it is clipped creating a straight line that will produce a noticeable pattern if the patch is used again. When this happens, make a new selection for the patch.

5. There are some lines that would be desirable to keep in the woman's dress. Switch the option for the Patch tool to Source, select the undamaged area of the fold, and drag down over the damaged area. Notice that the Patch tool retains the line and gets rid of the stain (FIGURE 6.44).

With the background cleaned up, all that's left to finish this repair are some minor dust spots on the woman.

6. Create a new empty layer. Select the Spot Healing Brush tool, set it to Darken and Sample All Layers (in the options bar), and brush over the light spots.

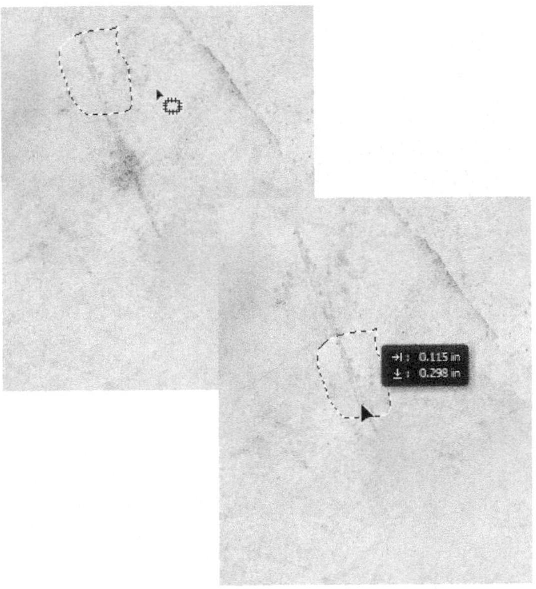

FIGURE 6.44 The Patch tool can also be used to replicate information. The patch keeps the line in the blouse while removing other stains.

Content-Aware Move Tool

The Content-Aware Move tool is useful to move or duplicate an object in an image. To use the tool, start by drawing around the object to be moved, then drag it to its new location. With Mode set to Move in the options bar, the previous location of the object in the photo is filled in. With Mode set to Extend, the object is duplicated in its new location.

ch6_three_in_chairs.jpg

This image was taken to demonstrate the angle of view encompassed by a panoramic camera. Using the Content-Aware Move tool, you can move the subjects closer together, allowing you to crop the image to a common print size (FIGURES 6.45 and 6.46).

1. Duplicate the Background layer.

2. Select the Content-Aware Move tool, set Mode to Move in the options bar, set Structure to 7 and Color to 0 (for minimal color blending), and select Transform On Drop. This option allows you to rotate or scale the part of the image you are moving before committing the move. The Structure and Color options are similar to the Patch tool.

FIGURE 6.45 Using the Content-Aware Move tool, the people can be brought closer together. @WP

FIGURE 6.46 The final crop presents an aspect ratio more suited to printing the image.

This tool has the option to work on an empty layer with Sample All Layers selected in the options bar. However, for this image Wayne achieved better results by using a duplicate layer.

3. Drag around the woman, including the shadow, to create a selection (FIGURE 6.47).

TIP When moving subjects, make a generous selection. The Content-Aware Move tool works better when extra background is included to complete its blend. A tight selection could result in a thin outline appearing in the previous location of the subject.

4. Position the cursor inside the selection and drag the woman closer to the man in the middle. Be careful not to overlap any material you would want to keep.

A transformation bounding box appears around the selection after you've moved it.

5. Move the cursor outside one of the corners and rotate the selection a little so that the edge of the lawn lines up better. Press Return/Enter to apply the transformation (FIGURE 6.48).

6. Choose **Select > Deselect** to deselect the selection (FIGURE 6.49).

FIGURE 6.47 A generous selection is made of the person on the left.

FIGURE 6.48 Before accepting the move, the person can be rotated.

FIGURE 6.49 After accepting the move, the original location is filled in.

FIGURE 6.50 There are areas where the blending is noticeable.

FIGURE 6.51 Touchups with the healing tools help to hide the imperfections and only need to be made in the areas of the image that will not be cropped.

7. Repeat steps 2 to 6 for the person on the right.

The result may not be perfect, but it's a good start (FIGURE 6.50).

8. Apply a few touchups with the Healing Brush tool to remove any obvious patch jobs in the image. Work only on the edges around the subjects, as that is what will be in the final image (FIGURE 6.51).

9. Finally, use the Crop tool to crop the image to 6 x 4 aspect ratio. Select Ratio from the Preset Aspect Ratio or Crop Size menu in the options bar, and enter 6 and 4 for the ratio settings (FIGURE 6.52).

The Content-Aware Move tool works best for solid or easy-to-duplicate backgrounds when a quick fix is needed.

Perspective Healing with Vanishing Point Filter

Repairing images showing perspective changes is challenging. When the spatial arrangement of the picture changes due to perspective, normal cloning and healing cannot accommodate for this. The Vanishing Point filter is able adjust cloning and healing in perspective after a perspective plane is defined.

FIGURE 6.52 The areas around the moved people are all that need to be touched up as the image is being cropped.

FIGURE 6.53 This old building had a number of windows bricked in. @*WP*

FIGURE 6.54 Healing in perspective makes it easy to put them back.

This image of an old building where windows have been filled with brick is a good example to demonstrate the power of this filter and its tools. Wayne used the information from the one complete window to replace the bricked-up windows (**FIGURES 6.53** and **6.54**).

ch6_vanishing_point_example.jpg

1. Create a new empty layer to work nondestructively.

2. Choose **Filter > Vanishing Point** or press Cmd-Option-V/Ctrl-Alt-V.

The first step is to establish the perspective plane so that the Vanishing Point tools can use the correct perspective.

3. Use the Create Plane tool to define the four corners of the perspective plane. Click the lower-left corner of the large center window. Then click the upper-left corner of the top window. Click in the upper-right corner of that window and then in the lower-left corner. A blue grid should appear (**FIGURE 6.55**).

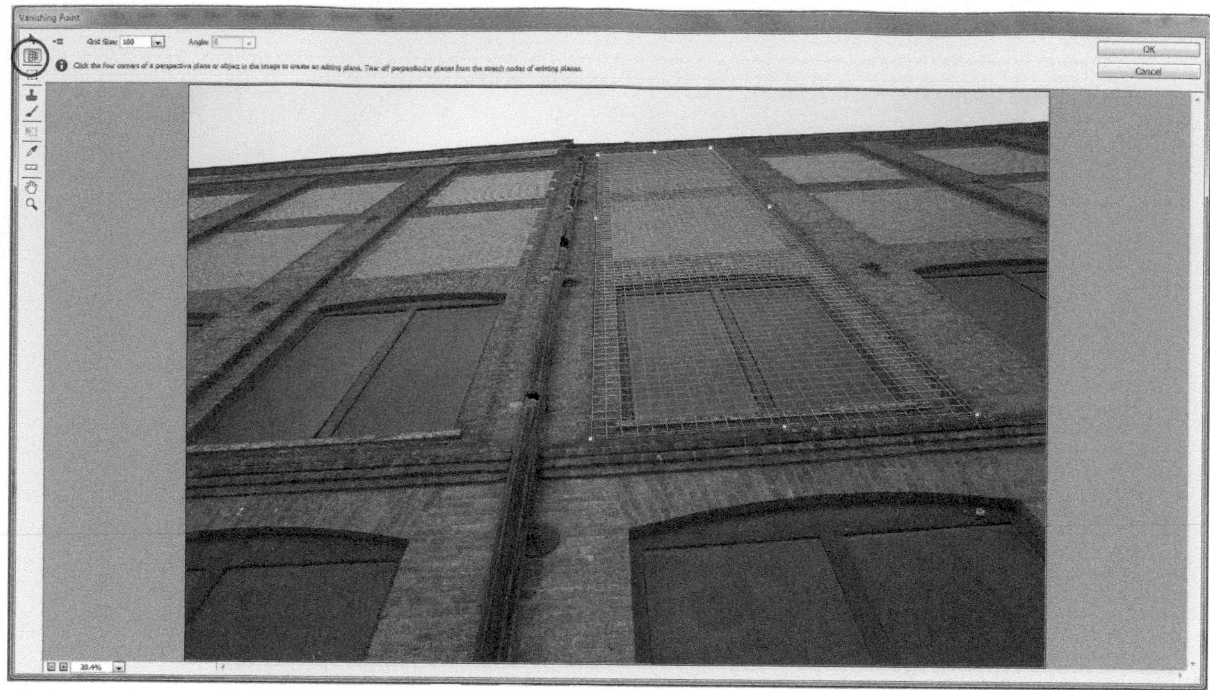

FIGURE 6.55 The Vanishing Point filter needs a perspective plane to establish how the Vanishing Point tools replace material.

A blue grid means the perspective is a valid perspective. A yellow grid means that you are close but need to make minor adjustments; if it is red, you need to make major adjustments or start over. Drag the corners of the grid to make adjustments to the perspective.

★ NOTE The Vanishing Point tools work even if the perspective plane is not blue, but the results will not be satisfactory unless the plane accurately reflects the perspective in the image.

+ TIP Use the Zoom tool to zoom in to the corners to position the handles more precisely. Double-click the Hand tool to fit the image in the Vanishing Point dialog box window again.

+ TIP Use the Delete/Backspace key to delete a grid.

4. With the plane still active, select the Edit Plane tool (black arrow), and drag the middle control handles on the left, right, and bottom off the grid to expand it across the entire image. If needed, press Cmd--/Ctlr-- to zoom out. It is OK for the grid to extend outside the image (FIGURE 6.56).

+ TIP Click inside the plane with the Edit Plane tool to select it if it's no longer active.

5. Select the Stamp tool. Set Diameter to 500 pixels, Opacity to 100%, and Healing to Off, and select Aligned. This tool works similarly to the Clone Stamp tool. Option/Alt-click to sample from the corner of the lowest full window.

6. Position the cursor in the same position in the bricked-in window above, and paint until the window brick is gone. Note that the brush won't appear as a circle because it now paints in perspective and is therefore squashed to match the perspective grid (FIGURE 6.57).

7. Return and sample again from the same point, and fill in the brick in the window above that. Repeat the process for the remaining bricked-in windows. Press the bracket keys to increase or decrease the brush

FIGURE 6.56 Once a grid has been established on a small area, it can be enlarged to take in the whole image.

FIGURE 6.57 The brick area can be filled in by starting to clone in the same relative position as the sample was taken from.

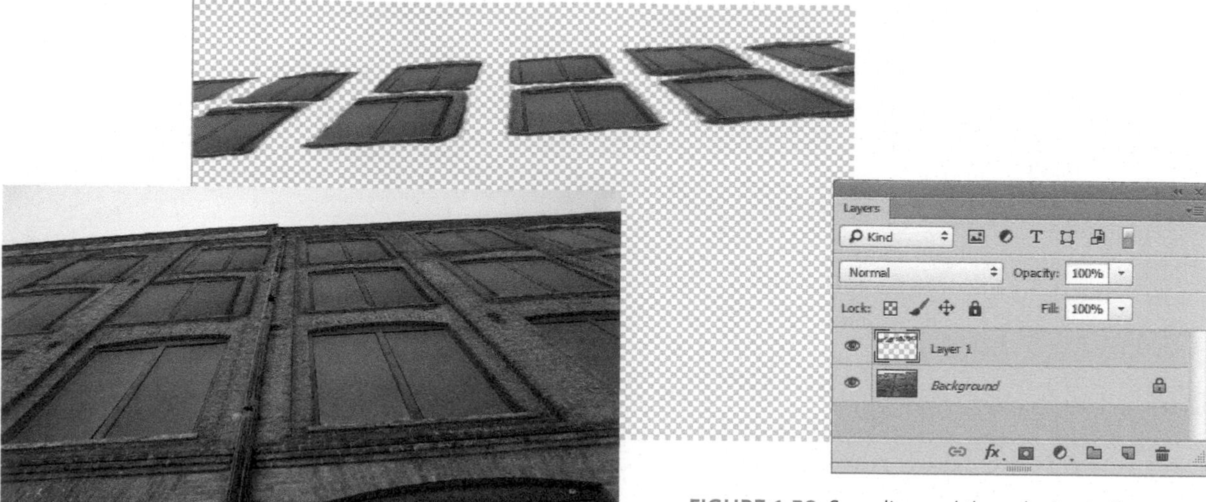

FIGURE 6.58 Sampling and then cloning in the same relative position makes filling in the brick easy.

diameter. When the lower-left corner is missing for bricked-in windows, sample from the right corner, and be sure to start cloning in the same relative position.

8. When complete, click OK. All the changes reside on a separate layer, making the whole process nondestructive—sweet (FIGURE 6.58)!

Content-Aware Fill

Have you ever waited for a person to get out of a scene you wanted to photograph? You may not have to. Content-Aware Fill can make removing people a cinch. It is such a valuable time saver that Wayne has made it his go-to feature for a lot of restoration work.

Content-Aware Fill, combined with a selection, can be one the easiest ways to remove something and simultaneously fill in a section of a photo.

Let's see how fast this feature can empty a crowded tourist attraction (FIGURES 6.59 and 6.60).

ch6_tourist_spot.jpg

1. One of the limitations of this feature is that it is destructive, so duplicate the Background layer. Start by making a selection around what you want to remove, including some of the background pixels outside the object.

2. Each person can be removed individually, but in this image it is possible to remove them all at once. Use the Lasso tool to draw a selection around each person in the image. Press Shift to add to an existing selection.

3. Choose **Edit > Fill**, and ensure that Contents is set to Content-Aware, Blending Mode to Normal, and Opacity to 100%. Click OK. It is that simple (FIGURE 6.61).

TIP If the results are not satisfactory, consider using the Content-Aware Fill command on the same area multiple times. The results vary each time. Additionally, if the command gives a partial result, make smaller selections each time for areas that still need further retouching, and repeat the command until you get the best result.

TIP To apply Content-Aware Fill to a selection, press Shift-Delete/Shift-Backspace to launch the Fill command. Check that Contents is set to Content-Aware, and press Return/Enter.

FIGURE 6.59 This scenic spot can be emptied with Content-Aware Fill. *@John Troisi*

FIGURE 6.60 Content-Aware Fill does a remarkable job of filling in areas.

TIP You can use a layer mask to define areas that Content-Aware Fill should not use for source material. See blogs.adobe.com/jkost/2017/04/content-aware-fill-control-the-source-in-photoshop-cc.html

FIGURE 6.61 Make a selection of what to fill in. Choose Content-Aware from the Contents menu.

SPOT HEALING BRUSH TOOL OR CONTENT-AWARE FILL

Picking the right tools for the job is something that you'll learn with experience. The power line in **FIGURE 6.62** is easy to remove where the line crosses the sky, but where it crosses over the building proves to be more of a challenge, as there are multiple patterns to maintain while getting rid of the wire. Photoshop offers multiple ways to tackle a problem. The Spot Healing Brush tool offers the option of working nondestructively on a separate layer. Content-Aware Fill can accomplish the same task, often in fewer steps, but needs to be performed on a duplicate layer to be nondestructive. Wayne's strategy for some images is to just work on a duplicate layer so he can switch back and forth between the two tools. If part of the image needs to be returned to its original state, it can be copy/pasted back in from the lower layer. Try the steps in the two methods listed below and compare the results (**FIGURE 6.63**).

 **ch6_old_north_church.jpg**

To use the Spot Healing Brush tool:

1. Click the start point with the brush.
2. Press Shift and click the end point to draw a straight line.
3. Repeat this for different sections of the power line until it is removed

FIGURES 6.62 An annoying cable blocks our view of Old North Church in Boston. ©*WP*

FIGURE 6.63 After using the Spot Healing Brush tool to remove the cable.

To use Content-Aware Fill:

1. With the Quick Mask tool option set to Color Indicates Selected Area, paint over the power line with a hard edged brush wide enough to cover the line.

2. Exit Quick Mask

3. Press Shift and Backspace to open the Fill dialog box. Select Content Aware and click OK. (**FIGURE 6.64**).

FIGURE 6.64 Returning to the same image of Old North Church, we find that Content-Aware Fill makes easy work of removing the power line.

FIGURE 6.65 This image cracked and split over time.
@Houser Family Archives

FIGURE 6.66 The tools presented in this chapter can tackle the job, along with a little patience.

Putting It All Together

The major tools for repairing damage have been covered, and as stated several times it may take a combination of all of them to restore a photo. This poor image was glued to a backing that did not expand and contract, causing the print to crack and split over the years (FIGURES 6.65 and 6.66).

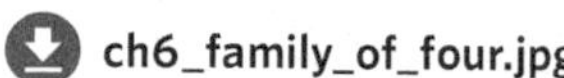

TRY IT With the tools covered so far, try to repair this image. In the detailed facial areas, use the Clone Stamp tool and the healing tools on the clothing and background. Try using the Patch tool with Content-Aware mode enabled to fix some of the wood paneling in the background; once you have a section fixed you can use it as a source to fix other parts. Content-Aware Fill might work well on patching some of the sections in the man's shirt.

DOCUMENT REPAIR

Part of our family heritage is the recording of major events, not only with images but with certificates and paper records. Birth, baptism, graduation, wedding, and even death certificates can be part of a family's legacy.

Faded Text on a Document

This letter (FIGURE 6.67) had a lot of sentimental meaning for one of Wayne's clients, and the text had severely faded. The result (FIGURE 6.68) was achieved by reconstructing the document and doing the old grade school activity of tracing.

Wayne's first thoughts were that some tonal corrections would be all that were needed. He added a Curves adjustment layer and tried to enhance the contrast in the letters by moving the black point to

FIGURE 6.67 The text in this document faded with age. *@Ogurcak Family Archives*

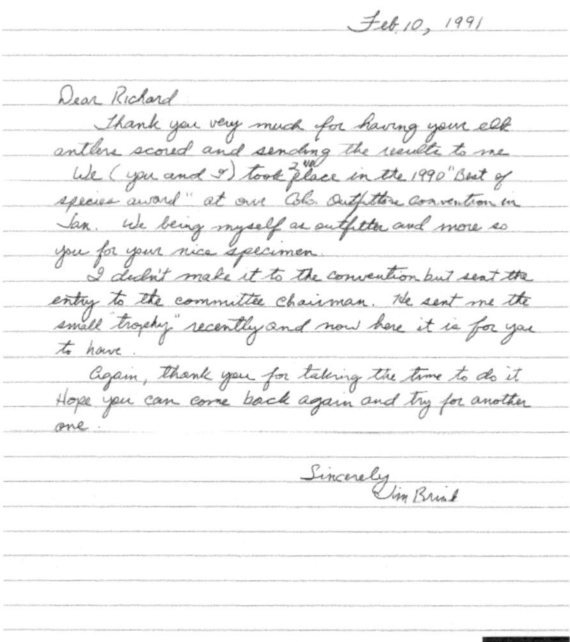

Feb 10, 1991

Dear Richard

Thank you very much for having your elk antlers scored and sending the results to me.

We (you and I) took 4th place in the 1990 "Best of species award" at our Colo. Outfitters Convention in Jan. We being myself as outfitter and more so you for your nice specimen.

I didn't make it to the convention but sent the entry to the committee chairman. He sent me the small "trophy" recently and now here it is for you to have.

Again, thank you for taking the time to do it. Hope you can come back again and try for another one.

Sincerely

Jim Brink

FIGURE 6.68 Digitally tracing over the text made for a good reproduction.

the start of the image information in the histogram. However, although adjusting the dark tones brought up the lettering, it also revealed the imperfections in the paper (FIGURE 6.69).

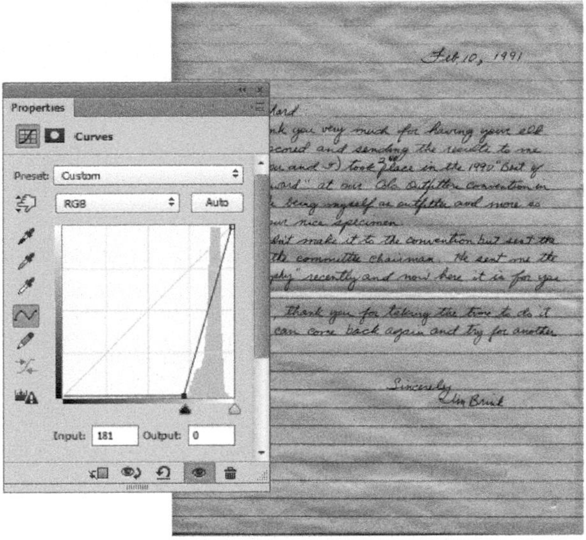

FIGURE 6.69 The Curves dialog shows how little tonal information there is to work with. Adjusting the dark tones brought up the lettering but also the imperfections in the paper.

To counterbalance this he brightened the paper by dragging the white point to the left, which resulted in the text becoming less legible (FIGURE 6.70).

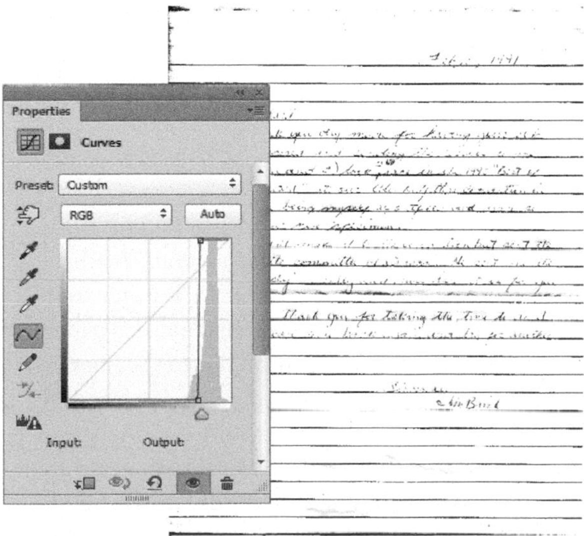

FIGURE 6.70 Brightening the paper made the text less legible.

The result was unsatisfactory. When the text was adjusted to become readable, the paper became too dark and noticeable. When the paper was adjusted to become white, the text was no longer as legible. And either adjustment removed the blue from the lines in the paper.

Wayne concluded it would be faster to re-create the document than to try to fix all the problems produced with tonal adjustments. He created an empty layer, named it *traced text,* and set the Pencil tool size to the same width as the text on the page. With the foreground color set to black, he traced the faded letters using a stylus on a drawing tablet (**FIGURE 6.71**).

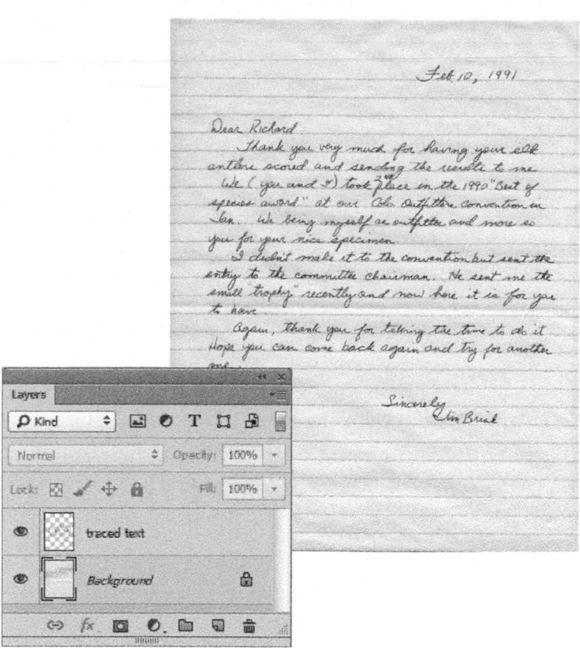

Feb. 10, 1991

Dear Richard

Thank you very much for having your elk antlers scored and sending the results to me. We (you and I) took 3rd place in the 1990 "Best of species award" at our Colo. Outfitters Convention in Jan. We being myself as outfitter and more so you for your nice specimen.

I didn't make it to the convention but sent the entry to the committee chairman. He sent me the small "trophy" recently and now here it is for you to have.

Again, thank you for taking the time to do it. Hope you can come back again and try for another one.

Sincerely,
[illegible]

FIGURE 6.71 The text was traced over on a separate layer.

Next he re-created the lined paper by adding an empty layer, named *Lines drawn,* and positioning it below the traced text layer. Using the Pencil tool, and sampling a color from the original lined paper by Option/Alt-clicking a line, he traced the lines on the paper by clicking at the beginning of a line along the edge of the paper and then Shift-clicking at end. He then added a new Solid Color fill layer below the Lines drawn layer (**Layer > New Fill Layer > Solid Color**), filling it with white (**FIGURE 6.72**).

FIGURE 6.72 The paper was created by drawing blue lines on a layer beneath the text, with a layer of white beneath that.

To make the new document look a little less fresh and crisp, he lowered the opacity of the traced text and lines and slightly blurred them.

Damaged Documents

Scanning larger documents in one piece might not be possible. Consider scanning the document in different sections, and use Photoshop to put them back together. Alternatively, it might be possible to photograph the original, as discussed in Chapter 1.

This poor document had been rolled up for years, had broken, and was taped back together, losing small pieces (**FIGURES 6.73** and **6.74**).

The document was larger than the scanner bed, so Wayne created three separate scans with a generous overlap to obtain all the pieces to rebuild the whole document. To prevent the scanner software from making autocorrects, disable any autocorrect features in your scanning software and scan the entire bed. Three separate images were created (**FIGURE 6.75**).

ch6_document_top.jpg
ch6_document_middle.jpg
ch6_document_bottom.jpg

FIGURE 6.73 This image was in bad shape. It was taped together and the text was faded. *@Buck Family Archives*

FIGURE 6.74 Cloning, healing, adjustment layers, and even some tracing make the document viewable again.

FIGURE 6.75 Scans of the top, middle, and bottom section of the document.

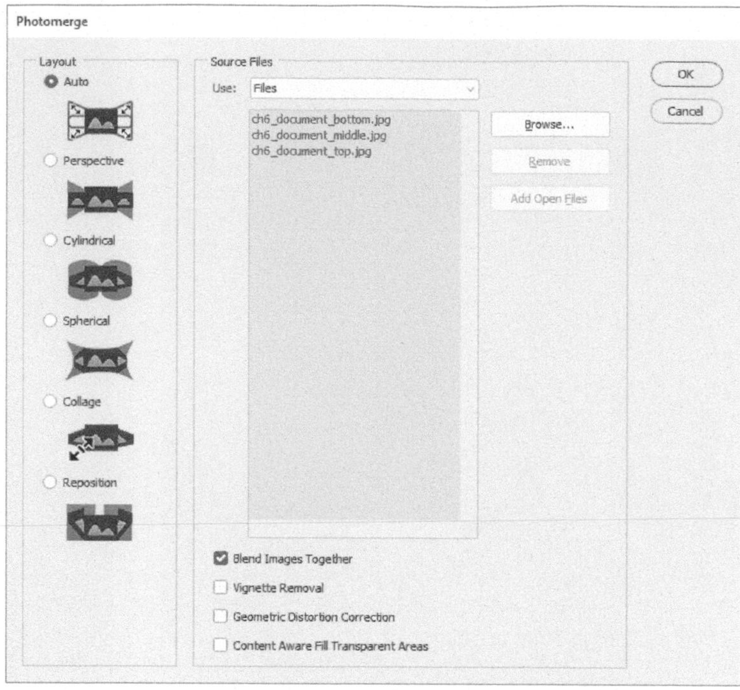

FIGURE 6.76 Use the Photomerge command to weld together several scanned portions of a document.

Let's go through the steps of putting this document back together.

1. Select **File > Automate > Photomerge.**

2. Click Browse and add the three images to the Source Files panel (FIGURE 6.76).

3. With Layout set to Auto, click OK.

4. A new document is created, with each file placed on its own layer masked and blended (FIGURE 6.77).

TIP Photomerge may not always be successful in piecing documents together, especially if the divisions in the scans involve text, which can become skewed or even removed. Should this happen, create an empty document large enough to accommodate the scans and manually align the pieces as much as possible. Choose **Edit > Auto Blend Layers** to align and blend the layers. If the result is still unsatisfactory, try changing the stacking order of the layers, which can yield different results.

5. Select the top layer, and press Cmd-Option-Shift-E/Ctrl-Alt-Shift-E to copy and merge the three parts into a new layer.

FIGURE 6.77 Photomerge creates a new document, with the three sections perfectly aligned.

6. Use the Crop tool, with Delete Cropped Pixels deselected in the options bar, to eliminate the extra material around the document (FIGURE 6.78).

FIGURE 6.78 The three layers are combined into one and the document trimmed to size.

7. Use any of the techniques covered earlier in this chapter (Content-Aware Fill, Patch tool, Clone Stamp tool, or healing tools) to repair the image. So that Content-Aware Fill can be used as an option, work on the merged layer rather than a new empty layer. This is still nondestructive editing, as the combined layer can be re-created; if some of the fixes need to be redone, the original information can be put back by copying and pasting from the lower layers (FIGURE 6.79).

The most important parts of the document are the two sections of text along the bottom (FIGURE 6.80). Unfortunately, they do not stand out very well and there is uneven fading in one section. Address each section separately, as the amount of correction needed is different.

FIGURE 6.79 The damage to the document is repaired.

FIGURE 6.80 The text is nearly unreadable.

8. Use the Rectangular Marque tool to select the dark box with the person's name in it.

9. Choose **Select > Color Range**. Deselect Localized Color Clusters if it is selected, and select the Eye-dropper tool in the Color Range dialog box. Click the gold text to sample it, and adjust the Fuzziness slider until the text inside your selection is chosen. Click OK. A selection of the text appears (FIGURE 6.81).

Because a selection is made prior to the Color Range command, the colors captured as part of the selection this command creates fall within the dark box.

FIGURE 6.81 Make a marquee selection of the text at the bottom of the document, and use the Color Range tool to select only the text.

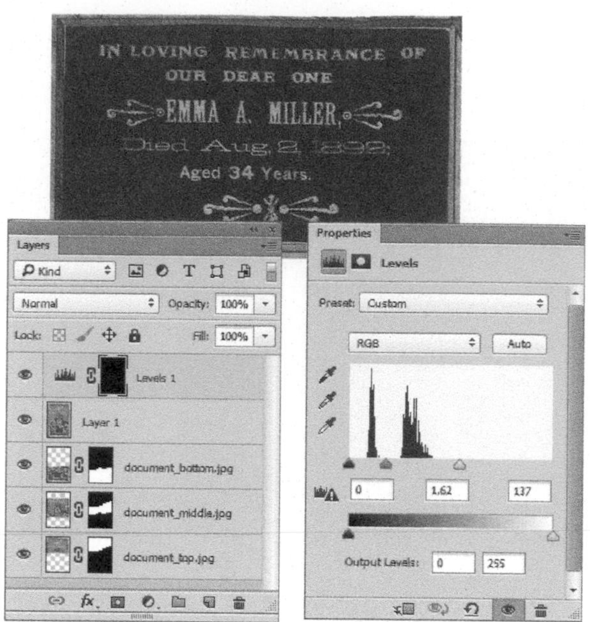

FIGURE 6.82 Brighten the text by applying a Levels adjustment layer to the selection.

10. Add a Levels adjustment layer. When a selection is active as you add an adjustment layer, a layer mask is automatically created so that only the text is affected by the adjustment.

11. In the Properties panel, drag the white point slider to 137 and the midtone slider to 1.62 to bring up the text (**FIGURE 6.82**).

12. Repeat steps 8–11 for the black panel at the bottom, this time dragging the whitepoint slider to 171 and midtone slider to 1.82 (**FIGURE 8.63**).

Unfortunately, because of the uneven fading, a little more work is needed.

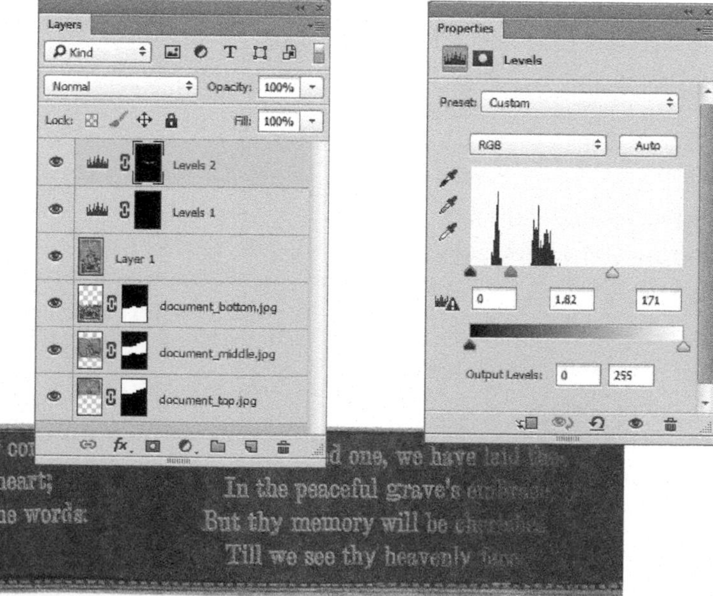

FIGURE 6.83 The amount of fading is not consistent, and a few letters are still not visible.

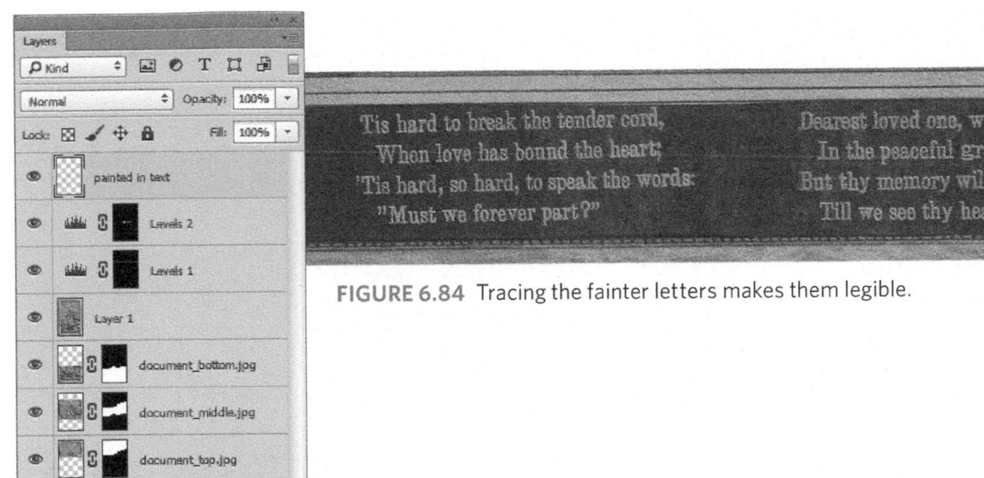
Layers
Kind
Normal
Opacity: 100%
Lock:
Fill: 100%
painted in text
Levels 2
Levels 1
Layer 1
document_bottom.jpg
document_middle.jpg
document_top.jpg
'Tis hard to break the tender cord,
When love has bound the heart;
'Tis hard, so hard, to speak the words:
"Must we forever part?"
Dearest loved one, we have laid thee
In the peaceful grave's embrace,
But thy memory will be cherished
Till we see thy heavenly face.

FIGURE 6.84 Tracing the fainter letters makes them legible.

13. Create a new empty layer, and name it *painted in text.*

14. Use the Eyedropper tool to click a gold letter and set the foreground color. With a small brush, paint over the faint letters to bring back the legibility (FIGURE 6.84).

REVERSING LENS ANOMALIES

Lenses with different focal lengths change our angle of view. Telephoto lenses make objects appear closer and compress the background in relationship to the subject, whereas wide-angle lenses take in a broader view. Zoom lenses, which accommodate a range of focal lengths, are very popular. As with any piece of equipment, quality may vary from outstanding (and most likely expensive) to very poor (and very cheap).

The better the lens, the less distortion your images should show, but it is the rarest lens that shows no hint of distortion. Common types of lens distortion include pin cushion, in which the image is pinched in, and barrel distortion, in which the image is bloated out.

Sometimes this distortion may go unnoticed, or it may be considered artistic or be accepted as an anomaly. Sometimes it can be distracting and unflattering, like the facial distortion that is commonly seen in selfies.

Correcting Lens Distortion

Photoshop has a Lens Correction filter to deal with common lens distortion. The filter has two options:

- **Auto Correction** makes corrections based on camera and lens information found in the file's metadata. Many camera and lens models are supported by the filter.

- **Custom** provides manual controls for removing distortion, chromatic aberration, and vignetting and for changing the vertical or horizontal perspective. This is useful when the image file you are working on contains no lens information or when the camera make or lens model are not supported by the filter.

★ NOTE If your camera and lens combination is not available, either use a similar lens profile or, for the technically adventurous, use the Adobe Lens Profile Downloader to create your own (https://helpx.adobe.com/photoshop/digital-negative.html#resources).

When a camera is tilted back to take in a subject, such as a tall building, there is often a type of distortion called keystoning. In this image it appears as if the church is falling backward. With a few steps in the lens correction filter, that effect can be corrected (FIGURES 6.85 and 6.86).

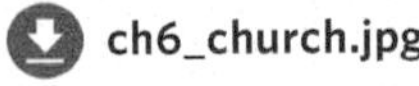
ch6_church.jpg

FIGURE 6.85 Wide-angle lenses and tilted cameras create distorted images. *@Cari Jansen*

FIGURE 6.86 The Lens Correction filter can correct for lens distortion.

1. Duplicate the Background layer to work nondestructively, and hide the Background layer.

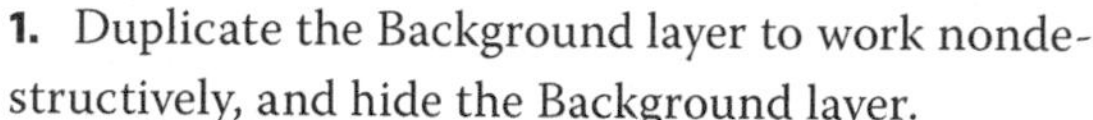

+ TIP To use this filter nondestructively and edit applied settings afterwards, convert the layer to a Smart Filter (**Filter > Convert for Smart Filter**) before applying the Lens Correction filter. In this example, the final steps cannot be done with a Smart Filter.

2. Choose **Filter > Lens Correction.**

3. In the Lens Correction dialog box, select Show Grid. Displaying the grid lets you see more easily how far the building is tilted.

+ TIP You can adjust the grid size to control the number of grid lines that appear. Use the Move Grid tool at the top left of the Lens Correction dialog box, and drag the grid so that it aligns with vertical lines in the image.

4. Click the Auto Correction tab, and deselect Auto Scale Image if it is selected.

5. Click the Custom tab, and drag the Vertical Perspective slider to –50. The building appears to be corrected (FIGURE 6.87).

FIGURE 6.87 Adjust the Vertical Perspective slider to straighten the tilt of the building. Use the grid as a guide.

FIGURE 6.88 Adjusting the Scale slider moves the top of the image back into view but leaves empty space at the bottom of the image.

TIP Select Auto Scale Image in the Auto Correction tab to ensure the image is scaled to fill the canvas. With the option deselected, you'll likely need to crop the image to remove transparent pixels later on, or you'll need to fill transparent areas using some of the retouching techniques covered in this chapter.

There is a tradeoff in using this filter. In exchange for making the correction, the area shown by the photograph is reduced. This may be problematic if the image is already tightly cropped. Notice that the flagpost on top of the building is running outside the frame.

6. Drag the Scale slider to 92% to bring the entire building back into view. Click OK to accept the correction (FIGURE 6.88).

The last step is to fill in the blank areas created by the filter. The quickest fix is to crop the image to a new size. But by using the Warp feature in Free Transform, a fair amount of information can be filled in.

7. Choose **Edit > Free Transform** or press Cmd-T/Ctrl-T. Click the Warp icon ( ) in the options bar. Drag the two lower-right handles so that the image is transformed out to the edge. Do the same for the two lower-left handles, coaxing the image out to the original edge. Press Return/Enter to apply the transformation (FIGURE 6.89).

FIGURE 6.89 The Warp option of the Free Transform tool fills in the right and left side. But there is still some area to fill.

The image is looking pretty straight and is filled in laterally, but it is still not the same dimension as the original. With one more tool, this can be corrected.

8. Choose **Edit > Content-Aware Scale** or press Cmd-Option-Shift-C/Ctrl-Alt-Shift-C. Drag the middle bottom handle down until the image fills the original canvas size. Press Return/Enter (FIGURE 6.90).

FIGURE 6.90 Content-Aware Scale can stretch a picture without distorting it.

TRY IT You might notice that the flagpole on top of the church is still a little stretched. Try selecting the top section of the pole with the Rectangular Marquee tool, ensuring you include plenty of sky above it and on either side. Then use the Content-Aware Move tool to move the pole down to shorten it.

LENS CORRECTION IN ACR

A variation of this filter is found in Adobe Camera Raw and Lightroom, with the only difference being the ability to correct for tilt (FIGURE 6.91).

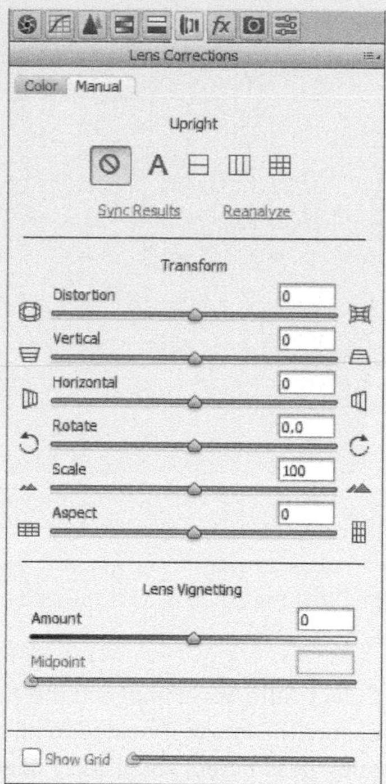

FIGURE 6.91 The Lens Correction feature is also found in Camera Raw and the Camera Raw filter.

Removing Curvature

Images that suffer very unnatural curvature from being taken with a wide-angle lens may get more correction assistance from the Adaptive Wide Angle filter, which addresses distortion from different angles at the same time. The filter can also make several corrections automatically by reading the metadata for the image.

This panoramic image originated on film and shows severe distortion from the camera not being level, making the mountain on the left look like it is tipping over and banking the road on the right. The Adaptive Wide Angle filter takes care of both problems rather easily (FIGURES 6.92 and 6.93).

FIGURE 6.92 This image shows severe distortion.

FIGURE 6.93 The Adaptive Wide Angle filter can straighten it out. ©*WP*

ch6_zion.jpg

1. Duplicate the Background layer. The Adaptive Wide Angle filter works nondestructively as a Smart Filter, but the final steps require the layer to be rasterized, so it is just as easy to work on a duplicate layer.

2. Choose **Filter > Adaptive Wide Angle** or press Cmd-Option-Shift-A/Ctrl-Alt-Shift-A. With no metadata to guide the filter, Fisheye correction is selected by default. Leave the Scale Factor set to 100%, leave the Crop Factor at 0.10, and adjust the Focal Length slider to maximum value (FIGURE 6.94).

★ NOTE The Crop Factor value defines how the image is cropped; it is often used in combination with Scale Factor to control the size of the transparent areas the filter creates.

FIGURE 6.94 Use the Fisheye setting and adjust the sliders so the image is not altered.

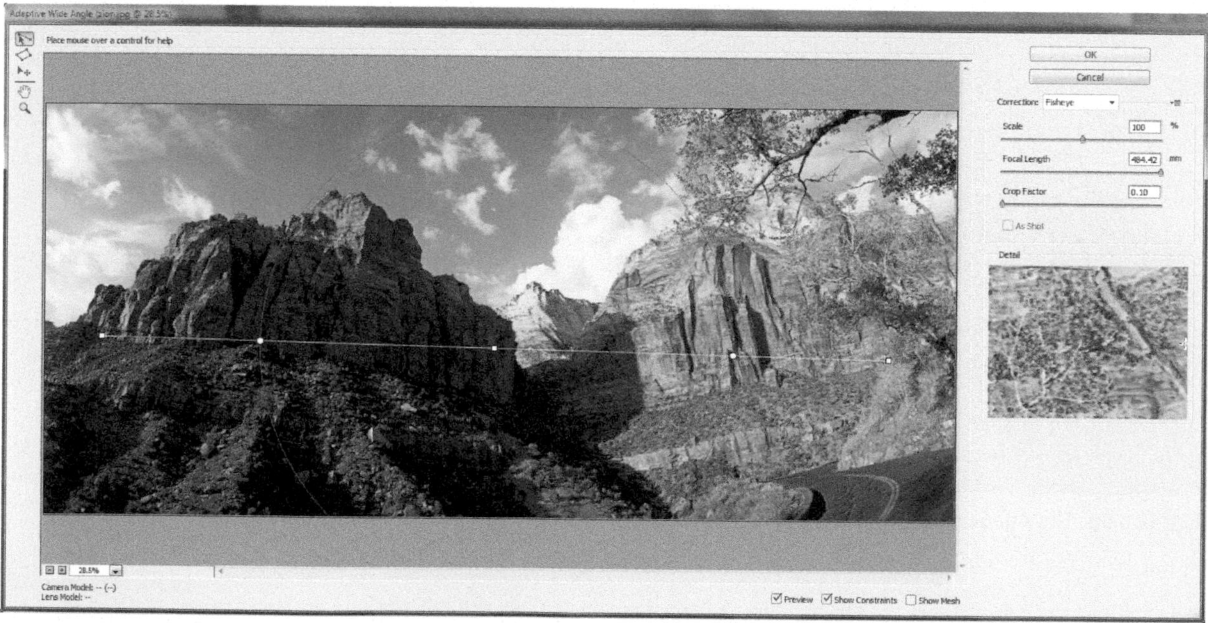

FIGURE 6.95 The Constraint tool draws a curved line between two points. This is the result after that curved line is straightened.

3. Select the Constraint tool in the top left of the panel. Click the left mountain where the green growth stops, and click again in the same relative positive on the mountain on the right (FIGURE 6.95).

TIP Click and then Shift-click to create a horizontal constraint line. To delete a constraint line, Option/Alt-click the line.

FIGURE 6.96 Bending the line by dragging the center handle straightens the image but also creates gaps.

4. A circle appears with a number of handles you can use to tweak the amount of correction. Drag the center handle downward a little to level the road on the right even further (FIGURE 6.96).

TIP To straighten curved areas in an image, you can drag shorter lines with the Constrain tool across the image. Once a section is straightened, you can select one of the dots on the circle and drag to rotate that section of the image to level it. You can also add multiple lines if needed.

5. Drag the Scale slider until you are happy with the size of the remaining transparent areas the filter generates. This fills in a large part of the gaps without significantly cropping the image (FIGURE 6.97). Click OK and hide the Background layer.

The remaining gaps can be filled in with Content-Aware Fill.

6. Select the Magic Wand tool, and deselect Contiguous in the options bar. Click in a transparent area to simultaneously select all the transparent areas. Expand the selection by choosing **Select > Modify > Expand** and enter 10 for the number of pixels. Click OK.

7. Choose **Edit > Fill** and change Contents to Content-Aware (FIGURE 6.98). Click OK for the fill to apply, and press Cmd-D/Ctrl-D to deselect the selection.

FIGURE 6.97 Using the Scale slider helps get the image closer to its original shape. There is still some filling-in to do.

FIGURE 6.98 Content-Aware Fill fills in the gaps with an expanded selection of the empty areas.

Upright Command

The Camera Raw filter interface inside Photoshop is nearly identical to ACR. Converted to a Smart Filter, the Camera Raw filter is nondestructive and allows the retoucher to make multiple major changes inside one interface.

One feature inside ACR and the Camera Raw filter that Katrin really likes is the Upright command, which is part of the Transform tool. The image perspective corrections in FIGURE 6.99, a Manhattan skyline, were made in a few short steps (FIGURE 6.100).

 **ch6_nighttime_skyline.jpg**

FIGURE 6.99 This image shows severe distortion, with all the buildings tilting toward the center. © *KE*

FIGURE 6.100 The Upright command makes quick work of correcting the tilt.

FIGURE 6.101 Using the Upright command inside the Camera Raw filter or ACR can quickly straighten perspective distortion.

1. Convert the Background layer to a Smart Object by right-clicking it in the Layers panel and selecting Covert to Smart Object.

2. Choose **Filter** > **Camera Raw Filter** or press Shift-Cmd-A/Shift-Ctrl-A.

3. Select the Transform tool from the toolbar at the top of the dialog box.

4. Click the Full icon under Upright options. This fully straightens the tilting of the buildings on both sides of the image (FIGURE 6.101). Click OK to accept the Upright correction.

The last step is to crop the image; this feature is not part of the Camera Raw Filter but is in ACR.

5. Use the Crop tool to remove missing areas from the image, being sure that Delete Cropped Pixels is not selected in the options bar (to keep the edits nondestructive).

CLOSING THOUGHTS

Fixing images can be a little dull and repetitive, but it can also be a creative process—like trying to solve a puzzle by recycling parts of an image. In the next chapter, even larger areas to correct—and creative ways to do so—are addressed.

Chapter 7

REBUILDING AND RE-CREATING IMAGES

The worst images you will face are those that are so damaged by mold, fire, water, or neglect that entire portions of the image are either missing or damaged beyond recognition. In these disaster cases, asking the client for the original negative or a better print is futile, because there probably is none. The secret to replacing, rebuilding, and repairing the all-but-beyond-hope images is to beg, borrow, and steal image information from whatever is left of the original image or to find suitable substitutes to re-create missing backgrounds and body parts.

Images without damage can require rebuilding too, as when the person's expression is wrong, their eyes were closed, or the photographer missed the perfect moment. Even changing family dynamics can create interesting requests, like removing the groom from a wedding picture or the sad occasion of extracting a person from a group shot to make a portrait for a funeral.

Fortunately, digitally adding people, removing people, and replacing faces and heads is 100 percent pain free. Get ready to sharpen your digital scalpel and learn to

- Re-create backgrounds
- Rebuild a portrait
- Add or remove people

- Tackle light leaks and lens flare issues
- Create vignettes
- The tools and techniques we'll use include
- Masking
- Texture and sharpening filters
- Clone and Healing tools
- Selections and masking
- Content-Aware Scale

★ NOTE Many of the techniques used to remove dust and scratches in Chapters 5 and 6 will serve as the foundation for repairing some of the almost hopeless examples used in this chapter.

Before jumping into a project, take a few moments to visualize the result. Often, believability is a priority, and the goal is not to look like a supermarket tabloid cover. Planning is needed. Removing something from an image is not necessarily difficult, as the challenge can be what to put in the created empty space. Likewise, thought should be given to what will be covered up when a person or object is added and to whether the canvas size will need to be adjusted to make space. When working with images of different quality, the higher-quality image may need to be dumbed down to make components look like they belong together. Other considerations include differences in size and resolution, color and tone, grain structure, and angle of view.

CHANGING BACKGROUNDS

Even though the background of an image can seem unimportant (by definition it's not the main subject, right?), replacing an image's background can help tie together composited subjects or provide a solid foundation for the repair of a badly damaged photo. How well changes blend together is the key to the successful rebuilding of an image. And that often depends on good masking skills. Telltale giveaways of "Photoshopping" are visible lines along composited edges or hard lines created by the mask of an adjustment layer. Creating a believable mask can be one of the most time-consuming tasks in Photoshop, and there are many sophisticated ways to do so, as I covered in *Photoshop Masking & Compositing, Second Edition*. In this chapter, I sometimes deal with simpler techniques. Keep in mind that most selection tools are only starting points for making a good mask, and additional steps are often needed to make them credible. To be efficient, balance the amount of time spent on getting every detail right against the size of the final output, which may not show it. And lastly, remember the masking mantra of "black conceals, white reveals."

Combining Images

There are times that images just don't happen naturally, as is the case with these two three-year-olds who would not stand still long enough to get them both in the same frame and looking at the camera (FIGURE 7.1). We don't mean to say that either of these girls will serve as the background, strictly speaking, but the techniques of selecting and masking used here are fundamental to background replacement. Follow these steps to make a believable composite from two separate images of the hyperactive girls (FIGURE 7.2).

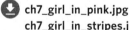

ch7_girl_in_pink.jpg
ch7_girl_in_stripes.jpg

1. Start by opening the image ch7_girl_in_stripes.

+ TIP When adding elements to an image, use one of the Place commands to make the addition a Smart Object, allowing for nondestructive scaling.

2. Choose **File > Place Embedded** and select ch7_girl_in_pink. The second image will open on a layer above the background. The large X across the image, as seen in FIGURE 7.3, indicates that you can scale the image as needed.

3. Click Commit or press Return/Enter to accept the size. The layer will become a Smart Object and can be scaled nondestructively if needed (FIGURE 7.4).

FIGURES 7.1 and 7.2 Before and after. © *WP*

FIGURE 7.3 The large X over the placed image indicates that the layer can be scaled as desired.

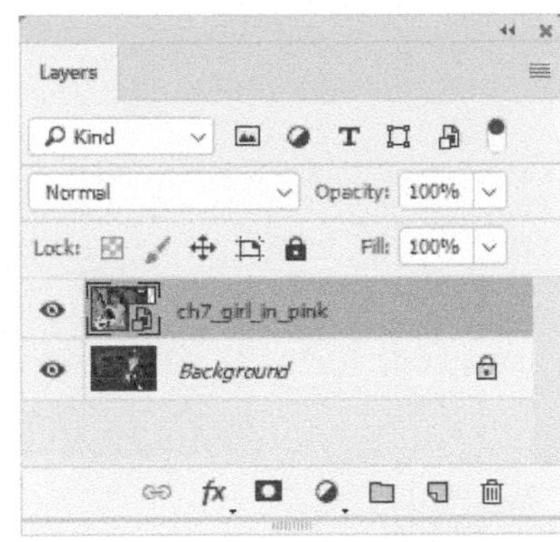

FIGURE 7.4 The additional icon on the Layers panel thumbnail indicates that the layer is a Smart Object.

4. Select the Quick Selection tool and make a selection of the girl, chair, and stuffed animal. The tool may tend to grab a little more than desired. Hold down Option/Alt to subtract from the selection until you get a selection like FIGURE 7.5.

FIGURE 7.5 The Quick Selection tool makes a fast initial selection of the girl in pink.

5. On the Layers panel, click the Add Layer Mask icon or choose **Layer > Layer Mask > Reveal Selection**, which will hide the area that was not selected and reveal the girl in the Background layer (FIGURE 7.6).

FIGURE 7.6 Adding a mask hides everything not selected.

6. Select the Move tool (V) and slide the layer to the left so that the stuffed animal is framed by the corner of the image.

7. Turn off the visibility of the lower layer and you will see the mask needs a little more work (FIGURE 7.7). Select the Brush tool (B), change the color to black, and use a soft edge to finish the selection running along the side of the face, shirt, and arm.

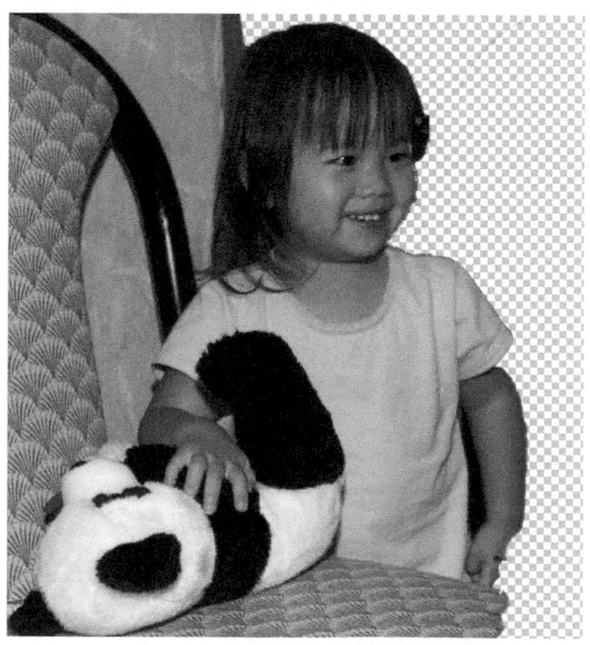

FIGURE 7.7 The mask needs a little more attention to make the combination believable.

8. With a just a minor amount of additional masking you can make the girl in pink appear to be behind the girl in stripes. Select the "girl in pink" layer mask and brush away enough of her arm and shirt to have the lower layer give the appearance of the girl in pink being slightly behind the girl in stripes (FIGURE 7.8).

FIGURE 7.8 Masking can create the illusion that the girls are changing positions.

9. There is a difference in the exposure of the two images, which results in a lack of realism. Create a Curves adjustment layer above the Background layer, and adjust the midtones to make the Background layer a little darker. Create a second Curves adjustment above the upper layer and be sure to select the Clip to Layer option so that only that layer is affected (FIGURE 7.9). Nudge the midtones up a little so the two layers have a similar exposure.

+ TIP Place Embedded and Place Linked produce the same result; the difference between the two choices is how Photoshop handles the placed file. Place Embedded incorporates the entire file inside the PSD file, making it larger. Place Linked makes a reference to the file and only uses the information needed for the current file. Both methods have their merits, but if you envision that the placed file might ever be moved, it is simpler to choose the Place Embedded option.

FIGURE 7.9 Adding a Curves layer to each girl's image layer allows the tonal imbalance to be corrected.

RE-CREATING BACKGROUNDS

Re-creating or rebuilding backgrounds can be as straightforward as lifting a person off the original image and placing her onto a blank background or as involved as finding suitable replacement back ground images to create a brand new environment. Backgrounds can come from a variety of sources, including other photographs, stock photography, the Library of Congress, digital files you created in Photoshop or Adobe Illustrator, and even cloth, textures, or objects you've scanned with a flatbed scanner. Wayne has gone as far as shooting an image from atop a mountain to create an aerial backdrop when asked to put a stationary plane into the air.

When you are replacing or re-creating backgrounds, you can choose from several working options:

- Clone the existing background over the damaged area.
- Mask out the background and replace it with a new one.
- Lift the object or person off the original picture and place it onto a new background.
- Rearrange people or objects to minimize distracting backgrounds.

Your first option of cloning or healing the existing background over damaged areas is self-explanatory, and as long as you work on an empty layer with the Clone Stamp and the Healing Brush tools, you can't get into trouble. The additional approaches are explained in the following sections, giving you a great deal of creative flexibility.

Masking Out the Background

Just as a painter is not limited to making creations that are photo authentic, neither is a photographer limited to photojournalist imagery. This scenic image looks a little ho-hum with the plain blue sky (FIGURE 7.10). Replacing it with an interesting cloud formation taken elsewhere, the image becomes more interesting (FIGURE 7.11). Follow these steps to swap a boring background with one that is more attention-grabbing.

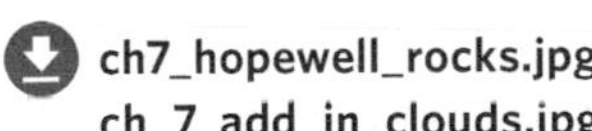

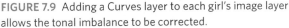

ch7_hopewell_rocks.jpg
ch_7_add_in_clouds.jpg

1. Open the ch7_hopewell_rocks.jpg file, and double-click the Background layer name in the Layers panel to open the New Layer dialog. Click OK, which renames the layer Layer 0 and unlocks the layer (required for some of the following steps).

FIGURES 7.10 and 7.11 Before and after. © *WP*

2. With the Quick Selection tool, select the sky and the area down to the edge of the water, as shown in FIGURE 7.12.

FIGURE 7.12 The Quick Selection tool makes fast work of selecting the sky.

3. Hold down Option/Alt and click the Add a Layer Mask button at the bottom of the Layers panel. This will reverse the mask, hiding the old skyline and keeping the rocks and shoreline. And if you forgot to press the modifier key before adding the mask, you can just as easily invert the mask by pressing Cmd-I/Ctrl-I. Either way, the result should look like FIGURE 7.13.

FIGURE 7.13 The background is masked and ready for replacement.

4. Click the Lock Image Pixels and Lock Position icons in the Layers panel to protect the image from destructive mistakes (FIGURE 7.14).

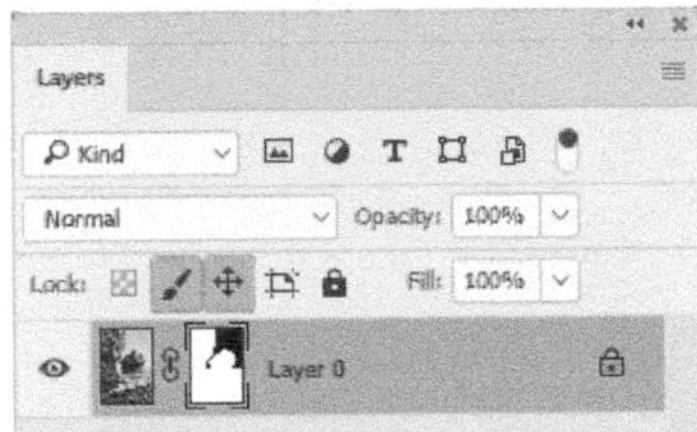

FIGURE 7.14 Locking pixels and position to avoid unwanted changes

5. Choose **File > Place Embedded**, select ch7_add_in_clouds.jpg, and click Place. Press Return/Enter to accept the file (FIGURE 7.15).

FIGURE 7.15 A placed layer becomes a Smart Object.

6. Because there was only one layer, the placed file is on top of the layer stack. In the Layers panel, change the order of the layers by dragging the placed layer below the original layer (FIGURE 7.16).

7. Be sure the cloud layer is selected, and with the Move tool (V) drag the image around so the wispy clouds look like they are emanating from the rock in the center of the shot. When they are in that position, you can see the horizon from the added image.

FIGURE 7.16 The placed layer is moved behind the layer containing the foreground.

8. Because there is no perspective by which to judge this image, it can be stretched to fit. Press Cmd-T/Ctrl-T to enable the Free Transform tool. Drag handles from the top or bottom to stretch the clouds to cover the area as needed (FIGURE 7.17). Note that the handles will be outside the image and you may have to zoom out a bit for this step. You can move the layer around by dragging inside the bounding box of the Free Transform tool. Press Return/Enter or click the check mark in the options bar to accept the transformation.

FIGURE 7.17 The added cloud image is stretched to fill in the area that was masked.

★ NOTE Transforming the layer may look like a destructive maneuver, but it isn't. Because the placed layer is a Smart Object, the Free Transform tool can be reopened and the original dimensions or aspect ratio returned. However, it would take fewer steps to just duplicate the cloud layer or simply repeat the steps to place the image.

9. The edges of the mask are a little too crisp, giving the rocks an unnatural appearance. Click the mask to select it, choose **Filter > Blur > Gaussian Blur**, and set Radius to 1.0 to remove the sharp edge (FIGURE 7.18).

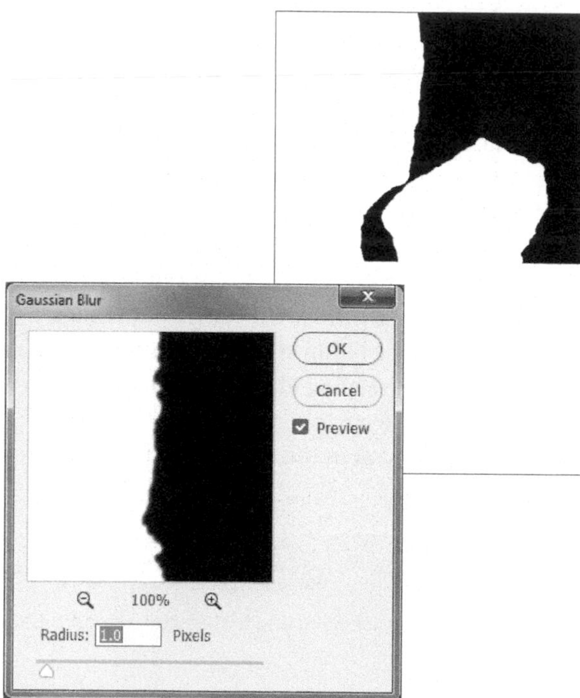

FIGURE 7.18 Blurring the edge of the mask helps blend the two images.

10. The transition between the water and the sky on the horizon is still noticeable despite the blurring from the filter. Select the Rectangular Marquee tool, select the edge of the mask where the two areas meet, and in the Gaussian Blur filter increase the effect to 20 pixels to blend the two areas. Deselect (Cmd-D/Ctrl-D) when satisfied (FIGURE 7.19).

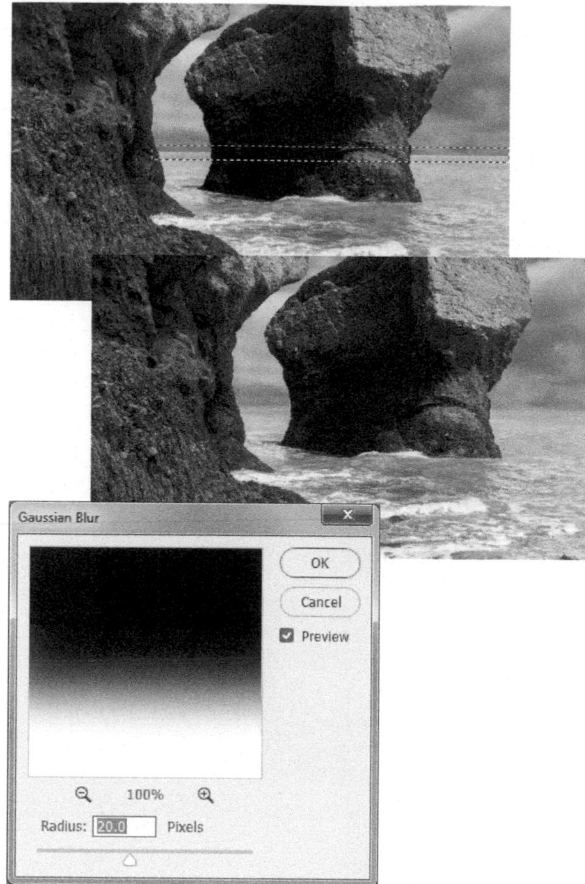

FIGURE 7.19 Selectively blurring the horizon further hides the abrupt transition.

Concentrating on the Essential

The power and finesse of the Healing Brush and Clone Stamp tools are both a blessing and a curse. The ability to invisibly repair and replace damaged image information seems magical. Yet the magic's siren call can lead you to waste time and effort on image areas that are better cropped away or replaced.

The woman in FIGURE 7.20 really liked her pose and expression in the impromptu photo, but the cluttered background, which included a sleeping cat, was distracting. Rather than wasting a lot of time covering up the background, the subject was separated from the background through masking, and a digital studio backdrop was created (FIGURE 7.21). Follow these steps to turn a snapshot into a more formal-looking portrait.

FIGURES 7.20 and 7.21 Before and after. © *WP*

ch7_studio_background.jpg

1. Use the Quick Selection tool to make an outline of the woman. The tool may have trouble discerning between the subject and the background. Hold down Option/Alt and drag over those areas to subtract from the selection. Pay attention to the area around the earring, being sure to exclude the center of it, as shown in FIGURE 7.22.

FIGURE 7.22 The Quick Selection tool creates a good initial selection.

2. Click the Add Layer Mask icon to create the mask. The Background layer is renamed Layer 0 and is unlocked. In the Layers panel, click the Lock Image Pixels and Lock Position icons to keep your work nondestructive (FIGURE 7.23). The mask reveals that the selection is not perfect; it will be addressed once a new background has been created.

FIGURE 7.23 Selecting Lock Image Pixels and Lock Position protects the original Background layer from destructive editing.

3. Add a new empty layer and move it underneath the first layer (FIGURE 7.24).

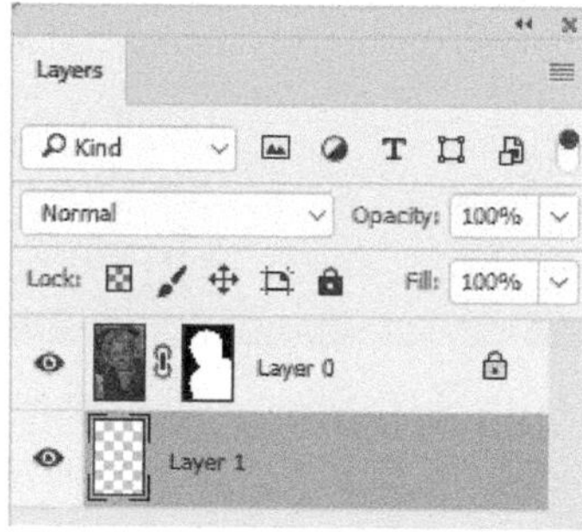

FIGURE 7.24 An empty layer behind the subject will be the start of the new backdrop.

4. Using a color already found in the image makes a more believable composite. Select the Eyedropper tool (I) and choose a shade of gray found in the sweater. Press the X key to switch foreground and background colors. In the Tools panel, click the Set Foreground Color icon and change the color to white.

5. Select the Gradient tool (G) and select Radial Gradient on the options bar. Click between the woman's eyes and drag up and out past her head, as shown in FIGURE 7.25. This creates the effect of a studio light on the wall behind the subject. This step also points out the need to improve the mask. The mask does not need to reveal every stray hair, but there is a noticeable edge that needs to be addressed.

FIGURE 7.25 A radial gradient will create a studio backdrop look.

6. Click the mask on Layer 0 to open the layer's Mask Properties panel. Then click the Select and Mask button or (double-click the mask icon) to open the Select and Mask workspace.

Drag the Feather slider to 3.4 pixels, which creates a soft edge. As the feathering expands the selection, drag the Shift Edge slider to –71%, which contracts the mask. In the Output Settings section, choose New Layer with Layer Mask from the Output To menu and click OK (FIGURE 7.26). A new layer and new mask are generated; the older layer is turned off and is preserved in the event you need to revisit the original mask (FIGURE 7.27). More time can be spent to produce a much more detailed mask, but again, gauge the time spent finessing the mask against the eventual print or display size of the final image.

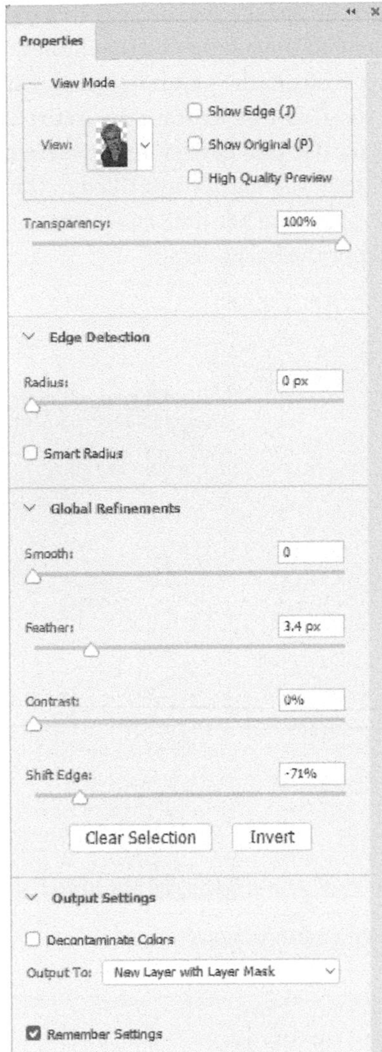

FIGURE 7.26 The Properties panel for theSelect and Mask interface provides more options than the Mask Properties panel, but any changes you make are destructive.

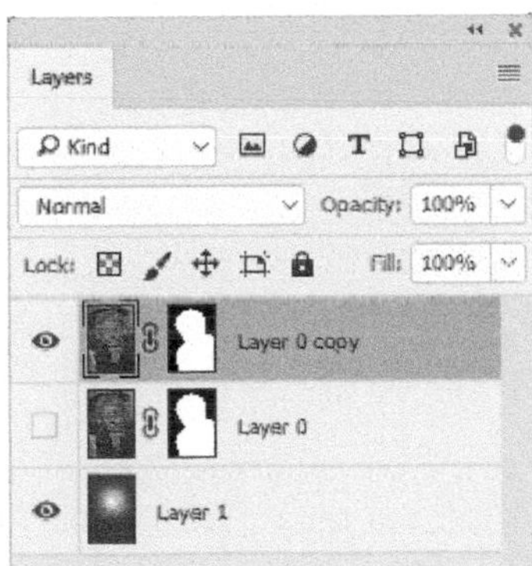

FIGURE 7.27 A new layer and a new mask are generated.

TIP Changes made in the Mask Properties panel can be undone, but changes made using the Select and Mask workspace are permanent.

7. Finally, add a little contrast to the image by creating a Levels adjustment layer and sliding in both the black and white points, as shown in **FIGURE 7.28**.

FIGURE 7.28 The addition of a little contrast finishes the job.

TIP A Gradient Fill adjustment layer can also be used to make the background. The Gradient Fill offers precise and readjustable options, but requires a few more steps than a simple drag with the Gradient tool.

Background Creation with Layer Styles

Lorie Zirbes (of Retouching by Lorie) has an extensive background in traditional as well as digital retouching. She pulled out all the stops using her artistic skills to restore this horribly damaged image

(FIGURES 7.29 and 7.30). Part of that process included abandoning the original background and creating a new one using layer styles.

She created an empty layer and filled it with 50% gray because some layer styles need tonal information in order to be visible. Choosing Gradient Overlay from the Add Layer Style menu, she created a light blue gradient that would complement the subject and then lowered the opacity for the next step to work. To add texture to the new background, she added Pattern Overlay from the Layer Style menu and chose Washed Water Color paper from the Artist Surfaces pattern library (FIGURE 7.31). With the background set (FIGURE 7.32), she masterfully filled in the rest of the damage, spending her time concentrating on the subject and not the background.

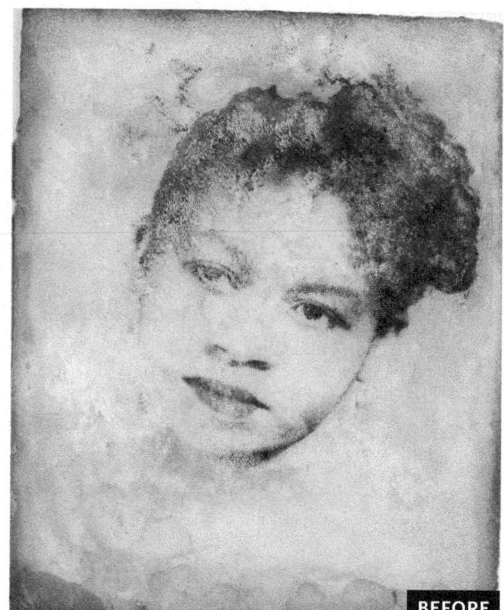

FIGURES 7.29 and 7.30 Before and after.
© *Blanco Family Archives*

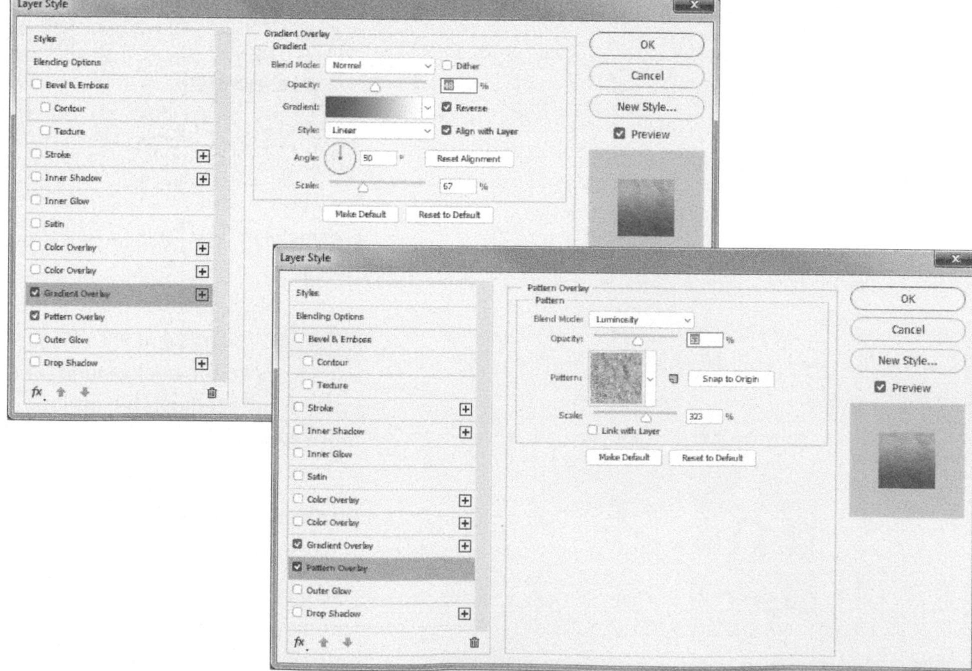

FIGURE 7.31 Combining the Gradient Overlay and Pattern Overlay layer styles to generate a textured background

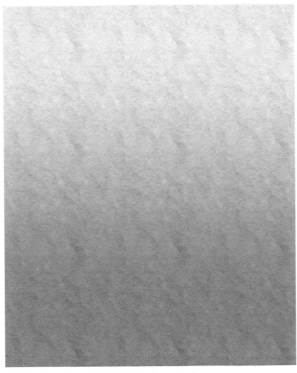

FIGURE 7.32 The finished background

FIGURES 7.33 and 7.34 Before and after. © *Browne Family Archives*

Using Outside Resources

Another dramatic example of restoration by Lorie Zirbes is shown with this water-damaged print (FIGURE 7.33). Initially, it looked hopeless, but she realized that the wedding couple could be repaired but that she would have to look elsewhere for material to replace the background. Lorie re-created part of the background using the technique described in the last example but then used a stock photo to complete the restoration (FIGURE 7.34).

Here are the steps she used in the repair.

1. She converted the image to black and white to simplify the repair and hide the discolorations (FIGURE 7.35).

FIGURE 7.35 Extracting a channel or converting to grayscale can help hide some damage.

2. Then she painstakingly cloned and healed the damage to the wedding couple and the floor (FIGURE 7.36).

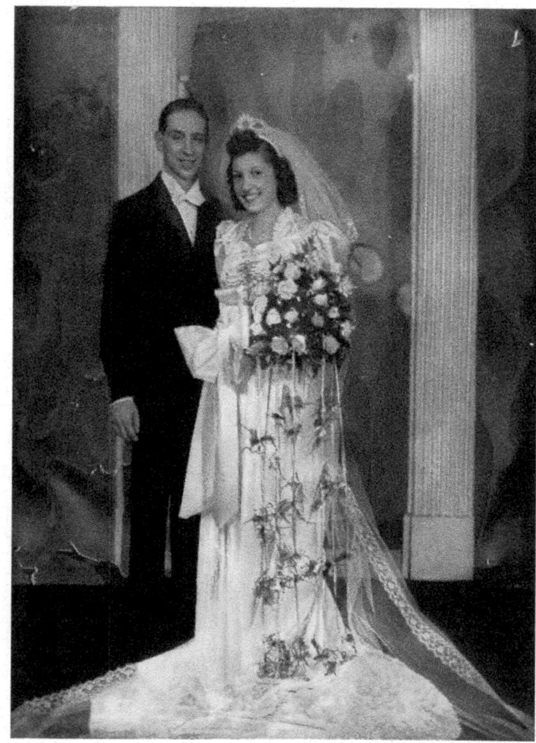

FIGURE 7.36 The wedding couple and floor were fixed through cloning and healing.

3. Next she masked out the background that was severely damaged, but kept the arches (FIGURE 7.37).

FIGURE 7.37 The severely damaged background is masked away for replacement instead of repair.

4. She liked the idea of drapes in the background and found a stock photo on the web to use. She placed curtains behind the couple, which eliminated the need for masking (FIGURE 7.38).

FIGURE 7.38 A stock photo of drapes was used for the new background.

5. To fill in the archway, she created a new layer between the curtains and the couple. With the Rectangular Marquee tool she selected an area that needed to be filled and then filled the selection with gray. Using layer styles she chose both a pattern and gradient to fill in the area (FIGURE 7.39).

FIGURE 7.39 Layer styles were used to create a faux wall.

6. Lastly, she brought the image back to life by hand-coloring using the techniques in Chapter 4 (FIGURE 7.40).

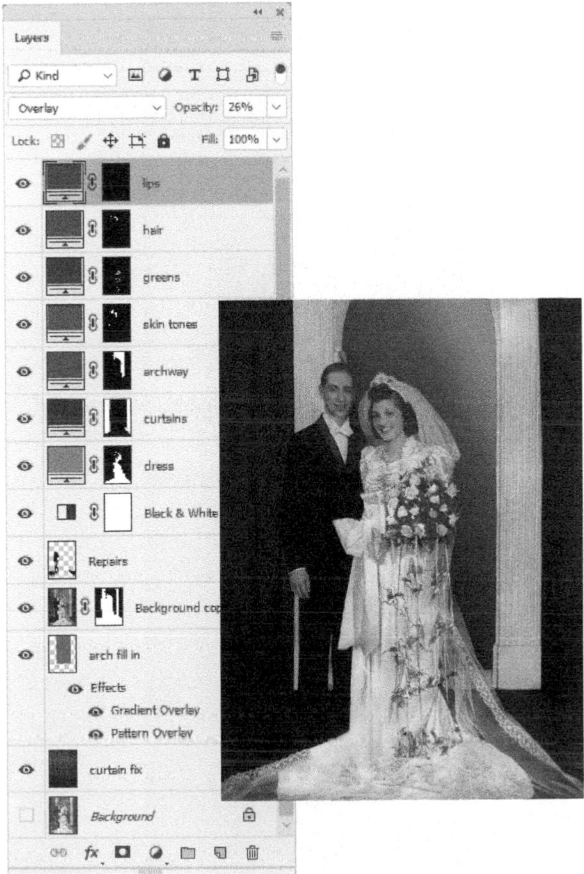

FIGURE 7.40 The finished image with its Layers panel

Film Grain and Digital Noise

Film grain and digital noise appear as small particles in an image. Although some photographers may find those particles desirable for providing a gritty look, it was and is the bane of those photographers who want clean, clear photographs. Grain (FIGURE 7.41) is associated with film-based images and becomes noticeable when an image is enlarged. It is most visible in high-speed films or film that has been push processed or underexposed. Noise (FIGURE 7.42) is a newer problem and is related to digital images. The sensor in a digital camera converts light into an electrical charge, which is boosted when higher ISO settings are used. Just as with film, the higher the ISO, the more likely it is that noise will be visible.

FIGURE 7.41 This film-based astrophotography image shows extreme graininess from a long exposure. © *WP*

FIGURE 7.42 This modern image shows digital noise from using a high ISO setting. © *WP*

Even though grain and noise are created differently, both result in a random pattern of particles interwoven into the image. Regardless, noise can be a friend or a foe, depending on your point of reference. Chapter 5 showed methods for reducing noise in images. But using noise in the restoration process can make an image look more authentic and less sterile.

Hiding Low Resolution

In the following example, the added background has a very smooth appearance, which may not always be the best choice for an image, particularly if there is already grain or noise. If the difference is noticeable, then the credibility of the image can come into question. Noise can add a sense of realism as well as help blend composited images of differing resolutions.

The image in FIGURE 7.43 was taken with a 1.3 MP camera, which does not provide enough resolution to make a detailed 8 x 10, let alone a cropped portion of it. Wayne was requested to make a portrait of the gentleman for a final memorial tribute. The final step of adding noise helped hide the softness and the JPEG artifacts made visible through resizing (FIGURE 7.44).

Cropping the image to a 4:5 ratio and using the Image Size command to resample the image to the needed size was the first and easiest step (FIGURE 7.45). The reflections were removed and an adjustment layer added to tone down the suit coat, where noise and artifacts were noticeable (FIGURE 7.46). The background was masked and a new background created (FIGURE 7.47). Because of the low resolution and interpolation, the image has a very smooth and soft look (FIGURE 7.48). As a final step, Wayne made an empty layer, filled it with 50% gray, and added noise to help hide some of the limitations.

FIGURES 7.43 and 7.44 Before and after. © *Bernie Synoracki*

FIGURE 7.45 The image was cropped and sized for output.

FIGURE 7.46 The reflections were removed and the coat darkened.

FIGURE 7.47 The background was masked out and a new background created.

FIGURE 7.48 The image has a very smooth look to it due to the low resolution and the amount of resizing.

Adding Texture

This image of a happy wedding couple (FIGURE 7.49) suffers from a plastic look to the skin due to a low-resolution file. Follow these steps to create a non-destructive noise layer that will give the image some texture. But first, use the Red Eye tool to easily get rid of those glowing reflections. The Red Eye tool is destructive, so if a before state is desired, duplicate the Background layer. Saving the final layered file will create a new document while automatically keeping the original image intact (FIGURE 7.50).

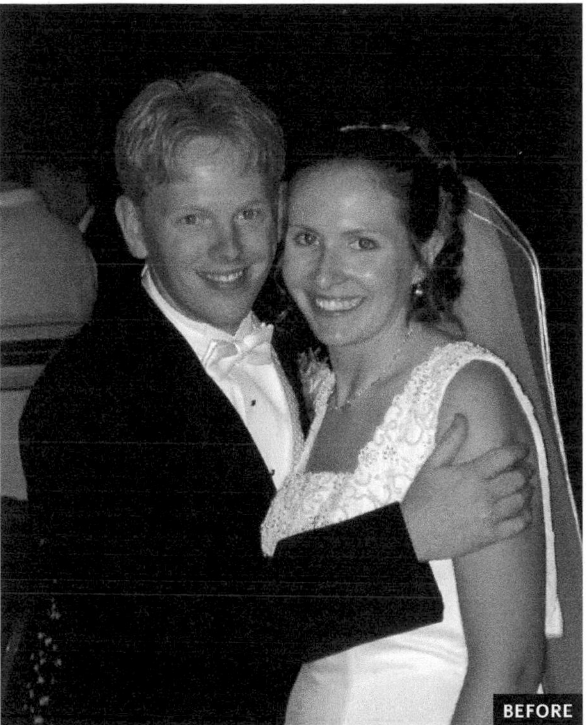

FIGURES 7.49 and 7.50 Before and after. © *WP*

TIP The Red Eye tool works in two ways. First it can be used like an eyedropper; just click inside the red area. The second way is to drag over the eye just like you would when using the Rectangular Marquee tool, but this method recognizes only one eye at a time.

ch7_bridal_couple.jpg

1. Select the Red Eye tool, nested under the Spot Healing Brush in the Tools panel. Zoom in if needed and click each red eye (FIGURE 7.51).

FIGURE 7.51 The Red Eye tool makes fast work of getting the red out.

2. In the Layers panel, add a new layer. Choose **Edit > Fill** and in the Fill dialog box choose 50% Gray from the Contents menu and Overlay from the Blending Mode menu. Click OK.

3. Convert the layer to a Smart Object by choosing **Filter > Convert For Smart Filters**. You can also right-click the layer in the Layers panel and choose Convert to Smart Object.

4. Choose **Filter > Noise > Add Noise**. There is no rule of thumb for adding noise, other than to experiment. The Noise filter has a slider for choosing Amount, a choice of Uniform or Gaussian Distribution (random pattern), and a checkbox for Monochromatic which adds only random gray specks when selected. Don't be concerned if the noise appears a little pronounced. For this image, slide the Amount to 10% and click OK (FIGURE 7.52).

FIGURE 7.52 Creating a basic noise layer

5. Choose **Filter > Blur > Gaussian Blur**. Starting with a low radius, soften the noise until it blends in and looks natural without disappearing. Click OK (FIGURE 7.53).

FIGURE 7.53 Using the Gaussian Blur filter to refine the noise

FIGURE 7.54 It's subtle, but the addition of texture hides the plastic look of the low-resolution file.

The added noise helps establish a realistic look. The results are subjective, and a favorable result will take some balancing between the two filters (FIGURE 7.54).

Here are some other tips for noise layers.

- Use noise to help dumb down sharper-looking layers in composites.
- Use the Soft Light or Hard Light blending modes for variety in textures.
- Use a lower layer opacity for a more subtle effect.
- Use the non-monochromatic option to create colored noise, which can create a more realistic look, especially in old color images.

Reconstruction from Other Images

Sometimes an image can be so destroyed that there is nothing to pull from inside the image and replacement information may need to be found elsewhere. That is what Lorie Zirbes did to fix FIGURE 7.55. This poor image, part of a collage of images, suffered a coffee spill. Through some borrowing of parts as well as some stock photography, Lorie was able to reassemble it (FIGURE 7.56).

1. Repairing the background was a simple matter of masking it and creating a new one with layer styles on an empty layer behind it (FIGURE 7.57).

FIGURES 7.55 and 7.56 Before and after. © *Hall Family Archives*

FIGURE 7.57 The background was replaced by a new layer with layer styles applied.

2. Repairing the foreground took a little more effort to keep the pattern for the blanket. Lorie selected a portion of it that was in good shape and replicated it to fill in the foreground (FIGURE 7.58).

FIGURE 7.58 Filling in the blanket required the reuse of a good portion.

3. When it came to the head and missing arm, there was not much information that could be cloned to make up for the missing areas. Between having another image from the same photo shoot (a stroke of good luck) and borrowing a hand that she found on the web, Lorie was able to fill in the damage (FIGURE 7.59).

FIGURE 7.59 This image provided the material for the arm and head top.

4. She copied the top of the head of the undamaged image and pasted it into the damaged one. She masked away the excess material, and using the Transform tool and temporarily lowering the opacity, she was able to match the head shapes, as seen in FIGURE 7.60.

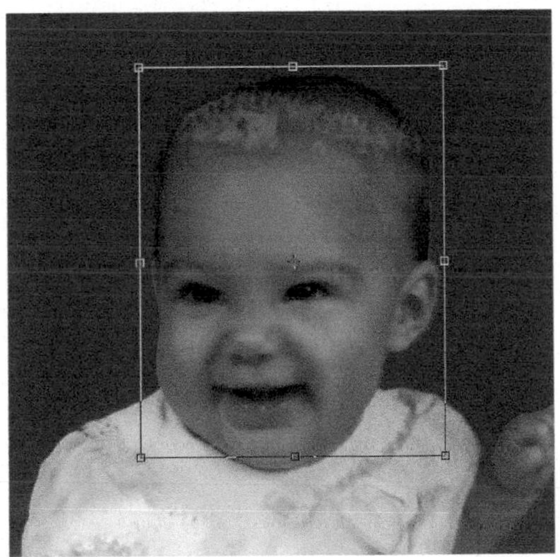

FIGURE 7.60 Lowering the opacity of the added layer assists the registration of the two layers.

5. Then she copied and flipped the arm from the other photo. Again she used a mask to blend the new arm into the existing image (FIGURE 7.61).

FIGURE 7.61 An arm copied from another picture and flipped horizontally nearly completes the restoration.

6. With the arm in place, Lorie was able to fill in the rest of the dress (FIGURE 7.62).

FIGURE 7.62 Sampling from the undamaged dress provided material to do the final work.

7. Lorie was not content just to move the arm from the other image. She went one step further and found a baby hand in stock photo images and used the fingers, matching color and dimension (FIGURE 7.63).

FIGURE 7.63 Extended fingers were added so that the image would not look so similar to the one the arm had been borrowed from.

When faced with such badly damaged examples, you may need to think outside the box (or outside the image) for answers.

REMOVING AND ADDING PEOPLE

It is a common request to alter the number of people in an image, whether adding or subtracting. Removing or adding people often means changing a major portion of the image, and it poses a difficult challenge.

Filling the Void

When it comes to "erasing" a person from an image, the difficulty lies in what to do with the vacancy. Sometimes it may just be a matter of using information already in the image or pulling information from another photo.

The bride in this photo always liked her and her husband's expressions, but the distracting head of the man in the foreground spoiled it (FIGURE 7.64). Wayne was asked to remove the person. The customer had other images from the day, and by borrowing material from one of them as well as recycling other information, he was able to fill in the area created by removing the man (FIGURE 7.65). Here are the steps he took.

FIGURES 7.64 and 7.65 Before and after. © *Moss Family Archives*

1. The red channel was extracted and made into a new file, as it had the best contrast and simultaneously eliminated the aged yellowed look, as seen in FIGURE 7.66. The technique was described in Chapter 4.

FIGURE 7.66 The red channel was used to create a new file, which removed the aged look.

TIP Working in grayscale will reduce the overall file size, as there are fewer channels compared to RGB or CMYK. Consider this option if there is no reason to keep color information

2. The man in the foreground was masked (FIGURE 7.67), which made it easier to see what needed to be filled and to plan a course of action.

FIGURE 7.67 The void to fill is nearly a quarter of the image.

3. Another image provided a usable shoulder of the wedding dress (FIGURE 7.68). The shoulder was copied from the red channel of that image, pasted into the first image, and scaled to match the existing shoulder; he masked the areas that weren't needed (FIGURE 7.69).

FIGURE 7.68 Another image from the wedding provided material to fill the void.

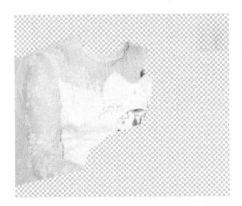

FIGURE 7.69 The bride's shoulder was copied from a separate image.

4. To complete the dress, he duplicated the layer, flipped it horizontally, and masked out any extra that was not needed.

5. On an empty layer above, he cloned and healed to cover the seam created by the joining of the two sections (FIGURE 7.70).

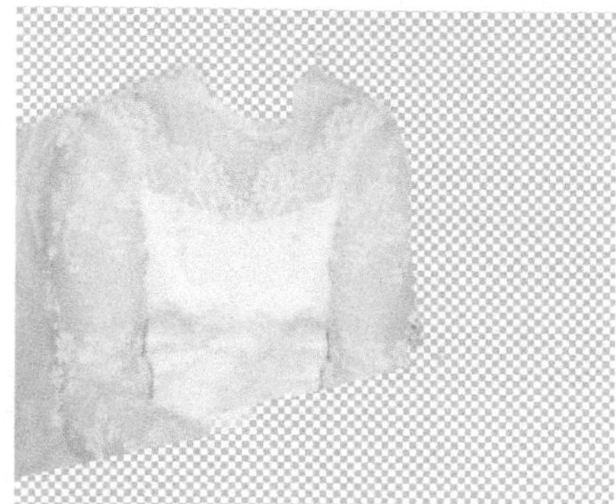

FIGURE 7.70 Repairing to cover the visible seam

6. With the bride completed, part of the table was copied to a new layer and moved to keep the perspective in alignment.

7. The cake copied from the other image, along with a little cloning, provided enough material to fill the remaining space. A clipped Levels adjustment layer was needed for the cake brightness to match the table (FIGURE 7.71).

FIGURE 7.71 The void was filled by duplicating part of the table and the cake from another image.

8. Finally, a Levels adjustment layer, as seen in FIGURE 7.72, was added for a bit more contrast.

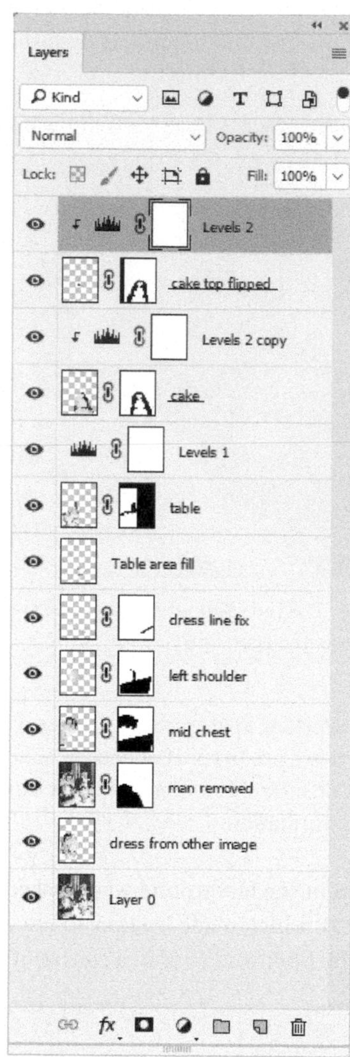

FIGURE 7.72 The Layers panel shows the number of layers used in the final image.

Rearranging a Snapshot

This picture of a picture (FIGURE 7.73) was taken with a phone camera and presented to Wayne with a request to make a 5 x 7, remove two of the neighborhood children (FIGURE 7.74) so that the remaining children would just be family members, and, if possible, keep the cars (to help date the image). The result is seen in FIGURE 7.75.

FIGURES 7.73, 7.74 and 7.75 Before and after. © *Hill Family Archives*

ch7_rearrage_snapshot.jpg

1. One of the children can be removed by cropping the image to the desired size. Select the Rectangular Marquee tool (M). In the options bar, choose Fixed Ratio from the Style menu and enter 7 for Width and 5 for Height. Drag from the lower-right corner until the five children on the right and the cars are selected, as shown in FIGURE 7.76. By cropping, the problem of the image not having square corners is resolved.

FIGURE 7.76 Define the area for the final image.

2. If rulers are not visible, press Cmd-R/Ctrl-R. Drag a guide from each ruler and place them on the marching ants of the marquee. Deselect the selection by pressing Cmd-D/Ctrl-D. FIGURE 7.77 shows the guides and the area that will be the final image.

FIGURE 7.77 Guides mark the area of the final image.

3. Duplicate the Background layer and turn off the visibility of the original. Create a layer mask and with the Brush tool (B) set to black, hide the boy with the raised arm (FIGURE 7.78).

FIGURE 7.78 Remove the second child through masking.

4. With the Lasso tool, make a selection of the girl with the bow in her hair and the girl with the printed shirt. Copy the selection (Cmd-C/Ctrl-C), and then paste (Cmd-V/Ctrl-V) it on a new layer. With the Move tool (V), slide the two girls to the right, covering the boy holding up his arm, as shown in FIGURE 7.79.

FIGURE 7.79 The two girls are copied to their own layer and moved to where the boy was.

5. If your selection is a little generous, create a layer mask for the copied girls and mask any excess information that overlaps the girl in the large hat, as in FIGURE 7.80.

FIGURE 7.80 Excess material is masked away.

6. There is a small area next to the added girl that needs to be filled. Create an empty layer behind the Background copy layer. Using the Clone Stamp tool, choose All Layers from the Sample menu on the options bar and fill in the area remaining area that had been occupied by the boy. Note that by cloning on a layer behind the Background copy layer, there is no concern for covering any material visible in the foreground (FIGURE 7.81).

FIGURE 7.81 Cloning on a layer behind keeps the foreground intact.

7. The hand from the first removed child is still visible. Create an empty layer on top of the copied girls and clone it out (FIGURE 7.82).

FIGURE 7.82 The hand of the girl that is going to be cropped is covered through cloning.

8. The image is a little orange from both age and the incandescent light under which it was taken. Create a Hue/Saturation adjustment layer, select the Colorize checkbox, and set Hue to 32 and Saturation to 11 to give the image an old-fashioned sepia look (FIGURE 7.83).

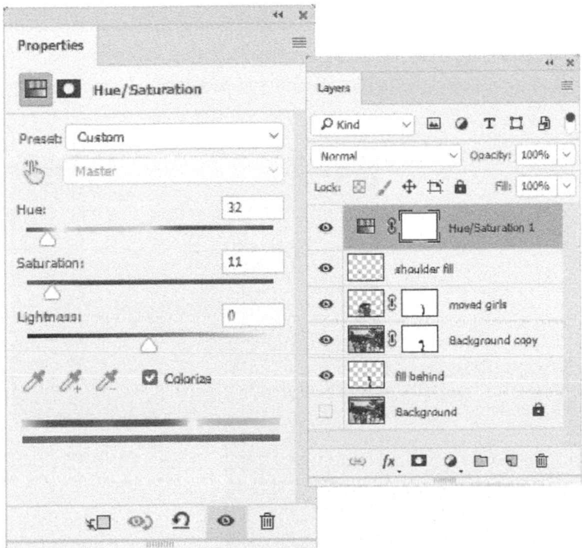

FIGURE 7.83 Use a Hue/Saturation adjustment layer to add a sepia color.

9. Select the Crop tool (C), be sure that Delete Cropped Pixels is deselected and that **View > Snap** is enabled, and drag the crop marks to the guides created earlier. Press Return/Enter or click Commit.

TRY IT Here's another example from Lorie Zirbes. Go ahead and remove the partial third person in the image so it is just a photo of the couple. All the information needed is already contained in the image (FIGURES 7.84 and 7.85).

ch7_cruise_couple.jpg

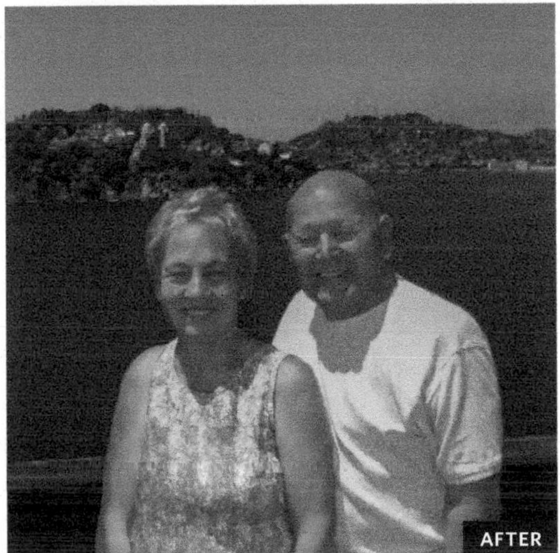

FIGURES 7.84 and 7.85 Before and after. © *Kaminsky Family Archives*

Adding People to Images

The reasons for adding people to images are as diverse as those for removing. Often the reason may be that there is no other way get the picture. Our busy lives keep us from being in two places at the same time. Families now are separated not only by countries but by continents. And sadly, the person being added to an image may no longer be living.

Working with Existing Images

Phil Pool, of Omni Photography, has had many occasions to create group photographs that did not really happen. One request was to make a family photo of the children from their graduation images (FIGURE 7.86). This posed several challenges in that there was a large age gap between the ages, the oldest child's graduation image was on 2¼ film, and sadly one child had passed away (FIGURE 7.87).

FIGURE 7.86 Three high school graduation pictures to be composited into a group family photo. © *Phil Pool - Omni Photography*

As luck would have it, Phil had taken two of the three graduation photos and had used similar lighting. Starting with the son who had passed way, Phil planned to make the group shot look as real as possible. He staged a shot of the mother leaning on the father and then substituted the son for the father (FIGURE 7.88). He photographed the father separately, as seen in FIGURE 7.89. Phil had used the same lighting setup for the daughter but from the opposite direction. By flipping the image horizontally, he was able to match the lighting of the other images (FIGURE 7.90). All the components were masked, he used a single image of the backdrop, and he changed the bright blue of the shirt to be less noticeable.

FIGURES 7.87 The final result with the parents. © *Phil Pool - Omni Photography*

FIGURE 7.88 A staged shot made for a more realistic composite. © *Phil Pool - Omni Photography*

FIGURE 7.89 The father was photographed separately.

FIGURE 7.90 Flipping the image of the daughter horizontally made the lighting direction match the other images.

Bringing the Family Together

In this second image from Phil (FIGURE 7.91), he used his skills to create a family portrait from a series of separate images when time limitations did not allow for all the members to be present in the same room. By using the same lighting arrangement for each subgroup of family members and shooting against a white background, he was able to overcome any technical issues of the different images coming together.

Phil mentally laid out the group shot and then took the individual shots with the plan of putting them together, as shown in FIGURE 7.92.

FIGURE 7.91 This family photo is a composite of four different photo shoots. © *Phil Pool - Omni Photography*

FIGURE 7.92 Each separate group was masked and successively composited. © *Phil Pool - Omni Photography*

Phil did not intend to shoot full-length images and concentrated on the waist up. This made the composite less complex. To cover the disparities among the bottom edges of the group portraits, he created a white vignette around the bottom. Vignetting techniques are covered later in this chapter.

FIGURES 7.93 and **7.94** Before and after. © *Hemmendinger Family Archives*

Adding a Missing Person

These tourists took turns photographing each other but wished they could all be in the same image (**FIGURE 7.93**). Follow these steps to pull a person from one image and place them in another; you'll also make corrections to the visual distortions created by a wide-angle lens and crop the image to a common photo size (**FIGURE 7.94**).

 **ch7_tourist1.jpg**
ch7_tourist2.jpg

1. Open the ch7_tourist 1.jpg file. Duplicate the Background layer for safekeeping, and turn off the visibility of the original.

2. Open the second image, ch7_tourist2.jpg. Make a selection with the Marquee tool (M) of the woman in the red jacket. Copy the selection (Cmd-C/Ctrl-C). Switch to the first image and paste (Cmd-V/Ctrl-V), as seen in **FIGURE 7.95**. The Place command could be used, but it will inflate the file size unnecessarily and some steps require the layer to be rasterized.

FIGURE 7.95 The woman in the red jacket is copied and pasted from the other image.

3. Use the Quick Selection tool to make an initial selection of the woman, and click the mask icon to hide the background. The woman has light shining off her face, which is similar to the others. With the Move tool (V), slide her into the space between the two men so that it looks like the light is hitting her in the same manner (**FIGURE 7.96**).

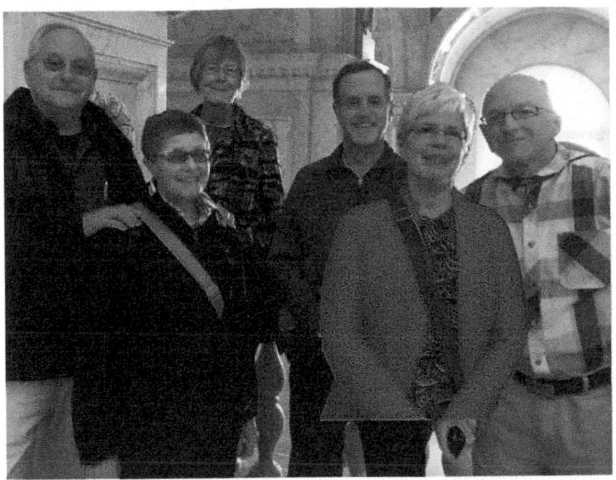

FIGURE 7.96 The added woman masked and put into position

4. The woman looks a little larger than the rest of the group and some of the next few steps are destructive, so duplicate the layer as backup and turn off the visibility of the lower layer.

5. Return to the duplicated layer and choose **Edit > Free Transform** (Cmd-T/Ctrl-T). Hold down Shift to constrain proportions, and shrink the woman slightly so her head size is comparable to the others (FIGURE 7.97). Press Return/Enter to accept the transformation.

FIGURE 7.97 The woman is scaled to match the other subjects.

6. The edge of the mask needs a touchup. Select a small, soft-edged brush and create a smooth transition between her and the background.

7. The men on either end of the photo show visual distortion from the use of a wide-angle lens. Content-Aware Scale can be used to correct it, but it needs to be applied selectively. Select the duplicate of the Background layer, select the Rectangular Marquee tool (M), and make a selection of the entire right side of the image, including the man, as seen in FIGURE 7.98.

8. From the Edit menu choose Content-Aware Scale (or press Cmd-Shift-Option-C/Ctrl-Alt-Shift-C). Click the handle to the right of the man's left arm, dragging to the left and stopping when the distortion on his face and shoulder is minimized (FIGURE 7.99). Press Return/Enter to accept. Press Cmd-D/Ctrl-D to deselect.

FIGURE 7.98 Select only the man to avoid scaling the entire image.

FIGURE 7.99 Content-Aware Scale reduces the distortion created by the wide-angle lens.

9. The desired final image size is 8x10, and determining the boundaries can help in reducing some of the work. The photographer who took the other shot did not compose in the same manner, so the added woman's torso does not extend to the bottom of the image. In addition, her hands are not included, but the hands of the other subjects are visible. Select the Marquee tool (M), and under Style, choose Fixed Ratio. Enter

10 for the width and 8 for the height. Start in the upper-right corner of the image and drag down to the left until the man on the left is mostly included, as shown in FIGURE 7.100.

10. If the rulers are not visible, press Cmd-R/Ctrl-R to make them visible. Switch to the Move tool (V), and from each ruler drag a guide to an edge of the selection. Press Ctrl-D/Cmd D to deselect (FIGURE 7.101).

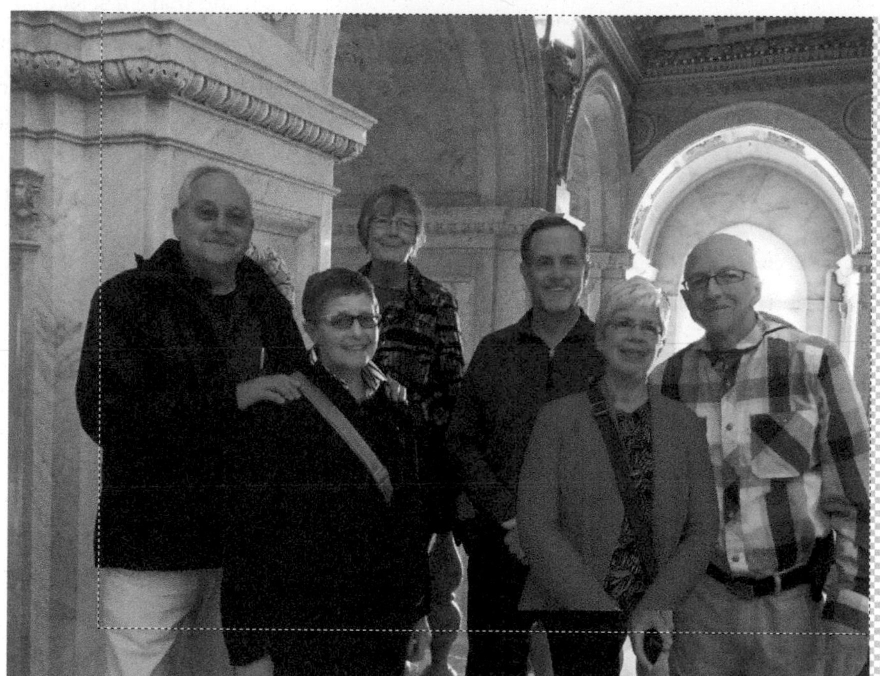

FIGURE 7.100 The Rectangular Marquee tool becomes a reference for setting guides.

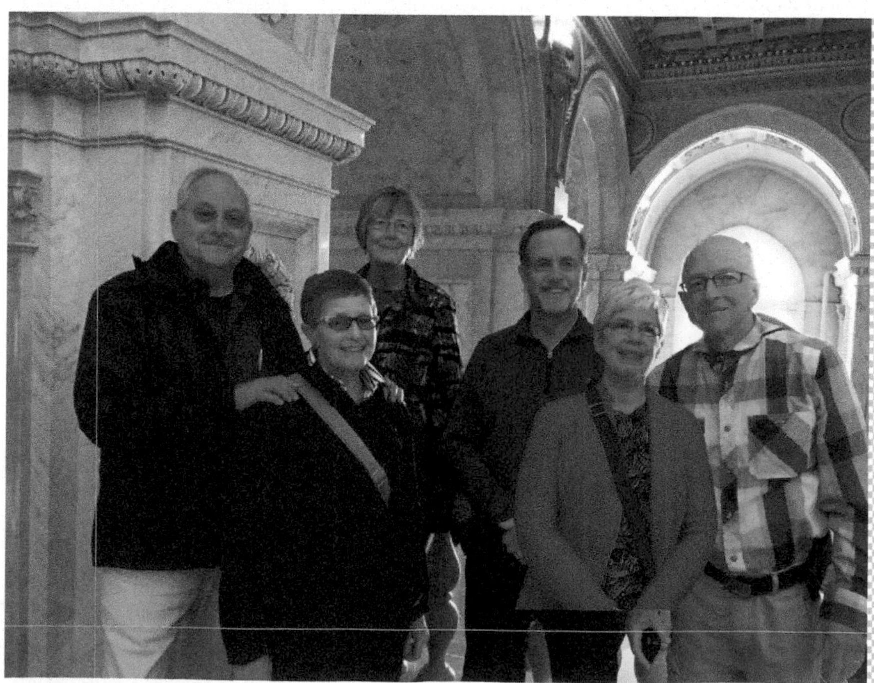

FIGURE 7.101 Guides are used to define the area of the image that will be kept.

11. The man's shoulder on the left side of the image seems a bit large. Select the Rectangular Marquee tool, choose Normal from the Style menu, and make a selection of the left side of the image, including the shoulder, as seen in FIGURE 7.102.

12. Choose **Edit > Content-Aware Scale**. Drag the handle on the left of the image to the right until the arm is mostly inside the vertical guide. Press Return/Enter to accept (FIGURE 7.103). Press Cmd-D/Ctrl-D to deselect.

FIGURE 7.102 The left side of the image is selected to include the man's shoulder.

FIGURE 7.103 Content-Aware Scale reduces the visual distortion.

TIP You could crop to an 8x10 ratio with Delete Cropped Pixels deselected to keep your work nondestructive, but it would not be as easy to compare your before and after results.

13. The woman in red needs to extend to the bottom guideline. Content-Aware Scale does not work on layer masks, so the next step is destructive. Being sure that the mask is final, right-click the layer mask and choose Apply Layer Mask. Make a selection of just the woman's shoulder and below (FIGURE 7.104).

FIGURE 7.104 Select only the red jacket to avoid distorting the woman's face.

14. Again use Content-Aware Scale to stretch the woman's torso to the guide, as seen in FIGURE 7.105. Note that marching ants switch from the area defined with the Rectangular Marquee tool to the information inside the selection. Pull the handle down to stretch the red coat to the guide (FIGURE 7.106).

FIGURE 7.105 Content-Aware Scale changes the selection to the information inside the initial selection.

FIGURE 7.106 The red coat is stretched to fill the frame.

15. In elongating the coat, Content-Aware Scale made the woman look a little heavier and her right arm is a little distorted. Press Cmd-T/Ctrl-T to start Free Transform. Hold down Cmd/Ctrl while dragging inward from the lower-left corner to return a normal perspective, as shown in **FIGURE 7.107**.

FIGURE 7.107 Free Transform corrects the distortion caused by stretching the coat.

16. The lens distortion also makes the woman in the back row look farther away than she really was. Enlarging her will correct this effect. Select the duplicate of the Background layer, and select the woman with the Quick Selection tool (**FIGURE 7.108**).

FIGURE 7.108 The Quick Selection tool easily selects the woman in the background.

17. Copy and paste the selection, which creates a new layer.

18. Start the Free Transform tool with Cmd-T/Ctrl-T and hold down Shift to constrain the proportion. Drag a corner handle to enlarge the woman until her face is similar in size to the others. Press Enter to accept the change. With the Move tool, nudge her into the same relative position (**FIGURE 7.109**).

FIGURE 7.109 Use Free Transform to enlarge the woman, making her more to scale.

19. Because the woman was enlarged, some of that layer is now hiding the person in front of her. Create a layer mask by clicking Add Layer Mask icon. Select a soft-edged brush set to black, and mask away the area that covers the foreground.

20. Crop the image using the guides as reference.

FITTING A PRINT TO A STORE-BOUGHT FRAME

A common misconception about the popular print sizes of 4x6, 5x7, and 8x10 is that they are just progressively larger versions of the same image area. While it is true they are progressively larger, they all have different aspect ratios. The 8x10 is an exact enlargement size of the 4x5 negative. But most photographers are accustomed to the aspect ratio of 35mm film, which is 2:3 and has carried over into digital photography. This has perplexed many new photographers who do not understand that the 2:3 ratio upsizes to 8:12, so 2 inches are missing in an 8x10 print. Keep this in mind when taking photographs. If different aspect ratios, or more specifically different-sized prints, are anticipated, don't crop tightly in-camera to allow for the differences in aspect ratio.

Planned Addition of a Person

It is all too often a difficult task to coordinate getting a group together. Such was the case for this group of music students when one member could not be present (FIGURE 7.110). With a little planning, the group shot left space for the missing student. That student was photographed later. Shooting in a studio, the photographer has more control of the image. Working outdoors, under different lighting conditions, presents different challenges. Follow the steps to see small details that make the end result believable (FIGURE 7.111).

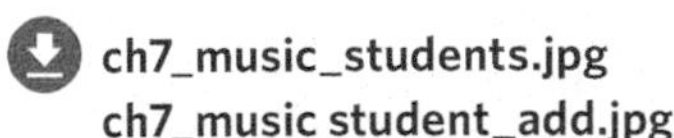

ch7_music_students.jpg
ch7_music student_add.jpg

FIGURES 7.110 and 7.111 Before and after. © *WP*

1. Open the file ch7_music_students.jpg, choose **File > Place Embedded**, and open ch7_music _ student_add.jpg, which will become a Smart Object (FIGURE 7.112).

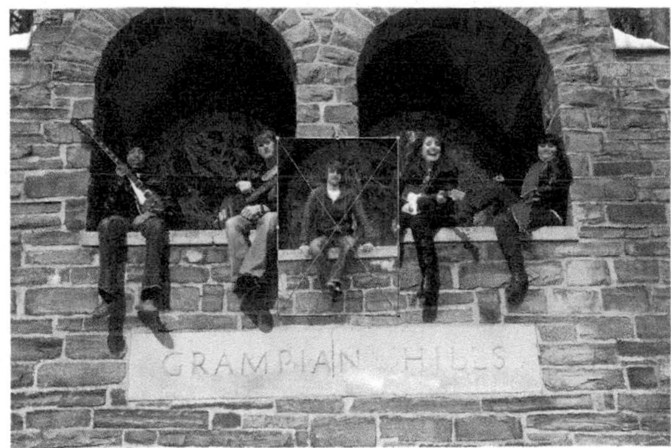

FIGURE 7.112 The added person placed inside the original image

2. Lower the opacity of the layer to about 75% and move the added person roughly into position. The person is slightly tilted and will need to be upsized a bit. Use the ledge as a guide to correct the tilt, and rotate the image by clicking outside a corner handle of the bounding box. The mouse pointer will display a double-headed arrow, as seen in FIGURE 7.113 (make sure that Show Transform Controls is selected in the options bar). Rotate the image slightly so the ledge direction matches. Hold the Shift button to constrain proportions, and scale the added person to match the size of the others (FIGURE 7.114). Press Enter to accept the new size, and return the layer opacity to 100%.

FIGURE 7.113 Tilting the image to match the Background layer

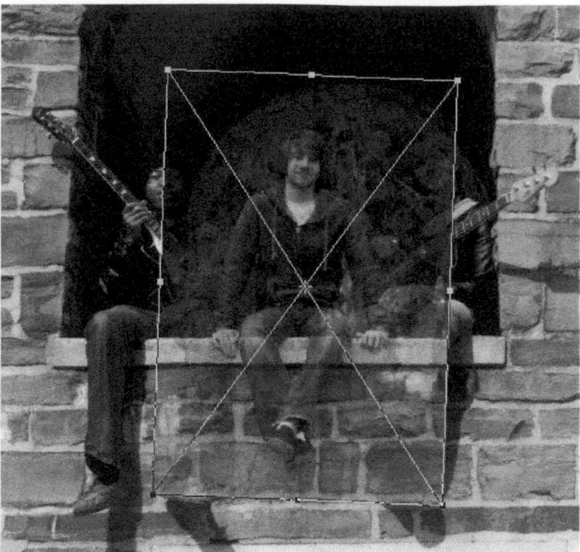

FIGURE 7.114 Scale the image to match the other subjects.

3. Use the Quick Selection tool to make a beginning selection of the added person. The tool will have a little difficulty making the selection. as there are areas where the contrast is not so noticeable. Hold down the Shift key to add to the selection, and hold down Option/Alt to subtract. Don't be concerned with getting the hands; get a selection as shown in FIGURE 7.115.

FIGURE 7.115 The subject is selected to mask out the background.

4. Click the Add Layer Mask icon in the Layers panel to make the background vanish (FIGURE 7.116).

FIGURE 7.116 The subject appears to be in front of the other two subjects.

5. Having the added person appear to be in front of the other two students does not look natural. Select the Brush tool (B), and with a soft-edged brush set to black, mask away the areas that make the added person look to be in front (FIGURE 7.117).

FIGURE 7.117 Careful masking gives the perception that the added person is behind the other two students.

6. With the added person in place and masked, perceptive eyes will pick up that the added person has no shadow like the others. Create an empty layer

underneath the added person layer. Cmd/Ctrl-click the Layer Mask icon, which will create a selection in the empty layer. Fill the selection with black by selecting **Edit > Fill > Contents > Black** or, if your foreground color is set to black, use the shortcut Option-Delete/Alt-Backspace. Press Cmd-D/Ctrl +D to deselect (FIGURE 7.118).

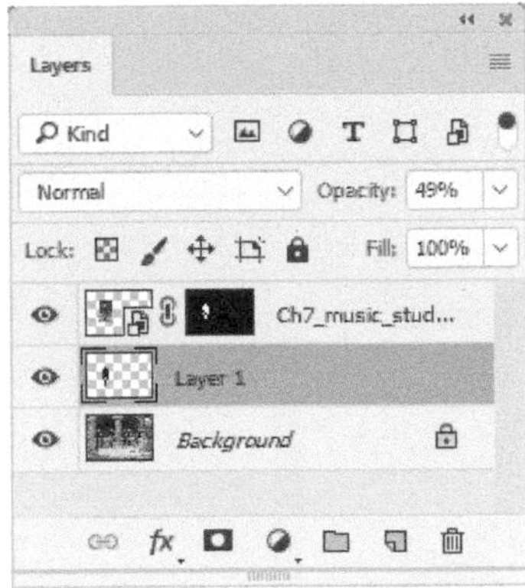

FIGURE 7.118 A shadow layer is made behind the added person.

7. The shadow is not immediately visible because it is directly behind the layer above it. Select the Move tool (V) and position the shadow at the same relative distance from the student as the other students' shadows (FIGURE 7.119).

FIGURE 7.119 The shadow is moved into the same relative position as the other subjects'.

8. Lower the opacity of the layer to 50% so that the transparency of the shadow matches that of the existing shadows (FIGURE 7.120).

FIGURE 7.120 Lowering the opacity of the shadow matches it to the others.

9. Create a layer mask for the shadow layer, and mask away any shadow above the ledge or touching the pant leg of the adjacent student (FIGURE 7.121).

FIGURE 7.121 Excess shadow is hidden through a mask.

10. The shadow length does not quite match the others. Use the Free Transform tool (Cmd-T/Ctrl-T) to stretch the shadow to match the others, as seen in FIGURE 1.222.

FIGURE 7.122 Free Transform is used to stretch the shadow to match.

11. There was no shadow in the added image because the image was taken on an overcast day. This makes the added person look a little flat. Create a Curves adjustment layer, click the Clipping icon so the change affects only the added person, and adjust the midtones (FIGURE 7.123).

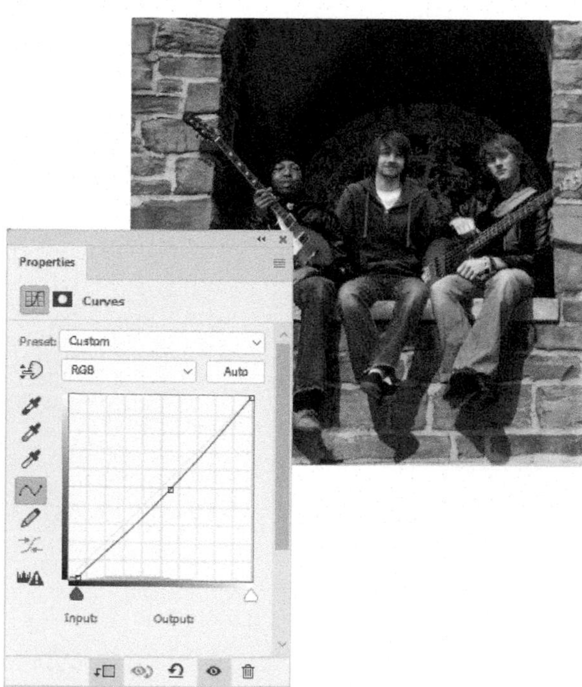

FIGURE 7.123 Curves adds some missing contrast.

12. The face is missing color. Create a Vibrance adjustment layer, again click the Clipping icon, and increase Vibrance to 32 to push the color level similar to the other subjects (FIGURE 7.124).

FIGURE 7.124 Vibrance punches up the color.

Scale to Fit

The Content-Aware Scale tool can be very useful in resizing a photo without cropping. This image of a fishing village needed to fit a precut mat (FIGURE 7.125). Cropping would have removed some of the interesting elements in the image, but Content-Aware Scale was able squeeze in everything and keep all the charm (FIGURE 7.126).

ch07_peggys_cove.jpg

1. The image measured 14 inches wide but needed to fit a 12.5-inch mat. With the rulers visible (Cmd-R/Ctrl-R), drag a vertical guide to the 14" mark, as seen in FIGURE 7.127.

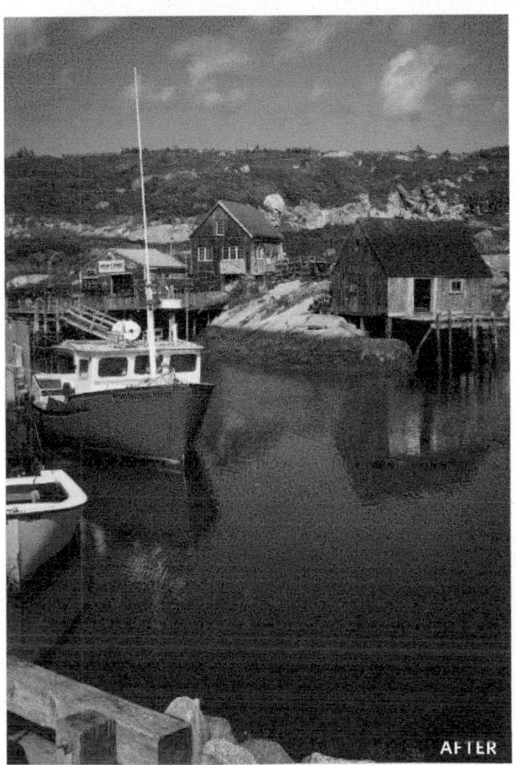

FIGURES 7.125 and 7.126 Before and after. © *WP*

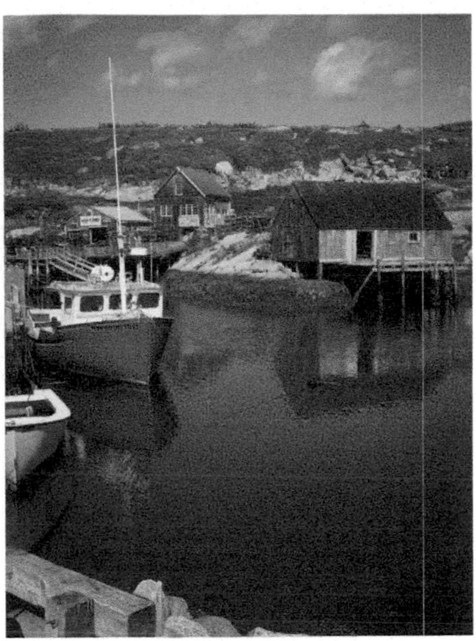

FIGURE 7.127 Use a vertical guide to mark the final dimension needed.

2. Duplicate the Background layer and turn off the visibility of the original.

Content-Aware Scale can distort an image, especially when the entire image is scaled, as seen in the jagged rooflines in FIGURE 7.128. To keep this from happening, apply Content-Aware Scale to a portion of the image.

FIGURE 7.128 Content-Aware Scale can create distortion when applied to the entire image.

3. Select the Marquee tool (M), and with Style set to Normal, select the entire right side of the image, taking in most of the old lobster shack (FIGURE 7.129).

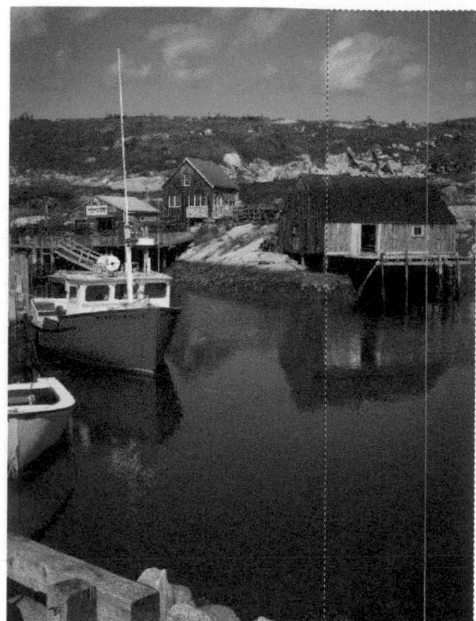

FIGURE 7.129 Use the Marquee tool to limit the scaling to a smaller portion of the image.

4. Choose **Edit > Content-Aware Scale**. Drag the handle on the right side of the bounding box inward until the edge of the image aligns with the guide. Press Return/Enter or click the check mark icon in the options bar to accept the change (FIGURE 7.130).

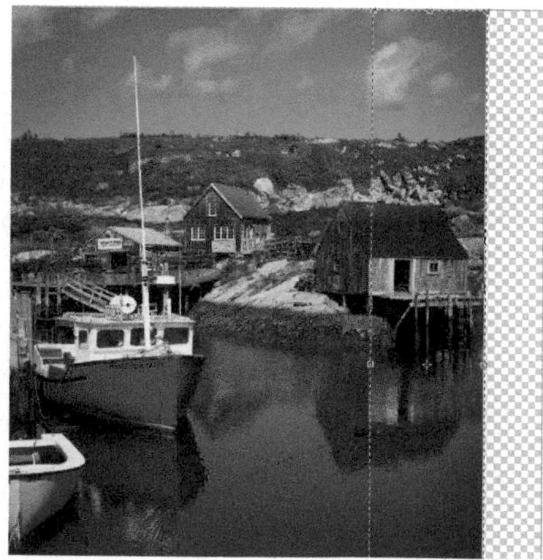

FIGURE 7.130 Content-Aware Scale allowed the shack to be shrunk successfully.

The image can then be cropped without permanently losing any information (make sure that Delete Cropped Pixels is deselected).

REDUCING REFLECTIONS AND LIGHT LEAKS

Light is the very foundation of photography, yet it can also be one of photography's biggest problems. Too much light, too little light, or light in the wrong place can create unique and challenging problems.

Reducing Reflections

Taking pictures of or through windows is challenging. To reduce reflections while taking the picture, use a polarizing filter. But sometimes the moment calls out for the shot to be taken regardless of the outcome. Such was the case with this couple, who saw the camera and struck a quick pose (FIGURE 7.131). Unfortunately, the reflection in the window is distracting and reshooting it would have ruined the spontaneity. The reflection was removed with adjustment layers, and Straighten Layer was used to straighten out the image (FIGURE 7.132).

FIGURES 7.131 and 7.132 Before and after. © *Pamela Herrington*

ch7_happycouple.jpg

1. To darken the reflection, start by selecting the interior of the window with the Lasso tool. Holding down the Option/Alt key, which toggles the Polygonal Lasso tool, start in the lower-right corner, working your way around to the young man. Release the Option/Alt key, which returns the tool to the Lasso tool, and make a freehand selection of the couple, returning to the corner of the window where the selection started, as seen in FIGURE 7.133.

FIGURE 7.133 Starting the selection with the Polygonal Lasso and finishing it with the standard Lasso tool

2. Add a Levels adjustment layer, and move the black slider to the right until the window reflection just about disappears, as in FIGURE 7.134. Leaving a hint of the reflection maintains environmental context and interest.

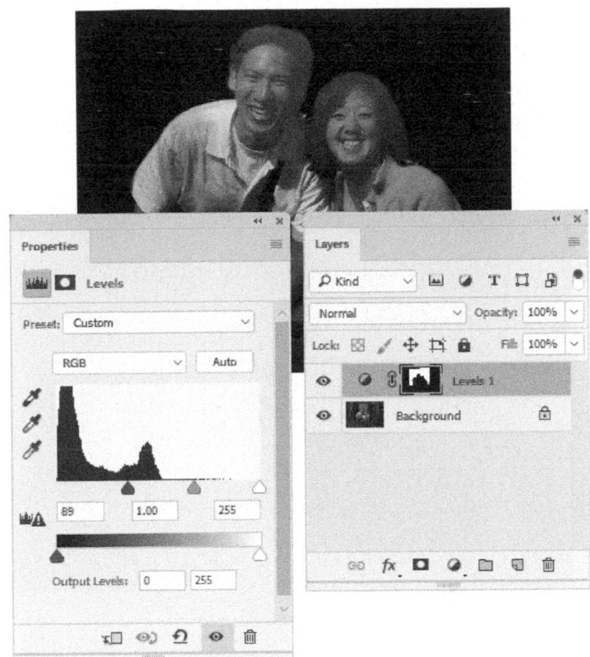

FIGURE 7.134 Increasing the black levels reduces most of the glare.

3. If the edge of your selection is too harsh, click the layer mask and in the Properties panel set the Feather slider to 5 to soften the transition (FIGURE 7.135).

FIGURE 7.135 Soften the edges of the layer mask with the Feather slider in the Properties panel.

4. To darken the couple, select them with the Elliptical Marquee tool (**FIGURE 7.136**), add a Curves adjustment layer, and darken the shadows, as seen in **FIGURE 7.137**. Use the Feather slider in the Properties panel with a setting of 5 to soften the transition.

FIGURE 7.136 Selecting just the couple

FIGURE 7.137 Darkening the couple and softening the transition removes a lot of the glare.

5. Add a new layer and use the Spot Healing Brush set to Sample All Layers to remove any remaining specks and clean up the window (**FIGURE 7.138**).

FIGURE 7.138 The lights visible in the background are removed.

6. Use Cmd-Option-Shift+E/Ctrl-Alt-Shift-E to merge all the layers up to a new "work in progress" layer. Turn off the visibility of lower layers.

7. Select the Ruler tool, nested underneath the Eyedropper tool, and draw a line following the bottom of the window frame (**FIGURE 7.139**). Select Straighten Layer in the options bar, which will correct the tilt in the image (**FIGURE 7.140**).

FIGURE 7.139 The Ruler tool has the option to straighten a layer.

FIGURE 7.140 Straightening an image will create transparent areas.

8. Crop (C) the image to eliminate the transparent corners created by straightening, as seen in FIGURE 7.141.

FIGURE 7.141 Crop the image to a new size to get rid of transparent areas.

Of course it is better to compose the best picture in front of the lens, but sometimes speed and spontaneity are more important than formal compositional rules, which is where Photoshop comes into play to help create the better image.

Correcting Lens Flare

Lens flare is caused by light bouncing off and around the inside of the lens barrel and can in most cases by avoided by shielding the lens from direct sun or by using large lens shades. Sometimes lens flare can be considered an artistic addition to an image (there is a Lens Flare filter in the Render group of filters), but many times it is distracting.

Repairing Extreme Lens Flare

With extreme lens flare, (FIGURE 7.142), you may need to rework image density, then duplicate information, and perform cloning and healing to turn the ruined photo into the final image (FIGURE 7.143).

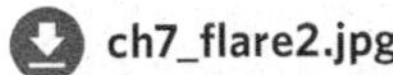

FIGURES 7.142 and 7.143 Before and after. © *KE*

1. Flare always reduces contrast, and improving the contrast is the first step in rebuilding the image. Add a Curves adjustment layer, and Option/Alt-click the Auto button to open the Auto Color Correction Options dialog box. Click the Enhance Per Channel Contrast button and select Snap Neutral Midtones; click OK (FIGURE 7.144).

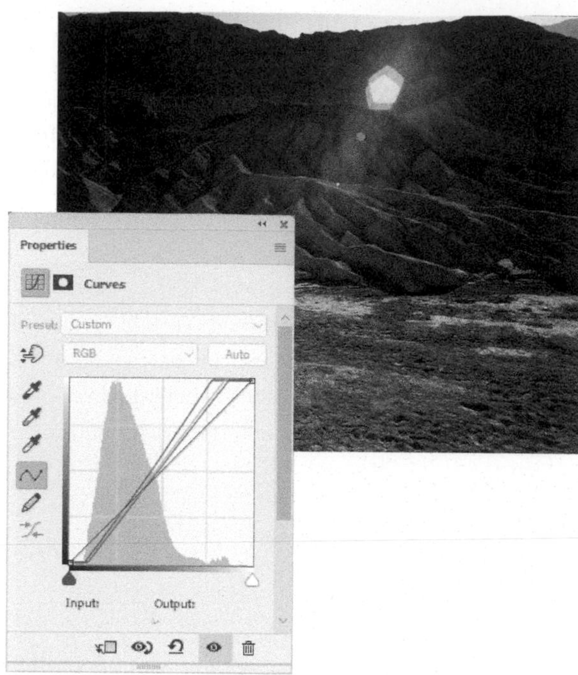

FIGURE 7.144 Improving the overall contrast

2. Select the large flared-out area with a 10-pixel feathered Lasso tool, and add a Curves adjustment layer to darken the area, as seen in FIGURE 7.145. Refine the transition by painting on the layer mask.

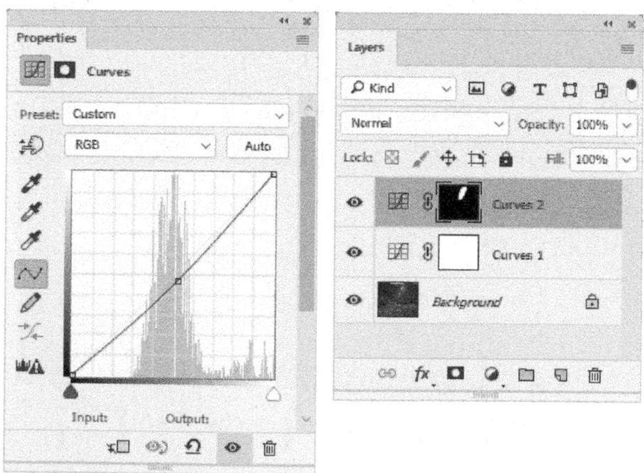

FIGURE 7.145 A masked Curves layer lets us darken a portion of the image.

3. Copy and merge the layers into a new one using the keyboard shortcut Cmd-Option-Shift-E/Ctrl-Alt-Shift-E.

4. With the Patch tool, make selections of each part of the reflections and move the selection to a suitable area for fill, as shown in FIGURE 7.146. Use the Healing brush or Clone Stamp tool to touch up any areas that need it.

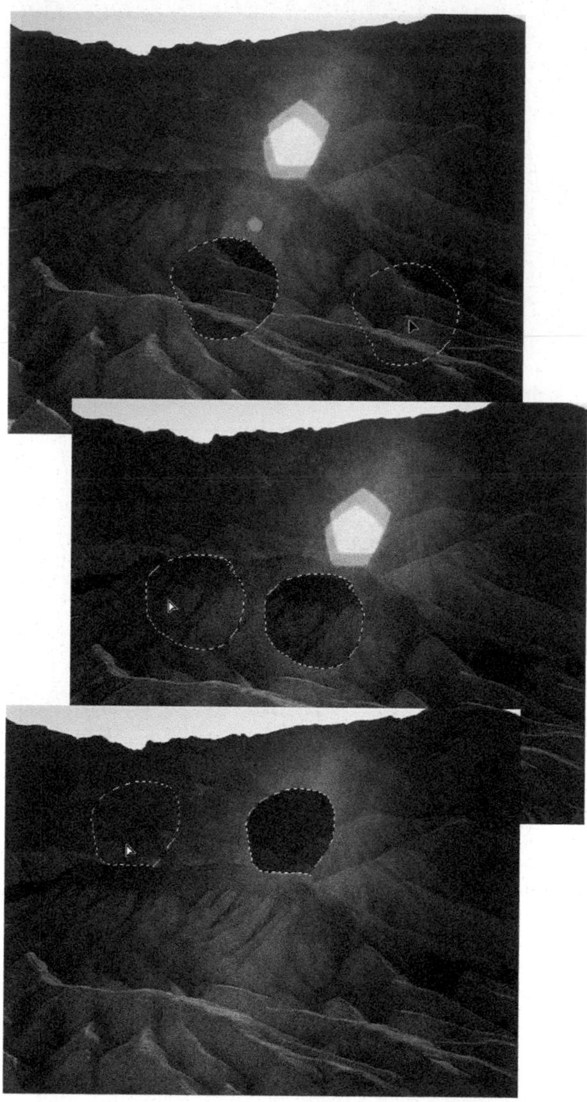

FIGURE 7.146 The Patch tool removes most of the glare.

5. There is still some haze left from the flare (FIGURE 1.47). Create an empty layer and set the blending mode to Soft Light (FIGURE 7.148). With the Brush tool (B) set to black and Opacity set to 8%, paint over the haze, reducing its brightness.

FIGURE 1.47 A haze still remains after the reflections are removed.

FIGURE 7.148 Burn in the last of the haze.

Repairing Light Leaks

Correcting overall color casts, as described in Chapter 4, can alleviate many problems, but often the actual color information in the file is badly damaged by light leaks, chemical staining, or dye coupler failure, causing severe color splotches or radical color shifts.

The damage seen in FIGURE 7.149 could have been caused by opening the camera before the film was entirely rewound or by light leaks in the camera or on the film roll. Using the best channel information, dodge and burn layers, and multiple Solid Color layers, the charm of the moment in time has been brought back to life (FIGURE 7.150). Of course, a repaired image will never be as perfect as one that wasn't damaged to begin with.

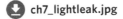

 **ch7_lightleak.jpg**

FIGURES 7.149 and 7.150 Before and after. © *Ehrman Family Archive*

1. Inspect each color channel (Cmd/Ctrl with 3, 4, and 5) to ascertain where the most damage is. Notice that the blue channel contains useful information (FIGURE 7.151). Due to the extreme damage suffered by the photo, I decided to convert it to a black and white image and then recolor it rather than trying to resurrect the color.

FIGURE 7.151 The blue channel shows the best information.

2. Add a Channel Mixer adjustment layer, select Monochrome, and move the Blue slider to 100% while setting the Red and Green sliders to 0. This reduces the streaks a great deal (FIGURE 7.152).

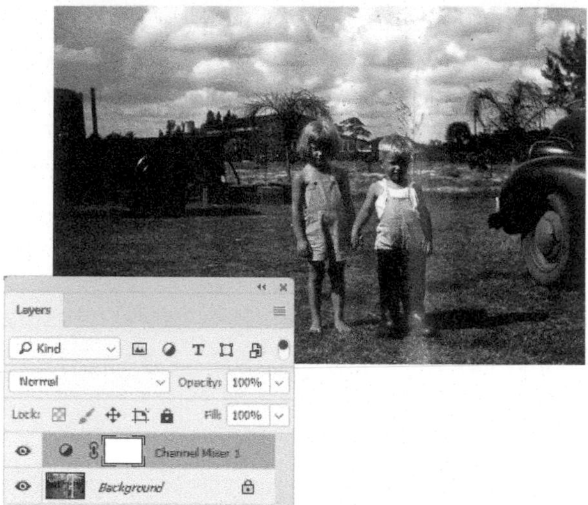

FIGURE 7.152 A Channel Mixer adjustment layer with Monochrome selected conceals most of the damage.

3. To improve the density, choose **Layer > New > Layer**, change Mode to Overlay, and select Fill with Overlay–neutral color (50% gray). Use a soft, low-opacity black brush to darken the remaining lighter streaks (FIGURE 7.153). If your own images have darker streaks, simply paint with white to lighten them appropriately.

FIGURE 7.153 Painting on a neutral layer set to Overlay blending mode to balance density

TIP Filling the layer with gray just helps identify where work has been done; it has no effect on the results.

4. Create a Work in Progress (WIP) layer by pressing Cmd-Option-Shift-E/Ctrl-Alt-Shift-E, then use the Spot Healing Brush and Clone Stamp tool to remove the most distracting dust on the children and in the foreground.

5. To remove the dust in the sky, select the sky with a 3-pixel feathered Lasso and choose **Filter > Noise > Dust & Scratches**. Set both Radius and Threshold to 2. After deselecting, use the Healing Brush to repair any remaining streaks in the clouds (FIGURE 7.154).

FIGURE 7.154 Dust spots and the clouds were repaired on a Work in Progress layer.

To color the image while maintaining flexibility, use Solid Color layers, as described here.

6. Start with the sky and make a rough selection of the area. Create a Solid Color layer, choose a light blue color, and click OK. Change the blending mode to Color. Use a soft-edged white brush to add more to the selected area, and use black if you spill outside the area you want to color. If the blue is too strong, reduce the layer opacity or double-click the layer thumbnail and choose a new blue.

7. Create separate layers for the grass, skin tones, clothes, hair, boots, and dirt. For added realism, sample colors from the original Background layer to use when coloring the image (FIGURE 7.155).

FIGURE 7.155 Seven Solid Color layers later, the image looks similar to its initial color.

NOTE When hand-coloring, put the least important areas lower in the layer stack, as the top color takes precedence.

8. After working with this image for a few minutes, I noticed that the car on the right side still maintained some of the original color. To add a heightened sense of realism, duplicate the Background layer and place it on top of the layer stack. Option/Alt-click the Add Layer Mask button to add a black layer mask, and use a soft-edged white brush to paint back the original car (FIGURE 7.156).

FIGURE 7.156 Reusing the color of the original image

9. To hide the last vestiges of the light leaks, choose **Layer > New > Layer**, set the blending mode to Overlay, and select Fill with Overlay–neutral color (50% gray). Use a soft, low-opacity black brush to darken the remaining lighter streaks, and use a white brush to lighten darker streaks (FIGURE 7.157).

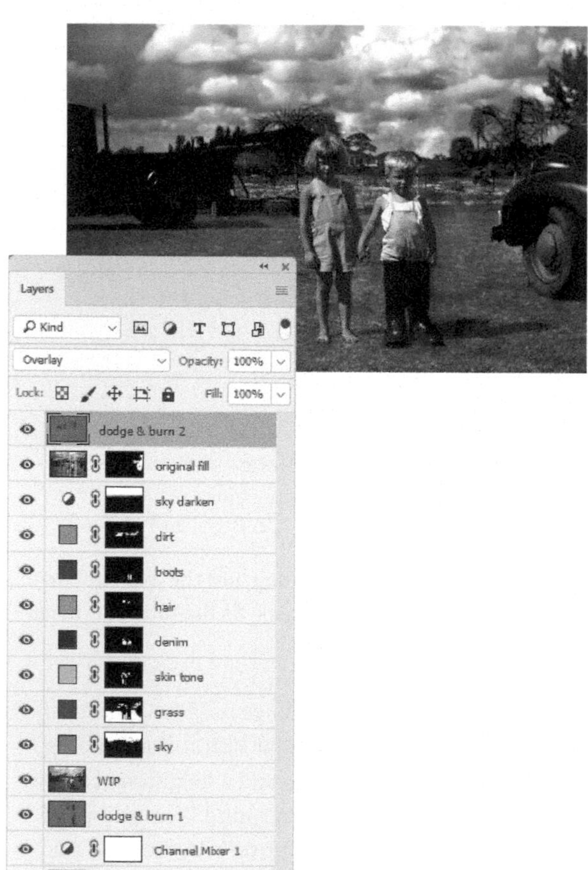

FIGURE 7.157 A final dodge and burn layer removes the last of the light leaks.

Finishing Touches: Vignetting

A vignette is the darkening or lightening of the corners of an image. Traditionally, it was done with a fade to black or white, but any color can be used. An unintentional vignette (FIGURE 7.158) is usually the result of a limitation in the photo equipment, which can be caused by a mismatched lens hood or an APS-designed lens on a full-frame camera. Done deliberately, it is a creative technique that draws the eye of the viewer toward the subject (FIGURE 7.159).

FIGURE 7.158 This unintended vignette was the result of using a lens hood that was the wrong size. © *John Troisi*

FIGURE 7.159 Vignettes draw the viewer's eye to the subject of the photo and away from any distractions in the background. © *WP.*

WHAT IS APS?

Ever wonder why the sensors in most digital single lens reflex cameras are referred to as APS sized? In the mid 1990s a joint venture between Kodak, Fujifilm, Nikon, Canon, and Minolta produced a new film format called Advanced Photo System (APS) that addressed one of the biggest perceived consumer challenges: properly loading a 35mm camera. This cartridge film was self-loading and could record image information similar to metadata. The customer never saw the film, as it stayed in the cartridge even after being processed. Commercially, it was a flop, with Kodak abandoning it just eight years after introduction. Technologically, it was a success, proving that a quality image could be made from a negative smaller than 35mm. That smaller size became the standard size for SLR sensors. The C was added to the designation to indicate the "classic" negative size of 25.1x16.7 mm.

In darkroom days, the vignette effect was accomplished through dodging and burning techniques or the use of a physical mask while the photo paper was being exposed. Things are much simpler to do in Photoshop, and there are number of ways to create a vignette, which often puts a nice finishing touch on an image.

Doing It Yourself

To create a vignette without a uniform appearance, use the Dodge and Burn tools. This method can be time intensive but offers the most control over the results (FIGURES 7.160 and 7.161).

ch7_horse_rider.jpg

1. Create an empty layer and change the blending mode to Overlay.

2. Select a large, soft-edged brush, one that will cover the corners of the image in fewer strokes. Start with a low opacity setting, below 10%, and paint black or white, depending upon desired result, to build up the effect (FIGURE 7.162). You can easily erase and start again if you don't like the results.

FIGURES 7.160 and 7.161 Before and after. © *WP*

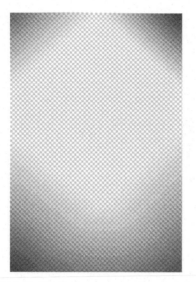

FIGURE 7.162 Burning in the corners on a separate layer keeps the changes nondestructive.

A variant of this method is to substitute the Gradient tool for the Brush tool and use the Foreground to Transparent preset.

1. Create an empty layer and set the blending mode to Overlay.

2. Select the Gradient tool, in the options bar select Linear Gradient, and choose the Foreground to Transparent preset. This preset is important because it allows for multiple gradients to be made on the same layer instead of one replacing the other (FIGURE 7.163).

FIGURE 7.163 With the Foreground to Transparent preset, multiple gradients can be added to the same layer.

3. Press D to reset the Color Picker to the default colors. Set the foreground color to the type of vignette desired.

4. If you don't want the corners to be absolute black or white, start the gradient outside the image. Drag partway toward the subject. Repeat for the remaining corners. If the corners are still too dark, just lower the opacity of the layer (FIGURE 7.164).

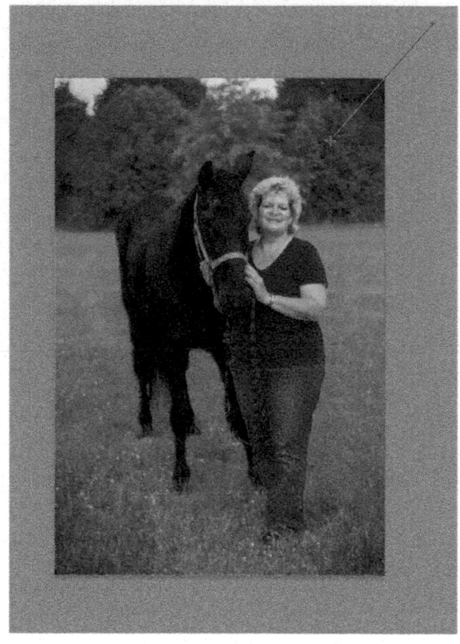

FIGURE 7.164 Starting the gradient outside the image keeps the corners from becoming totally black.

Using the Camera Raw Filter

The simplest way to create a vignette is to use the options in the Camera Raw filter on the Effects tab. There is a slider for controlling the intensity of either a dark or light vignette. Other options include Midpoint, which controls the width of the vignette. Be sure to convert the layer to a Smart Object/Smart Filter first to keep the changes nondestructive (FIGURE 7.165). If you want to apply a vignette to a multiple-layer file, start by creating a Work in Progress layer (WIP) layer: with the top layer selected, press the keyboard shortcut Shift-Cmd-Option-E/Shift-Ctrl-Alt-E to copy and merge visible layers to a new layer.

+ TIP The Custom tab in the Lens Correction filter also allows you to create a vignette but has fewer options.

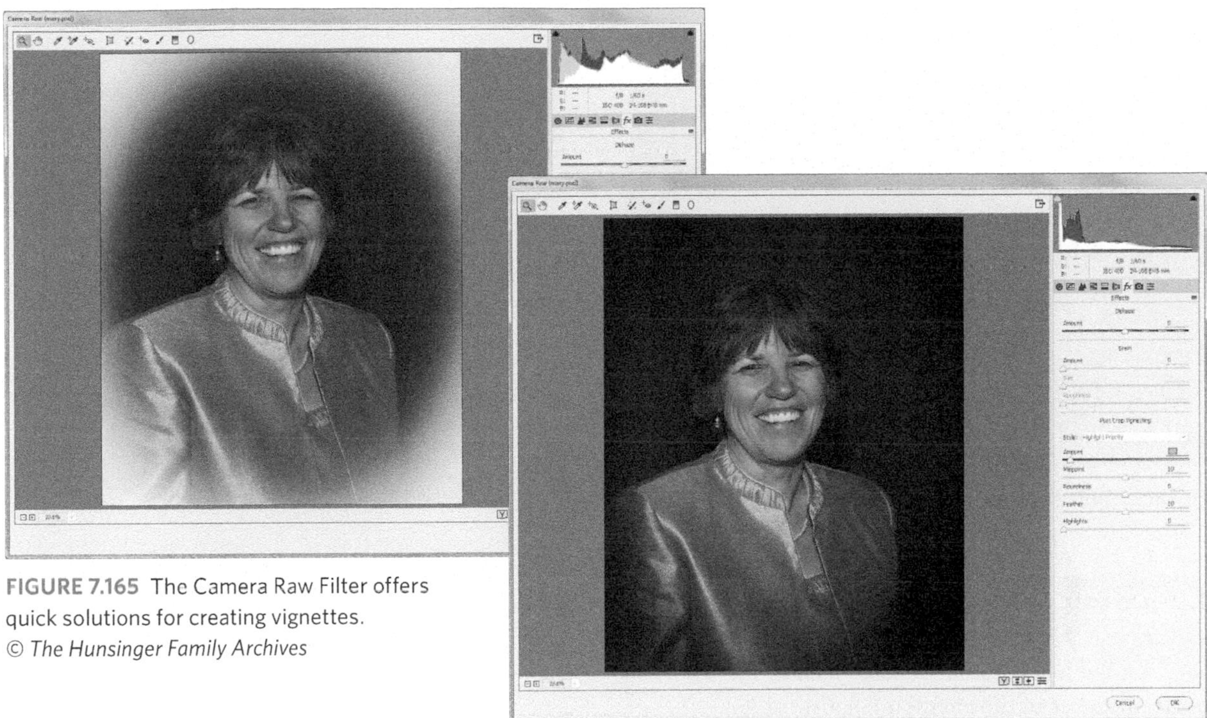

FIGURE 7.165 The Camera Raw Filter offers quick solutions for creating vignettes. © *The Hunsinger Family Archives*

Using Solid Color

The Solid Color fill layer works well when the desired vignette fades to a color that matches a colored mat, but it's also an easy way to create a conventional one (FIGURES 7.166 and 7.167).

1. With one of the marquee tools, select the area where you would like the vignette to begin. Often the Elliptical Marquee tool is best. If you press the spacebar while holding down the mouse button, you can move the selection (FIGURE 7.168).

ch7_man_in_chair.jpg

TIP Photoshop often provides multiple ways to accomplish the same task, and an alternative method of making a selection for a vignette is to hold Option/Alt while dragging out an ellipse from the center of the object you want to highlight.

FIGURES 7.166 and 7.167 Before and after. © *WP*

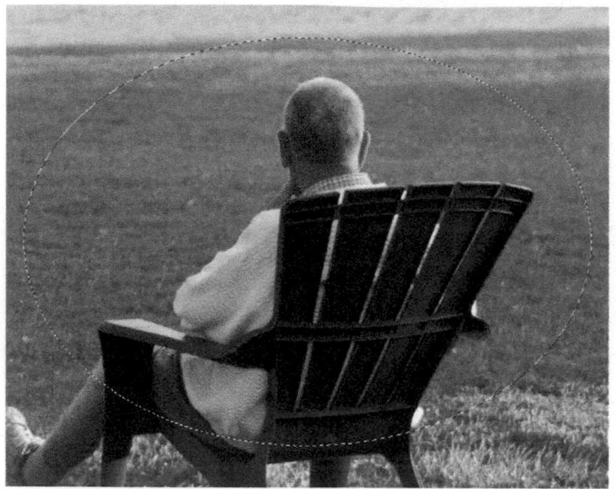

FIGURE 7.168 A rough selection made with the Elliptical Marquee tool

2. Open the Create Fill or Adjustment Layer menu and choose Solid Color. You can choose any color you like, but let's create the effect seen in the family portrait earlier in the chapter. Choose white.

3. The effect is the opposite of what is desired. Make sure the mask is selected, and invert it by pressing Cmd-I/Ctrl-I. You could invert the selection before this step, but it will make more work should you decide to unlink the mask and move it (FIGURE 7.169).

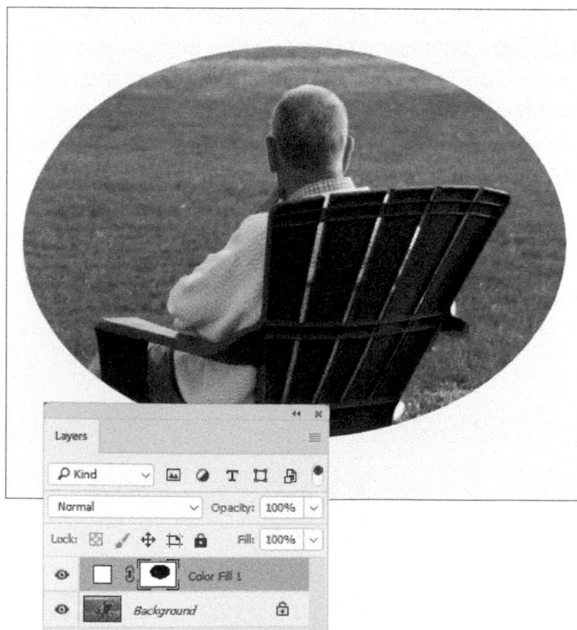

FIGURE 7.169 The initial effect has a hard edge.

4. With the mask still selected, drag the Feather slider in the Properties panel to refine the edge of the vignette. Adjusting to 111 pixels creates a nice fade that can be readjusted at any time (FIGURE 7.170).

FIGURE 7.170 Using the Mask Properties panel for feathering keeps the effect nondestructive.

+ TIP When fading to black or another dark color, lower the opacity of the adjustment layer if the corners are too dark.

+ TIP If the mask is not exactly where you want it, click the Link icon between the thumbnail and the mask to unlink the mask, and use the Move tool to reposition it.

Using a Hue/Saturation Adjustment Layer

One last technique combines the Lightness slider of a Hue/Saturation adjustment layer with the Feather slider on the Layer Mask Properties panel. This method offers a lot of flexibility for changing the effect (FIGURES 7.171 and 7.172).

ch7_butterfly.jpg

FIGURES 7.171 and 7.172 Before and after. © *WP*

1. Make a selection of the area where you would like the vignette to start. You can use the Elliptical Marquee tool for a more uniform look or just make a random selection with the Lasso tool, as seen in FIGURE 7.173.

FIGURE 7.173 An irregular selection of the subject is made.

2. Invert the selection by pressing Shift-Cmd-I/ Shift-Ctrl-I.

3. From the Layers panel, open the Create New Adjustment or Fill Layer menu and choose Hue/ Saturation. Drag the Lightness slider right or left to make a light or dark vignette (FIGURE 7.174).

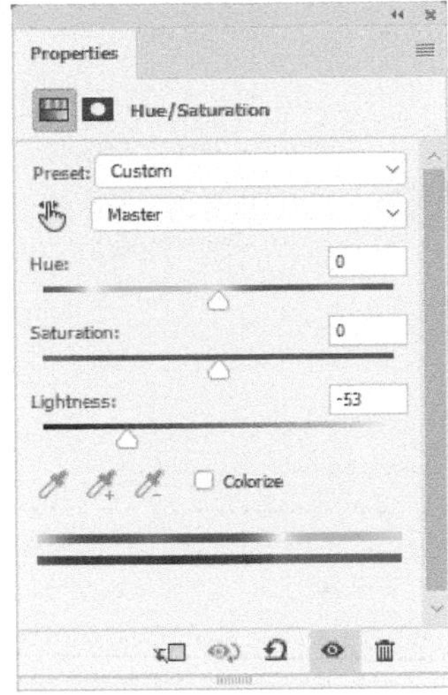

FIGURE 7.174 Using a Hue/Saturation layer to darken the unmasked area

4. The mask will have a sharp edge. Click the mask, and in the Layer Mask Properties panel use the Feather slider to make a smooth transition into the vignette (FIGURE 7.175).

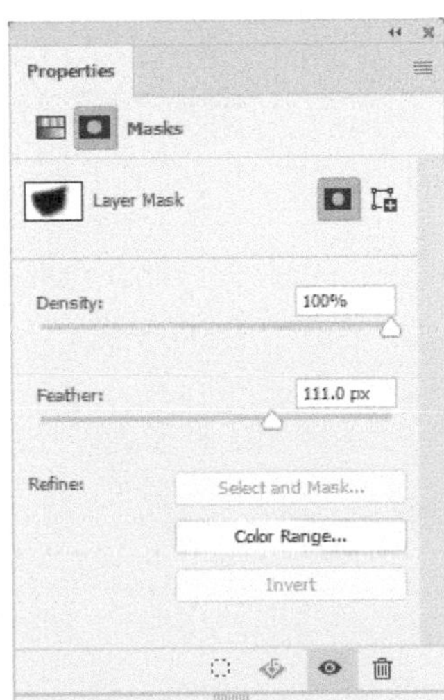

FIGURE 7.175 Use the Feather slider in the Properties panel to soften the edge of the vignette nondestructively.

One advantage to this method is the ability to tweak the vignette. The settings are saved and can be adjusted later by revisiting the Hue/Saturation layer and its mask.

CLOSING THOUGHTS

Replacing, rebuilding, and re-creating missing image elements requires creative problem-solving skills, the willingness to dig around in a file to look for useful material, and the ability to appropriate suitable pieces from other photographs and scenes. The search will result in new images that are much more pleasing and meaningful to display and cherish.

Part IV

PROFESSIONAL RETOUCHING

QUIFY • CAFFEINE • PERSPECTIVE CROP • COLOR CORRECTION • SHARPENING • RETOUCH STRATE
YER MASK • SEPIA TONING • HANDLING DELICATE ORIGINALS • DUST & SCRATCHES FILTER • CO
IGE • NOISE FILTERS • CONTENT AWARE MOVE • NOISE REDUCTION • FOOD RETOUCHING • LOCAL CO
RECTION • PRODUCT RETOUCHING • CONTENT AWARE SCALE • WHITE BALANCE • NONDESTRUCT
ING • RESTORATION WORKFLOW • HEALING TOOLS • CURVES ADJUSTMENT LAYER • TRANSFORMATIO
OPPING • DODGE AND BURN • ENVIRONMENT AND LIGHTING • PERSPECTIVE CORRECTIONS • EXPOSU

Chapter 8

PORTRAIT RETOUCHING

Good retouching requires starting with a vision of the ultimate goal for the image. If you're a retoucher working on images for clients, this means starting off with a discussion about the vision the photographer or client has for that particular photo. And it requires using a flexible workflow that enables you to adjust the various aspects of your retouching so you can easily dial in the look the client wants without having to redo a lot of work.

With portraits, the goal should be to bring out the best in the subject, enhancing their features while making them look refreshed and relaxed. The recommended approach when retouching portraits is to minimize the distractions and make the image a positive reflection of the subject.

In this chapter you'll learn how to work with color, contrast, and detail to make people look their best while keeping their individuality. The topics and techniques we'll concentrate on are:

- Developing a retouching strategy
- Removing distractions and improving contours
- Improving skin texture and important facial features
- Adding a creative interpretation
- Lightroom and plug-ins as alternatives to Photoshop

! CAUTION If, by chance, you jumped to this chapter first, please understand that the very first step of working with any digital image is to apply global exposure and color correction in either Adobe Camera Raw or Photoshop, as explained in earlier chapters. We recommend starting the image enhancement workflow by establishing correct tone and color foundations, before moving on to correcting and enhancing portraits as described in this chapter.

STAGES OF RETOUCHING

When retouching portraits one of the first things to keep in mind is the difference between how we perceive a photograph and how we perceive a person in real life. A photograph is a two-dimensional representation in which the shape and details of a person's face are limited to variations in tonality and color. In contrast, when we see that same person in real life we get a much more accurate idea of the actual shape and features of their face.

Good photographers understand this and use appropriate lighting to create a portrait that compliments the subject. By the time we get to the retouching stage, the lighting has already been set, but we do have an extensive set of tools that allow us to not only clean up the skin, eyes, and features but to enhance the lighting as well.

The first job of the retoucher is to work with the client to be sure you understand how they want the final image to appear and how extensive your retouching needs to be. While everyone wants to feel and look their best, not everyone will want the full Hollywood beauty treatment. It's important to have a clear discussion with the client to match their expectations with their budget so you'll know how much work you need to do.

One good strategy for doing this is to develop a retouching scale, as shown in FIGURE 8.1 (the original) and FIGURES 8.2 through 8.5.

This four-level approach makes it easy to show your clients what they can expect and how much it will cost them to have you do this work. For instance, level 1 usually involves basic color correction and blemish removal, which can be accomplished quickly, whereas levels 3 and 4 involve much more detailed work as well as artistic touches that can significantly add to the time needed to finish the work.

Clear communication about the client's expectations and budget will help you work efficiently and profitably.

Level 1

Includes color correction, removing obvious blemishes, and light work reducing lines and wrinkles on the subject's face. This level should take 5 to 10 minutes per image (Figure 8.2) and can often be accomplished in Lightroom or Adobe Camera Raw (ACR).

Level 2

Expands on the work done in level 1, going a bit further to enhance the features of the subject. Includes smoothing skin, further reduction of wrinkles and lines, removing distracting stray hairs, enhancing eyes, and reducing glare on skin. This level usually takes an additional 20 to 30 minutes (Figure 8.3).

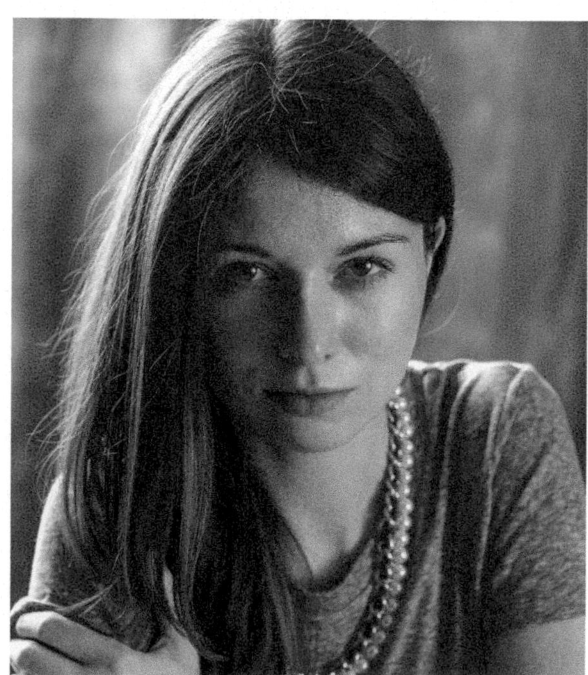

FIGURE 8.1 Original © *George Simian*

FIGURE 8.2 Level 1

FIGURE 8.3 Level 2

FIGURE 8.4 Level 3

FIGURE 8.5 Level 4

Level 3

This more advanced level of work includes smoothing the hair, removing crosshairs, adding drama to the eyes, enhancing the lighting with burning and dodging, enhancing the lips, paying additional attention to the color and tonality of the image, and giving extra care to the overall look and feel of the image. This level of work requires careful attention and can take 45 to 60 minutes per image (Figure 8.4).

Level 4

This level involves creative effects such as adding a subtle glow to the subject's face, further enhancing detail in the hair or make-up, and color treatments such as black and white conversion or color grading, which gives an image a cinematic appearance. This level allows you to add a more personal interpretation to the image, and while not every client will want such treatments, this level of work can be more personally satisfying, giving you a greater opportunity to be creative with your work. The time needed for this level can vary greatly, depending on how far you take the effects (Figure 8.5).

DEVELOPING A PORTRAIT-RETOUCHING STRATEGY

Although every image is different, basic portrait retouching involves some common tasks. Approaching these tasks in an organized way can help you work faster and more efficiently.

Before you jump into spotting and cloning away, take a moment to look over the image and make some mental notes about what needs to be worked on. Some retouchers find it helpful to add an empty layer, using a brush to make notes about what needs to be done.

As you form your plan, use the following steps to map out an efficient strategy for successfully completing the job.

- **Assess the image** to determine what features of the person you need to emphasize or tone down to help the person look their best. This will be influenced to a large degree by the ultimate purpose for the photograph. Will this image be used for a high school senior portrait, or is it a more casual photo such as a lifestyle image? Is the photo of a company president or a portrait of a bride on her wedding day? Each circumstance will need to be weighed when it comes to determining your approach and how far you will take the retouching.

- **Identify and remove distractions** that pull the viewer's eye away from the subject. One technique for identifying these is to defocus your eyes and take note of anything that seems to be begging for attention or explanation.

These distractions could be branches running through a person's neck, as shown in FIGURE 8.6, or bright background spots that compete with a person's face. Removing the distractions puts the viewer's focus on the subject, not the background (FIGURE 8.7).

- **Refine the contours** of the body, face, and neck. They should be smooth and graceful so they flatter the subject. Often, bulges and extra lines are caused by the pose, the clothes, or a little extra weight the person is carrying. As you assess the image, let your eyes follow the person's contours and make note of anything that seems distracting or unflattering. The main issues to look for are flyaway hairs, bulges in clothing, double chins, and folds of skin near the neck or armpits.

- **Enhance facial features** such as the eyes, lips, nose, and skin. Eyes are especially important because they can be so expressive. Care should be taken to retain the natural texture and shape of the skin so that it doesn't end up overly blurred and plastic looking. The goal should be to ease the lines, remove blemishes, and smooth the skin to make the person look well rested and relaxed, as in FIGURES 8.8 and 8.9. The lines under her eyes and on her cheeks have been lightened just a touch, and the shadow below her nose has been reduced as has the intensity of the hot spots on her forehead and shoulder. Additionally, the bit of white strap peeking out from under the black strap on the right side has been eliminated.

FIGURES 8.6 and 8.7 Before and after. © *Brent Bigler*

FIGURES 8.8 and 8.9 Before and after. © *KE*

• **Refine the lighting and focus** to draw the viewer's eye to the subject and to compliment the subject's face. In the example in FIGURES 8.10 and 8.11 the background has been darkened to pull the focus back onto the subject, and some subtle dodging and burning was applied to bring out the highlights in her hair and help shape her face. A little darkening of the background here not only focuses attention on the subject but also adds a sense of drama.

• **Evaluate** the results by zooming out so you can see the entire image at once. After spending a good deal of time working on an image, it also helps to take a brief break so you can view it with fresh eyes. Having someone you trust look at the image can be very helpful, as when we're focused so closely on the small details it can be very easy to miss, say, a color cast. If you are working as a retoucher for a client, such as a photographer or an art director, send JPEGs for their feedback to make sure you're on track and covering all the issues they care about.

FIGURES 8.10 and 8.11 Before and after. © *KE*

Working in Layers

After you've taken a few minutes to evaluate the image and form your plan for what needs to be retouched, be sure to take advantage of Photoshop's ability to work in layers. Here are three tips to keep in mind:

• **Use layers to make your job easier.** Some retouchers make their files bigger and more unwieldy by making several copies of the Background layer on which they do spotting and retouching. An easier way is to make a new, empty layer for each part of the job. By doing your retouching on an empty, separate layer, it's easier to adjust the opacity, erase parts and start over, or use a mask to blend the retouching with the image.

• **Name your layers!** By giving your layers names that remind you what they are for, you'll be able to keep track of what layer is doing what. This is very important when it comes to making those inevitable last-minute adjustments.

• **Do not flatten layers unless it's really necessary.** It's almost guaranteed that you'll need to go back and adjust things later. Flattening the layers locks in the work done and makes it more difficult to adjust later on. Exceptions to this are when you may need to blur or sharpen the entire image as part of the work. Whenever possible, leave blur and sharpening steps for last and take advantage of Smart Filters for greater flexibility.

Dennis's Retouch Workflow

Here is an overview of the basic workflow Dennis uses when working on portraits for clients:

1. Evaluate the image and make notes. Make a new layer, called *Retouch 1.* This layer is for all the little things that will need to be removed.

2. Use the Spot Healing Brush or Healing Brush tool remove the spots and blemishes that need to be taken out and are easy to remove. More difficult areas, such as lines around the eyes or mouth, will be tackled on a separate layer so that you can rework those areas without having to re-do the easy spots.

3. Create layers for all the areas that need more extensive work or that you may need to adjust the strength of separately. For instance, use a separate layer to reduce or remove forehead wrinkles. By retouching these completely out and lowering the layer's opacity, you can achieve the right level of wrinkle reduction. The same goes for removing distractions or cleaning up parts of the background.

4. Accentuate the eyes. Use an adjustment layer with a mask that isolates the eyes, allowing you to brighten them and reduce any redness or color cast. Be careful not to push them so far that they become glowing zombie eyes. Where needed, add a touch of sharpening to help focus the viewer's attention on the eyes.

5. Brighten and color correct the teeth. Use an adjustment layer with a mask to brighten the teeth and remove any yellowing or discoloration.

6. Perform final color correction and sharpening. Leaving these steps for the last allows you to fine-tune your work. If you correct colors before doing the retouching work, you may find yourself in the position of pushing and pulling the color, or having to redo the retouching work when you need to adjust the colors later on.

Layers Workflow in Action

ch8_mckenna.jpg

As an example of working in layers, let's look at the retouching steps for this image of a young woman (FIGURES 8.12 and 8.13).

1. Add an empty layer and use a small, hard-edged brightly colored brush to note and circle all of issues and details you need to correct, including; dark spots on her face, flyaway and distracting hair on her forehead and left cheek, red veins in her eyes and shadows under her eyes (FIGURE 8.14).

TIP Keep the retouch notes layer on the top of the layer stack and toggle the layer visibility on and off while retouching to check progress.

FIGURES 8.12 and 8.13 Before and after. © *George Simian*

FIGURE 8.14 Before starting, take a moment to make note of the issues that need to be addressed.

2. Add a new layer, called *Retouch* (**Layer > New > Layer**). This layer is for removing or reducing the spots, blemishes, and stray hairs that pull the focus away from her eyes and expression.

3. Select the Spot Healing Brush tool. In the options bar, select Sample All Layers and set the source sampling type to Content-Aware. Size the brush to be a tad larger than the blemish you are removing. Working on the Retouch layer, use the Spot Healing Brush tool to remove the blemishes and distracting hairs (FIGURE 8.15).

If, on your own images, the Spot Healing Brush tool is not creating the desired results, switch to the Healing Brush tool or the Clone Stamp tool with the hardness set to 75% to remove the objectionable bits.

+ TIP If the Sample All Layers button doesn't appear on your options bar, you're using the narrow version of the options bar. To use the normal options bar, open the Preferences dialog and go to Workspace > Condensed. Deselect the option Enable Narrow Options Bar and click OK. You'll have to restart Photoshop for the change to take effect.

FIGURE 8.15 After initial retouching to remove the blemishes and stray hairs on the forehead and cheek

4. Add a new layer, named *Stray Hairs*. This layer is used to remove the flyaway hairs that distract the viewer.

5. Use the Spot Healing Brush, Healing Brush, or Clone Stamp tool to remove the stray hairs around her head (FIGURE 8.16). Make the brush size a bit wider than the hair, and set the Hardness to 75%.

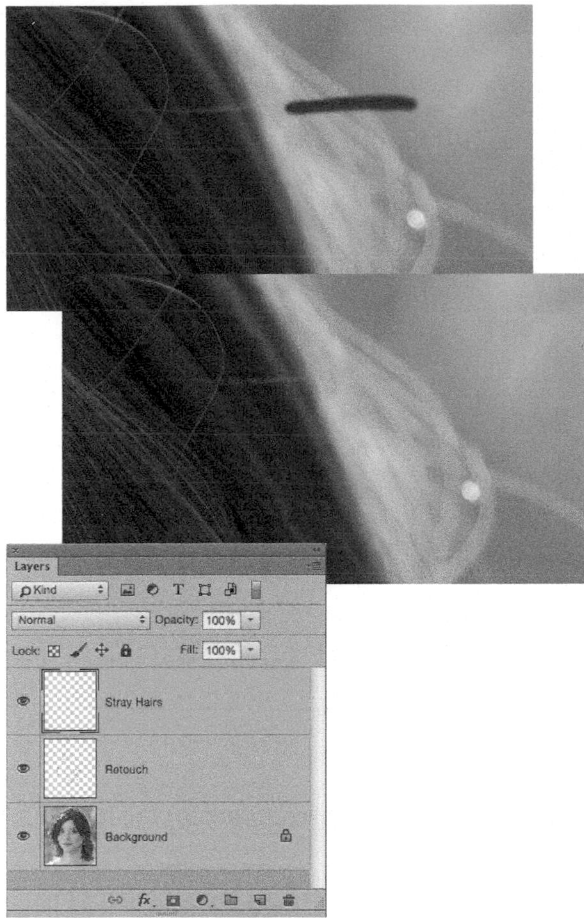

FIGURE 8.16 Distracting flyaway hairs removed

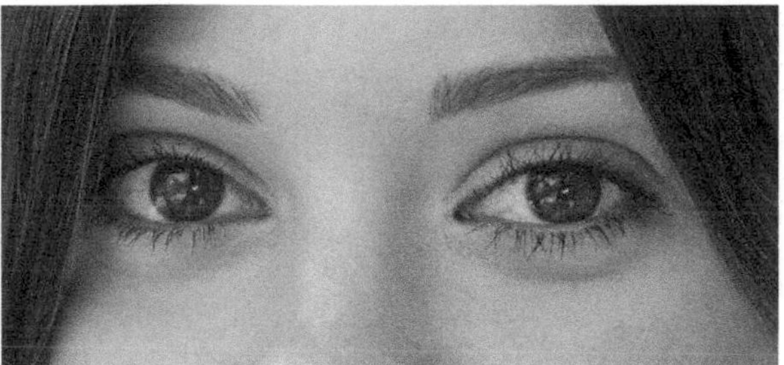

Before

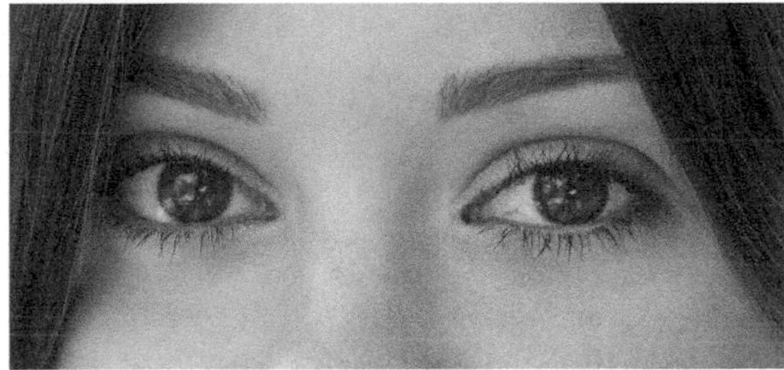

100%

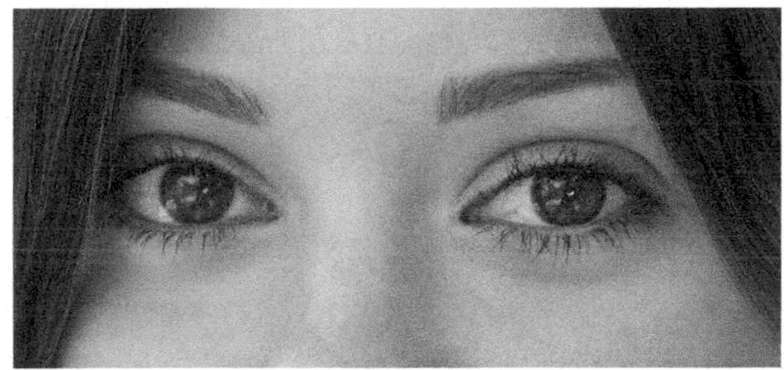

40%

FIGURE 8.17 Changing the layer's opacity from 100% to 40% after removing the lines under her eyes makes the retouched areas look less fake.

6. Add a new layer, named *Under Eyes*. Using the Healing Brush tool, with options set to sample Current & Below, to remove the lines under her eyes, sampling from just below the lines. Be careful when brushing near the eyelashes on the bottom of her eye, as painting too close can produce dark smears.

7 Change the layer's opacity to 40% to soften the lines a little but not so much that the area looks fake (FIGURE 8.17).

Removing the lines completely by retouching on a separate layer allows you to tone down the effect by changing the opacity of this layer—always handy when the client asks for a different strength than you initially set.

8. Add a layer named *Clean up eyes*. Use the Spot Healing Brush tool with a small brush size to remove the red veins visible in the whites of her eyes. The smaller brush size works well on small areas that require precision. FIGURE 8.18 shows the results.

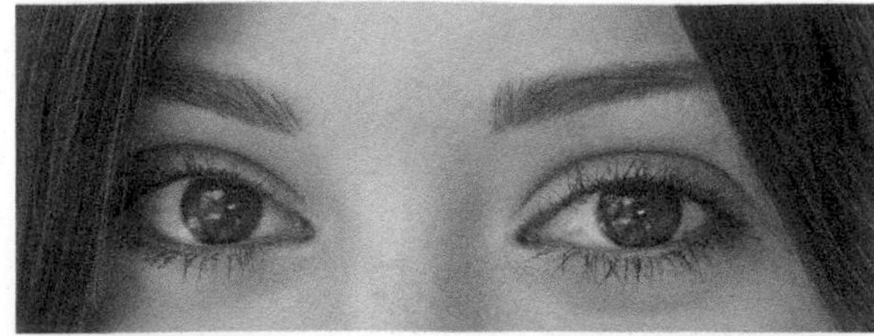

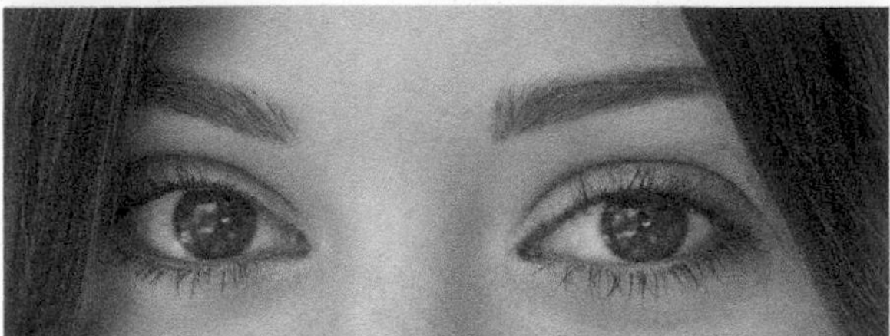

FIGURE 8.18 Close-up showing the red veins, and the result after cleaning up the whites of the eyes with the Spot Healing Brush tool

9. To enhance her eyes and brighten them up, start by selecting the eyes. An easy way to create a selection of her eyes is to use a Quick Mask and use the Brush tool to paint over her eyes (FIGURE 8.19). Tap Q to enter Quick Mask mode. Using the Brush tool set to 50% hardness, paint with black over the eyes.

The red overlay in Quick Mask mode indicates areas that won't be part of the selection. Thus, painting over the eyes, as in this example, is the opposite of what we need.

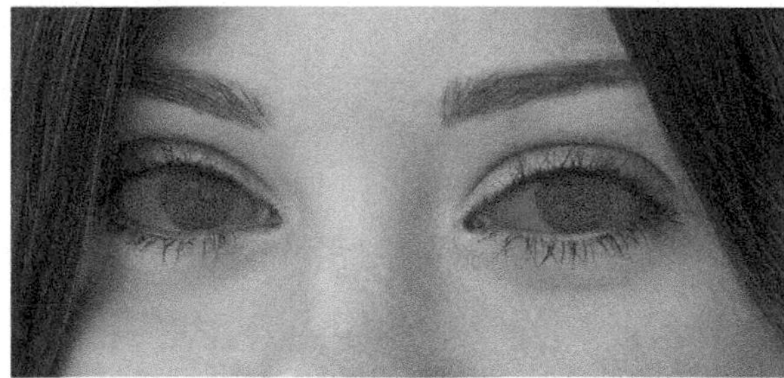

FIGURE 8.19 Use the Brush tool to paint a Quick Mask over her eyes.

10. Press Cmd-I/Ctrl-I to invert the Quick Mask. Tap Q to exit Quick Mask mode and turn the temporary mask into a selection.

11. With the selection active, add a Curves adjustment layer (**Layer > New Adjustment Layer > Curves**), named *Eyes Crvs*, and in the Properties panel, pull the RGB curve up slightly to lighten her eyes, as shown in FIGURE 8.20. The result should look like FIGURE 8.21. (Dennis abbreviates the word curves to Crvs when naming layers.)

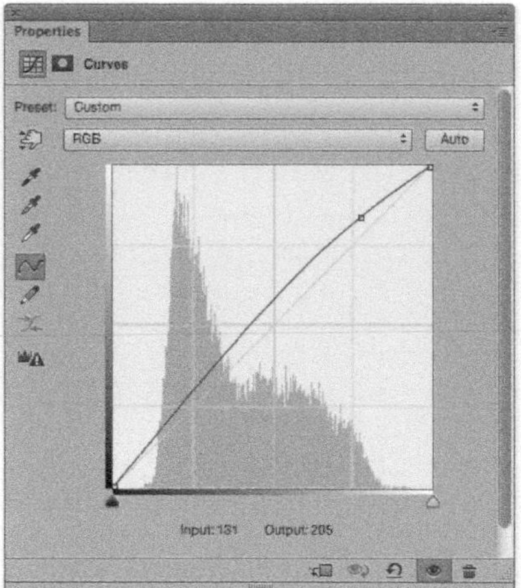

FIGURE 8.20 Brightening the eyes

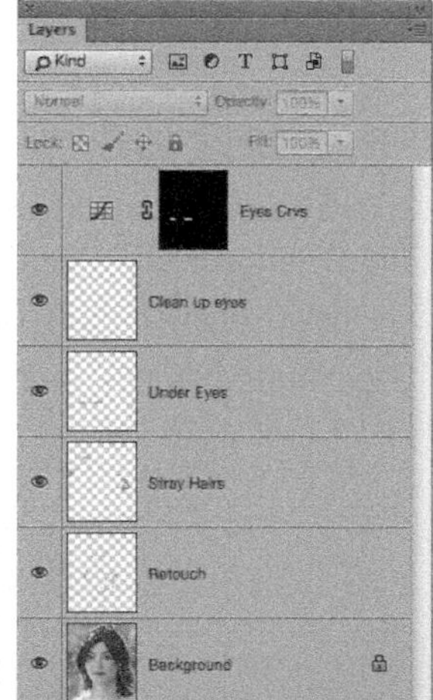

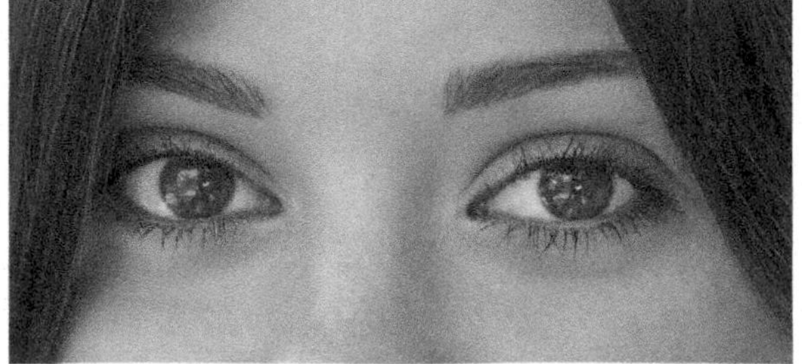

FIGURE 8.21 Eyes brightened with the Curves adjustment layer

12. The final step in this workflow is the color correction step. Add two Curves adjustment layers, named *Color Crvs* and *Contrast Crvs*.

13. Set the blending mode in the Color Crvs layer to Color, and in the Contrast Crvs layer to Luminosity.

14. Select the Color Crvs adjustment layer. In the Properties panel select the red curve. Select the On-Image Adjustment tool, move the cursor over her cheeks, and click to set a point on the red curve. Tap the Up Arrow key to nudge the point up a few ticks, and add a little red to the image. Select the blue curve, use the On-Image Adjustment tool to set a point on the blue curve, and use the Down Arrow key to nudge it down a few ticks to pull some blue out of the skin tones (**FIGURE 8.22**).

15. Select the Contrast Crvs adjustment layer. Place two points on the RGB Curve: one three-quarters of the way toward the black point (lower-left corner) and the other a quarter of the way toward the white point (upper-right corner). Pull up on the point near the white point a little, and pull down on the point near the black point about the same amount to add a little contrast to the image (**FIGURE 8.23**).

The final image is seen in **FIGURE 8.24**.

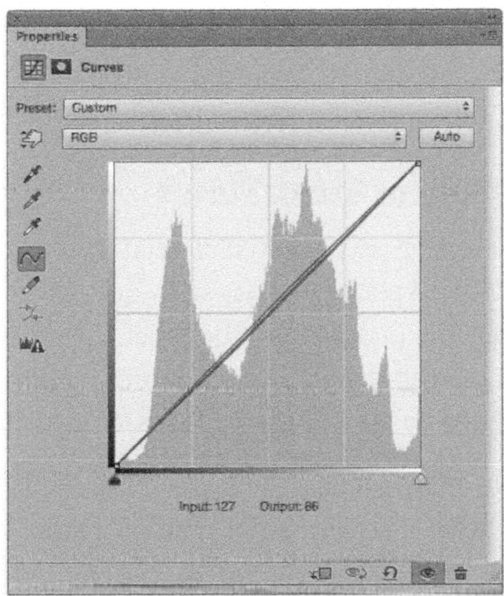

FIGURE 8.22 The color of the image has been warmed up by adding a small amount of red and subtracting a small amount of blue.

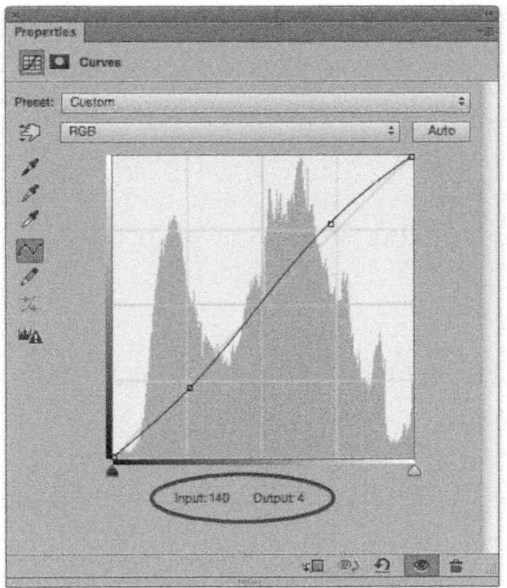

FIGURE 8.23 A slight amount of contrast has been added.

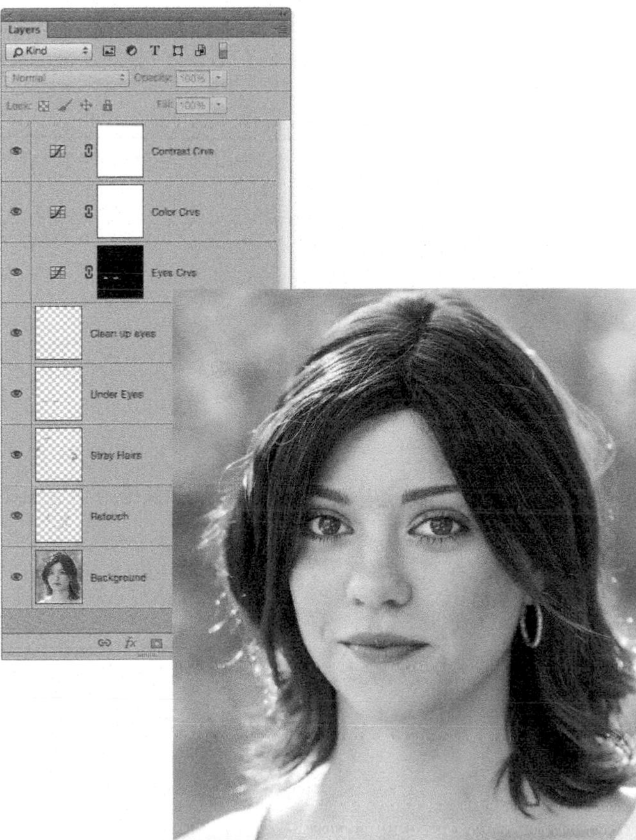

FIGURE 8.24 Retouched and color-corrected image

CHOOSING YOUR TOOLS AND WHAT TO LOOK FOR

Each retouching tool has its own strengths and weaknesses. Dennis finds the Spot Healing Brush tool the easiest to use, and he'll usually start with that before moving on to the Healing Brush tool or Clone Stamp tool. The key is to recognize when you are not getting the results you need.

With the Spot Healing Brush and Healing Brush tools, the biggest issues to look for are losing texture in the area you're working on (**FIGURE 8.25**) and the transition between contrasting colors or tones smearing (**FIGURE 8.26**).

For the Clone Stamp tool, the biggest issue you need to look for is when gradations, texture, or color don't match up properly (**FIGURE 8.27**).

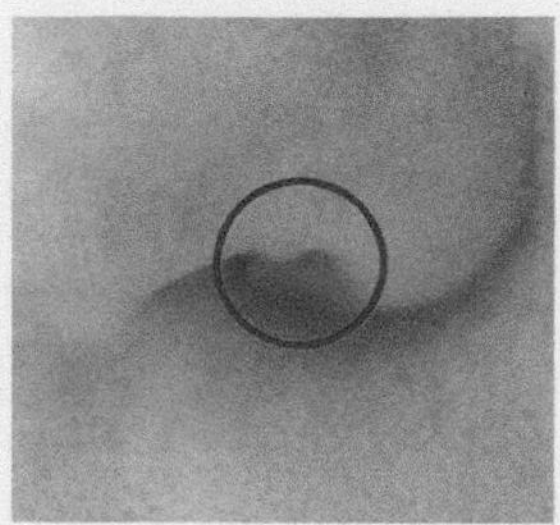

FIGURE 8.26 Sometimes the Spot Healing tool can give you a smeary-looking result when you come too close to a border between dark and light tones.

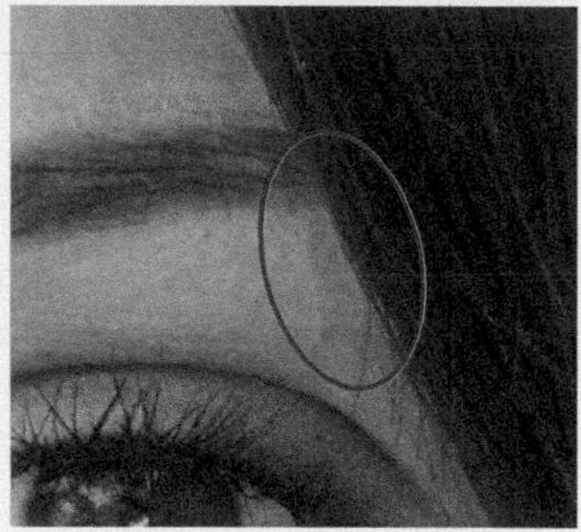

FIGURE 8.27 Be sure that the color, tone, and texture you're cloning blend properly.

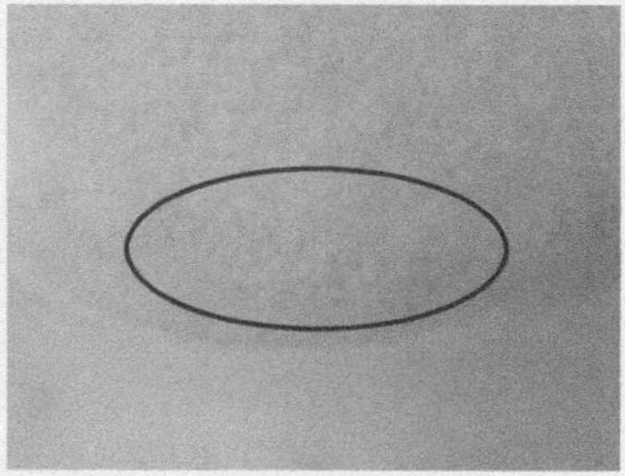

FIGURE 8.25 When working with the Healing Brush tool, avoid creating patterns or textures that do not belong.

REMOVING DISTRACTIONS

One of the most essential steps for creating good photographs of people is to notice whether anything in the background is competing with the subject. As you look through the viewfinder, scan the entire frame for anything that would distract the viewer's attention from the subject. The simplest way to deal with this is to move either the camera or the person to minimize the distraction.

Unfortunately, you don't always have the option to move the camera or person, but Photoshop offers several tools that can help. The primary methods for dealing with distractions are cropping; cloning something over the area to hide the distraction; blurring, darkening, or lightening the background; and replacing the background with a new one.

The Beauty of Blank Plates

Well before computer-driven special effects, filmmakers layered plates of glass with images on them into shots. The plates would be carefully positioned between the camera and the rest of the scene so that they covered an area of the frame with, say, a mountain or a building.

Today, seasoned professional photographers make use of a similar idea by shooting extra plates of the location they're photographing. They can then cover up or replace some unwanted element in the background.

This concept comes in especially handy when taking photos in public spaces, where we don't have control over who might be creeping into the frame.

Photographer Mark Rutherford faced this when shooting a campaign on the streets of San Francisco. In FIGURE 8.28 you can see the person in the dark outfit to the left of the model. Removing that person by cloning or stretching the background would be quite a challenge for even the most experienced Photoshop artist.

FIGURE 8.28 The person to the left of the model adds a distracting element. © *Mark Rutherford*

Thinking ahead, Mark made sure to grab several extra shots of the background from the same vantage point and focus effect. One of those blank plates is seen in FIGURE 8.29.

FIGURE 8.29 Blank plate shot without passersby in the frame © *Mark Rutherford*

Mark was able to easily layer this plate on top of his model shot to hide the person walking (FIGURE 8.30).

FIGURE 8.30 Bringing in the blank plate as a layer in Photoshop is the first step to hiding the pedestrian on the left.

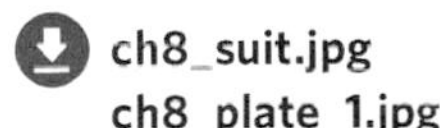

ch8_suit.jpg
ch8_plate_1.jpg

1. Open the shot of the model and the blank plate in Photoshop.

2. In the image with the model, choose **Image > Canvas Size.** Select Relative, set Width to 1 inch, and click the middle-right anchor to add an additional inch to the left of the image (FIGURE 8.31).

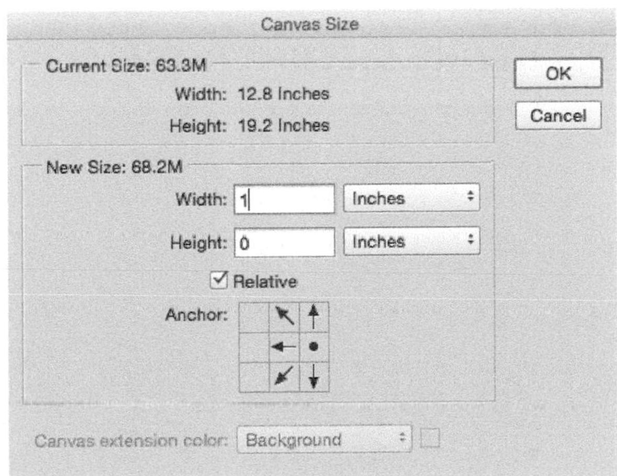

FIGURE 8.31 Make the canvas wider using Image > Canvas Size.

Adding extra canvas gives more room to the left of the model, which is a little closer to the left edge of the image than we'd like.

3. Choose **Window > Arrange > 2-Up Vertical** to show the images side by side.

4. Using the Move tool, drag the plate image onto the model image. Rename the plate image layer *Plate 1*, and close the plate image. Move the Plate 1 layer roughly into position, as shown in **FIGURE 8.32**.

FIGURE 8.32 Plate 1 roughly placed over the photo of the model

5. To see how well the Plate 1 layer lines up with the background, change its blending mode to Difference (**FIGURE 8.33**). Using this blending mode allows you to more easily line up the Plate 1 image against the background. Wherever the images match up with each other, you'll see black. Wherever they are different, you'll see rainbow result.

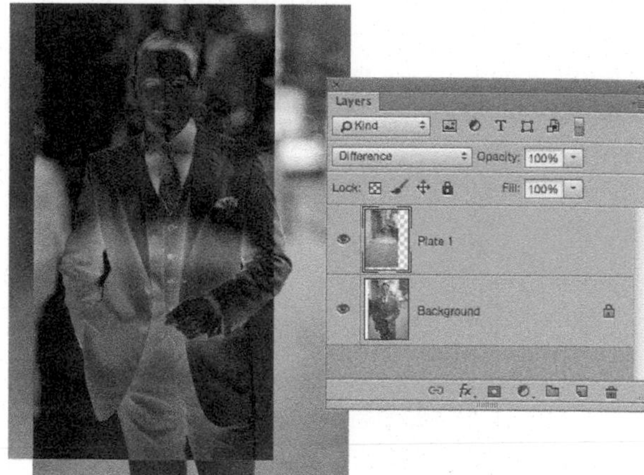

FIGURE 8.33 Use the Difference blending mode to see how the features in Plate 1 match up with the features in the image below.

6. Select the Plate 1 layer and choose **Edit > Free Transform**. Resize and move the Plate 1 layer until it lines up pretty well with the similar features in the background, as shown in **FIGURE 8.34**. Drag the bottom center handle down to increase the height of the Plate 1 layer so that the bottom lines up with the bottom of the canvas, and press Return/Enter. Change the blending mode to Normal.

There is no need to obsess over exact position—this is a background that should not call attention to itself.

FIGURE 8.34 Plate 1 scaled to better fit with the existing background

7. Hide the Plate 1 layer, and using the Quick Selection tool set to Sample All Layers, select the model. Show the Plate 1 layer again, and select the layer. Choose **Layer > Layer Mask > Hide Selection.**

8. With the Brush tool, paint with black over the right side of the mask, as seen in FIGURE 8.35. Pay extra attention to the edges of the model to make sure the edges blend neatly.

FIGURE 8.35 Carefully mask out Plate 1 to reveal the model.

The final step is to add color correction to the Plate 1 layer so that the density and color more closely match the original background.

TIP To quickly add an adjustment layer and set its name, blending mode, and other settings, Option/Alt-click the New Adjustment Layer icon in the Adjustments panel.

9. Choose **Layer > New Adjustment Layer > Curves,** and name the layer *Color Crvs*. Select Use Previous Layer to Create Clipping Mask to ensure that the adjustment layer affects only the Plate 1 layer and finally set the Mode to Color.

The color of the new plate looks a little warmer than the rest of the image, so we'll cool it off just a touch by first adjusting the Color Crvs adjustment layer.

10. Select the Color Crvs layer, and select the red curve in the Properties panel. Add a point a third of the way from the white point, and pull down slightly to remove some red. Select the blue curve, add a point at about the same place as you did for the red curve, and pull up a similar amount. FIGURE 8.36 shows the fine curves adjustments Dennis used to refine the color of the new plate to better match the model layer.

FIGURE 8.36 Adjust the color of Plate 1 to more closely blend in with the existing background.

11. Add another Curves adjustment layer by Option/Alt-clicking the Curves adjustment in the Adjustments panel. Name the new adjustment layer *Lum Crvs*. Set its blending mode to Luminosity, and again select Use Previous Layer to Create Clipping Mask. Select the RGB curve, and pull the middle of the curve up until the brightness closely matches the rest of the background (FIGURE 8.37).

FIGURE 8.37 Lighten Plate 1 using a Curves adjustment layer.

+ TIP To ensure that an adjustment layer affects only the layer directly underneath it, select the adjustment layer and choose **Layer > Create Clipping Mask**. Alternatively, Option/Alt-click the dividing line between the adjustment layer and the layer below it.

Flattering Contours

Photographs invite us to look more closely at a person than we would in real life. Something about a still image seems to say, "Come take a closer look—no one will ever know you are staring at me!" No wonder we notice things in a photo that we would not when dealing with a real person.

When it comes to photos, all we have to work with are light (also referred to as tonality) and color. Keep this in mind when working on a photograph of a person. One of the reasons people say "The camera adds 10 pounds" is that the way the light shapes someone is our primary clue to how heavy or thin they are.

Painters take advantage of the fact that lighter tones seem to come forward while darker tones recede. Photographers, too, take advantage of this fact with their careful use of lights, reflectors, and background relationships.

Experienced retouchers keep these relationships in mind when working on portraits, using dodging (lightening) and burning (darkening) in addition to warping tools like the Liquify filter to refine the shape of the subject.

Flattering the Couple

Let's take a look at how these principles apply to the real-world example in FIGURES 8.38 and 8.39.

FIGURES 8.38 and 8.39 Before and after. © *Phil Pool*

In this shot we see a happy couple with wide smiles. It's great to see the photographer capture such a genuine moment, but as you can see, the man's smile shows too much of his gums, and she could use a little bit of slimming. In retouching this image we'll use the Liquify filter and burning and dodging layers.

ch8_couple.jpg

1. Use the Rectangular Marquee tool to select an area around his mouth, as shown in FIGURE 8.40. Press Cmd-Option-J/Ctrl-Alt-J to copy this area into a new layer, named *Upper Lip*.

FIGURE 8.40 After merging the Background and Retouch layers into a copy, select the area around his mouth.

TIP Using Cmd-Option-J/Ctrl-Alt-J to copy a selection to a new layer opens up the New Layer dialog box, so that you can immediately name the layer. In contrast pressing Cmd-J/Ctrl-J means you'll need to rename the new layer in a separate step.

2. Select the Upper Lip layer and choose **Layer > Smart Objects > Convert to Smart Object**.

3. Choose **Filter > Liquify**. Ensure that Advanced Mode is selected, as well as Show Backdrop. Select All Layers from the Use menu and Behind from the Mode menu so you see the mouth as part of the entire image. Select the Forward Warp tool, and set the size of the brush to about three times the width of the upper lip. Gently nudge his upper lip down to cover his gums, as shown in FIGURE 8.41. Press OK.

4. While we're working on him, let's brighten up his eyes a little. Tap Q to enter Quick Mask mode. With the Brush tool, paint black over the lenses of his glasses. Press Cmd-I/Ctrl-I to invert the mask, and Tap Q to exit Quick Mask mode and convert the mask into a selection.

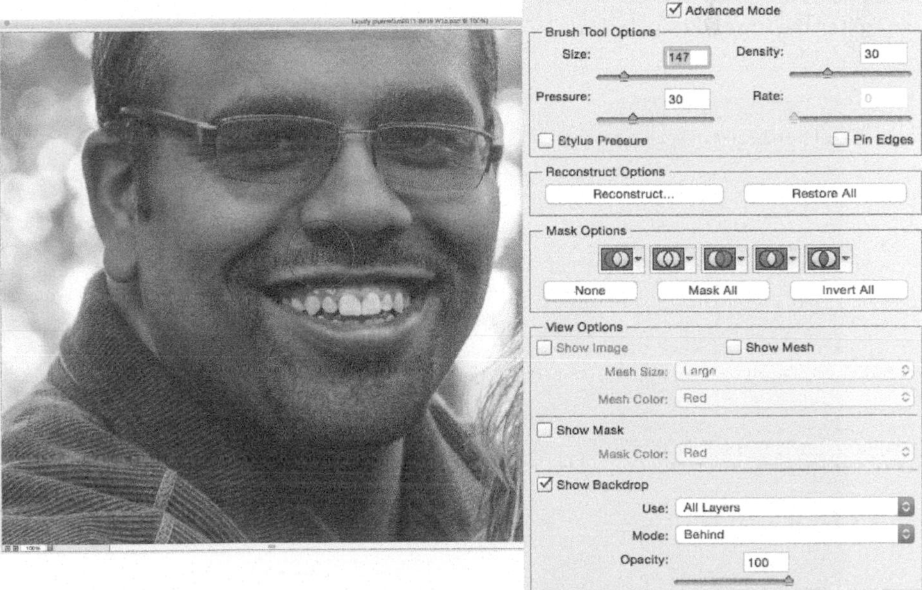

FIGURE 8.41 Use the Liquify filter to gently nudge his upper lip down to cover more of his gums.

5. Add a Curves adjustment layer, name it *Brighten Glasses Crvs*, and pull the RGB curve up, as shown in FIGURE 8.42.

6. To keep your layers organized, select the Upper Lip and Brighten Glasses Crvs adjustment layers and choose **Layer > Group Layers** to group them. Name this layer group *Him*.

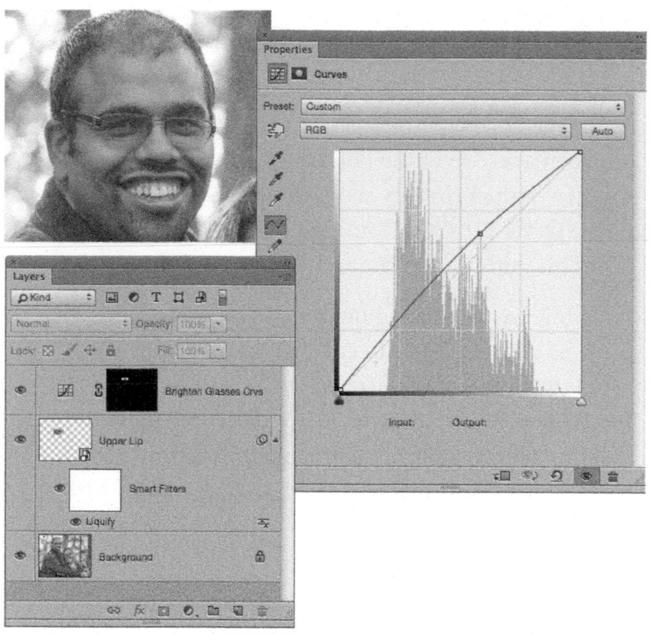

FIGURE 8.42 Pull up the RGB curve in the Curves adjustment layer to lighten the lenses on his glasses.

7. Moving on to slimming her, select the Background layer and use the Polygon Lasso tool to select an area around her head and shoulders, as seen in FIGURE 8.43. Press Cmd-Option-J/Ctrl-Alt-J to copy this selection into a new layer, named *Slim Her*. Move this layer above the Him layer group.

8. Convert the Slim Her layer to a Smart Object. Using the Liquify filter with the Forward Warp tool set to a medium brush, as seen in FIGURE 8.44, gently nudge in the areas around her neck and cheeks.

FIGURE 8.43 Select her head and shoulders using the Lasso tool.

FIGURE 8.44 Use the Liquify filter to gently nudge her neck and cheeks in a little.

9. We'll use burning (darkening) and dodging (lightening) to enhance the shape of her face. Create a new Hue/Saturation adjustment layer, named *Shaping H/S*. Set blending mode to Multiply. Set the opacity to 30%. In the Properties panel, move the Saturation slider to –40%. Select the layer for the Shaping H/S layer and press Cmd-I/Ctrl-I to invert the mask. Use the Brush tool to paint white into the mask in the areas around her cheeks and neck, as indicated by red in FIGURE 8.45. This darkens and shapes the neckline.

10. Create a new layer, name it *Light on Face*, and set the blending mode to Soft Light. This is a dodging (lightening) layer. Using the Brush tool set to around 30% to 40% opacity, paint with white on her forehead, cheeks, and chin to contour her face, as indicated by the red areas in FIGURE 8.46.

11. Select the three layers you've added, and choose **Layer > Group Layers**. Name the layer group *Slimming*.

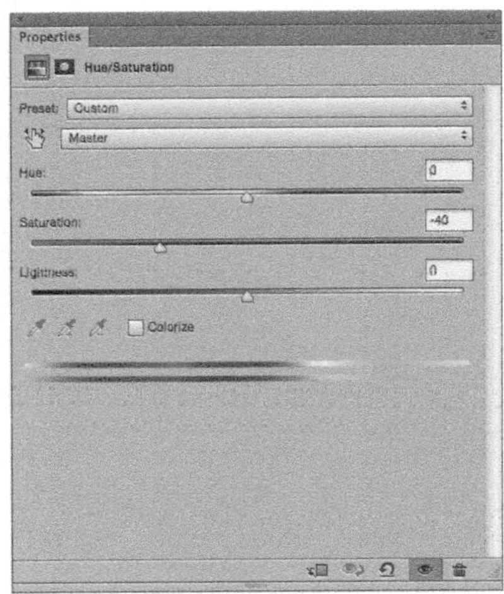

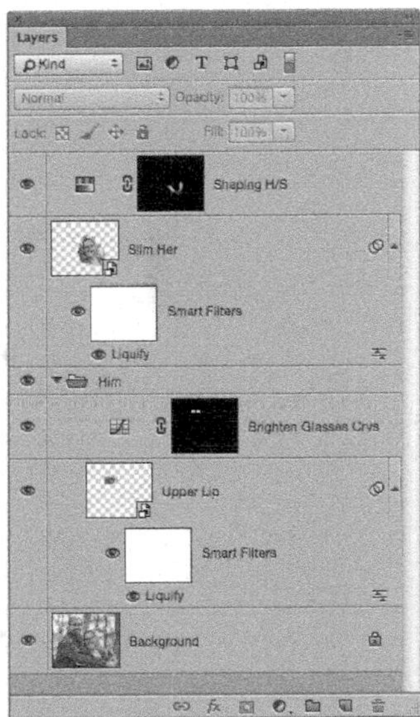

FIGURE 8.45 Use a Hue/Saturation adjustment layer set to the Multiply blending mode to burn in her cheeks and neck. The red areas indicate where to brush in the Shaping H/S layer.

FIGURE 8.46 The red areas indicate where to paint white into the Light on Face layer.

12. The hair above her forehead could use a little help matching the color of the rest of her hair. Above the Slimming layer group, add a new layer, named *Color on hair.* Set the blending mode to Color. Select the Brush tool, and set Opacity to 100% in the options bar. To select the color of the rest of her hair as the paint color, press Option/Alt to access the Eyedropper tool and sample the color of her hair to the right of her face. Paint this color over the hair above her forehead. To keep this area from looking too monochromatic, slide the opacity of this layer to around 70% (**FIGURE 8.47**).

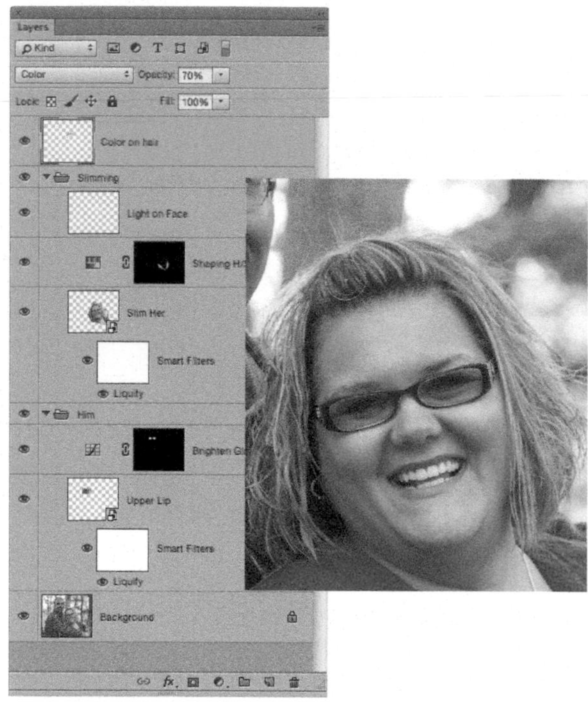

FIGURE 8.47 Choose a color from the hair on the side of her head, and paint that color into the "Color on hair" layer.

13. Next, we'll lighten her hair. Set the foreground and background color back to default by pressing D. Use Quick Mask mode to create a selection over the hair above her forehead. With the selection active, add a new Curves adjustment layer, named *Hairline Crvs,* and adjust the RGB curve as shown in **FIGURE 8.48**. In case everything but her hair is getting lighter, select the layer mask and invert it.

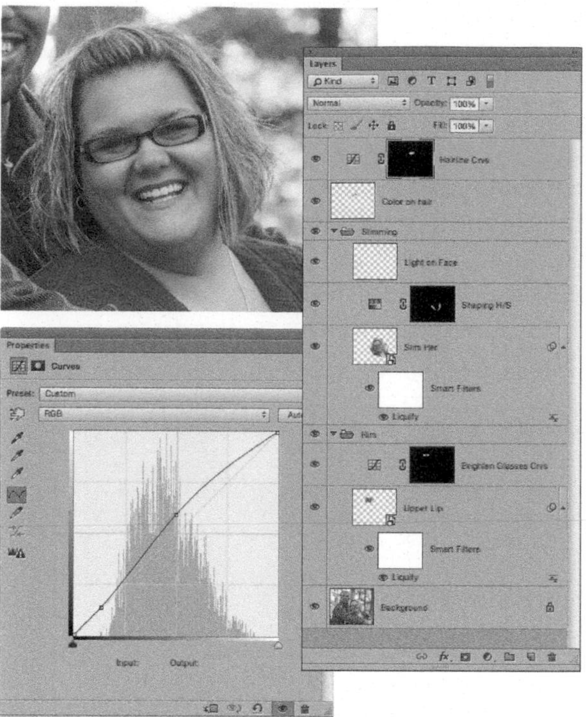

FIGURE 8.48 The hair above her forehead has been lightened with a Curves adjustment layer.

14. Her eyes could use a bit of brightening as well. Repeat step 13, this time selecting the lenses of her glasses. Name this layer *Glasses Crvs* and pull up on the RGB curve, as shown in **FIGURE 8.49**.

15. Select the Slimming layer group and the three layers added above that and choose **Layers > Group Layers**. Name the layer group *Her.*

Take a moment to assess the color and contrast of the image. We can see a little bit of a red color cast to the image, and it could use a little bit of contrast as well. So next we'll do an overall color correction to adjust the color and contrast while also bringing the focus back onto the couple.

FIGURE 8.49 Using another Curves adjustment layer to brighten the lenses of her glasses

16. Add a Curves adjustment layer and set the blending mode to Color. Name this layer *Color Crvs*. Ensure that the layer is positioned above the Her layer group. Select the red curve and pull down, as shown in FIGURE 8.50.

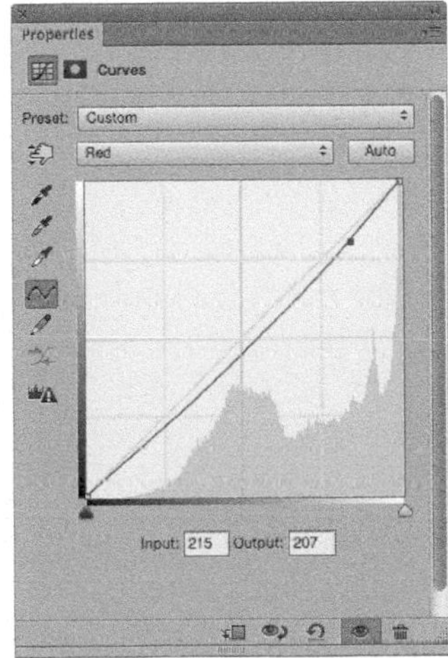

FIGURE 8.50 Use a Curves adjustment layer set to the Color blending mode to pull some red out of the image.

17. Add another Curves adjustment layer, named *Lum Crvs*, with blending mode set to Luminosity to add some contrast to the image and give it a bit of "snap." Create a gentle S curve by pulling the shadows down and the highlights up a little, as shown in FIGURE 8.51.

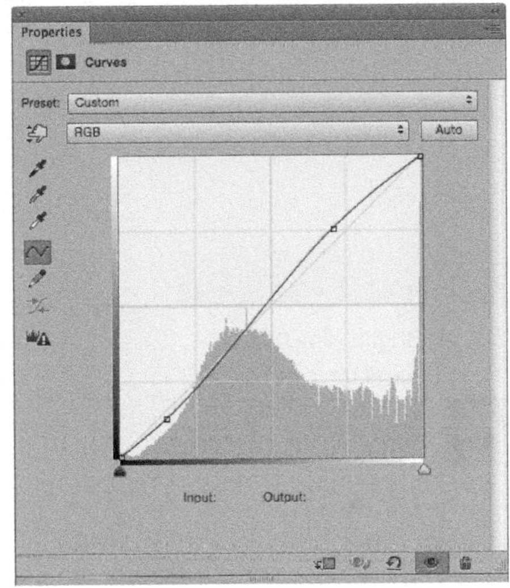

FIGURE 8.51 Use another Curves adjustment layer set to the Luminosity blending mode to add a little contrast to the image.

18. Finally, lighten the background so the couple stands out a little better. Add one more Curves adjustment layer. Name the layer *Background Crvs*. Leave the blending mode set to Normal. Pull up on the RGB curve, as shown in FIGURE 8.52. To keep this layer from affecting the couple, select the *Background Crvs* layer mask and use the Brush tool to paint black over the couple.

Most people think that the Clone Stamp and Healing Brush are the top retouching tools, but as you can see, working with light and dark to shape an image is very effective.

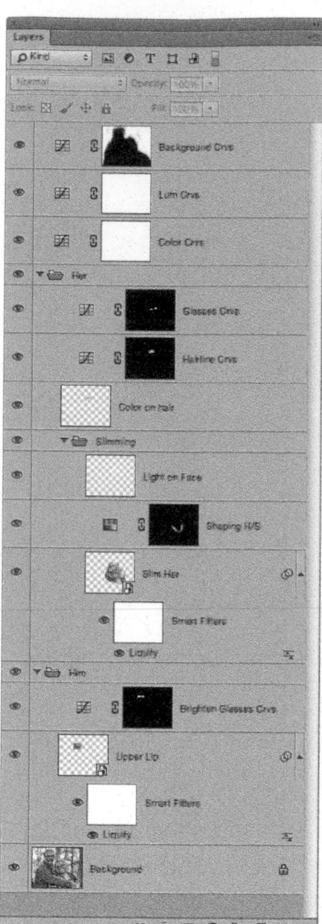

FIGURE 8.52 Brightening the background around the couple

THE IMPORTANCE OF SKIN

If the eyes are the windows to the soul, then skin might be a window to the life experiences of the individual. Along with features such as eyes and expression, we notice the skin and recognize when something is off or not quite right with it.

That's why retouchers have to strike a careful balance between concealing blemishes, balancing skin tones, and softening wrinkles without making the person look like a plastic doll.

This means the texture of the skin is just as important to pay attention to as blemishes or the lines around the eyes. The trick is to keep the level of texture appropriate for the age of the subject and the type of photograph.

A NOTE ON DODGING AND BURNING

Experienced retouchers often use layers that lighten (dodge) and darken (burn) the image as a way of smoothing out the unevenness in skin.

One way to do this is to create two Curves adjustment layers that lighten and darken the image while carefully painting in the layer masks to control the effect.

Another way you can dodge or burn is to create a new layer above the image with blending mode set to Overlay or Soft Light. To dodge (lighten) parts of the image, paint with a light color, for example white, onto the empty layer. To burn, paint with a darker color, such as black onto the empty layer.

Whichever technique you use, the key to successfully dodging and burning your image is to work carefully using a brush with a low opacity and flow so that you can gently build up the effect, making it easier to blend in with the rest of the image.

The Teenage Years

Photographers who specialize in high school senior portraits know very well the challenges presented by teenage skin. Fortunately, Photoshop gives us lots of tools that make it simple to clean up the blemishes teenagers are often plagued by.

Like many of the other tasks we've looked at so far, the strategy for removing blemishes involves working in steps. The first step is to clean up what you can using the Spot Healing Brush tool, Healing Brush tool, and Clone Stamp tool on a new layer. Follow that up with dodging and burning to even out the texture while smoothing the surface of the face (**FIGURES 8.53** and **8.54**).

The Spot Healing Brush tool auto selects and blends the new image information very well, and in many cases it does a great job. When you're working with the Spot Healing Brush tool, there are three things to pay attention to in the options bar (**FIGURE 8.55**):

- Make sure the Sample All Layers option is selected. This allows you to do your retouching on an empty layer, making it easy to rework an area by erasing and trying again.

- There are two options for Type: Content Aware and Proximity Match. In general, Content Aware does a better job respecting the borders between light and dark areas. With this option selected, you'll usually get better results when brushing over dark-to-light transition areas, for example, where the white of the eyes meets the lower eyelid. Content Aware may result in a slight loss of texture, which would require rebuilding with the addition of subtle noise, as addressed in the following example.

- The Proximity Match option does a good job matching the texture of the healed area with the surrounding texture but can yield smeary results when you venture too close to adjacent dark and light borders.

When Dennis is wrestling with problems like cleaning up blemishes, he starts off by using the Spot Healing Brush tool with the Content Aware option; if he notices a loss of texture, he switches to Proximity Match.

FIGURES 8.53 and **8.54** Before and after. © *Bobbi Lane*

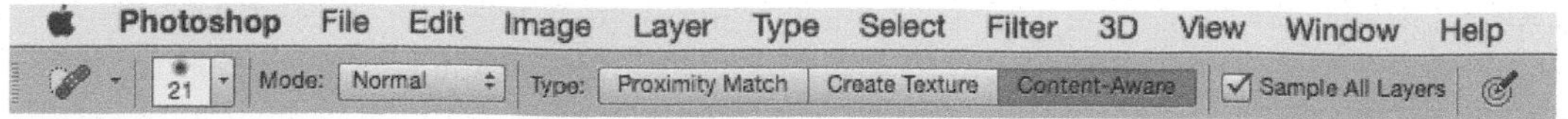

FIGURE 8.55 Spot Healing Brush tool options

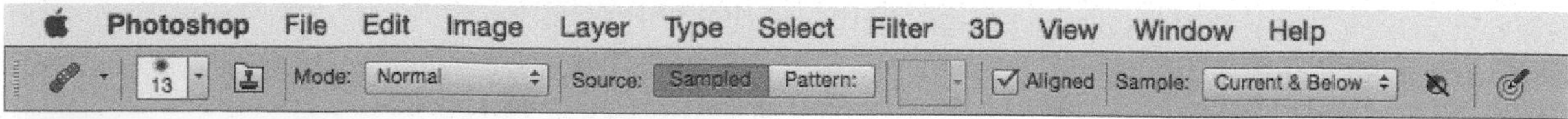

FIGURE 8.56 Healing Brush tool options

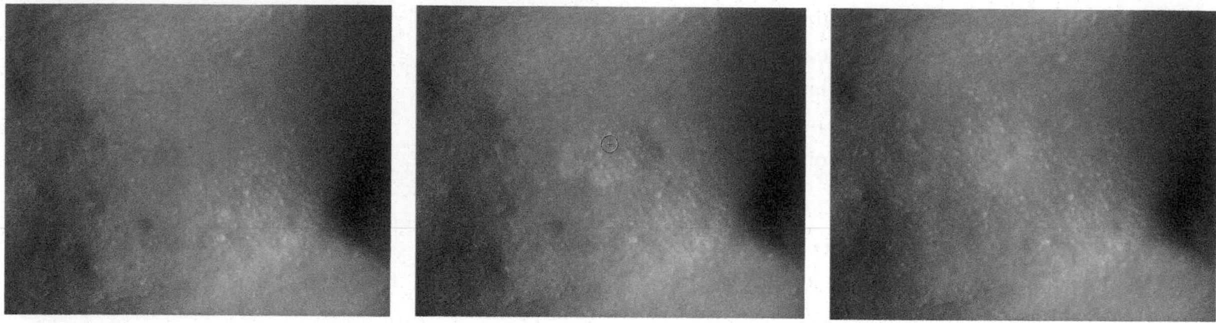

FIGURE 8.57 From left to right are the original image, the area being worked on with the Healing Brush and and example of the repeating pattern that can come from sampling the same area too many times.

If neither option gives him results he likes, he switches to the Healing Brush tool, and in the options bar sets Source to Sampled, and Sample to Current & Below (FIGURE 8.56). This allows him to work on an empty layer while the tool samples the layers below.

ch8_teenskin.jpg

1. Add a new layer and name it *Retouch*. Use the Spot Healing Brush tool to remove the major spots caused by the blemishes.

2. If the results are not blending properly, try switching to the Healing Brush tool; set the sample source spot by pressing Option/Alt on the area you want to sample from, and paint over the blemish to remove. Frequently changing the sample source location will help you blend your work and avoid the dreaded snakeskin pattern (FIGURE 8.57).

3. After removing the majority of the blemishes, move on to the dodging stage. Add a Curves adjustment layer, name it *Dodge Crvs*, and pull up on the RGB curve to lighten the image, as shown in FIGURE 8.58. Select the layer mask, and press Cmd-I/Ctrl-I to hide the adjustment layer's effect.

4. Using the Brush tool with Opacity and Flow options set to around 30%, paint with white on the layer mask so that you will be able to gently build up the effect while blending it in with the surrounding area. Zooming in and out while working helps you see what areas need to be lightened. If you see you've gone too far with this step, you can easily back off on the effect of the layer by tapping X to swap the Foreground and Background colors and then painting with black to undo the lightening.

5. Add another Curves adjustment layer, and pull down on the RGB curve, as shown in FIGURE 8.59. Name this layer *Burn Crvs*, and invert the layer mask. With the same settings for the Brush tool, paint white on the layer mask to darken the lighter areas left by the blemishes you removed in step 1.

Adding a subtle hint of noise can help blend the retouching and hide small imperfections created by the retouching.

FIGURE 8.58 Dodge Crvs layer settings (Properties panel), red areas indicating where the Dodge Crvs layer has been painted in, and the result after dodging

FIGURE 8.59 Burn Crvs layer settings, red areas indicating where the Burn Crvs layer has been painted in, and the result after burning

6. Option/Alt-click the New Layer icon at the bottom of the Layers panel to add a new layer, name the layer *Noise*, set the blending mode to Overlay, and select the option "Fill with overlay-neutral color (50% gray)" (FIGURE 8.60). Choose **Filter > Noise > Add Noise** and add a small amount of monochrome noise to the layer (FIGURE 8.61). Click OK.

New Layer
Name: Noise
OK
Use Previous Layer to Create Clipping Mask
Cancel
Color: None
Mode: Overlay Opacity: 100 %
Fill with Overlay-neutral color (50% gray)

FIGURE 8.60 Noise layer settings

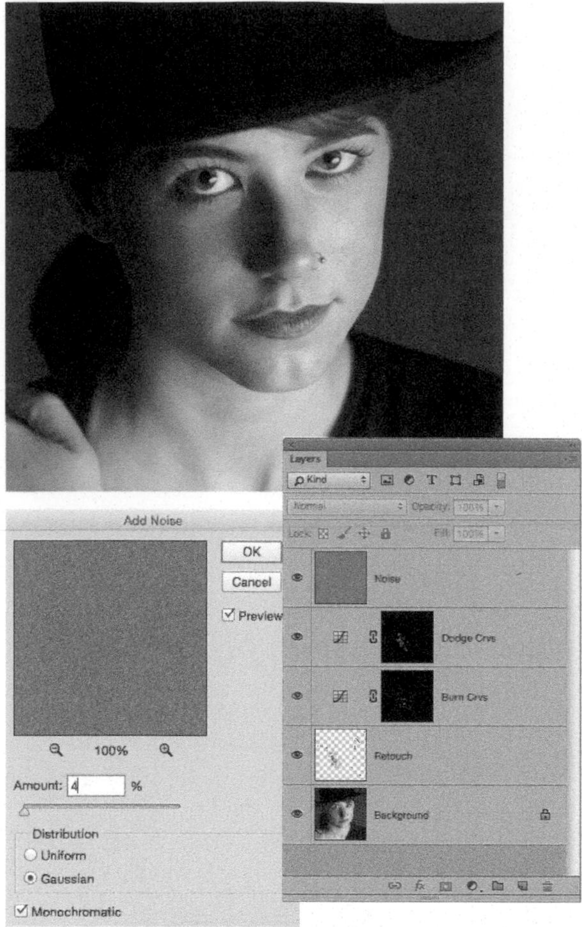

FIGURE 8.61 Adding a hint of monochrome noise blends and conceals tell-tale retouching artifacts.

★ NOTE The proper amount of noise will vary based on the resolution of the image and the amount of noise or grain already present in the image. With digitally captured images, this is usually somewhere from 2% to 4%.

Mature Skin

As we gain maturity, our experiences are written on our faces as lines and wrinkles that hopefully tell the tale of a life well lived. But that doesn't mean we want those experiences to be the first thing someone notices about us.

Like teen skin, mature skin presents the retoucher with a challenge: how to reduce the lines that age brings without making it look like the person made too many trips to the plastic surgeon.

The strategy for dealing with this challenge is very similar to the one used for dealing with teen skin. After doing the basic cleanup, the wrinkles are addressed. This can be done on one or many layers.

In the previous example we looked at how burning and dodging was done with two Curves adjustment layers. In this example we'll see how it can be done using the Soft Light blending mode (**FIGURES 8.62** and **8.63**).

FIGURES 8.62 and **8.63** Before and after © *Pavel Kubarkov/ Adobe Stock*

1. The first step in turning back the clock is to soften the lines on the face. Add a new layer and name it *Lines softening*. Using the Healing Brush tool, work on removing the lines on the face by using a nearby area of "clean skin" as your source for the Healing Brush tool. Continue carefully working on the lines around the face, frequently setting new source points for your Healing Brush so you don't get a repeating pattern.

Retouchers often use separate layers for each section of the face. For simplicity's sake, we're using one layer here. Using several layers means you can easily set the opacity for each layer separately, allowing for more finesse when needed.

2. When you've removed all the lines on the face, slide the opacity of the layer to around 50% to tone down the effect for a more realistic-looking result. The goal here is to flatter the subject while keeping it within the realm of reality (FIGURE 8.64).

3. The next step in our process is to do some dodging to lighten the darker sides of the wrinkles. Add a new layer, set the blending mode to Soft Light, and name the layer *Dodge Soft Light*. Select the Brush tool, and set the foreground color to white by tapping the D key and the X key. In the options bar, set both Opacity and Flow to 25%, and paint white on the shadow side of the wrinkles and folds on her face (FIGURE 8.65).

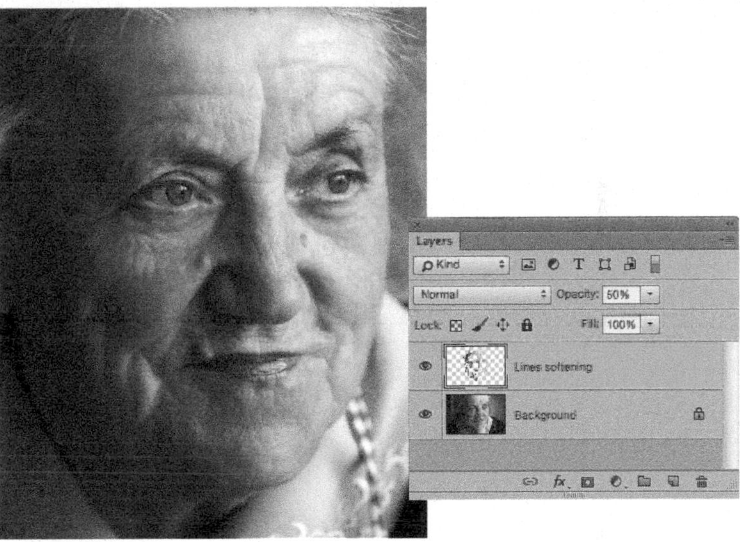

FIGURE 8.64 The lines on the face have been retouched using the Healing Brush. The version in the left has an opacity of 100%; the version on the right has the opacity turned down to 50% to soften the effect.

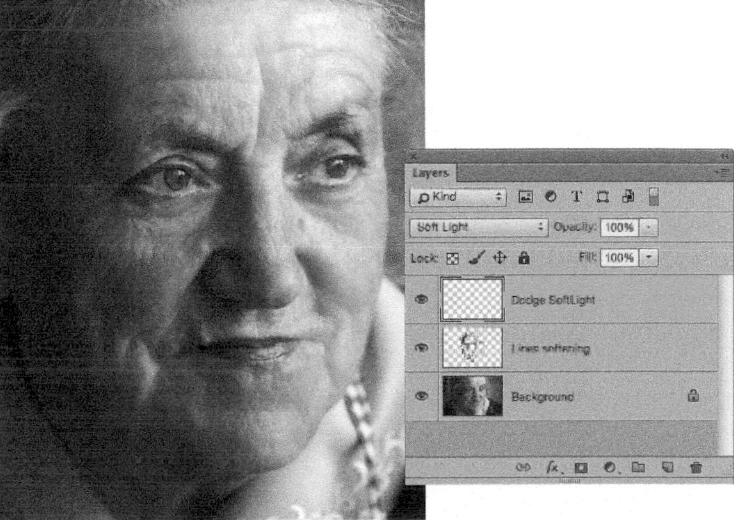

FIGURE 8.65 The green areas indicate where the shadows were dodged to smooth the wrinkles and folds on the face.

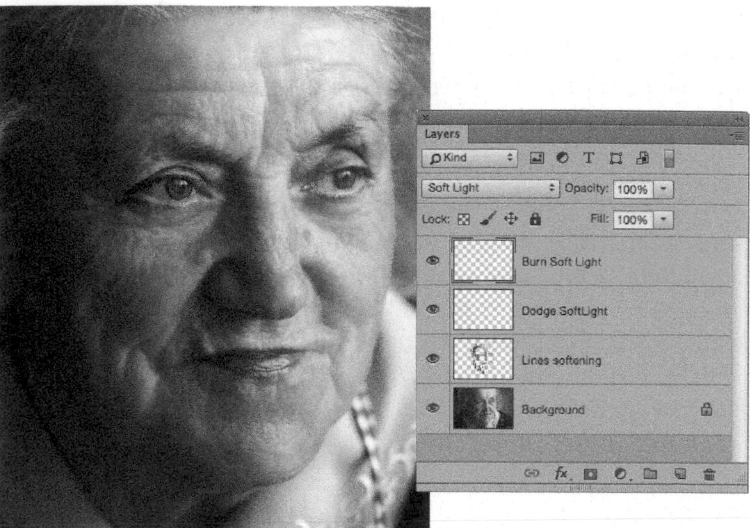

FIGURE 8.66 The green areas indicate where the highlights were burned to smooth the wrinkles and folds on the face.

4. Burning the lighter parts of the wrinkles and folds will complete the task. Add another layer, set the blending mode to Soft Light, and name this layer *Burn Soft Light.* As with the dodging layer, use the Brush tool with a low Opacity and Flow setting, and paint black over the the lighter parts of the wrinkles (FIGURE 8.66).

Color Correcting Skintone

The color of the skin is very important to pay attention to. When it comes to color correcting skin, take the overall environment and lighting conditions into account. Depending on the time of day, the surroundings, and the angle of the sun, the light hitting the scene may be warmer or cooler, and a person's skin will reflect those conditions.

For instance, if your subject is standing on the beach with the setting sun lighting their face, their skin will reflect that beautiful warm light. And if your subject is standing in the shadows on a snowy, overcast day, your subject will reflect the cooler blue light in that scene. It is perfectly natural for skin color to shift a little warmer or a little cooler depending on the scene it's being photographed in.

Although some variation in the warmth or coolness of the skin color can be appropriate, the most important color balance for skin is green/magenta. When the skin is too green, the subject tends to look nauseated. And when the skin is too magenta, the person can look flushed or sunburned. Neither of these looks makes for good-looking people, so it's important to watch this balance carefully.

Getting the Red Out

The gentleman in FIGURE 8.67 has skin that is unevenly colored and has a bit too much magenta in some patches, making his skin looked irritated. To address this issue, we'll use a tip, picked up from Photoshop guru Lee Varis, that takes advantage of the controls found in a Hue/Saturation adjustment layer (FIGURE 8.68).

ch8_red_face.jpg

TIP The default size of the Hue/Saturation controls may be too small, making it difficult to do fine adjustments on the color range controls. Dragging the lower-left corner of the Properties panel will let you "stretch out" the window, giving you both more room to work with and finer control.

FIGURES 8.67 and 8.68 Before and after. © *Bobbi Lane*

FIGURE 8.69 Sliding the Hue slider far to the right makes it easy to see which colors are being affected. Moving these sliders allows you to dial in the range of colors you need to adjust.

1. After doing the basic cleanup on the image with the Spot Healing and Healing tools, add a Hue/Saturation adjustment layer and select Reds from the preset color range menu. To make it easier to see which colors you're working with, slide the Hue slider most of the way to the right. This will shift the reds in the image in a dramatic way, making it obvious which colors are being affected (FIGURE 8.69).

2. Drag the center of the color range a little to the left to pick up more of the magenta in his cheeks and neck. By watching the effect this move has on the colors in the image, you can see when you're very close to the right range of colors (FIGURE 8.70).

3. Drag the inner-left slider to the right and left, watching how this affects the range of colors selected. Do the same with the inner-right slider. Do the same with the two outer sliders, watching to see how well the selection blends in with the rest of the colors on his face (FIGURES 8.71 and 8.72).

4. With the color range selection dialed in, pull the Hue slider back to the neutral position and then nudge it to the right to pull some of the magenta out of his cheeks and neck; in this example, +9 seems about right. Pull the Saturation slider to the left to desaturate these colors a little; –10 gives a good result here (FIGURE 8.73).

+ TIP Looking at the color ramp where the color sliders are will give you a good idea of which direction to go in making this adjustment. As you can see, the warmer yellow/reds lie to the right and the cooler magenta/reds lie to the left of the color range.

5. Finally, since this adjustment seems to be affecting his lips, select the Brush tool and paint with black over his lips on the layer mask to restore the original color.

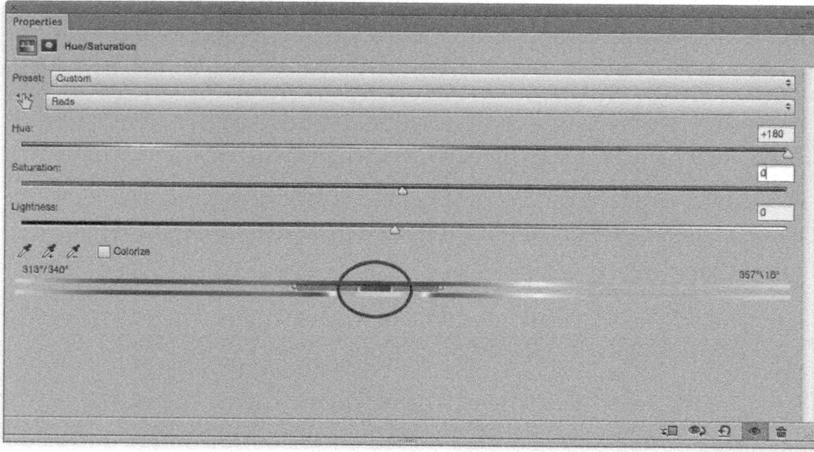

FIGURE 8.70 The sliders on the inside control the primary range of colors being affected.

FIGURE 8.71 The sliders on the outside control the feathering of the selected range of colors.

FIGURE 8.72 With the color range sliders dialed in, you can zero in on the areas that have too much magenta.

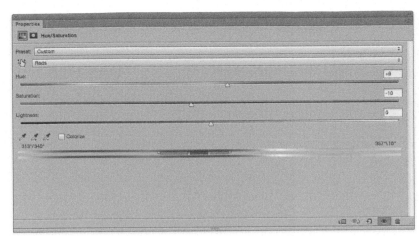

FIGURE 8.73 Final adjustments used to pull a little magenta out of the cheeks and neck

Color Correcting Skin

Using the "divide and conquer" technique discussed in Chapter 4 to improve color and tonality can result in a much better color balance for the skin.

 **ch8_blonde.jpg**

Before plunging into the color correction on this image, let's take a moment to evaluate the color and tonality of the image so we can form a plan that will help us as we work.

The first thing we notice is that the overall color is a bit too warm, almost orange. Since orange is a combination of red and yellow, we can address this by decreasing red and increasing blue.

The next thing we notice is that the tonality of the image is a bit flat. Adding a little contrast can give the image more snap and make it more dynamic (FIGURES 8.74 and 8.75).

The idea behind the divide and conquer technique is to use two adjustment layers so that you can address the color and the tonality (or contrast) separately.

Since both adjustment layers address different aspects of the corrections, the layer order does not matter; it makes no difference which layer is on top.

1. Add two Curves adjustment layers, one with blending mode set to Color and the other set to Luminosity. Name the layers *Color Crvs* and *Lum Crvs*.

2. Starting with the Color Crvs layer, select the red curve, select the On-Image Adjustment tool, and move your cursor over her skin to see where on the red curve most of her skin color lies. Click the area between her eyes to set a control point on the curve, and press the Down Arrow key to nudge this point down a few clicks to pull some red out of the image (FIGURE 8.76).

FIGURES 8.74 and 8.75 Before and after. © *Bobbi Lane*

FIGURE 8.76 After setting a control point on the red curve, pull it down slightly to pull some red out of the image.

3. Select the blue curve, and use the On-Image Adjustment tool to move your cursor over her skin to see where most of the skin color lies on this curve. Click the area between her eyes to set a control point on the curve, and press the Up Arrow to move this point up a few clicks to add some blue to the image (FIGURE 8.77).

FIGURE 8.77 Pull up on the blue curve to add a little bit of blue.

FIGURE 8.78 Brighten the image while keeping the shadows solid with the Lum Crvs layer.

4. Select the Lum Crvs layer. Brighten the image while adding a subtle contrast by pulling up on the highlight quartertones in the RGB curve, as shown in FIGURE 8.78. Add another point around the darker three-quartertones, and pull this down a little to keep the shadows looking solid.

5. The teeth could use a touch of whitening. Tap Q (Quick Mask mode) and use the Brush tool to paint black over the teeth, and tap Q to create a selection for the teeth.

6. Choose **Select > Inverse,** add a Curves adjustment layer, and name it *Teeth Crvs*. Use the On-Image Adjustment tool to set a control point on the RGB curve, and pull up a little to brighten the teeth. Select the red curve and pull a little red out. Finally, select the blue curve and pull it up a touch to add a little blue (FIGURE 8.79).

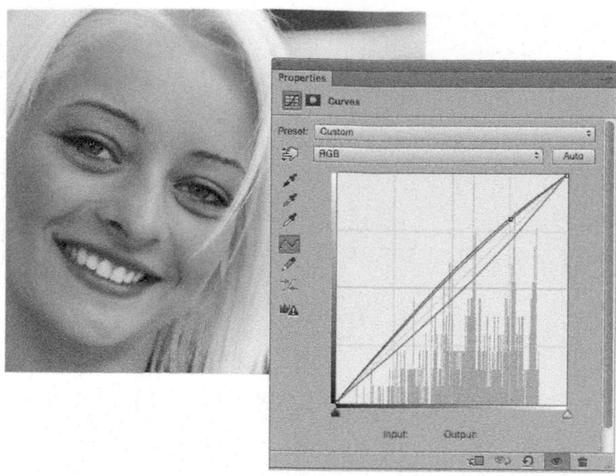

FIGURE 8.79 Color correct the teeth with another Curves adjustment layer.

7. Brightening her eyes will finish the color correction. Use Quick Mask to paint a selection over her eyes. Tap Q to enter Quick Mask mode and paint with black over her eyes. Press Cmd-I/Ctrl-I to invert the mask and tap Q to activate the selection. Add a Curves adjustment layer and name this layer *Eyes Crvs*. Click the RGB curve near the highlight quartertones, and pull up a little to brighten her eyes (FIGURES 8.80 and 8.81).

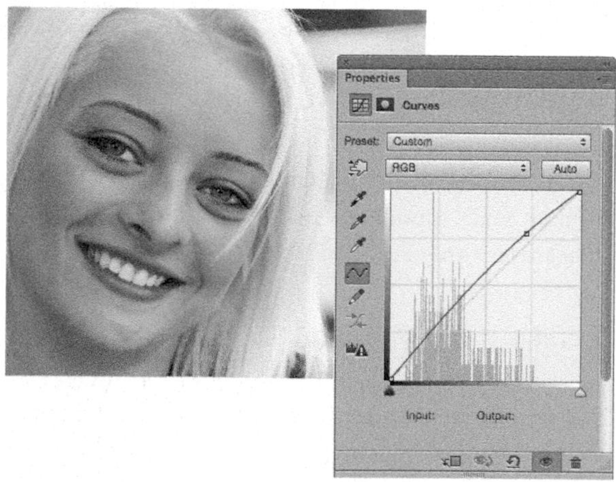

FIGURE 8.80 Brighten the eyes with one more Curves adjustment layer.

FIGURE 8.81 After color correction

Enhancing Facial Features

The more detailed sections of the face, such as the eyes, mouth, and hair, will all benefit from carefully applied Photoshop love.

Eyeball Fundamentals

The eyes can be the most important feature of a person's face. Many of the clues we get about a person's mood and health come from the eyes. By carefully working on the eyes, we can make the portrait more intriguing while pulling focus away from less important parts of the image.

Remember that our eyes are spheres that need moisture to feel comfortable and healthy. Over-retouching the eyes can make them lifeless and uninteresting. To avoid this over-worked look, take care to maintain the highlights that make the eyes look moist, keep the red tones near the tear ducts (on the inside corners of the eyes), and keep the lighter areas in the iris opposite the highlight (FIGURE 8.82).

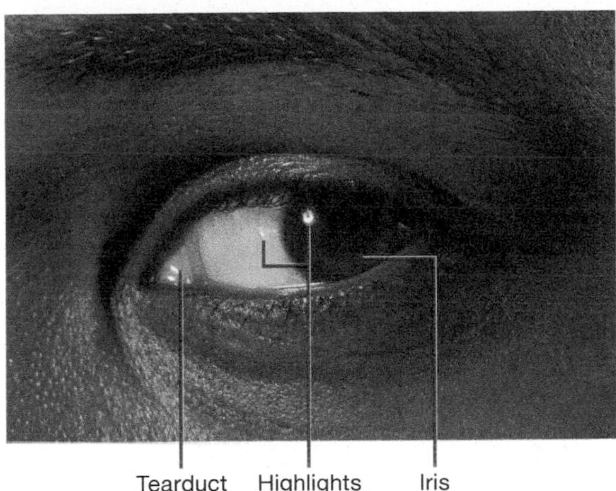

FIGURE 8.82 Our eyes are round and translucent, allowing light to play off their surface. © *KE*

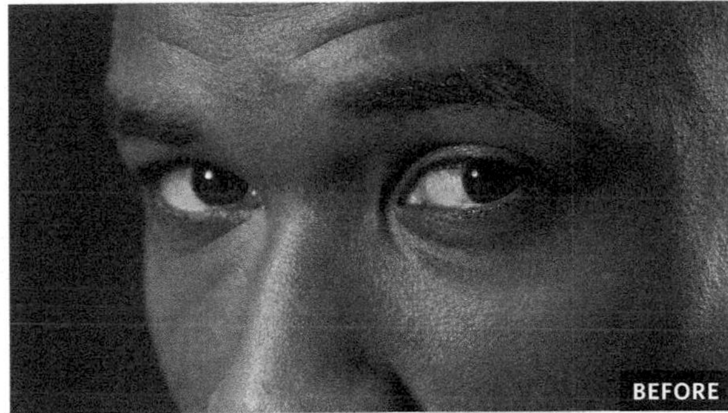

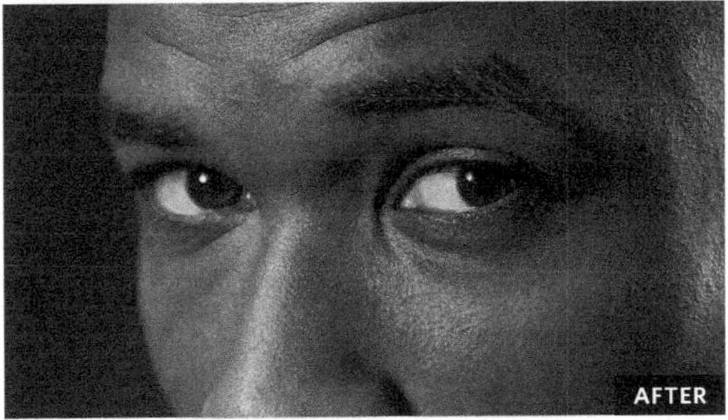

FIGURES 8.83 and 8.84 Before and after. © *KE*

Basic Eye Cleanup

The usual workflow for retouching a person's eyes is to first clean up any red veins or stray eyelashes and to even out and brighten the eye whites (FIGURES 8.83 and 8.84). It's also nice to add a touch of highlight to the irises to give them more liveliness.

ch8_male_eyes.jpg

1. Add a new layer and name it *Clean whites of eyes*. Using the Spot Healing Brush tool set to Sample All Layers and Content, retouch out the red veins in the whites of the eyes. Also clean up the errant eyelashes that come down over the eye whites (FIGURE 8.85).

2. The next step is to even out the color of the whites. Add another new layer, set the blending mode to Color, and name this layer *Even color in whites of eyes*. Select the Brush tool, set a low opacity (around 50%), sample the color of the eye that's closest to white, and paint this color over the rest of the white part of both eyes (FIGURE 8.86).

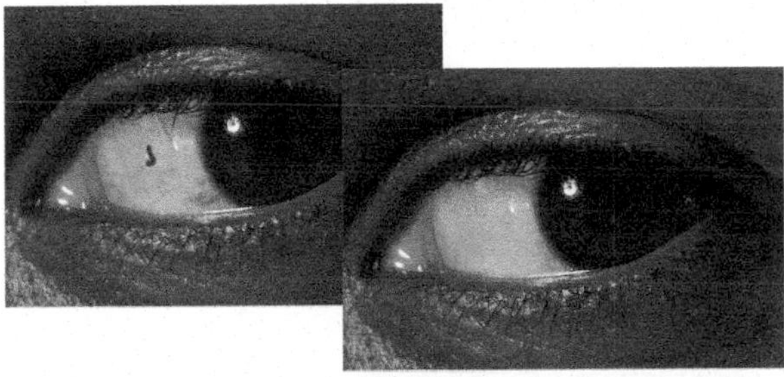

FIGURE 8.85 Use the Spot Healing Brush tool to clean the whites of the eyes.

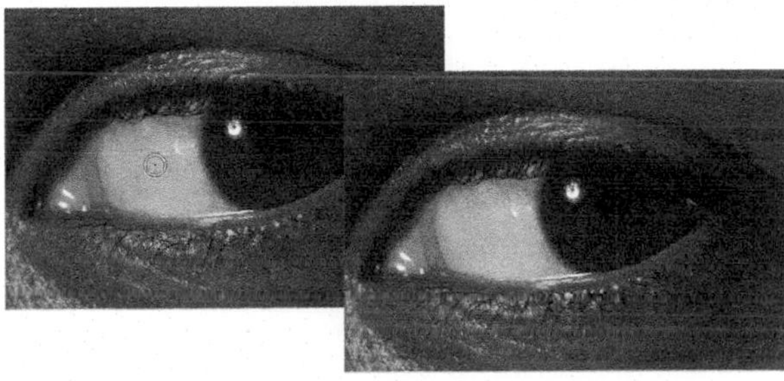

FIGURE 8.86 Even out the color of the whites of the eyes.

3. To brighten the eyes, set the opacity of the Brush tool to 100% and tap Q to enter Quick Mask mode. Paint black over the eyes, invert the Quick Mask, and tap Q to create your selection.

4. Add a Curves adjustment layer. Name the layer *Brighten Eyes Crvs*. Select the On-Image Adjustment tool, move your cursor over the whites of the eyes, and click to set a control point on the RGB curve. Pull up on the RGB curve to gently brighten the eyes. Select the red curve, and pull down slightly to remove some red. Next select the blue curve and pull up on it a little to remove the yellowish color (**FIGURE 8.87**).

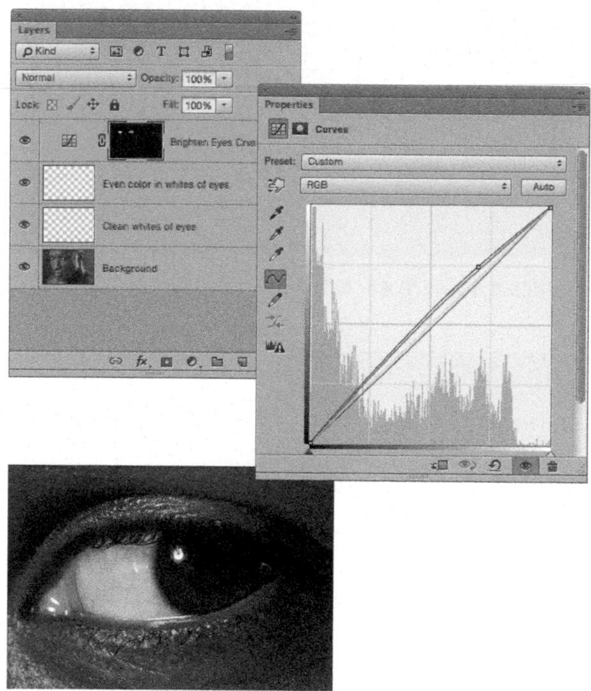

FIGURE 8.87 Brighten the eyes with a Curves adjustment layer.

5. Add more life to the irises by adding a new layer. Name this layer *Light in pupil S/L*. Set the blending mode to Soft Light. With the Brush tool set to a low opacity, around 30%, paint white over most parts of the irises. Reduce the layer's opacity if the effect looks too strong (**FIGURE 8.88**).

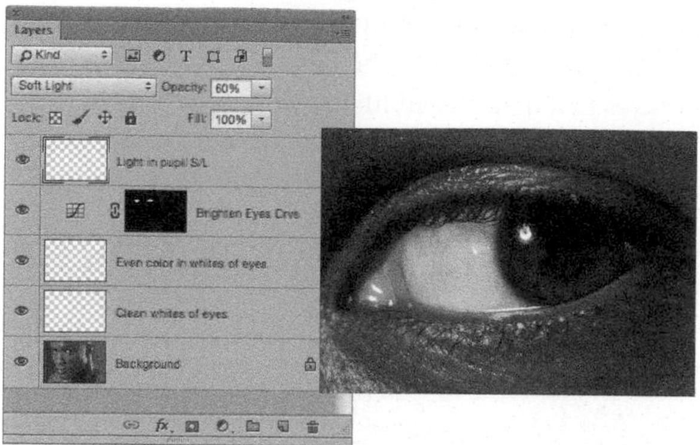

FIGURE 8.88 Layers used

Enhancing Eyebrows and Eyelashes

The eyebrows and eyelashes frame the eyes and can go a long way toward making a person's eyes look dramatic and interesting. So in addition to making sure the eyes are clean and bright, it often pays to give these areas a little care as well (**FIGURES 8.89** and **8.90**).

ch8_enhance_eyes.jpg

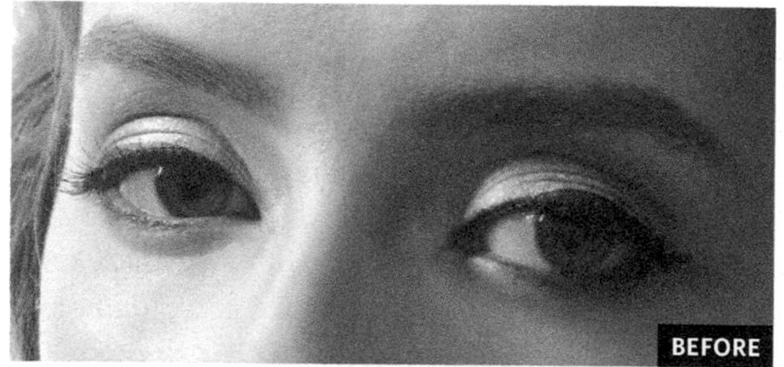

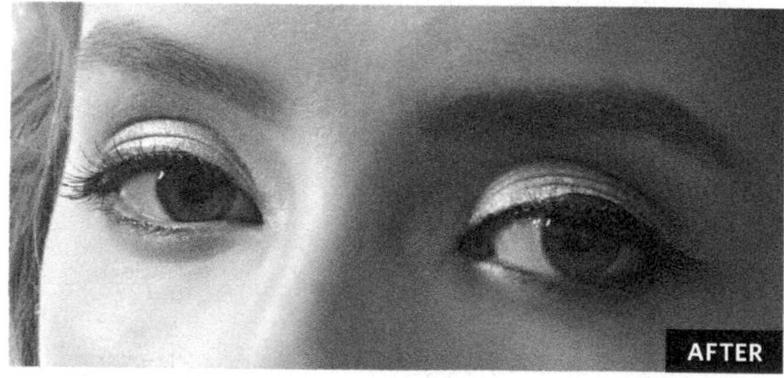

FIGURES 8.89 and **8.90** Before and after.
© *Mark Rutherford*

1. Create a new layer, named *Eyebrow cleanup,* and use the Spot Healing Brush tool set to Sample All Layers and Type to Content-Aware, and clean up the edges of the eyebrows and retouch out the lighter hairs (**FIGURE 8.91**).

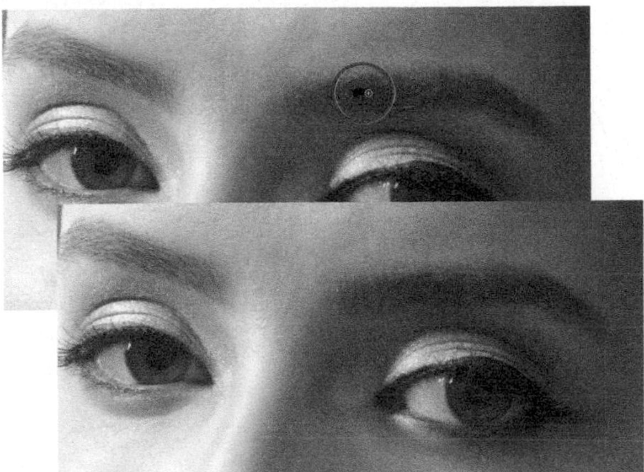

FIGURE 8.92 Clean up the eyebrows with the Spot Healing Brush.

2. Add a new layer, named *Eyebrow paint.* With the Brush tool set to a very small brush size, carefully sample the color of the eyebrows. Use short, curved strokes to paint in a few more hairs over the eyebrows to fill them in (**FIGURE 8.92**).

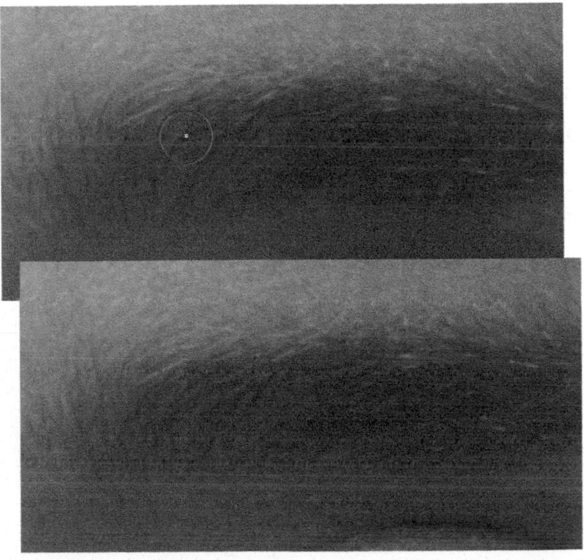

FIGURE 8.92 Fill in the eyebrows with the Brush tool, using a very small brush and short, curved strokes.

3. Select the top layer. Press Option/Alt and choose **Layers > Merge Visible** to merge all layers into a new layer. Name this layer *Sharper Eyes.* Convert this layer to a Smart Object and choose **Filter > Sharpen > Unsharp Mask.** Set Amount to 10, Radius to 60, and Threshold to 4 to emphasize the larger details in the eyes. Add a layer mask to this layer, and paint black in the mask to blend in the edges of the sharpened eyes with the rest of the image (**FIGURE 8.93**).

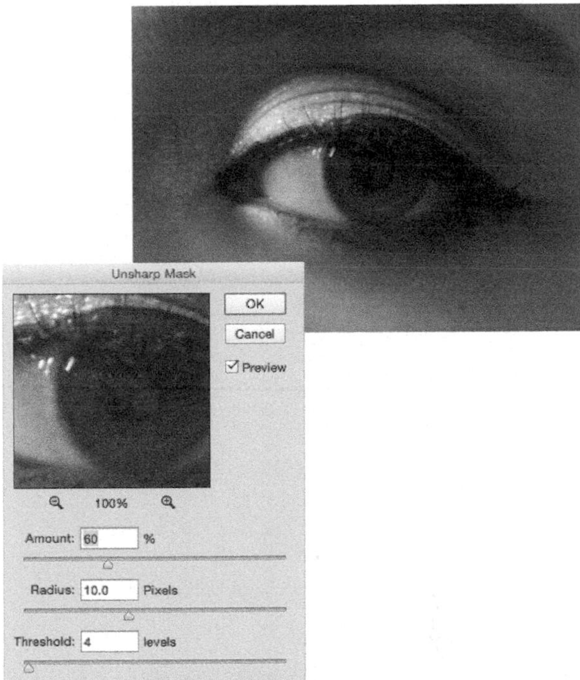

FIGURE 8.93 Sharpen the eyes with the Unsharp Mask filter, using a low amount and a high radius.

4. The final touch is to add a little digital mascara to her eyelashes to give them a touch more drama. Add a new layer, named *Eyelashes.* Set the Brush tool to about the same width as one of the narrower eyelashes. Sample the color of her eyelashes, and trace over the eyelashes that could use a little boost. Using short, curved strokes, add a few extra eyelashes on both the upper and the lower eyelids, as seen in **FIGURE 8.94**.

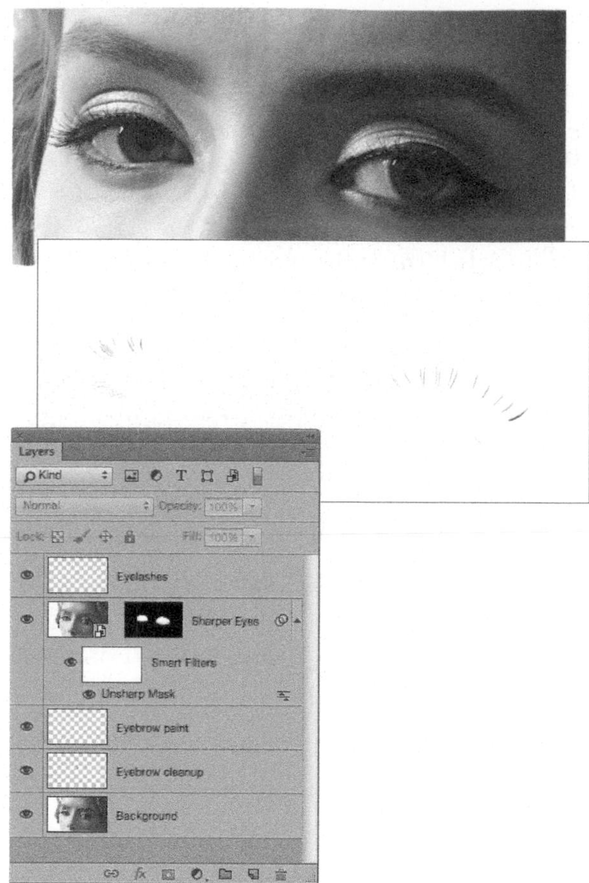

FIGURE 8.94 Eyes and eyebrows detailing completed

FIGURES 8.95 and 8.96 Before and after. © *WP*

The Dreaded Red Eye

Every now and then, we get those dreaded red eyes that make the subject look demonic.

In FIGURE 8.95 we see a happy couple at their wedding. As happens too often in portraits, their eyes have bright red pupils. Luckily, Photoshop has a very easy way to fix this problem, allowing us to exorcise the demons and restore their eyes to a normal appearance (FIGURE 8.96).

This marvelous tool works by detecting and desaturating the red in the pupils. Unfortunately, if you have a photo of a pet with a green-eye look, you'll have to use the Sponge tool to desaturate the green-eye.

1. To work nondestructively, duplicate the Background layer (Cmd-J/Ctrl-J).

2. Using the Red Eye tool, drag over the pupils one at a time to remove the red, as seen in FIGURE 8.100.

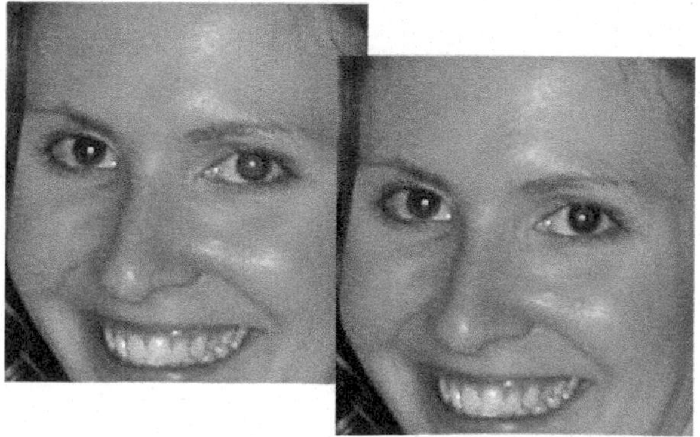

FIGURE 8.97 Using the Red Eye tool to fix red pupils. © *WP*

Digital Dentistry

The mouth often reveals the mood of the subject, and a nice smile makes a good impression. Performing a little digital dentistry is a common challenge. The trick here is to do so in a way that gives the subject a nice smile without being too heavy handed. As with most tasks in portrait retouching, a light touch goes a long way.

In FIGURE 8.98 you can see that the gap between the man's front teeth is a little wider than an orthodontist might prefer. With two simple steps, we close the gap and give him a nice, bright smile (FIGURE 8.99).

FIGURES 8.98 and 8.99 Before and after. © *Phil Pool*

ch8_teeth.jpg

1. Use the Lasso tool to draw a selection around his right front tooth, and press Cmd-J/Ctrl-J to copy the selected tooth to a new layer. Name the layer *Rt Tooth*, and use the Move tool to move it to the left to cover about half the gap. Add a layer mask to this layer, and use a small Brush tool to paint black on the mask to blend the edges of the moved tooth with the existing teeth and lips (FIGURE 8.100).

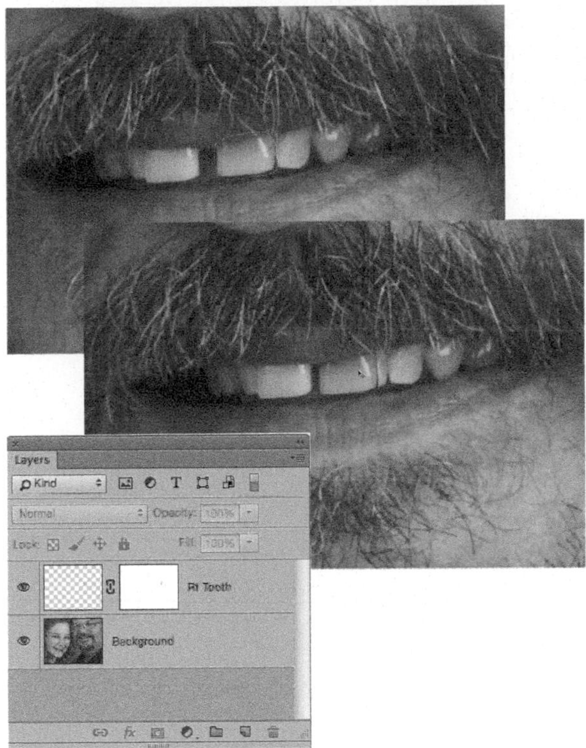

FIGURE 8.100 Copy his right front tooth and move it to the left.

2. Select the Background layer and repeat step 1, this time selecting the left front tooth and naming the layer *Lft Tooth*. Move this tooth to the right to finish closing the gap between the front teeth. Add a layer mask to this layer and use the Brush tool to paint black in the mask so that the new tooth blends in with the rest of the mouth (FIGURE 8.101).

After closing the gap in his teeth, it becomes noticeable that not all the teeth are the same color.

TRY IT Using the same techniques you learned to even and brighten the color of the eyes earlier, create a layer with blending mode set to Color and even the color of the teeth. Then add a Curves adjustment layer with a layer mask that isolates the teeth, and brighten the teeth. Practice creating two layer groups, one for his teeth corrections and another for hers.

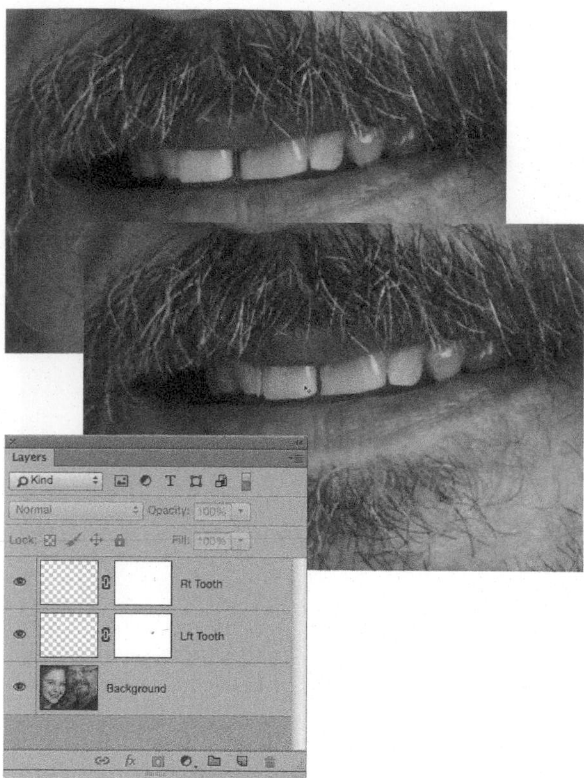

FIGURE 8.101 To finish closing the gap, copy his left front tooth and move it to the right.

The Digital Nose Job

One's nose never stops growing, and as we grow older it can become a more prominent feature, pulling attention away from the eyes and mouth.

Reducing the nose by copying it and using either the Warp transformation or the Liquify filter will usually be sufficient. On occasion, as with a profile shot, some cloning may be necessary to complete the task (**FIGURES 8.102** and **8.103**).

ch8_nosejob.jpg

1. With the Rectangular Marquee tool, select an area around the nose, including a little extra so you'll have enough to blend the new nose with the rest of the image. Press Cmd-J/Ctrl-J to copy this selection to a new layer. Name this layer *Nose* and convert it to a Smart Object (**FIGURE 8.104**).

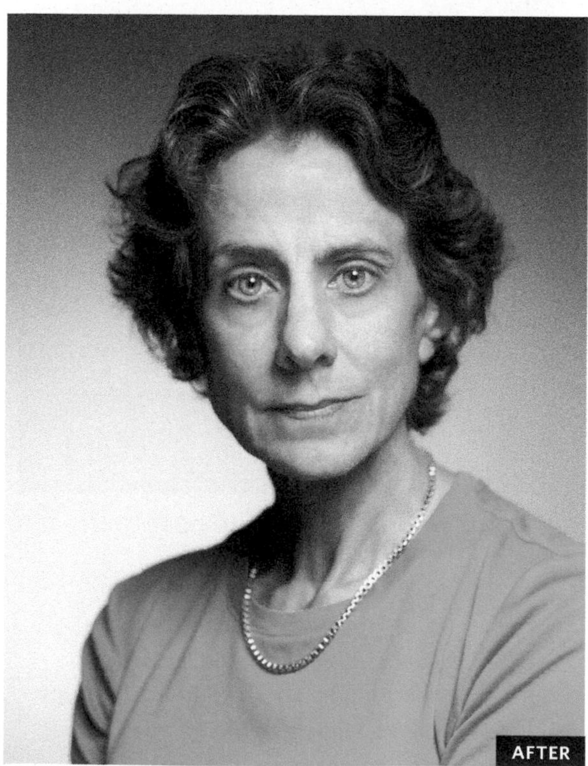

FIGURES 8.102 and **8.103** Before and after
© *Marko Kovacevic*

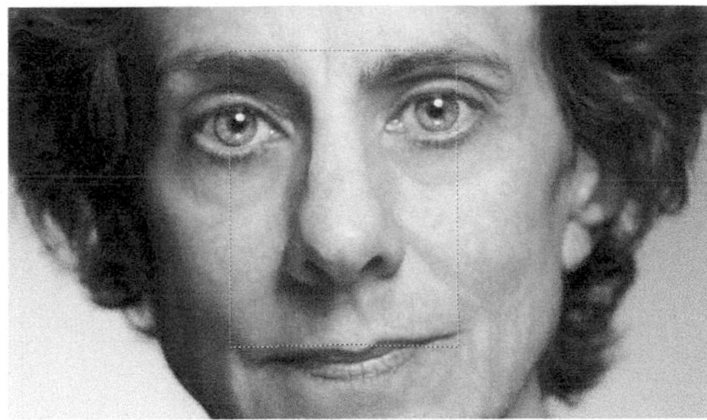

FIGURE 8.104 Use the Marquee tool to select an area around the nose.

2. Choose **Edit > Transform > Warp**. In the warp transformation mesh, click the area at the bottom of the nose and pull up to shorten the nose. Bring in each nostril a little bit to narrow the nose as well, as seen in FIGURE 8.105. Press Return/Enter to commit the transformation.

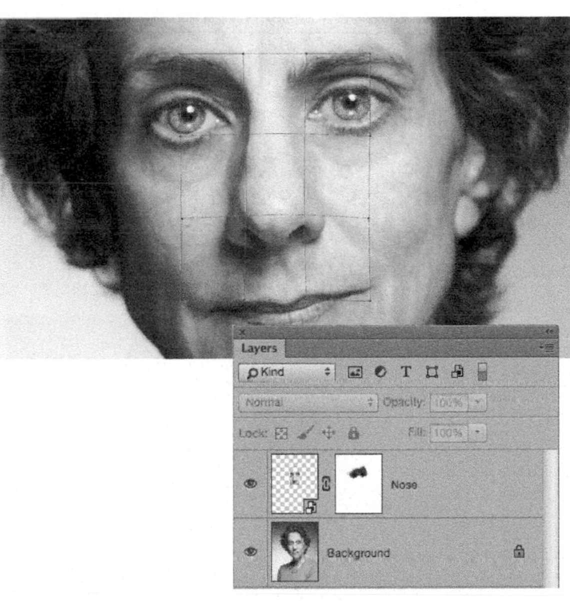

FIGURE 8.105 Use the warp transformation to squeeze in and shorten the nose.

3. Add a layer mask. Using the Brush tool with a soft edge, paint black into the mask around the edges of this layer to blend the new nose with the rest of the face. Pay extra attention to the way it blends in with the eyes to be sure they are not distorted.

The Digital Surgeon

Expressions and poses can be fleeting especially in photographs with multiple people in them! And sometimes the right pose and the right expression are in different frames. Photoshop makes it easy to combine the right pose with the right expression by compositing one shot with another.

When a photo has two or more subjects, it's inevitable that not everyone will be smiling at the same time. In FIGURE 8.106 the bride and the flower girl were a frame or two off from being in perfect sync. Thanks to Photoshop the bride will be able to enjoy a happy memory after all (FIGURES 8.107 and 8.108).

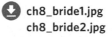

ch8_bride1.jpg
ch8_bride2.jpg

FIGURE 8.106 The expressions of the bride and the flower girl are not the best they could be. © *Phil Pool*

FIGURES 8.107 and 8.108 Before and after. © *Phil Pool*

1. With both images open, choose **Window > Arrange > 2-Up Vertical**. Using the Move tool, drop the photo with the flower girl smiling (bride1) on top of the shot of the bride smiling (bride2). Make sure that the Flower Girl layer is on top, and name it *Smiling Girl*. Close the bride1 image.

2. Change the layer's blending mode to Difference. Use the Move tool to position the head of the flower girl so that the edges of her left cheek line up closely with each other in both pictures. Ideally, the left side of the girl's cheek should align with her cheek in the Background layer, minimizing the amount of coverup work you'll need to do afterward (FIGURE 8.109). With the new head in the correct position, change the blending mode back to Normal.

FIGURE 8.109 Use the Difference blending mode on the top layer to make it easier to position the flower girl's layer over the bride's layer.

3. Add a layer mask to the Smiling Girl layer, press Cmd-I/Ctrl-I to invert it, and fill it with black. This hides the layer. Using the Brush tool with a soft-edged brush, paint white into the layer mask to reveal the new head.

Where her hair overlaps at the back of the head, use a larger brush to create a softer transition. Where her chin and cheek meet the bride's dress, zoom in and use smaller brush to carefully work on the edge for a sharper transition, giving you a nice, clean edge (FIGURE 8.110).

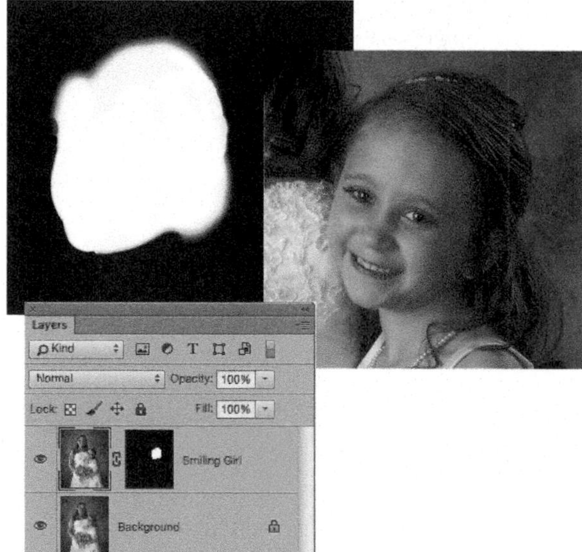

FIGURE 8.110 The layer mask should be sharper at the chin and cheek but can be softer where the hair overlaps.

TIP To invert a layer mask, as you add it Option/Alt-click the Add Layer Mask icon at the bottom of the Layers panel. To invert a layer mask after it was added, select the mask and click Invert in the Properties panel with the mask is selected, or press Cmd-I/Ctrl-I.

4. Refine the transition by tapping X to toggle the foreground and background color, and paint with black or white onto the mask. After working on the mask to reveal the new head, there is a small area to the left of the girl's head that needs a bit of work. Add a new layer, and using the Clone Stamp tool to carefully clone some of the bride's hair and dress to refine the blend (FIGURE 8.111).

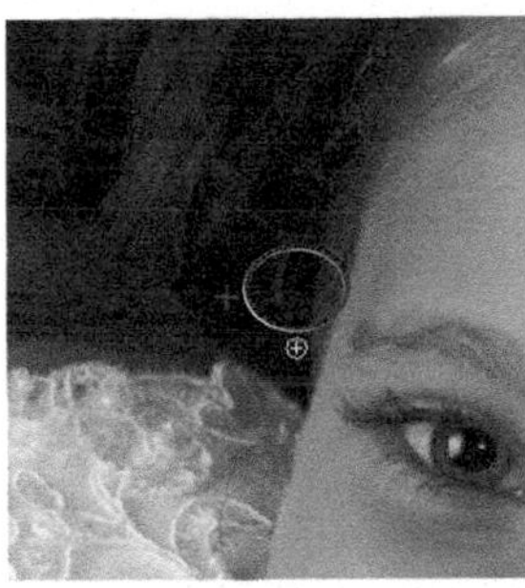

FIGURE 8.111 After the new head has been positioned and masked, one small area to the left of the flower girl's head needs to be fixed.

ADDING CREATIVE INTERPRETATION

Level 4 of the retouching process involves adding creative effects, including subtle glows or color treatments that give the image an artistic interpretation. This is one of area in which retouchers can express themselves and set their work apart from everyone else's.

Inspirations for these artistic interpretations can be found on countless sites on the web. Keep up on trends and looks that are on the upswing for image effects that will make your work shine.

Ad industry sites such as www.foundfolios.com and www.dripbook.com are great resources. And every year the well-regarded magazine Communication Arts (www.commarts.com) sponsors a photography competition that features the very best from across the world. Additionally, www.behance.com and www.instagram.com are terrific resources for inspiration.

Dennis used a combination of techniques to add a creative touch to FIGURE 8.112. The first step involved adding a little light to the model's face, giving her skin a subtle glow. He then added a split-tone color treatment and finished it off by adding a touch of contrast to the model while lightening the background (FIGURE 8.113).

ch8_splittone.jpg

Step One: Adding a Glow

1. After doing the initial rounds of retouching, view the Red, Green, and Blue channels in the Channels panel to see which one has the most detail in the skin tones. Usually, this will be the Blue channel.

2. Click the Blue channel in the Channels panel to select it (FIGURE 8.114).

FIGURES 8.112 and 8.113 Before and after. © *George Simian*

FIGURE 8.114 Blue channel

3. Drag the Blue channel onto the Create New Channel icon at the bottom of the Channels panel to create a copy of the Blue channel.

4. Choose **Image > Adjustments > Curves**. In the Curves dialog box, drag the black point approximately a third of the way to the right and click OK. This will boost the black values in the channel, helping to restrict the glow to the highlights in the image (FIGURE 8.115).

5. Cmd/Ctrl-click the Blue copy channel to turn it into a selection. Show the Layers panel, and add a new layer, named *Glow Blue Channel*. Set its blending mode to Soft Light. With the selection active, fill it with white (**Edit > Fill**).

FIGURE 8.115 Blue copy channel with the blacks boosted

6. Deselect the selection by pressing Cmd-D/Ctrl-D. Option/Alt-click the Layer Mask button at the bottom of the Layers panel to create a black layer mask. With a very soft, white brush, paint on the layer mask over her face and neck to reveal the glow in those areas (FIGURE 8.116).

FIGURE 8.116 With the Blue channel glow

7. Choose File > Save As to save the image as a Photoshop file, and keep the image open to continue the split toning treatment.

Step Two: Adding a Split-Tone Color Treatment

Split-tone color treatments involve shifting the color in the shadows one way and the highlights another way. For this split-tone treatment, we'll add blue to the shadows and red to the highlights and refine the overall image toning.

8. Add a Curves adjustment layer, set its blending mode to Color, and name the layer *Color Crvs.*

9. Select the blue curve and pull the black point up a bit; pull the white point down about the same amount. Notice that I pulled the Curves up along the very outside of the Curves dialogue box.

10. Select the red curve, and move the black point of this curve to the right about the same amount you moved the blue curve points; slide the white point to the left the same amount.

11. To desaturate the image, select the RGB curve and pull the white point down about a third of the way (FIGURE 8.117).

FIGURE 8.117 Split-tone color curves

12. Add a little contrast to the model by adding another Curves adjustment layer. Set the blending mode to Luminosity, and name the layer *Lum Crvs.* Add a control point to the RGB curve about three-quarters of the way to the top, and pull up slightly. Next, add another control point to the curve about three-quarters of the way to the bottom, and pull it down approximately the same amount (FIGURE 8.118).

FIGURE 8.118 Add contrast to the model by pulling up on the highlights and down on the shadows.

13. To keep the contrast boost from affecting the background, click the layer mask and paint black over the areas in the background.

14. Add another Curves adjustment layer, set its blending mode to Luminosity, and name the layer *Background Lum Crvs*. Pull up on the RGB curve to lighten the image.

15. Finally, select the layer mask for the Background Lum Crvs layer and paint black over the model to keep this layer from affecting her (FIGURE 8.119).

FIGURE 8.119 Lighten the background with another Curves adjustment layer.

TIP To simultaneously duplicate and invert a layer mask press Opt/Alt while dragging one layer mask onto the mask slot of other layers.

RETOUCHING PORTRAITS IN LIGHTROOM

Lightroom and Adobe Camera Raw (ACR) include powerful tools for handling many common retouching tasks. These tools pack quite a punch when it comes to editing and retouching portraits nondestructively, and they make it easy to go back and refine edits if you later decide to make additional improvements.

Much of this power comes from the ability to use Adjustment Brush tools that combine many adjustments, including Exposure, Contrast, Clarity, and Sharpness. This allows you to lighten, shift color, and soften all at the same time. Once you become familiar with the way these tools work, you can accomplish a lot quickly, making this a good option when you need to retouch very quickly.

Lightroom is well known for its strengths as a cataloging and nondestructive image processor. With the Spot Removal, Adjustment Brush, and Linear and Radial Gradient tools, you can complete many standard portrait-retouching tasks in Lightroom.

In terms of retouching, Lightroom shines. You can clean up a portrait during image development, many times when the person is still in the studio. Best of all, since Lightroom saves all changes in its XMP (extensible metadata platform) file, the actual image is never changed, so it's easy to return to an image hours, days, or even months later to improve a particular edit.

Lightroom's portrait-retouching workflow is similar to Photoshop's, with the biggest difference being that there are no layers in Lightroom. Because Lightroom saves the information for every brush stroke, adjusting any particular brush stroke is as simple as reselecting the Adjustment Brush or Spot Removal tool, clicking the pin where the brush stroke was applied to activate it, and adjusting the sliders or deleting the stroke (FIGURES 8.120 and 8.121).

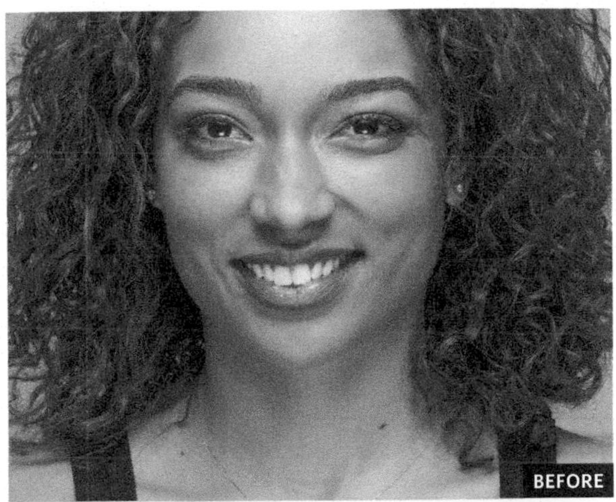

FIGURES 8.120 and **8.121** Before and after. © *KE*

In **FIGURE 8.122** each gray dot represents a place where the Spot Removal tool was used. The pins reappear in Develop mode when you click the Spot Removal tool. Click any pin to activate that spot, and you can adjust the Spot Edit settings and the source point for that brush stroke.

In this example, the Spot Removal tool was used to remove the lines under her eyes, with the Heal setting selected. Reselecting the spot allows you to drag down the Opacity slider to 25%, bringing back some of the original lines and creating the right amount of softening to the lines.

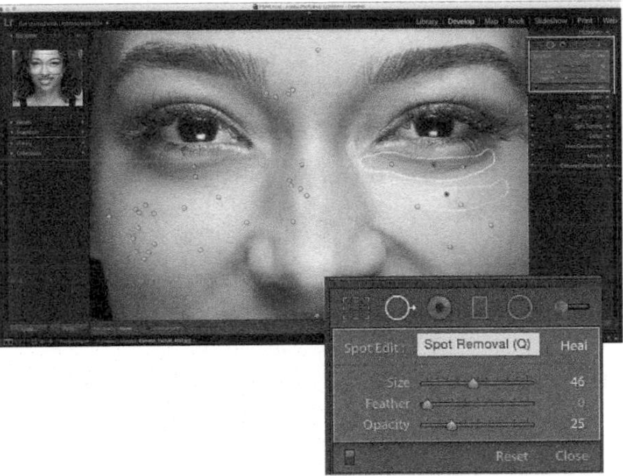

FIGURE 8.122 The tool overlay, indicated in red, lets you see the brush strokes you've made for the tool you're working with.

After going through the image to remove or reduce any spots or lines that need adjusting, the next step is to choose the Adjustment Brush tool and whiten the eyes or change the lip color.

The work that can be done with the Adjustment Brush tool is almost unlimited. It's even possible to add a bit of color to the brush stroke by clicking the rectangle to the right of the Color option beneath the sliders (**FIGURE 8.123**). If you need to lighten and soften an area at the same time, try increasing the Exposure setting while decreasing the Clarity slider.

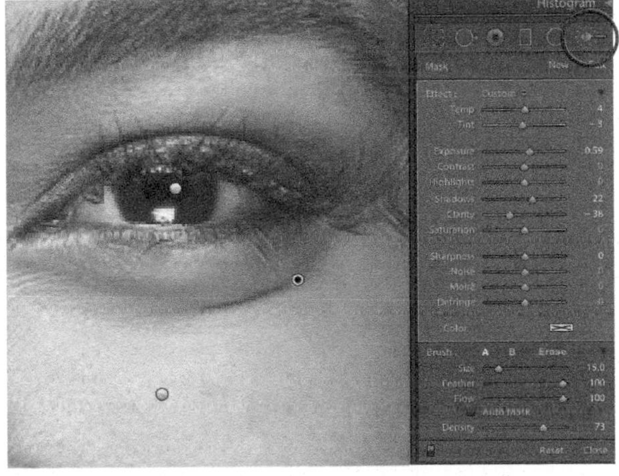

FIGURE 8.123 Adjustment Brush controls

Adjusting every slider each time you need to adjust something would be a daunting task. Fortunately, Lightroom makes it easy to save the settings for your favorite adjustments as presets. From the Effect pop-up menu, choose Save Current Settings as New Preset (**FIGURE 8.124**).

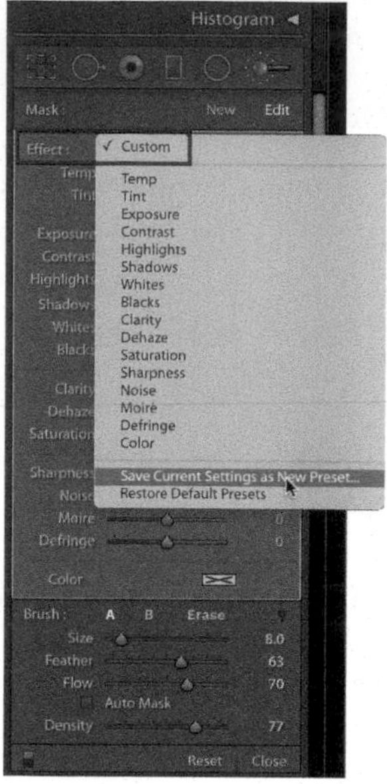

FIGURE 8.124 You can save your custom Adjustment Brush settings and reuse them later.

There are some really great Lightroom Adjustment Brush presets available on the Internet. One of the most extensive sets is Portrait Adjustment Brushes—Mega Pack 1, created by Kristi Sherk (www.sharkpixel.com/store/lightroom-presets/portrait-adjustment-brushes-mega-pack-1/).

To import local Adjustment Brush presets, click the Presets tab in the Preferences dialog box and then click the Show Lightroom Presets Folder button. Inside this folder, locate the Local Adjustment Presets folder and copy the presets into it (**FIGURE 8.125**).

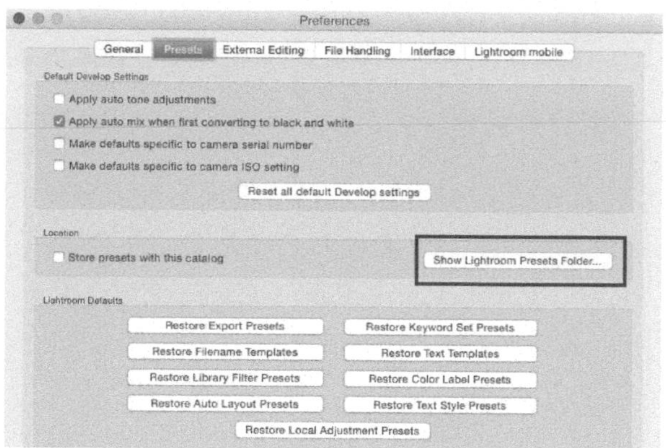

FIGURE 8.125 The Show Lightroom Presets Folder button

BEWARE THE BLUR

Good retouchers know that very few shortcuts will lead to a great result. When it comes to retouching portraits, the key is to make the subject look natural and refreshed while avoiding the over-retouched, "plastic skin" look. As humans, we're hard-wired to recognize faces, and we are especially sensitive to recognizing when something looks "off" or unnatural about a person's face.

Many of the skin-smoothing actions and techniques being promoted on the web these days rely on combining blurred and sharpened versions of an image. In **FIGURE 8.126** the disconnect between the softened skin and the lines defining her features is obvious. This look is the telltale sign of overly blurred skin. The challenge when using any technique is to keep the effect subtle enough that no one will notice it.

FIGURE 8.126 Heavy-handed blurred-skin technique

THIRD-PARTY PLUG-INS AND APPLICATIONS

Retouching portraits can be challenging, and especially so for those who have to retouch many portraits in a short time. In these situations, efficiency and quickness become high priorities.

Filling the need for those with such demands, several companies offer plug-ins or stand-alone applications that provide powerful tools to speed your workflow. These solutions offer various levels of control over skin smoothing, color correction, and even face sculpting, allowing you to easily reshape the face and eyes or even lengthen the neck.

The plug-ins we'll take a look at here are Digital Anarchy's Beauty Box, Imagenomic's Portraiture, On1's Perfect Portrait, and Anthropics Technology's Portrait Professional.

The skin smoothing in these plug-ins and applications seems to work by combining blurred and sharpened layers to achieve the desired smoothness while retaining enough detail to look believable. And the challenge when using them is to keep the effects subtle enough that you improve the image but don't wind up with overdone, plastic-looking skin. That's why we strongly recommend you first get comfortable retouching portraits by hand before delving into plug-ins. The more familiar you are with manual techniques, the better able you'll be at achieving a realistic effect with the plug-ins.

Digital Anarchy Beauty Box

Like most of the skin retouching plug-ins, Beauty Box offers a variety of sliders, allowing you to control smoothing, detail retained, contrast, and color correction.

When the sliders are moved too far, it's very easy to wind up with overly smoothed skin, so be judicious. That said, it's possible to improve the look of the skin with Beauty Box.

For those looking for a quick way to apply color effects, Beauty Box comes with a number of presets, from the out-of-this-world Blue Love to the dramatic Sunkissed (FIGURE 8.127).

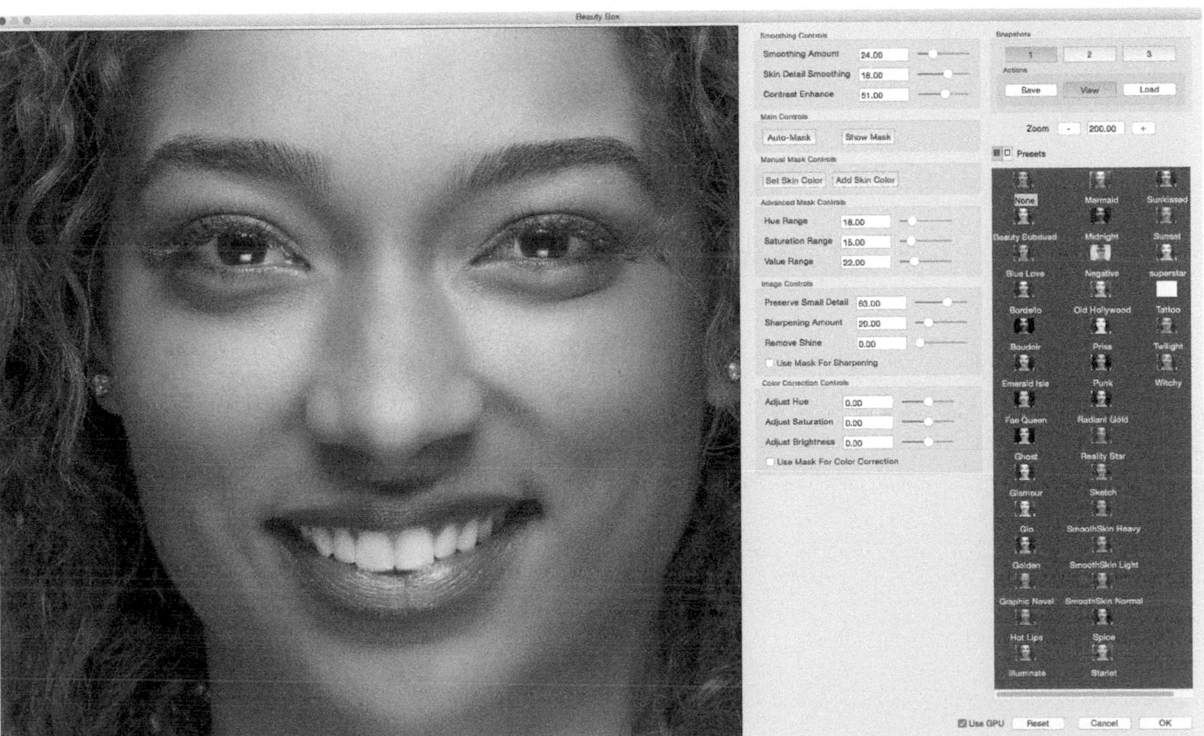

FIGURE 8.127 Beauty Box interface

Imagenomic Portraiture

The workflow for Portraiture also starts off with selecting skin tones so that you can restrict the smoothing to the areas that need it. Once the Skin Tones mask has been finessed, you control the smoothing in the Detail Smoothing section, with sliders for Fine, Medium, and Large detail. The Threshold slider acts as master control over the others.

The interface offers simple controls that, with restraint, can help you get a nice result quickly (FIGURE 8.128).

On1 Perfect Portrait

With Perfect Portrait, you begin by helping the program identify the eyes and mouth, moving control points to make sure those areas are properly selected.

In addition to smoothing and color correction tools, Perfect Portrait also gives you a nice Retouch Brush that works similarly to Photoshop's Spot Healing Brush tool. By retouching the blemishes and spots with this tool first, you can use lower settings on the smoothing controls (FIGURE 8.129).

FIGURE 8.128
Portraiture interface

FIGURE 8.129
Perfect Portrait interface

FIGURE 8.130 Portrait Pro interface

Once the eyes and mouth have been properly identified, the Eyes and Mouth controls allow you to dial in the amount of whitening, sharpening, and color enhancement you feel is needed.

When you've achieved a pleasing look with the adjustments, you can also save your own presets, speeding up your workflow—especially handy when you're working with a lot of images from a single shoot.

Anthropics Technology Portrait Pro

Like the other plug-ins, Portrait Pro starts by identifying the facial features in the image. In FIGURE 8.130 the panel on the left shows the blue outlines Portrait Pro uses to define the shape and position of the features on the face. It uses this information to more accurately calculate the results when you use the face-sculpting and skin-lighting controls, as it approximates the way the face works in 3D.

Portrait Pro also has controls for enhancing makeup, making it easy to give the eyes a more dramatic look, even allowing you to add eyeliner and mascara with a few sliders.

CLOSING THOUGHTS

Portrait retouching can be one of the more challenging types of retouching. Beginning with a good plan and working in layers can make this work more manageable. Above all, remember that the goal of good portrait retouching is to flatter the subject while keeping the work of the retoucher invisible. Ideally, the subjects should recognize themselves, and viewers should not be thinking "Great retouching!"

Chapter 9

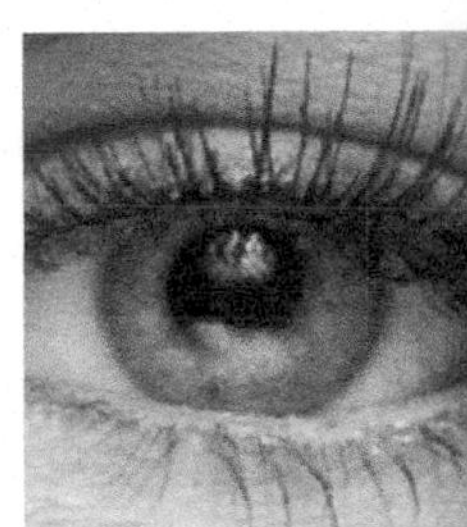

BEAUTY RETOUCHING

Idealized images of perfect women and men surround us daily. We see these pixel-perfect photos staring at us from the covers of magazines while waiting in line at the market and in the ads we're confronted with inside those same magazines on the web. While these images are often beautiful, it's important to realize they very often represent an unattainable standard.

Being blessed with great genetics and health is not enough for even the most famous models these days. Increasingly, the images you see in these publications have been extensively worked over in Photoshop, perfecting every little bit. As much as we admire the work done in creating beautiful images, we also recognize that these images represent more fantasy than truth. The images in beauty and fashion magazines and ads are the culmination of several factors: great models, great photography, great lighting, and great retouching. This chapter is dedicated to discussing many of the techniques used in the retouching of these photos, but in many ways they are not so different from the techniques discussed in Chapter 8.

As Dennis says, the techniques we use in Photoshop are like a basic set of Lego blocks that we keep reconfiguring and combining to solve the challenges an image presents. The primary difference between the work done on a typical portrait and that done on a typical beauty image is a matter of the degree and care taken in working on the shot. At the highest level, beauty retouching demands carefully working to achieve the final look needed without taking shortcuts that might be acceptable for jobs that are not subject to such high standards.

Here we'll take a close look at the techniques used by the top pros to make the beautiful perfect and the less than perfect beautiful.

In this chapter you learn how to

- Develop a retouching/working strategy
- Balance skin color and tone
- Perfect skin and hair
- Use frequency separation to refine skin color and texture
- Enhance the shape of the face with lighting

TYPES OF BEAUTY RETOUCHING

Beauty retouching usually falls into three categories: commercial, portrait, and editorial. Commercial images are ones meant to sell something, usually cosmetics or hair- or skin-care products. These images can also be used for selling jewelry—for instance, showing the model wearing a ring or necklace.

For these types of images, great emphasis is placed on making the skin and features look absolutely flawless and less emphasis is placed on showing the personality of the model.

Beauty portrait images, as seen in FIGURE 9.1, can include shots of celebrities or models and are more about showing the personality of the model while bringing it as close to perfection as possible. Again, great care is taken to make the skin look flawless while balancing that with the distinguishing features of the subject.

Finally, editorial images, as seen in FIGURE 9.2, can be a much broader category. They are usually more about telling a story, whether as a single image or as a series of images. These can also include fashion images where the intent is simply to show the clothing in the best possible light.

Many retouchers find working on editorial images more enjoyable, as there is often more freedom for creativity with color schemes and applying "looks" to make the images more interesting.

FIGURE 9.1 Example of a beauty portrait. © *Scott Nathan*

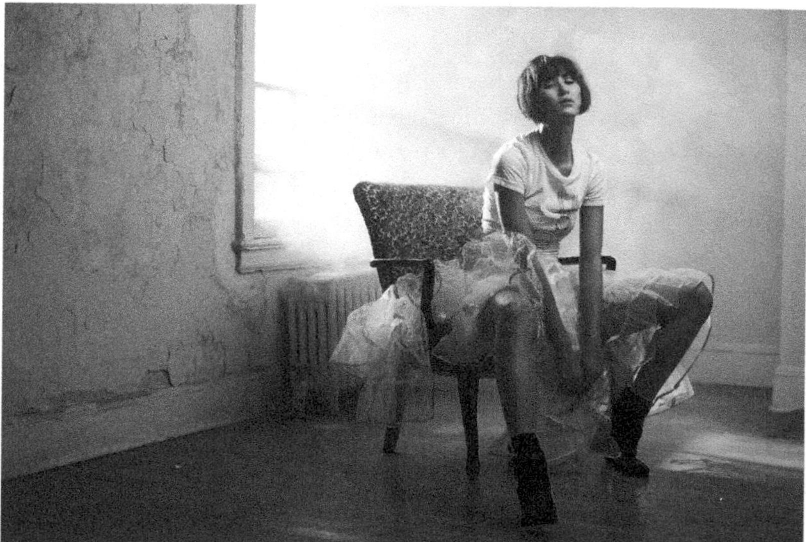

FIGURE 9.2 Example of an editorial image. © *Kent Meister*

DEVISING A WORKING STRATEGY

While the first impulse when a new image comes into your studio for retouching might be to just plunge in and start spotting and cleaning your way through the shot, it's important to first take a step back to evaluate the image and make sure you and the client are on the same page regarding what work needs to be done.

Working with the Client

Whether you're a photographer doing your own retouching or a professional retoucher, clear communication with the client is essential. You could say of all the skills a retoucher needs, the ability to listen and communicate clearly is the most important.

Clients use so many vague terms when talking about an image, and the look they want it to have, that it can be a challenge to discern exactly what they mean.

For instance, the term "perfect skin" is used by most clients with beauty images, but what that means can vary quite a lot from client to client. For some it might mean smoothed skin with very subtle texture, and for others it may mean "keep every pore."

Knowing your client and their tastes is essential when retouching any job, but even more so when working on a "high-end" project such as beauty retouching. Familiarity with their goals will also make it easier to offer suggestions or ideas for adding something special to the image. Your suggestions will often be much appreciated!

Markups

When Dennis is sent a new photo for retouching, he'll first have a discussion with the photographer or client to learn as much as he can about their vision for it. Then he'll do some quick research on the subject of the photo or the brand of the client to become familiar with their aesthetic before he begins the retouching process.

The most important part of this stage is making sure you have the clearest idea possible as to what the client would like to see done. Experienced retouchers will think through the amount of time they expect the work to take and will get the client to approve an estimate before starting on the image. Often the estimates will include a broad description of the work to be done along with the agreed-upon deadline for delivering the final file.

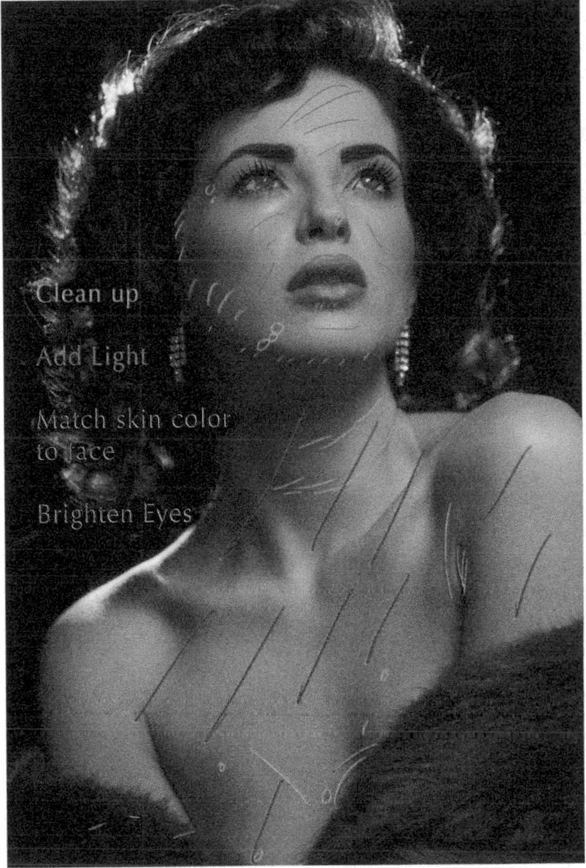

FIGURE 9.3 An image that has been marked up by a client

Many times the client will provide the retoucher with a marked-up copy of the image with notes outlining the issues they would like addressed (FIGURE 9.3). This provides the retoucher with a checklist of sorts that serves as a reminder for the work that needs to be done.

Deadlines, Approvals, and Revisions

Since professional retouching is a deadline-driven business, an essential part of the initial work order is making sure you know when the client is expecting to have the final retouched image delivered to them. There is nothing quite like getting a panicked call from the client early in the morning asking where their image is when you thought you had another couple of days to complete the work.

Additionally, it is important to set reasonable limits with the client regarding how many rounds of revisions are included in the initial estimate. As many professional retouchers know, some clients will expect you to do endless rounds of revisions before they approve the final image. Once the client understands that any revisions beyond what was agreed upon in the estimate will increase their cost, they'll have an increased passion for brevity.

Image Rights

Finally, once the job is done and the retouched image has been delivered to the client, it is very important to make sure you have clearance to show your work on the web or in your portfolio. With most commercial retouching jobs the client will want to wait until the advertising campaign or the magazine spread runs before letting the retoucher share the image publicly.

Discussions on image rights aside, this comes down to good business practices. Well-paying projects are not easy to come by, and the last thing you want to do is upset a client because you shared an image before they were ready to have it shown.

This also includes any "befores." While many people like to see before/after comparisons so they can appreciate the retouching that went into the "after" image, many times the subject or client has good reasons for not wanting the unretouched images shown to the public.

THE BEAUTY-RETOUCHING WORKFLOW

As mentioned, the basic techniques used in retouching beauty images are the same as those covered in Chapter 8. The primary difference is the degree to which they are applied and the scrutiny the clients may give your work. This is why doing high-end work means not taking shortcuts and using a sound workflow that makes it easier to finesse the result.

In Chapter 8 we discussed working in layers, and as you'd expect, this strategy is every bit as important when retouching beauty images as it is for portraits. Properly using layers and layer groups enables you to work efficiently while also allowing you the flexibility to make any revisions the client may ask for.

The Big Picture

The first step in working on the image is to take a moment to look at the shot, sweeping your eyes across the image to see if anything stands out to you. Follow the line of the image's composition and see if you notice any distractions that could take attention away from the "hero" part of the image. For instance, if this shot is to be used as an advertisement for nail polish you'd want to make note of anything that pulls attention away from the model's nails.

Among the issues to consider are:

- Is the overall tone and color balance of the image correct?
- Is the model's pose making a part of her body look awkward or misshapen?
- Are the contours of the body and clothing smooth?
- Are the important parts of the shot properly focused?
- Are the colors and tones of the face and body in agreement?
- Is anything in the background too distracting?

Ideally, an experienced photographer will address many or all of these issues "in camera" by making sure the makeup, lighting, pose, and background are all working together to make a great image. But as you can imagine, especially during a location fashion shoot some details might be missed or beyond the control of the photographer.

The Details

The next step is to zoom in to get a closer look at the image, usually zooming in to 100% to 200% view and then scrolling through the image to note all the smaller details that may need to be worked on (**FIGURE 9.4**).

FIGURE 9.4 Common image problems (from left to right): "peach fuzz" on the chin, skin tones of body and face not in agreement, a stray hair across the eye

Among the details to check are:

- Are there any dust specks or stray bits of lint that need to be removed?
- Are there any stray hairs on the face that need to be removed?
- What blemishes, wrinkles, or shadows need to be reduced or removed?
- Is the makeup properly applied?
- Do the eyes need cleaning up, sharpening, or both?
- Are there any distracting, out-of-place hairs in the hair (otherwise known as "cross hairs) that need to be cleaned up?
- Is there any "peach fuzz" around the jawline that needs to be minimized?

With practice, this process becomes faster and more second nature. The goal is to accomplish the photographer's or client's vision as nearly as possible, making the subject look flawless while keeping the retouching invisible. Forming a plan before you begin, even if it's just in your head, will help make this all easier.

The Workflow

Many of the techniques and strategies used in retouching beauty images are very similar to those we discussed in Chapter 8. The key is to use layers effectively, do your retouching on "empty layers," do your burning and dodging using either neutral layers or adjustment layers, and (of course) never change the Background layer (this is also known as "working nondestructively").

The basic beauty retouching workflow is:

1. Perform general cleanup and spotting.
2. Balance facial symmetry.
3. Perfect the skin.
4. Enhance eyes, lips, and hair as necessary.
5. Reshape/rebuild the body.
6. Refine clothing.
7. Balance color/tone selectively to make sure the face, neck, and chest match.
8. Finesse lighting and focus.
9. Prepare the final deliverable.

MATCHING TONE, COLOR, AND CONTRAST

One issue frequently encountered when working on beauty images is making sure the skin tone and color agree between the face and chest. In FIGURE 9.5 the makeup on the model makes her face look lighter and slightly cooler than her shoulders and chest. The shoulders need to be color corrected to match the tones and color of her face.

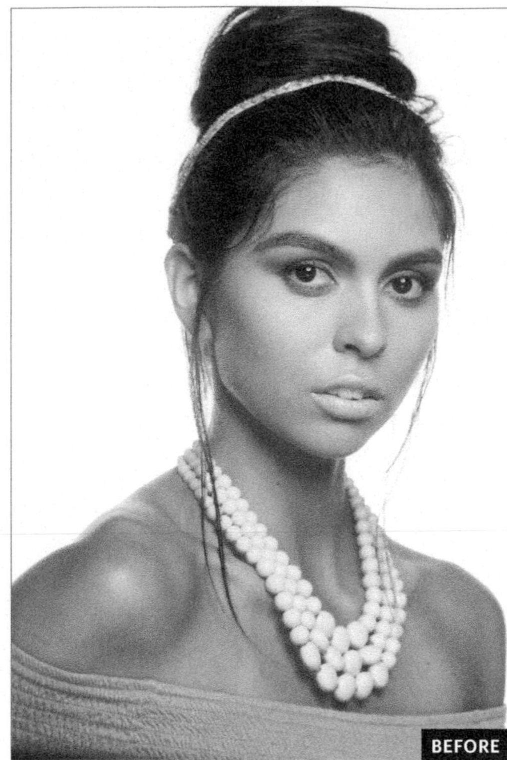

FIGURES 9.5 and 9.6 Before and after.
© *Julia Kuzmenko-McKim*

An additional goal of retouching this image was to highlight the yellow necklace, and to really make this image work the lips should match the necklace (FIGURE 9.6). We'll accomplish this by selecting each problem area individually and using each selection as the layer mask for a unique Curves adjustment layer.

1. Add an empty layer and use a small, hard-edged brightly colored brush to note and circle the details you need to correct (FIGURE 9.7). Note that the face and shoulders are different tones, some spots on the skin need to be retouched, and the lipstick should match the necklace.

TIP When making notes on images, it can be helpful to use different colors for different types of corrections.

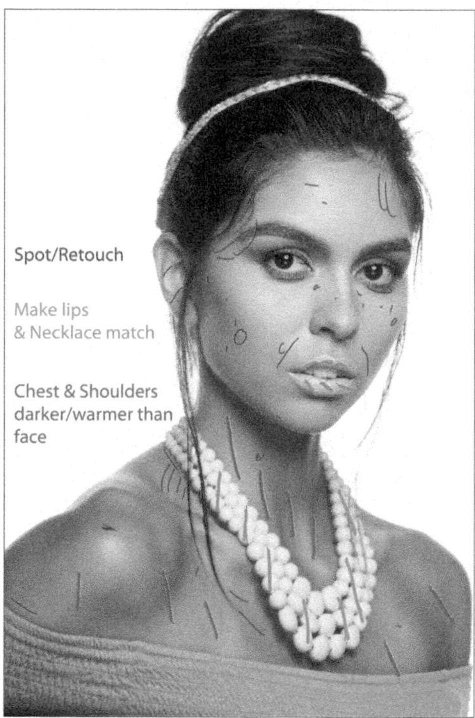

FIGURE 9.7 The marked-up image

2. With the Quick Selection tool, drag over the shoulders and neck to select them, as seen in FIGURE 9.8. This will allow you to adjust the colors of the shoulders independently of the face and necklace.

FIGURE 9.8 Use the Quick Selection tool to select her shoulders and neck.

3. Since we don't want the necklace selected as well, Option/Alt-drag over the necklace to deselect it. Continue selecting and deselecting as needed to make sure you've selected all of the shoulders, chest, and neck without the necklace, face, or dress (FIGURE 9.9).

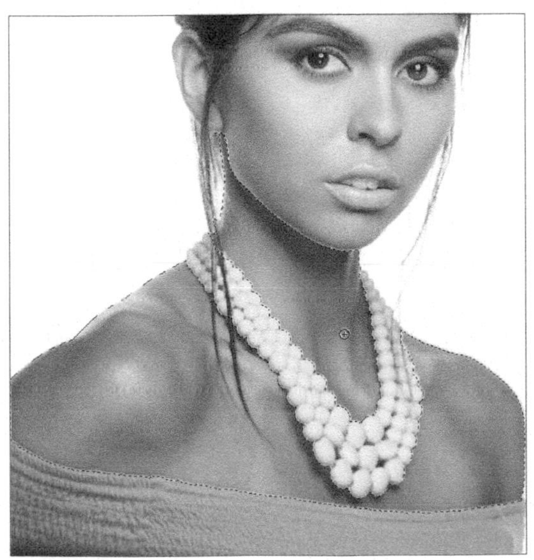

FIGURE 9.9 Delete the necklace from the selection.

4. With the shoulders selected, add a Curves adjustment layer and name it *Shoulder Crvs*. The active selection should automatically add a layer mask, making sure only the shoulders will be affected. Add a point in the middle of the RGB curve, and pull up just enough to lighten the shoulders so they're closer in tone to the face.

5. Since the shoulders also have a little more yellow in them, we need to add some blue to bring the color there closer to the color of her face. Open the Channel menu to the left of the Auto button and choose the blue curve. Add a point on the middle part of the curve and nudge the point up by tapping the Up Arrow key a couple of times to add a touch of blue (FIGURE 9.10).

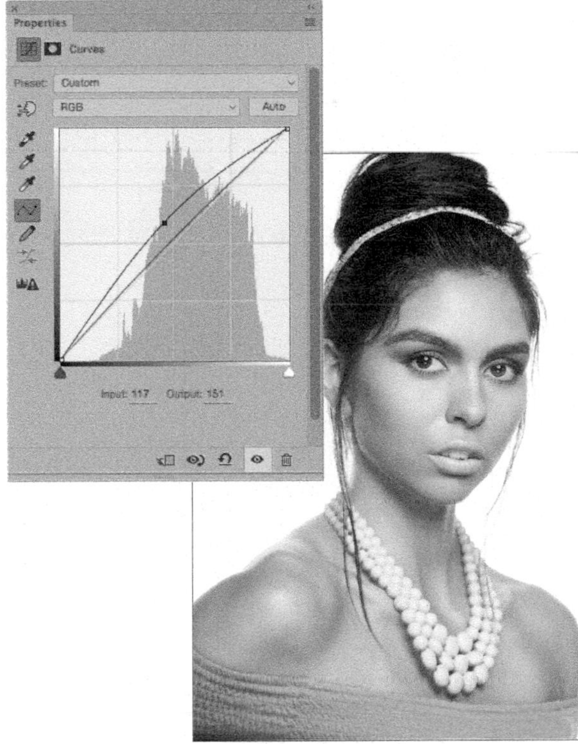

FIGURE 9.10 Use a Curves adjustment layer to bring the shoulders closer in color and tone to her face.

6. Next we'll work on getting the lips to match the color of the yellow necklace. Tap Q to enter Quick Mask mode, and then select the Brush tool. Tap D to set the foreground color to black and, using a brush that is about half as big as the upper lip's thickness, paint a selection over her lips. Press Cmd-I/Ctrl-I to invert the Quick Mask, tap Q to activate the selection, and add a Curves adjustment layer. Name the new layer *Lips Crvs*.

7. Using the On-Image Adjustment tool, click the lips to set a control point on the RGB curve and pull up a little bit to lighten the selected area. Then select the blue curve, use the On-Image Adjustment tool to set a control point, and pull down to shift the lips toward yellow.

Getting the right balance takes a bit of finesse, so it may be necessary to go back and forth between the RGB curve and the blue curve to adjust the lips to the desired color. Your final Curves adjustment should look something like FIGURE 9.11.

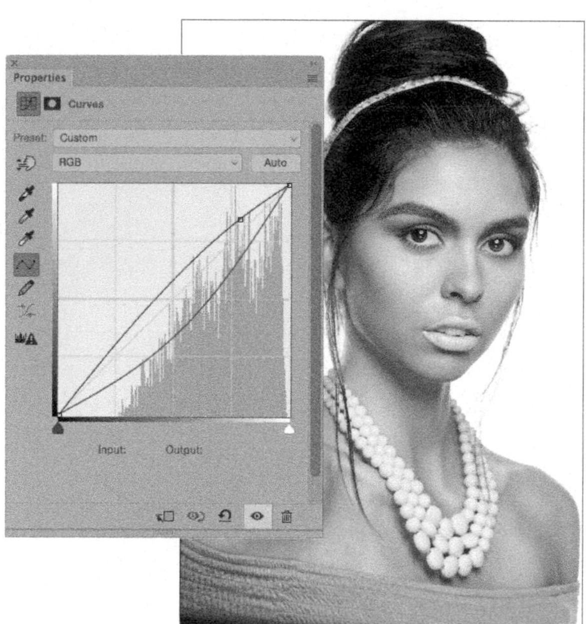

FIGURE 9.11 Use a Curves adjustment layer to shift the color of her lips so they match the yellow necklace.

8. The final step is to add a touch of overall color correction. The skin tones look a little too saturated and a tiny bit too warm. To correct this, add one more Curves adjustment layer and set the blending mode to Color. Name this layer *Overall Color Crvs.* Then select the RGB curve and drag the right end of the curve (at the white point) down a small amount, about one-tenth of the way, to slightly desaturate the image.

9. Select the blue curve and use the On-Image Adjustment tool to set a control point by clicking her camera-left cheek between the highlight and shadow marking her cheekbone. With the control point set, tap the Up Arrow key once or twice to shift the colors slightly toward blue, as in FIGURE 9.12.

FIGURE 9.12 Apply a final color correction with a Curves adjustment layer set to the Color blending mode.

PERFECT SKIN

Making sure skin looks flawless is a big part of the job a retoucher is expected to handle. With high-end beauty images, much greater attention is given to all the small details, especially when it comes to maintaining good skin texture.

Interestingly, this usually means sticking to basic techniques such as healing, cloning, and burning or dodging. Filters that smooth the skin with some form of blurring are shunned, as they inevitably lead to undesirable results such as skin that is too smooth (plastic looking) or whose texture is much too even across all the areas of the face.

We strongly recommend that you read Chapter 8, particularly the section "Developing a Portrait-Retouching Strategy," before you plunge into this more advanced workflow. That way, you'll be familiar with the principles and basic techniques required so you can concentrate on the skills you need for the more demanding task of beauty retouching.

Just about anyone would be proud to have the skin and features seen in FIGURES 9.13 and 9.14, but in the world of high-end beauty images it is not good enough to be merely extraordinary. In addition to a few minor blemishes here and there, we can see a little bit of unevenness in the skin below and around

FIGURES 9.13 and 9.14 Before and after. © *Dante Dauz*

her mouth. And on close inspection it becomes apparent that the eye on the left of the image is not quite as open as the one on the right, while her mouth is skewed slightly up on the left.

To summarize the process:

- Examine the image carefully to determine where to make changes. Add a new layer and mark up the areas that need correction (see Figure 9.19).

- Add another layer for each aspect of the image that you work on, beginning with removing localized blemishes and other distracting elements.

- Dennis's preference is to start off with the Spot Healing tool, as it will usually remove the objectionable spots with the least effort. Again, the key here is to carefully watch the results and when you notice something that doesn't quite blend in properly, switch to another tool, usually the Healing Brush tool, to take care of the problem. (See the section "Choosing Your Tools and What to Look For" in Chapter 8 for more on this technique.)

- When retouching stray hairs (FIGURE 9.15), begin by tracing over the offending hair with the Spot Healing tool or the Healing Brush tool. When the hair runs over fairly even skin tone, this works very well. But when the hair runs over an area with a lot of detail, for instance over an eye, great care needs to be taken to re-create the detail covered up by the hair.

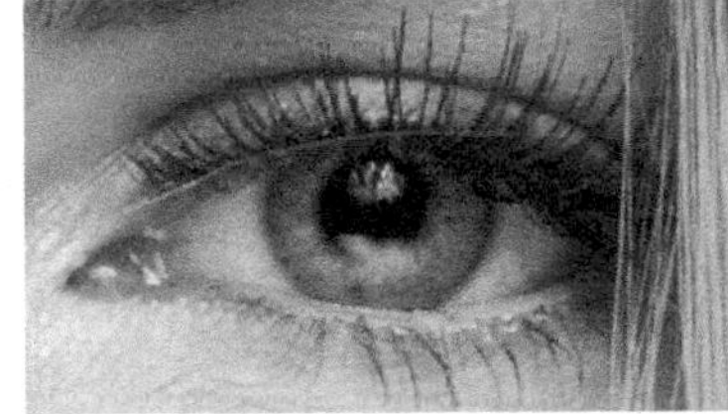

FIGURE 9.15 A strand of hair has strayed across this eye.

- When the basic spotting and healing is done, the next areas to work on are the lines below her eyes (FIGURE 9.16). Since the goal is to keep this looking natural, the approach here should be to tone down the darker lines so that they are not as noticeable but are still there nonetheless. (The degree to which these lines are lightened is always a subjective matter, and usually the final decision will lie with the client.)

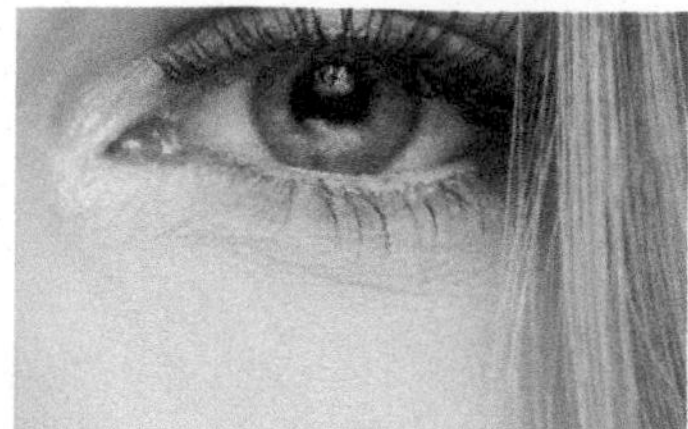

FIGURE 9.16 We'll soften the crinkles under her eye.

- Her eyebrows look a little thin at the ends near the center of her forehead, so they'll need to be filled out by painting (FIGURE 9.17).

FIGURE 9.17 This eyebrow is a bit scanty.

- Some areas of her face have bright spots and shadows that make the skin look uneven. Subtle dodging and burning can smooth out these irregularities, so we'll first get rid of the shadows by using a Curves adjustment layer to brighten the image. Then we'll add a layer mask to control where the effect is applied.

- Because not all the tones that make the skin look uneven are shadows, it's often necessary to darken, or "burn," some of the lighter tones. On shots that have been properly lit and exposed there will not be nearly as many of these areas as those that need to be dodged. Mostly these are just small highlights that attract a little too much attention or make the skin look too shiny. We'll use a Hue/Saturation layer to darken the image, and then we'll use a layer mask to apply the burning only to certain areas.

- After smoothing the surface of the model's skin, improve the symmetry of her features by leveling her mouth (FIGURE 9.18) and adjusting the left eye to balance the right eye.

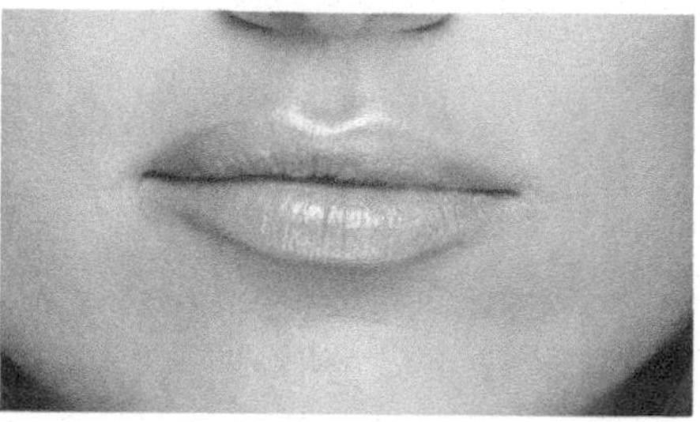

FIGURE 9.18 Straightening her mouth will make her face more symmetrical.

1. Add an empty layer to the image and use a small, hard brush to note items that need correction. FIGURE 9.19 shows the notes Dennis made before starting the retouching work on this image. The red lines and circles indicate the stray hairs and minor blemishes, and the straight blue lines confirm that her features are not quite symmetrical.

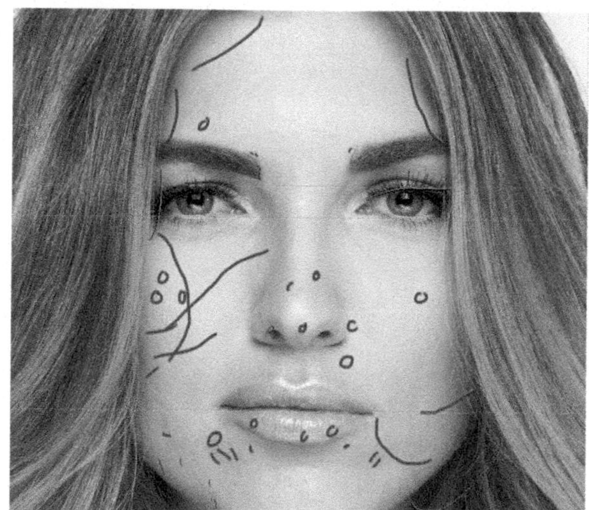

FIGURE 9.19 Marked-up photo with red indicating areas that need retouching. The blue guides show that the eyes are not quite symmetrical and that the mouth is slightly tilted up on the left.

2. Create a new layer named *Retouch* and, as discussed in Chapter 8, use the Spot Healing Brush tool, the Healing Brush tool, and the Rubber Stamp tool to take care of all the small blemishes and stray hairs that are relatively easy to remove with these tools.

3. Use the Spot Healing Brush or the Healing Brush to remove stray hairs. However, be alert for cases where you need to retouch out a stray hair that runs

over an eye, as seen in FIGURE 9.20. The result blends in where there is skin, but where it runs over the eyelashes we get a grayish line that looks nearly as bad as the hair itself.

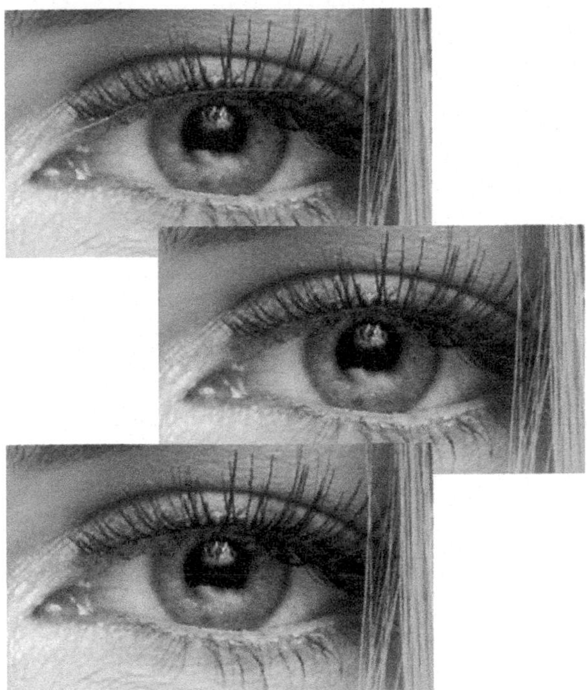

FIGURE 9.20 To remove the stray hair over areas such as this eye, it's sometimes necessary to use a very small brush to paint out the offending hair.

4. Zoom in very closely and switch to the Brush tool. To complete the removal of the stray hair, Dennis used a 1-pixel brush to paint in the proper colors for the eyelashes. Dennis used the Eyedropper tool, setting the sample size to "point sample," to accurately sample the appropriate colors as he painted in the eyeliner and eyelashes where the stray hair crossed over the area.

5. To lighten the lines below the model's eyes, create a new layer and name it *Lines around eyes*. Then start by setting the Spot Healing Brush tool to a size that just covers one of the lines under the eye (in this example Dennis used a 4-pixel brush) and trace over the lines below her eyes. Again, since the goal here is to just tone them down a touch it's not necessary to remove them completely. FIGURE 9.21 shows a close-up view of the area below her eye being retouched.

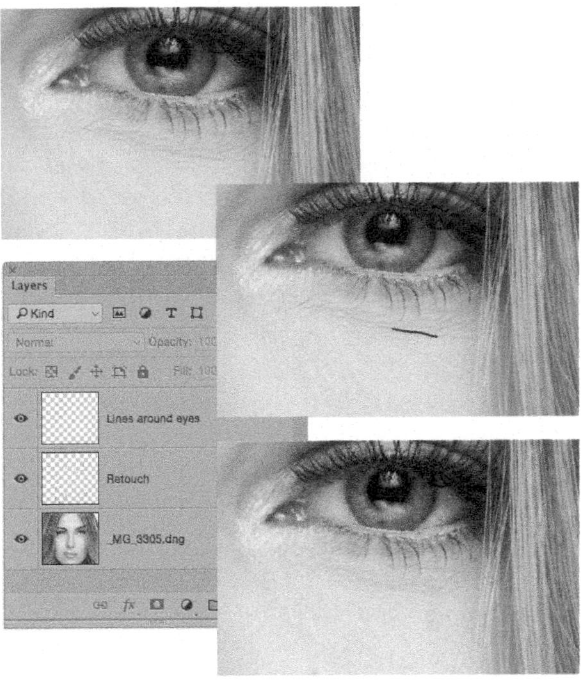

FIGURE 9.21 Retouch the lines around her eyes just enough to tone them down, not remove them.

6. To fix the eyebrows, create a new layer and name it *Eyebrows*. Select the Brush tool and set the size to something close to the size of the individual hairs on her eyebrows—in this case, 2 pixels. To make sure your painting matches the existing brows, Option/Alt-click one of the eyebrow hairs to sample the color. Paint in a few hairs using curved brush strokes to fill in the ends of each eyebrow, as shown in FIGURE 9.22.

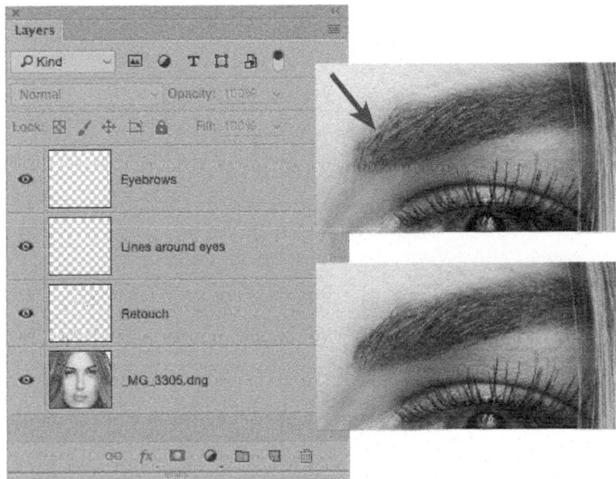

FIGURE 9.22 Fill in the areas where her eyebrows appear a little thin.

HELPER LAYERS

As we've discussed both here and in Chapter 8, dodging and burning is a big part of the retouching workflow when it comes to making skin look as good as possible. The challenge many folks face as they work on improving their D&B techniques is that often it can be hard to see what needs to be dodged and what needs to be burned.

Enter the "helper layer." Basically this is an adjustment layer that turns the color image black and white, showing the image as simply tones that are lighter or darker. By temporarily hiding the color information, many users find it easier to see a shadow or highlight that looks out of place and needs to be toned down.

There are several ways to accomplish this, but Dennis prefers the method suggested by noted retoucher Pratik Naik: using a Black & White adjustment layer set to the Color blending mode. When creating this layer the default settings work just fine and no adjustments are needed in the layer's Properties panel (**FIGURE 9.23**).

Do note that it is important not to change the contrast of the image, which could lead to overworking the dodging and burning. This is why the blending mode of the helper layer should be set to Color.

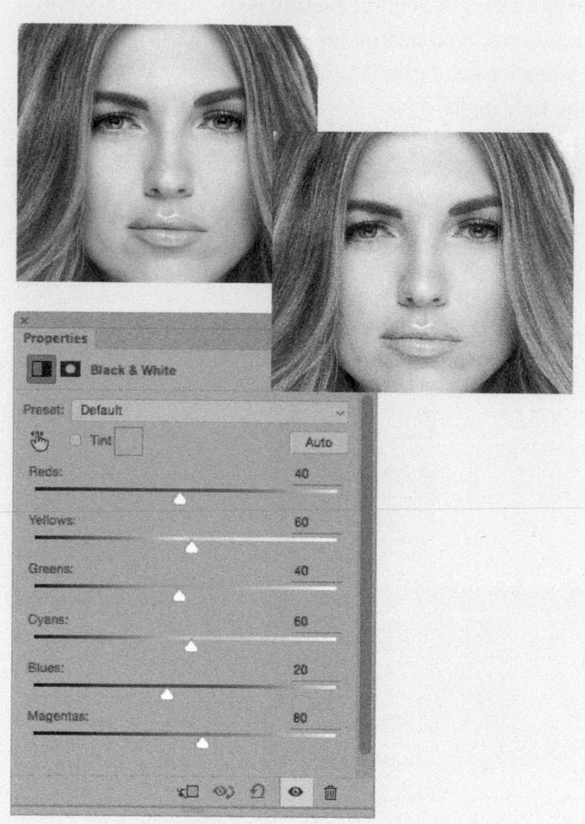

FIGURE 9.23 Use a Black & White adjustment layer to temporarily hide the color.

7. To take care of the small shadowed areas, create a Curves adjustment layer and name it *Dodge Crvs.* In the Properties panel, click near the middle of the RGB curve to add a control point on the curve and pull up slightly to lighten the image, as shown in **FIGURE 9.24**. Next select the layer mask for this layer and fill the mask with black by pressing Cmd-I/Ctrl-I to invert it.

Then use the Brush tool to paint white into the mask to reveal the effect. To give yourself more control over your dodging, set the brush opacity and flow to 30% each. Using a low opacity and flow allows you to gently build up the effect while adding just enough to smooth out the shadows caused by the unevenness of her skin. The size of the brush you're using as you work will need to vary depending on the size

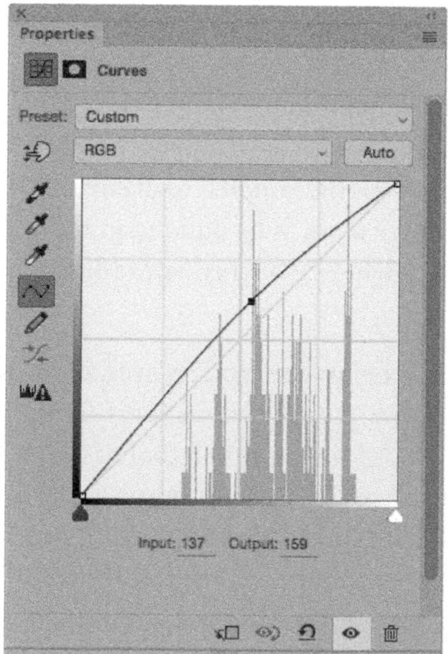

FIGURE 9.24 Pull up slightly on the RGB curve and use the layer mask to control where the dodging effect shows up.

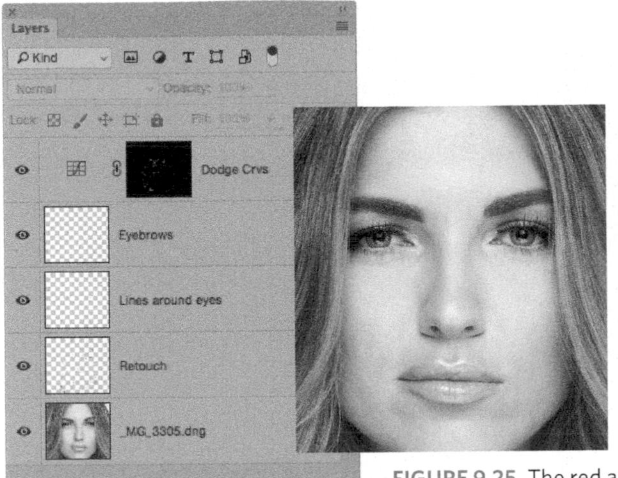

FIGURE 9.25 The red areas in the middle image show where the dodging effect was brushed in.

of details you're working on. For small details it's useful to use a brush that is a little smaller than the spots you're working to lighten. For larger areas you will need a larger brush to make easier to blend in the effect.

FIGURE 9.25 shows how Dennis used this technique on the image of the blonde woman. In the second image the red areas indicate where Dennis applied the dodging effect. Notice how in some places he used a very small brush, while in others he used a larger one to cover a bigger area.

8. To tame overbright highlights, create a new Hue/Saturation adjustment layer, name it *Burn H/S*, set the blending mode to Multiply, and set the opacity to 50%. In the Properties panel move the Saturation to –40%, as seen in FIGURE 9.26. (This helps avoid the increase in saturation that often occurs when burning parts of an image.)

Select the layer mask for the Burn H/S layer and press Cmd-I/Ctrl-I to invert the mask. Make sure the Brush tool has the same settings as in the previous step, and paint white on the highlights that need to be toned down. If the effect looks too strong you can lower the opacity of the adjustment layer, or dial down the opacity and flow of the brush to give you more control over how quickly the effect builds up.

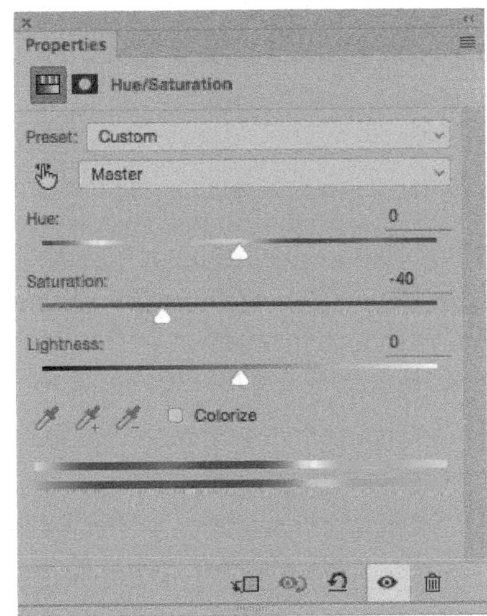

FIGURE 9.26 Use a Hue/Saturation adjustment layer with the blending mode set to Multiply to burn or darken tones on the skin that are too bright.

FIGURE 9.27 shows a close-up of the camera left eye of the model; Dennis darkened the distracting highlights on the skin around her eye.

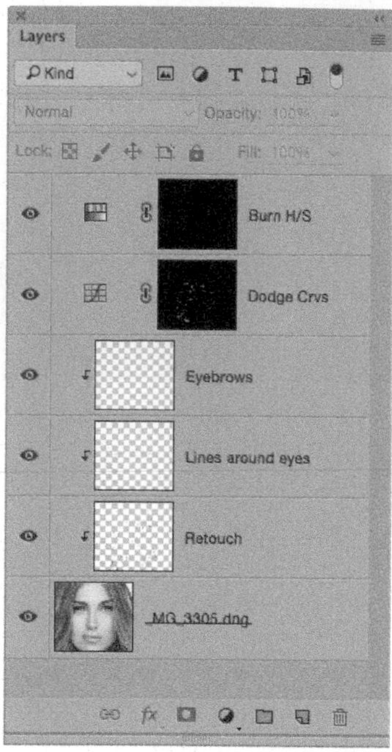

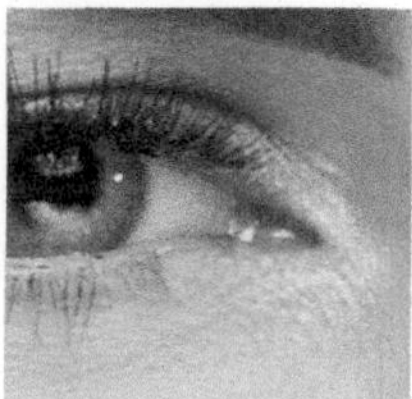
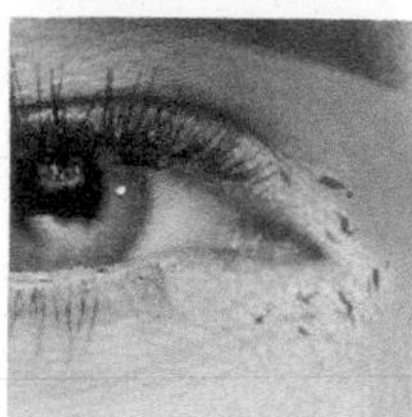
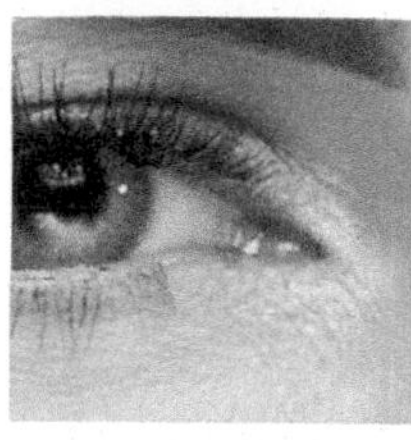

FIGURE 9.27 The image on the top shows a close-up of the eye before burning, the red areas in the middle image show where the image was burned, and the image on the bottom is after the burning has been applied.

9. As noted in the markup stage, her mouth is skewed slightly higher on the left than on the right, so let's balance the sides of her mouth. In the Layers panel, press Option/Alt while choosing **Layers > Merge Visible** to merge them into a new layer (this layer is temporary, so don't bother to name it).

10. Use the Rectangular Marquee tool to draw out a selection around the mouth. Be sure to include a generous area around the mouth to make it easier to blend the result of our edit with the original image. With the selection active, press Cmd-J/Ctrl-J to copy this selection to a new layer. Name this layer *Mouth* and then choose **Layer > Smart Objects > Convert to Smart Object.** (Doing this will make it easier to edit the results of any warping or transformation you make.) We're done with the merged layer, so you can delete it to reduce the size of the file.

11. Choose **Edit > Transform > Warp,** and drag the left corner of her mouth down slightly to straighten it, as seen in FIGURE 9.28. Press Enter on your keyboard to accept the result.

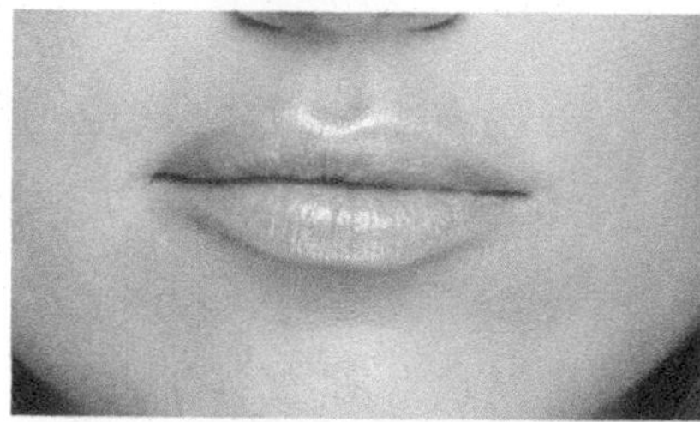
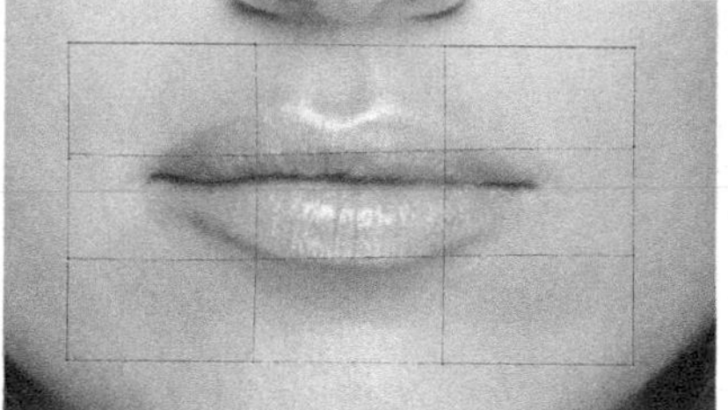
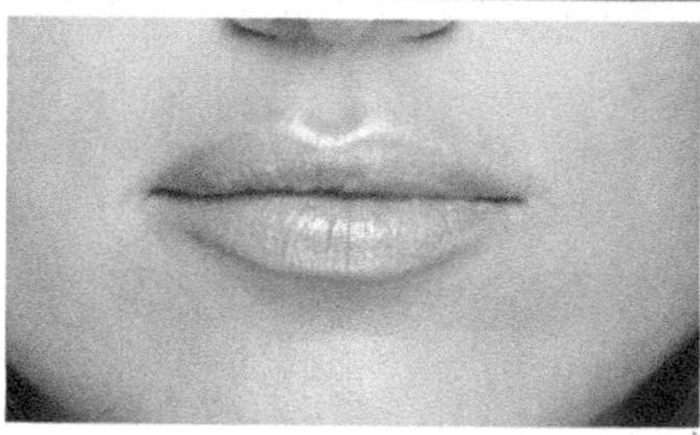

FIGURE 9.28 Use the Warp command to pull the left corner of the mouth down slightly.

To be absolutely sure the edges of the warped layer are not visible, add a layer mask to the Mouth layer and use the Brush tool to paint with black around the model's mouth to blend the layer smoothly with the rest of the image.

12. To adjust the size of her left eye, begin by pressing Option/Alt while choosing **Layers > Merge Visible** to merge all the layers into a new layer.

13. Use the Rectangular Marquee tool to draw out a selection around her camera-left eye. Be sure to include enough around the eye to make it easier to blend the edited portion with the rest of the image later. With the selection active, press Cmd-J/Ctrl-J to copy it to a new layer. Name this layer *Camera Left Eye* and choose **Layer > Smart Objects > Convert to Smart Object.**

14. Choose **Filter > Liquify** to open the Liquify filter. Then select the Forward Warp tool and set the size of the brush to about the same size as her pupil. Gently nudge the eyelid up just enough to open her eye so it balances out better with her right eye, as shown in FIGURE 9.29.

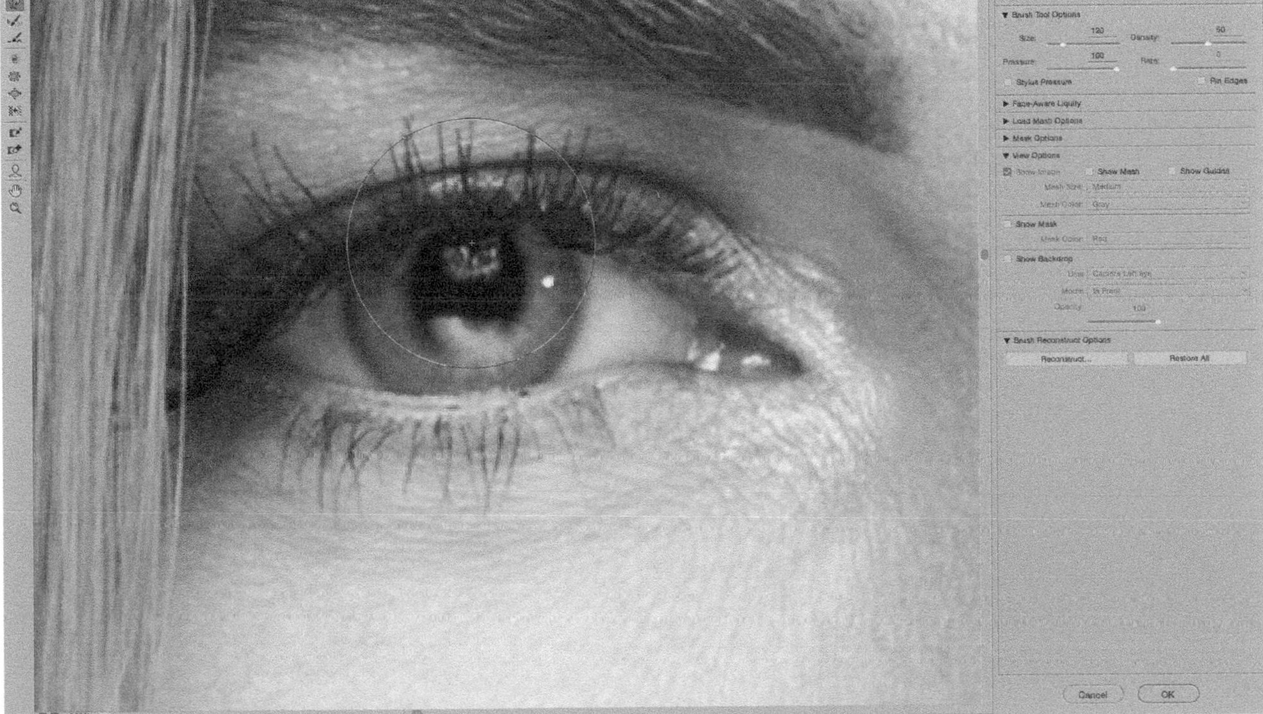

FIGURE 9.29 Use the Liquify filter to open her left eye slightly and improve the symmetry of her eyes.

15. If the pupil looks a bit stretched after this adjustment, the fix for that is simple. Select the merged layer you made for the previous step, and use the Rectangular Marquee tool to draw out a selection around her right pupil. Then press Cmd-J/Ctrl-J to copy this into a new layer, name the layer *Camera Right Pupil*, and move it above the Camera Left Eye layer in the Layers panel.

16. Select the Move tool and slide the Right Pupil layer into position over her left eye. Since she is facing the camera almost straight on in this photograph, the new pupil should fit well enough to cover the stretched one. Then add a layer mask to the Right Pupil layer, invert the layer mask, and use the Brush tool to carefully paint white into the layer mask, revealing the minimum amount needed to hide the stretched pupil (**FIGURE 9.30**).

TIP Temporarily reduce the opacity of the Right Pupil layer so the Camera Left Pupil layer is visible underneath. This will to help with aligning the eyes. Raise the Opacity value back to 100% when you're done.

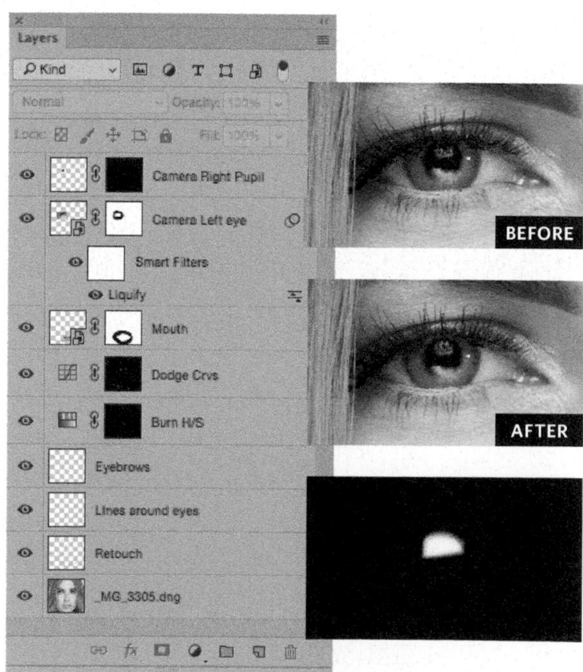

FIGURE 9.30 Fix the droopy eye by layering a copy of the other eye over it and blending in the new layer.

FREQUENCY SEPARATION

Over the last few years frequency separation has become the latest "wow technique" that seems to be the answer for all things related to skin retouching. Indeed this can be a very powerful technique, but one that needs to be wielded more like a scalpel than a samurai sword.

Used properly it can be an effective tool for solving problems that would otherwise be much more problematic or time consuming. But as with any powerful tool, it can also be used in a heavy-handed way that results in unnaturally perfect faces strangely disconnected from their texture in a way that most high-end clients find off-putting. (See the section "Beware the Blur" in Chapter 8.)

Briefly put, frequency separation is a process that lets you separate the details of the image from the colors and tones, allowing you to work on them separately. You'll start with two identical layers and wind up with one layer that has had a blur applied to it and one that looks a lot like it's had the High Pass filter applied to it.

This second layer, when set to the correct blending mode, provides most or all of the detail in the image. In setting up this second layer, you'll use the Apply Image command (on the Image menu) to subtract the non-blurred layer from the blurred layer. The goal is to wind up with a layer that is mostly neutral gray but that includes the detail information that was lost in the blurring of the first layer. This is useful because if we set the layer to the Linear Light blending mode, the gray areas become invisible but the detail information is restored.

With the blurred layer sitting below the detail layer (which is set to Linear Light blending mode), the result looks exactly like the image did before these layers were created. The advantage here is that by separating the color and tone information from the detail information we can solve a lot of problems that would otherwise be difficult to solve, as you'll see.

Since the blurred layer has the color and tone information, it's commonly called the "low-frequency" layer. And since the other layer has all the fine detail, it's commonly called the "high-frequency" layer.

Working with these two layers allows you to lighten shadows and bring tone back into blown-out highlight areas without affecting the detail. It also allows you to quickly retouch lines or add skin texture where it's been lost.

TIP Use this technique only for the issues that would otherwise be too difficult or time consuming. If your goal is to create high-end commercial or editorial images, never use this technique in place of basic retouching or dodging and burning.

The process for creating these layers is at once both simple and highly technical, which explains why there are so many Photoshop actions available that shortcut the process, automating the steps for you. Once you've practiced the steps for creating the two layers the technique uses, however, it will become second nature to you and you will have greater control over the results.

In FIGURE 9.31 the highlights on the subject's forehead and the tip of his nose are a bit blown out. Darkening these areas while keeping local detail is normally a challenging task, but frequency separation can make it much easier.

Likewise, the dark areas and line under his eyes could be retouched and dodged using conventional techniques, but you'd be in danger of losing the skin texture. Frequency separation can help here too, as you can see in FIGURE 9.32.

Creating the Frequency Separation Layers

1. Before starting the frequency separation process, do all the conventional retouching you can. This will make the technique more of a surgical scalpel and less of a blunt hammer.

2. Open the Layers panel and select all the layers you've created so far. Press Option/Alt while choosing **Layers > Merge Visible** to merge all the layers into a new layer. Make a duplicate of this layer by pressing Cmd-J/Ctrl-J. Name the first layer *Low* and the second layer *High*. Be sure the High layer sits just above the Low layer in the Layers panel.

FIGURES 9.31 and 9.32 Before and after. © *KE*

3. Select both the Low and High layers in the Layers panel, and place them into a layer group by choosing **Layer > Group Layers.** Name this layer group *Frequency Separation.*

4. Select the Low layer in the Layers panel, and apply the Gaussian Blur filter to the layer by choosing **Filter > Blur > Gaussian Blur.** The amount of blur depends on several factors, the most important being how much is needed to lose the detail in the skin. Other factors, such as the resolution of the image, will affect the amount of blurring needed as well.

Dennis chose to add three pixels of Gaussian Blur, as seen in FIGURE 9.33. The amount you need to add might be different, depending on the resolution of the image you're working on.

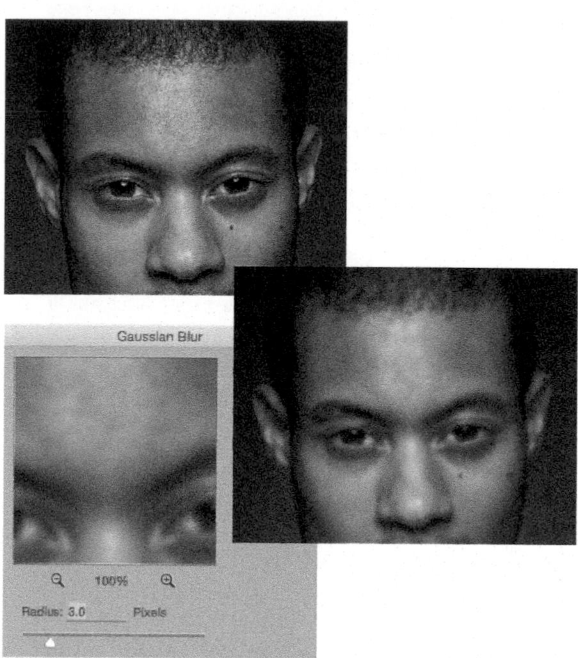

FIGURE 9.33 Apply the Gaussian Blur filter to the Low layer (we've temporarily turned off visibility for the High layer).

5. Next comes the fun part: creating the detail layer. Select the High layer in the Layers panel and then choose **Image > Apply Image.** This opens the dialog box seen in FIGURE 9.34 (don't worry if the options in your dialog box don't exactly match the ones shown here).

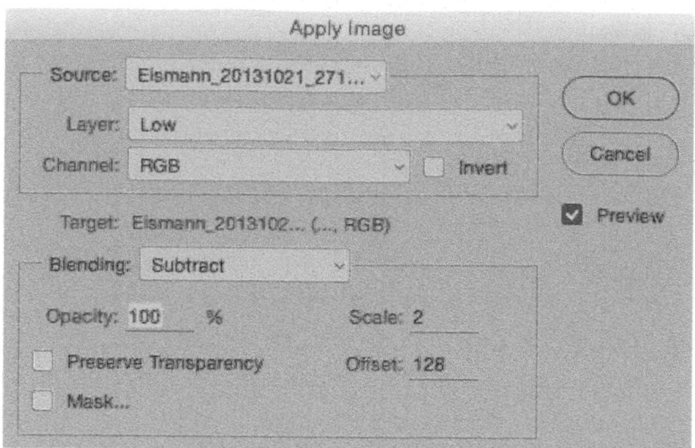

FIGURE 9.34 The Apply Image command is used to create the detail layer as part of the frequency separation technique.

6. In the Apply Image dialog box the file you're working on should be chosen by default from the Source menu. Next choose Low from the Layer menu; this is the layer that the calculations will be based on. The Channel menu should remain at the default RGB setting to make sure that we're using all the information in the blurred Low layer. Choose Subtract from the Blending menu, and keep Opacity at 100%.

Scale is limited to a value between 1 and 2. Set this to 2. (Values of less than 2 give results that are too strong for the frequency separation layers to work properly.) Because the goal is to wind up with a layer that is mostly gray but that retains the detail we lost in the blurring stage, set Offset to 128, or neutral gray, and click OK. The result should look like FIGURE 9.35.

FIGURE 9.35 The High layer before and after the Subtract operation

7. Finish this stage of the process by setting the blending mode for the High layer to Linear Light.

If you've made these layers correctly you should see no difference when the Frequency Separation layer group is toggled on or off in the Layers panel.

Working with the Frequency Separation Layers

With the image separated into "low" and "high" frequencies, take a moment to look at each layer separately. While lots of users are familiar with the look of the blurred layer, not as many will recognize the look of the high-frequency layer, which is very similar to, but not exactly like, the results you might get from the High Pass filter.

The Linear Light blending mode, like the Overlay and Soft Light blending modes, affects the contrast of the layers below. The parts of the upper layer that are lighter than 50% gray will lighten the image, and the parts that are darker than 50% gray will darken the lower layer. The Linear Light blending mode has a much stronger effect than the Overlay blending mode, and when it's used to combine the High layer with the blurred layer it adds back just the right amount of detail to replicate the look of the original image.

Now that the broader tones and colors are separated from the texture and detail of the image, many tasks become much simpler. For instance, you can easily tone down the really bright areas of our subject's forehead by adding a layer, between the Low and the High layers, on which you paint a little color. This leaves all the texture in those areas undisturbed. Add more layers to take care of problems like shadows, splotches of color, and so on. Remember to follow Dennis's principle of using a different layer for each type of problem you need to fix.

Likewise, you can use retouching techniques such as healing or cloning on the High layer to simply add or remove detail without disturbing the color or tone of the image.

Working on Skin with Frequency Separation

First, a word of caution: it's very easy to go too far with this technique! When using it, keep two principles in mind: subtlety makes for better, more natural-looking results, and never add more blur to the low-frequency layer. The latter is the most common cause of unnatural-looking images. (See "Beware the Blur" in Chapter 8.)

1. Select the Low layer in the Layers panel and add a new layer; name it *Reduce highlights*. We'll use it to tackle the hotter highlights on the subject's forehead and nose.

2. Select the Brush tool and set both the opacity and the flow to around 30%. This lets you add paint to the layer gradually so that it blends better with the rest of the face. Press Option/Alt and sample the skin color near the areas you'll be working on. Then adjust the size of your brush so it will comfortably cover the areas that need toning down. For the forehead in this shot Dennis used a 140-pixel brush, as seen in FIGURE 9.36. Gently paint the color over the blown-out highlight on the forehead just enough to bring in some more tone while keeping the shape of the forehead.

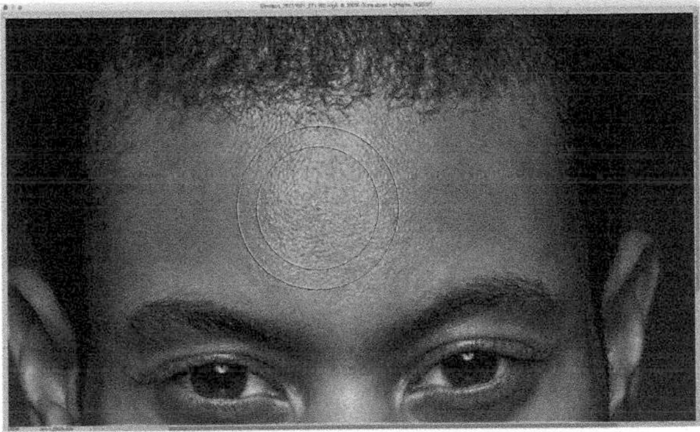

FIGURE 9.36 Dennis used a 140-pixel brush to add tone back into the hot highlight on the forehead.

3. To work on the highlight on the tip of his nose, make your brush smaller (Dennis used a 40-pixel brush); gently add in a little tone to knock back the highlight a bit. If, after painting tone into these areas, you feel you went too far, adjust the opacity of the layer to dial down the effect.

FIGURE 9.37 shows the forehead and nose areas before and after toning down the highlights.

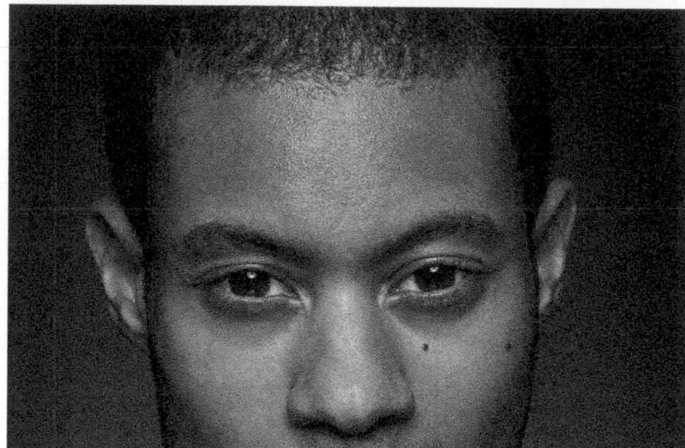

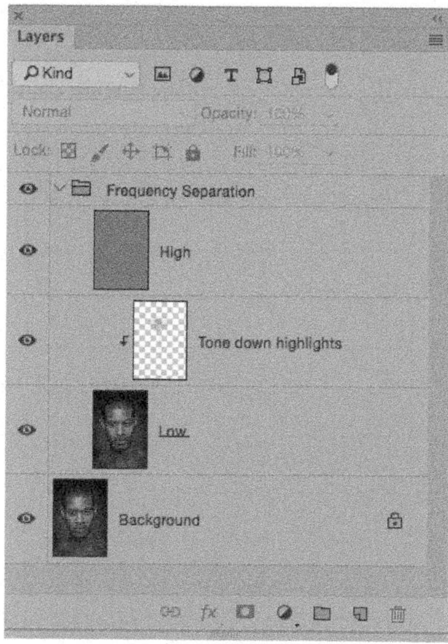

FIGURE 9.37 Reducing the highlights on the forehead and tip of the nose by painting on a new layer above the Low layer

4. Add a new layer above the Reduce highlights layer and name it *Under eyes*. You'll use this layer to lighten the dark areas under his eyes in much the same way as in step 1, except in this case we'll sample a lighter color to paint with.

5. Select the Brush tool and adjust the size of the brush so you can easily cover the area under his eyes with one or two strokes (about 30 pixels in this case). Press Option/Alt and sample the lighter color on his cheeks just below the dark areas under his eyes. Set the brush to a low opacity (about 30%–40%) and paint with the lighter color under his eyes. Take care to blend the paint so that you avoid making drastic changes to his face.

6. Finally, since subtlety is very important in producing natural-looking work, lower the opacity of the Under eyes layer until you've brought back enough of the original tone and color to make the area look natural. For this layer Dennis used an opacity of 30%, and you can see the result in FIGURE 9.38.

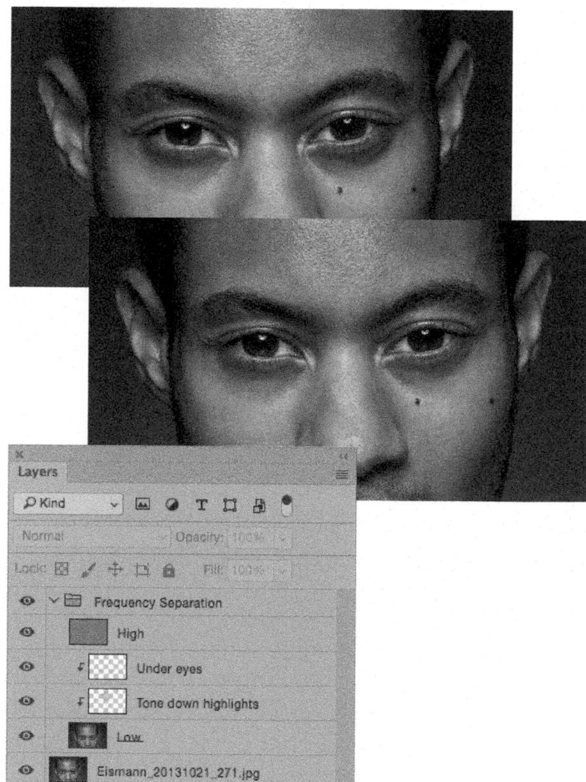

FIGURE 9.38 Using a separate layer for lightening under the eyes allows you to adjust the strength of the effect.

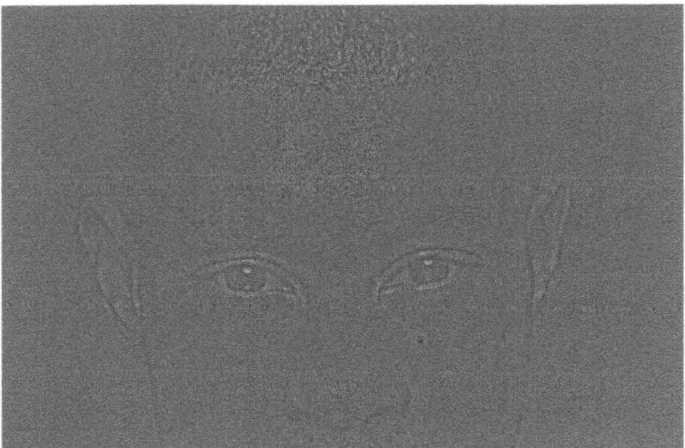

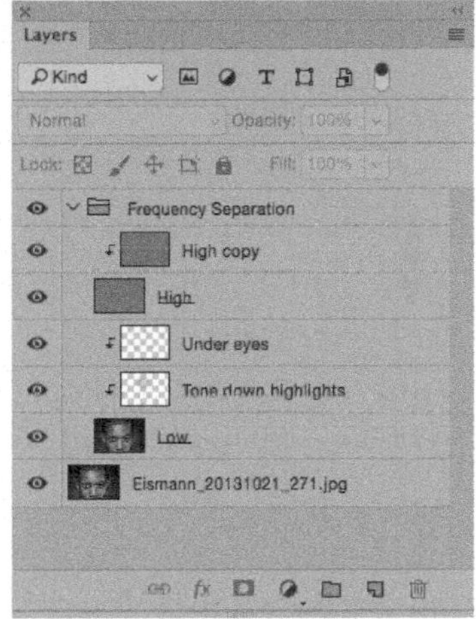

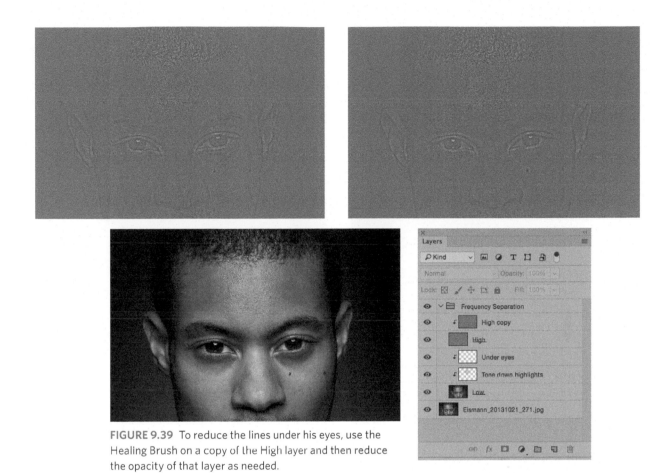

FIGURE 9.39 To reduce the lines under his eyes, use the Healing Brush on a copy of the High layer and then reduce the opacity of that layer as needed.

7. Select the High layer in the Layers panel and make a copy by pressing Cmd-J/Ctrl-J. Clip this layer to the original High layer by pressing Cmd-Option-G/Ctrl-Alt-G, and change the blending mode to Normal. With the tones nicely adjusted under his eyes we still have to deal with the lines in that area.

8. Select the Healing Brush tool and set the sampling mode to Current Layer. Use a brush that's just large enough to cover the lines, around 10 pixels. Then Option/Alt-click his cheek to sample the texture, and with a few strokes brush over the lines under the eyes to eliminate them. Reset the sampling area as needed in case you accidentally wind up sampling the moles or other unwanted textures.

9. Finally, lower the opacity of this layer to about 50% to bring back enough of the lines to keep a natural-looking result. Most of the time these lines just need to be minimized, as seen in FIGURE 9.39, not eliminated entirely.

Smoothing Wrinkles with Frequency Separation

In addition to being a very helpful skin-retouching technique, frequency separation can be a very powerful tool for retouching tasks such as smoothing wrinkles on clothing. Other methods for smoothing wrinkles involve dodging and burning, or lots of work with the Healing Brush, but used properly frequency separation can work wonders in a fraction of the time.

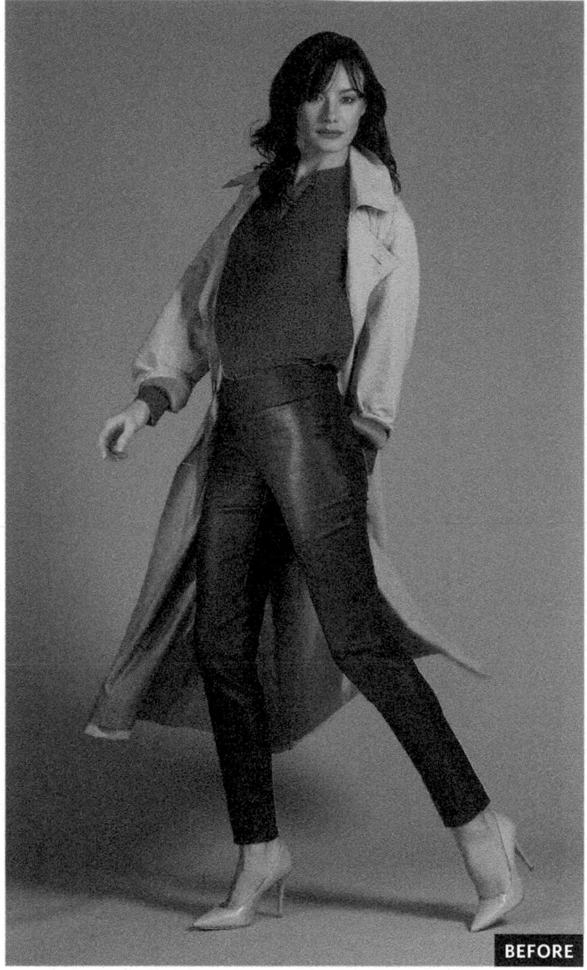

FIGURE 9.40 Before. © *Anthony Nex*

FIGURE 9.41 After. © *Anthony Nex*

Smoothing wrinkles in clothing and fabric is a common task that retouchers face. In FIGURES 9.40 and 9.41 you can see that the wrinkles in the dark leggings have been smoothed using frequency separation. The steps are similar to the procedure you've just worked through.

1. Select the Background layer in the Layers panel and press Cmd-J/Ctrl-J twice. Name the first copy *Low* and name the second copy *High* (FIGURE 9.42). Select both of these layers and press Cmd-G/Ctrl-G to place them in a layer group. Name this layer group *Frequency Separation*.

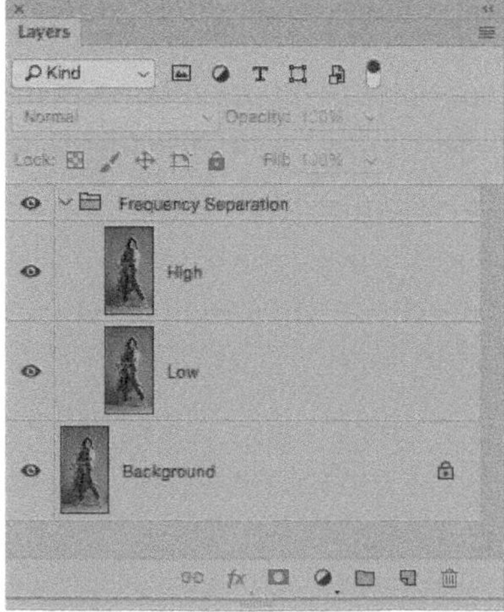

FIGURE 9.42 Create two copies of the Background layer and put them in a layer group.

2. Select the Low layer and add just enough Gaussian Blur to eliminate the sharper texture in the leggings. In this case Dennis used a Gaussian Blur setting of 4 pixels, shown in FIGURE 9.43.

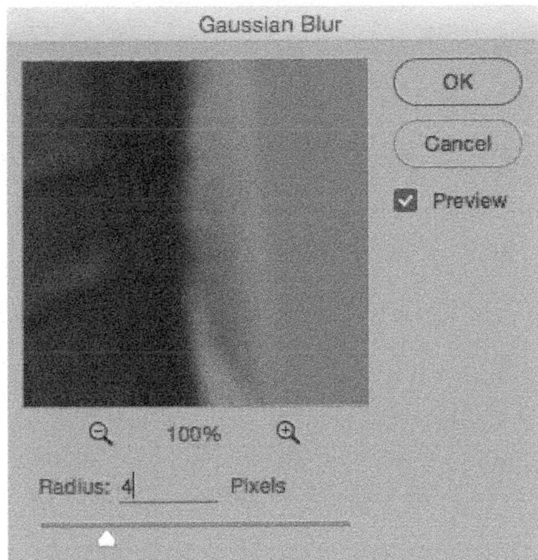

FIGURE 9.43 Add just enough Gaussian Blur to lose the texture on the leggings.

3. Now select the High layer and choose **Image > Apply Image.** Choose Low from the Layer menu and choose Subtract from the Blending menu. Finally, set Scale to 2 and Offset to 128, as shown in FIGURE 9.44. Click OK.

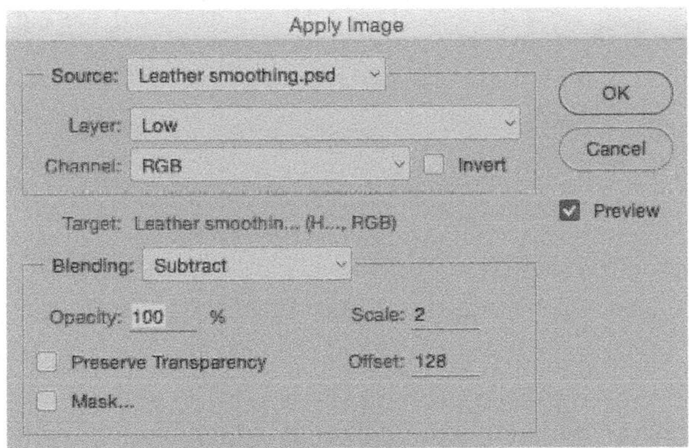

FIGURE 9.44 Use the Apply Image command to subtract the Low layer from the High layer.

The High layer should now look like FIGURE 9.45. Set the blending mode for this layer to Linear Light. Then turn the Frequency Separation layer group on and off. If the layers were created correctly, you should see no difference as you turn them on or off.

FIGURE 9.45 The High layer will contain all the fine detail in the image.

4. Select the Low layer and add a new layer. Name this layer *Smooth Wrinkles*. You'll use the Brush tool to paint on this layer to remove the majority of the wrinkles. Turn off the High layer temporarily (to make it easier to see what you're doing) and make sure you have selected the Smooth Wrinkles layer.

5. Select the Brush tool and set the opacity of the brush to a relatively low amount; Dennis favors using something between 30% and 40%. This helps your paint to blend in subtly without changing the image radically. Zoom in close enough to see the wrinkles, and Option/Alt-click to sample a color above or below a wrinkle. Gently brush several strokes of this color over the blurry wrinkle until it has been nicely blended with the surrounding area. Continue working over the garment this way until you have smoothed the wrinkles out, as shown in FIGURE 9.46.

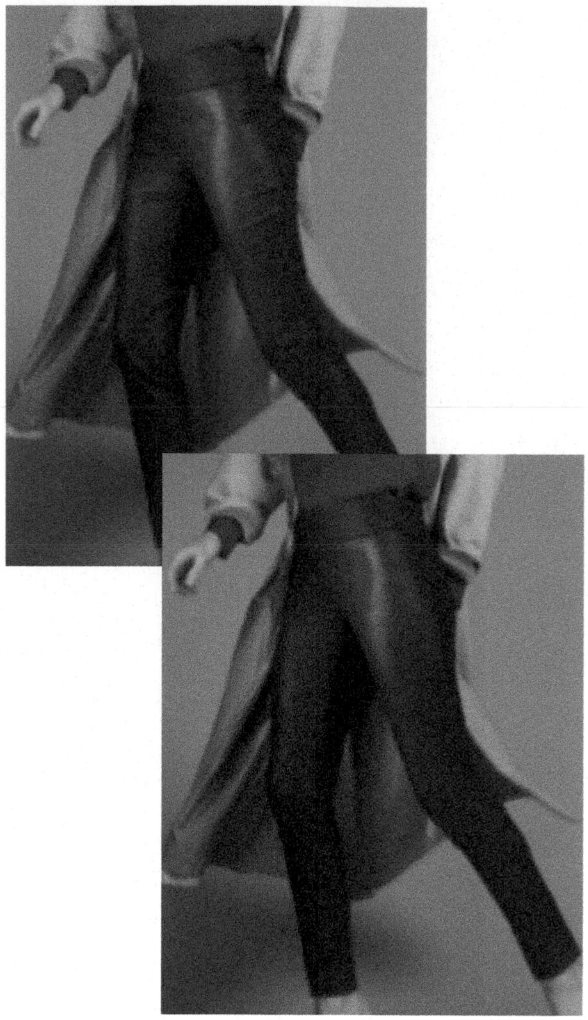

FIGURE 9.46 Before and after painting on the Smooth Wrinkles layer to smooth out the wrinkles on the Low layer

Turning on the High layer, you'll see that now the image appears to have sharper wrinkles, as seen in FIGURE 9.47. This is because the sharper detailed information for the wrinkles is on the High layer. In the next step we'll smooth those out too.

FIGURE 9.47 With the blurry part of the wrinkles smoothed, the wrinkles now look sharper.

6. Select the High layer and make a copy by pressing Cmd-J/Ctrl-J. Clip this copy of the High layer to the original by pressing Cmd-Option-G/Ctrl-Alt-G, and set its blending mode to Normal. (Working on a copy of the High layer makes it easier to go back in case you make a mistake or go too far.)

7. Turn off all the layers except the High and High copy layers to make it easier to see the wrinkles that need to be retouched out. Then with the High copy layer selected, select the Healing Brush tool, Option/Alt-click an area adjacent to a wrinkle, and carefully blend out the wrinkles.

From time to time turn the other layers back on to check your progress. When you're satisfied that you've sufficiently smoothed the wrinkles out, toggle the Frequency Separation layer group on and off to check your results.

Because perfectly smooth clothing can look as though the person travels with an iron and constantly presses their clothes, restoring some of the original wrinkles can help make the image look more natural. In this case, sliding down the opacity of the Frequency Separation layer group to around 80% looks pretty good, as you can see in FIGURE 9.48.

FIGURE 9.48 Lower the opacity of the Frequency Separation layer group to achieve a more natural-looking result.

8. With the wrinkles smoothed, the small bumps around her legs and hips that were created by the wrinkles now look out of place. Add a new layer above the Frequency Separation layer group and name it *Lose Bumps*. Then using the Clone Stamp tool, carefully retouch the bumps that look out of place. Your final result should look something like FIGURE 9.49.

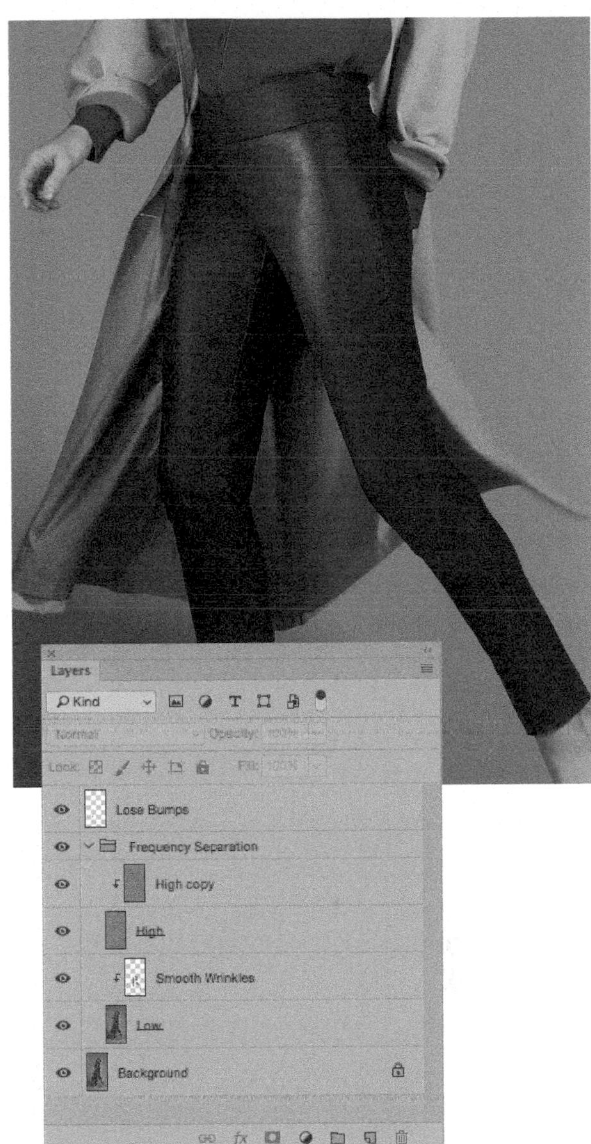

FIGURE 9.49 Close-up view of the smoothed leggings

ENHANCING THE LIGHTING

One of the last steps in finessing the image is adding a little dramatic effect to the image by tweaking the look of the shadows and highlights. After the retouching, the skin work, and the color corrections have all been done, a few quick steps to enhance the lighting can really make the image pop.

FIGURES 9.50 and 9.51 Before and after. © *Rick Rose*

Doing this on shots like the one shown in FIGURES 9.50 and 9.51 usually involves adding a subtle glow to the highlights on the face and a little more contrast to the hair. Often the highlights or shadows of the hair are also manipulated a little.

Adding a Glow

Adding the glow can be done in a number of ways, but the most commonly used technique involves manipulating a copy of one of the channels, usually the Blue channel, to emphasize the distribution of light and dark tones. Then that channel is used to create a selection on a new layer that is then filled with white. That new layer is then set to the Soft Light blending mode. Let's take a closer look at how this is done.

FIGURE 9.52 shows the Red, Green, and Blue channels from the photo of the blonde woman. Since we're looking to isolate the highlights on the face, the channel that has the most shadows on her face will usually be the best starting place. In most images this is the Blue channel, just as it is here.

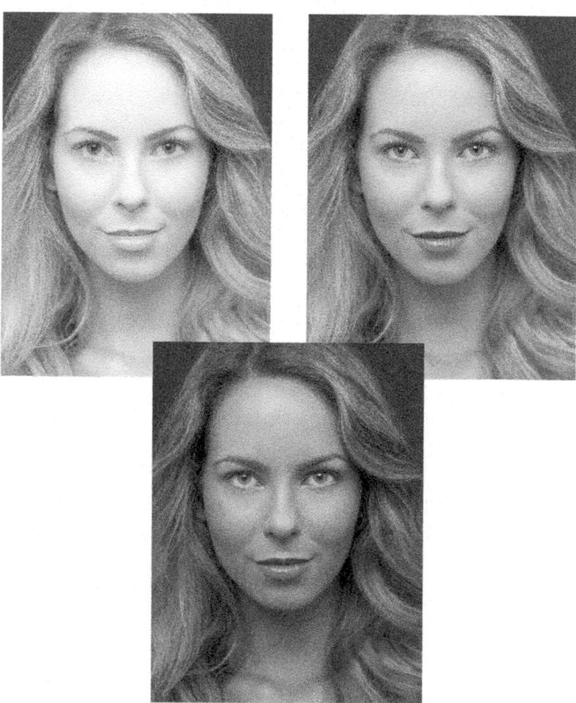

FIGURE 9.52 Look through the Red, Green, and Blue channels to see which one has the most shadows in the skin area.

1. Make a copy of the Blue channel by opening the Channels panel and dragging the Blue channel over the Create New Channel icon at the bottom of the panel (FIGURE 9.53). (This technique for copying channels is often called "channel pulling.")

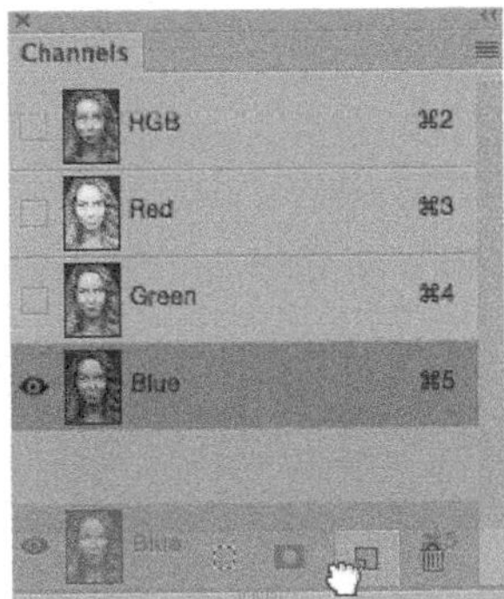

FIGURE 9.53 Start by duplicating the Blue channel.

2. Select the Blue copy channel and choose **Image > Adjustments > Curves.** Because our goal is to isolate the highlights in this channel, the Curves command lets us make a quick adjustment to exaggerate the lights and darks.

3. In the Curves dialog box, drag the black point on the curve about one-third of the way to the right to push more of the shadow values to black (FIGURE 9.54).

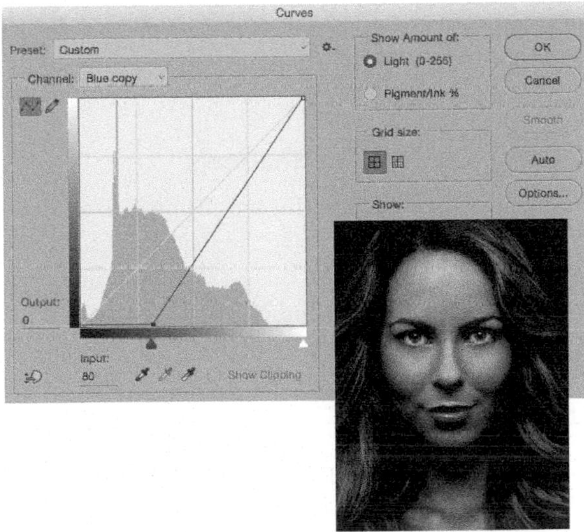

FIGURE 9.54 Use the Curves dialog box to darken the shadow values in the Blue copy channel and isolate the highlights.

4. Switch to the Layers panel and add a new layer named *Glow*. Set its blending mode to Soft Light. Then Cmd/Ctrl-click the Blue copy channel to load it as a selection (the brighter parts of the channel will determine the selected area). Make sure the Glow layer is selected in the Layers panel and fill the selection with white.

5. Deselect the selection, then choose **Layer > Layer Mask > Hide All** to add a layer mask. Since we want the effect to show only on her face, use the Brush tool to paint with white over the parts of her face where you want to reveal the glow. In doing this step be sure to set the opacity and flow of your Brush to 100%. Remember to keep the glow out of her eyes so the whites of her eyes don't become too bright.

Next, because the effect can be a bit too strong at times, slide the opacity of the layer down to about 60%. After you've added the glow to her face the result should look similar to FIGURE 9.55.

FIGURE 9.55 The result of adding a soft glow to her face

Adding Light to the Hair

The next step in enhancing the lighting is to "pop" the highlights on her hair. This can be easily done with a variation on the technique we just used for adding a glow to the face. In this case we'll look for the channel that seems to give us the best chance to isolate the highlights in her hair. The color and tone of her hair will affect which channel we find this in, but for blondes this will usually be the Blue channel.

1. Open the Channels panel and duplicate the Blue channel, then choose **Image > Adjustments > Curves** to open the Curves dialog box. Our goal is to darken the shadows of the hair while not darkening the highlights too much, so drag the black point in the Curves dialog box to the right, as seen in FIGURE 9.56. Note that this time the black point has not been moved nearly as far as when adjusting the channel in the "Adding a Glow" section.

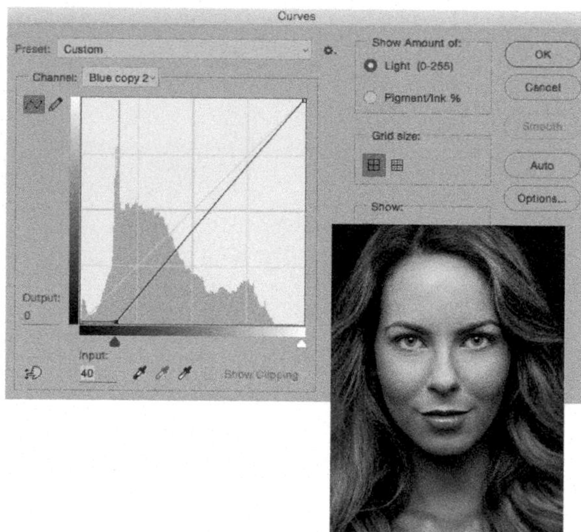

FIGURE 9.56 A slightly darkened copy of the Blue channel is used to bring out the highlights in her blonde hair.

2. Cmd/Ctrl-click the Blue copy 2 channel to load it as a selection. Add a new Curves adjustment layer, name this layer *Light in her hair Crvs,* and set the blending mode to Screen.

The highlights in her hair are now being lightened by this layer, but the effect is showing up all over the image, so we need to add another mask that will let us limit this effect to just her hair.

3. Select the Light in her hair Crvs layer and choose **Layer > Group Layers.** Then click the layer mask icon at the bottom of the Layers panel to add a mask to this layer group. Invert the layer mask by pressing Cmd-I/Ctrl-I. Select the Brush tool and set the foreground color to white. Paint on the layer mask over the parts of her hair where you want the lightening effect to be visible, as shown in FIGURE 9.57.

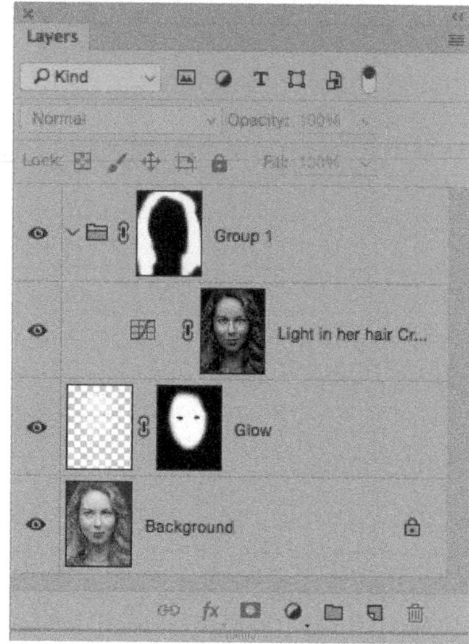

FIGURE 9.57 Place the Light in her hair Crvs layer into a layer group so you can use a layer mask to control where the effect shows.

Adding Contrast to Shadows

The final step in making this image pop is to add a touch of drama by darkening the shadows just a little. As with the other steps in this process we'll manipulate a copy of the Blue channel to accomplish this. The twist here is that instead of using the channel to isolate the highlights we'll use this copy to isolate the shadows in the image.

1. Make one more copy of the Blue channel and then choose **Image > Adjustments > Curves** to open the Curves dialog box. Drag the white point of the curve to the left about one-third of the way to force more of the lighter tones in the channel to become white, as seen in FIGURE 9.58. Since we're looking to keep this effect out of the highlights, invert the channel by pressing Cmd-I/Ctrl-I.

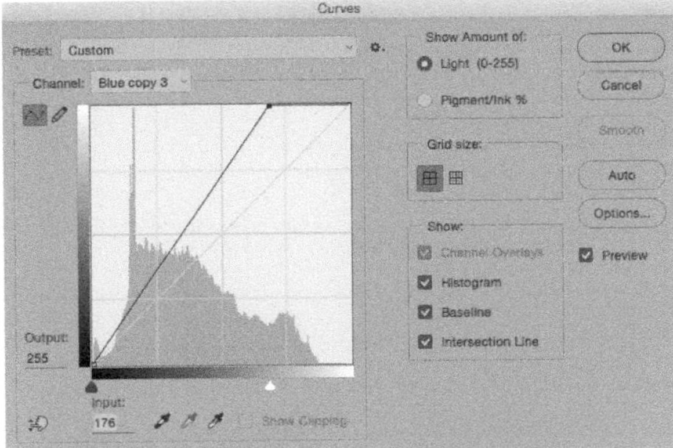

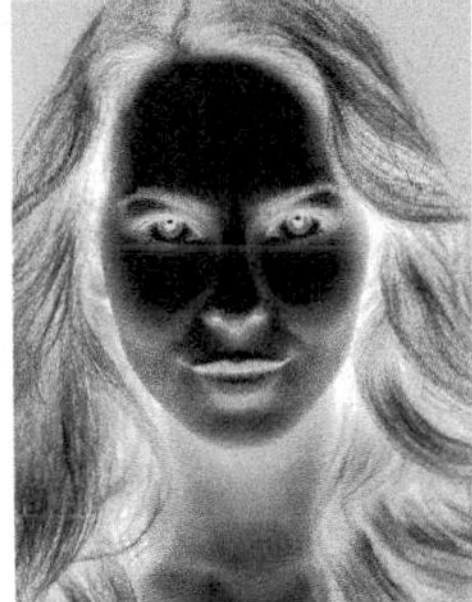

FIGURE 9.58 Drag the white point to the left to force the lighter values in the Blue channel copy toward white, and then invert that channel.

2. Cmd/Ctrl-click the inverted channel in the Channels panel and choose **Layer > New Adjustment Layer > Curves.** Name this adjustment layer *Enhance Lighting Crvs* and set the blending mode to Soft Light. In this case the Soft Light blending mode is doing the work for us, so there is no need to make any adjustments to the curves themselves. Be sure to drag this layer above the layer group you made in the previous step so that layer group's mask will not affect this layer.

3. Since this effect can be a little too strong, dial down the strength by lowering the opacity of the layer to 40%. The final image can be seen in FIGURE 9.59.

FIGURE 9.59 Deepening the shadows a little adds the finishing touch to this image.

CLOSING THOUGHTS

Beauty retouching builds on the skills you develop when retouching portraits but requires much closer attention to detail, and to balancing the color and tone of the various parts of the image while maintaining realistic texture in the skin. So while the techniques are very similar to the ones we looked at in Chapter 8, their application is done in a much more careful manner. In the end the goal is to craft a flawless image that looks perfect yet real.

Chapter **10**

PRODUCT, FOOD, AND ARCHITECTURAL RETOUCHING

Beautiful images have a wide variety of subjects. In the last two chapters we discussed beauty as it applies to images of people. Here we'll take a look at three different kinds of images: product, food, and architectural.

Each of these genres involves not only good photography but also lots of retouching. We'll take a look at some of the typical techniques used in retouching these kinds of shots.

As with shots of people, retouching shots like these is all about the lighting and the details. Many of the techniques are similar to what we covered in the previous chapters—they're just adapted to fit the different subject matter.

In this chapter you learn how to

- Create a clipping path around a product
- Remove and replace labels on products
- Create drop shadows for products
- Make food shots look irresistible
- Remove unwanted objects in real estate photos
- Combine exposures in architectural shots to balance windows and interiors

PRODUCT RETOUCHING

Product photography, like beauty and fashion photography, is primarily about selling the product by making it look as clean and interesting as possible. The range of issues that product retouching can cover could easily fill a book, but some of the most common tasks that product retouchers are asked to handle are stripping out the product (making a clipping path), cleaning it up, and replacing the labels.

In addition to many of the tools and techniques we discussed in earlier chapters, product retouching frequently makes extensive use of the Pen tool. Typically, the Pen tool is used to draw around the product a path that can then be used to create a clean mask, allowing you to "strip out" the product and define any parts that may need to be selectively cleaned up or enhanced in some way.

Let's use a simple shot of a bottle to take a look at how these challenges can be taken care of (**FIGURE 10.1**).

PEN TOOL POWER

For this book we're assuming you already have some familiarity with the Pen tool. If you'd like to read more about this powerful tool's features and how to use them, we refer you to the section "Pen Tool Power" in Chapter 12 of the second edition of Katrin's book *Photoshop Masking & Compositing*.

You can easily download a copy of this chapter by opening a web browser and going to www.peachpit.com/store/photoshop-masking-compositing-9780321701008.

To access the correct chapter follow these steps:

1. Click the Sample Content tab, about halfway down the page.
2. Click "Chapter 12 The Pen Tool" (it has a faint highlight to show that it's a link) to open the Files List page for the book.
3. On the Files List page, click Pentool Webfiles.zip and PSMaskingCompositing_PenTool.pdf.

The work we'll be doing on this shot involves stripping out the bottle, placing it against a new background, and replacing the old label with two new ones. In addition, the top needs to be replaced with one on which the tab is not visible, and the color and lighting need to be enhanced to make the shot "pop" a bit more (**FIGURE 10.2**).

FIGURES 10.1 and **10.2** © *David Blattel*

ch10_bottle.jpg
ch10_bottle top.jpg
ch10_bottle_background.jpg
ch10_KEP-labels.psd

Before beginning the work, let's take a moment to think about the strategy we'll use to accomplish all these tasks. Stripping the bottle out will require a mask. It's also going to take a few layers to remove and replace the label, and to put a new top on the bottle.

Placing the Bottle on a New Background

Knowing we're going to need at least a handful of layers, it makes sense to use a layer group with a mask for the bottle and the various layers. By using a mask on the layer group we'll need only one mask to make sure the work we do on the bottle affects only the bottle itself.

1. Open ch10_bottle.jpg in Photoshop.

Since we've already decided to use a layer group, let's start by turning the Background layer into a regular layer and putting it in a layer group.

2. Double-click the Background layer in the Layers panel. When the New Layer dialog box opens, name this layer *Bottle*. With the Bottle layer selected, put it in a layer group by pressing Cmd-G/Ctrl-G. Name this group *Bottle Group*.

3. Now we'll move on to making the mask for the bottle. Select the Pen tool and draw a path around the bottle, as shown in FIGURE 10.3. When you finish drawing the path, go to the Paths panel, double-click the Work Path name, and rename it *Outline*.

TIP Give each path a descriptive name that helps you remember what it's for. That will come in especially handy for images that use a lot of paths.

FIGURE 10.3 Put the bottle into its own layer group, and then use the Pen tool to draw a path around it.

4. With the Outline path selected in the Paths panel, open the panel menu and choose Make Selection. In the Make Selection dialog box, choose the amount of feathering you want for the selection (FIGURE 10.4). The ideal amount of feathering depends a great deal on the resolution of the image; the bigger the image, the bigger the feather you might need. In this case, a feather radius of 1 pixel should work fine.

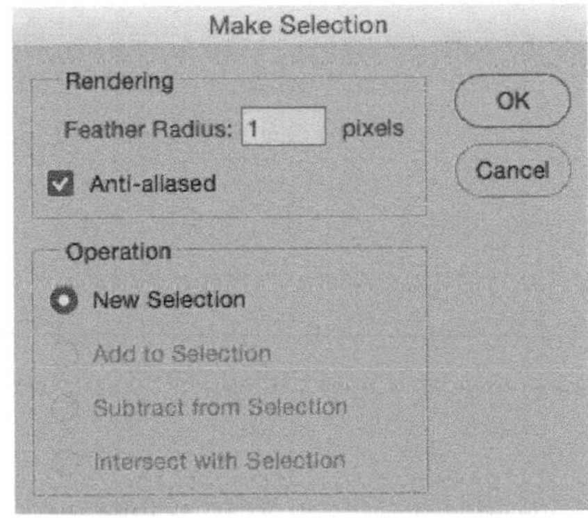

FIGURE 10.4 Use the Make Selection dialog to turn the path into a selection.

5. Turn the selection into a layer mask by going to the Layers panel and clicking the Add Layer Mask button, as seen in FIGURE 10.5.

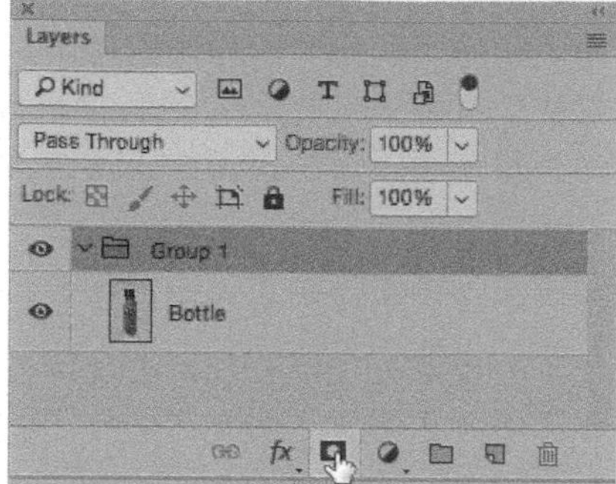

FIGURE 10.5 Turn the selection into a layer mask.

Once Bottle Group's mask has been made, we need to check the edges to be sure the mask "fits" just right. Dennis finds one of the best ways to do this is to put a layer filled with a bright, contrasting color behind the layer so that it's easier to see any gaps or parts of the mask that might need to be addressed.

6. Choose **Layer > New Layer,** name the new layer *Mask Test,* and click OK.

7. Select red for your foreground color and fill the Mask Test layer with the foreground color by pressing Option-Delete/Alt-Backspace. Go to the Layers panel and pull the Mask Test layer below Bottle Group so you can see the bottle on top of the red color.

Now that we have a strong contrasting color behind the bottle, check to see how accurate the mask is by zooming in and panning around the bottle, looking for any parts of the original background that might still be showing. Use the Brush tool on the layer mask to correct any mistakes in the layer mask. When you're sure the layer mask is working properly, delete the Mask Test layer by dragging it onto the trash icon at the bottom of the Layers panel.

8. With the bottle nicely masked it's time to drop in the background we'll be using for this shot. Open the file ch10_bottle_background.jpg, and select the Background layer in the Layers panel. Press the Shift key while dragging the Background layer from the bottle background image onto the tab of our bottle image window. Make sure the new background layer is below Bottle Group in the Layers panel, and name it *Background.*

★ NOTE Pressing Shift while dragging the layer from one image to another will make sure the copied layer will be centered in the destination image.

9. Before getting rid of the old label on the bottle, make sure the bottle is nice and clean. Make a new layer, name it *Retouch,* and make sure it is clipped to the Bottle layer by pressing Cmd-Option-G/Ctrl-Alt-G while it is selected in the Layers panel.

Then use the Spot Healing tool, the Healing Brush tool, and the Clone Stamp tool to zoom in and retouch any stray spots or specks that should not be on your nice, clean bottle.

Replacing the Label

With the bottle cleaned up, we'll use a merged copy of the Bottle and Retouch layers to give us an easy way to remove the old label.

1. Select both layers in the Layers panel and press Cmd-Option-E/Ctrl-Alt-E to merge them into a copy. By default this layer will be named *Retouch (merged),* and since this will only be a temporary layer there is no need to rename it.

2. Make sure you have the Retouch (merged) layer selected in the Layers panel, and then use the Rectangular Marquee tool to draw out a selection that covers the open space between the upper and lower parts of the label, as shown in FIGURE 10.6.

FIGURE 10.6 Use the Rectangular Marquee tool to select the area between the upper and lower parts of the label.

3. With this selection active, copy this part of the merged layer to a new layer by pressing Cmd-J/Ctrl-J. Name this new layer *Lose Label* and convert it to a Smart Object by choosing **Layer > Smart Object > Convert to Smart Object.** Once this is done, you can trash the Retouch (merged) layer, keeping your layer stack more efficient.

4. Choose **Edit > Free Transform** to stretch the Lose Label layer so it covers all of the old label, as seen in FIGURE 10.7. Stretching the layer a little more than necessary can make it easier to hide the borders of this stretched layer, making for a better blend with the bottle.

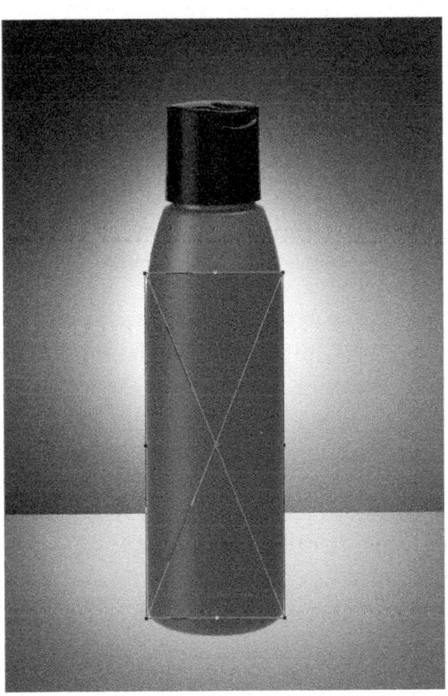

FIGURE 10.7 Stretch the Lose Label layer so that it hides the old label.

5. Add a layer mask to this layer, and use the Brush tool to paint black in the layer mask to blend this layer in with the rest of the bottle.

Since we stretched this layer quite a bit, we need to zoom in to see if there are any telltale "stretched pixels" that will give away our shortcut. In this case we can solve that by making use of the Gaussian Blur filter. And since our Lose Label layer is a Smart Object, any blurring we do with this filter will be easily adjustable if we later decide the blurring needs tweaking.

6. Choose **Filter > Blur > Gaussian Blur** and use just enough blur to hide the stretched pixels. FIGURE 10.8 shows that in this case an amount of 4 pixels looks about right.

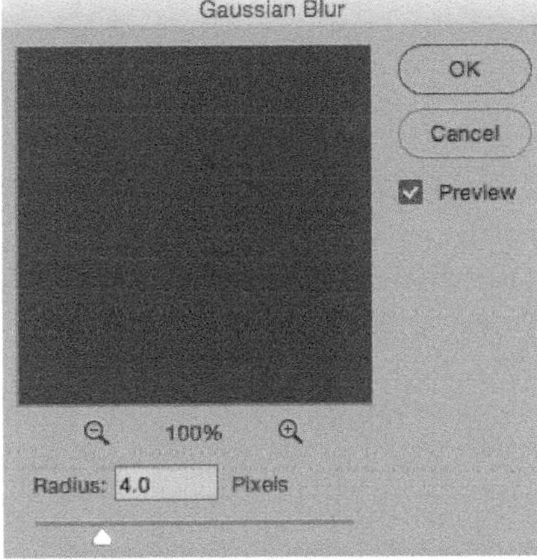

FIGURE 10.8 Adding a Gaussian Blur of 4 pixels helps hide the stretched look of the pixels.

Because the lighting on the bottle falls off a bit toward the bottom, the upper part of the stretched Lose Label layer is noticeably darker than the upper part of the bottle, so we need to lighten it so that it matches better.

7. With the Lose Label layer selected in the Layers panel, add a Curves adjustment layer by choosing **Layer > New Adjustment Layer > Curves.** Name this layer *Lighten Top Crvs,* and select Use Previous Layer to Create Clipping Mask so that this Curves adjustment layer will affect only the Lose Label layer.

Add a point near the middle of the RGB master curve, and pull up just enough to make the upper part of the Lose Label layer match the density of the upper part of the bottle. FIGURE 10.9 shows we don't need to pull up very much.

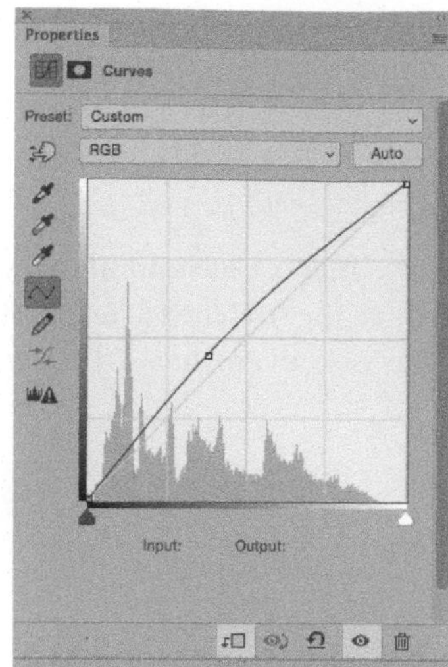

FIGURE 10.9 Use a Curves adjustment layer to lighten the top of the Lose Label layer so that it matches the density of the top of the bottle.

8. Select the layer mask for this layer and invert it by pressing Cmd-I/Ctrl-I to hide it. Then use the Brush tool to paint white in the layer mask; use a large brush, around 800 pixels or so, to reveal the lightening effect on the upper part of the layer so that it blends nicely with the rest of the bottle.

Replacing the Bottle Cap

1. Before we add the new labels we need to replace the black top of the bottle. Open the file Ch10_Bottle top.jpg. In the Layers panel, select the Background layer in the "Bottle top" image, and press the Shift key while dragging and dropping this layer onto our Bottle image. Name this layer *Cap.*

2. Make sure the Cap layer is on top of the layer stack inside the Bottle Group layer group. This will make it easier to be sure we're covering up the old cap. When positioning a new layer, it helps to be able to see all the layers we're trying to line up. For now, turn off the layer mask for Bottle Group by Shift-clicking Bottle Group's layer mask.

3. Select the Cap layer and set the blending mode to Difference. Then select the Move tool and use the arrow keys to nudge it into position, as shown in FIGURE 10.10.

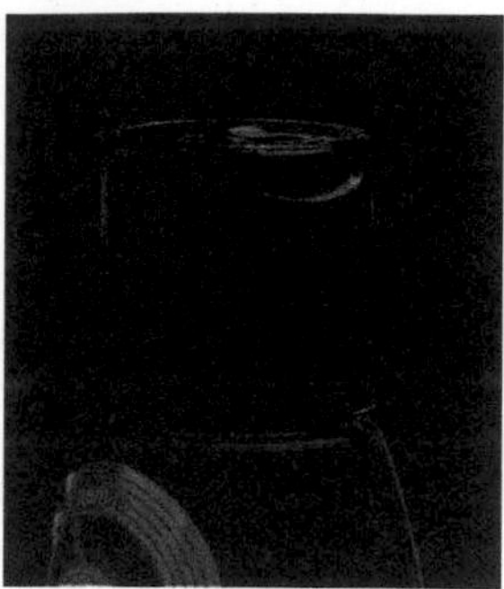

FIGURE 10.10 The shot on the left shows the cap slightly out of position, while the one on the right shows it in the right position.

4. With the cap correctly positioned, change the blending mode back to Normal and then turn the layer mask back on for Bottle Group. Now we need to make a mask for the new cap so it covers up only the old one, not the cleaned-up bottle. Use the Pen tool to draw a path around the new cap. Create a selection from the path, and turn the selection into a layer mask for the Cap layer.

5. To clean up the new cap, create another layer and name it *Retouch.* Clip it to the Cap layer and then use the Spot Healing tool, the Healing Brush tool, and the Clone Stamp tool to clean the new cap.

Adding New Labels

1. Open the file ch10_KEP-labels.psd. You will find two layers, each one containing a different label. Considering that both labels need to be wrapped around the bottle and placed in the same position, we can save a considerable amount of work by placing them at the same time. This can be done very effectively by placing the labels into a single Smart Object, with each label a different layer.

2. Make sure only one of the label layers is visible (so we see only one at a time), select both layers in the Layers panel, and choose **Layer > Smart Object > Convert to Smart Object.** Rename the Smart Object *Labels.*

3. Copy the Labels Smart Object and paste it into our bottle image. Position it over the bottle and choose **Edit > Free Transform** to scale the labels so they fit nicely on the bottle.

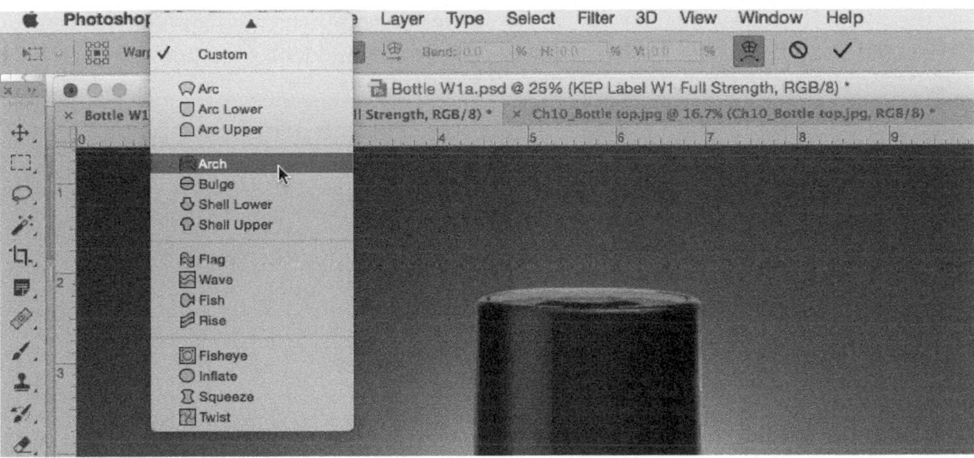

FIGURE 10.11 Choose Arch from the Warp Style menu.

4. Next, we need to warp the label so it wraps around the bottle, making it look like it really belongs. Choose **Edit > Transform > Warp** and on the options bar choose Arch from the Warp Style menu (FIGURE 10.11). (Choosing Arch provides uniform distortion without a lot of wobbling that can make the label seem oddly warped.)

The default Arch warp curves the label in the wrong direction, but adjusting the Bend value (also in the options bar) will correct that. A positive Bend value (as it has by default) warps the label upward. Since we need the warp to go down, following the shape of the bottle, we need a negative value.

5. We want a subtle warp, so a value of –8 should work.

Since the perspective of the bottle shows more curvature at the bottom than at the top, we'll need to adjust the warp of the label so the bottom of it follows that curvature better.

6. Open the Warp menu again and choose Custom to reveal the mesh and control points for the transform. The control points for the bottom curve are just below the ends of the second and third vertical lines in the mesh. Drag down slightly on both handles to give the labels a bit more curve at the bottom (FIGURE 10.12). When you're satisfied the labels are fitting on the bottle properly, press Return/Enter to apply the warp.

FIGURE 10.12 Drag the control points at the bottom of the warp mesh to increase the warp at the bottom of the bottle.

After applying the warp, your label should look something like FIGURE 10.13.

FIGURE 10.13 After you apply the warp, your label should better follow the lines of the bottle.

Adjusting the Lighting

The last step in making the label look like it really belongs on the bottle is to match the lighting on the label to the lighting on the bottle itself.

As we've discussed, a bit of burning and dodging will darken and lighten the "object" in imitation of the way the light should be affecting it. Since our label is black we won't really need to darken it. All that's needed in this case is to add a hint of highlight to the label, in keeping with the vertical highlight on the bottle.

1. Add a new layer, name it *Lighting,* and be sure to clip it to the Labels layer. Set its blending mode to Overlay. Then select the Brush tool and adjust the size of the Brush to match the width of the highlight on the left side of the bottle, about 300 pixels. Make sure the foreground color is white, and paint a stroke of "light" down the label where the highlight lies on the bottle. When your lighting has been added to the label it should look something like FIGURE 10.14.

FIGURE 10.14 Adding a highlight to the label

Now we need to add a shadow to the bottle so it looks like it's really sitting on the "table" part of our background.

Looking closely at photos of real objects and at the shadows in those photos helps us imagine how our shadow should look. In this case we will create a relatively simple drop shadow. These shadows often have two parts: a softer shadow that grades outward from the object, and a darker, harder shadow right where the object makes contact with the table. Re-creating this kind of shadow is simple to do with two layers, one for the softer shadow and one for the core shadow.

2. Make a selection by Cmd/Ctrl-clicking Bottle Group's layer mask icon in the Layers panel. Then select the Background layer, create a new layer, name it *Soft Shadow,* and fill it with black. Make a duplicate of this layer and name it *Core Shadow.* Position the Core Shadow layer just above the Soft Shadow layer in the Layers panel and temporarily turn off visibility for it.

3. Select the Soft Shadow layer and add a Gaussian Blur to soften the shadow. The goal is to make it nice and soft, so use an amount of 40 pixels. Then select the Move tool and nudge the shadow down by tapping the down arrow key a couple of times.

4. Select the Core Shadow layer in the Layers panel and add a smaller amount of Gaussian Blur, 10 pixels. With the Move tool selected, nudge it down a touch so we catch enough of the blurred edge to make it look like a real shadow.

Looking at the results, we see that the strength of the shadows needs to be reduced a bit. Lowering the opacity of the layers will take care of that.

5. Set the opacity of the Soft Shadow layer to 40% and the opacity of the Core Shadow layer to 60%.

6. We now see our shadows spilling out all around the bottle instead of just at the bottom where it sits on the table. To fix this, select both shadow layers in the Layers panel and put them in a layer group by pressing Cmd-G/Ctrl-G. Name this layer group *Shadows.*

7. Add a layer mask to the Shadows layer group by Option/Alt-clicking the Add Layer Mask icon at the bottom of the Layers panel. (Holding Option/Alt automatically fills the mask with black, hiding the shadows.)

8. Reveal the shadows by choosing a 300-pixel brush and painting white in the layer mask at the bottom of the bottle, being sure to let the shadows show up on the table but not around the sides of the bottle. If your core shadow spills too much to the sides of the bottle, add a layer mask to its layer and paint black in the mask to hide it where it's not needed.

At this point your image should look similar to FIGURE 10.15.

Our bottle still looks a little dull. We can give the shot a little more "pop" by increasing the saturation and contrast of the bottle. This is easily done by adding two new adjustment layers: a Hue/Saturation layer and a Curves layer.

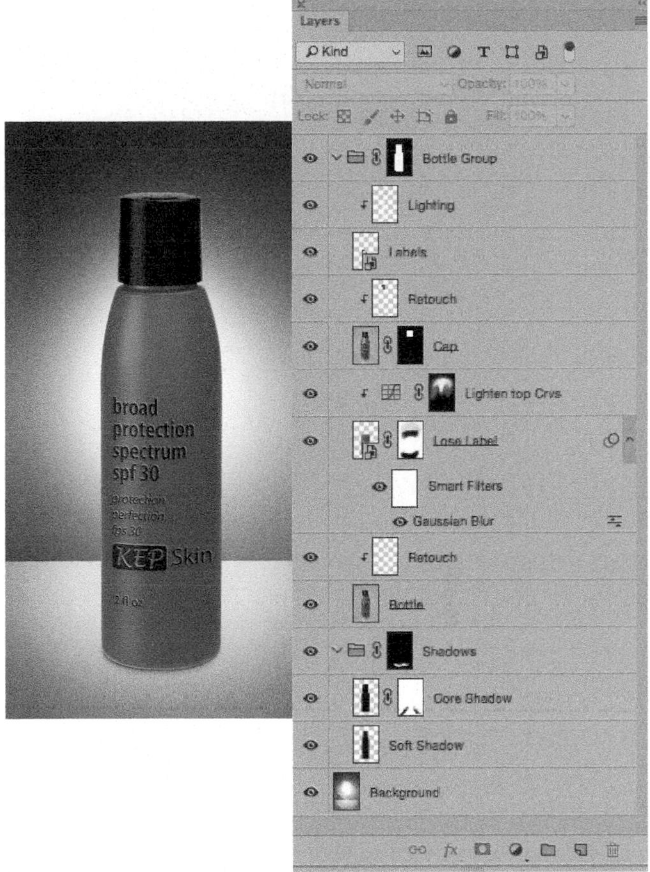

FIGURE 10.15 Using two layers in a layer group, we can add both a soft shadow and a core shadow, making it look as if the bottle is really sitting on the table.

9. We want the "pop" to affect only the bottle, so before adding the adjustment layers be sure to select the Lighting layer that sits on top of the Labels layer. Choose **Layer > New Adjustment Layer > Hue Saturation** and move the Saturation slider to +20.

10. Choose **Layer > New Adjustment Layer > Curves.** Since we don't want this layer to affect the saturation, set the blending mode to Luminosity. Then set two control points on the RGB curve: one a quarter of the way up from the bottom, for the shadows, and the other about three quarters of the way up, for the highlights. Drag down on the control point for the shadows and up on the one for the highlights, as seen in FIGURE 10.16.

FIGURE 10.16 Add contrast to the bottle with a Curves adjustment layer set to the Luminosity blending mode.

This is all looking pretty good, but you'll recall that we need two different labels on our bottle. Instead of having to do all these steps again for the second label, remember that our Labels Smart Object was made from two layers, one for each label.

11. The beauty of stacking these labels in a single Smart Object is that all we have to do to switch labels is double-click the Labels Smart Object. This opens up the Smart Object as a separate file that has two layers: KEP Broad Spectrum and KEP Full Strength, as shown in FIGURE 10.17. So far, the layer that's been visible is KEP Broad Spectrum.

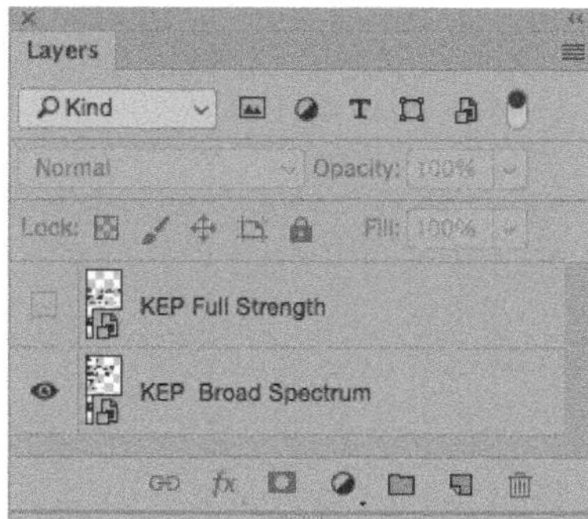

FIGURE 10.17 The Labels Smart Object has two layers, one for each label.

12. Turn off visibility for KEP Broad Spectrum, turn it on for the KEP Full Strength layer, and press Cmd-S/Ctrl-S to save the changes. This will automatically update the Smart Object, swapping the label on the bottle with the new one. Because these layers have been properly lined up with each other, when we switch the labels they'll wind up in the right position on the bottle. FIGURE 10.18 shows our final bottle with the two labels.

FIGURE 10.18 Switch labels by changing active layers in the Labels Smart Object.

FOOD RETOUCHING

Food retouching can be a discipline all its own. There are retouchers who base their entire career on adding the final touches that make shots of tender morsels look delicious. The goal for food retouching, as with beauty and product retouching, is to make your subject look as good as possible. As one retoucher/blogger put it, "You want to make your viewer hungry!"

As you might have guessed by now, the techniques and workflow for retouching these kinds of shots are pretty similar to what we've looked at throughout this book. The complexity of the final Photoshop file will vary according to what needs to be done, but it usually involves using layers to clean up stray bits and using adjustment layers with masks to correct or enhance the color. Additional elements may be composited to help cover up something or to bring in something extra to make the final shot a masterpiece.

In Chapter 9, we looked at the importance of communication with the client. Good communication is just as important here, because there are so many directions a retoucher can take that it's tremendously helpful to have a good understanding of what the photographer or client is envisioning for the project.

Photographer Teri Campbell provides a great example of how helpful it can be to have good notes on what the photographer wants. FIGURE 10.19 shows a marked-up photo Teri sent to Dennis, with notes that gave him a very clear idea of Teri's vision for the shot.

FIGURE 10.19 An image marked for retouching by photographer Teri Campbell © *Teri Campbell*

The notes accompanying the marked-up shot said, "The biggest thing that needs to be done to this image is to add red to the bacon. I also think the graham cracker on the s'more is a little too cold/bland, especially when compared to the ones in the background—could use some warmth and maybe density."

Most of the work the client is asking for involves color correction. Inevitably, there are always stray bits or imperfections that need to be cleaned up as well. As in previous examples, the first steps are to open the image, zoom in so you're viewing it at 100%, look it over, and make a few of your own notes about what might need to be done.

For instance, as it sits under the lights, chocolate tends to get whitish specks popping up. To make the chocolate look as desirable as possible, these specks need to be cleaned up. And whenever you have food, you're going to have crumbs. In some circumstances, like with this shot, some crumbs make the food look inviting, but too many will make the table it's sitting on look messy.

Much of the work of the retoucher is to strike a balance between what to leave and what to take out. In FIGURE 10.20 Dennis has circled many of the specks and stray bits that need to be retouched out. Depending on how large the image will be when shown, you may decide to go a little further.

FIGURE 10.20 The red circles show where specks and stray crumbs need to be cleaned up.

FIGURES 10.21 and 10.22 show the s'more before and after the stray bits are cleaned up and the various color adjustments made.

FIGURES 10.21 and 10.22 Before and after.

ch10_smores.jpg

1. With the image open in Photoshop, create a new layer for the cleanup work and name it *Retouch.*

2. Select the Spot Healing Brush tool and make sure that Content Aware and Sample All Layers are selected in the options bar, as discussed in Chapter 8. Zoom in to 100% view and work your way through the image, starting in the upper-left corner and scrolling a screen's worth at a time, retouching out the unwanted specks and stray bits. If you don't get the results you need from the Spot Healing tool, switch to the Healing Brush or Clone Stamp tool. If you need to work on the very tiny details, zoom in closer. After working your way through the image this way, zoom back out so you can see more of the image and look it over for anything else that stands out as distracting or out of place.

3. Now we can move on to making the bacon "pop." Press the Q key to enter Quick Mask mode. Select the Brush tool and tap the D key to set the foreground color to black. Set the brush size to about 200 pixels and the hardness to 0 to make sure you will have a soft transition at the edge of your mask.

4. Use the Brush tool to paint black over the bacon in the sandwich. Since the default mode for the Quick Mask is to show red where it is black, you should see semi-transparent red covering the bacon, as in FIGURE 10.23. When you've covered the bacon, invert the Quick Mask by pressing Cmd-I/Ctrl-I, and turn it into a selection by tapping the Q key once more.

FIGURE 10.23 Use Quick Mask mode to paint a selection for the bacon.

5. With the selection active, add a Vibrance adjustment Layer by choosing **Layer > New Adjustment Layer > Vibrance.** Name this layer *Bacon Vibrance.* Then slide the Vibrance slider to +32 and the Saturation slider to +35, as seen in FIGURE 10.24.

TIP Vibrance intelligently increases saturation in the more muted colors of the image and does not affect the more saturated colors as much.

FIGURE 10.24 Use a Vibrance adjustment layer to increase the saturation of the bacon.

6. A little more brightness would help the bacon look even more delicious. Since we already made a selection of the bacon when we created the Vibrance adjustment layer, we can reload the selection by Cmd/Ctrl-clicking the Bacon Vibrance layer's mask.

7. Add a Levels adjustment layer by choosing **Layer > New Adjustment Layer > Levels.** Name this layer *Bacon Levels.* Then move the black point slider to 11, the middle slider to 1.20, and the white point slider to 230, as in FIGURE 10.25.

FIGURE 10.25 Brighten the bacon with a Levels adjustment layer.

Next we turn our attention to the graham cracker part of our s'more. As the client requested, the graham crackers need to be warmed up a bit. To do this we'll use the Quick Mask again to paint a selection of both parts of the cracker.

8. Tap the Q key, and use the Brush tool to paint black over the top and bottom parts of the cracker (FIGURE 10.26). When you're satisfied you've covered all of the cracker, invert the mask by pressing Cmd-I/Ctrl-I, and tap the Q key once more to activate your selection.

FIGURE 10.26 Use Quick Mask mode to paint a selection of the graham crackers.

9. With the selection active, add a Curves adjustment Layer by choosing **Layer > New Adjustment Layer > Curves.** Name this layer *Graham Crvs.* Choose Red from the channel menu (to the left of the Auto button), and pull up on the middle part of the curve to add red to the crackers. Next take out some of the blue by choosing the Blue channel and pulling down a little bit. Finally, to keep the crackers from getting too bright, choose the RGB channel and pull down on the middle of the curve. When you're done, your Curves Properties panel should look like FIGURE 10.27.

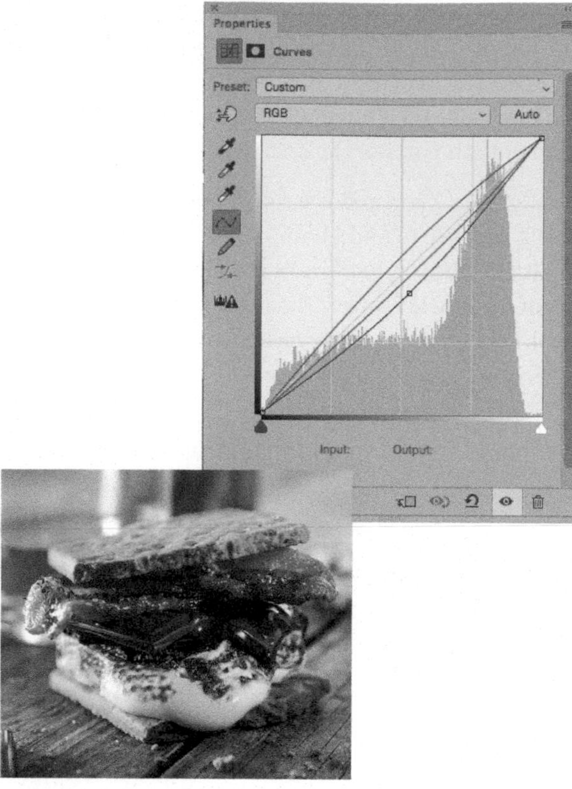

FIGURE 10.27 Use a Curves adjustment layer to add warmth to the graham crackers.

The final task for this shot is to make it even more enticing by adding a little light here and there. In our discussion on beauty retouching in Chapter 9, one of the last steps in the retouching workflow was enhancing the lighting. Our goal here is the same—by selectively dodging the details, we can heighten the sensuousness of the food and make it just that much more irresistible.

10. Add a Curves adjustment layer and name it *Dodge Crvs*. Then add a control point around the middle of the RGB curve and pull up on it a bit, as shown in FIGURE 10.28.

11. Hide the effect of the layer by inverting the Dodge Crvs layer mask (Cmd-I/Ctrl-I), and select the Brush tool. Tap the D key to set the foreground color to white. In the options bar, set Opacity and Flow to 20% to 30%, and use a very small brush to paint white in the mask where you'd like to bring in a little more light.

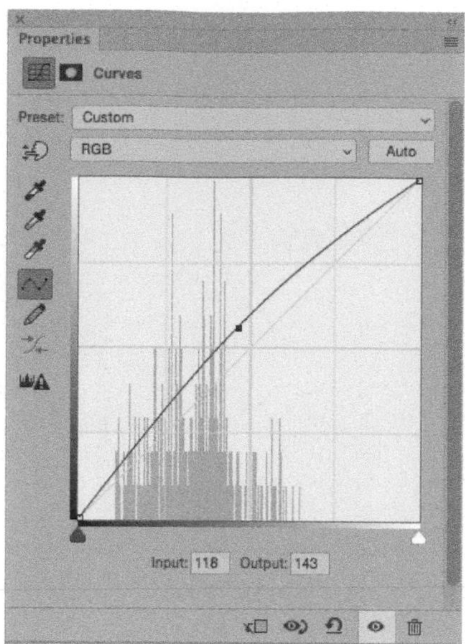

FIGURE 10.28 Use a Curves adjustment layer to enhance the lighting.

The size of your brush will vary a fair amount, depending on the features you're trying to highlight. In some instances you may be using a very small brush—maybe 8 to 10 pixels—to emphasize the highlights on the chocolate squares. Your brush will be larger—perhaps 50 or 60 pixels—when pushing the light on the edges of the crackers. FIGURE 10.29 shows red where Dennis added this effect to our shot.

FIGURE 10.29 The red areas are where Dennis used this layer to dodge.

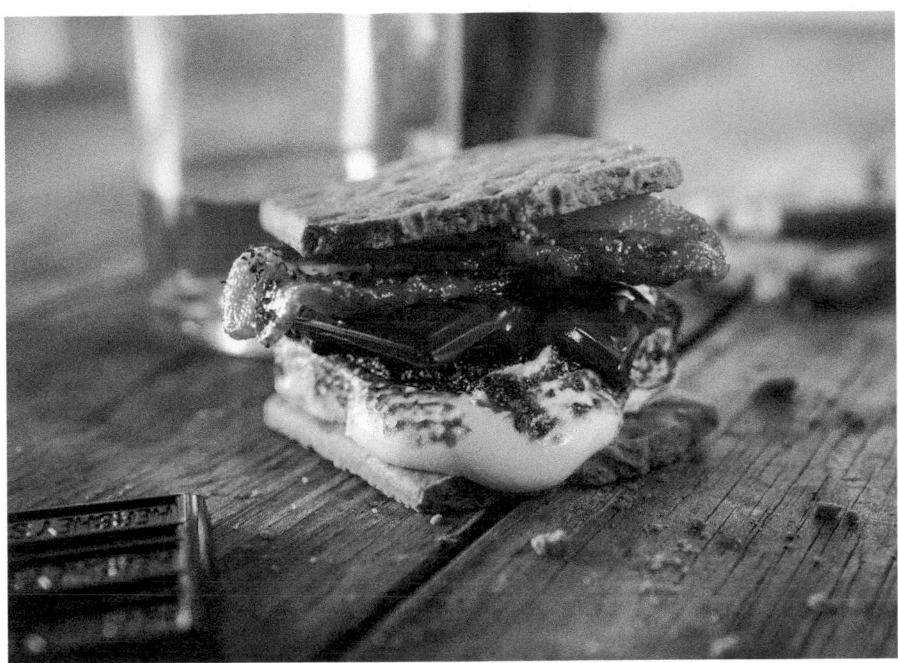

FIGURE 10.30 After retouching and color correction

Enhancing the lighting with the dodging layer finishes the work on the image. To recap, after doing a quick round of cleanup, we added life to the bacon with a couple of adjustment layers, warmed up the color on the graham crackers, and brought in extra light on the edges of the chocolate, bacon, and graham crackers (FIGURE 10.30).

ARCHITECTURAL RETOUCHING

We see architectural photos nearly every day. In everything from real estate listings to high-end magazines featuring the work of master architects and builders, this genre of photography may be one of the most common there is.

The uses for these shots fall into two basic types: real estate, meant to show off and sell the property, and architectural, meant to show off the beauty of the space and the masterful work done in creating it.

Typically, the budgets for these two sub-genres vary quite a bit. Usually shots meant for real estate will have a much smaller budget, which can mean you're asked to do more basic work on the shots—for instance, removing For Sale signs or overhead wires.

Meanwhile, architectural shots can be far more involved. This can mean combining different exposures, such as one for the interior and one for the windows, producing a balance that would be challenging to achieve in-camera.

Here we'll take a look at one example of each. The first shot is a view from the street of a beautiful home that needs to have the For Sale sign removed. And the second is an interior shot of a room with big sliding windows; it required that two exposures be composited to achieve a properly balanced photograph.

Real Estate Shots: Losing the For Sale Sign

In FIGURE 10.31 we see a shot of a beautiful home for sale. Shots like this are used to help attract buyers by picturing the inside and outside of the home from angles that emphasize its best aspects.

The retouching requests for shots like this are usually fairly simple, as the clients don't often have a large budget for retouching. They involve things like removing the For Sale sign on the right and the power wires on the left. FIGURE 10.32 shows the resulting image.

FIGURES 10.31 and **10.32** Before and after. © *William Short*

Removing elements frequently means carefully rebuilding parts of buildings, fences, and so on. Ideally, the photographer will shoot "plates" showing what's behind the things you need to remove (see the section "The Beauty of Blank Plates" in Chapter 8). For those times when you don't have the benefit of these plates, you will need to pay careful attention to detail and to the patterns or features of the buildings so you can re-create what's missing.

Let's take a quick look at the sign and see what we're in for.

In FIGURE 10.33 we can clearly see the challenge ahead of us. Fortunately, the sign covers part of the house next door, so we're not worried about the features of our "hero house." But if we want our work to be unnoticeable, we still need to pay careful attention.

FIGURE 10.33 A closeup view of the sign we need to remove

Three features need to be rebuilt in removing the sign. Things like bushes are pretty easy to rebuild with the Clone Stamp tool. But the garage door and the side of the garage have clear features that will have to be re-created. We have some small samples of what these features look like. Looking closely, we can see just enough of an example of what we need for the garage door on the right side of the pillar next to the For Sale sign.

And the side of the building to the left of the garage door looks like we should be able clone it straight down to extend it below where the bush would be covering it up.

TIP When working on more complex tasks, such as removing the For Sale sign, break the work into steps and use different layers for each step.

ch10_home.jpg

The first step is to rebuild the garage door covered up by the sign. We can see that the white pillar just to the right of the sign and the frame of the garage door form a sort of rectangle.

1. Use the Pen tool to create a path tracing the edge of the pillar on the right and the inside of the doorframe on the left. In FIGURE 10.34 the red line shows where Dennis drew this path.

FIGURE 10.34 Use the Pen tool to draw a path that defines the garage door.

2. Cmd/Ctrl-click the path in the Paths panel to turn it into a selection. Then add a new layer and name it *Garage Door*. With the selection still active, click the Add Layer Mask button at the bottom of the Layers panel to turn the selection into a layer mask, making it easy to control where your cloning will show.

3. Select the Clone Stamp tool and pick a small brush, about 11 pixels in this case. Find a point you can use as the source for your clone. It should have an easily definable feature that is similar to a point in the area you want to clone to. Here, the upper-left corner of the window just to the right of the pillar is a good match for the upper-left corner of the window to the left of that pillar, as seen in **FIGURE 10.35**.

FIGURE 10.35 Rebuild the garage door by carefully lining up the source and destination points for the Clone Stamp tool.

4. To reconstruct the windows on the door covered up by the sign, Option/Alt-click the source point and begin to draw on the equivalent spot to the left of the pillar. Keep an eye on your source cursor to the right of the pillar. When your painting brings it too close to the pillar (when pieces of the pillar start to show up under your brush), Option/Alt-click the source point again to reset the cloning.

Continue to redraw the windows by repeating this process across the door, keeping in mind that we'll be adding another layer with the cloned bush on top of this. **FIGURE 10.36** shows how Dennis rebuilt this part of the image.

The next step is to continue rebuilding the area behind the sign. The brown clapboard siding next to the garage door needs to be extended down a bit and the bushes need to be built up. As we add in the bushes, they will start to cover up the part of the garage door we just re-created.

FIGURE 10.36 Continue rebuilding just enough of the door so that you can build up the bush over the door to cover up the sign.

5. Add another layer and name it *Frame & Bushes*. Again, use the Clone Stamp tool to carefully rebuild the siding along the garage door downward so that it extends a bit below the line of windows on the garage door. Then, using the bushes to the left of the sign as a source, work on cloning the bushes upward to cover up the rest of the sign while taking care to blend in with the rest of the bushes. Do not worry about the top of the bushes yet; we'll take care of that in the next step. **FIGURE 10.37** shows how Dennis built up this area.

FIGURE 10.37 Add another layer and continue to build up the area covered by the sign.

The final touch is to build up the top of the new bush so it has a natural, organic look. Take a moment to zoom in to study the natural edges of the bush, especially along the tops of the bushes you'll be looking to match. These edges tend to be uneven, with a few branches and leaves reaching up here and there. Using a round brush to re-create this look will be problematic.

This is where the options Photoshop offers in the Brushes panel (**Window > Brushes**) come in handy. To begin, we need to find a brush that has a nice leafy shape. Among the default Photoshop brushes, one has a shape that looks something like a maple leaf, as seen in FIGURE 10.38. Since the leaves on our bush are pretty small, this should work fine with a few adjustments. Even though we normally think of these brushes as something we'd use with the Brush tool, we can also use these brushes with the Clone Stamp tool.

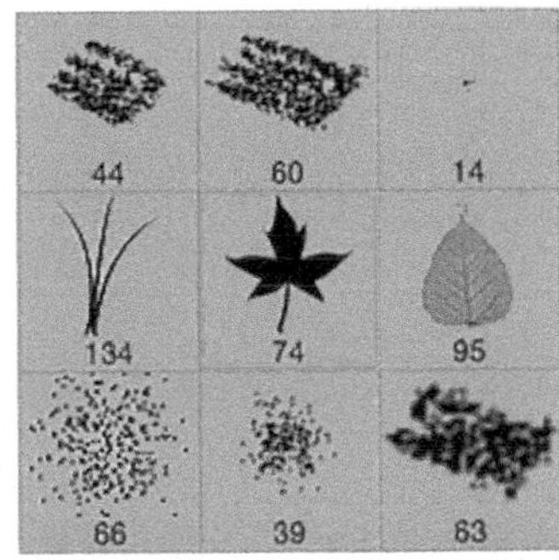

FIGURE 10.38 The maple leaf-shaped brush is among the brushes that ship with Photoshop.

+ TIP To see these brushes in Photoshop CC 2018, you may need to load them manually. Open the Brushes panel, open the panel menu (in the upper-right corner), and choose Legacy Brushes. Then you should be able to find the one used here, called Scattered Maple Leaves.

Since we're looking for a more random, leafy edge to our bush, the first thing we need to adjust is the size and the spacing on the brush we've chosen. The size should be pretty close to the size of the actual leaves on the bush.

6. Make sure you have the Clone Stamp tool selected and that you've chosen our leaf brush. To gauge the size, hover the cursor over the image where the bush will be built up to see how the size of the brush matches. In this case, Dennis set the size to 7 pixels. To create more space in between each leaf, turn up the spacing of the brush to 100%.

Make sure Shape Dynamics is turned on. This will vary the size and the angle of the brush, helping give us a natural-looking distribution of leaves with different sizes.

Click the Scattering option to turn it on, and set Scatter to 450%, Count to 4, and Count Jitter to 100%. These settings help randomize the placement of our leaves.

To give yourself some control over the opacity of the brush, select Transfer and, in the Opacity Jitter section, choose Pen Pressure from the Control menu. (Note that this will only work if you're using a stylus with a pressure-sensitive tablet, such as those made by Wacom.) FIGURE 10.39 on the next page shows the options we've used to set up our brush.

7. Start cloning the bush upward, rebuilding the top of the bush as needed. Remember to keep resetting your sample point from time to time so you don't wind up with an exact copy of any identifiable features of the bush.

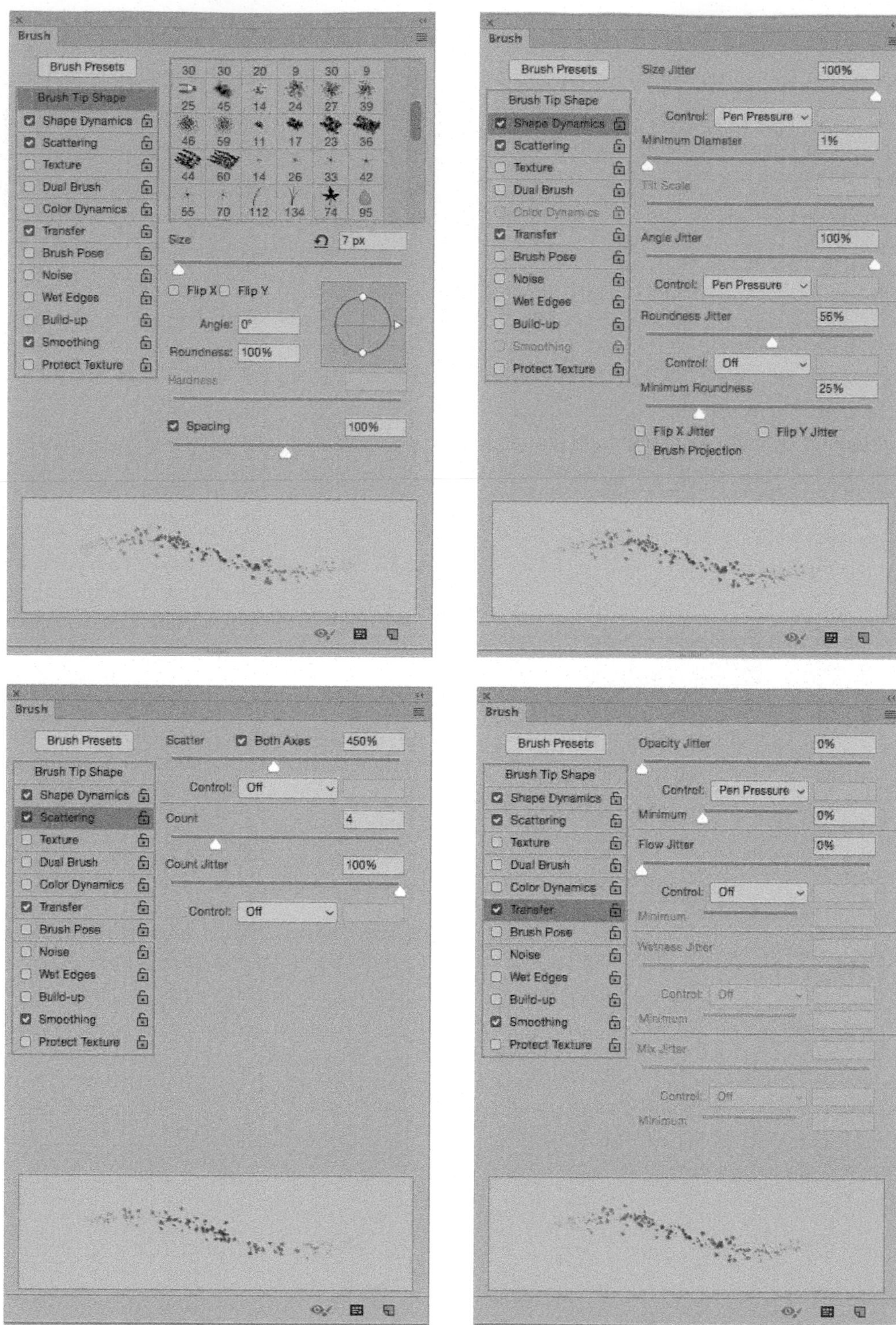

FIGURE 10.39 Use these settings with the leaf brush to get a natural-looking result.

Be sure to add in a few "branches" along the top extending up over the garage door. This will help hide any imperfections where you rebuilt the garage door and will make the top of the bush more believable. FIGURE 10.40 shows a closeup of the bush Dennis rebuilt to cover up the For Sale sign.

FIGURE 10.40 Use the Clone Stamp tool to rebuild the top of the bush.

The final step is to remove the wires extending from behind the house into the bushes on the far left of the shot. The clear blue sky makes this step simple.

8. Before working on this area be sure to reset the Clone Stamp tool to your preferred brush settings and set the size to about 15 pixels. Then add a new layer and name it *Lose Wires*. Option/Alt-click a point on the edge of the roof without wires to select your clone source, and then find the point where the lines extend beyond the side of the house; this will be your destination point (FIGURE 10.41).

FIGURE 10.41 Line up the sampling point with the destination point, using the edge of the roof to keep the roofline straight.

9. Click at the destination point, and then hold the Shift key while clicking at the other end of the wire just before it disappears behind the trees. This will cause the Clone Stamp tool's brush stroke to paint a straight line covering up the wire.

Repeat this for the other two wires. Then carefully work with the Clone Stamp tool to clean out the wires where they meet the trees. Continue working in this way where the wires extend to the left behind the trees until they are completely gone.

When you're done the image should look something like FIGURE 10.42.

FIGURE 10.42 The house exterior after removing the sign and wires

Interior Shots: Combining Exposures

When shooting interiors it's very common to have to combine two images of the scene: one exposed for the interior and the other exposed for the windows. This lets you get a good balance between the two areas of the image. If the photographer uses a tripod to lock down the camera position, combining these different frames is a relatively simple matter in Photoshop (FIGURES 10.43 and 10.44).

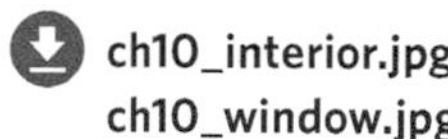

ch10_interior.jpg
ch10_window.jpg

1. With the interior shot and the window shot both open, arrange the windows so you can see both images at the same time. With the window shot active, find the Layers panel. Hold down Shift and drag the Background layer onto the interior image and release the mouse button. This adds the window image as a new layer in the interior image file. Name this new layer *Windows*.

Holding the Shift key will line up both images so their centers are aligned. If the camera did not move in between frames, this should mean everything is lined up properly.

FIGURES 10.43 and 10.44 Before and after. © *William Short*

2. To double-check the alignment between the two layers, select the Windows layer in the Layers panel and set the blending mode to Difference. This blending mode makes it easier to see how two layers line up.

In this case, since the exposures for the two layers are different, the image won't be completely black, but you will see a clear outline wherever any features are not lined up properly. These images are aligned for the most part, but the glowing fringe around the plants in the garden shows they probably moved in the wind between exposures (FIGURE 10.45). If there are any telltale borders along straight lines, you can bring the layers into alignment by selecting the Move tool and tapping the arrow keys to nudge the top layer into place. Once the layers are properly lined up, change the blending mode back to Normal.

The next task is to draw a path around the windows that we can use to make a layer mask.

FIGURE 10.45 Use the Difference blending mode to make sure the layers are lined up correctly.

3. Select the Pen tool and carefully trace around the windows, keeping just to the glass side of the frames. Be sure to catch the small hole in the large leaf on the plant by the lower corner of the far left window. Save this path and name it *Windows*. In FIGURE 10.46 the red line shows where Dennis traced the path he used for this step.

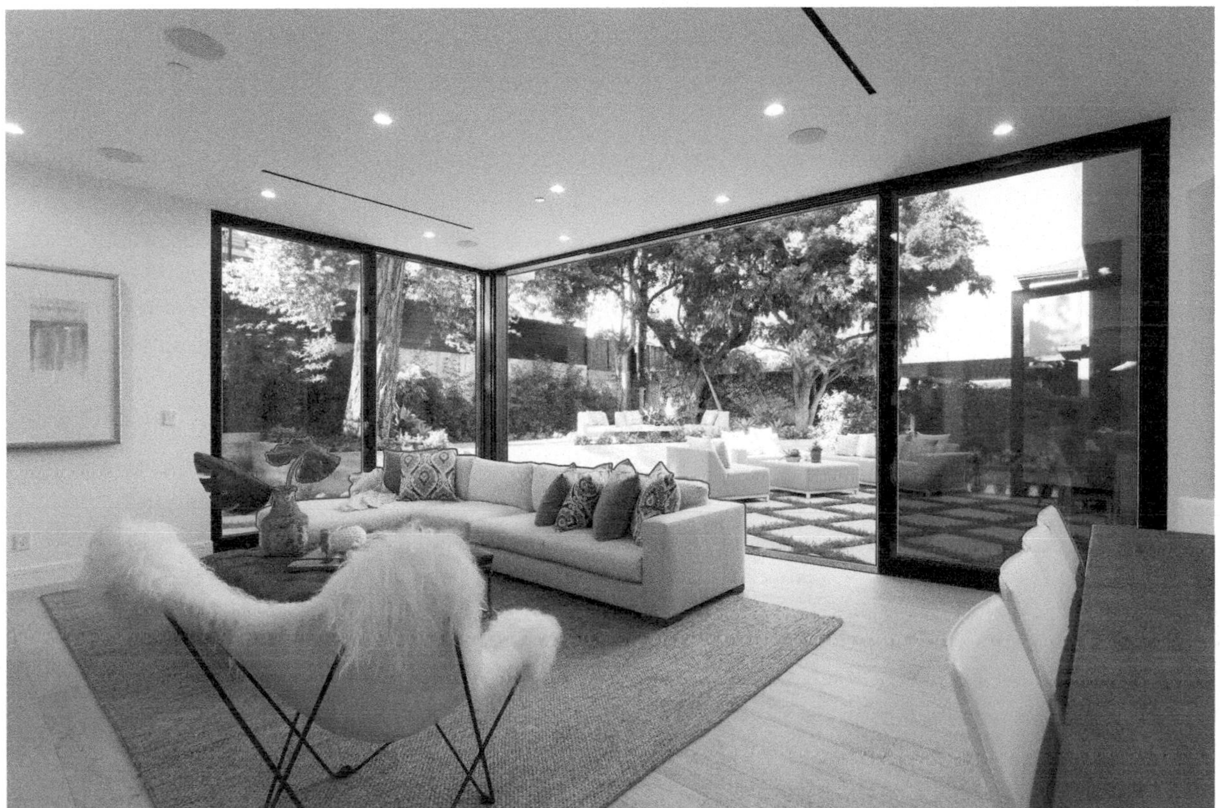

FIGURE 10.46 The red line shows the path created with the Pen tool.

4. Turn the Windows path into a selection by selecting it in the Paths panel, opening the panel menu, and choosing Make Selection. In the Make Selection dialog box, set Feather Radius to 1 and click OK to make the selection active.

With the selection active, select the Windows layer in the Layers panel, and click the Add Layer Mask button at the bottom of the panel to turn your selection into a layer mask. You should now have something very much like **FIGURE 10.47**.

TIP After creating a layer mask from a path, it's always a good idea to zoom in to check the edges of the mask and make sure there are no unwanted halos or areas that need cleaning up. The edges can be refined by carefully painting black or white with the Brush tool as needed on the mask to make sure everything fits just right.

FIGURE 10.47 With the Windows layer masked in

Looking at the composited image, we see it's getting pretty close. With a little color correction on the layers we'll have a finished image.

5. Add a Curves adjustment layer just above the Background layer so we can cool off the color of the room just a bit. Name this layer *Interior Crvs*. In the Curves Properties panel, choose Red from the channel menu, add a point to the middle of the curve, and pull it down a little. Next choose the Blue channel and pull up on the middle a bit. **FIGURE 10.48** shows the adjustments Dennis made to the curve he used.

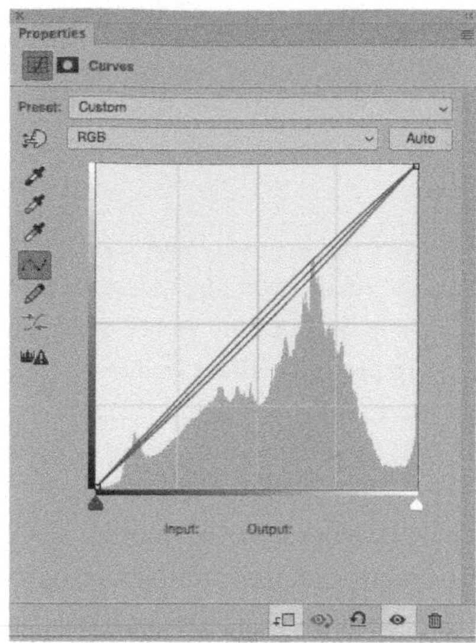

FIGURE 10.48 Add a Curves adjustment layer just above the Background layer to cool off the color of the room.

The light hitting the table, the chairs, and the wall on the right is warmer than the light in the rest of the room. This is a pretty common situation, especially in a room with mixed lighting from outside windows and inside lamps. Photoshop lets us unify the lighting pretty easily.

6. Use the Pen tool to trace a path around the table and chairs. Save this path and name it *Table & Chairs*. Then Cmd/Ctrl-click the path in the Paths panel to turn it into a selection. With the selection active, add another Curves adjustment layer. Name this layer *Chairs Crvs*. This adjustment layer, like the one we just made, should be above the Background layer and below the Windows layer so that it affects the room but not the windows.

Since the light on this side is warmer, we need to cool it off by reducing the red while adding a little blue. Choose the Red channel and drag down the middle of the curve slightly; then choose the Blue channel and drag up on it a bit more than you did the Red channel, as shown in **FIGURE 10.49**.

It's now more obvious that the wall near the tables and chairs was affected by that warm light as well. Here, the warm light falls off gently as the lighting of the rest of the room takes over. So we'll use a soft mask to blend the correction.

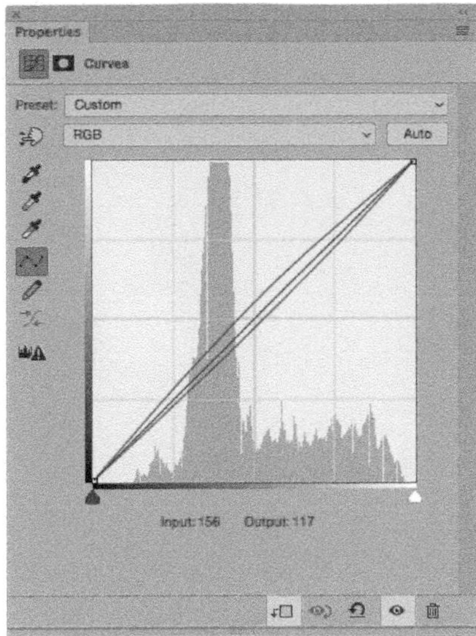

FIGURE 10.49 Use another Curves adjustment layer to counter the warmer light hitting the chairs and table on the right side.

7. Tap the Q key to enter Quick Mask mode, and use a large, soft brush, about 350 pixels wide, to paint black over the far edge of the wall where you notice the warmer light tinting it. (Be sure to set the opacity and flow for the Brush tool to 100% for this step.) Invert the Quick Mask by pressing Cmd-I/Ctrl-I, and tap the Q key one more time to turn the mask into a selection. Now add another Curves adjustment layer and name this one *Wall Crvs*. With the Curves Properties panel open, make an adjustment to the curves that's similar to what we did in the previous step. (The same light is affecting this area, so the adjustment will be pretty much the same.)

The final step in bringing the room and windows into proper balance is to add a little color adjustment to the Windows layer. This time we'll warm up the color while brightening it a little as well.

8. Select the Windows layer in the Layers panel. Then add a new Curves adjustment layer. In the New Layer dialog box, select Use Previous Layer to Create Clipping Mask so that this layer will affect only the Windows layer, as shown in FIGURE 10.50. Name this new layer *Windows Crvs*.

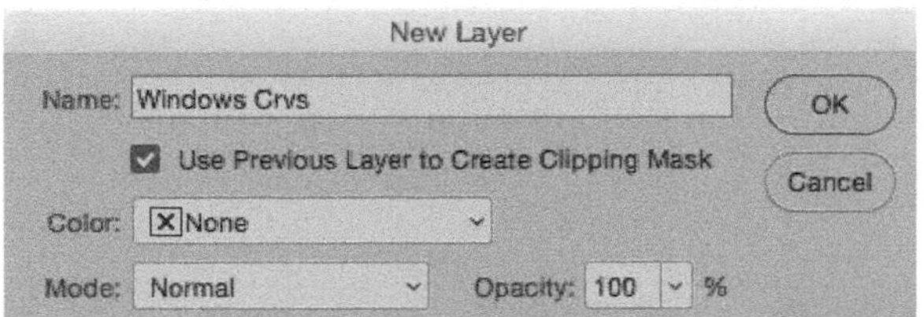

FIGURE 10.50 Clip the new Curves layer to the Windows layer.

9. Make the needed adjustment by pulling up a little on the middle of the RGB curve. Then choose Red from the channel menu and add a point in the middle of the curve. Use the up arrow key on your keyboard to nudge it up slightly. Finish the adjustment by choosing the Blue channel and pulling down on the curve a little more than you moved the RGB curve up. When you're done, your curves should look like those in FIGURE 10.51.

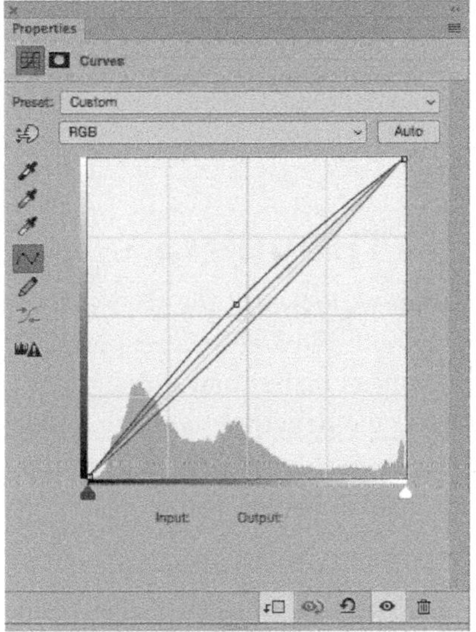

FIGURE 10.51 Use a Curves adjustment layer to adjust the color and brightness of the Windows layer.

With this color correction completed, the exterior seen through the windows and the interior of the room should be nicely in balance with each other (FIGURE 10.52).

FIGURE 10.52 The room and the windows have been brought into balance.

CLOSING THOUGHTS

In this chapter we looked at the process for retouching product, food, and architecture photos. Even though the subject matter may differ greatly, the basics of using file structure (how you build your layered files), retouching tools such as the Healing Brush and Clone Stamp tools, and color correction are very similar.

As Dennis likes to say, Photoshop techniques are like basic building blocks that we can put together and reconfigure to assemble or enhance images, creating some pretty cool artwork. The key is in building your familiarity with the various tools and their uses while training your eye to recognize whether you're getting the results you need.

APPENDIX

CONTRIBUTORS

This book would never have come to fruition without the generous sharing of images and techniques by these very talented professionals. We thank the following for allowing us to share their images with you by including them with the downloadable files.

Sonya Adcock

Sonya Adcock Photography
Fine art photography
Pennsylvania, USA
sonyaadcockphotography.com
sonyaadcockphotography@gmail.com

David Blattel

David Blattel Photography
Topanga, CA
davidblattel.com
david@davidbattel.com

Teri Campbell

Teri Studios
Cincinnati, OH
teristudios.com
sherry@teristudios.com

Alan Cutler

PhotoRescuer
Photograph & document restoration; semi-professional photography
Potomac, MD
Photo & Document restoration: www.photorescuer.com
Photography: alanjcutler.zenfolio.com
alancutler@verizon.net

Allen Furbeck

Allen Furbeck—Painting and Photography
New York, NY
af111.photoshelter.com
mail@allenfurbeck.com

Marko Kovacevic

Marko Kovacevic Photography
Brooklyn, NY
www.markokovacevic.net
mk@markokovacevic.net

Bobbi Lane

Design X
Carver, MA
bobbilane.com
bobbi@bobbilane.com

Richard Lynch

Propictrix
Articulated image correction
Gandia, Spain
photoshopdocs.com
photoshoplayers@gmail.com

Rod Mendenhall

Rod Mendenhall Fine Art Photography
www.rodmendenhall.com
www.rodmendenhall.com/Other/About-RMP

Operation Photo Rescue

Worldwide non-profit volunteer organization that restores images damaged by natural disaster
President Margie Hayes, El Dorado, KS
www.operationphotorescue.org

Phil Pool

Omni Photography
Digital portraiture and wedding photography, image restoration
West Burlington, IA
www.omniphotobyphil.com
www.omniphotobyphil.com/contact.html

Mark Rutherford

Mark Rutherford Photography
www.mrutherford.com
www.mrutherford.com/contact

Mark Segal

Mark D. Segal Photography
Toronto, Ontario, Canada
markdsegal.com
mgsegal@rogers.com

William Short

William Short Photography
Architectural, editorial, and documentary photography
Los Angeles, CA
www.williamshortphotography.com
bill@williamshortphotography.com

George Simian

Commercial photography and education
Los Angeles, CA and Bali, Indonesia
georgesimian.com
georgesimian.com/contact

Amanda Steinbacher

Amanda Steinbacher Photography, LLC
Newborn and Milestone Photography
North Central PA
amanda@steinbacher.photography

John Troisi

Freelance landscape photography
Williamsport, PA
humblejn@comcast.net

Lorie Zirbes

Retouching by Lorie
Old photo restorations & full color tints, creative montages, portrait & commercial retouching
www.retouchingbylorie.com
artistlz@aol.com

IMAGE CONTRIBUTORS

Thank you to these photographers, museums, and companies for allowing us to feature their images on the pages of this book. Your generosity and understanding made this book possible.

Tom P. Ashe
Beckleman Family
Blanco Family
David Blattel
Brent Bigler
Browne Family
Buck Family
Teri Campbell
Cyan Jack
Claster Family
Dante Dauz
Davis Family
Rick Day Photography
Eckhart Family
Ehrman Family
Alexander P. Eismann
Eismann Family
Goldberg Family
Hall Family
Haskett Family
Hemmendinger Family
Hendrick Family
Pamela J. Herrington
Hildenbrand Family
Hill Family
Houser Family
Hunsinger Family
Cari Jansen
Kaminsky Family
Pavel Kubarkov/Adobe Stock
Julia Kuzmenko-McKim
Mody Family
Moss Family
Scott Nathan
Anthony Nex
Ogurcak Family
Palmer Family
Piper Family
The Right Image
Smith Family
Stephen Rosenblum
Grace Rousso
School of Visual Arts (SVA) Photography Department
George Simian
Bernie Synoracki
Wiedersheim Family

INDEX

D

K

L

M

T

U

V

W

X

Z